LANGUAGE AND COGNITION IN BILINGUALS AND MULTILINGUALS

Language and Cognition in Bilinguals and Multilinguals

An Introduction

Annette M. B. de Groot

Psychology Press
Taylor & Francis Group

NEW YORK AND HOVE

Published in 2011
by Psychology Press
270 Madison Avenue New York, NY 10016

www.psypress.com

Published in Great Britain
by Psychology Press
27 Church Road Hove, East Sussex BN3 2FA

Psychology Press is an imprint of the Taylor & Francis Group, an Informa business

Typeset in Times by RefineCatch Limited, Bungay, Suffolk, UK
Printed in the USA by Sheridan Books, Inc. on acid-free paper
Cover design by Hybert Design

10 9 8 7 6 5 4 3 2 1

Library of Congress Cataloging-in-Publication Data
A catalog record for this book is available from the Library of Congress

ISBN: 978–1–84872–901–8

To the memory of my parents
    Johan de Groot (1917–2008)
    Cher de Groot-Fransen (1921–2001)

To the memory of my twin sister
    Jeannette de Groot (1951–1994)

For my son Jan Kraak

Contents

About the Author

Annette de Groot is Professor of Experimental Psycholinguistics at the University of Amsterdam. She moved to Amsterdam in 1987 after completing a master's degree in General Linguistics and a doctorate in Psycholinguistics at the University of Nijmegen, The Netherlands, and following a Research Fellowship awarded to her by the Netherlands Organization for Scientific Research. In Amsterdam she first held the position of Associate Professor of Cognitive Psychology and, since 1995, her current position. Her work has concentrated on word recognition and the structure of the mental lexicon, the psychology of reading, and bilingualism and multilingualism. Her present research focuses on bilingualism, with a special interest in bilingual word processing, foreign language vocabulary learning, and simultaneous interpreting. She has been a member of the Editorial Boards of *Memory and Cognition*, and *Psychonomic Bulletin & Review*. Currently she is a member of the Editorial Board of *Bilingualism: Language and Cognition*, and of the Advisory Board of *Interpreting*. With Judith Kroll she co-edited *Tutorials in Bilingualism: Psycholinguistic Perspectives* and the *Handbook of Bilingualism: Psycholinguistic Approaches*.

Preface and Acknowledgements

For about four decades following its emergence around 1950, psycholinguistics—the field of science that examines the mental processes and knowledge structures involved in acquiring, understanding, and producing language—had a strong monolingual orientation. In a prototypical experiment native speakers of a language were asked to perform some task in that language while it was implicitly assumed they did not speak any other language, or the possibility they might do so was simply taken for granted. Although this monolingual bias still characterizes mainstream psycholinguistics, from about 1990 a clear shift of focus toward the bilingual and multilingual language user can be witnessed. Two insights have arguably caused this change of focus: the awareness that a large part of mankind speaks more than one language and that a person's multiple languages interact with one another even when one of them is selected for current use. Therefore, in order to obtain a faithful account of man's linguistic abilities, the study of human language processing could not remain stubbornly monolingual.

And it did not. Journals exclusively dedicated to the study of bilingualism have been founded, workshops on bilingualism are being organized, and quite a few books on bilingualism have appeared since around 1995. But among those books, one is clearly missing: a comprehensive text that covers many of the topical sub-areas within the psycholinguistic study of bilingualism; that integrates these sub-areas into a coherent whole; that is written at an introductory level; and that reflects the fact that in the field, in addition to the more traditional behavioral methods, brain research is becoming increasingly popular. Most of the books published so far concern edited volumes with a relatively restricted scope (e.g., foreign language vocabulary acquisition, or sentence processing in bilinguals) and some are monographs dealing with just one topic (e.g., bilingualism in development, or translation and simultaneous interpreting). Instead, the *Handbook of Bilingualism: Psycholinguistic Approaches*, edited by Judith Kroll and myself and published by Oxford University Press, has a broad scope, but it does not qualify as an introduction. The contributions to that volume were all reviews of one specific sub-area of study written by experts and aiming at an audience of graduate students and researchers in the field. This same description applies to an earlier volume we edited together, *Tutorials in Bilingualism: Psycholinguistic Perspectives*, published by Erlbaum, except that it contained fewer contributions.

The topics covered by the present text are largely the same as those dealt with in the above two volumes, but this time they are presented at an introductory level, aiming at a less advanced readership: far less prior knowledge is assumed, methods and tasks are explained in relation to theory, and more illustration materials and a glossary are included. Furthermore, I have worked with the same "model of the reader" in mind all through, trying to use the same balance between depth and scope when presenting each individual theme. Finally, I have used a uniform structure for the majority of the chapters: They start with an introduction and preview of the topics to be dealt with, continue with a *Methods and Task* section and, next, a number of sections that each treats a different theme and the associated evidence, and they conclude with a summary of the main findings. Chapter 1 does not follow this format because it is only meant to set the stage for the rest of the book, explaining what psycholinguistics is about and providing some standard terminology and definitions and a preview of the chapters to come. Chapter 8 lacks a summary because it introduces relatively few new topics but focuses exclusively on the brain basis of bilingualism and multilingualism.

The reader will notice that this book's chapters are generally quite long. The fact that little prior knowledge is assumed is partly responsible for this. Further reasons are that I wanted to provide some history as well—relating the bilingual (and multilingual) studies to be presented to the monolingual psycholinguistic studies they derive from—and be up to date at the same time. Especially meeting this last goal posed quite a challenge because new articles are appearing at an accelerating pace.

Many people have supported me, in many different ways, since I first started to work on this book about four years ago and I am grateful to all of them. First of all there are my colleagues in the field who contributed importantly by providing information, sharing their ideas, and nourishing my views on bilingualism, through their published work and in personal contacts: Jubin Abutalebi, Panos Athanasopoulos, Teresa Bajo, Ellen Bialystok, David Birdsong, Lera Boroditsky, Laura Bosch, Anna Bosman, Mirjam Broersma, Ingrid Christoffels, Dorothee Chwilla, Vivian Cook, Albert Costa, Annick De Houwer, Ton Dijkstra, Giuli Dussias, Wouter Duyck, Jim Flege, Wendy Francis, Cheryl Frenck-Mestre, Daniel Gile, Jonathan Grainger, David Green, François Grosjean, Marianne Gullberg, Lynne Hansen, Jan Hulstijn, Sonja Kotz, Wido La Heij, Batia Laufer, Renata Meuter, Barbara Moser-Mercer, Michel Paradis, Aneta Pavlenko, Antonio Rodriguez-Fornells, Ardi Roelofs, Rosa Sánchez-Casas, Núria Sebastián-Gallés, Peter Starreveld, Janet van Hell, Walter van Heuven, and Jyotsna Vaid.

One person is noticeably missing in this list, the reason being that the fleeting inclusion of her name among those of my other valued colleagues would not do justice to the significant impact she has had, and still has, on my academic career and beyond. Of course the person I am hinting at is Judy Kroll, who I first met in 1989 and since built up a professionally productive and privately enriching relationship with. Even though my life in academia steered away in a different direction after I decided to broaden my perspective by joining the University of Amsterdam administration, our close collaboration in the past has never stopped to inspire me and this book would not have been written without it. Thank you Judy for all that!

I am also indebted to a number of people I first met in the more remote past. They mentored me during the initial stages of my academic career and some of them I became and stayed friends with to this very day: Jan Elshout, Ken Forster, Gerard Kempen, Remmert Kraak, Pim Levelt, and Ar Thomassen.

The following students have contributed very tangibly to this book and I am deeply grateful to them. Nick Naber always knew where I was getting at when I gave him some general instructions regarding the illustrations I wanted to include in the book and then designed and produced all of them on the basis of these fuzzy indications. Geoffrey Cramm embellished the figures of the brain as designed by Nick. Arien op 't Land took upon her the rather unrewarding task of obtaining the publication rights of the figures that

I borrowed from other publications and Hilde Smedinga's eagle eyes spotted many typing errors and other infelicities in the list of references and corrected them. Finally, Ingrid Singer helped me compiling the chapters' summaries.

A next group of people to thank are a couple of my colleagues, former and present, at the University of Amsterdam. When my adventurous sojourn in the university administration ended, Rector Paul van der Heijden and Chairman Sijbolt Noorda granted me a sabbatical that enabled me to start working on this book and the administrators of the Department of Psychology, Agneta Fischer, Gerard Kerkhof, and Klaas Visser, saw to it that I landed safely again in the Department at the conclusion of this sabbatical. Johan van Benthem is probably unaware of the fact that he also had a role to play in me reaching the finish; suffice to say that he did. I would like to thank Nol Verhagen for his role in the great collection of journals and books the University of Amsterdam community has access to. I am also grateful to the Department's secretarial staff, and especially to Hubert Eleonora and Anna Bogerd, for supporting the logistics of the entire enterprise.

I started my sabbatical in Tuscany, where Elda and Fernando Giannini guarded my health and general well-being and Italy's unparalleled cultural treasures took care of the rest. These treasures were my reward after each week of unremitting labor. And then there were the friends that boosted my spirits in times of looming despair. I enjoyed an occasional lunch with Walter Hoogland, a drink with Sander Bais, a concert with Harm Pinkster, and a meal with Lief Keteleer. Special thanks go to three of my friends: Ruud Bleijerveld, Kees Roza, and Marjan Freriks. In need of a place to retreat to for a couple of weeks halfway into the project, Ruud and Kees generously offered me their home in the German Eifel that, with some force of imagination, can be seen to resemble Tuscany, and in the years to follow they bestowed their hospitality upon me in their Amsterdam home over grand meals. On many Friday evenings I met with Marjan in her home, spending them according to an agreeable division of labor: she cooked, I ate (in which she joined in), and we both discussed the week's noteworthy events.

I am also grateful to the staff at Psychology Press, and especially to Editors Cathleen Petree and Paul Dukes for their pleasant and effective guidance and to Production Manager Mandy Collison and Editorial Assistant Lee Transue, who provided advice and help during the final stages of the project.

And then, of course, there is my wonderful family, which provides attentive and loving company whenever I need it. But there is another reason why I am indebted to my family, each of its members: Lives are largely shaped by one's relatives of three generations, one's own, the previous one, and the next. I dedicate this book to the main representatives of these three generations: my parents, my twin sister Jeannette, and my son Jan.

Annette M. B. de Groot
Amsterdam, May 2010

Introduction and Preview

Bilingualism has become an omnipresent phenomenon in our modern society of large-scale migration, international markets and finance, backpacking youngsters, and a scientific community in need of a lingua franca to disseminate its achievements among its members. The awareness that bilingualism is not at all exceptional any more and may not have been so for a long time has recently led to a steep growth in the number of studies on the implications of being bilingual for language use and cognition in general. This book brings together the results of many of these studies. It presents the theories and views on bilingualism that motivated these studies and emerged from them, but it also explains the research methods and tasks that were used to address these theories and views in specific experiments. Because of this latter feature this book qualifies as an introduction to the study of bilingualism. However, it presupposes some basic knowledge of the research area of cognitive psychology and, specifically, the psychology of language (or "psycholinguistics"). The issues that will be dealt with are largely based on those addressed in the study of psycholinguistics, but they are approached from the perspective of bilingual language users.

In this introduction I will first describe what psycholinguistics is about and show how it has provided the basis for the study of bilingualism. Next I will present the colorful variety of language users who are all called bilingual. I will then introduce a number of central themes in the study of bilingualism and, hence, in this book. This will be followed by a brief section on conventional nomenclature in the field and I will conclude with a brief preview of the chapters to come.

But first some words are in order on the title of this book: "Language and cognition in bilinguals and multilinguals: An introduction". The vast majority of the studies to be discussed tested bilinguals; that is, people who know and use two languages. Relatively few studies will be included that examined multilinguals—people who know and use three or more languages. This reflects the fact that relatively few of these studies have been conducted and reported. Because of the unbalance between bilingual and multilingual studies, I considered the alternative, smoother, title "Language and cognition in bilinguals: An introduction", but for a couple reasons I decided against it. The first is simply that it would not do justice to that fact that some multilingual studies are in fact included. But a more principled reason is that the theories, processes, and mechanisms that will be dealt with apply, I believe, to both bilingualism and multilingualism. A multilingual language system is potentially noisier than a bilingual language system, but the mental processes and mechanisms that handle this increased level of noise are presumably no different from those involved in dealing with the extra noise in a bilingual system as compared with a monolingual system. To the extent that these claims are true, this book is as much about multilingualism as it is about bilingualism, and in many places where I talk about bilinguals and bilingualism one might take these to imply multilinguals and multilingualism as well. Furthermore, as we shall see below, some people considered bilingual according to one definition of bilingualism may be considered multilingual by another (because they also possess some knowledge of at least one further language and can put it to effective use, which counts as an additional language for one theorist but not another). Finally, it is not unusual to call a particular study a bilingual one because two specific languages of the participants are being examined while the fact is ignored that the participants might also possess at least some basic knowledge of one or more other languages.

PSYCHOLINGUISTICS AND THE STUDY OF BILINGUALISM

Psycholinguistics is an interdisciplinary field of study that connects the disciplines of psychology and linguistics. Briefly, linguistics is the field of science that describes the knowledge that underlies language, whereas psychology is the field of science that explains behavior in terms of mental processes. Psycholinguistics combines these two orientations by examining the mental processes and types of knowledge involved in understanding and producing language, in both its oral and written forms. In other words, it deals with the linguistic skills of listening, speaking, reading, and writing, trying to discover the cognitive machinery and knowledge structures that under-

lie these skills and what role they play in linguistic behavior. In addition, psycholinguistics is concerned with how we acquire these skills.

While exhibiting any of the above-mentioned four skills, the language user makes use of knowledge units of various different types, each of them relating to a separate domain of linguistic study: phonology, morphology, syntax or grammar, vocabulary, orthography, and pragmatics. Phonological units ("**phonemes**") are the smallest sound units of a language and the corresponding field of study (phonology) attempts to discover the sound system of a language; that is, what sounds it contains and how these combine into larger sound units. Morphological units ("**morphemes**") are the smallest linguistic units that bear meaning and the corresponding field of study (morphology) investigates the way these meaning units can combine into words. Syntactical knowledge is knowledge about the way words can combine into sentences and the corresponding domain of study (syntax) tries to identify the rule system that underlies permissible word order and sentence structure in a language. A language user's vocabulary consists of all the words he or she knows. Knowing a word minimally involves knowing its spoken form and its meaning, but for literate language users it also implies knowing how it is spelt. A word's spelling is called its "orthography", but this name is also used for spelling in general (especially in alphabetic writing systems, in which the orthographic units, the letters, represent phonemes). In addition it is used to refer to the field of study that investigates the rules of spelling of a language—how exactly orthographic units map onto phonological units. Finally, pragmatics concerns the study of how people use language differently in different contexts, taking world knowledge and knowledge about the specific communicative circumstances into account in choosing the exact wording. They might, for instance, use slang words when interacting with their peers in an informal setting but choose more formal vocabulary when talking to their superiors, or they might choose to use some indirect form of language such as irony to maximize the communicative effect. Whereas linguistics is primarily concerned with describing these various sources of knowledge, psycholinguistics focuses on how we exploit them in using language.

In addition to discovering how language is acquired and used, psycholinguistics tries to discover the relation between language and non-linguistic cognition, specifically the relation between language and thought. Across the centuries, various views on the relation between language and thought have been advanced, such as the idea that thought is internal speech, that language is a tool to communicate thought, that language guides thought, and that language influences thought (see Whitney, 1998, for an overview). The view that language influences thought also incorporates the idea that specific languages influence thought in specific ways, with the effect that speakers of different languages might think and perceive the world differently.

Even now, psycholinguistics is characterized by a strong monolingual bias: The participants who are asked to perform some language task in some experiment are typically native speakers of the test language and it is implicitly assumed—possibly mistakenly—that they lack knowledge of any other language(s). Alternatively, the investigators might be well aware that the participants might speak one or more other languages in addition to their native language, or that they are native speakers of two languages, but this possibility is simply ignored or taken for granted. The monolingual orientation of psycholinguistics has arguably led to an incomplete conception, possibly even a false one, of human linguistic ability and language processing, because knowing more than one language may have an impact on the way each individual one of them is mentally represented and processed. If forced to single out the most salient result emerging from the study of bilingualism/multilingualism to date, I would choose the ubiquitous effect of the language(s) currently not in use on the one selected for current use. In addition, acquiring a new language is influenced by prior knowledge not only of the first language but of all further languages of which the learner has at least some knowledge. A further consequence of the monolingual bias in

psycholinguistics is that not all means have been exploited to become informed on the relation between language and thought: If specific languages influence thought in specific ways, a person who masters more than one language may live in different worlds of thought depending on the language currently used. Alternatively, this person's way of thinking may be based on a merger of the worlds of thought associated with the separate language he or she speaks.

The insight that, as compared with monolingualism, bilingualism may alter language acquisition, representation, and processing as well as thought (and, as we shall see, other aspects of non-linguistic cognition), has in recent years led to a steep rise in studies on language use and cognition in speakers of more than one language. In this book I discuss many of these studies and attempt to integrate the wide range of miscellaneous findings that have emerged from the various sub-disciplines within this field of study into a coherent whole. The study of bilingualism deals with largely the same topics and the same linguistic domains and skills as covered by traditional psycholinguistics, and can therefore be regarded a branch of psycholinguistics. But because the study of bilingualism has only quite recently started to gain momentum it has not yet grown as many branches as its source, traditional psycholinguistics, and some of the sub-areas that have started to emerge have not yet had the chance to develop into anything more than a tender twig.

The study of bilingualism can be dissected into three main areas of study that map directly onto the three main lines of study within traditional psycholinguistics. The first examines how language users understand (or comprehend) language input; the second how they produce language output. The main difference between the traditional psycholinguistic studies and the bilingual studies is that only the latter address these topics from the bilingual perspective, testing bilinguals and posing the question of how the fact that they speak more than one language influences the way they process language. The third main line of study is language acquisition and can be divided into two sub-areas. One of them deals with the simultaneous acquisition of two languages from birth and how it compares with acquiring just one language. The second is concerned with acquiring a second language after a first one is already partly or fully in place.

As mentioned above, language comprehension and production both occur in two modalities depending on the nature of the input and output: speech or writing. Taking both dimensions of classification (comprehension/production; speech/writing) into account, four linguistic skills can be distinguished: listening, reading, speaking, and writing. The first three of these have established a clear presence on the agenda of bilingualism researchers, but studies on the writing skills of bilinguals are still sparse. Another noteworthy feature of the state of the art in bilingualism research is that relatively many of both the comprehension and the production studies that have been performed have investigated the processing of words instead of larger linguistic units such as complete sentences or texts. For example, the majority of the bilingual speech production studies conducted so far have examined the production of single words out of context. Finally, looking at the current state of the study of bilingualism from the viewpoint of the various types of linguistic knowledge distinguished above, it appears that (aspects of) vocabulary, phonology, and syntax have received ample attention while studies on morphology and pragmatics are still rare. The content of this book reflects this imbalance.

DEFINING AND CLASSIFYING BILINGUALS

Which language users count as bilinguals? An obvious and common answer to this question is that any person who speaks more than one language is a bilingual, but this answer does not take into account the wide range of differences between individuals who fit that definition. For instance, it does not do justice to the fact that one can speak a language at different levels of fluency. Does the above definition imply that the level of fluency in both languages is nativelike or does it allow for lower levels of fluency in one of the languages or perhaps in both and, if so, what minimal level would be required to be included? Is this minimum level of fluency required for all of the four linguistic skills distinguished earlier or does it suffice, for instance, to be able to just speak in both languages or to just read in both languages? In fact, in bilingualism research a wide range of more specific definitions of bilingualism can be encountered. These vary from only considering a person bilingual if he or she masters two languages at the same level of fluency and with the same level of control as native speakers of the two languages—as if a bilingual person is two monolinguals in one person—to regarding people who only possess some minimal competence in one of the four linguistic skills as bilingual. According to the first of these definitions the bilingual population is a very small one, if only because of the fact that the language selected for current use is influenced by all of the other languages known by this speaker (see above). According to the second definition even people who are in an initial stage of second language learning count as bilingual.

Bilinguals are classified according to a number of dimensions (see e.g., Butler & Hakuta, 2004; Hamers & Blanc, 1989). Each of these dimensions will be explained briefly here and detailed further elsewhere in this book. One of them is a classification according to their relative competence in both languages. So-called "balanced bilinguals" possess similar degrees of proficiency in both languages, whereas "dominant bilinguals" (or "unbalanced bilinguals") are those with a higher level of proficiency in one language than in the other. Balanced bilingualism does not necessarily imply a high competence in both languages. For instance, a child who masters two languages to equal degrees is said to be a balanced bilingual even though in neither language has he or she reached full competence yet. Therefore a further distinction to make is according to the level of fluency or proficiency in, especially, the second language. Bilinguals who have attained a (near-) native level of proficiency in this language are called "proficient bilinguals"; those who have not are called "non-proficient bilinguals".

Three other dimensions concern the age at which second language acquisition starts (the so called "age of acquisition" variable), the way words and their meanings are organized in bilingual memory, and the social status of each of the languages. The age of acquisition dimension splits up the bilingual population into "early" and "late" bilinguals. Early bilinguals are those who acquired both languages in childhood, whereas late bilinguals became bilingual beyond childhood. In its turn, early bilingualism is divided into early "simultaneous" and early "consecutive" or "sequential" bilingualism. Early simultaneous bilinguals have been exposed to both languages from birth, whereas early consecutive/sequential bilinguals have first been exclusively exposed to one language, their native language, and from some later point in time during early childhood have started to receive bilingual input. In some classifications late bilingualism is also split up into two subgroups—adolescent and adult bilingualism. This subdivision relates to the view, held by some scientists in the field, that adolescence marks a critical boundary in language-learning ability.

The classification that splits up bilingualism according to bilingual memory organization distinguishes between "compound", "coordinate", and "subordinative" bilingualism. In bilinguals of the compound type the two word forms of a translation-equivalent word pair map onto one and the same meaning representation in memory, whereas in coordinate bilinguals each term in such a word pair maps onto a separate meaning representation. In subordinative bilingualism, as in compound bilingualism, there is also just one meaning representation for both elements of a translation-equivalent word pair, but this time the word form of the weaker language does not map directly onto this meaning representation but via the word form of the stronger language. These three forms of bilingualism have been related to different contexts of acquisition. For instance, it has been hypothesized that compound bilingualism emerges when a child grows up in a home where the two languages are spoken interchangeably, and that coordinate bilingualism emerges

when there is a strict separation in the use of the two languages.

A division that splits up bilinguals according to the status of their two languages is one between "additive bilinguals" and "subtractive bilinguals". Additive bilingualism is thought to arise in circumstances wherein both languages are socially valued, whereas subtractive bilingualism results from a situation in which one of them, usually the child's native language, is devalued in his or her environment and there is social pressure not to use it. Additive bilingualism is considered to be beneficial for cognition and cognitive development, whereas subtractive bilingualism is thought to hamper them. The distinction between additive and subtractive bilingualism has also been referred to as one between "elite" and "folk" bilingualism, respectively.

This enumeration of dimensions according to which bilinguals can be categorized is by no means exhaustive (see Butler & Hakuta, 2004, and Hamers & Blanc, 1989, for further divisions) but will do to make the point that the bilingual community are a colorful lot. One should therefore think twice before generalizing a conclusion based on the results of a study testing bilinguals of a specific type to another type, and it behoves the author of any bilingual study to provide details about the type of bilinguals tested.

CENTRAL THEMES, CONCEPTS, ASSUMPTIONS, AND QUESTIONS

Arguably the most central set of assumptions in both general psycholinguistics and in the study of bilingualism is that linguistic knowledge units like words, phonemes, and, perhaps, grammatical rules each have a representation in long-term memory, and that language processing involves the concerted activation and deactivation of subsets of these memory representations. This set of assumptions applies to both language comprehension and language production. Take for example word recognition, perhaps the most thoroughly examined language subskill in the study of bilingualism. Each word representation in our mental lexicon (and each component part of this representation) is assumed to be activated at some baseline level. If a particular word is presented for recognition, it boosts the level of activation of the corresponding lexical representation. If the activation of this representation surpasses some critical threshold level, the corresponding word is recognized. Similar activation processes, but now incited by the intention to express a particular content of thought instead of from an input presented to our ears or eyes, lead to word production.

A word presented for recognition increases the level of activation of not only "its own" lexical representation, but also that of representations of words similar in form (spelling or sound, depending on the modality of input) to the input word. Because the level of activation in one or more of these simultaneously activated representations may also approach the critical threshold, this leads to competition in the word recognition process. Similarly, the conceptualization of a particular content to put into a word activates not only the lexical representation of the targeted word but also those of words with a similar meaning as the target word. This leads to competition in the word production process.

Bilingualism researchers have wondered about the implications of these views on the activation dynamics of word recognition and word production for bilingual speakers. Bilinguals possess two stocks of lexical representations, one for each language. Does a spoken or written word (in comprehension) or a specific conceptual content (in production) give rise to activation in both of these lexical subsets, or can bilinguals somehow "switch off" the contextually inappropriate language? If the latter holds, what mental mechanism is involved in switching off the non-intended language? If the former holds, this implies that bilinguals must experience more competition during word recognition and word production than monolinguals do, and this must have consequences for performance. A further question, then, is how bilinguals resolve the extra-fierce competition and manage to correctly recognize or produce the intended word.

As we shall see, these questions have dominated a substantial part of the bilingualism research to date. The question of whether or not elements of the non-target language are co-activated with elements of the target language has been extended from the vocabulary domain to other domains of language such as phonology and grammar. The question of how bilinguals resolve the extra-fierce competition within their mental language system has led to the insight that bilinguals possess a very effective control system which sees to it that linguistic performance meets their current goal; for instance, to now speak in this specific language, not the other. Subsequent research has revealed that, presumably, the control system in question is not exclusively dedicated to language control but is likely to be a general executive control system that is implicated in the control of behavior in general. This, in turn, has led to the hypothesis that, as compared with monolinguals, bilinguals might be experts in (some aspects of) executive control because they exploit the underlying cognitive machinery incessantly to always use the intended language. These, in a nutshell, are some of the most important themes of this book.

A further central question in traditional psycholinguistics (and in linguistics) is whether humans have an innate capacity for learning language. Human languages, especially their grammars, are extremely complex systems and yet children start to exhibit knowledge of the underlying rule system within a matter of about 2 years. This feat has led a substantial part of the scientific community to assume that the human capacity for language learning is at least partly innate. Other researchers reject this idea and believe that language learning is enabled by general learning mechanisms that are exploited for learning in other domains of cognition as well. In this book an echo of this debate can be heard in, especially, the discussion on language development in monolingual-to-be and bilingual-to-be children, and in the review of studies on age of acquisition effects on (first and) second language learning. An important conclusion to draw from the studies on language development is that children have remarkably good general perceptual skills that bootstrap language acquisition, and that these skills on their own might suffice to explain children's rapid language development. The age of acquisition studies clearly show that if one starts learning a language at a young age, ultimate linguistic performance is generally better than when language learning starts relatively late in life. This superior ultimate performance of those who start young may inform the present "nature–nurture" debate, because it might result from an innate language faculty that is present early in life but is dismantled at some point before adulthood (see e.g., Pinker, 1994). Other effects of acquisition age that have been assumed are that language acquisition differs between early and late learners, that early and late learners process language differently, and that the network of brain structures that are recruited during language processing differs between them. These themes are also all dealt with in this book.

SOME NAMING CONVENTIONS

For convenient reading, in this book the first and native language is often referred to briefly as L1 (for Language 1) and the second language is called the L2. The number conventionally refers to the order of acquisition and any languages to be acquired later are numbered accordingly (L3, L4, etc.). In the case of unbalanced bilingualism, the L1 is often, but not always, the stronger one of a bilingual's two languages. I will use these same conventions throughout. Whenever in a specific study the L1 and dominant language are not one and the same (as might be the case for an immigrant who has resided in the new country for quite some time), I will explicitly clarify which language is the stronger one. A distinction is sometimes made between a second language (L2) and a foreign language (FL). Where this is done, "foreign" means that the L2 in question is not an official language of communication in the country where it is learned or used. For instance, English learned in a school in Japan or Italy is a foreign language for the students in those English

classes. In this book I will generally use the more neutral term L2, except in Chapter 3, which largely deals with L2 vocabulary learning in typical school settings. Of many of the studies presented in this book I will explicate the two languages involved in the participants' bilingualism. For example, I may talk about the Spanish–Catalan participants in a particular study or the French–English ones in another. Generally, in these cases the language mentioned first is the participants' L1 and, at the same time, strongest language, and the one mentioned second their L2 and weaker language. Exceptions to this rule will be noted.

In many situations bilinguals have to use one specific language while trying to prevent intrusions from the other language. The language to use in a specific setting is variously called the "target" or "targeted" language, the "intended" language, the "selected" language, the "language-in-use", the "chosen" language, or the "response" language (and still further names might be used as well). Conversely, the language *not* to use in a specific setting is referred to as the "non-target" or "non-targeted" language, the "non-intended" language, the "non-selected" language, the "language-not-in-use", the "non-chosen" language, or the "non-response" language (and, again, still further names occur). In this book I will use some of these terms, but most often I will talk about the target (or targeted) and non-target (or non-targeted) language.

PREVIEW OF THE CHAPTERS

The first chapter to follow this introduction, Chapter 2, consists of two parts. The first compares language development in monolingual-to-be and bilingual-to-be infants. It focuses on phonological and lexical development in the first years of life as witnessed from infants' performance on speech perception tasks. Due to the availability of relatively new experimental techniques to assess infants' perceptual skills, in this research area in particular substantial progress has been made in recent years. As a result, our understanding of the development of speech production has greatly increased as well (because the development of speech perception and speech production go hand in hand). The second part of Chapter 2 deals with the question of why L2 users who started to learn the L2 when they were young generally achieve a higher level of proficiency than late learners. One popular explanation of this phenomenon will be highlighted in the discussion: that during some bounded period early in life humans possess a heightened sensitivity to language and that, for a language to be acquired fully, the period of acquisition should coincide with this period of heightened sensitivity.

Chapter 3 examines late foreign vocabulary acquisition and the ensuing types of representations in the bilingual mental lexicon. Late foreign vocabulary learning differs substantially from vocabulary learning in L1 acquisition. One of the differences is that in L1 vocabulary learning a word's form, its meaning, and the link between the two must all be learned. In foreign vocabulary learning the meanings of many of the words to be learned are already largely in place. After all, the learner already knows the meaning of many L1 words and these are largely similar to those of the corresponding foreign words. The only thing that needs to be done in the initial stage of foreign vocabulary learning is to connect the new foreign forms to the corresponding extant meanings. The most popular methods that are used to make this connection, the keyword method and paired-associate learning technique, are presented and their efficacy will be discussed. In addition it will be explained why some types of words are easier to learn than other types, and attention will be devoted to later stages of learning, in which the meanings of the foreign words are gradually refined and become more nativelike. Finally, various views on the structure of bilingual lexical representations and how they relate to levels of foreign language fluency will be presented.

Chapter 4 largely deals with the question, introduced above, of whether a spoken or written word input causes activation in both of the language subsystems in bilingual memory or only in the contextually appropriate subsystem. The evidence suggests that co-activation in the non-targeted subsystem is ubiquitous if the word is presented out of context. Further questions to be dealt with are whether a linguistic context might constrain this nuisance co-activation and what type of memory representations (phonological, orthographic, semantic) are simultaneously activated in both language subsystems. In addition, a couple of bilingual word recognition models will be discussed that account for evidence of co-activation. The chapter concludes with a discussion of bilingual language comprehension beyond the level of the word, addressing the question of how bilinguals parse syntactically ambiguous sentences and process semantic and syntactic anomalies.

Chapter 5 first presents models of monolingual and bilingual speech production, zooming in on the word production component contained by the complete process. Subsequently, it focuses once again on the question of whether simultaneous activation occurs in a bilingual's two language subsystems, but this time from the viewpoint of word production instead of word recognition. The majority of the pertinent studies have used versions of two classes of tasks to examine this question: picture naming and color naming. The evidence from both classes of tasks will be reviewed. In addition, a set of studies will be discussed that have investigated bilingual word production using word translation. The chapter concludes with a discussion and account of the speech accents that characterize the speech of the vast majority of non-native speakers.

Bilinguals are generally quite good at avoiding intrusions of the language they currently do not want to use: Code switches into the other language are rare. Conversely, in situations where they need to switch between their two languages, for instance in translation settings, they can do so. These skills, to maintain a language or to switch between languages, are together known as bilingual "language control". Chapter 6 presents various views on how bilinguals exert language control and reviews the evidence for each of them. A central assumption in most of these views is that the activation level of the elements in a bilingual's two language subsets can be regulated such that those of the target language become more activated and those of the non-target language deactivated. The mechanism assumed to take care of these regulatory processes in the most topical of these views is the general executive control system introduced above. The chapter concludes with a discussion of the way control is exerted in what is arguably the most difficult type of linguistic behavior: simultaneous interpreting.

One of the topics discussed in Chapter 7 is language loss, of both the L1 and L2. Two further ones concern aspects of the influence that each of a bilingual's or multilingual's language exerts on the other(s). One of these topics is which one of two earlier languages affects learning a third language most, and why it is that earlier languages have differential effects on learning a new one. The second concerns the influence of later languages on the first, in the domains of phonology, grammar, and semantics. The remaining parts of this chapter deal with effects of bilingualism on non-linguistic cognition; specifically, on thought, general intelligence, and cognitive control.

Finally, Chapter 8 deals with the study of the bilingual brain. One of the questions examined in this chapter is what parts of the brain are recruited when bilinguals process language, and whether these might differ from those involved when monolinguals process language. It is well known that the two hemispheres of the human brain are not equally involved in language processing but that in the vast majority of monolingual language users the left hemisphere dominates language processing. This is known as left "lateralization" of language. One of the specific questions addressed in this chapter is whether language might be lateralized differently in bilinguals, as some researchers have assumed to be the case. Furthermore, this chapter reviews studies that have tried to identify the brain structures involved in bilingual language control—the ability of bilinguals to maintain the use of one language if such is demanded by the current circumstances and to switch between the two languages under circumstances where switching is required. As we shall see, this line of research suggests that bilinguals exert language control by exploiting the brain structures that subserve general executive control.

2

Early Bilingualism and Age of Acquisition Effects on (First and) Second Language Learning

INTRODUCTION AND PREVIEW

On the face of it, acquiring a language is an easy thing to do. After all, it does not take long before newborn children start to utter the sounds of their native language and, some months later, their first words. Yet linguistic competence requires the mastery of an extremely complex linguistic system which appeals to many sub-skills that all exploit a large database of knowledge. Tens of speech sounds and thousands of words must be learned, as well as phonological and grammatical constraints on combining and ordering them in words and sentences and, ultimately, ways of organizing sentences in coherent discourse. Word learning on its own is already a multifaceted process, involving the learning of the words' phonological forms (that is, their sound patterns), the awareness that these forms carry meaning, the linking of the sound patterns to meaning, and the understanding that words generally refer to whole classes of objects, people,

and events rather than to individual entities and that they can do so even under circumstances in which the words' referents are not actually present in the environment.

One feature of the speech signal in particular complicates language learning; namely, the fact that the primary meaning-bearing components of language, its words, do not occur as discrete packages of information in the speech signal. Visual records of speech fragments produced by means of a technical device called a **spectrograph** show that the breaks in a speech signal do not correspond straightforwardly to word boundaries. Often the pauses in the signal fall within words and, conversely, many boundaries between words are not marked by a clear speech break. Pauses in the speech signal are thus unreliable cues for developing a lexicon. A further cumbersome characteristic of the speech input is that one and the same **phoneme** (and, as a consequence, one and the same word) is realized in an endless variety of ways in actual speech, depending on speaker characteristics (e.g., male or female; child or adult), speech rate, and the adjacent sounds. How then does the infant manage to unearth the relevant phonemes and the first words from this noisy input so soon after birth, and what are the skills and mechanisms that get vocabulary acquisition going? These questions become all the more intriguing when we realize that newborn children growing up in a bilingual environment do not take much longer to acquire the phoneme inventories and some vocabulary of both ambient languages than it takes infants growing up in a monolingual context to acquire the corresponding knowledge structures of their one native language.

Since Eimas and his associates introduced a sensitive new technique to assess the ability of infants to discriminate speech sounds (Eimas, 1974, 1975; Eimas, Siqueland, Jusczyk, & Vigorito, 1971), and other researchers developed clever new versions of this technique, our knowledge about the way infants gradually come to master the sound system(s) of their native language(s) and, in parallel to this development, start to recognize and produce words, has tremendously increased. The technique in question will be explained next, in the Methods and Tasks section, together with other methods that are used to investigate this chapter's themes: early bilingualism and **age of acquisition** (AoA) **effects** on (first and) second language learning and proficiency. In the first part of this chapter current insights into the development of language in monolingual- and bilingual-to-be infants will be presented. The focus will be on phonological and early lexical development as manifested in speech perception tasks; that is, tasks that assess the infants' ability to recognize phonemes and sound patterns that correspond to words. In addition some attention will be devoted to the development of the ability to link word forms to meaning. The reason for dealing primarily with speech perception, not speech production, is that choices had to be made and that especially the research area of infant speech perception has recently witnessed substantial progress. The insight that speech perception and speech production do not develop independently from one another, but that the infant's gradual advances in

native language speech perception bootstrap speech production, is another reason to highlight infant speech perception.

Whereas the first part of this chapter examines early bilingualism during development and, accordingly, the participants in the studies to be reviewed are always infants or toddlers, the second part compares second language ability in "early" and "late" adult bilinguals; that is, in adults who began to learn their second language when young or relatively late in life. Innumerable studies have addressed the question of whether and how the age at which one starts to acquire a second language affects the level of proficiency that is ultimately reached in it. I will organize the discussion of this work around the popular "critical period hypothesis", which holds that during some bounded period early in life humans possess a special sensitivity for linguistic input and that for a language to be acquired fully its acquisition should coincide with this period of heightened sensitivity. The critical period hypothesis applies to the learning of any language, including the first, and studies that examined the effect of acquisition age on first language learning will also be discussed in this section. Whereas the chapter's first part focuses on phonology and early lexical skills, its second part primarily deals with grammar. The question of how age of acquisition affects second-language speech accent will be dealt with in Chapter 5.

In addition to examining infants or toddlers versus adults, a further difference between the studies covered in this chapter's two main sections concerns the type of early bilinguals that are examined in both areas of study. The participants in many of the developmental bilingual studies are infants who are exposed to bilingual input from birth, a situation that has been coined **bilingual first language acquisition** (BFLA) or "2L1" by Meisel (1989, 2001) and that is also referred to as **simultaneous bilingualism**. The development of bilingualism in these children, who can be said to have two native languages, differs from early second language acquisition or **sequential** (or "successive") **bilingualism**, where the development of the native language is well under way the moment the child gets introduced to a new, the second, language. The early bilingual adults partaking in studies that look at the role of age of acquisition on ultimate attainment are typically of this kind. In sequential bilingualism, by the time the child is first exposed to the second language, phonological, lexical, and grammatical knowledge about the native language will partly be in place already, the more of it the later the child starts receiving bilingual input. This situation is known to give rise to transfer between the two languages and, especially, from the native onto the second. On the other hand, in BFLA the two languages appear to develop relatively independently from one another (e.g., De Houwer, 2005; Genesee, Nicoladis, & Paradis, 1995; Meisel, 2001). A further difference between BFLA and early sequential bilingualism relates to the fact that, in tandem with increasing brain weight, general cognitive skills improve during maturation. The implication is that also as a consequence of improved general cognition, second language development in sequential child bilingualism proceeds differently from language acquisition in BFLA. Age-related differences in cognitive skills—both the improvement thereof during maturation and cognitive decline beyond a certain age—should also be taken into account when evaluating the findings from studies on the role of age of acquisition on ultimate L2 attainment.

METHODS AND TASKS

The primary research method used to assess the speech perception abilities of newborn children makes use of the fact that babies pay more attention to novel stimuli, visual and aural, than to stimuli they have perceived before (e.g., Melson & McCall, 1970). This phenomenon was exploited in the development of the **habituation paradigm** or **familiarization paradigm** in which, in the habituation phase, young infants are repeatedly presented with one and the same stimulus, say a speech sound. When this sound is first presented, it will arouse the infant's attention. Attention will subsequently gradually lessen during the

habituation phase and eventually be back at some low baseline level. A test phase then follows in which a new speech sound is presented which, if the difference between the new and old stimulus is detected at all, will arouse the child's attention again. A control condition may also be included in which one and the same sound is presented during habituation and test. In this condition attention should remain at the same low level as reached at the end of habituation.

To apply this paradigm in the study of speech perception in babies a technique is required that is sensitive enough to detect fluctuations in attention in children this young. One such technique measures the rate at which infants suck on an artificial pacifier, a high rate indexing attention and a low rate indexing that they have lost interest. Eimas et al. (1971) first used this technique in an experimental procedure (called the **high-amplitude sucking paradigm**, HAS) that they developed to find out whether young infants, just as adults, perceive speech sounds in phonemic categories. This phenomenon, called **categorical perception**, implies that listeners can hear the difference between two speech sounds that represent two different phonemes but fail to discriminate a pair of speech sounds that are variants of one and the same phoneme. This even holds if the acoustic differences between the two phonemes on the one hand and the two variants of one phoneme on the other hand are equally large. Figure 2.1 illustrates the HAS paradigm, with the infants' sucking rate on the y-axis and the time from the start of a trial's habituation phase on the x-axis. In the example the trial's total time lasts 9 minutes and consists of 5 minutes of habituation followed by 4 minutes of testing. The dashed line represents the moment at which, following habituation, a new speech sound is presented to an experimental group of infants but not to a control group. Figure 2.1 shows a situation in which the experimental group noticed the difference between the speech sounds presented during habituation and testing, as evidenced by the increased sucking rate, indexing renewed attention, upon the presentation of the new sound.

Employing this procedure, Eimas and his associates (1971) demonstrated categorical

FIGURE 2.1

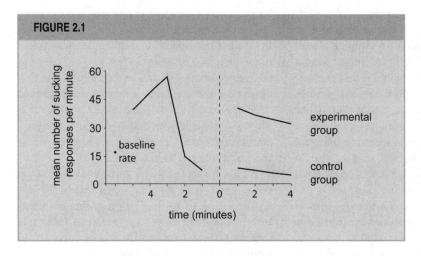

Mean number of sucking responses as a function of time since trial onset and experimental condition. Total trial time is 9 minutes. The dashed line indicates the moment the experimental group is presented with a new speech sound. The baseline sucking rate is also indicated. Adapted from Eimas et al. (1971) with permission from AAAS.

FIGURE 2.2

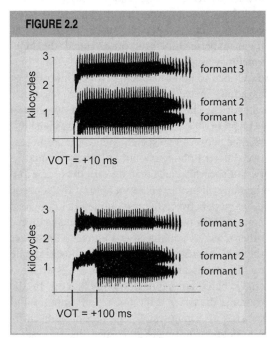

Spectrograms of two synthetic plosives, one with a VOT of +10 ms, the other with a VOT of +100 ms. The formants are bands of relatively intense acoustic energy in the speech spectrum. From Eimas et al. (1971). Reprinted with permission from AAAS.

perception of (synthetic, machine-made) **plosives** that only differed from one another in **voice onset time** (VOT) in 1- and 4-month-old infants. VOT is the time between the release of the air and the moment the vocal cords start to vibrate when a plosive is uttered. It is illustrated in Figure 2.2, which shows **spectrograms** of two synthetic plosives, one with a VOT of +10 ms and the second with a VOT of +100 ms. A spectrogram is a visual record of a speech fragment produced by a spectrograph and shows an analysis of the speech fragment in the constituent sound waves and how they develop over time. The horizontal and vertical axes of a spectrogram represent time and frequency of the constituent sound waves, respectively. The intensity of the speech sound at any moment in time is indicated by the degree of blackness of the marks on the paper— the higher the intensity, the blacker the markings. The black bands in Figure 2.2, called **formants**, thus represent frequency bands of relatively intense acoustic energy in the speech spectrum.

The investigators found that the sucking rate increased at test when the two plosives presented during habituation and at test, respectively, had VOTs that are contrastive in English (which means that two plosives that only differ in this one respect represent different phonemes, in the present case the phonemes /p/ and /b/). The increased sucking rate at test indicates that the infants could discriminate between these two plosives. In contrast, the sucking rate remained low at test when, again, two different plosives were presented during habituation and at test, however the two now had VOT values that are not contrastive in English but are manifestations of one and the same phoneme. This suggests that the infants failed to discriminate between this pair of plosives. Importantly, this result occurred despite the fact that the VOT difference between the non-contrastive pair of plosives was equally large as the difference between the plosives of the contrastive pair. In subsequent studies Eimas generalized these findings to other so-called "minimally contrastive" pairs of consonants, such as a contrast between plosives in their **place of articulation** (Eimas, 1974; e.g., /p/ versus /t/) and the contrast between /r/ and /l/ (Eimas, 1975). Because consonants cannot be uttered separately from a vowel, in all experiments of this type the unit of presentation is a **syllable**, consisting of the critical consonant and a vowel, the latter being identical for the two consonants in a contrasting pair. For instance, the contrast between /p/ and /b/ is tested with the synthesized syllables /pa/ and /ba/.

Infants' increased attention to novel stimuli can also be detected with other experimental procedures. One is the **heart-rate paradigm**, which exploits the fact that an increase in attention is accompanied by an increase in heartbeat (e.g., Lasky, Syrdal-Lasky, & Klein, 1975). Changes in a cardiogram that occur the moment a new speech sound is presented thus suggest that the infant has noticed the change. A technique that has more recently become popular is a visual fixation habituation procedure sometimes called the **preferential looking technique**. It makes use of the fact that infants look at the place where an interesting new sound comes from and stop looking when the novelty of the sound wears off. As in the high-amplitude sucking and heart-rate paradigms, the infants are generally first familiarized with one type of speech stimulus, for instance a phoneme (embedded in a syllable, e.g., /ba/). The speech stimulus is accompanied by some visual stimulus, typically presented on a TV screen, to attract the infant's attention. The source of the speech stimulus is located near the TV screen. The infant's looking time at the screen is registered for each trial—a trial consisting of the repeated presentation of the speech stimulus. The underlying assumption is that looking time is a reflection of listening time which, in turn, is a reflection of attention time, and that as a consequence of habituation the looking time will

decrease when the infant gets used to the concurrent speech sound. (Because looking time serves as a measure of listening time and it is the latter that the researcher is interested in, the technique is also called the **preferential listening technique**). At the onset of the familiarization phase the looking time per trial will be relatively long because of the novelty of the presented speech sound. The habituation phase is ended the moment looking time drops below some preset minimum duration. At that point either one of two new speech stimuli is presented; for instance, a new variant of the phoneme presented during habituation or an exemplar of a different phoneme. An increase in looking time indicates discrimination between the sounds presented during habituation and test. If looking time does not recover at test one may conclude that the test stimulus is not perceived as different from the stimulus presented during habituation.

This general procedure has not only been used to chart the speech sounds that infants can and cannot discriminate at various ages, but also to discover whether and when infants can discriminate between languages. It has also been used to find out how word learning in infants comes about, including the prerequisite ability to segment the speech stream into words (see Werker & Byers-Heinlein, 2008, for a review). Some of the studies that employed the preferential looking paradigm will be presented in more detail in the sections to come. As you will see, the exact procedure used differs between studies. For instance, the stimuli presented during familiarization, if uttered by real speakers and not generated by a speech synthesizer, may be delivered by one and the same speaker or by different speakers. The latter procedure mimics the fact that in natural speech different instantiations of one and the same linguistic unit typically differ somewhat from one another due to speaker variability and co-articulation. A further difference between studies using this paradigm concerns the duration of the familiarization phase. In the habituation procedure as described above the infant controls the duration of this phase: Familiarization stops the moment looking (= listening) time drops below some predetermined level. In another version of the procedure the duration of familiarization is fixed for all participants within a study. Depending on the duration of this fixed period and, thus, the number of exposures to the familiarization stimulus, the infant may show a listening preference for the novel or for the familiar stimulus. Specifically, it has been noticed that after a relatively short familiarization period the infant may show a familiarity preference at test, listening longer to the familiar stimulus than to the novel stimulus. In contrast, the infant may show a novelty preference after a relatively long familiarization procedure, listening longer to the novel stimulus (Saffran, 2001). But the crucial finding in these studies is the occurrence of a difference in listening time for familiar and novel stimuli, not its direction. A final difference between studies to mention here is that the preferential looking procedure (or any other of the above habituation procedures) does not always require an initial familiarization phase as part of the experiment, because prior linguistic experience in a natural language environment may also serve as the familiarization phase. For instance, to examine whether, say, 10-month-old infants recognize particular frequently occurring words, one may simply compare listening times, as assessed by means of the preferential looking technique, for these words and a set of words unlikely to be known at that age.

A related technique is the **head-turn procedure**, which also comes in various versions and was originally developed by Kemler-Nelson et al. (1995). This time, speech sounds are emitted from *two* loudspeakers positioned left-front and right-front of the infant and, as in the above paradigms, a test phase is preceded by a familiarization phase. In the familiarization phase of the original version the infant learns to turn his or her head towards a light that flashes near the one or the other loudspeaker while a stimulus set is emitted continuously from both loudspeakers. A familiarization trial starts with the flashing of a light that is centered between the two speakers and extinguishes when the infant looks in the direction of this light. At that moment the side light near one of the speakers begins to flash. After the infant has made a criterion head turn of

30 degrees toward this light it continues flashing until the infant looks away from it again for a certain duration. At this moment the trial ends. After familiarization a test phase follows wherein stimuli are played from only one loudspeaker at the time and this time stimulus presentation is contingent on the infant's behavior: When the infant turns his or her head toward the flashing side light, a stimulus is presented from the loudspeaker on that side. The presentation of the stimulus and the flashing of the light both stop when the infant fails to maintain the head turn for a predetermined amount of time. The stimuli presented at test are either the ones presented during familiarization (or related to them in some way or other) or unfamiliar ones. If the test phase shows a difference in looking (= listening) time between the stimuli presented duration familiarization on the one hand and the new stimuli on the other hand it can be concluded that the infant notices the difference between them. This procedure has also successfully been used with stimuli of various kinds: phonemes, words, and complete sentences.

To examine the development of a particular linguistic ability a cross-sectional design is typically employed in which groups of infants are selected that differ in age but are matched with respect to relevant background variables such as the parents' socioeconomic status. The studies that focus on language development in bilingual (more precisely, bilingual-to-be) children typically include monolingual (to-be) control groups so that differences in the language development of monolingual and bilingual children can be assessed. Incidentally, "monolingual" in these studies does not always imply that the children in question are exclusively exposed to their native language, nor does "bilingual" imply that the children concerned receive balanced bilingual input. Many of the bilingual studies are carried out in bilingual communities where language-pure exposure does not occur. For instance, in Wales some exposure to English cannot be prevented so that children from Welsh monolingual families are exposed to some English as well. Similarly, in Catalonia exposure to Spanish cannot be completely prevented. What "monolingual" means in these studies is that exposure to the one and the other language is extremely unbalanced, say 95% versus 5%. Instead, "bilingual" means that the dual language exposure is more balanced, say minimally 40% for each language.

A requirement of many of the studies that focus on vocabulary development is that information is available on how many and what words are likely to be known by the participating infants or toddlers. This information is needed to select the experimental materials and to properly match bilingual infants to monolingual controls. Instruments that are often used for these purposes are the infant and toddler versions of the American-English MacArthur Communicative Development Inventory (CDI; Fenson et al., 1993, 2000) adapted to the language under study (see e.g., De Houwer, Bornstein, & De Coster, 2006). A CDI concerns a list of words arranged in various categories that the participants' parents or other caregivers check off, indicating which ones they believe the child understands, or understands and produces. In bilingual studies CDIs in both languages are used and dominance differences in lexical knowledge between the participants' two languages can be established. Furthermore, Total Conceptual Vocabulary size (TCV) in bilingual infants can be determined by first calculating the sum of the words reported to be known in each of the languages separately and then subtracting from this summed score the number of translation-equivalent pairs among this total set (e.g., Conboy & Mills, 2006; Pearson & Fernández, 1994). A procedural decision that must be made prior to running an experiment is whether the stimulus materials will be delivered in **child directed speech** (CDS or **motherese**) or in speech with which adults are typically addressed. CDS is characterized by exaggerated intonation and clear articulation, is spoken slowly and, if the stimuli concern sentences at all, the sentences are typically very short.

In addition to using the above behavioral methods, the linguistic skills of infants and toddlers can, and have, also been studied by registering "event-related potentials" (**ERPs**) while they are presented with language materials of some type. This technique is described more completely in later chapters (Chapters 4 and 8). Here it suffices to say that the presentation of a particular stimulus induces small voltage changes in the electroencephalogram (**EEG**). These voltage changes, which can be positive (indicated by P) or negative (indicated by N), are the ERPs. One and the same stimulus can give rise to several ERPs that take different amounts of time from stimulus onset to develop. An ERP is often named after its polarity (that is, whether it is positive or negative) and its "latency", the time it takes to develop. For instance, the P200 is an ERP with a positive polarity that takes about 200 ms following stimulus onset to develop. ERPs are very sensitive measures of cognitive activity, sometimes pointing up some ongoing cognitive process that behavioral measures fail to detect.

Obviously, the central manipulation in studies examining the relation between the onset age of L2 acquisition and L2 language proficiency is the age of acquisition manipulation: Groups of participants are tested on a specific linguistic ability, say L2 grammar, the different groups consisting of participants that first started to learn the L2 within different age ranges (e.g., 3–6, 13–16, and 23–26 years). Other studies have not compared the performance of discrete age of acquisition groups but have correlated age of acquisition and performance scores of a large number of individuals that together cover a large part of the whole age of acquisition spectrum. Ideally, all participants in these studies have used the language under study a large number of years so that it can safely be assumed they have reached their ultimate level of proficiency in it and do not still qualify as learners. Furthermore, wherever possible potentially confounding variables, such as the chronological age of the test takers, their length of residence in the L2-speaking country, their educational level, and their amount of daily L2 use, should be controlled for. To examine age of acquisition effects on first language learning, the linguistic skills of deaf people can be assessed while varying the age at which they first started to have full access to a language, typically sign language. A second method that has been used is to study the rare cases of people deprived of language during childhood because of physical isolation from other human beings.

EARLY BILINGUALISM IN DEVELOPMENT

Categorical speech perception in infants

The introduction of the high-amplitude sucking paradigm and the related techniques described above has boosted research into infants' perceptual abilities and these efforts have been rewarded with a greatly increased understanding of how speech perception develops during the first year of life. An important first finding was already briefly described above—that, just as adults, infants exhibit categorical perception of speech sounds. Eimas and his collaborators (1971) presented their 1- and 4-month-old infant participants, born of English-speaking parents, with a number of machine-synthesized instances of the **bilabial** plosives /p/ and /b/ (with a vowel added onto the critical plosive), manipulating the plosives' VOT value. The VOT values included in their study were −20 ms, 0 ms, +20 ms, +40 ms, +60 ms, and +80 ms. The minus and plus signs indicate that the vocal cords start to vibrate before and after the moment the air is released, respectively. A VOT of 0 ms indicates that the release of the air and the onset of the vocal cords' vibration coincide. Earlier studies had shown that adult speakers of English identify bilabial plosives with VOT values below +25 ms as /b/ and those with VOT values above +25 ms as /p/. In other words, the first three of the above six speech sounds are perceived as voiced /b/, the last three as voiceless /p/.

The infants within each age group were divided in three subgroups. One subgroup was familiarized with the +20 ms stimulus and, after habituation, tested with the +40 ms stimulus. The stimuli presented during habituation and test thus fell on opposite sides of the adult phonemic boundary. The habituation and test stimuli presented to a second subgroup both fell on the same side of the phonemic boundary (−20 ms and

0 ms, or +40 ms and +60 ms). A third subgroup was presented with exactly the same sound during habituation and test. The important finding was that only the first of these subgroups of infants, in both age groups, showed release from habituation at test, as evidenced by an increase in sucking rate the moment they were presented with the test stimulus. This finding suggests first, that, just as adult listeners, infants this young perceive speech sounds in categories, only detecting differences between speech sounds that are linguistically meaningful. Second, it suggests that the boundary between the two phoneme categories that are perceived as different from one another coincides with the adult boundary.

The study of Eimas et al. (1971) inspired many new ones testing other minimal contrasts between speech sounds, including the two already mentioned above: between plosives that only differ in their place of articulation (e.g., /p/ versus /t/, both voiceless; Eimas, 1974) and between the /l/ and /r/ (Eimas, 1975). These studies have revealed that infants can discriminate many speech sound categories, including these two further distinctions tested by Eimas and his collaborators and differences between vowel categories (e.g., Trehub, 1973). Other discriminations appear more difficult for infants this young, such as the minimal contrast between pairs of **fricatives** such as /v/ and /f/ or /z/ and /s/.

Because of the tender age of the participants in these studies it has been suggested that the ability to perceive speech sounds in phonemic categories is innate. If correct, all infants should initially be sensitive to the same phoneme boundaries irrespective of the language that surrounds them. Interestingly, the number of the critical boundaries on a given speech dimension, and hence the number of phonemic categories, differs between languages. In a cross-linguistic study of 11 natural languages, Lisker and Abramson (1964) showed that some languages cut up the VOT continuum into three categories, distinguishing between speech sounds with a "short voicing lag" (where the vocal cords start to vibrate very soon after the air is released), those with a "long voicing lag" (where they start to vibrate relatively late after air release), and those with a "voicing lead" (where the vocal cords start to vibrate relatively long before air release). The authors showed that some of the examined languages exploit all three of these VOT values, whereas others only exploit two of them. In the latter type of language the intermediate short voicing lag always occurred, accompanied by either the long voicing lag or the voicing lead (the latter occurring, for instance, in Tai, where a boundary exists somewhere between VOT values of −60 ms and −20 ms, a contrast that is not distinctive in English). In addition to a difference in the number of phoneme boundaries, the exact locus of the boundary or boundaries differs between languages. For instance, whereas the boundary between voiceless and voiced consonants lies near a VOT value of +25 ms in English, in Spanish it lies somewhere between the values of −20 ms and +20 ms. In other words, a voiceless plosive is spoken with a longer VOT in English than in Spanish.

Using the heart-rate paradigm, Lasky et al. (1975) addressed the question of which contrasts on a VOT continuum ranging from −60 ms to +60 ms Spanish infants, varying in age between 4 and 6.5 months, could detect. The results showed they could detect a difference between a VOT of −60 ms and one of −20 ms, suggesting that they were sensitive to the Tai boundary. In addition, they could detect a difference between VOT values of +20 ms and +60 ms, demonstrating sensitivity to the English boundary between voiceless and voiced speech sounds. Interestingly, when the habituation and test stimuli had VOT values of −20 ms and +20 ms, respectively, no increase in heartbeat was observed at test, suggesting that the difference, contrastive in the participants' native language Spanish, could not be detected yet. This combination of findings suggests, first, that the ability to discriminate between contrastive speech sounds is indeed innate, because how else can it be explained that contrasts that are linguistically relevant in some languages (here, Tai and English) but that do not occur in the native language (here Spanish) can be perceived at all? Second, it suggests that this predisposition does not extend to all of the contrasts occurring in natural languages, because if it would, the native Spanish contrast between VOT −20 ms and VOT +20 ms should also have been perceived. The fact that it was not indicates that in acquiring the relevant phoneme contrasts of the native language there is a role for learning through language exposure as well. A third conclusion to draw from the above results is that 6.5 months of exposure to the ambient language (here Spanish) does not suffice for (all) of the native language's contrasts to be acquired.

The precise nature of the apparently innate ability to perceive a number of phonemic contrasts is a source of dispute among scientists. Some hold the view that the phenomenon of categorical perception only applies to language and not to other forms of perception and that it is unique to humans, and does not apply to other species (e.g., Eimas & Miller, 1991). This view instantiates the more general view that the linguistic ability of *Homo sapiens* is enabled by a special innate language faculty that is independent of general cognition. Other scholars assume that categorical perception is not unique to language and the human race but results from general perceptual abilities of the auditory system of mammals. These scientists' reason for taking this stance is that categorical perception in humans has also been observed for non-speech sounds (Jusczyk, Pisoni, Walley, & Murray, 1980) and that non-human mammals such as chinchillas and macaques have been shown to perceive the same speech contrasts as humans do (e.g., Kuhl & Miller, 1978). As argued by Kuhl (1986, 2004), the match between the boundaries between phonetic categories in natural languages on the one hand, and the way humans and non-humans categorize speech sounds on the other, is not accidental. She assumed that during their development the world's languages have primarily exploited the auditory discontinuities to which the mammalian auditory system is especially sensitive, showing a tendency to place the phoneme boundaries at the points of highest auditory sensitivity. In agreement with this view, and getting back to the studies of Eimas et al. (1971) and Lasky et al. (1975) presented above, Gerken (1994) hypothesized that on the voicing continuum English has exploited the peak of highest auditory sensitivity of the auditory system in creating the phoneme boundary between voiced and voiceless plosives (e.g., /b/ versus /p/) and that this is why infants in both an English and a Spanish environment are sensitive to the English boundary. For one reason or other, during the development of Spanish this peak of highest sensitivity was not used to create the boundary between voiced and voiceless plosives but, instead, a point of lesser sensitivity. This is the reason why 4- and 6.5-month-old Spanish infants do not yet perceive the Spanish contrast. Further exposure to Spanish is required for them to discover the critical boundary.

The above discussion leads to two questions that have engaged researchers in this area of study after the discovery of the phenomenon of categorical perception and its constraints: First, do humans continue to perceive phonetic distinctions that are contrastive in some languages but not in the ambient language, and if not, at what age does the ability to perceive these contrasts decline? For example, are English adults still sensitive to the Tai boundary on the VOT continuum despite the fact that it is not distinctive in English? Second, how long does it take humans to develop sensitivity for contrasts that are linguistically meaningful in the ambient language but that are not innate? For example, when do Spanish infants become sensitive to the boundary between VOTs of −20 ms and +20 ms, which they do not yet perceive at 6.5 months of age but will have to learn at some point in order to come to perceive and produce Spanish properly?

A third question is particularly relevant in view of our special interest in bilingualism: Does the learning of contrasts that are linguistically meaningful in the ambient language(s) but not innate, and the unlearning of innate contrasts that are not functional in the ambient language(s), differ between children growing up monolingual and those growing up bilingual? Evidently, children growing up in a bilingual environment must come to acquire the sound systems of both their native languages, a state of affairs that may delay the acquisition process and especially so if the two systems exploit different phoneme boundaries. The double acquisition

process in children growing up bilingual may, in addition to delaying the learning process, lead to two systems that differ from the corresponding systems of monolingual speakers. Alternatively, the two emerging systems may resemble the corresponding monolingual speakers' systems but interact with one another during speech perception and production (see pp. 363–365 for evidence from production studies). Early (and late) sequential bilingualism confronts the special problem that non-native phonetic contrasts that were initially perceived but subsequently lost may have to be relearned because they are meaningful in the second language.

A substantial amount of research has addressed the first two of the above questions. In the next section I will first outline the major results of this work and briefly discuss some of the mechanisms that have been proposed to account for the perceptual changes involved. Next, I will address the third question, discussing the little bilingual work there is in more detail.

The unlearning of non-native phoneme contrasts and the learning of native phoneme contrasts

The collected studies show that the unlearning of non-native phoneme contrasts and the learning of native phoneme contrasts that are not perceived from the outset go hand in hand, and that many of the perceptual changes involved occur during the first year of life. Table 2.1 presents the various developmental steps encompassed in the "universal language timeline" of speech perception development as envisioned by Kuhl (2004). According to this timeline infants under about 6 months of age can perceive phoneme contrasts of all languages (but, as we have seen, not necessarily *all* contrasts of all languages). After 6 months of age the perception of non-native contrasts declines and the ability to perceive contrasts specific to the native language increases (e.g., Werker, Gilbert, Humphrey, & Tees, 1981; Werker & Tees, 1984). The latter happens sooner for vowels than for consonants. The increase in native language perceptual ability not only involves the learning of contrasts not

TABLE 2.1

Universal language timeline of speech perception and speech production development

Speech perception	Speech production
0–5½ months: Infants discriminate phonetic contrasts of all languages	**0–3 months:** Infants produce non-speech sounds
	3 months: Infants produce vowel-like sounds
From 6 months: Statistical learning (distributional frequencies) and language-specific perception for vowels	
	7 months: Canonical babbling
From 8 months: Statistical learning (transitional probabilities) and detection of typical stress patterns in words	
From 9 months: Recognition of language-specific sound combinations	
	From 10 months: Language-specific speech production
From 11 months: Decline in foreign language consonant perception and increase in native language consonant perception	
	12 months: First words produced

Adapted from Kuhl (2004).

present initially but also the sharpening of the boundaries between the native phonetic categories that are present from the outset (see e.g., Kuhl, Williams, Lacerda, Stevens, & Lindblom, 1992). By the time infants are about 11 months of age they have largely lost the ability to discriminate between pairs of contrastive foreign speech sounds, especially if they concern consonants, behaving like the adult speech listeners in their language community. Discriminatory ability for foreign language vowel contrasts lasts longer (Polka & Werker, 1994). This develop-

mental pattern has been observed for infants growing up in different language environments and has been tested with a varied set of phoneme contrasts (see Werker, 1989, for a review).

In addition to the points in time at which native and foreign phoneme contrasts start to appear and disappear, respectively, Table 2.1 shows the times at which other perceptual abilities emerge—for instance, the sensitivity to the ambient language's **phonotactics**; that is, the specific sequences of sounds that do and do not occur in the language. Although the developmental change in infants' speech perception is not yet completely understood, it is generally believed that the developing perceptual skills bootstrap language acquisition in general. The fact that landmarks in the development of speech production during the first year of life closely follow specific perceptual landmarks (see Table 2.1) supports this idea. A final point stressed by Kuhl (2004) and other authors (see e.g., Kuhl, Tsao, & Liu, 2003; Sebastián-Gallés & Bosch, 2005) is that the decline in infants' sensitivity to non-native contrasts and the increase in sensitivity to native contrasts both result from perceptual reorganization processes caused by linguistic experience. In other words, the decreasing sensitivity of infants to foreign phonetic contrasts also indexes growth in phonetic development.

Still, linguistic experience does not result in the loss of discrimination ability for *all* non-native contrasts. The earliest study to demonstrate a lasting ability to discriminate between particular pairs of non-native speech sounds examined the perception of dental versus lateral click consonants in isiZulu, the native language spoken by the Zulu people (Best, McRoberts, & Sithole, 1988). Both English-speaking adults and infants up to 14 months of age (the oldest infants tested) detected the difference between these consonants. Attempts to explain the developmental change in perceiving non-native speech contrasts must take this variability into account. Best and McRoberts (2003) contrasted three such accounts. One of them distinguishes between "fragile" and "robust" contrasts (Burnham, 1986). Robust contrasts involve distinctions that are acoustically salient and common across languages, whereas fragile contrasts are non-salient and occur only rarely in the languages of the world. According to this view, the ability to discriminate robust contrasts remains intact irrespective of whether they occur in the ambient language. In contrast, fragile contrasts can only be maintained if they occur in the language environment. As noted by Best and McRoberts, a problem with this account is that it is circular, because the notions of fragility and robustness are hard to define independent of the development of the behavioral responses to the contrasts in question (that is, independent of whether or not the contrast continues to be perceived, as suggested by the experimental evidence).

A second account that takes variability in the decline of foreign language phonetic contrasts into consideration (Tees & Werker, 1984) holds that non-native contrasts continue to be perceived if they occur as **allophones** of one and the same phoneme in the language environment, but are lost if they do not. Best and McRoberts (2003) queried this account on the basis of counter-evidence. Recall that in Spanish the boundary between voiced and voiceless plosives (for instance, between /b/ and /p/) lies between VOTs of −20 ms and +20 ms whereas in English it lies around a VOT of +25 ms. Yet Spanish voiced and voiceless plosives do occur in English, but as allophones of one and the same (voiced) phoneme. Despite their occurrence as allophones, English listeners have been shown to experience problems in discriminating between pairs of Spanish voiced and voiceless plosives.

The third account of why the sensitivity to non-native contrasts is variable across such contrasts is framed within the perceptual assimilation model (PAM) developed by Best (e.g., Best, 1994; Best et al., 1988). The central premise of the model, from which it derives its name, is that "mature listeners have a strong tendency to perceptually assimilate non-native phones to the native phonemes they perceive as most similar" (Best & McRoberts, 2003, p. 186). The model predicts that the discrimination of non-native contrasts depends on the way the two elements in a contrasting pair are assimilated to the extant native phonemic categories. If both are assimi-

lated to one and the same native category and, at the same time, they are considered to be equally good representatives of this category, the two elements in the non-native contrastive pair are perceived as similar to one another; in other words, they cannot be distinguished from one another. If instead one element of the contrasting pair is assimilated to one native phonemic category whereas the other is assimilated to a different native category, discrimination is easy and performance near ceiling. An intermediate situation arises if the two elements in the non-native pair are assimilated to one and the same native category but at the same time are not considered as equally good exemplars of the native category. In this case discrimination ability lies in between that in the above two cases: Sometimes the two phones in a non-native contrastive pair are regarded as similar to one another; at other times they are judged to be dissimilar. A special feature of PAM is that it defines perceptual similarity in terms of the way movements of the articulatory apparatus shape the speech signal. Specifically, it is assumed that sounds that are produced by similar movements of the articulatory organs are perceived as similar.

Employing the visual fixation habituation procedure described earlier (p. 15), Best and McRoberts (2003) examined the predictions of PAM regarding the perception of a set of non-native consonant contrasts (occurring in isiZulu and in Tigrinya, a language spoken in Ethiopia) by 6–8- and 10–12-month-old English-learning infants. The specific hypothesis tested was that the ability to discriminate non-native contrasts remains intact if the two contrastive speech sounds are produced by different articulatory organs (e.g., lips, larynx, and velum) but that it declines if one and the same articulatory organ is involved in producing them. The results confirmed this hypothesis by showing that infants in both age groups could detect the difference between contrastive non-native sounds produced by different articulatory organs and that discrimination of these contrasts was equally good in both groups of infants. In contrast, the younger group outperformed the older group on the contrasts that involved a single articulatory organ, suggesting a decline in performance with aging.

Apart from once again demonstrating that the decline in discriminating between non-native contrastive speech sounds is not a uniform phenomenon affecting all non-native contrasts equally, these results also support PAM's tenet that speech perception and speech learning exploits articulatory information in addition to acoustic information. As assumed by the authors, attending to the articulatory gestures produced by native speakers provides infants (with intact eyesight) with an additional, visual, source of information next to the acoustic information during speech learning. This hypothesis is supported by the well-known finding that infants are sensitive to the congruence or incongruence between talking faces on the one hand and audible speech signals on the other (e.g., Kuhl & Meltzoff, 1982; Rosenblum, Schmuckler, & Johnson, 1997). It is also consistent with the observation that 4- and 6-month-old infants from monolingual homes can discriminate between their native language and a non-native language just by looking at silent video clips of speakers reciting sentences in two different languages (Weikum et al., 2007). At 8 months they have lost this ability, while bilingual-to-be infants tested on their two native languages exhibit it at both 6 and 8 months (they were not tested at 4 months). Of course, lip reading in the deaf also corroborates the hypothesis.

Best and McRoberts (2003) thus demonstrated that the developmental decline in perceiving foreign language contrasts is not a unitary phenomenon but depends on specific acoustic/articulatory characteristics of the foreign sounds involved. A study by Rivera-Gaxiola, Silva-Pereyra, and Kuhl (2005) goes one step further by showing that the discrimination of specific non-native contrasts, which at first sight seems to be lost, still appears to be intact at some level. Reviewing the literature, these authors observed that event-related potentials (ERPs) provide a more sensitive marker of speech perception abilities than do the common behavioral measures such as looking time, head turning, or sucking rate. This is suggested by the fact that a

couple of studies testing the perceptual abilities of adults have shown evidence of non-discrimination of non-native contrasts when behavioral testing methods were used, whereas the same participants demonstrated the ability to still perceive these contrasts when ERPs served as the measurement technique. Conversely, studies in which the perception of new speech sounds is being trained show evidence of speech sound learning in the ERPs earlier on during training than behavioral measures do. In other words, ERP measurements suggest that the insensitivity to non-native contrasts sets in later, and the sensitivity to new sounds earlier, than previously thought on the basis of just the behavioral data. Accordingly, the authors hypothesized that the above infant studies, which all employed behavioral measures, might have underestimated the longevity of the ability to perceive non-native contrasts and overestimated the time it takes to learn not-innate native contrasts.

To test this possibility, Rivera-Gaxiola et al. (2005) examined infants' discrimination of native and non-native speech contrasts by means of the ERP technique. The participants in this study were American infants tested twice, at 7 months and 11 months of age. At both moments in time they were presented with (many instances of) three consonant-vowel syllables differing in VOT and perceived as either /da/ or /ta/, the syllables' VOT values being −24 ms, +12 ms, and +46 ms. As we have seen before, the boundary between voiced and voiceless consonants differs between Spanish and English: It falls in between VOTs of −24 ms and +12 ms in Spanish but between VOTs of +12 ms and +46 ms in English. In other words, the syllable with a VOT of +12 ms is voiceless in Spanish but voiced in English. The experimental procedure used concerned a "double-oddball" paradigm in which the ambiguous +12 ms VOT syllable was presented as the "standard" stimulus 80% of the time and each of the remaining two "deviant" stimuli were presented 10% of the time, the presentation order being randomized. The critical question was whether and at what age the infants could distinguish between the standard on the one hand and one or both deviants (the "oddballs") on the other hand, as evidenced by differences between the brain responses to the standard and deviants. A difference between the ERPs to the +12 ms standard and the +46 ms deviant would suggest sensitivity to the native (English) contrast. A difference between the ERPs to the +12 ms standard and the −24 ms deviant would indicate sensitivity to the non-native (Spanish) contrast.

In agreement with the behavioral data reported in the literature, the analysis of the neural responses of all participants combined suggested that at 7 months of age the infants discriminated both the native and the non-native contrast. This was suggested by a different ERP response to the standard on the one hand and both oddballs on the other hand in a time window from 250 to 550 ms after stimulus onset. Furthermore, a larger amplitude of the ERP to the deviant contrastive in English (+46 ms) at 11 months of age than at 7 months suggested that between 7 and 11 months of age infants' sensitivity to native language contrasts increases. In contrast, at 11 months of age nowhere over the entire time window tested did the ERP signals to the standard (+12 ms) and the non-contrastive deviant (−24 ms) differ significantly from one another, suggesting, again in agreement with the behavioral data, that by this age infants have lost the ability to perceive the non-native contrast. However, further data analysis proved this conclusion premature. During an examination of the ERP signals of the individual participants it became clear that the group as a whole was made up of two subgroups, showing different brain responses to the non-contrastive deviant. In about half of the infants this deviant aroused an early positive component in the ERP signal as compared with the standard, whereas the remainder of the infants showed a slightly later negative component for this deviant. Plausibly, the opposite brain responses to the non-contrastive deviant in these two subgroups cancelled one another out in the overall analysis. An analysis of the data for the separate subgroups of 11-month-olds confirmed this hypothesis by showing that the difference between the brain response to the standard and to the non-contrastive deviant was statistically sig-

nificant for both groups. It thus seems that 11-month-olds have not yet lost the ability to perceive the non-native contrast between Spanish voiced and voiceless plosives. Exactly why the brain responses of 11-month-olds may exhibit this sensitivity in different ways across individual participants is a question that needs further research.

To summarize, loss of the ability to discriminate non-native contrasts is variable, depending on the acoustic and articulatory characteristics of the contrasting speech sounds. In other words, not all non-native phonetic contrasts are lost. Furthermore, discrimination of non-native contrasts that appears to be lost when relatively insensitive behavioral measures are employed may turn out to still be intact when ERP patterns are used to index discrimination ability. Both findings suggest good news for the sequential bilingual, who after first being immersed in an exclusively or predominantly monolingual environment for some time starts to receive input in a second language and must come to learn the sound system of this new language. The residual sensitivity to non-native contrasts as detected by means of the ERP methodology suggests that regaining sensitivity to contrasts apparently lost does not have to start from scratch but may build on dormant memory traces. A final finding emerging from the above studies is that learning the sound system of the ambient language and the unlearning of innate non-native contrasts develop in parallel, suggesting that the language learners' increasing insensitivity to non-native phonetic contrasts is the direct consequence of their exposure to the native language and the phonetic knowledge that emerges from this exposure. According to Rivera-Gaxiola et al. (2005), the process involved in both increased sensitivity to the native language sound system and decreased sensitivity to foreign sounds is a gradually increasing "neural commitment" of brain tissue to the speech patterns of the ambient language. The corollary is a gradual decrease in the availability of neural tissue to subserve non-native speech. As we will see toward the end of this chapter, the ubiquitous age of acquisition effects that are observed in adult second language speakers and in all domains of language—not only in phonology but also in morphology and syntax—have also been attributed to this phenomenon of neural commitment to native language structures.

Early bilingualism: Reversing decreased phonetic sensitivity and doubling phonetic development

As described above, exposure to the native language and the native language phonetic structuring that comes with it lead to a decrease in discriminatory ability for non-native phonetic categories. What are the consequences of this typical phonetic development for the child in a sequential bilingual setting where it first experiences pure monolingual input to which some time later a second language is added? And how does the phonetic development of children growing up under circumstances of simultaneous bilingualism compare to that of children growing up in a monolingual environment? Now that research has revealed the general pattern of monolingual phonetic development, the first studies addressing these questions are beginning to appear. I will discuss these in the present section.

Sequential bilingualism

The consequences for early sequential bilinguals of the reduced ability to discriminate non-native speech sounds from about 11 months of age are obvious: By the time the child is introduced to the second language his or her perceptual ability has started to shift from a language-general to a language-specific pattern of phonetic discrimination and the child has generally become less sensitive to non-native phonetic contrasts, including contrasts that are distinctive in the second language to which the child is now exposed. To come to master the second language, sensitivity to these contrasts will have to be restored. To illustrate, a Japanese-born child who, at 12 months of age, can no longer perceive the difference between /l/ and /r/ (which in Japanese are instances of the same phonetic category) and

is subsequently exposed to L2 English will have to learn to discriminate between /l/ and /r/ again in order not to run into comprehension and production problems in English (where, e.g., *lip* and *rip* or *loom* and *room* mean different things). Plausibly, the later the onset of second language exposure, and therefore the further advanced native language phonetic development and neural commitment, the more effort it will take to restore the perceptual abilities required for proper perception and production of the new language.

Kuhl et al. (2003) examined the conditions that enable a reversal of the decline in foreign language phonetic discrimination during the first year of life. In 12 laboratory sessions of 25 minutes spread out over a period of 4 weeks, they exposed a group of 9- to 10-month-old American infants, from families where only English was spoken, to Mandarin Chinese. During these sessions four different native Mandarin Chinese speakers read children's books to the infants and played games with them. The number of Mandarin syllables heard by each infant over these sessions amounted to over 25,000. This experimental set-up was designed to closely mimic natural adult–infant interaction, the naturalness of the situation being enhanced further by the use of child directed speech. A control group of American infants of the same age was exposed to 12 similarly designed sessions but held in English and with native speakers of English interacting with the infants.

Following training, Mandarin speech perception ability of the two infant groups was tested, using a version of the head-turn procedure described earlier (p. 16). As experimental stimuli two computer-synthesized speech sounds were chosen that are contrastive in Mandarin but not in English. One of these sounds was an **affricate**, the second a fricative, and both were articulated in the **alveolar-palatal** region of the vocal tract. Prior studies had shown that adult native speakers of Mandarin show near-perfect discrimination of these two sounds whereas adult native speakers of English perform poorly on them. As usual, the head-turn procedure consisted of a habituation phase followed by a test phase. In the habituation phase the infants were trained to turn their heads when they heard a change from a repeated background sound (the fricative) to the target sound (the affricate). A test phase then followed in which the number of head turns upon a change in speech sound served as the dependent variable, each head turn indicating that the change in input was perceived. The question of interest was whether the infants who had been exposed to native Mandarin in the prior training sessions would exhibit heightened discrimination of the Mandarin contrastive pair as compared to the control group of infants trained in English. The results are shown in Figure 2.3, which also shows the results of a group of native Mandarin Chinese infants of the same age tested in their home country (Taiwan).

The results clearly indicate that the foreign language intervention to the infants in the experimental group had reversed their relative insensitivity to this Mandarin contrast: The infants in the Mandarin training group responded with more head turns to a change of input than those in the control group exposed to English during training, and in fact were as sensitive to this contrast as the infants of comparable age who had never been exposed to any other language than Mandarin.

A second experiment used the same head-turn testing procedure and tested the same two speech sounds but this time the Mandarin training sessions did not involve natural live adult–child interaction but the presentation of either

FIGURE 2.3

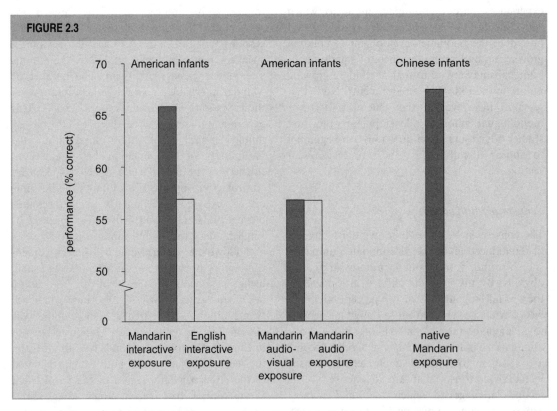

Mandarin Chinese speech discrimination in American 9- to 10-month-olds after exposure to Mandarin Chinese or American English in 12 sessions of natural live adult–child interaction (the two left bars) or to Mandarin Chinese in 12 non-interactive audio-visual or audio-only sessions (the middle two bars). The performance scores indicate the percentage of head turns upon a change from a Mandarin affricate to a Mandarin fricative or vice versa. The performance of a control group of native Mandarin Chinese infants is also shown (the right bar). Adapted from Kuhl et al. (2003). Copyright 2003 National Academy of Sciences, USA.

audio-visual Mandarin materials (to one infant group) or of audio-only Mandarin materials (to a second group). Interestingly, the performance of both these Mandarin training groups now equaled that of the live English training group in the first experiment (see Figure 2.3). The investigators concluded that a reversal of the typical developmental decline in foreign language speech perception in infancy requires true-to-life social interaction. (See Bijeljac-Babic, Nassurally, Havy, & Nazzi, 2009, for another demonstration of the efficacy of social interaction in early sequential foreign language learning.) It remains to be seen whether true-to-life social interaction is a necessary requirement for learning all perceptual aspects of foreign speech and for all sequential bilinguals. Plausibly the generally better cognitive skills of older second language learners can compensate for the suboptimal learning context that an audio-visual or audio-only learning environment provides.

Simultaneous bilingualism

A couple of recent studies have examined the development of native phonetic contrasts in infants growing up in a bilingual language environment from birth. These studies focused on the role of statistical distributional information in the ambient languages in the development of phonetic discrimination. In a study testing 6- and 8-month-old infants from monolingual English homes, Maye, Werker, and Gerken (2002) were among the first to show that infants can exploit statistical distributional information of speech sounds in the language input to build phonetic categories. In this study the researchers used the preferential looking procedure described earlier to first familiarize infants with eight stimuli on a continuum from the voiced to voiceless stop consonants /da/ and /ta/. The infants were divided over two familiarization conditions. One group was presented with a bimodal distribution of all eight stimuli, which meant that during familiarization stimuli near the endpoints of the continuum occurred more often than stimuli from the center of the continuum. The other group was presented with a unimodal distribution of the

same stimuli, meaning that stimuli from the center of the VOT continuum occurred relatively often. The authors predicted that the infants familiarized by means of the bimodal distribution pattern would develop two phonetic categories, while those familiarized with the unimodal pattern would develop a single phonetic category. The results obtained in the test phase supported this prediction by showing that only infants in the bimodal condition, in both age groups, discriminated tokens from the endpoints of the continuum.

Simultaneous bilingual infants are exposed to two speech systems that differ from one another in a number of ways, among others with respect to the distribution of the phonetic values of the systems' phonetic elements on the various acoustic dimensions (such as the VOT in plosives). Maye et al.'s (2002) discovery of sensitivity to the statistical distribution of speech sounds in the speech input as a mechanism for learning phonetic categories and contrasts thus gives rise to the question of how infants growing up in a bilingual setting from birth come to master the speech systems of their two native languages, and how this development compares to that of infants exposed to just one language. Plausibly, because of the relatively complex linguistic input, it takes longer for simultaneous bilingual-to-be infants to develop the two targeted phonetic systems than it takes monolingual infants to develop their single phonetic system, and the developmental trajectories may differ between these two groups of learners. These questions have been addressed in a small set of recent studies that together have examined the perception of a couple of vowel and consonant pairs in Catalan–Spanish (Bosch & Sebastián-Gallés, 2003a, 2003b) and French–English (Sundara, Polka, & Molnar, 2008) bilingual infants and matched monolingual control groups.

Using a version of the familiar head-turn procedure, Bosch and Sebastián-Gallés (2003b) examined the development in Catalan–Spanish infants of a vowel contrast that exists in Catalan but not in Spanish. Two age groups were tested, 4-month-olds and 8-month-olds. This choice of age groups was motivated by the fact that a shift from language-general to language-specific vowel perception has been shown to occur at around 6 months of age in monolingual infants (see Table 2.1). Comparable groups of 4- and 6-month-old infants from Spanish and Catalan monolingual environments were also tested so that the developmental pace and trajectory of the infants exposed to both languages from birth could be evaluated against a monolingual standard. In all then, six infant groups participated, three per age level. The vowel contrast under study concerned the vowels /e/ (as in *bait*) and /ɛ/ (as in *bet*). This vowel pair is contrastive in Catalan although acoustically no clear demarcation exists between manifestations of /e/ on the one hand and of /ɛ/ on the other hand. The Spanish phonetic system only contains /e/, which acoustically overlaps with both Catalan /e/ and /ɛ/ and whose prototypical exemplar is intermediate between the prototypical exemplars of the two Catalan

vowels. The experimental stimuli were different instances of /e/ and /ɛ/ (embedded in the disyllabic nonwords /deði/ and /dɛði/), thus imitating the natural variation in the way phonemes are realized in actual speech as a consequence of variables such as individual speaker characteristics and speech rate. All /e/ and /ɛ/ tokens used (18 of each) are shown in Figure 2.4 in a phonetic vowel space formed by the vowels' first and second **formants** (recall that formants are concentrations of acoustic energy in particular frequency ranges in speech sounds). As can be seen, the first-formant frequencies of all tokens formed a continuum; that is, there was no clear acoustic boundary between the /e/ tokens on the one hand and the /ɛ/ tokens on the other hand. During familiarization half of the participants were presented with /e/ exemplars and the other half with /ɛ/ exemplars. In the subsequent test phase all were presented with "same" and

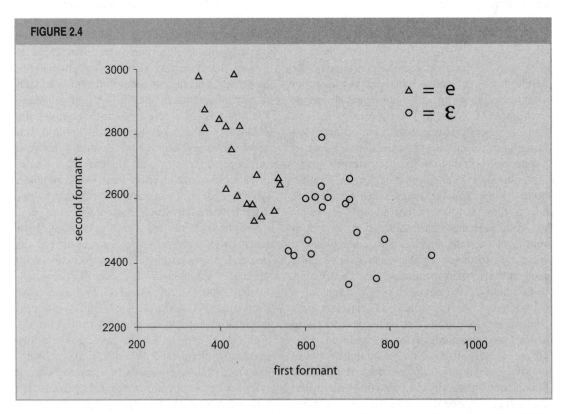

FIGURE 2.4

First- and second-formant mean values (in Hz) for all /e/ and /ɛ/ stimuli. Adapted from Bosch and Sebastián-Gallés (2003b). Copyright © 2003 SAGE Publications. Reprinted by permission of SAGE Publications.

"different" trials. On a same test trial the stimulus was a token of the same category (/e/ or /ɛ/) as presented during familiarization. On a different test trial the stimulus was a token from the other category.

The authors predicted that all three groups of 4-month-olds, including the Spanish monolinguals for which /e/ and /ɛ/ are not contrastive, would perceive the contrast, because at this age language-specific phonetic sensitivity has not yet emerged. Because language-specific perception should have developed by 8 months, the Catalan monolingual infants were predicted to have remained sensitive to the contrast, still showing discrimination at 8 months. In contrast, at 8 months of age the Spanish monolingual infants should have lost the ability to perceive the contrast because it is absent in the ambient language.

Regarding the bilingual-to-be infants the authors pondered that two factors might play a role in discrimination ability: continued versus discontinued exposure to the Catalan /e/–/ɛ/ contrast, and the distributional overlap between Spanish /e/ and Catalan /e/ and /ɛ/. If only continued exposure matters, the bilingual-to-be 8-month-olds should have developed two separate phonetic categories and, thus, perceive the contrast. After all, they had been exposed to Catalan from birth, albeit only part of the time. In contrast, the distributional overlap between Catalan /e/ and /ɛ/ and the acoustically intermediate Spanish /e/ might foster the emergence of a single phonetic category in the bilingual infants and the ensuing inability to perceive the contrast. The upper part of Figure 2.5 shows the results of this experiment. Specifically, it shows the average listening time for "same" and "different" trials in the experiment's test phase for all infant groups.

As shown, in agreement with the predictions, all three groups of 4-month-olds perceived the contrast. This suggests that, for infants this age, speech perceptual abilities are not yet influenced by the specific language(s) they have been exposed to. Also in agreement with expectation, the Catalan 8-month-old monolinguals but not the Spanish monolinguals this age discriminated between instances of /e/ and /ɛ/. (The small dif-

ference between same and different trials in the opposite direction in the Spanish group was not significant.) This suggests a lost sensitivity to a contrast that does not exist in the ambient language or, in other words, that all exemplars of both /e/ and /ɛ/ are perceived as realizations of a single phonetic category. Of special interest are the results observed for the bilingual 8-month-olds. These show that, despite having been exposed to Catalan at least part of the time, at 8 months these infants have lost the ability to perceive the difference between exemplars of the one or the other category, behaving like Spanish monolingual infants of the same age. This result gives rise to the question of how long it takes before sensitivity to the Catalan contrast is restored again. To answer this question the researchers tested a new group of Catalan–Spanish bilingual-to-be infants, now at 12 months of age. The data for this group clearly suggest that discrimination ability has been restored at this age (see the upper part of Figure 2.5).

The authors concluded that due to the overlapping distributions of instances of Spanish /e/ and Catalan /e/ and /ɛ/, bilinguals first develop a single extended phonetic category that includes all three vowels and therefore fail to discriminate between them. They suggested that this one category is ultimately separated into three (Catalan /e/ and /ɛ/ and Spanish /e/) as a result of either extended exposure to Spanish and Catalan or of progressed lexical development. In two further Catalan–Spanish studies Bosch and Sebastián-Gallés (2003a, 2005) similarly showed a differential developmental pattern for monolingual and bilingual infants, now testing the participants' ability to discriminate between the fricatives /s/ and /z/ and between the vowels /o/ and /u/ (as in *boat* and *boot*), respectively. As with the vowels /e/ and /ɛ/, the fricatives /s/ and /z/ are contrastive in Catalan but not in Spanish and instances of these phonemes show a distributional overlap. Instead, the vowels /o/ and /u/ are contrastive in both Spanish and Catalan, with their prototypical acoustic values differing somewhat between the two languages and, again, instances of the two phonemes exhibiting distributional overlap. The fricative contrast was

FIGURE 2.5

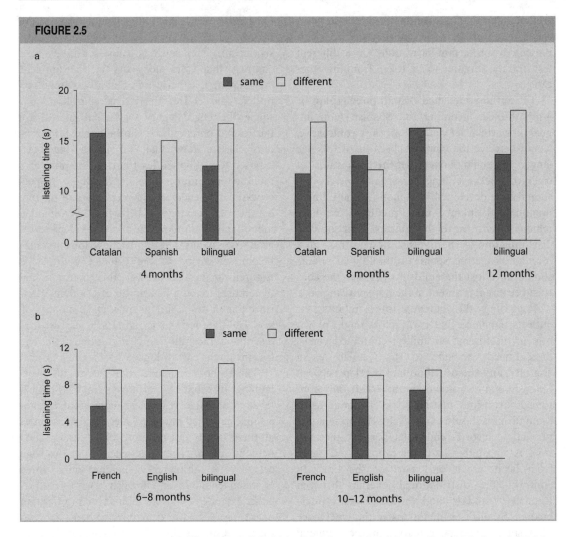

(a) Mean listening time to same and different (= switch) trials of Catalan and Spanish monolingual infants and Catalan–Spanish bilingual infants of different ages. Adapted from Bosch and Sebastián-Gallés (2003b). (b) Mean listening time to same and different (= switch) trials of French and English monolingual infants and French–English bilinguals of different ages. Adapted from Sundara et al. (2008) with permission from Elsevier.

tested on 4½-month-old and 12-month-old monolingual Catalan, monolingual Spanish and Catalan–Spanish bilingual infants. At 4½ months both the Catalan and Spanish monolingual infants and the bilingual infants could discriminate /s/ and /z/ (if the contrast occurred in word-initial position). At 12 months, however, the Catalan monolinguals still could, whereas the monolingual Spanish and the bilingual infants failed to do so. Unfortunately, no older bilingual

age group was tested to find out when discrimination ability of this contrast is restored again in bilinguals. The /o/ and /u/ contrast (Bosch & Sebastián-Gallés, 2005) was tested on 4- and 8-month-old monolingual and bilingual infants (the authors do not explicitly mention whether the ambient language of the monolingual-to-be infants was Catalan or Spanish, so presumably both Spanish and Catalan monolinguals were included among the monolingual group). At 4 months both the monolingual and bilingual infants could discriminate /o/ and /u/, but at 8 months only the monolinguals could do so. The authors mention that preliminary data from a group of 12-month-old Catalan–Spanish infants show evidence of discrimination again, so the same developmental pattern emerged as with the /e/–/ɛ/ contrast: initial sensitivity to the contrast, followed by loss of sensitivity (presumably because a single phonemic category is temporarily formed), followed by restored sensitivity.

It thus appears that cross-language distributional overlap of speech sounds delays the building of language-specific contrastive categories in bilinguals. Sundara et al. (2008) hypothesized that infants may be sensitive not only to distributional characteristics of the speech input but also to the frequency of occurrence of phonetic elements. If so, a high frequency of occurrence of particular phonetic elements might offset the adverse effect of cross-language distributional overlap on discrimination ability. In other words, bilingual and monolingual infants might show the same developmental trajectory on contrastive pairs consisting of speech sounds that both occur frequently in speech.

The researchers tested this hypothesis by comparing the ability of monolingual French, monolingual English, and bilingual French–English infants to discriminate between exemplars of French /d/ and English /d/ (presented as the onset in syllables that always contained the same vowel). The average French and English /d/ differ in their place of articulation. In French, /d/ is produced "dentally", that is, by putting the tongue to the back of the upper teeth, whereas in English it is realized by putting it somewhat further back in the mouth, on the so-called "alveolar ridge". These differences in place of articulation are reflected in acoustic differences between French and English /d/. The difference between dental /d/ and alveolar /d/ is phonemic in some languages but not in French or English: All realizations of dental and alveolar /d/ in both French and English instantiate one and the same phoneme /d/. Furthermore, exemplars of French /d/ and English /d/ show considerable

acoustic overlap. Still, English adults, but not French adults, can distinguish between the French dental /d/ and the English alveolar /d/. (Sundara and her colleagues suggested that a reason that English adults are sensitive to the distinction might be that French dental /d/ is perceptually similar to English /ð/.) Importantly, French dental /d/ and English alveolar /d/ occur very frequently in their respective languages. As hypothesized by the authors, thanks to the high frequency of occurrence of these speech sounds English–French bilingual-to-be infants exposed to both languages from birth might show the same developmental path as monolingual English controls, despite the fact that the distributions of French and English /d/ overlap.

Employing the visual fixation habituation procedure, three groups of 6–8-month-olds and three groups of 10–12-month-olds were tested: monolingual French, monolingual English, and simultaneous English–French bilinguals. During habituation half of the infants of each of the six groups heard repetitions of four different French /d/ tokens excised from words spoken by three different monolingual French speakers. The other half heard repetitions of four English /d/ tokens excised from words spoken by three different monolingual English speakers. At test, each participant heard some new /d/ tokens from the language of familiarization and some tokens from the other language. The question of interest was whether dental French /d/ and alveolar English /d/ were discriminated at test, as evidenced by relatively long listening times for trials involving a language switch as compared with same-language trials. Because language-specific consonant perception has not yet developed at 6–8 months of age, the infants in all three groups this age were expected to discriminate French and English /d/. The data, shown in the lower part of Figure 2.5, supported this prediction. Furthermore, monolingual English and French 10–12-month-olds were expected to behave in the same way as monolingual English and French adults, respectively—the English monolingual infants noticing the difference between French and English /d/ but the French monolinguals failing to do so. Again, the data confirmed these predictions (see Figure 2.5, lower part).

Of special interest was the pattern to be observed for the bilingual 10–12-month-olds. If cross-language distributional overlap on its own determines the time course of phonetic development, the bilingual 10–12-month-olds should fail to perceive the contrast, grouping the instances of French and English /d/ into a single category. If, however, a high frequency of occurrence of particular speech sounds counteracts the effect of distributional overlap on discrimination, the bilingual 10–12-month-olds should behave like their English monolingual peers and like English adults. This is in fact the pattern that emerged (Figure 2.5, lower right part).

In conclusion, the joint results of the above studies indicate that simultaneous bilingual infants develop some phonetic contrasts at the same pace and following the same trajectory as their monolingual peers, but that the development of other contrasts is delayed and follows a different route. They furthermore suggest that both cross-language distributional overlap of representatives of different phonetic categories and their frequency of occurrence in actual speech determine whether or not bilinguals show a different development from matched monolinguals for a specific phonetic contrast. More generally, these data show that infants are sensitive to statistical distributional information regarding phonetic units in the speech signal, and exploit this source of information in learning the phonetic categories of their language(s). As such, these results add to the growing body of evidence suggesting that statistical distributional learning plays a pivotal role in language learning in general, and challenging theories of language acquisition that assume language acquisition to be driven largely by innate linguistic universals (see Saffran, 2003, for a review). So far statistical learning has not only been shown to play a role in phonological development but also to contribute to the development of the lexicon (e.g., Saffran, Aslin, & Newport, 1996a) and grammar (Gomez & Gerken, 1999; Saffran & Wilson, 2003). It is to some of the relevant evidence that I will now turn.

Lexical development

Introduction

So far the discussion has primarily focused on the way infants growing up in a monolingual environment gradually attune to the phonetic system of their native language and, in parallel to this development, become less sensitive to foreign speech sounds and foreign phonetic contrasts. In addition, a few studies were reviewed that addressed the question of how phonetic development in infants exposed to just one language compares to that of infants that receive dual-language input from birth or soon thereafter. This joint research has revealed important insights into the emergence of language-specific phonetic categories and contrasts in infants, monolingual and bilingual. Given the fact that phonetic categories are the building blocks of words, this work pertains to lexical development as well. Yet it does so only indirectly, exploiting techniques and using stimulus materials especially developed to learn about the emergence of phonetic categories and contrasts, not words.

Other researchers have addressed the question of how infants acquire vocabulary more directly. The goal of some of them was to discover when and how infants start to detect sound patterns that correspond to words in fluent speech, an ability that is a prerequisite for acquiring vocabulary. As mentioned in the introduction to this chapter, word boundaries are typically not marked by breaks in the speech signal and, conversely, the acoustic information conveying a single word may be interrupted by one or more pauses within the word. How then do listeners segment the speech stream into words, the primary linguistic units to convey meaning? For adults, the fact that they have a vocabulary presumably contributes greatly to solving the segmentation problem because they can monitor the speech input for familiar sound patterns; that is, for sound sequences that match the phonological representations of words stored in their mental lexicon. This is not an option for infants because they have no lexicon yet, or only a very rudimentary one. The evidence suggests that caregivers do not generally facilitate children's vocabulary acquisition by providing them with words clearly separated from their linguistic context: Woodward and Aslin (1990; in Jusczyk & Aslin, 1995) have shown that even in situations in which mothers are explicitly asked to teach their infants new vocabulary the vast majority of the targeted words are not presented in isolation but in continuous speech.

What, then, are the cues to segmentation of the speech input, and at what age and through what mechanisms can infants exploit these cues and start recognizing the sound patterns of words in connected speech? Obviously, recognizing a word's sound pattern does not yet equal knowing the word in question, nor does it imply that the infant has some awareness that the sound patterns that he or she recognizes are linguistically meaningful. A word can only be said to be known if a connection has been established between its sound pattern—that is, its phonological form—and its meaning. The ability to link the form and meaning of words develops later than the ability to recognize the sound patterns of words in continuous speech. Furthermore, there is some evidence to suggest that the pairing of words to their meanings consists of two successive stages during which different learning mechanisms are operative and that result in different types of word–meaning linkages (Nazzi & Bertoncini, 2003). In the first stage an associative lexical acquisition mechanism links phonetically underspecified sound patterns to specific objects through the repeated co-occurrence of sound pattern and object. In the second stage a referential lexical acquisition mechanism pairs phonetically specified sound patterns with categories of objects rather than single objects. Nazzi and Bertoncini regard the word–meaning connections resulting from the first, associative, stage as "proto-words" and those resulting from the second, referential, stage as genuine words. Only after a word has been learned at the referential level is there an understanding that words refer to things and events and that, to do so, these referents need not be present in the environment.

It is well known that, following the emergence of the first words around 12 months (see Table 2.1), the vocabulary of infants initially grows very slowly, with just one or two newly produced words a week. Around 18 months a sudden steep growth in vocabulary, the so-called "vocabulary spurt" or "lexical spurt", is observed (e.g., Benedict, 1979; Nelson, 1973). Nazzi and Bertoncini (2003) hypothesized that this vocabulary spurt reflects a qualitative shift from the associative to the referential mode of word acquisition, the latter allowing an increase in cognitive economy and, thereby, a reduction in cognitive load: If a particular sound pattern is connected to a category of objects, far fewer word–meaning pairings have to be learnt (namely, one for the whole category of objects) than when words are paired with separate objects. In addition, the reduced cognitive load would allow the infants to attend to the words' phonological forms more carefully than before, thus gradually replacing the phonetically underspecified word forms by more precisely specified ones.

In the next sections I will discuss a number of studies that examined when and how infants start to recognize the phonological forms of words in the speech stream and subsequently connect these to meaning. In so doing I will move from a couple of monolingual and cross-language investigations to the specific case of infants exposed to two languages.

Segmenting the speech stream

Statistical bootstrapping. Employing the head-turn procedure, Jusczyk and Aslin (1995) tried to find out at what age infants start recognizing the sound patterns of words in connected speech. The investigators first familiarized a group of 7½-month-olds from American-English homes with two monosyllabic words by presenting both of them repeatedly until some predetermined familiarization criterion was attained. At test, four passages, each consisting of six sentences, were presented. Two of these passages each contained six repetitions of one of the two words presented during familiarization. The remaining two passages each contained six repetitions of two novel words, one novel word per passage. The authors reasoned that if the infants noticed the similarity between the words presented during familiarization and testing, this should show in different listening times at test for the passages containing the familiar words and those containing the novel words. Such a result was indeed obtained: The average listening time for the passages containing familiar words was more than a second longer than for the passages containing unfamiliar words. Accordingly the authors concluded that at 7½ months infants can isolate from fluent speech words they have before been familiarized with by just listening to them being repeated in isolation. A replication of this experiment with 6-month-olds showed equally long listening times to passages containing familiar and unfamiliar words, suggesting that the ability to detect familiar sound patterns in fluent speech develops some time between 6 and 7½ months.

As mentioned earlier, child directed speech does not generally consist of words presented in isolation, so the ability to match words first presented in isolation to these same words presented in fluent speech later may not help infants greatly in learning to identify words in continuous speech. Jusczyk and Aslin (1995) therefore performed a further experiment that more closely mimics the segmentation problem faced by infants. A new group of 7½-month-olds served as participants. This time the order in which the infants encountered the passages and the isolated words was reversed so that they were now first familiarized with two words presented in passages. At test they listened to four different lists of isolated words, two lists consisting of repetitions of either one of the two words that had occurred repeatedly in the passages and the remaining two consisting of repetitions of either one of the two novel words. The infants listened significantly longer to the former two lists than to the latter. As concluded by the authors, this finding constitutes strong evidence that 7½-month-olds have developed the ability to recognize the sound pattern of words in fluent speech.

But what exactly is the mechanism underlying this ability? Saffran et al. (1996a) suggested that a statistical learning mechanism similar to the one involved in the development of phonetic categories and contrasts (pp. 27–32), plausibly even the very same mechanism, plays a pivotal role in bootstrapping this particular aspect of lexical development. They tested this idea by familiarizing a group of 8-month-olds from an American-English language environment with 2 minutes of fluent synthesized nonsensical speech. The speech stream consisted of four three-syllabic nonsense words (*pabiku*, *tibudo*, *golatu*, and *daropi*) repeated in a random order (e.g., *tibudodaropipabikutibudogolatudaropigolatu* . . .). It did not contain any pauses, stress differences between the syllables, nor any other prosodic cue signaling the boundaries between the "words". The only cue that pointed at the word boundaries was the sequential ("transitional") probabilities of the neighboring syllables, these always being 1.0 within words but much lower between words (.33). For instance, *ti* is always followed by *bu*, *bu* is always followed by *do*, but *do* may be followed by *go*, *da*, or *pa*. At test the infants were presented with repetitions of two of the four "words" presented during training (e.g., *pabiku* and *tibudo*) and with repetitions of two syllable triads that were created by joining the final syllable of one of the words to the first two syllables of a second word (e.g., *tudaro* and *pigola*, called "part-words" by the authors). Inspecting the above speech stream the reader will discover that the infant has also encountered these part-words while listening to the input, but much less often than the syllable triads imitating words. If at test the infants responded differently to the words than to the part-words, this would mean they had extracted from the input the relative frequencies of the transitions between syllables (high within words; low between words). A difference in listening times for the words and part-words was indeed obtained, supporting the idea that infants exploit a learning mechanism that detects sequential probabilities as a tool in developing a lexicon.

In a later study Saffran (2001) strengthened this conclusion by showing that infants treat the output of statistical speech learning—that is, the sequences of syllables they have become familiar with—as potential words and not simply as sound

y be expected
rence between
ct of list type

simultaneous
ic sensitivity,
subsequently
alan–Spanish
had all been
om birth. A
l was how
tactic sensi-
re tested: a
an average
of 60% and
ninant group
e time and to
epending on
several out-
exposure to
of bilingual
ve as their
ver, *amount*
t to find a
pes of lists
r the two
ct for the
e Spanish-
dominance
-dominant
nolinguals
rformance
roup may
guals. The
pper panel
r the two
rticipants.
ype effects
ning-time

ominance
pattern:
dominant
been on
monolin-
ype effect
In con-
ominant

us (in
ognize
tonal
nly if
to the
to con-
hanism
is study
n et al.,
merican
nonsense
d "part-
n (as in
h context
o) or in a
Foo dray
he syllable
ning were
instead of
which they
nse, should
during test-
as potential
ct listening
e of context
stening time
biku versus
d when they
xts but not
ical contexts.
ed that "...
the statistical
tead, they are
und sequences
ssible words in
01, p. 165).
showed that
ial probabilities
of syllables,
(2003) gathered
e to the sequen-
phonemes. This
age learners to
's phonotactics;
issible phoneme
nal constraints.
al constraints pre-
nge than learning

transitional probabilities of syllables because syllables are more salient perceptual units than phonemes. Using the head-turn procedure, Chambers and her colleagues first familiarized a group of 16½-month-old infants from American-English speaking homes with 25 CVC syllables (C = consonant; V = vowel). These syllables instantiated a particular (artificial) set of phonotactic constraints: Five consonants only occurred in syllable-initial position (e.g., /b/ and /m/) and five different consonants only occurred in final position (e.g., /p/ and /g/). At test the infants heard *novel* CVC syllables that either respected the phonotactic constraints of the syllables presented during training (that is, their initial and final consonants were members of the syllable-initial and syllable-final set, respectively; e.g., /bɛg/) or that violated them (e.g., /pim/). Listening times were longer for the illegal syllables than for the legal ones, suggesting that the participants discriminated between the two types of stimuli. This discrimination ability was not based on familiarity or unfamiliarity at the level of the syllables as wholes because all of the syllables presented at test were new. It therefore seemed legitimate to conclude that during training the participants had discovered the phonotactic system underlying the training set.

Other studies have shown that this sensitivity to sublexical phonotactic constraints is in fact already in place in infants much younger than those tested by Chambers et al. (2003) and that it may coincide with infants' sensitivity, at 8 months, to sequential probabilities of syllable-sized speech segments (Saffran et al., 1996a; see above) and with their ability to isolate familiar monosyllabic word forms from fluent speech (Jusczyk & Aslin, 1995). Jusczyk, Friederici, Wessels, Svenkerud, and Jusczyk (1993) presented American and Dutch infants of about 9 months of age with a series of Dutch and English word lists. Each list contained words in one language only and all of the presented words were abstract and had a low frequency of occurrence, so that it was unlikely any of them was familiar to any of the participants (examples of the English words used are *kudos*, *aglow*, *butane*, and *scutcheon*). The majority of the English words violated the phonotactic constraints of Dutch, containing sound sequences that do not occur in Dutch. Conversely, the majority of the Dutch words violated the phonotactic constraints of English, containing sound sequences alien to English. The results, obtained by means of the head-turn procedure, showed that the American infants listened significantly longer to the lists of English words than to the lists of Dutch words, suggesting that at 9 months of age American infants have become sensitive to the phonotactics of English. The Dutch infants showed the opposite pattern, listening longer to the Dutch lists. As shown in a separate experiment, this discrimination ability was not yet present in American infants at 6 months of age, suggesting that sensitivity to a language's phonotactics develops between 6 and 9 months.

In a more recent Catalan–Spanish study Sebastián-Gallés and Bosch (2002) provided converging evidence as well as a first indication that growing up bilingual does not inevitably delay phonotactic development. In a first experiment they presented 10-month-old infants growing up in either Catalan-speaking or Spanish-speaking monolingual families with lists of nonwords, all with a CVCC structure. (Infants were considered monolingual if their exposure to a single language ranged from 80% to 100%; the average exposure to the other language was estimated to be about 5%.) Catalan contains CC clusters in word-final position whereas Spanish does not. Half of the lists presented to both the Catalan and Spanish infants consisted of nonwords with legal Catalan end clusters (e.g., *birt* and *kisk*). The other half contained nonwords with illegal Catalan end clusters (e.g., *ketr* and *datl*). Because Spanish does not have consonant clusters in word-final position, in Spanish all nonwords were illegal. The results indicated that at 10 months infants from Catalan monolingual homes can discriminate between legal and illegal consonant clusters: They listened significantly longer to the lists containing legal nonwords than to those containing illegal nonwords, thus demonstrating sensitivity to the phonotactics of their native language. Because both types of nonwords are equally illegal in Spanish, infants from the

Spanish monolingual families ma[...] not to show a listening time diffe[...] the two types of lists and a null eff[...] was indeed obtained.

In order to find out how [...] bilingualism influences phonotact[...] Sebastián-Gallés and Bosch (2002)[...] replicated this experiment with Ca[...] bilingual-to-be 10-month-olds who[...] exposed to the two languages fr[...] second question they addresse[...] language dominance affects phon[...] tivity. Two groups of infants we[...] Catalan-dominant group with [...] exposure to Catalan and Spanish [...] 40%, respectively, and a Spanish-do[...] exposed to Spanish about 60% of th[...] Catalan about 40% of the time. D[...] what causes phonotactic sensitivity, [...] comes are conceivable. If it is merely[...] Catalan that matters, both groups [...] infants may be expected to beha[...] Catalan monolingual peers. If, howe[...] of exposure matters, one may expe[...] larger difference between the two t[...] for Catalan monolinguals than f[...] bilingual groups, and a larger eff[...] Catalan-dominant group than for th[...] dominant group. Finally, if language [...] is the critical factor, the Catalar[...] bilingual infants and the Catalan m[...] may behave similarly, whereas the p[...] of the Spanish-dominant bilingual [...] resemble that of the Spanish monolin[...] results are shown in Figure 2.6. The u[...] presents the average listening times f[...] types of lists for all four groups of pa[...] The lower panel shows the average list-t[...] for all groups; that is, the average list[...] difference between the two list types.

These data suggest that language d[...] in particular determined the respons[...] Despite the fact that the Catalan-[...] bilinguals' exposure to Catalan had [...] average 35% lower than the Catalan [...] guals' exposure (60% vs. 95%), the list-t[...] was equally large for these two group[...] trast, the list-type effect for the Spanish-[...]

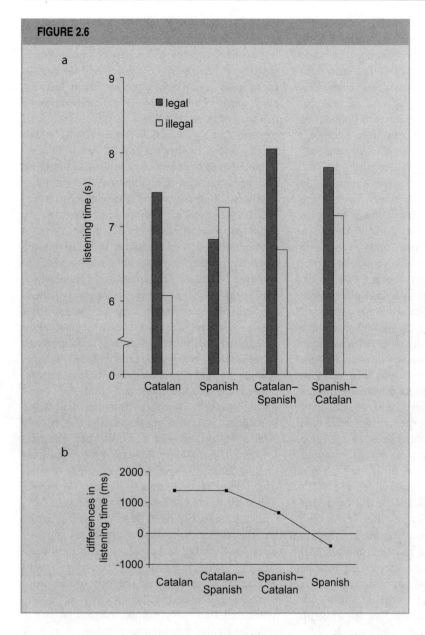

(a) Mean listening times of Catalan monolingual, Spanish monolingual, Catalan–Spanish bilingual, and Spanish–Catalan bilingual 10-month-olds to lists of CVCC nonwords with CC endings that are legal or illegal in Catalan. All CC endings are illegal in Spanish. Adapted from Sebastián-Gallés and Bosch (2002). (b) The corresponding list-type effects for all four groups; that is, the differences in listening time for lists with legal Catalan CC clusters and lists with illegal Catalan CC clusters. From Sebastián-Gallés and Bosch (2002). Copyright © 2002 American Psychological Association.

bilinguals was not statistically reliable, indicating that these infants behaved like their monolingual Spanish peers (for which the effect in the opposite direction was also not significant). These findings suggest that, just as monolingual infants of 10 months of age have become sensitive to the phonotactics of their one native language, bilingual infants this age have developed this sensitivity for their dominant, but not yet their non-dominant, language.

To summarize, the combined results of the above studies converge on the conclusion that at about 8 months of age infants recognize recurring syllable sequences in speech and soon thereafter recurring phoneme sequences. The mechanism that underlies this skill is a statistical learning device that is sensitive to sequential probabilities of speech units. This learning mechanism is effective even with speech that contains no other (prosodic) cues to the recurrent patterns than sequential probabilities of the speech units. This ability to detect repeated speech patterns provides infants with a means to discover word boundaries in continuous speech and can thus bootstrap vocabulary acquisition: A syllable sequence of high sequential probability is likely to be a word, and one of low sequential probability presumably contains a word boundary somewhere in the middle. Similarly, a particular phoneme sequence of high sequential probability is likely to belong to one and the same word, and a phoneme sequence of low sequential probability presumably marks a boundary between two words. That such statistical learning indeed plays a role in launching vocabulary acquisition is supported by the additional finding that infants treat the familiar sound patterns they have extracted from continuous speech as *linguistic* units (Saffran, 2001). The above studies furthermore demonstrated that at around 9–10 months of age infants growing up in a monolingual environment have had sufficient language exposure for statistical learning to have differentiated between phoneme sequences that occur in their native language (the "legal" sequences) and those that do not (the "illegal" sequences; Jusczyk et al., 1993; Sebastián-Gallés & Bosch, 2002). But of special interest is Sebastián-Gallés and Bosch's finding that 10-month-olds growing up in a bilingual environment are as good as their monolingual peers at discriminating between phoneme sequences that are legal or illegal in their dominant language, the language they are exposed to most. It indicates that growing up bilingual does not inevitably delay the development of language-specific phonotactic knowledge. In addition, it suggests that the development of phonotactic knowledge is not linearly related to amount of exposure to the phonotactic constraints in question.

Prosodic bootstrapping. A separate line of studies suggests that, in addition to the above statistical learning device, infants make use of a further mechanism that helps them to segment continuous speech into words, thus bootstrapping vocabulary acquisition. The device in question is sensitive to the rhythm of speech and appears to be in place even before the statistical learning mechanism. Three classes of languages can be distinguished on the basis of their rhythmical patterns (see e.g., Nazzi & Ramus, 2003): stress-based (e.g., English, German, and Dutch), syllable-based (e.g., French, Spanish, and Italian), and **mora**-based (e.g., Japanese). A large number of studies have shown that adults exploit the specific rhythmical pattern of their native language to segment the speech stream, using a segmentation procedure which is based on the metrical unit that is typical for this language. For instance, Mehler, Dommergues, Frauenfelder, and Segui (1981) have shown that the syllable is the unit of segmentation used by French adult native speakers. Syllable-based segmentation is effective in French because this language has relatively clear and unambiguous syllable boundaries and a syllable-based timing pattern. Subsequent studies indicated that for adult native speakers of other Romance languages, Portuguese, Catalan, and Spanish, the syllable is also the primary segmentation unit (Morais, Content, Cary, Mehler, & Segui, 1989; Sebastián-Gallés, Dupoux, Segui, & Mehler, 1992). In contrast, native adult speakers of Dutch (Vroomen, Van Zon, & De Gelder, 1996) and English (e.g., Cutler, Mehler, Norris, & Segui, 1986) exploit the fact that the majority of words in these languages carry stress on the first syllable. Speakers of these languages find it hard to detect a real word embedded in nonsense if the end of the word is a strong (stressed) syllable (Cutler & Norris, 1988) and frequently mistake non-initial strong syllables to be word-initial syllables (Cutler & Butterfield, 1992). Finally, Japanese adults use the mora to segment their native language (Otake, Hatano, Cutler, & Mehler, 1993). Interestingly, English monolinguals also exploit stress-based segmentation on French words and, conversely, French monolinguals apply syllable-based segmentation to English words (Cutler et al., 1986). In other words, monolingual language users seem to transfer their native language segmentation procedure to a language that does not encourage it.

The above cross-language segmentation patterns give rise to the question of how bilinguals segment their two languages. Do bilinguals behave like monolinguals in each language such that, if their two languages differ in rhythmical type, they exploit one segmentation routine while listening to their one language and the other while listening to their other language? Another possibility is that they develop only one segmentation routine and apply it also to the language for which it is not optimally suited. Addressing these questions, Cutler and her colleagues (Cutler, Mehler, Norris, & Segui, 1989, 1992) examined speech segmentation in a group of highly proficient French–English bilinguals. All of them were judged to be native speakers of both languages by monolingual native speakers of these languages and they were all tested in both languages. The overall data, collapsing across all participants, produced a pattern that in neither language condition replicated the behavior of the corresponding monolingual group and that was generally hard to interpret. To be able to better understand what was going on, the authors subsequently subdivided the participants into two groups by language preference and analyzed the data for these two groups separately. The assignment of a participant to one or the other group was based on the answer to the following question: "Suppose you developed a serious disease, and your life could only be saved by a brain operation which would unfortunately have the side effect of removing one of your languages. Which language would you choose to keep?" (Cutler et al., 1992, p. 390). The pattern of results emerging from the subsequent analyses provided a mixed answer to the above question, suggesting that, depending on which language is the dominant one, bilinguals may either behave like two monolinguals within one person or apply one and the same segmentation procedure to both languages: The French-dominant participants performed like French monolinguals (employing syllable-based segmentation) when they had to segment French materials and like English monolinguals (using stress-based segmentation)

while processing English materials. The English-dominant participants, however, behaved like English monolinguals in both language conditions, showing stress-based segmentation in both of them.

To account for these results Cutler and her colleagues (1989) assumed syllabic segmentation to be a special, "marked" (non-default) language-processing routine that language users only develop and apply if their native (or in the case of bilinguals, their dominant) language encourages it. The authors claimed that most languages, including English, do not encourage syllabic segmentation and that speakers of these languages therefore develop more common, "unmarked", segmentation routines. The present bilingual evidence suggests that bilinguals dominant in the language that favors the marked, syllable-based procedure can develop and use an unmarked (stress-based) segmentation procedure in addition to the marked procedure, but that those dominant in the language that encourages an unmarked segmentation procedure cannot develop the marked procedure in addition to the unmarked procedure.

An obvious prerequisite of using a language's specific rhythm to segment speech is that the speech perceiver is sensitive to language rhythm. A number of recent infant studies, both monolingual and bilingual, have examined at what age this sensitivity is in place and how it develops. This joint work has shown that at birth newborns can discriminate languages of different rhythmical classes but fail to discriminate languages of the same rhythmical class (see Nazzi & Ramus, 2003, and Sebastián-Gallés & Bosch, 2005, for reviews), suggesting the sensitivity to language rhythm is innate. Nazzi, Bertoncini, and Mehler (1998), for instance, observed that newborns from monolingual French-speaking families discriminated between stress-timed English and mora-timed Japanese but not between English and Dutch, both stress-based. In this study cues to discrimination other than the languages' rhythmical patterns were removed so that sensitivity to differences between the languages' rhythms could unequivocally be designated as the source of this ability. Further studies have shown that this ability is not specific to humans but is also present in other mammals, as demonstrated in research testing tamarin monkeys and rats (e.g., Toro, Trobalón, & Sebastián-Gallés, 2003).

In the months following birth, infants' knowledge of their native language increases and this influences their discriminative ability regarding other languages. Mehler et al. (1988) found that 2-month-old American babies from English-speaking homes could discriminate between English and Italian but failed to distinguish French from Russian. Similarly, Christophe and Morton (1998) observed that 2-month-old English babies discriminated between English and Japanese but not between French and Japanese even though in both cases the two languages belong to different rhythmical classes. At first sight these findings suggest that infants this age distinguish between their native language on the one hand and foreign languages on the other hand, but two further experiments by Christophe and Morton, each again testing groups of English 2-month-olds, indicated that the complete story is somewhat more complex. One of these experiments showed that a subgroup of the participants failed to discriminate between native English and foreign Dutch, whereas the second indicated that a subgroup of the participants succeeded in discriminating between foreign Dutch and foreign Japanese. Both these findings thus suggest that a subgroup of 2-month-olds with English as their mother tongue considered Dutch as native, presumably because these two languages are both stress-timed and prosodically similar in a number of other respects as well. It thus appears that the infants in this subgroup have not yet developed sufficiently fine-grained phonetic knowledge of English to be able to use other than **suprasegmental** prosodic information in discriminating between languages. A second subgroup considered Dutch as foreign, suggesting that they have already started to develop more detailed, **segmental**, knowledge regarding native English, and to use it in language discrimination.

Employing a so-called "visual orientation" procedure Bosch and Sebastián-Gallés (1997) were the first to compare the ability of monolingual and bilingual infants to discriminate between a pair of rhythmically similar languages, one native, the other non-native. Across two experiments, three languages were tested, all syllable-timed: Catalan, Spanish, and Italian. In one experiment 4-month-olds growing up in monolingual Spanish or Catalan homes were presented with Catalan and Spanish sentences. On each separate trial a Catalan or a Spanish sentence was played from one of two laterally positioned loudspeakers and across trials the loudspeaker emitting the sentence and the sentence's language were randomized. Per trial the infant's orientation time was measured; that is, the time it took the infant to start looking in the direction of where the sound came from. Prior research had shown that infants' orientation time to familiar stimuli is usually shorter than to unfamiliar stimuli. The question of interest was whether 4-month-olds have become sufficiently familiar with the ambient, native language to be able to distinguish it from a rhythmically similar non-native language, as would show from faster orienting to sentences in the native language. The results provided an affirmative answer to this question: The infants from Catalan homes oriented faster to Catalan sentences than to Spanish sentences and the infants from Spanish homes oriented faster to Spanish sentences than to Catalan sentences. In a second experiment 4-month-old infants from Catalan–Spanish bilingual homes were presented with Catalan *or* Spanish sentences (depending on their maternal language) and with Italian sentences. An orientation time difference between familiar Catalan or Spanish on the one hand and unfamiliar Italian on the other hand occurred, although surprisingly, orienting time was *longer* for the familiar language. The reason may be—so the authors conjectured—that when hearing familiar language material bilingual infants first try to determine which of their native languages is being spoken and only then start looking at the speech source. Importantly though, the fact that the two language conditions led to different orienting times indicates that 4-month-old bilingual-to-be infants can also discriminate between two languages of the same rhythmical class, one native, the other non-native.

The above orientation procedure makes use of the fact that the participants have been exposed to one but not the other of the test languages *prior to* the actual experiment through naturalistic language exposure. This procedure is unsuitable to examine whether bilingual infants can discriminate between their two native languages, to both of which they have been previously exposed. Experimental materials in *both* languages would thus give rise to a feeling of familiarity and, consequently, to equally long orienting times (see Bosch & Sebastián-Gallés, 1997, for evidence). Bosch and Sebastián-Gallés (2001) therefore used a different procedure to discover whether Catalan–Spanish bilingual 4-month-olds can also discriminate between their two, rhythmically similar, native languages. They exploited a version of the familiarization procedure described earlier, in which an experimental test phase is immediately preceded by an experimental familiarization phase. The participants were first familiarized with two speech passages in one language, the infants with Spanish-speaking mothers listening to Spanish passages and those with Catalan-speaking mothers listening to Catalan passages. Familiarization lasted until the infants had accumulated 2 minutes of sustained attention to the presented materials. When this criterion was reached the test phase started. During testing four new passages were presented, two in the same language as presented during familiarization and two in the other language. Presentation time continued until the infant ceased to look into the direction of the loudspeaker emitting the test materials. The results showed different listening times for the language presented during familiarization and the novel language: The infants presented with Catalan during familiarization listened more briefly to Catalan than to Spanish and the reverse pattern was observed for the infants familiarized with Spanish. A control experiment testing groups of age-matched monolingual Catalan and Spanish infants showed that these "novelty effects" were equally large as those obtained for the monolingual groups. These results thus indicate that at 4 months of age

bilingual-to-be infants can discriminate between two rhythmically similar native languages and that, despite the relative complexity of bilingual speech learning, infants growing up with two languages do not lag behind their monolingual peers in developing language discrimination abilities.

To summarize, immediately after birth babies can discriminate between rhythmically different languages but not between rhythmically similar languages. At 2 months, some infants from monolingual homes can discriminate between their native language on the one hand and foreign languages on the other hand, even if the foreign language has the same rhythm as the native language, whereas others treat a foreign language with the same rhythm as the native language as native. These findings suggest that some 2-month-olds have already started to develop detailed segmental knowledge regarding their native language and use it in language discrimination. It appears that the infants in the other subgroup are not this advanced yet and still have to rely on suprasegmental, prosodic information in discriminating between languages. At 4 months, infants from both monolingual and bilingual homes can discriminate between their native language and a rhythmically similar foreign language. This suggests that by this time all infants have begun to acquire phonetic knowledge specific to their native language and use it in language discrimination. This conclusion is corroborated by the finding that 4-month-olds from bilingual homes also successfully discriminate between two rhythmically similar native languages.

Word form recognition and linking word to meaning

So far we have seen that from a very young age babies are sensitive to speech rhythm and to the sequential probability of speech units, syllables and phonemes, and these abilities were assumed to provide them with clues to word boundaries in continuous speech and to thus bootstrap vocabulary acquisition. Having determined that the mechanisms underlying this ability—the prosodic and statistical learning devices—are operational at birth or soon thereafter, a next step is to ascertain how many months of naturalistic language exposure it takes infants to start recognizing sound patterns that correspond to actual words. A word's sound pattern must probably be encountered a minimum number of times to give rise to a feeling of familiarity. It will be clear that reaching this minimally required number of encounters will be spread out over a much longer period of time than the duration of a familiarization phase in the laboratory (as in Saffran et al., 1996a, and Saffran, 2001, in which the habituation phase typically only lasts a few minutes) and longer than the period of naturalistic exposure it takes to become familiar with recurrent **sublexical** phonotactic sound sequences (at about 9 to 10 months; see the above studies of Jusczyk et al., 1993, and Sebastián-Gallés and Bosch, 2002). In other words, phonotactic knowledge is likely to precede lexical knowledge. The ground for this claim is that a particular sublexical pattern recurs across many different words and its frequency of occurrence is therefore larger than the occurrence frequency of a particular word. Because the frequency of occurrence of each individual word will generally be smaller for infants growing up in a bilingual environment than for infants growing up monolingual, it plausibly takes longer for a bilingual than a monolingual child to start recognizing it. The first study reviewed in this section examined at what age monolingual and bilingual infants start to detect familiar word forms in speech on the basis of prior naturalistic language exposure; that is, at what age word form recognition emerges. The remainder of this section looks at a more advanced aspect of lexical development in infants; namely, the ability to associate a particular phonological form with meaning.

Vihman, Thierry, Lum, Keren-Portnoy, and Martin (2007) examined the emergence of word form recognition by testing groups of English monolingual infants of four different ages: 9, 10, 11, and 12 months. In addition, one group of English–Welsh bilingual 11-month-olds was tested. (In fact, Welsh monolingual infants were also tested but there was reason to believe they were not as monolingual as the English monolinguals and their data will therefore be ignored here.) From CDIs produced by the infants' families (see p. 17 for details), two sets of disyllabic English words and two sets of disyllabic Welsh words were selected. One set per language, called the "familiar" set, consisted of words judged to be known by on average 35% of the infants (e.g., *nappy*, *apple*, *naughty*). The other set, called "unfamiliar", consisted of words that were considered unknown to all infants (e.g., *nettle*, *juncture*, *wacky*). The experiment consisted of two parts. The first part used a version of the head-turn paradigm: Two loudspeakers were mounted on a wall, one on either side of the participant. On each trial one of the word sets (e.g., familiar English) was played from one of the loudspeakers and across trials presentation side (left or right) and type of word set played (familiar or unfamiliar) were randomized. Per trial the time the infant kept looking in the direction of the word-playing loudspeaker was registered. There was no experimental familiarization phase. A difference in looking time between the familiar and unfamiliar word conditions would indicate that as a consequence of prior naturalistic language exposure the infants had come to recognize at least some of the word forms of the familiar set and, therefore, that word form recognition had started to emerge. The English monolingual infants were tested on the English materials only; the bilingual infants on both language sets. In the second part of the study electrophysiological responses (ERPs) to the same stimulus words were collected in order to see how word learning affects neural responses to word stimuli. In this part of the study all stimuli were presented to the participants in a random order.

Of all four English-monolingual age groups only the 11-month-olds showed a significant difference in looking time between the familiar and unfamiliar conditions, the familiar words being listened to longer than the unfamiliar words. The bilingual infants, all 11-month-olds, showed a reliable familiarity effect in both languages, and the size of this effect was comparable to that of the 11-month-old monolinguals. These findings suggest that word form recognition emerges at

11 months and that it is not noticeably delayed in bilinguals as compared with monolinguals. The authors hypothesized that the reason the familiarity effect was not observed at 12 months is that when word learning is well under way a word's familiarity is no longer a sufficient reason for a child to pay special attention to it. These conclusions were corroborated and qualified by the electrophysiological data, which showed differences in the ERP signals to familiar and unfamiliar words. Like the familiarity effect in the head-turn data, this familiarity effect was significant (in some time windows of the signals; see the original study for details) for both the 11-month-old English monolinguals and the bilinguals, but disappeared at 12 months. It is illustrated in Figure 2.7 for one electrode position (but it occurred over more electrodes). For the bilinguals only the effect for the English materials is shown, but it occurred in Welsh as well and was statistically equally large in both languages. The authors interpreted it as an "oddball" effect, the relatively few stimuli that

were actually familiar to the infants (none of the "unfamiliar" words and only 35% of the "familiar" words; see above) drawing their attention. This attention allocation is reflected in deflections in the ERP signal. The reason the effect has disappeared in 12-month-olds plausibly is that at this age more words, also a number of the previously unfamiliar ones, have become familiar. In other words, there are no oddballs any more.

Interestingly, the familiarity effect in the ERP signals was also significant in the monolingual 10-month-olds. Unfortunately, because only 11-month-old bilinguals were tested it is impossible to tell whether 10-month-old bilinguals would also have shown it, thus exhibiting word form recognition at that age. Still, the conclusion seems warranted that if word form recognition is delayed at all in bilingual infants, the delay is a modest one. A final conclusion echoes one drawn earlier (see p. 23, namely that ERPs provide a more sensitive marker of cognitive abilities— word form recognition in this case—than

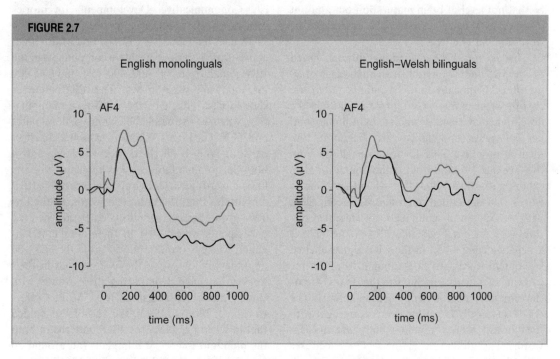

FIGURE 2.7

Event-related potentials elicited by familiar (black wave) and unfamiliar (gray wave) English words at electrode AF4 in English monolingual and English–Welsh bilingual 11-month-olds. Adapted from Vihman et al. (2007). Copyright © Cambridge University Press. Reproduced with permission.

behavioral measures do. This is suggested by the fact that the brain responses but not the behavioral responses already show evidence of word form recognition at 10 months.

Like Vihman et al. (2007), Conboy and Mills (2006) examined the brain responses of bilingual infants—Spanish–English bilinguals this time—to different types of spoken words, but in a number of respects the two studies differed critically from one another. The primary aim of the latter researchers was to tease apart the roles of language experience and brain maturation in the neural responses to familiar and unfamiliar words. They argued that children growing up bilingual provide the perfect opportunity to contrast the roles of these two variables because typically they are exposed to their two languages to uneven degrees. At the same time, it is one and the same brain, in a single maturational state, that houses both languages. So if bilingual infants' brain responses to word stimuli differ between their dominant (high-experience) and weaker (low-experience) language, the conclusion must be that not level of brain maturation but amount of prior experience underlies the emergence of word familiarity effects.

The age of the participating infants varied between 19 and 22 months, with an average of 20 months. This means that the infants tested are past the stage of mere word form recognition, the developmental stage examined by Vihman and her colleagues, and have clearly begun to link form to meaning. This, for instance, shows from the fact that 19-month-old monolingual toddlers exhibit a so-called N400 effect when they listen to words that are either congruent or incongruent with the content of simultaneously presented pictures (Friedrich & Friederici, 2004). (The N400 is a negative component in the ERP signal elicited by content words, which is thought to reflect the working of a neural mechanism that takes care of the semantic integration of words in context. The effect is typically larger for words congruent with the context than for contextually incongruent words. This difference is the N400 effect; see pp. 162 and 173–175 for more details.) Children's vocabulary spurt around 18 months (see above) is a further indication that the infants tested by

Conboy and Mills have begun to link word forms to their meanings. The test words were one group of known words and a second of unknown words. Whereas in the study by Vihman and colleagues every individual child knew only a subset of the "familiar" words, the present authors developed an individuated word set for each child so that all words from the "known" set (and none from the "unknown" set) were indeed known by the child (note that this a priori rules out an interpretation of any effect of the known–unknown manipulation to be observed in terms of a simple oddball response to the one or other word group). The participants were split up according to their Total Conceptual Vocabulary size (TVC; see p. 17) and the researchers examined each child's brain responses to stimuli in both the dominant and the weaker language. If language experience shapes the neural response, the ERPs for one and the same child (at one and the same brain maturational level) may be expected to differ between the dominant and weaker language. Language dominance was determined by English and Spanish Communicative Development Inventories provided by the children's parents.

In their data analysis Conboy and Mills (2006) concentrated on three negative components in the ERP signal: from 200–400, 400–600, and 600–900 ms following word onset. The ERP analyses showed clear effects of the word-type manipulation, which were qualified by language dominance and TCV. The high TVC group exhibited an effect of word type in all three time windows and in both the dominant and weaker language, with the known words always eliciting more negative ERP amplitudes than the unknown words. In the low TVC group these same effects emerged when the participants were tested in their dominant language, whereas it only showed up in the 600–900 ms time window when they were tested in their weaker language. Comparing these results with similar monolingual studies (e.g., Mills, Coffey-Corina, & Neville, 1997), the authors concluded that in several respects the ERP patterns of both the high and low TCV bilinguals (all around 20 months of age) resembled those of 13–17-month-old normally developing monolinguals and 20-month-old monolingual late talkers. This suggests that word acquisition is somewhat delayed in bilingual infants as compared with normally developing monolingual infants. In addition, the different response patterns for the dominant and weaker language within the low LVC group indicates that amount of language experience affects brain processes independent of brain maturation.

Conboy and Mills (2006) hypothesized that the difference between the ERP brain responses to known and unknown words that they observed indexes differential processing of meaning and not merely differential word form recognition. This account receives support from a study by Mills, Plunkett, Prat, and Schafer (2005), in which 20-month-old monolingual infants were first trained to associate two novel nonsense words (*bard* and *wug*) to two novel artificial objects. Two other novel nonsense words (*gaf* and *sarl*) were not paired with objects during training but simply repeated. The paired and unpaired novel words were presented equally often during training. After training the participants were presented with all four novel words, those paired with an object and the unpaired ones, while their EEGs were recorded. The finding of special interest here is that the paired and unpaired nonsense words showed exactly the same negative deflections in the EEG as the known and unknown words, respectively, in Conboy and Mills's study, including a larger deflection for the paired words. The critical difference between the paired and unpaired nonsense words in Mills and colleagues' study is that the former words had been assigned a meaning whereas the latter remained meaningless and, probably, it is this difference that brought about the differential brain response to both types of nonsense words. From here it is only a small step to conclude that the different ERP signals to the known and unknown words in Conboy and Mills's study also reflect a difference between the two in meaningfulness.

The above results indicate that at some point before they are 20 months old monolingual infants have started to form associative connections between words and their referents (Friedrich & Friederici, 2004; Mills et al., 2005) and that this also holds for bilinguals of a similar age,

especially in their dominant language (Conboy & Mills, 2006). Three studies resembling Mills et al.'s (2005) investigation but measuring behavioral responses instead of ERPs delimit the lower age boundary of this ability in monolinguals (Werker, Cohen, Lloyd, Casasola, & Stager, 1998; Werker, Fennell, Corcoran, & Stager, 2002) and in simultaneous bilinguals (Fennell, Byers-Heinlein, & Werker, 2007). Across these three studies infants of different age groups were first familiarized with two word–object pairs (Word A–Object A; Word B–Object B), the object of each pair shown on a video screen and the (nonsense) word played repeatedly from a speaker just below the screen. The age groups in Werker et al. (1998) involved infants of 8, 10, 12, and 14 months, whereas the age groups in the remaining two studies involved toddlers of 14, 17, and 20 months. In Werker et al. (1998) the two words to be paired with the objects were totally dissimilar (*lif* and *neem*) whereas in the remaining two studies they were similar (*bih* and *dih*). After habituation—which lasted between about 5 to 10 minutes—the participants were tested on "same trials" and "switch trials" (e.g., Word A–Object A vs. Word A–Object B). The researchers argued that if the infants had learned the associative links between the words and corresponding objects, the incorrect pairings in the switch trials should surprise them, resulting in longer looking times for the switch trials. In contrast, if they had not learned the word–object links, looking time should not differ between the two types of trials.

The 14-month-olds in Werker et al. (1998; dissimilar words; monolinguals), but not the younger age groups, showed longer looking times for the switch trials than for the same trials. Werker et al. (2002; similar words; monolinguals) found equally long looking times for same and switch trials in the 14-month-olds and different ones in the 17- and 20-month-olds. Finally, Fennell et al. (2007; similar words; bilinguals) observed equivalent looking times for same and switch trials in both the 14-month-olds and the 17-month-olds, whereas the 20-month-olds exhibited different looking times for the two types of trials. These results indicate that 14-month-old monolingual toddlers are able to simultaneously attend to the sound pattern of a word and to an object associated with this sound, while at the same time establishing a connection between the two. Within a short time span (of about 5 to 10 minutes) they can do this for (at least) two word–object pairings, on condition that the two words have dissimilar phonological forms. According to the authors this finding challenges the standard view that "prior to the vocabulary spurt, it is a very slow and laborious process for infants to learn to associate new words with objects" (Werker et al., 1998, p. 1301). The equally long looking times of the monolingual 14-month-olds on same and switch trials in Werker et al. (2002) suggest that the mental resources—attentional, perceptual, and memorial—of 14-month-olds do not yet suffice for all of the component processes to be executed successfully in parallel if the two words to pair with their respective objects are very similar and thus require very detailed perceptual analysis. An account in terms of the inability of toddlers this age to perceive the difference between the two similar words is not plausible because 14-month-old infants, and even younger ones, have no problem whatsoever discriminating two words differing in only one sound in simple speech perception tasks (see p. 18). Three months later, at 17 months, monolingual but not bilingual toddlers manage to perform the task successfully with a pair of similar words. Finally, at 20 months, bilingual toddlers catch up with their monolingual peers. As suggested by the authors, the developmental delay in bilinguals may be due to a lesser phonetic perceptual precision resulting from the fact that they have to acquire a double stock of phonetic segments. This lesser phonetic precision may increase the computational load involved in the word–object association task. In conclusion, it appears that attending to the phonetic details of words while at the same time linking these words to objects develops somewhat more slowly in bilinguals than in monolinguals. However, as noted by Fennell et al. (2007), this may not noticeably delay word learning in children growing up bilingual because the initial lexicon of infants contains very few similar-sounding words and, consequently, perceptual imprecision will hardly ever lead to a misunderstanding.

In the preceding sections we have followed the development of language in infants all the way from their ability to discriminate native and non-native phonetic contrasts at birth to recognizing words in their native language and forming associative connections between words and their meanings, a stage that appears to coincide with a vocabulary spurt around 18 months. The focus in our discussion has been on comparing these developing abilities in infants growing up monolingual and bilingual. In a number of cases, this comparison has revealed a developmental delay in the bilingual-to-be infants (Bosch & Sebastián-Gallés, 2003a, 2003b, 2005; Fennell et al., 2007), but about equally often the bilingual infants behaved similarly to their peers of the same age (e.g., Bosch & Sebastián-Gallés, 2001; Sundara et al., 2008; Vihman et al., 2007), and if a delay occurred at all, the bilinguals caught up with the monolinguals a couple of months later. It thus seems legitimate to conclude that the degree to which bilingual-to-be infants and toddlers trail behind their monolingual-to-be peers is negligibly small and often zero. This conclusion is corroborated by studies examining the development of vocabulary (e.g., Junker & Stockman, 2002; Pearson & Fernández, 1994; Pearson, Fernández, & Oller, 1993, 1995) and morpho-syntactic knowledge (e.g., De Houwer, 2005) in children covering a larger age range (between 8 and 30 months) than those tested in the above studies. These studies, in which the bilingual children's vocabulary knowledge was assessed in both their languages, have shown that their productive vocabulary *in the two languages together* equaled that of their monolingual age-mates and that their receptive vocabulary *in each of the languages* was comparable to that of their monolingual peers (studies that have used single language measures typically underestimate the vocabulary abilities of bilingual children; see Pearson, 1998, for a review). The Pearson and Fernández study has furthermore indicated that the vocabulary spurt occurs around the same age in bilingual children as in age-matched monolingual children. At the same time these and other studies (e.g., Genesee et al., 1995; Meisel, 2001) have shown that the long-held view (e.g.,

Volterra & Taeschner, 1978) that during the initial stages of language development bilingual children's linguistic system is undifferentiated by language is wrong. Instead, they suggest that children growing up bilingual separate their two languages from the start. In conclusion, it appears that a bilingual language environment is no serious source of confusion in language development nor does it appreciably delay language development.

AGE OF ACQUISITION EFFECTS AND THE CRITICAL PERIOD HYPOTHESIS

Introduction

Young children are generally believed to be better at language learning than adults and in some respects they demonstrably are. Many have posited the existence of a critical period during development to explain this age effect on language learning. The **critical period hypothesis** (CPH), as succinctly defined by Birdsong (1999, p. 1), states that "there is a limited developmental period during which it is possible to acquire a language, be it L1 or L2, to normal, nativelike levels. Once this window of opportunity is passed, however, the ability to learn languages declines." The hypothesis instantiates the more general notion that the development of some forms of behavior requires a specific type of stimulation to occur during a specific, bounded, period of time. One prototypical example to illustrate this idea is the case of birds such as the chaffinch that must be exposed to the male song of its species within 10 and 15 days after hatching in order to develop a similar singing skill. Another is the case of imprinting in ducklings, who for a limited period of time after hatching become irrevocably attached to the first moving object they descry, be it the mother duck, a crocodile floating by, or a twig swayed by the wind. A final example concerns a visual critical period in cats, the proper development of the visual cortex requiring the occurrence of early visual experience.

The critical period hypothesis for language learning enjoys a widespread interest among the general public and various specialized groups of people: linguists, psychologists, biologists, foreign language teachers, and language policy makers. This general interest as well as the most popular, neurobiological, explanations of the hypothesis can be traced back about 50 years, to the work of the Canadian neurosurgeon Penfield and the German-born Harvard psycholinguist Lenneberg. Penfield (1963; Penfield & Roberts, 1959) attributed the superior language-learning skills of young children to the fact that the child's developing brain still has a high level of plasticity whereas with aging the brain becomes progressively rigid. According to him, this progressive stiffening sets in after the age of 9 (Penfield & Roberts, 1959, in Singleton, 2005). He based these conclusions on differences between children and adults in the success of language recovery after speech areas of the dominant left hemisphere have been damaged by disease or injury (the linguistic skills of children recovering better after brain injury than those of adults), and on the related differential success of children and adults in transferring speech mechanism from the injured dominant hemisphere to the intact minor hemisphere (Singleton, 2005). The decreasing plasticity beyond early childhood has been suggested to result from progressive "myelination" (the coating of the axons of neurons by **myelin**, a fatty substance that speeds up the conduction of electrical signals).

Lenneberg (1967) popularized and extended these ideas, associating the critical period with a stage of progressive lateralization of brain functions, a process that he believed to end in puberty. According to him, at birth the two hemispheres are similar ("equipotential"), but as a consequence of maturation lateralization takes place gradually in childhood and during this process the brain's dominant hemisphere, usually the left, becomes specialized for language. This period of lateralization is the assumed critical period. The lateralization process is accompanied by a process of decreasing brain plasticity and its termination in puberty ends a state of organizational plasticity. To support these claims Lenneberg resorted to the same sources of evidence that Penfield came up with to substantiate his views, for instance the differential recovery from aphasia in children and adults.

A further popular explanation of the advantage of the young in language acquisition is that early in life humans possess a special language faculty, often called **universal grammar** (UG), which consists of innate knowledge regarding the forms that the grammars of natural languages may take. This language faculty is thought to be intact during a limited number of years and to subsequently become inoperative. It has been suggested that the neural substrate subserving the language faculty is demolished at some point because it consumes relatively large portions of the body's oxygen and calories (Pinker, 1994). The moment this neural tissue has done its job and language has been successfully acquired it becomes superfluous and might as well be dismantled, freeing resources to be used for other functions. In terms of this view, during the formation of human's biological make-up, evolution or the Creator seems to have overlooked the fact that the learning of second and further languages beyond childhood is a rather commonplace phenomenon.

The relatively good recovery of language functions following brain damage in children as compared to adults only provides indirect support for the hypothesis that there is a critical period early in life during which humans are especially well equipped to acquire language. Such findings merely suggest that areas in the brain that are not predisposed for language can take over language functions after damage to the areas that normally subserve language and that the young brain especially possesses this capacity. Instead, the hypothesis would receive direct support if it could be demonstrated that a language cannot be acquired successfully when learning only starts after closure of the putative critical period. Such support has been gathered in two lines of studies that both examined the rather exceptional cases of first language acquisition beyond early childhood and in the absence of obvious brain injury. The first of these concerns studies of children having grown up under circumstances of extreme deprivation, linguistically,

but typically also in a number of other respects: socially, emotionally, and physically. The second involves studies of the linguistic abilities of deaf individuals born to hearing parents, who are often not exposed to proper language until they start to attend schools for the deaf where they acquire sign language. I will present both these sources of evidence in the next section.

In the subsequent section I will discuss evidence gathered in studies on second language acquisition. The core of the approach pursued in these studies is to compare the degree of ultimate success in speakers of a second language who started learning the language at different ages. The critical period hypothesis in its most common form (the "maturational state" hypothesis) predicts that not only the first language but also a second and further languages cannot be fully acquired after closure of the critical period or, at least, that second language learning after offset of the critical period proceeds differently from, and is more effortful than, second language learning within the language-sensitive time window early in life. According to a second conception of the hypothesis (the "exercise" hypothesis, to be detailed below) a second language can be successfully acquired after the offset of the critical period as long as the human language-learning capacity is exercised early in life (as, of course, it is in most individuals).

Age of acquisition effects in first language acquisition

Late first language acquisition under circumstances of extreme deprivation

As mentioned, one way of studying first language acquisition beyond early childhood is to examine language development in individuals who have suffered severe linguistic deprivation as children. According to a strong version of the critical period hypothesis, children who are not exposed to linguistic input during the putative critical period will fail to acquire any language when later in life this state of linguistic isolation is discontinued. The most extreme of these cases concern so-called "feral children", and can be subdivided into three groups. A first group concerns children who supposedly have been raised by animals such as wolves, monkeys, dogs, and gazelles. Because in most of these cases wolves have been claimed to be these children's caretakers, these children as a class are called "wolf children". The website "feralchildren.com" lists a large number of these cases, discovered between AD 250 and present times. As acknowledged there, the evidence for many of these cases is virtually non-existent and it is possible that a large number of them concern mere folk tales or hoaxes. Nevertheless, a number of them are quite well documented and appear authentic.

One fairly well-documented case (e.g., Singh & Zingg, 1942/1966) concerns two girls who were discovered in 1920 in Midnapore, India, and were called Kamala and Amala. They were found together in a wolves' den. Kamala was estimated to be between 6 and 8 years old, Amala a couple of years younger. After their discovery the missionary Joseph Singh took them into the orphanage where he was in charge and started to train them to develop humanlike behavior, including language. Whereas various aspects of Kamala's non-linguistic behavior showed good progress over the years, her language skills improved extremely slowly. After about 3 years she mastered a vocabulary of approximately a dozen words and following another couple of years of training she mastered about 40, a number that a normal 2-year-old may acquire in a single week and smaller than the number of (sign language) words some chimpanzees have been reported to master at similar ages (Fouts, Fouts, & Van Cantfort, 1989; Gardner & Gardner, 1969, 1975). The words that Kamala did master were phonologically underspecified (saying, for instance, *bak* and *poo* for *baksa*, "box", and *pootool*, "doll") and her linguistic expressions were characterized by a lack of grammar. Amala, the younger girl, was reported to have made better progress but fell ill and died within a year of her admission into the orphanage, an event that caused a great setback in Kamala's development. Whether Kamala's level of language performance had reached its ultimate

limit with the above linguistic accomplishments is a question that will never be answered because in 1929, at an estimated age of 16, she caught typhoid and died.

A second group of feral children concerns those who are thought to have lived in isolation in the wild. Feralchildren.com lists about 20 such cases, again many of them of uncertain credibility. The best known, and well–documented, case is that of a boy to be named Victor, the wild boy of Aveyron. He was first seen in the woods of Saint Sernin sur Rance in the south of France, near Toulouse, at the end of the 18th century. After having been captured and having escaped several times, he emerged from the woods on his own on January 8, 1800, and was taken into custody. He was estimated to be about 12 years old then. A medical student, Jean-Marc Itard, took it upon himself to try to civilize him, taking great pains to teach him to speak. Initially Victor showed some progress in reading simple words and understanding but his progress soon came to a halt and after working with him for 5 years with disappointing results, Itard quit his efforts. The only words that Victor reputedly ever learned to speak were *lait* ("milk") and *O Dieu* ("oh God").

A third category concerns children who are not literally feral but whose behavior in some respects resembles that of feral children. The category encompasses children who grew up in or around their own home where their care involved little more than the absolute minimum to keep them alive. From an early age they were kept in confinement in a room or cellar, or even in a pigsty, dog kennel, or hen house, or they were not literally held in confinement but simply neglected. As a consequence, they were exposed to relatively little linguistic input (see the website feralchildren.com for many such cases, and Skuse, 1993, for a review). One of these children is Oxana Malaya, a Ukrainian girl who spent a large part of her childhood, between the ages of 3 and 8, in a dog kennel behind her house where she developed the behavior of her animal companions. A British Channel 4 television documentary shows her running about on all four limbs, barking, growling, and sniffing at her food.

Again, many of these cases are poorly documented and it is not always clear to what extent the child in question had been linguistically deprived prior to being discovered.

The best-documented case of a child growing up in confinement and under circumstances of severe linguistic deprivation and neglect is undoubtedly that of Genie, a girl who was discovered in 1970 in a Los Angeles suburb. From the age of 20 months until she was 13 years and 7 months old she had been locked up in a small bedroom, much of the time strapped naked onto a potty chair, and lived there in nearly total isolation and with nothing to do. Because of her father's intolerance to noise there was virtually no speech in the house, and Genie was not allowed to make any sounds herself. Her contact with other people was limited to the very brief periods of time her father, mother, or brother fed her baby food. Upon being discovered she was first put into the children's hospital in Los Angeles. The only speech she used shortly after being admitted to the hospital were the phrases *stop it* and *no more*, and she only appeared to recognize her own name and the word *sorry*. A team of physicians, psychologists, and therapists was soon formed that started to rehabilitate her and investigate her abilities. Victoria Fromkin, a psycholinguist at the University of California in Los Angeles, was asked to join the team to assess Genie's linguistic abilities and development. Fromkin brought along Susan Curtiss, a graduate student, who for the next 7 years of her life spent much of her time examining Genie's linguistic development. Thanks to the efforts of Curtiss, Fromkin, and some of their colleagues, detailed reports exist about Genie's linguistic development during these years (e.g., Curtiss, 1977, 1988; Curtiss, Fromkin, & Krashen, 1978; Fromkin, Krashen, Curtiss, Rigler, & Rigler, 1974).

Poignant as it is, the case of Genie is especially interesting in the present context because her linguistic (and social, nutritional, and physical) deprivation ended at about the time in life (at the age of 13) that Lenneberg (1967) assumed to mark the offset of the critical period for language acquisition. A strong version of the critical period hypothesis thus predicts that Genie, after her ordeal ended, should not show any signs of a linguistic ability despite the intensive efforts to teach her language skills. Victor was estimated to be of about the same age as Genie when he was discovered but we do not know for sure what his actual age was. Furthermore, nothing is known about the circumstances under which Victor grew up, nor about the reasons why he ended up alone in the woods. It is not unlikely he was abandoned because he was abnormal in the first place and, indeed, Victor is sometimes regarded the first documented case of autism. For these reasons, his utter lack of speech even after a lengthy period of intensive language training hardly counts as evidence that a critical period for language acquisition exists. Although much is also unknown about Genie's abilities before she was locked up, on the whole we know much more about her than about Victor, including the fact that, when tested in the years following her discovery, she demonstrated a high level of skill on tasks that exploited various forms of non-verbal intelligence, for instance on tasks that assess spatial abilities. As described by Curtiss (1988, p. 369):

> Her mental age [. . .] increased 1 year for each year post-discovery. Within 4 years of her discovery, she had clearly attained most aspects of concrete operational intelligence, including both operational and figurative thought [. . .] and had demonstrated not only fully developed but superior abilities in the domain of visual and spatial function (e.g., Gestalt and part/whole abilities; spatial rotation; spatial location; conservation of spatial features; and knowledge about visual and spatial features, such as size, shape, and color).

The answer to the question of whether Genie, despite her state of language deprivation during the putative critical years, shows a capacity to learn language, depends on exactly which domains of linguistic functioning are thought to reflect the essence of language. Within a few months after she was discovered she began to produce single words, and a couple of months later she had acquired a productive vocabulary of 100 to 200 words and had started to combine words. Her vocabulary included all sorts of words, such as words referring to colors, numbers, emotional states, and words that expressed subtle meaning distinctions (*pen* vs. *marker*; *jumper* vs. *dress*; Curtiss, 1988). It was also clear that her one-word utterances and the word combinations that she produced were not imitations but that she construed them herself. These results suggest that she was fully able to acquire referential-lexical knowledge and, hence, that nothing was wrong with her semantic development. However, Genie's development of morphology and syntax lagged far behind that of normally developing children and remained atypical in several ways. Even after years of training she experienced great problems with inflectional morphology; that is, the ability to add **affixes** to the roots of words. (Examples of affixes are the plural **morpheme** -s (*roof/roofs*), the possessive -*s* (*sister's*), tense morphemes (*grab/grabbed*), and case endings.) In addition, she experienced problems with word order, prepositions, pronouns, and the use of auxiliary verbs (e.g., *be*, *do*, *can*, *will*, *may*), and was unable to transform active sentences into their passive form. She also showed a disproportionately large discrepancy between her comprehension and production skills. The upper part of Table 2.2 shows the utterances with which Curtiss (1988) illustrated Genie's lack of grammar.

Genie's poor grammatical performance (including **morphology**) but good lexical-semantic performance suggests that a late start of first language acquisition, in adolescence, is an impediment for syntactic development but not for semantic development. If semantic development is considered the exclusive domain of language, this overall pattern of data supports a weak version of the critical period hypothesis: Some aspects of language can apparently only be learned within a critical, bounded period early in life (grammar and morphology) whereas the acquisition of other aspects of language is not confined by a developmental time window (semantics). If, however, grammar and morphology are considered the quintessential components of human language, whereas other

TABLE 2.2
Sentences produced by Genie and Isabelle

Genie:
  I like hear music ice cream truck.
  After dinner use mixmaster.
  Like kick tire Curtiss car.
  Ball belong hospital.
  Genie Mama have father long time ago.
  Think about mama love Genie.
  Dark blue, light blue surprise square and rectangle.
  Teacher say Genie have temper tantrum outside.
  Father hit Genie cry longtime ago.
  Genie have Mama have baby grow up.

Isabelle:
  Why does the paste come out if one upsets the jar?
  What did Miss Mason say when you told her I cleaned my classroom?
  Do you go to Miss Mason's school at the university?

Sentences produced by Genie and Isabelle who both had been deprived of linguistic input during childhood, Genie until she was 13 years old, Isabelle until she was 6.5 years old. Genie's expressions are characterized by a lack of grammar, Isabelle's by a good mastery of grammar. The Genie examples are from Curtiss (1988); the Isabelle examples from Pinker (1994).

aspects of language are not regarded unique to language but, instead, to be manifestations of other, non-linguistic, abilities (e.g., acquiring vocabulary may reflect memorizing and association skills or general intelligence), then Genie's case seems to support a stronger (or even a strong) version of the critical period hypothesis. Apparently, some specialist morpho-syntactical acquisition device had become corrupted by the time Genie was finally allowed to start developing language. Interestingly, brain research and tests specifically designed to find out what hemisphere is involved while performing tasks that tap various forms of cognitive functioning (p. 413) revealed that Genie's language was not lateralized in the left hemisphere, as it is in the far majority of right-handed people (e.g., Curtiss et al., 1978). Instead, (right-handed) Genie appeared to use the right hemisphere for both language and non-language functions. In fact, whatever task she performed there was almost no brain activity in the left hemisphere. This led the investigators to assume that language acquisition triggers hemispheric specialization and that the brain tissue normally committed to language—that is, the left hemisphere—functionally atrophies if it is not exposed to linguistic input early in life.

Pinker (1994), a fierce supporter of the view that a critical period exists for grammar learning, underscored this position by comparing Genie's poor grammatical performance with the excellent morpho-syntactic skills of Isabelle, another girl who experienced extreme linguistic deprivation as a result of years of confinement early in life. Together with her deaf-mute mother, Isabelle had been locked up by her grandfather in a darkened room from birth. When Isabelle was 6.5 years old both of them escaped from their imprisonment. Although she had learned to communicate with her mother through a system of gesture, when Isabelle was first tested immediately after her confinement ended she had a mental age of about 19 months and no language whatsoever. An intensive training program was developed to socialize her and she developed language at an astonishingly rapid pace: 18 months after her liberation Isabelle mastered over 1500 words and spoke in grammatically complex sentences (see Table 2.2). As argued by Pinker, the salient difference between the excellent syntactical skills of Isabelle and Genie's poor grammar resulted from the fact that Genie started her linguistic training after the closure of the critical period, whereas Isabelle started it well before this point of closure. However, unlike Genie, Isabelle had not been fully deprived of communication with another human being during her confinement. This may partly account for her successful grammatical development.

Conclusions. Suggestive as the above case studies may be, they do not unequivocally settle the question of whether a critical period for language learning exists. The evidence based on children claimed to have been raised by animals or to have somehow survived in the wild on their own is severely compromised by the fact that the children in question all suffered other forms of deprivation in addition to a lack of language input (for instance, social and nutritional deprivation) and that these may be the cause of their failure to acquire language after their circumstances normalized. Furthermore, the reason

why these children were left to nature's care is unknown. It is plausible that they were abandoned or neglected because they were abnormal in the first place, and that this is why they failed to learn language. Genie also suffered other types of deprivation in addition to her greatly impoverished exposure to language: She was not fed properly, lacked a supportive social environment and cognitive challenges, and her movements were severely constrained. It is conceivable that some or all of these aspects of her detention aversely affected her later linguistic development, although admittedly this would not explain the observed discrepancy between Genie's lexical-semantic development on the one hand and her syntactic development on the other, nor would it explain why similar forms of non-linguistic deprivation did not keep Isabelle from developing a fully fledged grammatical system after her ordeal ended.

A further point of concern is that in at least one more recent publication serious doubts are raised as to whether the Genie case has been presented in a sufficiently balanced way. Jones (1995) scrutinized all of Genie's spontaneous utterances as included in the original publications, the far majority of them being reported in Curtiss (1977) and having been gathered during the first 4 years that Curtiss worked with Genie, between June 1971 and June 1975. In addition, Jones studied all original publications based on Genie's linguistic behavior. Examining this work he noted a shift in the assessment of Genie's linguistic accomplishments, the year 1977 marking a turning point. All publications up until that year (Curtiss, 1977; Curtiss, Fromkin, Krashen, Rigler, & Rigler, 1974; Fromkin et al., 1974) presented Genie's productive language development as one in which in all linguistic domains—phonological, morphological, syntactic, and pragmatic—clear progress could be observed, and dated charts were included in which Genie's progress in the acquisition of morphology and syntax was presented step by step (Curtiss, 1977). To illustrate Genie's morphological and syntactic knowledge, Jones (1995) listed a number of Genie's utterances as selected from Curtiss (1977). They are shown in Table 2.3.

TABLE 2.3

Sentences produced by Genie 1974–5

Curtiss is dancing.
I want think about Mama riding bus.
I want you open my mouth.
Teacher is boss at school.
Coffee on the table is spill[ed].
I am thinking about Miss J. at school in hospital.
M. said not lift my leg in the dentist chair.
Mr. W. say put face in big swimming pool.
I do not have a toy green basket.
I do not have a red pail.

Sentences produced by Genie between June 1974 and June 1975,
as selected by Jones (1995) from Curtiss (1977). The sentences are
listed in order of occurrence.

It is obvious from even a cursory look at these utterances that they are much more elaborate in morphology and syntax than those listed in Table 2.2. As illustrated by Jones with several quotations from the original publications, the authors of the pre-1977 publications were of the opinion that these already relatively complex utterances in fact underestimated Genie's morphological and syntactical skills because of a large disparity between her **competence** and **performance**. In agreement with these observations, the authors concluded that Genie's linguistic performance manifests the mastery of syntax to at least some extent.

Despite the fact that they are based on the same data, the post-1977 publications (e.g., Curtiss, 1988; Curtiss et al., 1978) presented a much more negative evaluation of Genie's syntactic accomplishments, judging it to be primitive and underdeveloped. These claims were illustrated by selections of Genie's utterances that were, according to Jones (1995), highly biased, excluding all those that clearly suggest the presence of morphological and syntactical knowledge. On the basis of his analysis Jones concluded that the post-1977 claims that Genie was unable to acquire the morphology and syntax of English and that her utterances remained uninflected and telegraphic are either misleading or false. Unfortunately, it is not likely that the controversy surrounding the Genie case will ever be resolved because the study of Genie's language

development came to an abrupt halt when quite suddenly her mother no longer allowed her to be a subject of study. It will therefore never be known whether after this point her language, and specifically her grammatical skills, progressed any further.

A further and larger category of late first language learners, deaf children of hearing parents, offers a stronger test of the critical period hypothesis than the above cases of severely neglected children because, apart from experiencing linguistic isolation, the former generally grow up under normal circumstances. It is to some research that examined the linguistic abilities of these individuals that I will now turn.

Late first language acquisition in deaf individuals born to hearing parents

Similarity between sign language and spoken language. Because hearing parents of deaf children typically do not know any sign language, first language exposure of children born to these parents is often delayed until they enter a school for the deaf where they start to learn sign language. For various reasons sign languages are now considered real languages (Carroll, 2004). One of them is that spoken languages and sign languages are structurally similar in a number of respects. Taking American Sign Language (ASL) as an example, one of its similarities to spoken languages is that, just as words in the latter are composed of a relatively small set of smaller, meaningless elements (the language's phonemes) that are combined in regular ways, the signs of ASL are composed of a relatively small set of subcomponents. The components in question all instantiate different values of three parameters: hand configuration (e.g., open palm or closed fist), place of articulation or location (the body part near which the sign is made; e.g., near the cheek or near the upper arm), and the exact movement of the hand (e.g., upward or sideways; e.g., Klima & Bellugi, 1979). A pair of signs that differ from one another in just one parameter can refer to different things or events, just as in spoken languages words that differ from one another in a single phoneme mean different things (e.g., *dog* versus *fog*). A further similarity is that, as many natural spoken languages, sign languages have a rich morphological system. For instance, a typical ASL verb of motion can contain no fewer than seven independent morphemes that are articulated simultaneously (Singleton & Newport, 2004).

A further similarity is that the first stages of language development have been found to be similar in sign language and spoken language. For instance, deaf infants born to deaf parents who master ASL appear to engage in manual "babbling" around 12 months of age, combining values of the ASL parameters handshape, location, and movement into signs that do not exist in ASL but that are nevertheless permissible within that system (Pettito & Marentette, 1991). This behavior resembles that of hearing infants of speaking parents, who by 11 to 12 months combine phonemes into permissible but non-existing sequences of sounds, as if they are practicing the language's sound system. Furthermore, just as children at the two-word stage in spoken language development signal the meaning of two-word utterances by the order of the component words, in children with ASL as their native language a two-word stage can be identified in which sign order is used to indicate meaning. Yet a further source of evidence that spoken and sign languages are governed by the same principles is that "slips of the hand" in sign production are of the same types as the "slips of the tongue" that occur in speech production, suggesting similar language production processes. In general, the comprehension and production of sign language require processing operations similar to the decoding and encoding operations in spoken language processing (e.g., Klima & Bellugi, 1979; Supalla & Newport, 1978). Finally, largely the same brain structures are involved in sign language and spoken language (e.g., MacSweeney et al., 2002; MacSweeney, Capek, Campbell, & Woll, 2008; see Chapter 8 for details about these structures). In sum, parallels between sign language and spoken language have been revealed in terms of their linguistic structure, acquisition, processing, and neurocortical substrate. Deaf children who have access to sign language can

thus rightfully be said to have access to real language.

Age of sign language acquisition and ultimate attainment. The age at which deaf children of hearing parents are first exposed to sign language varies greatly, depending on such factors as when the child's deafness is detected, if and when special schooling facilities are available, and when it has been established that the child will not be able to acquire language via audition, augmented by hearing aids, cochlear implants, and lipreading (Mayberry, 2007). In contrast, deaf children of deaf parents (about 10% of the deaf population; Schein & Delk, 1974) are often exposed to sign language from birth because their parents are fluent in it. Combined with the above observation that sign languages are proper languages, this state of affairs offers a natural arena to examine the possibility of the existence of a critical period for first language learning, namely by comparing the linguistic skills of deaf people who differ from one another in the age at which they were first exposed to sign language.

Several studies using this methodology have shown an inverse relationship between age of first exposure ("age of acquisition"; AoA) to sign language and ultimate level of proficiency in this language. In one of these studies, Newport and Supalla (in Johnson & Newport, 1989) tested participants with a minimum of 40 years of experience in American Sign Language (ASL) as their primary language on their comprehension and production of ASL verb morphology. The fact that all participants had used ASL for so many years guaranteed that the researchers tapped their participants' ultimate level of ASL proficiency and not some stage at which they could still be considered learners of the language. The participants were split into three groups: "native learners", "early learners", and "late learners". The native learners had deaf parents and had been exposed to ASL from birth, whereas the early and late learners had hearing parents and had first been exposed to ASL between the ages of 4 and 6 (the early learners), and at the age of 12 or later (the late learners). On virtually all of the morphemes tested and on both the comprehension and production tests the results showed a linear decline in performance with increasing age of acquisition. The native learners outperformed the early learners and the early learners scored better than the late learners. Nevertheless, the late learners, despite first being exposed to ASL around the closure of the putative critical period, demonstrated some knowledge of ASL verb morphology.

Similarly, Boudreault and Mayberry (2006) tested three groups of adult deaf ASL signers on a grammatical judgment task. All participants had used ASL as their primary language daily for minimally 12 years and none of them had successfully acquired a spoken language prior to learning ASL. In other words, all participants were L1 learners of ASL. One group, the group of "native controls", had been exposed to ASL from birth. Those in the second group were first exposed to it between the ages of 5 to 7, when they were first enrolled in a school for deaf children. The participants in the third group were first exposed to ASL when they enrolled in a school for deaf children between the ages of 8 and 13. Prior to this they had attended schools where the oral method was used, which prohibits the use of sign language and relies on speech and lipreading instead.

Various types of grammatical and ungrammatical ASL syntactic structures were presented (in signed form) on a computer screen and the participants had to decide for each signed structure whether or not it was grammatically correct. The selected structure types were of different levels of difficulty and are normally acquired at different stages of ASL acquisition: simple affirmative sentences that contained uninflected signs only; negative sentences that again only contained uninflected signs but included a negation; sentences that contained verbs inflected for person and number; question structures that consisted of uninflected signs only and included a question marker; "relative clause" sentences that consisted of two clauses; and "classifier" structures that, unlike any of the other types of structures, contained a **classifier**.

Large AoA effects on response accuracy were observed. This held for all types of structures, and

the effects of acquisition age did not interact with structure type. The results are summarized in Figure 2.8 in terms of so-called A′ scores, which take guessing into account. A′ scores vary from 0.5, indicating that the syntactical rule in question is completely unknown, to 1.0, indicating that the rule is mastered.

As can be seen, the native ASL learners outperformed the other groups on all types of structures and the group that had only started to learn ASL between the ages of 8 and 13 performed worst on all structures. It can also be seen that in all three groups performance was relatively poor on two of the relatively complex structure types, the question and relative clause structures, and that the latest learners' performance on these structures in fact approached chance. Nevertheless, as was the case for verb morphology in the study of Newport and Supalla discussed above, the late learners clearly also acquired some ASL syntax.

Late learning of a spoken first language in a deaf person and the role of homesign. The results of the above two studies clearly suggest that the onset age of ASL learning affects ultimate attainment. However, they also indicate that a late start of ASL acquisition does not frustrate grammar learning completely, because even the late learners in Newport and Supalla's study, first exposed to ASL after the closure of the putative critical period, ultimately mastered some grammar. At first sight these results appear to refute the critical period hypothesis because according to the hypothesis no grammar learning should be possible after the critical age. However, a study by Grimshaw, Adelstein, Bryden, and MacKinnon (1998) provides an interesting new perspective on the above results. These authors noted that in studies on AoA effects on sign language acquisition, age of acquisition is typically defined as the age at which the participants were first enrolled in a boarding school for the deaf which uses sign language as the medium of communication, but that prior to their admittance into such a school they have not experienced complete linguistic isolation. Instead, most of them received some previous schooling in

FIGURE 2.8

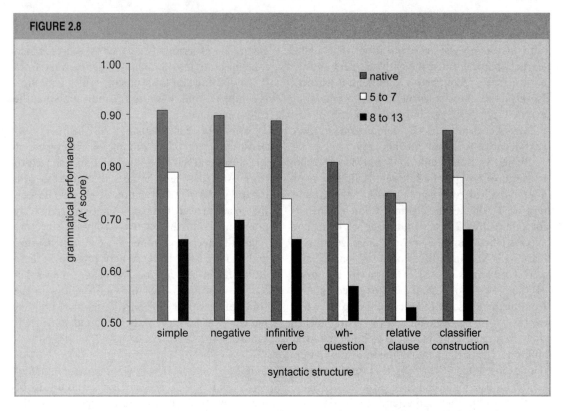

Mean accuracy on a grammatical judgment task in American Sign Language (ASL) as a function of age of first ASL exposure and type of sentence structure. The participants had first been exposed to ASL from birth (native), between 5 and 7 years, or between 8 and 13 years. A′ scores of 0.50 indicate chance performance. Data from Boudreault and Mayberry (2006). From Mayberry (2007). Copyright © Cambridge University Press. Reproduced with permission.

either a regular school or in day classes for the deaf and may have acquired some linguistic skills as a result of this. Furthermore, prior to being exposed to proper sign language the participants in these studies communicated with both their family members and their peers by using "home-sign", a system of gestures that deaf children who are not exposed to natural language spontaneously develop to be able to communicate with their environment.

Although homesign systems lack many of the syntactical subtleties of full languages, spoken or signed, they are not completely devoid of structural regularities and are similar to full languages in some respects (Goldin-Meadow, 2003, 2005; Goldin-Meadow, Butcher, Mylander, & Dodge, 1994). Among the properties that homesign systems share with real languages is the consistent

ordering of signs within a sentence to mark particular thematic roles. Another is the property of "displaced talk": Just as in real languages, homesign is used to communicate about the past, present, and hypothetical future (see Table 2.4 for a complete list of the properties shared by homesign systems and proper languages).

Because of these similarities with real languages, homesign systems are considered a type of proto-language and their spontaneous creation and rapid development provide a window on how natural languages are created and evolve over generations (Botha, 2007; Goldin-Meadow, 2005; Sandler, Meir, Padden, & Aronoff, 2005). Because homesign shares features with real language, the use of homesign can be regarded a preparatory stage of later language acquisition and, plausibly, it especially provides a basis for later sign

TABLE 2.4

Properties of natural languages that also characterize homesign systems

Property	As instantiated in homesign
Words	
Stability	Sign forms are stable and do not change capriciously with changing situations
Paradigms	Signs consist of smaller parts that can be recombined to produce new signs with different meanings
Categories	The parts of signs are composed of a limited set of forms, each associated with a particular meaning
Arbitrariness	Pairings between sign forms and meanings can have arbitrary aspects, albeit within an iconic framework
Grammatical functions	Signs are differentiated by the noun, verb, and adjective grammatical functions they serve
Sentences	
Underlying frames	Predicate frames underlie sign sentences
Deletion	Consistent production and deletion of signs within a sentence mark particular thematic roles
Word order	Consistent orderings of signs within a sentence mark particular thematic roles
Inflections	Consistent inflections on signs mark particular thematic roles
Recursion	Complex sign sentences are created by recursion
Redundancy reduction	Redundancy is systematically reduced in the surface of complex sign sentences
Language use	
Here-and-now talk	Signing is used to make requests, comments, and queries about the present
Displaced talk	Signing is used to communicate about the past, future, and hypotheticals
Narrative	Signing is used to tell stories about self and others
Self-talk	Signing is used to communicate with oneself
Meta-talk	Signing is used to refer to one's own and others' signs

From Goldin-Meadow, 2005. Copyright 2005 National Academy of Sciences, USA.

language learning. According to this view, the late sign language learners examined in the above and similar studies (Emmory, Bellugi, Friederici, & Horn, 1995; Mayberry & Eichen, 1991) did not start the language acquisition trajectory from scratch. Therefore the above-chance performance on the grammatical tasks that they exhibited may not challenge the critical period hypothesis but reflect a form of preliminary sign language learning prior to the closure of the critical period.

In a single-case study Grimshaw et al. (1998) examined a purer example of late first language acquisition. Their subject, E.M., was a profoundly deaf 19-year-old man from rural Mexico with hearing parents. He had not received any formal education, nor had he been in contact with other deaf persons, before he was 12 years of age. His preparatory linguistic experience was therefore much more limited than that of the participants in the above studies, being limited to the homesign communication with his family members. At age 15 E.M. left the family home to stay with relatives in Canada and soon afterwards got binaural hearing aids that allowed him to hear speech at a normal conversational level. Since that time he had been overhearing spoken Spanish within the family but did not receive any formal language instruction, nor did he attend school. In other words, his oral linguistic input resembled that of young hearing children acquiring a first spoken language at home. At the time of testing this situation had lasted about 4 years. A number of non-verbal intelligence tests administered between the ages of 8 and 19 had all demonstrated a low-average level of intelligence, leading toward the conclusion that E.M.'s cognitive development had not been severely hampered by his linguistic isolation.

Grimshaw and his collaborators assessed E.M.'s comprehension and production abilities in Spanish at various moments during 4 years after he was fitted with hearing aids. His comprehension was assessed with Spanish versions of a set of tests that had also been administered to Genie (p. 50). Each test assessed passive knowledge of some specific aspect of grammar such as verb tense and conjunction, and it was administered several times over the years. Even though, unlike Genie, E.M. had not experienced other forms of deprivation than linguistic isolation and his intelligence was within the normal range, his performance was generally poor and on about half of the tests it still did not differ from chance when the last comprehension test was taken 34 months after he was first exposed to spoken Spanish. He still did not understand verb tense, negation, pronouns, or prepositions, nor did he show any systematic improvement on these subtests over time. Another salient characteristic of his performance on the comprehension tests was that it varied greatly over the different test sessions. An earlier session might show above-chance performance and the next might show chance performance again. In fact, the linguistic skills of E.M. were generally rather similar to those of Genie. Both manifested a paucity of grammatical knowledge, and Genie also showed the variability in performance typical of E.M.'s behavior. A noteworthy characteristic of E.M.'s language production was that after 48 months of exposure to Spanish (when the last production test was taken) he showed a **mean length of utterance** (MLU) of less than two words, a stage that in normal language development is reached at 20 months (at 48 months normally developing children have an MLU of 4.4). Other features of E.M.'s linguistic behavior were that he never went through a stage of experimenting with language sounds comparable to the babbling stage in normal development and never asked questions regarding language, thus exhibiting poor **metalinguistic awareness**. In conclusion, E.M.'s mastery of spoken Spanish after having had access to it for 4 years was extremely modest and far weaker than the linguistic mastery of the late ASL learners in the above studies.

The authors concluded that the case of E.M. supports the existence of a critical period for first language acquisition and that the difference in the amount of prior linguistically relevant experience might have been the cause of the discrepancy between the linguistic performance of E.M. on the one hand and the late ASL learners on the other hand. In support of the above suggestion that homesign provides a better foundation for the acquisition of a manual than a spoken language they report the case of Anna, a deaf homesigner with a history similar to E.M. Her linguistic isolation ended when, aged 16, she started to learn ASL rather than a spoken language. In contrast to E.M.'s poor progress with spoken Spanish, Anna advanced from homesign to ASL at a rapid pace. This result suggests that the late ASL learners in the above studies indeed started the language-learning task better prepared than E.M. Still, an alternative explanation of the relatively poor performance of E.M. must be considered: E.M.'s mastery of spoken Spanish was only tested up until 4 years after first being exposed to it, whereas in the ASL studies the participants were tested after a much longer period of ASL exposure. It is plausible that E.M.'s mastery of Spanish when tested for the last time had not reached its ultimate level yet. In conclusion then, although informative, this study also did not provide an optimal test of the critical period hypothesis.

Summary and conclusions

The evidence assembled in the above two lines of studies provides suggestive but not unequivocal support for the existence of a critical period for language acquisition. The evidence gathered in studies that looked at first language development in children who grew up isolated from other human beings is compromised by the fact that, in addition to linguistic deprivation, other forms of hardship have plausibly contributed to their poor linguistic performance. This possibility frustrates a firm conclusion that linguistic proficiency imperatively demands linguistic exposure during a delimited period early in life. The evidence collected in the ASL studies must be considered with caution as well because the late first language learners in these studies do not appear to have started learning the targeted language from scratch the moment they gained full access to it. This may be the reason why grammar learning was evidently not completely beyond their reach. In contrast to the deaf late ASL learners, E.M. had experienced relatively little relevant preparatory linguistic experience the moment he started to learn spoken Spanish. At first sight, in support of the critical period hypothesis, his poor grammatical skills in Spanish therefore suggest that linguistic isolation during the putative critical years prevents the successful attainment of the syntax of this language later in life. Yet there is a reason to believe that his Spanish ability was assessed at a time when it might not have reached its ultimate level. All in all then, on the basis of the above evidence it cannot be decided whether or not a critical period for language learning exists. The only conclusion that *can* legitimately be drawn from it is that early learners are at an advantage, a conclusion that is strengthened further by the research presented in the next sections. In those sections I will also explain why it is that the verification of the critical period hypothesis requires more than the mere demonstration that acquisition age affects ultimate linguistic proficiency.

All of the above studies dealt with the rather exceptional case of late first language acquisition. A further area of research addresses the question whether a critical age for language learning exists from a different angle; namely, by looking for age of acquisition effects on *second* language acquisition in the hearing population. Second language users with normal hearing abound worldwide and the age at which they start to acquire their second language varies greatly. This combination of facts is undoubtedly the reason why studies of this type by far outnumber those that focus on first language acquisition. I will review part of this evidence from second languages hereafter, but as a bridge to that discussion I will first present a couple of clever hybrid studies that looked at the effect of the age at which a first language is acquired on later second language learning. To anticipate, the results of these studies suggest that the human ability to learn language remains intact throughout life as long as it is fed by early linguistic experience. If it is not nourished in this way, the proficient use of languages learned later in life seems beyond reach.

Second language acquisition after delayed first language learning

Mayberry (1993) also exploited the fact that first language learning is delayed in a large part of the deaf population and provided a strong indication that to come to master a language fluently, early linguistic experience is indispensable. What is more, she showed that to become fluent in a particular language, early experience in *any* language will do. She compared the grammatical performance of two groups of ASL signers on a task that required them to recall complex ASL sentences. Both groups were late learners of ASL who started to acquire it between the ages of 9 and 13. For one group ASL was the first language. The second group consisted of people who had been born with normal hearing but had lost it between the ages of 9 and 13, after which they had started to learn ASL as an L2. Even though the ASL onset age was the same for the two groups of learners, test performance was substantially better for the L2 ASL learners than for the late L1 ASL learners (82% vs. 43% correct, respectively). Apparently the fact that the L2 learners but not the late L1 learners had had access to spoken language as young children made the difference, as if the triggering of some language acquisition machinery early in life keeps it operational for the rest of life. Conversely, if it is not triggered during this critical phase, it gets corrupted and later language learning becomes a laborious enterprise that must exploit other means than the hypothesized machinery dedicated to language learning.

Mayberry and Lock (2003; see also Mayberry, 2007) extended this experimental result from sign language to spoken language, looking at the effects of early linguistic experience, or the lack thereof, on late acquisition of (the written version of) English. They had four groups of participants perform a task that assessed their knowledge of various types of English sentence structures. The participants in one group, the "native controls", were normally hearing native speakers of English. The second group, the "early spoken language" group, consisted of participants with normal hearing who had acquired a spoken language other than English from birth (Urdu, French, German, Italian, or Greek) and had been enrolled in schools where English was the language of instruction at a mean age of 9 years, ranging from 6 to 13. The third group, the "early sign language" group, consisted of people who were born profoundly deaf and had acquired ASL as a first language from birth. They started to be exposed to L2 English from the moment they enrolled in preschools and elementary schools between the ages of 4 to 7 (5 on average). The participants in the fourth group, the "no early language" group, were deaf individuals born to hearing parents who started to attend schools for the deaf where sign language was used between the ages of 6 and 13 (9 on average). Before they enrolled in these schools they had only had a negligible amount of access to language. From the moment they started to attend these schools, they were also taught English (which implies that the participants in this group were late simultaneous first language learners and not pure late L2 English learners). Note that their age of first exposure to English was the same as for the "early spoken language" group. At the time of testing, the average number of years of English use varied between 23 and 26 across the four groups and all participants had been using English for at least 11 years. In other words, it may be assumed that at the time of testing they all had attained their ultimate level of English proficiency.

The task performed by the participants concerned a grammatical judgment that assessed their knowledge of five types of English sentence structures. For each type of structure, pairs of grammatical and ungrammatical sentences were created. These were presented one at a time on a computer screen and participants indicated with a button press whether or not the presented sentence was grammatically correct. Table 2.5 gives examples of all sentence types and explains the type of violations used to turn grammatical sentences into ungrammatical ones. Figure 2.9 summarizes the results in terms of the A' scores mentioned earlier, where 0.5 indicates performance is at chance level and 1.0 indicates complete mastery of the sentence type in question.

In addition to the fact that the depicted results strongly resemble those of the L1 ASL learners presented in Figure 2.8, three results (which were substantiated by the statistical analyses) pop out from this figure: First, the two groups of English L2 learners with early language experience perform similarly despite the difference in the nature

TABLE 2.5

Examples of English syntactic structures and rule violations used by Mayberry and Lock (2003)

Syntactic structure	Rule violation	Example
Simple	Auxiliary changed from "be" to "have"	The girl is playing in the water *The girl have playing in the water
Dative	Indirect object placed before the verb	The father is giving the girl an apple *The father an apple is giving the girl
Conjoined clauses	Conjunction placed at end of sentence	The girl is eating while the man is sleeping *The girl is eating the man is sleeping while
Non-reversible passive	Deletion of passive marker "by"	The girl was hit by the ball *The girl was hit the ball
Subject-subject relative clause	Incorrect relative clause marker	The boy who is chasing the girl is happy *The boy whose is chasing the girl is happy

of their prior language experience (spoken versus signed). Second, the group not exposed to language early in life performed worst on all structure types. Third, the group of native controls performed best on all types of structures. Recall that the early spoken language group and the no early language group were first exposed to L2 English at exactly the same age (9 years on average). Apparently, the age of acquisition of an L2 is not the sole factor to determine what level of proficiency is ultimately attained in it. Instead, what appears to have caused the difference in L2 performance between these two groups is the fact that the former but not the latter had been exposed to another language early in life. The authors concluded that these findings suggest that "early language experience helps create the ability to learn language throughout life, independent of sensory-motor modality. Conversely, a lack of

FIGURE 2.9

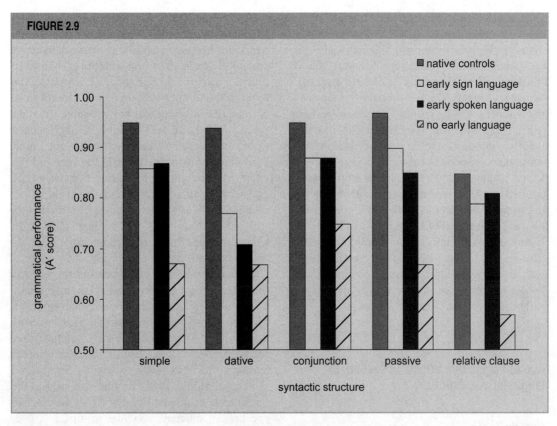

Mean accuracy on a grammatical judgment task in English as a function of early language experience and type of English syntactic structure. A' scores of 0.50 indicate chance performance. Data from Mayberry and Lock (2003). From Mayberry (2007). Copyright © Cambridge University Press. Reproduced with permission.

language experience in early life seriously compromises development of the ability to learn any language throughout life" (Mayberry & Lock, 2003, p. 382). Put differently: "[. . .] the timing of L1 exposure in early life affects the outcome of all subsequent language learning" (Mayberry, 2007, p. 543).

These quotes are strongly reminiscent of one of two versions of the critical period hypothesis that were considered by Johnson and Newport (1989) in an influential study on age of acquisition effects on second language learning that set the agenda for this line of research for years to come. They dubbed this version of the hypothesis "the exercise hypothesis". It ran as follows (1989, p. 64):

Early in life, humans have a superior capacity for acquiring languages. If the capacity is not exercised during this time, it will disappear or decline with maturation. If the capacity is exercised, however, further language learning abilities will remain intact throughout life.

I will shortly return to Johnson and Newport's study and to a selection of the wealth of further investigations that it provoked. But before doing so, one finding of Mayberry and Lock (2003) still begs some comment, namely the fact that, overall, performance was best for the native controls. Given the fact that all L2 English participants had been using English for at least 11 years, and may therefore not be expected to improve any more, this result is less trivial as it may seem at first sight. For some theorists this very difference in grammatical proficiency between native speakers and highly practiced late L2 users of a language constitutes the primary reason why they adhere to the critical period hypothesis (e.g., Abrahamsson & Hyltenstam, 2009). Other theorists, however, take the position that one may never expect speakers of more than one language to use language in the way native monolinguals do, because all extant languages within one and the same mind interact with one another. The poorer performance of L2 learners as observed in Figure 2.9 may simply result from interaction between the L1 and L2 language systems (both fully developed) during acquisition and/or use. Substantial evidence in support of this position will be presented in Chapters 4 through 7.

Age of acquisition effects in second language acquisition

Introduction

Unlike late first language acquisition, late second language acquisition is a common phenomenon and arguably more common than early second language acquisition. Accordingly, the study of age of acquisition effects on second language acquisition and use, being within reach of many language researchers, is a prolific research field that has produced a wealth of data, as well as a refined approach to tackle the question of whether a critical age for acquiring a second language exists. Arguments have been advanced about what types of evidence would support the critical period hypothesis, or provide evidence against it, and various domains of language, particularly grammar and phonology, have served as playgrounds to test it. Starting with the agenda-setting study of Johnson and Newport (1989), in this section these nuanced views on the critical period hypothesis will be expounded and some of the (counter)evidence will be discussed. One important source of (counter)evidence concerns

the exact shape of the age function that shows the relation between age of acquisition on the one hand and L2 performance on the other hand. A second source is the (im)possibility of nativelike ultimate performance in late L2 learners. The focus in the following discussion will be on these two sources of evidence, but a couple of other types of evidence will also be briefly touched upon, specifically the occurrence of non-nativelike performance in early learners and the effect of the typological distance between L1 and L2 on ultimate attainment. As in the above sections on late L1 acquisition, our discussion will concentrate on grammatical ability. In Chapter 5 age effects on L2 phonological ability will be covered.

In agreement with common current practice, only ultimate L2 attainment in relation to age of acquisition will be considered as critical evidence, not rate of progress during the various stages of acquisition. A number of early studies have shown that rate of acquisition is faster in older learners than in child learners. Snow and Hoefnagel-Höhle (1978), for instance, studied the naturalistic acquisition of Dutch by L1 English speakers of different ages (age groups 3–5, 6–7, 8–10, 12–15, and adults), assessing their progress at three different moments during their first year in The Netherlands. Participants in the 12–15 and adult groups progressed most rapidly during the first few months, and at the end of the first year the age groups of 8–10 and 12–15 outperformed the other groups of learners. The participants in age group 3–5 scored lowest on all of the tests, covering, among others, pronunciation, auditory discrimination, morphology, story comprehension, and storytelling. Long (2005, p. 289) generalized these findings and converging results from other studies into the following two conclusions: First, "adults proceed through early stages of morphological and syntactic development faster than children" and, second, "older children acquire faster than younger children". The above findings led Snow and Hoefnagel-Höhle to reject the critical period hypothesis, on the assumption that a special biologically determined language-learning endowment early in life implies relatively fast progress in young learners. Long and many others, however, have argued that what counts as proper evidence for or against the hypothesis is not how fast L2 learners with different onset ages improve but what their L2 performance looks like in the long run—in other words, what their ultimate attainment (or "end state" or "final state") is. This view is also adhered to in the studies to be presented below, as it was in the above studies on late language acquisition in deaf people.

Johnson and Newport (1989) considered two versions of the critical period hypothesis: the "exercise hypothesis" and the "maturational state hypothesis". The former was already presented in the quote that ended the previous section. The latter simply runs as follows: "Early in life, humans have a superior capacity for acquiring languages. This capacity disappears or declines with maturation" (Johnson & Newport, 1989, p. 64). Both versions of the hypothesis predict that for a first language to be learned completely it must be exercised early in life. However, they make different predictions regarding second language learning. The exercise hypothesis predicts that, as long as a first language is acquired early—as, of course, holds for the great majority of human beings—the ability to learn languages remains intact over life and, therefore, a similar level of fluency can be attained for languages learned later in life as for the first language. In other words, children and adults should show equal second language-learning skills. In contrast, the maturational state hypothesis assumes that, irrespective of whether a first language is acquired early in life, the language-learning capacity declines with aging as a consequence of maturational changes in the child's brain, from a state that benefits the learning of *any* language (be it the L1, L2, or any further language) to one that no longer offers this advantage. According to this version of the hypothesis, children are better at second language learning than adults are. As argued by Johnson and Newport, proving the maturational state hypothesis correct requires not only evidence that the ability to learn language diminishes over age but also evidence of a discontinuity in the age function that can be related to the closure of the period of brain maturation.

As they put it (1989, p.79):

> If the explanation for late learners' poorer performance relates to maturation, performance should not continue to decline over age, for presumably there are not many important maturational differences between, for example, the brain of a 17-year old and the brain of a 27-year old. Instead, there should be a consistent decline in performance over age for those exposed to the language before puberty, but no systematic relationship to age of exposure, and a leveling off of ultimate performance, among those exposed to the language after puberty.

Johnson and Newport (1989) tested these ideas in a study that looked at L2 speakers' knowledge of English morphology and syntax. A varied set of morpho-syntactical aspects of English were tested, 12 in all, such as its past tense and plural systems, its determiners and use of auxiliaries, and the way questions are formed in English. All participants, 46 in all, were Chinese and Korean native speakers who had immigrated to the United States between the ages of 3 and 39. Their age of arrival in the US was considered their age of first exposure to English or their age of acquisition. Because of this wide range in arrival age it was possible to determine the shape of the age function, including the predicted discontinuity.

To ensure that all participants had probably attained their end state of proficiency in English, included in the sample were only L2 speakers who attended university or had obtained a university degree and, furthermore, had been immersed in English for at least 5 years. In addition to the English L2 speakers, a group of 23 English native speakers were tested to provide a measure of baseline performance. The experimental task involved a grammaticality judgment to each of 276 spoken English sentences presented by means of an audiotape. Each sentence tested the presence or absence of one of the above mentioned types of morpho-syntactical knowledge. Grammatical and ungrammatical example sentences are shown in Table 2.6.

TABLE 2.6

Examples of grammatical and ungrammatical sentence pairs used by Johnson and Newport (1989)

1a. The farmer bought two pigs at the market
1b. *The farmer bought two pig at the market (plural violation)
2a. A bat flew into our attic last night
2b. *A bat flewed into our attic last night (incorrect past tense)
3a. The boys are going to the zoo this Saturday
3b. *A boys are going to the zoo this Saturday (incorrect determiner)
4a. Susan is making some cookies for us
4b. *Susan is making some cookies for we (incorrect pronoun)
5a. Kevin called Nancy up for a date
5b. *Kevin called Nancy for a date up (incorrect particle movement)
6a. Has the king been served his dinner?
6b. *Has been the king served his dinner? (incorrect position of the auxiliary)
7a. What do they sell at the corner store?
7b. *What they sell at the corner store? (omission of "do" insertion)
8a. Martha asked the policeman a question
8b. Martha a question asked the policeman (word order violation)

The results showed a strong relationship between age of arrival and grammatical knowledge ($r = -.77$), the early arrivals performing better than the later arrivals. Zooming in on the results of four separate age groups it appeared that the earliest arrivals (between the ages of 3 and 7) performed no differently from the native controls, whereas all three groups of later arrivals (with ages of arrival of 8–10, 11–15, and 17–39 years) performed worse. Furthermore, the latter three groups all differed significantly from one another, with those who arrived later performing more poorly than those who arrived earlier. As concluded by the authors, these findings suggest that it is possible to achieve native fluency in an L2 if one is immersed in it before the age of 7.

To test the above prediction of a discontinuity in the age function that could be related to brain maturation, the participants were subsequently divided into two age groups: those who had been first immersed in English between the ages of 3 and 15, and those for whom immersion started between the ages of 17 and 39. For the former group the correlation between age of arrival and performance was much higher ($r = -.87$) than for the latter ($r = -16$) and only the first of these correlations was statistically significant. These results are shown in Figure 2.10. A further noteworthy result was that the variance within the group of early arrivals was much smaller than in the group of late arrivals. Apparently, for L2 learners with an age of arrival below age 15, success in L2 learning is almost entirely determined by the age at which learning begins, whereas for those who are older at arrival other factors also play a role in what proficiency level will ultimately be obtained. Overall the authors concluded that their results support the maturational state version of the critical period hypothesis.

The shape of the age function: Mismatches between predictions and data

Two relatively recent investigations (Birdsong & Molis, 2001; DeKeyser, 2000) have tried to replicate Johnson and Newport's (1989) study using the same experimental materials but testing L2 English speakers with other L1 backgrounds. The results of neither study mimicked Johnson and Newport's findings in all respects. Yet DeKeyser, examining L2 English speakers with Hungarian as their native language, concluded that his data agreed with the findings of the original study and, accordingly, saw them as support for the (maturational state version of the) critical period hypothesis. In contrast, Birdsong and Molis (2001), testing native speakers of Spanish, had a special eye for the discrepancies between their findings and those of Johnson and Newport, and suggested that other factors than a bounded period of special language-learning ability early in life might bring about the age of acquisition effects.

In order to tackle a couple of concerns that had been raised regarding Johnson and Newport's (1989) study since its appearance in the literature, DeKeyser (2000) modified the original design in a number of respects. In Johnson and Newport's investigation the minimal length of

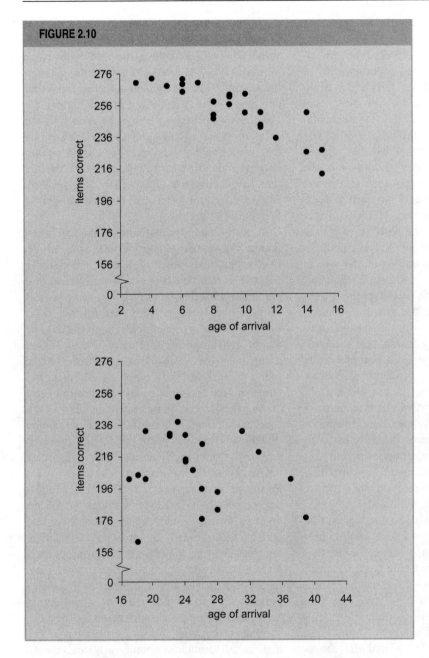

Number of items correctly responded to (out of a total of 276) by individual participants on a morpho-syntactical judgment test in English as a function of age of arrival in the United States. The top and bottom panels present the data for the participants who had arrived between 3 and 15 years and between 17 and 39 years, respectively. From Johnson and Newport (1989). Copyright © 1989, with permission from Elsevier.

residence of the participants in the US had been only 5 years. This may not have been long enough for some of the participants to have reached their ultimate level of English proficiency at the time of testing. Furthermore, age of arrival had been confounded with the participants' age at test taking and, consequently, the older test takers may have performed worse because of, say,

diminished attention skills and not because they had learned the L2 relatively late in life. Finally, differential ability to remain concentrated all through a rather lengthy test session may have contributed to the differential results for early and late arrivals. DeKeyser addressed these concerns by increasing the minimal length of residence in the US to 10 years, correcting for chronological age in the data analysis, and reducing the set of test items from 276 to 200.

But the most important procedural adjustment was that DeKeyser administered a language-learning aptitude test. His reason to do so was to test one specific view of the critical period hypothesis, dubbed the "fundamental difference hypothesis" by the scholar who first suggested it (Bley-Vroman, 1988). As argued by DeKeyser, this hypothesis could explain the large variability in the scores obtained by the late learners in Johnson and Newport's study, the performance of a number of them in fact overlapping with that of the early learners (see Figure 2.10). On the face of it, this finding is inconsistent with the predictions of the critical period hypothesis (see e.g., Birdsong, 2005, 2006), but the fundamental difference hypothesis provides a way to reconcile the existence of such successful late learners with the notion of a critical period for language learning early in life.

The fundamental difference hypothesis posits that in learning languages children exploit an innate language-specific mechanism for implicit, unconscious learning, and that this mechanism is no longer available for adult learners. To learn a second language, adults must therefore resort to explicit, conscious learning strategies that exploit the learners' general problem-solving capacities, including their ability to reflect on the structure of the targeted language. Adults who are good at this and, specifically, those with high verbal analytical skills, may attain a high level of proficiency in a second language despite the fact that they have no longer access to the assumed innate mechanism for implicit language learning. Conversely, those who lack a high level of verbal ability should never be able to attain a high level of proficiency in a second language. To test these predictions, DeKeyser administered the above-mentioned language-learning aptitude test, which was hypothesized to reflect the participants' verbal analytical skills.

In agreement with the hypothesis that good verbal analytical skills in late learners can compensate for the fact that an innate language acquisition mechanism is no longer accessible, the few late arrivals who obtained grammaticality-judgments scores within the range observed for the early arrivals had an above-average analytical verbal ability. Among the participants with an age of arrival of 17 or more, the correlation between the grammaticality-judgment score and the verbal ability score was a significant (but moderate) .33. For those who arrived before the age of 16 the correlation was a non-significant .07, suggesting that verbal ability plays no role when a second language is learned at a young age. It thus appears that the occurrence of successful late learners per se does not challenge the critical period hypothesis.

A further important finding was that, when taking the group of participants as a whole, DeKeyser (2000) observed a reasonably strong negative correlation between age of arrival and grammaticality test score ($r = -.63$), just as Johnson and Newport (1989) had (in their case: $r = -.77$). However, when splitting up the data by age of arrival (before and after 16), in neither group was the correlation significant: In the group of early arrivals a non-significant correlation of $-.26$ was obtained; in the group of late arrivals the correlation was a non-significant $-.04$. The latter finding replicates the analogous finding of Johnson and Newport. The former, however, deviates from their results in that these researchers observed a high correlation ($r = -.87$) for the group of early arrivals. This discrepancy is underexposed in DeKeyser's discussion of his findings. Yet, as argued by several authors and perhaps most ardently by Birdsong (2005, 2006), the absence of an age effect in the group of early arrivals constitutes a real challenge to the critical period hypothesis, and also Johnson and Newport (1989) had emphasized that a maturation account of language learning predicts a negative correlation between age of arrival and grammatical performance among early arrivals. In other words, it is not the occurrence of a significant correlation over the whole age spectrum per se that counts as critical evidence in support of the hypothesis. Instead, the hypothesis predicts the occurrence of specific discontinuities in the age function that can directly be related to maturational change. Specifically, it predicts the ("stretched Z"; Birdsong, 2005) age function

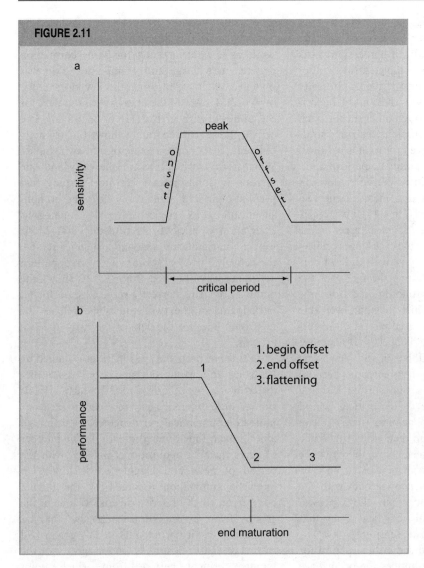

FIGURE 2.11

(a) Common view of the critical period hypothesis for language acquisition. A period of heightened sensitivity to linguistic input reaches a peak soon after its onset and decays gradually before it flattens out. (b) The "stretched Z" function relating age of acquisition to ultimate performance as predicted by the critical period hypothesis. Adapted from Birdsong (2005). By permission of Oxford University Press, Inc.

sketched in Figure 2.11b. This function is shown in relation to Birdsong's visualization of the standard conception of the critical period hypothesis for language learning (Figure 2.11a; Birdsong, 2005, 2006).

This view of the hypothesis holds that at some point early in life, and maybe already soon after or at birth, humans experience a heightened sensitivity to linguistic input that takes a brief amount of time to reach its peak level. The sensitivity peak lasts for a particular length of time, after which it declines gradually and then flattens out when brain maturation is completed.

This hypothesized state of affairs predicts that if the learner is immersed in the L2 environment during the full period of highest sensitivity (ending at Point 1 in Figure 2.11b, in which for simplicity sake the onset of heightened sensitivity is not shown), nativelike proficiency will ultimately be attained. If acquisition starts later and only coincides with part of the period of peak sensitivity (before Point 1), continuing into the stage during which sensitivity gradually decreases (between Points 1 and 2), or it only starts somewhere between Points 1 and 2, ultimate nativelike performance is no longer within reach, and the shorter the period of heightened sensitivity that is still exploited, the lower the level of ultimate performance will be. Finally, if immersion starts when brain maturation is completed (at or after Point 2), the learner has missed the opportunity to profit from heightened sensitivity and L2 learning has to come about through other means, such as the use of effortful conscious learning strategies. For these learners age of arrival is assumed to no longer correlate with ultimate performance.

In conclusion, the critical period hypothesis predicts an age function that includes the two discontinuities visualized in Figure 2.11b. DeKeyser's (2000) data do not meet these requirements because the grammaticality-judgment scores of his early arrivals did not correlate with arrival age, despite the fact that the participants within that group differed from one another in the extent to which they had been able to profit from the hypothesized period of heightened sensitivity. Birdsong (2005, 2006; Birdsong & Molis, 2001) argued that Johnson and Newport's results also deviated from the predictions because second language speakers who started learning the L2 after the closure of the critical period should never manage to acquire (near) native levels. Yet it was clear from their study that some do. However, as we have seen above, there may be a way to reconcile the incidental occurrence of nativelike performance in late learners with the hypothesis, by assuming that they possess exceptionally good verbal analytical skills that compensate for lost linguistic sensitivity.

If the notion of a bounded critical period for language learning indeed implies the occurrence of the above two discontinuities in the age function, it appears that the results of a couple of recent studies constitute a serious challenge for the critical period hypothesis. Like DeKeyser (2000), Birdsong and Molis (2001) conducted a replication of Johnson and Newport's study, using exactly the same methods and the same audiotape with spoken English sentences. The only difference between the two studies was that the L2 speakers' native language was now Spanish instead of Korean or Chinese. Even though one discontinuity in the age function was obtained, the general shape of the function

differed substantially from the one predicted by the hypothesis. Considering the group of participants as a whole, exactly the same correlation between arrival age and grammatical skill was obtained as in Johnson and Newport's study ($r = -.77$). However, the analyses on the data for the groups of early arrivals (16 or before) and late arrivals (after 16) separately showed a strikingly different pattern of results across the two studies. Whereas the correlations for the early and late arrivals in Johnson and Newport's study had been a high and significant $-.87$ and a non-significant $-.16$ respectively, the analogous correlation coefficients in Birdsong and Molis were a non-significant $-.24$ and a significant $-.69$, respectively. In other words, a reversed pattern of results was obtained. Figure 2.12 shows the numbers of items correctly responded to for all participants in the two studies as well as the regression lines for the data of the early and late arrivals.

In three respects the age functions obtained by Birdsong and Molis deviated from those predicted by the hypothesis: First, the early arrivals showed little difference between them in terms of ultimate grammatical performance, even though among them they differed greatly in the number of years their L2 acquisition coincided with the period of peak and heightened sensitivity to linguistic stimulation assumed by the theory. Second, an effect of arrival age is obvious in the group of late arrivals, despite the fact that L2 immersion of all participants in this group had started after the closure, at about age 15, of the putative critical period, from which point onwards age of arrival should no longer predict ultimate attainment. Third, there is no endpoint to the age-related decline in final-state performance of the late arrivals. In other words, the second discontinuity predicted by the hypothesis is missing in this age function. None of these findings can be reconciled with a view that age-of-arrival effects relate to a bounded maturational period early in life and, accordingly, Birdsong and Molis rejected the critical period hypothesis. A final noteworthy finding that speaks from Figure 2.12 is that the incidence of near-native performance differs greatly between the two

FIGURE 2.12

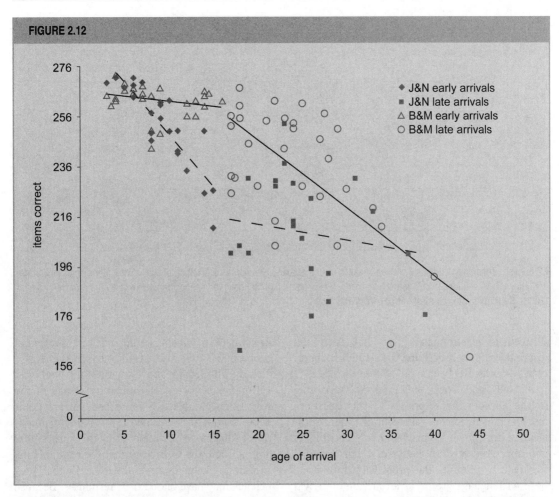

Number of items correctly responded to in Johnson and Newport (1989) and Birdsong and Molis (2001) as a function of age of arrival in the United States. The participants' L1 in Johnson and Newport's study was Chinese or Korean. In Birdsong and Molis' study it was Spanish. The regression lines concern the data of four subgroups of participants: the early and late arrivals in both studies. From Birdsong and Molis (2001). Copyright © 2001, with permission from Elsevier.

studies, in the sense that it is much higher in Birdsong and Molis's study. The authors suggested that the closer structural similarity between Spanish and English than between both Chinese and Korean on the one hand and English on the other hand may have caused this difference between the studies. Plausibly, the more similar the L2 is to the learners' native language, the more successful L2 acquisition will be.

A study by Hakuta, Bialystok, and Wiley (2003) challenged the critical period hypothesis for similar reasons. These researchers derived their data from the US Census information,

selecting from this database all respondents who could be identified as native speakers of Spanish (structurally relatively close to English) or Chinese (structurally distant from English) and had been residing in the US for minimally 10 years. The selected sample consisted of over 2 million native speakers of Spanish and over 300,000 native speakers of Chinese. Because the census database also contained information on the immigrants' educational background, the relation between this variable and English proficiency could also be determined. English proficiency ratings were based on a single question in

FIGURE 2.13

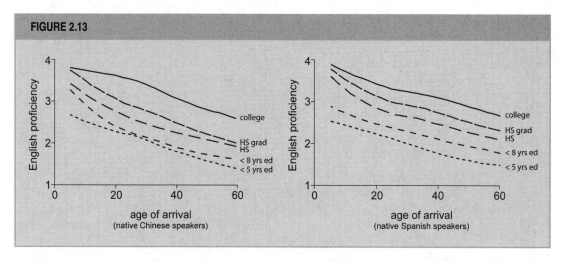

L2 English proficiency ratings of native speakers of Chinese and Spanish as a function of age of arrival in the United States and education level: less than 5 years, less than 8 years, some high school, high school, and some college. From Hakuta et al. (2003). Reprinted with permission from Wiley-Blackwell.

the census questionnaires, one that asked the respondents to self-describe their English ability on a 5-point scale: "not at all", "not well", "well", "very well", and "speak only English". According to the authors the responses to this question, involving a subjective assessment of English proficiency, are known to correlate reasonably highly with more objective measures of English ability. Figure 2.13 presents the proficiency ratings of both L1 language groups as a function of arrival age and educational level.

As shown, English proficiency clearly depended on both age of arrival and educational level: the higher the educational level and the younger the age at immigration, the higher the L2 English proficiency. To be able to discover discontinuities in the age functions mathematical modeling was applied to the data. Contrary to the predictions of the critical period hypothesis, no discontinuities were revealed. In addition to the effect of age of arrival and educational level, Figure 2.13 shows that Spanish native speakers had reached somewhat higher levels of proficiency in English than Chinese native speakers. This finding suggests that the degree of structural similarity between L1 and L2 might indeed be a further determinant of ultimate proficiency.

A potential weakness in Hakuta et al.'s (2003)

investigation (which could not be prevented because of their use of the census data) was already alluded to above, namely the fact that L2 proficiency was determined by means of the respondents' subjective assessment on a 5-point scale. Long (2005) pointed out a number potential problems associated with this procedure, among them the possibility that the respondents' expectancy with respect to their L2 English proficiency may have biased their responses: Because it is conventional wisdom that older L2 learners generally fare worse than younger learners and the respondents themselves plausibly also believe such to be the case, they may have taken their chronological age at arrival in their new country into account in their subjective assessment of their L2 proficiency level, choosing a point on the scale matching with this widespread belief (see also DeKeyser & Larson-Hall, 2005). With this possibility in mind it is important to note that the present two studies of Birdsong and Molis (2001) and Hakuta and collaborators (2003) are by no means the only ones that have failed to produce the discontinuities in the age function predicted by the critical period hypothesis. On the basis of a survey of 10 studies, Birdsong (2005, 2006) concluded, first, that age of arrival and ultimate L2 attainment consistently showed a negative correlation when the data for early and late arrivals were collapsed. (In Chapter 5 a couple of studies will be presented that show this same linear relation between arrival age and L2 ultimate attainment, but in the domain of phonology.) Second, when the data of early and late arrivals were considered separately, no clear pattern occurred, both groups showing a correlation between arrival age and attainment, neither group doing so, or either only the early arrivals or only the late arrivals showing a correlation. Because, for the critical period hypothesis to be supported, the data of the separate groups should *systematically* show the discontinuities predicted by the hypothesis, this result clearly constitutes a challenge for the hypothesis. At the same time, the consistent negative correlation obtained when the data of the early and late arrivals are combined into a single analysis shows that the age of acquisition effect is a genuine one that any valid theory of second language learning must take into account.

Further sources of counterevidence

Nativelike ultimate attainment in late L2 learners. As mentioned earlier, in addition to the exact shape of the age function, the occurrence of late L2 learners who perform in a nativelike way is a further source of evidence to consider in evaluating the critical period hypothesis. If success in language learning is fully determined by whether or not it coincides with a bounded period of special linguistic sensitivity early in life, not a single second language speaker who started L2 acquisition beyond the offset point of this period should manage to achieve a nativelike mastery of the L2 grammar. Conversely, the grammatical ability of all second language speakers who started L2 acquisition long before the offset point should be indistinguishable from native grammatical ability.

Contrary to the first of these predictions, since 1990 many studies have been published that report nativelikeness in late arrivals and their numbers do not warrant them being discounted as rare exceptions to the rule. Birdsong (2006) noted that earlier estimates of a 0–5% incidence

of nativelike L2 use in late arrivals were based on studies that may have tested L2 users who had not yet reached their L2 end state. In a review of studies that only included late arrivals with a long length of residence in the L2 country and who interacted with native speakers on a daily basis, he estimated the incidence of nativelike attainment to range between 5% and 15%, with an upper limit as high as 45% (Birdsong, 1999, 2006). Typically, the incidence is higher in the linguistic domain of morpho-syntax than in pronunciation, but also nativelike pronunciation is within reach of late L2 learners (see Chapter 5). These figures led Birdsong to conclude that nativelike learners cannot be dismissed as "peripheral". As he put it (1999, p.15):

> How many nativelike learners would be required for falsification of the CPH-L2A is, of course, debatable. It is safe to say, however, that a strict Popperian criterion, where one exception suffices to reject the hypothesis [. . .], is more than amply met. [. . .] Assuming a normal distribution, a 15% success rate corresponds to all of the area from roughly 1 standard deviation above the mean and higher; as such, these participants cannot be regarded as mere outliers in a distribution. [CPH-L2A is an abbreviation of the "critical period hypothesis of second language acquisition"; *AdG.*]

Yet some doubts remain regarding the strength of this type of evidence against the critical period hypothesis. We have already seen that exceptional verbal ability might compensate for a loss of access to a putative innate language-learning mechanism later in life (De Keyser, 2000). Furthermore, Abrahamsson and Hyltenstam (2009) argued that the measures by means of which nativelikeness is typically determined are not precise enough, and subsequently showed that detailed scrutiny of late learners' linguistic performance reveals that all of them differ from native speakers in at least one linguistic subdomain of L2. A cautionary note of a different nature is made by Long (2005), who observed that a number of studies demonstrating nativelike performance in late learners have used tests that do not reflect natural language use. Therefore the possibility cannot be ruled out that, had these studies employed more naturalistic tasks, the participants would not have passed as natives.

Non-nativelike ultimate attainment in early L2 learners.   A further source of evidence to weigh in this discussion is the occurrence of non-native ultimate attainment in L2 speakers exposed to the L2 early in life. According to the critical age hypothesis all early learners should be indistinguishable from native speakers. If this assumption is valid, the actual data challenge the hypothesis. In Chapter 5 some evidence will be presented of early L2 learners with a noticeable speech accent in this language. Here I will focus on the occurrence of a lasting grammatical accent in early L2 learners.

McDonald (2000) had native Spanish early and late learners of English (with an age of arrival to the US of 0–5 years and 14–20 years, respectively), as well as native Vietnamese early and child learners of English (with an age of arrival of 0–5 and 6–10, respectively), perform a grammaticality judgment test which contained the same types of grammatical and ungrammatical sentence structures as used by Johnson and Newport (1989; see Table 2.6). (Note that age of arrival for the late-learner groups was not matched across the two L1 conditions. The reason was that insufficient L2 English speakers with a Vietnamese L1 background and an arrival age between 14 and 20 years could be found.) All L2 speakers had resided in the US long enough to have reached their ultimate level of L2 proficiency. In addition, a group of native English speakers served as controls for all four of the L2 learner groups.

Despite being matched on arrival age, the two groups of early arrivals performed differently in relation to the other participant groups: An analysis of the data of the Spanish condition showed that the L1 Spanish early learners of English did not differ significantly from the native English speakers, whereas the L1 Spanish late learners of English performed more poorly than

both the native and early-learner groups. So far this is what the critical period hypothesis would predict. However, an analysis of the data of the L1 Vietnamese learners of English produced a totally different pattern of results: The performance of the early and child acquirers of English did not differ from one another and both performed worse than the native English speakers. In particular, the lasting grammatical accents in the early Vietnamese learners challenge the critical period hypothesis.

MacDonald (2000) suggested that the difference in structural distance between English and Spanish and between English and Vietnamese had caused the performance difference between the two groups of early learners. This idea was supported in a further analysis of the early arrivals' performance on the separate types of English structures. A preliminary contrastive analysis of the experimental materials had revealed that the tested structures were all largely similar in English and Spanish but that many of the English structures differed markedly from the analogous structures in Vietnamese. The additional analysis showed that especially the L2 English structures that differed from the corresponding L1 structures caused errors, thus resulting in the poorer performance of the Vietnamese early learners.

To conclude, early exposure to a second language is no guarantee that nativelike proficiency will ultimately be obtained, and once again it appears that structural (dis)similarity between L1 and L2 is one of the variables determining ultimate L2 attainment.

Nativelike brain responses in late L2 learners. Friederici, Steinhauer, and Pfeifer (2002) tested the critical period hypothesis by challenging the correlated, hitherto underexposed, assumption that late learners process language in a fundamentally different way from native speakers, exploiting different brain mechanisms. These authors had one group of adults, the "training group", learn an artificial spoken language, using a learning paradigm implemented on a computer. The artificial language in question, Brocanto, consisted of a small set of grammatical rules and a small set of lexical items that together instantiated six word classes. Whereas the training group received Brocanto training in grammar and vocabulary (by being presented with full-fledged Brocanto sentences during training), a control group of participants received vocabulary training only involving a paired-associate learning paradigm (see pp. 87–89 for details). After training, an experimental auditory test session followed in which the participants in both groups were presented with a large set of simple Brocanto sentences, half of them grammatical and the remaining half containing syntactic word category violations. The task was to judge whether the presented sentence was grammatically correct or incorrect in Brocanto, or whether a visually presented symbol, representing one of Brocanto's lexical items, corresponded to a word in the preceding sentence. During this experimental session ERPs were recorded. The ERPs were measured time-locked to the violating lexical item in an ungrammatical sentence and to the corresponding correct item in a grammatical sentence.

Syntactic violations are known to elicit two ERP components in native speakers, an early negativity that occurs from 100 to 200 ms after the violating word (the "N200") and a late positivity occurring about 600 ms after the violation (the "P600"). The early negativity is thought to reflect the disturbance of a rapid automatic parsing process that assigns an initial syntactic structure to the input sentence (e.g., Hahne & Friederici, 1999). The late positivity is assumed to index a controlled process of structural reanalysis and repair (e.g., Osterhout & Holcomb, 1992). The question posed by Friederici et al. (2002) was whether or not the brain responses of the participants in the Brocanto training group would reveal these same two components, arguing that an affirmative answer would challenge the critical period hypothesis (because the participants were *late* learners of Brocanto). The participants in the control group were not expected to show these brain responses because their training had not enabled them to acquire Brocanto's grammatical rules.

The data of the training group revealed a similar pattern of brain activation when processing Brocanto as observed in native speakers processing a natural language. Specifically, as compared to the corresponding words in the matched grammatical sentences, syntactic violations in ungrammatical sentences aroused the early negativity and the late positivity introduced above, suggesting similar processes of rapid automatic parsing and slower reanalysis and repair as assumed to occur when native speakers process syntactic violations. Neither of these two effects emerged in the brain responses of the untrained participants. Native and late L2 speakers of a language thus appear to process sentences presented in this language in a similar way. At variance with the critical period hypothesis, the most parsimonious conclusion to draw from this result is that early and late learners of a language exploit the same brain mechanisms when processing this language.

The results of Friederici et al. (2002) agree with those of a set of studies that compared the ERP responses during language processing by native and late speakers of natural languages. These studies have shown that the pattern of ERPs evoked in proficient L2 users is largely similar to the one occurring in native speakers (e.g., Hahne & Friederici, 2001; Ojima, Nakata, & Kakigi, 2005; see Steinhauer, White, & Drury, 2009, for a review). In contrast, comparisons of ERP patterns in non-fluent L2 users and native speakers have revealed differences between the two groups (Ojima et al., 2005). Similarly, recent brain-imaging studies employing the **PET** or **fMRI** methodology have shown that the same brain regions are activated when native and proficient L2 speakers process language (Perani et al., 1998), whereas comparisons of native and non-fluent speakers have revealed the activation of different areas between groups (Dehaene et al., 1997; Perani et al., 1996). The well-trained participants in the training group of Friederici et al. (2002) may be assumed to have reached a high level of proficiency in Brocanto and were, plausibly, comparable in Brocanto ability to the proficient L2 speakers in this set of studies testing natural languages. All these studies thus indicate that the L2 processing profile of late but proficient L2 speakers and the neural substrate involved resemble those of native speakers (see Abutalebi, Cappa, & Perani, 2005, Steinhauer et al., 2009, for discussions). The studies that suggested differential processing and cerebral representation of a language in native speakers and late L2 learners have possibly confounded L2 proficiency and age of L2 acquisition.

Summary and conclusions

So far several research findings have been presented that contravene the critical period hypothesis: The hypothesis predicts a pattern of discontinuities in the age functions that does not materialize. In addition, it falsely predicts that after many years of using the L2 all early learners but no late learners should perform at native levels. Furthermore, the hypothesis suggests that brain processes differ between native speakers and late L2 learners processing a language's grammar, but the evidence shows similar brain processes for these two types of language users as long as the late learners are proficient users of their L2. Finally, if a special sensitivity to linguistic stimulation during some bounded period early in life determines language-learning outcome, it is not immediately obvious why educational level and structural similarity between L1 and L2 would matter at all. Yet, as we have seen, these two factors do affect ultimate performance.

Taking a different approach, Singleton (2005) criticized the critical age hypothesis on the grounds that the collected evidence shows vast variability in three parameters that are central to the hypothesis: the assumed onset and offset points of the putative critical period; the linguistic domains assumed to be affected by it; the underlying causes that have been suggested. He showed, for instance, that the assumed offset of a special sensitivity for learning a language's **phonetics** and phonology varies between as early as age 1 and as late as puberty, and he lists no fewer than 14 different proposed causes of the hypothesized heightened sensitivity for language within a bounded period early in life (see Table 2.7)

TABLE 2.7
Assumed causes of a critical period for language learning

Neurobiological
   Diminution of cerebral plasticity
   Lateralization
   Localization
   Maturation timetables of brain cells
   Myelination
   Different spatial representation in the brain

Cognitive-developmental
   Need for theory after puberty
   Awareness of differences after puberty
   Interference of post-pubertal problem-solving cognitive structures
   Decline in capacity for implicit learning of complex abstract systems

Affective-motivational
   Strengthening affective filter
   Identification, super-ego, libidinous relations, narcissism
   Hardening ego boundaries
   Social and psychological distance

Adapted from Singleton, 2005 (see there for references).

Given this large variability Singleton (2005, p. 280) concluded that:

[. . .] the CPH cannot plausibly be regarded as a scientific hypothesis either in the strict Popperian sense of something which can be falsified [. . .] or indeed in the rather looser logical positivist sense of something that can be clearly confirmed or supported [. . .]. As it stands it is like the mythical hydra, whose multiplicity of heads and capacity to produce new heads rendered it impossible to deal with.

He then continued, observing that trying to generalize the various versions of the hypothesis into some summary form that applies to all studies fails as well because the outcome of such an enterprise would look something like the following rather inconclusive platitude: "For some reason, the language acquiring capacity, or some aspect or aspects thereof, is operative only for a maturational period, which ends some time between perinatality and puberty". This, he concludes, "is not a hypothesis either; it is at best an extremely vague promissory note" (Singleton, 2005, p. 280).

Age of acquisition effects: Alternative accounts

Giving the steadily increasing evidence that age of acquisition effects on L2 performance cannot be attributed to a special language-acquiring capacity that is only operational during a bounded period early in life, what else could it be that causes them? Recently several authors have advanced alternative accounts that reject the idea that language acquisition is driven by an age-constrained cognitive faculty dedicated exclusively to language. Instead they assume that language acquisition, just as other forms of learning, exploits general-purpose cognitive machinery and that the operation of this machinery is affected by age, favoring the young. For instance, McDonald (2000) attributed the grammar problems of late L2 learners discussed above to a difficulty that non-native language users have in rapidly decoding aurally presented L2 sentences, which, in turn, disrupts the operation of working memory (recall that in, e.g., the studies by Birdsong & Molis, 2001, and Johnson & Newport, 1989, the stimulus materials were presented aurally). Following a seminal study by Just and Carpenter (1992), a large number of studies have demonstrated that language processing exploits working memory and that performance breaks down the moment its capacity is exceeded for one reason or other. Capacity overload during native language processing may, for instance, occur when the input speech consists of extremely complex sentences or when the speech is input under noisy conditions or at an extremely rapid pace. In general, the higher the mental load, the larger the chance of a processing breakdown. In L2 speakers relatively slow input decoding (or output encoding, for that matter) adds to the load imposed on working memory and, thus, increases the chance of a breakdown.

According to McDonald (2000), language learners' decoding ability decreases linearly with increasing age of acquisition and this decrease continues after puberty. As a consequence, the later the onset age, the more often the L2 user's working memory capacity will be exceeded while processing L2 structures and, in turn, the larger the chance that an L2 grammatical structure will not be processed correctly. In addition to thus explaining the (unbounded) age effects on L2 grammatical ability, this account can explain the role of L1–L2 grammatical similarity observed by this and other authors (e.g., Hakuta et al., 2003; see Figure 2.13): Plausibly, L2 grammatical structures that have no close analogue in the L1 especially pose a high load on working memory and are therefore particularly vulnerable. Furthermore, a working memory account can explain why L2 users' grammatical performance is variable in the sense that a given linguistic structure can cause a problem under one set of circumstances but is correctly processed on other occasions (e.g., Jiang, 2004). The fact that the structure is processed correctly at least part of the time suggests that the associated knowledge is established in memory. The processing failure that nevertheless occurs once in a while is likely to result from a high momentary mental load caused by extra-linguistic factors. Finally, the present account can explain the finding that a nativelike grammatical skill is achieved by at least some late L2 learners: Working memory capacity is known to differ between individuals (e.g., MacDonald, Just, & Carpenter, 1992). Plausibly, the L2 users whose grammatical performance is indistinguishable from that of native speakers are the ones with a relatively high working memory capacity. In agreement with this suggestion, several studies have shown that L2 working memory span p. 330—a measure that is thought to reflect L2 working memory capacity—correlates with L2 grammatical skill (Harrington, 1992; Miyake & Friedman, 1998).

McDonald (2006) put these ideas to a test and obtained support for them, among others, by demonstrating that in circumstances that tax monolingual native speakers' working memory they perform similarly (in their one and only language) to late L2 learners (in their L2). (Working memory was taxed by, for instance, having the native speakers perform a grammaticality judgment task while the stimuli were presented with an overlay of white noise or while they were hurried up by a response deadline.) Interestingly, the decrements in performance selectively affected the types of structures that had been shown earlier to be especially vulnerable in L2 speakers. The similar behavioral profiles obtained for native speakers performing under taxing circumstances and non-native speakers support an account of the data in terms of limited working memory capacity and render implausible one in terms of some mental device exclusively dedicated to language learning and only operative during some delimited period early in life.

In a similar vein, Birdsong and Flege (2001) attributed the age of acquisition effects on the processing of sentences containing regular and irregular English verbs and nouns to an aspect of general cognition assumed to be affected by aging. In this study, Spanish and Korean native speakers performed a correctness judgment task in which they had to select the correctly inflected form of the verb or noun among five alternatives. Generally, performance was better for regular forms than for irregular forms and a strong effect of age of acquisition occurred for the irregular forms but not for the regular forms. In line with the results of McDonald (2000) discussed earlier, these data show that effects of acquisition age may differentially affect different types of structures (see also Flege, Yeni-Komshian, & Liu, 1999). But of special interest in the present context is the authors' suggestion (see also Birdsong, 2005, 2006) as to what causes this differential age of acquisition effect for irregular and regular forms. Cognitive psychologists make a distinction between declarative and procedural memory. Following Ullman (2001; Ullman et al. 1997), Birdsong and Flege assumed that declarative memory is involved in the learning and storing of facts (such as irregular forms) whereas procedural memory deals with the computation of rule-based knowledge (such as regular forms). They furthermore hypothesized that declarative memory is especially susceptible to aging, for instance because cortisol levels that increase with age lead to atrophy of the hippocampus that subserves

declarative memory (Birdsong, 2005). Consistent with this suggestion, skills that depend on declarative memory decline more noticeably with age than do procedural memory functions; hence the specific vulnerability of the irregular forms to increases in arrival age. A more general conclusion to draw from this analysis is that age effects on L2 performance may result from a more general process of aging of the L2 speaker's cognitive machinery that affects language and other cognitive functions alike.

The above two accounts of AoA-related declines in L2 performance in terms of general-purpose cognitive mechanisms (working memory and declarative memory, respectively) that gradually decay with aging can explain the continued linear decreases in performance in adulthood following a stage when, in early adulthood, the associated cognitive skills are at their peak. However, they fail to provide an explanation for the generally superb language-learning skills of very young children, whose cognitive abilities are generally still inferior to those of young adults. A third construal that assumes specific characteristics of general cognition to cause the age of acquisition effects focused on this specific part of the age function. Newport (1988, 1990) attributed the superior ultimate performance of L2 speakers who started acquiring the language at a young age to children's limited cognitive resources, a hypothesis that she dubbed the "less-is-more" hypothesis. In her words: "[. . .] language learning declines over maturation precisely because cognitive abilities increase" (Newport, 1990, p. 22). Because of its limited perception and memory skills, a young child is forced to process the linguistic input in relatively small units and this is assumed to facilitate certain aspects of the language-learning task. The author hypothesized that especially those aspects of language learning that require some type of componential analysis, such as the analysis of words into their component morphemes, benefit from these still-suboptimal perception and memory skills of young children. Adults process such input as unitary wholes, thus failing to discover its separate form components, each of which maps onto some aspect of meaning, so the idea goes. Evidence in support of this idea has been gathered in both computational simulations and in studies testing real participants (e.g., Cochran, McDonald, & Parault, 1999; Elman, 1993; Goldowsky & Newport, 1993).

In a more recent study that simulated effects of acquisition age on language learning in a connectionist network, Rohde and Plaut (2003) questioned the validity of much of this evidence and presented results suggesting that "starting small" and the associated limited cognitive resources may in fact generally hinder language acquisition. Accordingly, better in accordance with intuition, they concluded that "less is less" in language acquisition—that is, that the lesser cognitive skills of children are not advantageous for language learning. As an alternative to the less-is-more hypothesis, they attributed the superior ultimate L2 performance of young language learners to the fact that their brain resources are still largely uncommitted. As a consequence, neurons can be more easily recruited and the response characteristics of already participating neurons can be altered relatively easily. The older the learner, the more neural tissue is already committed to other knowledge and processes, and recruiting neurons to subserve new knowledge and tasks becomes increasingly difficult. As suggested by the authors, this explanation of age of acquisition effects also holds for skills other than language use, for example learning to play tennis or a musical instrument.

These suggestions regarding age of acquisition effects in second language learning accord with those advanced by Ellis and Lambon Ralph (2000), who modeled age of acquisition effects in monolingual vocabulary acquisition in a connectionist network. It is well known that words learned early in life are recognized and produced faster than words acquired later. Furthermore, the former are more immune than the latter to retrieval failures that increasingly occur with aging and to loss after brain damage in adulthood. Importantly, these age of acquisition effects have been shown not to be frequency effects in disguise, resulting from the fact that the cumulative frequency of early words is larger than of words acquired later (e.g., Morrison,

Ellis, & Quinlan, 1992; Morrison, Hirsh, Chappell, & Ellis, 2002). Ellis and Lambon Ralph successfully modeled these effects under circumstances of "cumulative" and "interleaved" learning. In this learning scheme, a second set of patterns to learn does not fully replace a first set in the sense that the moment the new set is introduced the old patterns are no longer presented. Instead, the new patterns are interleaved with old items so that there is continued exposure to the items acquired first. This learning scheme resembles monolingual vocabulary acquisition, where new words do not replace old words but are added onto the vocabulary acquired earlier. It also resembles L2 vocabulary acquisition in learners who continue to use their L1 regularly. Adopting a learning scheme that imitated this characteristic of natural vocabulary acquisition, the network reproduced the common age of acquisition effects, the items learned first showing an advantage over those learned second. Interestingly, a learning scheme in which the presentation of the first set of patterns was suddenly and completely discontinued the moment the new set was introduced led to "catastrophic forgetting", showing gradual and, ultimately, complete loss of the first set. In real life this phenomenon has been observed with adopted children who are suddenly cut off from their L1, and will be discussed in Chapter 7, pp. 356–358.

But of special interest in the present context was Ellis and Lambon Ralph's (2000) finding that analysis of the activation patterns in the network's units in the cumulative and interleaved learning condition indicated that the age of acquisition effects reflected a gradual reduction of the network's plasticity with the consequence that the items presented late failed to develop clearly distinguishable representations. As training continued, the network became increasingly committed to representing the patterns presented early. As a corollary it became harder for the network to assimilate new, late patterns. Based on these data the authors concluded that age of acquisition effects in adult lexical processing are likely to be caused by a similar decline in plasticity in the networks that subserve human lexical processing.

In a way, with the present interpretation of age of acquisition effects in terms of neural tissue becoming gradually more and more committed and, hence, less plastic, as a consequence of ever-increasing experience over the lifespan, we have come full circle. I started this discussion of age of acquisition effects briefly referring to the work of Penfield (1963) and Lenneberg (1967), who were the first to suggest that differential neural plasticity in children and adults might cause the effects of acquisition age on linguistic performance. In one crucial aspect, however, the present conception differs from the one advanced in these early studies. According to Penfield and Lenneberg, brain plasticity declines relatively abruptly at some point early in life, at the closure of some putative critical period. Instead, according to the present account the process of decreasing plasticity is a gradual one that continues over a lifetime, and the fact that knowledge and skills continually increase with aging is held responsible for this ever-declining plasticity: Knowledge and skills are represented in neural tissue and every new bit of knowledge and the acquisition of any further skill must somehow recruit brain tissue that is more likely to already be committed the older one gets. This clearly places the young child, whose brain is still largely a *tabula rasa* that stores relatively little content and procedures, at an advantage. In other words, it is the relative order of acquisition of knowledge and skills that determines learning success (within L1, within L2, across L1 and L2, and plausibly within and across any other, non-linguistic, cognitive domain(s); see also Hirsh, Morrison, Gaset, & Carnicer, 2003, who account for age of acquisition effects in L2 picture naming in late learners this way). Plausibly, adverse effects of aging on working memory or declarative memory add to these effects of increasing rigidity of the brain but, in theory, the present explanation of age of acquisition effects in, among others, second language learning does, on its own, a good job in accounting for the most reliable pattern observed across studies: that of a linear decrease in performance over the whole age range. The present chapter discussed evidence that this linearity holds for morphology and syntax. In Chapter 5 some studies will be presented that demonstrate it holds for phonology as well.

SUMMARY

- Speech perception in infants can be studied by exploiting the fact that babies pay more attention to novel stimuli than to familiar stimuli. This fact is used in the high-amplitude sucking paradigm, the heart-rate paradigm, the preferential looking technique, and the head-turn procedure. All these procedures typically (but not always) consist of an experimental habituation/familiarization phase followed by a test phase.
- Just like adults, infants exhibit categorical perception of speech sounds. This ability appears to be innate, as suggested by the fact that all infants are initially sensitive to the same phoneme boundaries, irrespective of what boundaries exist in the ambient language(s). Categorical perception may also apply to other cognitive domains than language and to other species than humans.
- The ability to perceive non-native phoneme contrasts declines during the first year of life. This loss of discriminative ability does not affect all non-native contrasts but depends on specific acoustic and articulatory characteristics of the foreign sounds involved.
- Event-related potentials provide a more sensitive marker of speech perception abilities than the more commonly used behavioral measures. For instance, adult studies have shown that the discrimination of non-native contrasts that appear to be lost when behavioral measures are employed, may turn out to still be intact when ERP measures are used to examine discrimination ability.

- Sequential bilingualism requires the reversal of the decreased sensitivity to non-native phonetic contrasts. There is some evidence to suggest that training sessions involving natural live adult–infant interactions are more conducive to the restoration of lost non-native contrasts in 9–10-month-olds than mere audio-visual or audio-only training.
- Cross-language distributional overlap of the speech sounds that instantiate particular phonetic categories in a bilingual infant's two languages may delay the emergence of contrastive phonetic categories, possibly because a single extended category for the phonemes of a contrastive pair is first built. This one extended category is subsequently gradually separated into different categories as a result of continued exposure to both languages.
- The adverse effect of cross-language distributional overlap of speech sounds in a bilingual infant's two languages on phonetic discriminative ability can be counteracted by a high frequency of occurrence of the overlapping speech sounds.
- At about 8 months of age infants can recognize recurring syllable sequences in speech and soon thereafter phoneme sequences. This ability provides infants with a means to discover word boundaries in continuous speech and can thus bootstrap vocabulary acquisition. The mechanism that presumably underlies this skill is a statistical learning device that is sensitive to sequential probabilities of speech units, both syllables and phonemes.
- At about 9–10 months of age infants growing up in a monolingual environment have had sufficient exposure to the ambient language for statistical learning to have differentiated between phoneme sequences that occur in their native language and those that do not.
- At about 9–10 months of age infants growing up in a bilingual environment have developed the phonotactics of their dominant language from naturalistic exposure to this language but the phonotactics of their non-dominant language are not quite developed yet. The former finding indicates that growing up bilingual does not inevitably delay the development of language-specific phonotactic knowledge.
- At birth, babies can discriminate between rhythmically different languages (e.g., English and Japanese) but not between rhythmically similar languages (e.g., English and Dutch).
- At 2 months some infants from monolingual homes can discriminate between their native language on the one hand and foreign languages on the other hand, even if the foreign language has the same rhythm as the native language, whereas others treat a foreign language with the same rhythm as the native language as native. These findings suggest that some 2-month-olds have already started to develop detailed segmental knowledge regarding their native language and use it in language discrimination. Others still appear to rely on suprasegmental, prosodic information in discriminating between languages.
- At 4 months infants from both monolingual and bilingual homes can discriminate between their native language and a rhythmically similar foreign language, and infants from bilingual homes can discriminate between their two native languages, even if they share the same rhythm. This suggests that by this time all infants have begun to acquire phonetic knowledge specific to their native language and use it in language discrimination.
- Differential head-turn responses to familiar and unfamiliar words suggest that word form recognition in monolingual and bilingual infants emerges at 11 months but more sensitive ERP responses to these same words suggest this ability is already present at 10 months in monolinguals and possibly also in bilinguals (the latter possibility has not yet been examined).
- There is some ERP evidence to suggest that the formation of word–meaning connections is somewhat delayed in bilingual-to-be infants as compared with monolingual infants and that this holds in particular for the weaker language of bilingual infants with a relatively low total conceptual vocabulary. Additional behavioral evidence suggests that attending to the phonetic

details of words in tasks that require the linking of words to objects develops somewhat more slowly in bilinguals than in monolinguals. Whereas monolingual infants have developed this ability between 14 and 17 months, bilingual infants master it between 17 and 20 months.

- The critical period hypothesis of language acquisition has been examined in three lines of study: (1) studies examining late first language acquisition in normally hearing children growing up under circumstances of extreme linguistic deprivation; (2) studies examining late first language acquisition in deaf children born to hearing parents; (3) studies that examine age of acquisition effects on second language learning.

- Studies examining the critical period hypothesis by scrutinizing the L1 linguistic development of so-called "feral" children are compromised by the fact that these individuals were not only deprived of proper linguistic input during the putative critical period but typically suffered other forms of deprivation as well during the critical years: emotional, social, physical, and nutritional.

- Studies examining the critical period hypothesis by looking at the linguistic development of late L1 learners of sign language are compromised by the fact that relevant preparatory linguistic experience, including the use of an elaborate and sophisticated system of homesign, has plausibly provided these learners with a foundation for later sign language learning. In other words, they did not start first language learning from scratch the moment they gained full access to it.

- Given two groups of equally old late learners of one and the same language, one that has normally acquired language early in life and the second having been deprived of language early in life, ultimate attainment will be substantially higher in the former group than in the latter. This finding supports the "exercise hypothesis" of language learning, which holds that early language experience creates the ability to learn language throughout life and that a lack of language experience early in life compromises the acquisition of any language throughout life.

- Because late second language learning is a far more widespread phenomenon than late first language acquisition, the majority of studies examining age of acquisition effects on language learning have tested second language learners varying in acquisition age.

- The "maturational state" version of the critical period hypothesis holds that early in life humans have a superior capacity for language learning which declines with maturation, even if the language-learning capacity is exercised early in life.

- The maturational state version of the critical period hypothesis predicts two discontinuities in the function that relates the onset age of L2 acquisition to ultimate L2 attainment. The discontinuities result from a temporarily heightened sensitivity to linguistic input early in life that is maximal for some number of years, then gradually decreases, and finally plateaus at some low level.

- A negative correlation between the onset age of L2 acquisition on the one hand and ultimate L2 attainment is consistently obtained across many studies, but contrary to the maturational state hypothesis no discontinuities can be observed in this age function.

- Contrary to the critical age hypothesis, some late L2 learners attain a nativelike proficiency in L2 and some early L2 learners fail to do so.

- Grammatical violations elicit the same pattern of ERP responses (the N400 and P600), and activity in the same brain regions, in proficient L2 speakers and native speakers, but different ones in non-fluent L2 users.

- A gradual decline in L2 performance with an increasing age of acquisition beyond early adulthood can be explained in terms of two general-purpose cognitive mechanisms, working memory and declarative memory, which peak in early adulthood but gradually decay afterwards. Because cognitive abilities such as working memory and declarative memory are still underdeveloped in early childhood, the generally superb language-learning skills of very young children cannot be explained this way.

- The "less-is-more" hypothesis has been advanced to explain the superior ultimate performance of L2 speakers who started acquiring the language in early childhood. According to this hypothesis, the superior performance of early learners results from the limited perception and memory skills of very young children. These resource limitations force the child to process the linguistic input in relatively small units and this is assumed to be beneficial for certain aspects of language learning.
- An account of age of acquisition effects in terms of gradually increasing neural commitment can, on its own, explain age effects over the whole age spectrum. It holds that the brain resources of young language learners are still largely uncommitted and can therefore be easily recruited for the learning task. The older the learner, the more neural tissue is already committed to other knowledge and processes and recruiting neurons to subserve new knowledge and tasks becomes increasingly difficult.

3

Late Foreign Vocabulary Learning and Lexical Representation

INTRODUCTION AND PREVIEW

Until rather recently both foreign language teachers and researchers focused their efforts on grammar and phonology more than on vocabulary. Yet it is obvious that vocabulary is of crucial importance to the foreign language learner. From the viewpoint of the beginning learner it may even be considered the most crucial language component: The chances of getting one's basic needs fulfilled in a foreign language environment are substantially better if the learner possesses some well-chosen basic vocabulary in the language concerned than when, instead, he or she masters the language's grammar flawlessly. Any learner who has struggled to make himself understood in a foreign language environment will eagerly admit this statement to be true. In addition to such anecdotal evidence, experimental evidence also points at the pivotal contribution of vocabulary to effective foreign language use, such as the finding that the size of the foreign vocabulary is a good predictor of success of reading comprehension in the language involved

(e.g., Laufer, 1992, 1997; Nation, 1993). Furthermore, from a wealth of studies on monolingual language comprehension and production it is well known that sentence-building processes start off with information retrieved from word representations in memory, suggesting the central role of vocabulary in language processing in general.

A language typically contains tens of thousands of words, and the thorough mastery of a word involves knowing many different types of information associated with it: phonological and orthographic, morphological, syntactic, semantic, articulatory, idiomatic, and pragmatic (e.g., Laufer, 1997). Any single one of these various types of knowledge may cover multifarious components. For instance, complete knowledge of a word's meaning involves both knowledge of the word's **referential meaning**—that is, knowledge regarding the entities or events in the external world to which it refers (this is also called a word's **extensional meaning**)—as well as knowledge of its relation to other words in the vocabulary, such as its **antonyms**, **synonyms**, and **hyponyms** (its "intensional" meaning; see e.g., Henriksen, 1999). In addition, true mastery of vocabulary not only requires the mere presence of the relevant knowledge in the learner's memory but, in addition, the swift availability of this stored information the moment its associated word is targeted in production or comprehension. In other words, lexical knowledge is not yet lexical competence; that is, the skill to use it fluently (see e.g., Jiang, 2000).

Acknowledging the central role of vocabulary in foreign language use, the learner thus appears to face a task of daunting dimensions and may wonder even before getting started whether it will be worth the effort. However, a swift conclusion that it will not be worthwhile would be premature, because there is an obvious way to reduce the task to manageable proportions. The solution is to not attack the task haphazardly, but to sequence it in such a way that the most useful words, those that occur most frequently in speech and writing, are learned first. Several studies have shown that adequate language comprehension requires the knowledge of only a relatively small number of carefully selected words. Laufer (1992) found that learners reach a sufficient level of comprehension in a foreign language when their vocabulary covers 95% of the words in a text, and Nation (1993) argued that a basic vocabulary of the 3000 most frequent word families, equaling about 5000 lexical items, suffices to reach this state. (A word's family consists of its base word and its derived and inflected forms.) The obvious conclusion to draw from this is that the words constituting this basic vocabulary should be the ones to focus on in what is called "direct" vocabulary instruction in the foreign language classroom (where "direct" refers to the fact that the vocabulary to be acquired is focused on explicitly). Equipped with the basic vocabulary thus learned, the learner can subsequently gradually add to it through immersion in the language, for instance by extensive reading in the target language and participating in a variety of natural communication settings involving fluent speakers of the language.

The research domain of foreign language learning includes work in all subdomains of language: phonology, vocabulary, grammar, and pragmatics. These joint research efforts are far too varied to be covered in a single chapter and choices will therefore have to be made. Because of the pivotal role of vocabulary in mastering a foreign language, this chapter will be devoted to the acquisition of foreign vocabulary and the type of knowledge structures that emerge in memory in the process. The Methods and Tasks section first describes the various acquisition methods that have been studied in the laboratory and that, in one form or another, are common practice in the foreign language classroom as well. In addition, it presents the major methods used to assess the breadth and depth of the extant foreign language vocabulary. The next two sections discuss the results obtained in the pertinent research. The first of these compares the efficacy of the keyword method and other instruction methods and details the conditions under which the former is most effective, and for whom. The keyword method is plausibly the instruction method that has attracted most attention in research on foreign language vocabulary learning and enjoys the reputation of being highly effective. The second section discusses studies that have employed the paired-associate paradigm, focusing on the effects of particular features of the vocabulary to be learned on acquisition rate and retention. The features considered are **word concreteness**, frequency of word usage, **phonotactical typicality**, and whether or not the new words to be learned resemble their L1 translations in form. In each of the subsequent three sections some mechanism or process is expounded that plays a major role in foreign language vocabulary acquisition. At the same time, each of them provides an account of one or more of the effects of the vocabulary features revealed before. Successively, these three sections (1) highlight the important role that prior knowledge plays in foreign language vocabulary acquisition; (2) explain the roles of phonological short- and long-term memory in foreign vocabulary acquisition; and (3) account for the pervasive effects of form similarity between the native and foreign word on learning the latter. I will subsequently present a view of word learning which holds that during its initial stages the learner attends more to the word's form than to its meaning, after which gradually meaning is attended to more. A similar developmental course is assumed in the revised hierarchical model of bilingual memory developed by Judith Kroll and her colleagues (e.g., Kroll & Stewart, 1994). This model, the models it emerged from, the data that support and challenge it, and alternative models of bilingual memory, are the topics dealt with next.

Up until that point in the discussion hardly any studies will have passed in review that one way or the other dealt with the role of context in foreign language vocabulary acquisition. Yet, as pointed out above, to acquire complete mastery of a new language's vocabulary, in addition to going through direct vocabulary training the learners will have to immerse themselves in the targeted language, for instance through reading veridical texts in that language. The effectiveness of vocabulary acquisition in context is the main theme of the final part of this chapter.

As mentioned, there is considerably more to acquiring a foreign language than mastering its vocabulary. Some of the subdomains of language neglected in this chapter will be covered elsewhere. For instance, in Chapter 2 the role of age of acquisition in ultimate grammatical attainment was discussed, and in Chapter 4 some aspects of grammatical development in late learners as revealed by the way they process sentences will be covered. Another important aspect of foreign (and second) language acquisition, the gradual formation of language subsets within the larger language system, is treated in Chapter 6, and information on the brain processes and structures involved in foreign language acquisition will be provided in Chapter 8. Finally, one part of Chapter 7 deals with a relatively new research field, third language acquisition and use, discussing, among others, the influence of the typological distance between the first, second, and third language on the learning process.

METHODS AND TASKS

The keyword method

Learners of a new language spontaneously use a variety of strategies to increase their vocabulary knowledge of this language, bringing in, for instance, their knowledge of the native language and of other languages they may already have mastered, or consulting dictionaries. They may also create mental images that contain the referent of the word to be learned interacting with the referent of a native language word that sounds similar to the foreign word. It has long been known that this form of mental imagery may facilitate foreign vocabulary learning. Desrochers and Begg (1987; in Ellis & Beaton, 1993a) traced this insight back to 1862, when the Reverend J. H. Bacon described the way he learned the French word *arbre* ("tree"): He imagined the arbor at the foot of his garden, which was shaded by a tree. The process of learning *arbre* this way contains the two steps that, in combination, were coined the **keyword method** of foreign vocabulary learning by Atkinson and Raugh, who were the first to study the method in the laboratory (Atkinson, 1975; Atkinson & Raugh, 1975; Raugh & Atkinson, 1975). The two steps are a first stage in which the foreign word (e.g., *arbre*) is linked to a native language word with a similar sound (*arbor*). This native language word is the so-called "keyword", and Atkinson and Raugh refer to this first step as creating an "acoustic link". In a second step (creating an "imagery link"), a mental image is then created in which the meaning of the keyword and the meaning of the new vocabulary item (which, of course, is also the meaning of the corresponding native language word) interact (the arbor shaded by the nearby tree). When at some later point the learner encounters the new foreign word (*arbre*), it will evoke the similar sounding native keyword (*arbor*), which in turn will arouse the "interactive image" of keyword (*arbor*) and the foreign language word's meaning ("tree"). The moment this happens the foreign word's translation can be retrieved.

As an alternative to the construction of an interactive image of the referents of the keyword and the new vocabulary item, the second step of the keyword method may involve what Raugh and Atkinson (1975) called "**verbiage**": the construction of a sentence in which the keyword and the native translation of the targeted foreign word are related to one another. This alternative form of mental elaboration with a keyword has been largely ignored in the research that ensued from Atkinson and Raugh's seminal publications. Yet anecdotal evidence suggests this form of keyword usage may be quite common: In need of a pair of scissors in my temporary Italian home and preparing to ask my Italian neighbor for one, I looked up the Italian for *scissors* in my dictionary: *forbice*. I then found myself spontaneously constructing the Dutch sentence *Een schaar is verboden voor kinderen* ("scissors are forbidden for children"). Subsequently I had no problem whatsoever recalling *forbice* and its associated meaning when turning up at my neighbor's door. To me, Dutch *verboden*—whose pronunciation vaguely resembles the pronunciation of Italian *forbice*—combined with its meaningful sentence context, served as an effective recall cue. I have chosen this example because of the form resemblance between Dutch *verboden* and English *forbidden*. The reader is thus likely to appreciate the retrieval process's workings from it (note that the equivalent English sentence would work as well). The example also shows that even a marginal sound overlap between the keyword (*verboden*) and the targeted new foreign word (*forbice*) suffices for the trick to work.

In the version of the keyword method developed by Atkinson and Raugh, the keywords were not generated by the learners themselves (as in the examples above) but provided by the experimenters. The learners were explicitly instructed to create, for each of the provided triads of foreign language word, native language translation, and keyword, an interacting image of the meanings of the keyword (*arbor*) and the native language translation of the foreign word (*tree*). Other versions of the method have been

developed since. In one of them the learners are merely told what keywords are and how they can be used to create interactive images that facilitate vocabulary learning. This version is the experimental analogue of the *arbor–tree* example, except that the participants do not have to discover the strategy by themselves, as the Reverend Bacon did. In yet a further version of the method, for every foreign language word to learn, both a keyword and a suitable interactive image are provided by the experimenter. The interactive images may be presented in auditory form (for instance, in the form of the sentence: *The Spanish for bed is cama. Imagine a camel lying on your bed*), or in the form of an actual picture (of a camel lying on a bed). Finally, pictorial support has been provided in the form of separate (non-interacting) pictures of the referents of keyword and new word. Figure 3.1 illustrates the "interacting picture", "separate picture", and "separate word" conditions (the latter being Atkinson's keyword provision condition) included in a study by Pressley and Levin (1978). In addition, two control conditions used in this study are shown. These concern the two **paired-associate learning** techniques to be discussed later.

The acquisition phase is followed by one or more tests that measure recall of the vocabulary acquired during training. Most often a **receptive cued recall** test is used, in which on each test trial one of the trained foreign words is presented (the "cue") and the participant is asked to give its translation in the native language. This method thus tests whether the new word is understood. Occasionally, productive knowledge of the new word is tested. On each test trial in **productive cued recall** a native language word is given as the recall cue and the participant is asked to produce its newly learned foreign equivalent. The assumed processing sequence that leads to the retrieval of the response in receptive testing is as follows: The foreign word's sound (/arbre/) activates the similar native keyword's sound (/arbor/) which, in turn, activates the keyword's meaning ("arbor"). The keyword's meaning then activates the interactive image (the arbor shaded by a tree), from which the foreign word's meaning ("tree") can be read off. At that point, the native word associated

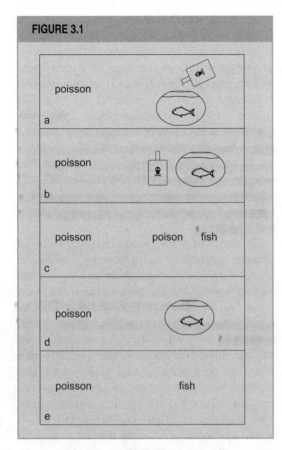

FIGURE 3.1

Versions of the keyword method (a, b, and c) and two paired-associate control conditions (d and e). a = interacting picture; b = separate picture; c = separate word; d = picture–word association; e = word–word association. Based on Pressley and Levin (1978).

with this meaning (*tree*) can be retrieved and produced as the response. In productive testing, the native stimulus word's sound (/*tree*/) activates the corresponding meaning ("tree"), which in turn activates the interactive image (the arbor shaded by a tree). This image includes the keyword's meaning ("arbor") and the keyword's sound (/*arbor*/) will subsequently become available. Finally, this sound will trigger the retrieval of the similar sound of the targeted foreign word (/*arbre*/). It may be obvious from this description of the component parts of the full retrieval process that both the learning by means of the keyword method and the subsequent retrieval of the vocabulary thus acquired are complex pro-

cesses, involving many mental processing steps. Indeed, at first sight the keyword method seems a more complex learning method than is paired-associate learning, to be discussed shortly. But despite its complexity it has been shown to be a highly effective method, as we will see in due course.

The stimulus materials in keyword studies generally exclude foreign language words that share a cognate relation with their native translations. **Cognates** are words that are identical to, or share a large part of their phonology (as well as their orthography, if the two languages concerned employ one and the same **alphabet**) with their L1 translation (e.g., the French *chaise*, for English *chair*; see pp. 121–122 for a more elaborate description of what cognates are). Presumably, the native language cognate form itself (*chair*) will generally share more phonology with the corresponding foreign word (*chaise*) than any other native word that could serve as keyword (e.g., *champion*). Therefore the most straightforward way to learn foreign cognate words is to create a direct acoustic link between the foreign word and its native translation, circumventing any more complex mediating process such as those required by the keyword procedure. During testing, the sound of a foreign cognate form (mediated by orthography, if testing involves the visual presentation of the recall cues) will directly activate the sound of its native language equivalent (in receptive testing), or the sound of a native language cognate form will directly trigger the sound of its foreign translation (in productive testing). It has been suggested (Ellis, 1995) that the keyword method is not optimally suited for learning abstract foreign words either, because it might be relatively hard to create interactive images for such words. However, studies that have applied the keyword method to the learning of both abstract and concrete words do not support this idea (e.g., Pressley, Levin, & Miller, 1981; Van Hell & Candia Mahn, 1997).

Paired-associate learning

Another common method of foreign language vocabulary instruction is the paired-associate learning technique that has been used in verbal learning and memory research for decades. In studies of this type, pairs of stimuli are presented during the acquisition phase. Following training, retention is again often assessed in a cued-recall test: On each test trial one of the elements of a trained pair (the cue) is presented and the participant is asked to come up with the second element. Alternatively, a recognition task is used during testing: Complete stimulus pairs are presented during testing and the participant must indicate for each pair whether or not it occurred as a pair during learning. The stimulus pairs as a whole and the separate elements within a pair may vary on a number of dimensions, such as the modality of presentation (auditory or visual) and the nature of the stimuli. Among the many types of stimuli used in paired-associate studies are line drawings of common objects and actual objects, nonsense shapes and nonsense words, single letters, numerals, and foreign words. Prior to training, the learners may be informed that their retention of the newly acquired materials will subsequently be tested, or the recall or recognition test may come as a surprise. Learning under these circumstances is called intentional learning and incidental learning, respectively.

Two versions of this common methodology have often been used in foreign language vocabulary acquisition research: **picture–word association** and **word–word association** (see Figure 3.1). In the picture–word association version, one of the terms in each stimulus pair is a foreign language word to be learned (*arbre*) and the second is a picture depicting its meaning (a picture of a tree). In the word–word association version the paired terms presented during training are two words: the foreign language word and its translation in the native language (e.g., *arbre–tree*). The foreign terms in these word pairs may be actual words in an existing language (*arbre*) or artificial words that do not occur as such in any natural language (*arbra*). The use of artificial foreign words enables the systematic investigation of effects that certain word features might have on acquisition and retention, such as the phonological and/or orthographic resemblance between the terms in a translation pair (in

other words, whether or not they are cognates). In addition, using artificial foreign vocabulary is a means to rule out any effect of (latent) prior knowledge of the new language the learner might already possess. The native and foreign terms of a translation pair may be presented in both orders (native–foreign or foreign–native). However, Griffin and Harley (1996) recommended the native–foreign presentation order. Their reason to do so was that they provided evidence that this order compensates for the relative difficulty of learning to use the new vocabulary in production as compared to learning to use it in comprehension.

In word–word association learning, often no specific instructions as to how to process the stimulus pairs are given and the participants are free to choose the learning strategy that suits them best. This is called **uninstructed learning** (or "unstructured learning" or "own-strategy learning"). At other times participants are instructed to silently rehearse the words in a pair until the next learning trial is presented (for instance, to say *arbre is tree, arbre is tree*, and so on), sometimes by writing them out on paper. This way an association between the new word's sound and meaning is assumed to be formed (as well as an association between the new word's sound and the sound of its translation in the native language). This learning method is known as **rote-rehearsal learning** (or "rote-repetition learning" or "rote learning"). Of these two forms of word–word learning, the uninstructed version is regarded as the most effective (Pressley, Levin, Kuiper, Bryant, & Michener, 1982b; Raugh & Atkinson, 1975). Nevertheless, the rote-rehearsal version is often favored in experimental studies, because it enables better control of what learning strategies the participants exploit, thereby reducing learning variability.

Of the two paired-associate learning methods, the picture–word method can be applied less widely than the word–word method for reasons that it is relatively difficult to draw pictures that unambiguously depict abstract words. As a consequence, studies that have employed the picture–word method have typically confined themselves to investigating the acquisition of concrete words. Recall that a similar limitation was said to hold for the keyword method, which was argued above to be unsuitable for the learning of cognates. The word–word paired-associate method does not suffer from any of these limitations. Another attractive feature of the word–word method is that it resembles a common form of foreign vocabulary acquisition outside the laboratory, namely looking up a' foreign word's native translation (or vice versa) in a bilingual dictionary. Even more so it resembles "list learning", which is a common (albeit not always popular) component of the foreign language curriculum: The learning materials usually include lists of translation pairs to be studied. Of course, for illiterates such as very young children, printed forms of the word–word method will not work. For them the picture–word technique (but with the foreign word presented in auditory form) may be a good alternative. In fact, this method also closely resembles a common, natural form of vocabulary acquisition, especially in young children, namely associating a spoken word to the corresponding object in the learner's environment or to a picture in a children's book.

Learning foreign vocabulary in context

The keyword method and the paired-associate learning techniques are both out-of-context ("decontextualized") methods in the sense that the target word occurs in isolation and not embedded in a larger (foreign language) linguistic unit, which is how we encounter words outside the laboratory. A third category of studies examines the acquisition of foreign words occurring as part of a sentence, text fragment, or complete text presented in the foreign language. This "context method" has been implemented in many different forms, depending on the specific questions posed. However, all of the chosen forms are motivated by the understanding that to acquire proficiency in a new language this language must become largely independent of the native language, that it must become "autonomous". To reach this stage, the learner must repeatedly encounter the targeted foreign words in their natural habitat, the foreign language

environment. This way a lexical network can gradually be built that reflects the relations that hold between the words in the target language (see pp. 296–302 on the emergence of language subsets), and knowledge—syntactic, semantic, and pragmatic—of the contextually appropriate (and inappropriate) use of words will be acquired.

The starting point of many of these "context studies" is the common thesis that most foreign words are learned from context, for instance while reading profusely in that language (e.g., Krashen, 1993; Nation, 1990). Context studies often copy real-life immersion situations relatively faithfully (as compared to the methods presented above), typically by looking at the acquisition of target words as they occur in actual texts (e.g., Hulstijn, Hollander, & Greidanus, 1996; Laufer, 2003b). The main questions these studies try to answer are to what extent vocabulary learning is incidental and what the favorable circumstances for **incidental vocabulary learning** are: What amount of vocabulary is picked up when learners are not involved in activities that are explicitly directed toward acquiring vocabulary and, therefore, do not explicitly focus on the meaning and form of individual words with the purpose to store them in memory (as when, for instance, they read a foreign language novel for the mere pleasure of it)? What text and learner characteristics affect the amount of such incidental learning? In contrast, **intentional vocabulary learning** is the learning that occurs when learners perform activities that are deliberately aimed at committing lexical information to memory. A number of researchers studying incidental vocabulary learning have included, in addition to "pure" reading conditions, conditions where reading was combined with vocabulary enhancement techniques such as the provision of glosses in the margin of the text. Even though these conditions explicitly draw attention to vocabulary, as long as the reader's goal is to comprehend the text, and *not* to commit the attended words to memory, they are still regarded incidental learning conditions. It may be obvious though that reading under the latter circumstances does not faithfully copy real-life reading settings.

The claim that most vocabulary is learned from context is based on the observation that instruction time in the foreign language classroom is too limited to teach more than a basic vocabulary through direct means and that near-native speakers of a foreign language possess a vocabulary that is considerably larger than this basic set. What it does *not* imply is that context learning is a more *effective* means of acquiring *specific* foreign vocabulary than other, vocabulary-focused, methods are. Yet some studies apparently assume such a claim to be implied, and subsequently challenge it by showing that word-focused methods are far more effective (e.g., Laufer, 2003b).

The goal of other context studies is not so much (or not primarily) to study the feasibility and limits of incidental vocabulary learning from context but, for instance, to compare the efficacy of the context method with the efficacy of one or more out-of-context methods such as the keyword method or rote-rehearsal learning (e.g., Prince, 1996; Rodríguez & Sadoski, 2000). Alternatively, they may be designed to answer the question of whether "meaning-inferred" vocabulary learning (where the learner infers a word's meaning from context) or "meaning-given" vocabulary learning (where the meaning is provided, often in the form of the foreign word's translation in the native language) is more conducive to learning (e.g., Mondria, 2003). As a consequence of these different goals, these studies bear a much fainter resemblance to real-life reading situations than those designed to test the thesis that most vocabulary is learned from context: Typically they do not present the target words in natural text but in one or more sentences created with the explicit purpose of focusing the learner's attention on meaning components that strongly suggest the target words' definition. Consider as an example the context sentences that Rodríguez and Sadoski provided to suggest the meaning of the English word *empennage* (meaning the tail of an airplane): (1) *After the plane crash, the only part that remained intact was the empennage*; (2) *From its nose to its empennage, the plane is about 150 feet long*; (3) *The plane empennage looks like a fish tail*. It may be obvious

that a typical, real-life text does not give away so much of a particular word's meaning this pointedly, nor does it give away its meaning over such a small fragment of text.

This classification of context studies is neither exhaustive nor does it do justice to studies that have combined the above approaches in a single study. Its purpose was to introduce some of the major questions addressed in these studies. Further on in this chapter a selection of the major findings of vocabulary acquisition studies that have employed at least one of the methods introduced so far—keyword learning, paired-associate learning, and context learning—will be discussed. In fact, many of these studies have used more than one method, contrasting the various methods' effectiveness. The primary focus of each of these studies determines to what section it will be assigned. But before presenting the evidence, I will first introduce some of the test methods that have been used to assess what vocabulary knowledge a particular foreign language learner possesses at a particular point in time and/or how fast this knowledge can be retrieved from memory. Two of these test methods were already introduced above: receptive and productive cued recall following a learning episode. Testing both what vocabulary is known and how fast it can be dug up from memory is important because skillful use of a foreign language demands the existence of a sufficiently large body of knowledge about the pertinent language, as well as the ability to access fluently the pieces of knowledge targeted at any point in time during language processing. Communication will falter or may even break down completely not only when a particular piece of sought-for knowledge is missing in the foreign language knowledge stock but also when it is there but can only be accessed and retrieved painstakingly.

Methods of assessing vocabulary knowledge

Vocabulary tests may be administered with many different purposes in mind and the test format varies with the examiner's specific goal. For instance, a test may be designed to assess

vocabulary breadth; that is, the number of words the learner knows to at least some extent. Alternatively, a test may attempt to reveal **vocabulary depth**; that is, the degree to which individual words are known, what different types of knowledge regarding a word (e.g., semantic, syntactic, morphological, pragmatic) a learner possesses (see Schmitt & Meara, 1997, for an example). A test may either be used to assess the number of vocabulary items acquired in a specific prior training episode (such as a session of learning by means of the keyword method, the paired-associate method or the context method), or to determine the state of the foreign language vocabulary that has resulted from all prior learning experiences with the target language, in the foreign language classroom and beyond. Furthermore, a test may be taken to determine the speed with which foreign language words can be retrieved from memory, or to become informed on the degree of interconnectedness of the elements in the foreign vocabulary. A test may be administered to get some idea of the general state of the foreign vocabulary or zoom in on individual items in the learner's lexicon. Finally, a specific test may combine a number of these different goals.

The test that presumably has been applied most widely is the cued recall test introduced above, which is typically used to assess the learning that has occurred in a specific prior learning episode. Of its two forms, receptive and productive cued recall, especially the former, the least demanding of the two, is popular. The cued recall test may be taken immediately after the examined training session (**immediate recall**), or at some later point, say 1 or 2 weeks later without intervening additional training having taken place between first training and testing (**delayed recall**). Incidentally, the formats of the receptive and productive cued recall tests are exactly the same as those of the "backward" (foreign to native) and "forward" (native to foreign) word translation tasks, respectively, which are often used in laboratory studies that attempt to find out how learners at various levels of proficiency in the foreign language map the foreign language word-forms onto their meanings (see pp. 136–137). These latter studies do not encompass an initial training phase but tap the state of the learners' vocabulary knowledge as it is the moment they arrive in the laboratory for testing, and without any reference to the specific learning experiences that led to the memory storage of the tested words. A further salient difference between the training studies and the translation studies is that in the latter retrieval time is the major dependent variable. In contrast, in the training studies the primary dependent variable is the recall score. In other words, whereas the training studies tend to focus on the amount of vocabulary learned, the translation studies focus on the acquired level of fluency in using it.

At low levels of foreign language proficiency the above versions of the translation task may constitute a real challenge to the test-takers. The reason is that they are both production tasks in the sense that the test-takers have to generate a response from within (note that this also holds for the receptive, foreign to native, version of the task). Therefore, two less-demanding versions of the translation task have been introduced for use with learners at relatively low levels of foreign language proficiency. One of them is **translation recognition**, in which pairs of words are presented, each pair consisting of a native language word and a foreign word. A given word pair may consist of actual translations, or the words in the pair are not translations of one another. The participant's task is to indicate for each word pair whether or not the two words are translations of one another. The translation recognition task is generally sensitive to the same stimulus manipulations (e.g., of word frequency and word concreteness) as is the productive version of the task (e.g., De Groot, 1992b; De Groot & Comijs, 1995). This suggests that it can be used as a valid alternative to the **translation production** task. The second relatively easy version of the translation task is what I have previously called **cued translation**: Each stimulus word presented for translation is accompanied by a cue that reveals part of the identity of the solicited translation, for instance, its first letter and a dot for each of the remaining letters (De Groot, 1992b). Like translation recognition, cued translation responds to the same stimulus manipulations as translation production and thus also seems to be an appropriate alternative to the production task.

A widely used test designed to assess the *breadth* of a learner's foreign vocabulary is Nation's Vocabulary Levels Test (e.g., Nation, 1990). It covers the 10,000 most frequent English words and estimates the proportion of words known at each of four frequency levels from the 2000 most frequent ones to the 10,000 most frequent ones (2000, 3000, 5000, and 10,000). A fifth level assesses the learner's knowledge of academic vocabulary. A word is considered known if it is correctly matched with its definition. The proportion of correctly matched items at each level (out of a total of 18 per level) is taken to be the proportion of words mastered within that frequency band. The total scores for the five levels are added up and the resulting overall score is considered an estimate of the learner's overall English vocabulary size. This test is both used as a diagnostic instrument and for placement purposes in language-teaching classrooms (Read, 2004).

Different versions of the **word association** task are used to assess one particular aspect of the *depth* of L2 vocabulary knowledge, namely the interconnectedness of a given word with other words in the learner's L2 lexicon (the "word web", as it is often called). In the most common *productive* version of this task, "discrete" word association, participants are presented with a series of prompt words, one by one, and are asked to say the first word that comes to mind after hearing or seeing the prompt word (see Meara, 1983, for a review). As an alternative to this version, the productive **continued word association** task could be used. In this task participants generate as many words as possible for each of the prompt words within a certain unit time. In a *receptive* version of the word association task, a target item is presented together with a set of other words. A number of the latter are clearly semantically related to the target whereas the remaining ones (the "distracters") are unrelated (Read, 1993), have a more loose relation to the target word (Schoonen & Verhallen, 1998), or are either unrelated or loosely related to the target

(Greidanus & Nienhuis, 2001). The learner's task is to indicate which of the words that accompany the target are related to the latter (or related to it relatively strongly). By varying the type of semantic relation between target and word set (for instance, the related words may be antonyms, synonyms, or hyponyms of the target; or the relation may be **syntagmatic** or **paradigmatic**), fine-grained information on the depth of the learner's knowledge can be disclosed.

Wilks and Meara (2002) and Wilks, Meara, and Wolter (2005) combined (a slightly different version of) this receptive word association task (or "association recognition task") with computer simulations based on graph theory (see Wilks & Meara, 2002, for details). Their goal was to obtain an estimate of the average number of links that connect each of the words in an L2 vocabulary of a certain size with the other words in this lexicon, thus assessing the density of the word webs. Perhaps the most important conclusion to draw from this work is that, despite the precision that is suggested by using simulation techniques, the data emerging from running the model may be way off target, especially when the wrong assumptions about the learners' performance on the association recognition task are built into the simulation model: When reconsidering a number of the earlier assumptions and then resetting the parameters of the model and rerunning it, an earlier estimate of 30 to 40 links for each L2 French word (in L1 English speakers who had studied French in school for about 7 years; Wilks & Meara, 2002) dropped to an estimate of about 7 per L2 word (Wilks et al., 2005).

The technique that is plausibly used most frequently in monolingual psycholinguistic studies that examine the connections between lexical entries in the mental lexicon is the **semantic priming technique**. In these studies each target word is preceded by a semantically related prime word or by either an unrelated prime word or some "neutral" context stimulus and the effect of the prime on target processing is measured. A target that follows a related prime is often responded to faster than a target preceded by an unrelated or neutral prime (and fewer errors are made to the former). This effect is called the **semantic priming effect**. It is often attributed to a process of activation spreading along the connection that exists in lexical memory between the representations of prime and target and that facilitates the process of accessing the target word's representation (but see pp. 138–139 for an alternative account). The very occurrence of such an effect thus suggests the existence of a link between the lexical representations of prime and target. Therefore the technique involves another way to study word webs in memory. To prevent any process other than spreading activation in memory causing the priming effect (such as a conscious semantic integration process that occurs *after* the target word's lexical representation has already been accessed; see De Groot, 1984, and Neely, 1991, for discussions), **masked priming** is occasionally applied. This involves visually degrading the primes (mostly by presenting them very briefly and embedding them in between two nonsensical masking signals) in such a way that they can no longer be identified or even detected. This way any priming process for which conscious perception of the prime is a prerequisite is impeded (for the process of spreading activation to take place the prime does not have to be consciously perceived).

Bilingual studies have mostly adopted the semantic priming methodology to study the connections between the L1 and L2 lexicons. In these studies (see pp. 138–141 for example studies of this type) the primes are words from the participants' one language and the targets are words from their other language. But occasionally the semantic priming technique has been employed to study learners' word webs within the L2 lexicon, presenting both primes and targets in the L2 and comparing the priming effects with those for the same words in native speakers of the language in question. To be able to attribute any priming effect to emerge to spreading activation within the L2 lexicon, in one of the pertinent studies the primes were masked and thus could not be consciously identified (Frenck-Mestre & Prince, 1997). Nevertheless, priming occurred for various types of prime–target relations (antonyms, synonyms, and collocations), but the exact priming

patterns that emerged depended on the L2 learners' level of proficiency. The facts that these effects occur and are sensitive to the proficiency manipulation prove that the technique is a valuable additional tool to study L2 lexical networks.

THE KEYWORD METHOD: SUCCESSES AND LIMITATIONS

General results and evaluation

In one of the seminal papers by Atkinson and Raugh that introduced the keyword method in the laboratory, Atkinson (1975) drew up a research agenda for subsequent studies on the efficacy of the keyword method by posing the following questions: In an experimental setting, is the method's effectiveness greater when the experimenter supplies the keywords or when the learners themselves generate them? Does learning by means of the keyword method lead to equally fast retrieval during recall of the newly acquired vocabulary as learning via other methods, for instance, rote rehearsal? Is the imagery component an indispensable part of the instructions or is an instruction to associate the keyword and the new foreign language word by generating a meaningful sentence connecting these two words equally effective (the "verbiage" version of the method presented on p. 86)? Is the keyword method equally effective in productive and receptive testing? These are obviously important questions because their answers provide relevant information on the scope of the method's success. For instance, a hypothetical finding that the method is only effective if the experimenter supplies the keyword would severely constrain the method's potential impact because learners usually do not have experimenters (or teachers) around to provide them with appropriate keywords. Similarly, the method's usefulness would also be limited if it leads to successful recall of many of the trained foreign words but the retrieval process is slower than the speed required for fluent communication.

The research that ensued from the pioneering work of Atkinson and Raugh picked up this research agenda and extended it by looking into possible interactions between learning method and learner characteristics, hypothesizing that the keyword method might be especially effective for young, beginning learners, for learners with a relatively low verbal ability, for learners with little experience in foreign language learning in general, and for learners with a high imaging capacity. Other studies have compared the efficacy of the keyword method with that of other methods such as paired-associate learning or context learning. Yet other studies have looked at the effect of qualitatively different keywords or have compared the efficacy of supplying the learners with either keywords only or with complete interactive images in the form of written or spoken sentences (where the learners have to create the mental image themselves on the basis of the verbal information), or in the form of actual pictures. Further questions that have been posed are whether the keyword method is as effective in learning in real-life learning settings such as an actual foreign language classroom as in learning under strictly controlled circumstances in a laboratory, and whether word knowledge acquired by means of the keyword method generalizes to other contexts, such as when the learned vocabulary occurs in actual text. Finally, one line of research has looked into the durability of the memory representations formed for the learned foreign language words, comparing short- and long-term retention following learning with the keyword method and using other methods. These are the questions that I will address in the sections to come.

Despite the fact that the keyword method seems a rather complex, even bizarre, procedure for learning foreign vocabulary, it can boast of triumphal successes. Sommer and Gruneberg (2002) noted that by then at least 60 studies had been published showing that this technique enhances retention, whereas only a handful of studies had failed to find an effect (for reviews comparing the keyword method with other methods such as rote rehearsal, uninstructed learning, and other control conditions, see Cohen, 1987; Hulstijn, 1997; Pressley, Levin, & Delaney, 1982a). The beneficial effects of the method have been demonstrated for different learner groups learning different languages, including Arab elementary school students learning English (Elhelou, 1994), L1 English American college students learning Russian (Atkinson, 1975; Atkinson & Raugh, 1975) or Spanish (Raugh & Atkinson, 1975; Sagarra & Alba, 2006), L1 English learners of German (Desrochers, Wieland, & Coté, 1991), Australian-English high school students learning Italian (Hogben & Lawson, 1997), elderly L1 English speakers learning Spanish (Gruneberg & Pascoe, 1996), and for L1 English learning-disabled adults (Gruneberg, Sykes, & Gillett, 1994) and learning-disabled adolescents (Gruneberg, 1989, in Gruneberg et al., 1994) acquiring Spanish.

Across these studies the learning settings varied between strictly controlled experimentation in the laboratory (e.g., Raugh & Atkinson, 1975) and more natural settings such as a classroom environment (e.g., Hogben & Lawson, 1997). These findings suggest the method can be successfully used in many different learning environments. This conclusion receives further support from the fact that the method's success extends beyond the learning of foreign language vocabulary to the learning of curricular content such as the capitals of states (Levin, Shriberg, Miller, McCormick, & Levin, 1980), the attributes of minerals (Morrison & Levin, 1986, in Elhelou, 1994), associating cities to their products (Roberts, 1983), learning the letters of a non-Roman foreign alphabet (e.g., Greek or Russian; Gruneberg & Sykes, 1996), and the learning of obscure (L1) words (McDaniel, Pressley, & Dunay, 1987).

As an illustration of how powerful the keyword method is as a strategy to acquire new vocabulary, consider a single-case study by Beaton, Gruneberg, and Ellis (1995) and Beaton (2005). These authors studied the retention of 350 Italian words in a university lecturer, referred to as NP, 10 years (Beaton et al., 1995) and 22 years (Beaton, 2005) after initial learning by means of a "Linkword" Italian course that employed the keyword method (Gruneberg, 1987/2004). In

Linkword (of which versions exist for many languages) the learners are presented with sets of new words, each of them embedded in a pair of sentences that relates the new item to its translation by means of a suitable keyword and that contains the explicit instruction to create an image of keyword and translation. An example is: *The Italian for chicken is pollo: Imagine using a chicken as a polo stick.* Other examples, with different target languages, are provided in Table 3.1 (examples taken from Beaton, Gruneberg, Hyde, Shufflebottom, & Sykes, 2005). As noted by Gruneberg and Pascoe (1996), this is a rather exceptional use of the keyword method. More often, only keywords instead of complete interactive images are given, or the participants are simply instructed to use keywords, which they have to generate themselves. Vocabulary teaching

with Linkword is integrated with a basic grammar: During training simple grammar is introduced at regular intervals, and the previously learned grammar and vocabulary is practiced in sentence-translation exercises. The method is not meant to replace other teaching methods but is complementary to existing classroom practices.

After starting training with Linkword, it had taken NP about 32 hours to first learn the targeted vocabulary of 350 Italian words (Beaton, 2005). Without any intervening use of Italian and using a conservative scoring criterion (the responses had to be completely correct), NP remembered 35% of the Italian words learned 10 years before, as determined in a productive written cued recall test. Immediately after only 10 minutes of relearning, he took a second productive recall test, now performing at 66% correct. This test was followed by a further 90 minutes of learning (both the target vocabulary and grammar sections). In the productive recall test that immediately followed this learning session the percentage correct recall had increased to 95%. A more lenient scoring procedure was performed as well, in which slight deviations from the target words were accepted. According to this scoring criterion, the percentages correct at the three recall tests were 52%, 76%, and 99%, respectively.

When tested again an additional 12 years later, without using any Italian in the intervening period, the corresponding recall scores at the three tests (following no relearning whatsoever, 10 minutes of relearning, and an additional 90 minutes of relearning, respectively) were 38%, 71%, and 90% using a conservative criterion, and 53%, 84%, and 98%, respectively, using the more lenient criterion. Control data of a participant having learned the same set of Italian words with a different method are lacking. It is therefore impossible to tell whether this high level of performance might have been equaled (or even surpassed) by any other learning method (see pp. 101–103 for a discussion of studies that looked at long-term retention following other learning methods). Notwithstanding this caveat, the level of recall performance of this learner decades after learning is impressive, and one can

TABLE 3.1

Examples of keyword images

1. The Polish for juice is SOC: imagine drinking juice through a *sock*.
2. The Italian for night is NOTTE: imagine having a *naughty* night out.
3. The Spanish for cow is VACCA: imagine a cow cleaning a field with a *vacuum*.
4. The French for fish is POISSON: imagine *poisoning* your pet fish.
5. The Greek for blood is KAN: imagine pouring blood from a *can*.
6. The Russian for eye is GLAZ: imagine you had a *glass* eye.
7. The Japanese for shorts is HAN ZUBON: imagine my *hands upon* your shorts.
8. The Spanish for rice is ARROZ: imagine *arrows* landing in your bowl of rice.
9. The Dutch for tooth is TAND: imagine you *tanned* your tooth in the sun.
10. The Hebrew for elephant is PEEL: imagine feeding an elephant orange *peel*.
11. The Vietnamese for hand is SAWN: imagine watching your hand being *sawn* off.
12. The Polish for herring is SLEDZ: imagine a herring sitting on a *sledge*.
13. The French for hedgehog is HÉRISSON: imagine your *hairy son* looks like a hedgehog.
14. The Greek for diarrhoea is THEARIA: imagine a soprano singing *the aria* from Tosca while suffering from diarrhoea.
15. The Spanish for fly is MOSCA: imagine flies invading *Moscow*.

The words to learn are in capitals. The keywords are italicized. Examples from Beaton et al. (2005). With permission from the authors. © Linkwordlanguages.com with permission.

only agree with Beaton (2005, p. 32) when he notes with subdued enthusiasm that:

> a level of recall close to 100 per cent for over 300 foreign words first encountered more than 20 years earlier, achieved at the expense of less than two hours of explicit study (plus testing time) at the end of each of two decades, represents an excellent return on the initial investment of cognitive effort.

The conclusion seems warranted that the keyword method (as implemented by Linkword) is an effective method of foreign vocabulary learning.

Despite its success, the keyword method has been received with skepticism, even with aversion, by linguists and teachers, if not by learners. Gruneberg and Morris suggested the linguists' aversion possibly results from their concern with higher-order aspects of language learning, which may blind them to the "basic advantages of enhanced methods of vocabulary learning" (Gruneberg & Morris, 1992, p. 181). One of the reasons teachers may oppose the method may be their concern that words not learned in context might not be understood when embedded in normal discourse (a criticism that might apply to other direct methods, such as paired-associate learning, as well). This fear seems unwarranted though, because at least two studies have demonstrated that learning by means of the context method did not produce better reading comprehension than did keyword learning (McDaniel & Pressley, 1984, 1989). Another reason may be the fear that memory retrieval of words learned by means of the keyword method will always require retrieving the image created during learning first. Sommer and Gruneberg (2002, p. 52) note that this fear is unwarranted because "the image rapidly drops out as learning is established".

In all then, from the above overview of the evidence it seems the keyword method is an effective, albeit cumbersome, method to learn foreign vocabulary. Yet it remains to be seen whether other, less laborious methods are not equally effective and, having the advantage of being simpler, are therefore to be favored over the keyword method. The next sections compare the keyword method with other methods, in so doing providing more fine-grained information on the efficacy of the keyword method. But first some words are in order on why the keyword method is as effective as it is.

The suggested explanations point at an important role of mental imagery during vocabulary learning. The best known of these explanations is one in terms of Paivio's **dual-coding theory**, which assumes the existence of both a verbal system and an image system in memory (e.g., Paivio, 1986; Paivio & Desrochers, 1980). The keyword method is thought to enhance learning and recall because the method exploits both the verbal system and the image system during learning (and the latter more so than other methods do): During learning, both a verbal and an image code of the new item are stored in memory. Assuming that these codes have additive effects, retrieval of the foreign word is facilitated (as compared to when just one code is stored) because both stored codes can support recall. An alternative explanation was proposed by Marschark and his colleagues, who suggested that image processing facilitates recall by increasing the relational and distinctive information of the items to be learned (where an item's distinctive information concerns information specific for the item concerned, and its relational information concerns the information relating it to the context in which it occurs; Marschark & Surian, 1989; Marschark, Richman, Yuille, & Hunt, 1987).

Refinements and qualifications of the keyword method's efficacy

The substantial research efforts that ensued from the promising first results of Atkinson and Raugh's early studies (Atkinson, 1975; Atkinson & Raugh, 1975; Raugh & Atkinson, 1975) have led to detailed knowledge about the conditions under which the keyword method is maximally effective. In addition, they have given some cause for caution and skepticism because of the fact that under certain circumstances the method produces poorer results than simple rote rehearsal or uninstructed learning. In this section I will present some of the relevant findings, providing answers to the research questions listed above (pp. 93–94).

Quality of keywords and keyword images

It goes without saying that the central component in the keyword method is the keyword itself and therefore that choosing good keywords is crucial for the method to work. Raugh and Atkinson (1975) listed three criteria for a good keyword: (1) It must sound as much as possible like the foreign word to be learned. (2) It must allow the easy formation of a memorable mental image (the "imagery link") in which the referents of the keyword and the L1 translation of the foreign word to be learned interact. (3) It must be unique (that is, different from the other keywords used in the test vocabulary).

What degree of sound similarity between keyword and foreign word is minimally required is unclear, but the examples provided in the literature suggest that even keywords whose sound vaguely hints at the targeted foreign words can be effective and that the shared sound part may occupy any position of the foreign words to be learned. Examples of English keywords for learning Russian vocabulary provided by Atkinson (1975) are: *strawman* for *straná* ("country"); *poised* for *póezd* ("train"); *saviour* for *séver* ("north"); *two rocks* for *durák* ("fool"); *Gulliver* for *golová* ("head"); and *tell pa* for *tolpá* ("crowd"). These examples show clear differences in the degree of sound overlap between keyword and foreign word. Apparently, the method allows for flexibility in sound similarity, proving its robustness. The provided examples also show that keywords do not have to be single words but that short phrases may serve as keywords as well (*two rocks* and *tell pa*). Furthermore, they illustrate that keywords may be of different grammatical classes (e.g., *poised* vs. *strawman*), and that also proper nouns may serve as keywords (*Gulliver*). Given this flexibility, it is likely that a suitable keyword can readily be found for any foreign word to be learned.

The second of the criteria for good keywords listed above implies that keywords that are easy to imagine lead to more successful learning than keywords that are hard to imagine. Indirect support for this claim comes from a study in which noun keywords for which an image can be created (typically keywords that refer to concrete entities) were presented to one group of English learners of German, and verb keywords to a second group (Ellis & Beaton, 1993a). In both cases, the keywords were embedded in sentences describing a complete interactive image and containing the explicit instruction to the participants to use imagery. Example sentences used in the noun-keyword condition were: *Imagine a sparrow on a station barrier* (for learning *Sperre*, which is German for *barrier*) and *Imagine trousers wrapped round a garden hose* (for learning *Hose*, the German word for *trousers*). The corresponding sentences in the verb-keyword condition were: *Imagine you spare a penny at the station barrier*, and *Imagine dirty trousers and hose them down*. These sentences were presented visually on the screen, together with the German word to be learned and its English translation. The results of this experiment are presented in Figure 3.2.

Both in a productive-testing condition (in which, for instance, *barrier* was presented as recall cue and the participants had to produce the corresponding German word, in this case *Sperre*) and in a receptive-testing condition (cue: German *Sperre*; response: English *barrier*), recall scores were higher for the noun-keyword group than for the verb-keyword group. A plausible cause of this effect of grammatical class is that the referents of verbs are harder to imagine than those of concrete nouns. Importantly, with receptive testing, the noun-keyword condition showed higher recall scores than two control conditions, one in which the participants had been allowed to choose their own learning strategy (uninstructed paired-associate learning), and a second in which they had been asked to repeat the German–English translation pairs out loud (rote rehearsal). In contrast, with productive testing recall scores were higher in these two control conditions than in both keyword conditions. The results of this study thus suggest that concrete nouns are more effective keywords than verbs, and that the keyword technique's efficacy depends on the testing

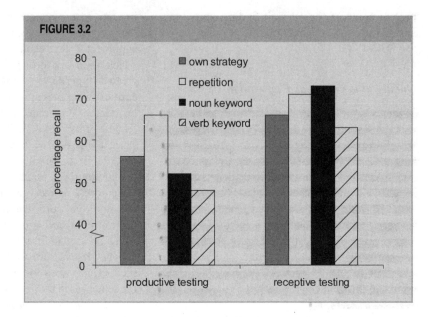

FIGURE 3.2

Recall scores as a function of learning method and testing method. From Ellis and Beaton (1993a). Copyright © 1993 The Experimental Psychology Society, used with the permission of Taylor & Francis.

procedure. More specifically, it depends on whether comprehension or production of the newly acquired vocabulary is tested.

Other researchers have qualified these conclusions. Gruneberg and Pascoe (1996) compared the efficacy of the keyword method with that of uninstructed paired-associate learning in elderly native English speakers learning Spanish. As Ellis and Beaton (1993a), they embedded the keywords in sentences that described complete interactive images. This time—but adopting a somewhat more liberal criterion for scoring a response as correct—superior results for the keyword method were obtained not only with receptive testing but also with productive testing. A similar result with liberal scoring had been obtained earlier for younger age groups (Pressley, Levin, Hall, Miller, & Berry, 1980). Both studies thus indicate that the keyword method may outperform the uninstructed method both when learning new vocabulary for comprehension as well as when learning it for production.

The disparate findings regarding productive learning between these studies may be due to any of the differences that may exist between them (*exact* replications are rare), however minor they may seem at first sight. Gruneberg and Pascoe (1996) suggested a difference in the quality of the keyword images used across the two studies might be the culprit, some of the keywords used by Ellis and Beaton possibly being of inferior quality. Beaton et al. (2005; Experiment 3) tested this hypothesis, selecting from the set of materials used by Ellis and Beaton a subset of relatively good keyword images, as based on ratings by an independent group of participants. When only these were subsequently used in an acquisition study, the results showed better recall performance for the keyword learners than for a control group of rote-repetition learners, both on a productive and a receptive recall test. The authors concluded that learning using the keyword method is generally superior to learning by means of rote repetition, provided that the keyword images are of good quality.

The role of learner characteristics: Prior foreign language learning experience and verbal ability

Several sources of evidence suggest that the keyword method's efficacy depends on a number of learner characteristics. One of them is amount of prior foreign language learning experience, either in the target language itself or in other foreign languages. A second, perhaps, is the learner's verbal ability. Van Hell and Candia

Mahn (1997) compared the performance of two learner groups. One group consisted of L1 Dutch learners of Spanish who were naive with regard to Spanish but had taken English, French, and German classes in the past. The second group consisted of L1 American-English naive learners of Dutch who had not had any prior training in any other foreign language. All participants in both groups were university undergraduates and they were randomly assigned to a keyword condition or a rote-rehearsal condition. In the keyword condition the keywords were provided (rather than self-generated) but the participants had to generate the interactive images themselves. Both cued recall scores (receptive testing) and retrieval time served as dependent variables.

The Dutch learners of Spanish showed better recall performance following rote-rehearsal learning than following keyword mnemonics: Cued recall scores were higher and retrieval times were shorter for the rote-rehearsal group. In contrast, the American-English learners of Dutch recalled the same proportion of Dutch words in the two learning conditions, but also for these learners retrieval time was shorter in the rote-rehearsal condition. In conclusion, for experienced learners, rote rehearsal was clearly more effective than keyword mnemonics on both measures. Considering the amount of learned vocabulary, it appears that for inexperienced learners the two methods were equally effective. Yet, when taking retrieval time into account as well, for inexperienced learners too, rote rehearsal seems to be the superior method. Additional evidence to suggest that rote rehearsal is more effective than keyword mnemonics for experienced learners has since been provided by Rodríguez and Sadoski (2000). These authors showed that for L1 Spanish learners of English L2 who had already acquired an above-average English vocabulary, rote rehearsal was more effective than the keyword method when learning additional English vocabulary. This time, however, for learners with less than average English vocabulary knowledge the keyword method was the more effective of the two.

The above finding that rote-rehearsal learning leads to faster recall than keyword learning appears to be robust, because Wang and Thomas (1999) also observed this effect in a study that examined the learning of Tagalog (the national language of the Philippines) and that employed a recognition test instead of cued recall to assess the amount of learning. It refutes the suggestion by Atkinson (1975) that the method of learning does not affect retrieval time. Specifically it suggests, contrary to Sommer and Gruneberg's (2002) claim presented earlier, that recall of a word learned by means of the keyword method requires the prior recall of the keyword and the interactive image constructed during training. In other words, it involves a relatively long retrieval path. Rote learning plausibly involves the formation of more direct connections between the two terms of a translation pair so that during testing a shorter retrieval path can be taken.

Van Hell and Candia Mahn's (1997) study thus indicated that, as compared to rote rehearsal, the keyword method might actually be an inferior method of foreign vocabulary learning by university students, especially when they are experienced foreign language learners. This suggestion casts doubt on the proposed explanation of the results of two earlier studies that also tested university students. McDaniel and Pressley (1984) and McDaniel and Tillman (1987) observed no difference in mean level of recall for a keyword group and an own-strategy control group whereas earlier studies of this research group had provided an overwhelming amount of evidence of the keyword method's superiority. To account for this unexpected result they hypothesized that, irrespective of the learning instructions, high verbal-ability students always adopt a learning strategy similar to keyword mnemonics. University students are possibly a rather select group of individuals, with arguably a generally high verbal ability. Belonging to this population of verbally gifted individuals, the participants in the own-strategy experimental group may have chosen to adopt the keyword method. As a result, they performed equally well on the recall test as those in the keyword group. This account thus remains faithful to the conviction that the keyword method is a superior strategy for learning foreign vocabulary and adds the assumption that learners with a high verbal ability do not need to be instructed to use the method but apply it spontaneously. The important contribution of Van Hell and Candia Mahn's study is that it suggests the keyword method is not the optimal method under all circumstances and for all learners. Furthermore, it indicates that the learning strategies adopted by the participants in their rote rehearsal and keyword conditions differ from one another despite the fact that, as university students, they presumably all have high verbal skills.

Subsequent research provided more direct evidence against the hypothesis that learners of high verbal ability always spontaneously adopt the keyword technique when learning foreign vocabulary. Hogben and Lawson (1997) had Australian-English high school students learn Italian words either with the keyword method or in an own-strategy condition in a classroom setting. Prior to learning the students completed a test that provided a measure of their verbal ability. If high verbal-ability students always use keyword mnemonics, whether or not instructed to do so, the experimental manipulation (keyword method versus own-strategy method) may be expected not to have an effect on students with high verbal ability. The results did not confirm the hypothesis. Specifically, high verbal-ability students in the keyword condition outperformed high verbal-ability students in the own-strategy control group (see Lawson & Hogben, 1998, for converging evidence), suggesting the superiority of the keyword method even in learners with a high verbal ability. These results can be reconciled with those of Van Hell and Candia Mahn (1997) if we assume that the participants in Hogben and Lawson's study (high school students) had less prior foreign language learning experience than those tested by Van Hell and Candia Mahn (university students). Irrespective of the correctness of this hypothesis, the above discussion seems to warrant the conclusion that the efficacy of the keyword method depends on at least one learner characteristic, namely, the amount of prior foreign language learning experience.

To conclude this section, one further result obtained by Van Hell and Candia Mahn (1997)

deserves mention, namely the fact that, with an equal amount of practice, the recall scores for the experienced foreign language learners were substantially higher than for the inexperienced learners (see Hansen, Umeda, & McKinney, 2002, for a similar effect). The difference occurred irrespective of the learning method, suggesting that the experienced learners were also the better learners. This clearly is a manifestation of the **Matthew effect**, a phenomenon that has been demonstrated in various knowledge domains (e.g., in the domain of reading; Stanovich, 1986) and also in more profane aspects of life, for instance the acquisition of material fortune. The essence of the phenomenon is summarized in the maxim "the rich get richer", or in the words of the eponymous apostle: "For unto every one that hath shall be given, and he shall have abundance: but from him that has not shall be taken away even that which he hath" (from Merton, 1968, p. 58, who applies the phenomenon to [mis]allocation of credit for scientific work).

Applied to the present result, the data show that the more prior knowledge of foreign languages has previously been acquired, the easier it is to accumulate still more. It is easy for any learner of a foreign language to recognize this to be the case. For this learner of Italian, for instance, knowing the French words, *hiver* ("winter"), *bouillir* ("to boil"), and *nouveau* ("new")—as well as the English words *to boil* and *new*—greatly facilitated the learning of their Italian counterparts *inverno*, *bollire*, and *nuovo*. Similarly, to learn that the Italian equivalent of the Dutch word *eergisteren* ("the day before yesterday") is *altro ieri* ("the other yesterday") was a piece of cake after I had gained the knowledge that *ieri* and *altro* in Italian mean "yesterday" and "other", respectively. Also my native Dutch appeared helpful: Remembering the Italian *dimenticare* ("to forget"; *vergeten* in Dutch) was easy the moment the awareness dawned that it must be related to Dutch *dement* ("demented").

These anecdotal examples illustrate that the experienced foreign language learner possesses an immense stock of relevant prior knowledge with which to tackle the task of learning yet further vocabulary. But there is experimental support for it as well. Gibson and Hufeisen (2003), for instance, gave a particularly stunning demonstration of the Matthew effect. They had trilingual and multilingual learners of either German or English translate a text in Swedish, an *unknown* language to all participants in the study, into one of their foreign languages. Even though the cognitive load was lessened by a picture that visualized parts of the text's content, the results may still be considered impressive: Overall translation accuracy was 76%. In addition to lexical similarities, the participants used metalinguistic knowledge (conscious knowledge about the structure and form of linguistic elements) and world knowledge to figure out the correct translation, and the more languages known, the more successfully these knowledge sources were exploited. Similarly, Sanz (2000) demonstrated that Catalan–Spanish bilinguals are better learners of L3 English than Spanish monolinguals learning English as an L2, even when potentially confounding variables such as motivation to learn English and exposure to that language were controlled for. From studies that have focused on transfer phenomena during processing (rather than learning) a foreign language, we know this exploitation of prior knowledge holds for other language components, such as grammar, as well (see, e.g., Bates, McNew, MacWhinney, Devescovi, & Smith, 1982; McDonald, 1987; and see MacWhinney, 1997, 2005, for two versions of the competition model, which was developed to account for these transfer phenomena). Above we have seen that for experienced language learners paired-associate learning is a more effective learning method than the keyword method. Arguably, a reason for this is that in paired-associate learning experienced learners have more freedom than in keyword learning to exploit their rich linguistic knowledge base, the latter method constraining the learner more than the former.

Long-term retention of new foreign vocabulary

Although occasionally passing an exam may be the sole reason for a student to expend effort in acquiring foreign vocabulary, most students will also be motivated by the prospect of being able to actually use the new vocabulary in the long term in real-life communication settings. The latter will be the primary motivation for those learners who are planning a trip to a country where the language in question is the major means of communication, and who feel more comfortable possessing some basic knowledge of it, as well as for learners who plan to settle in that country. In all these cases the goal of learning is that the new vocabulary gets stored in memory permanently, not transiently. For this reason, in evaluating a method's efficacy it is imperative to know the durability of the acquired vocabulary.

In a series of studies, Wang and Thomas compared the long-term efficacy of the keyword method to that of other methods, collecting recall data both immediately after training and after a delay (Thomas & Wang, 1996; Wang & Thomas, 1992, 1995a; Wang, Thomas, Inzana, & Primacerio, 1993; Wang, Thomas, & Ouellette, 1992). Across these studies, various versions of the keyword method and various control methods were used, the vocabulary to be learned was taken from different languages (French and Tagalog), and the learning took place under both an incidental learning set (where during learning the participants are not aware that their long-term retention will be tested afterwards) and an intentional learning set (where they are informed beforehand their recall will be tested after a delay).

A consistent finding across all these studies was that, when tested after a delay instead of immediately after training, keyword learners performed worse than rote learners or demonstrated a steeper forgetting slope. Conversely, immediately after training keyword learners often outperformed learners in the control conditions, evidencing a faster acquisition rate in the keyword condition. The upper and middle panels of Figure 3.3 show the results of two representative experiments with university students as participants. In one of them (Thomas & Wang, 1996, Experiment 1), the control condition concerned learning through rote rehearsal. In the second (Wang & Thomas, 1995a, Experiment 2), the participants in the control condition had to deduce the foreign word's meaning from two

FIGURE 3.3

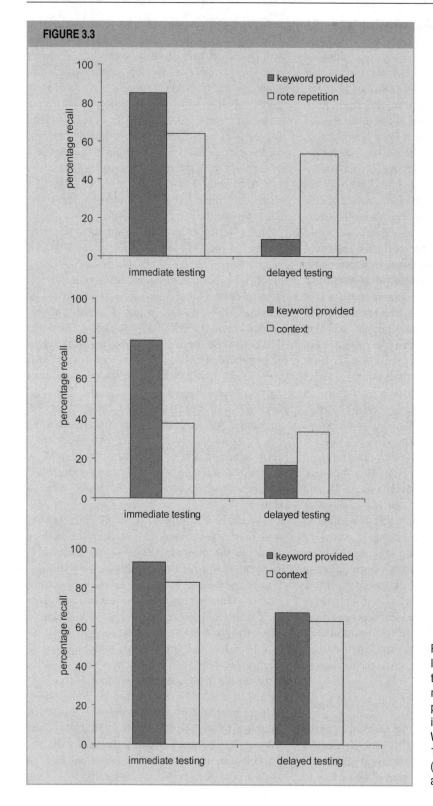

Recall scores as a function of learning method and time of testing, after two (upper and middle panels) or five (lower panel) learning trials per item. Based on Thomas and Wang (1996, Experiment 1) and Wang and Thomas (1995a, Experiments 2 and 3).

sentences, each of which provided a strong clue regarding its meaning (e.g., *The warrior pulled his claymore from its sheath. He used his claymore and shield to slay the dragon*). In the keyword condition of both experiments, the experimenters provided the keywords, and in both studies delayed testing took place 2 days after learning.

Crucially, in designing their experiments, in one respect these researchers deviated from earlier studies that had looked at delayed retention of the learned words and that had demonstrated a keyword method advantage both immediately after training and after a delay. In these earlier studies each participant had been tested both on the immediate test and on the delayed test. But because the immediate recall test provides an additional opportunity to learn (on trials where recall actually succeeds), in this design the degree of learning and the time of recall, immediately after learning or delayed, are confounded variables. As a consequence of the differential acquisition rates in keyword learning on the one hand and rote-rehearsal and context learning on the other hand (see the immediate testing conditions in Figure 3.3), this design favors keyword learners (who show relatively high immediate recall scores). Wang and Thomas got rid of this confounding variable by using a between-participants design, in which different groups of participants participated in the immediate and delayed recall conditions. This way, they matched the number of learning opportunities in the immediate and delayed recall conditions, thus obtaining a purer assessment of the various learning methods' effectiveness in the long term. This seemingly minor change in the design apparently caused the comparatively steep decrease of the recall scores in the keyword condition between the two moments of testing. The finding suggests that learning strategies that boost immediate performance do not under all circumstances confer advantages in the long term as well, a fact that language teachers should be well aware of (Wang & Thomas, 1995b).

In a further experiment, Wang and Thomas (1995a, Experiment 3) manipulated the frequency with which the new vocabulary items were studied prior to the first recall test, hypothesizing that additional practice might counteract the relatively large susceptibility of the keyword method to forgetting in the between-participants design. In other words, extended practice may have the effect that foreign words learned with the keyword methodology also become consolidated in memory so that they are no longer more prone to long-term forgetting than words learned with other methods. The data in the upper and middle panels of Figure 3.3 were based on two learning trials per item. For comparison, the lower panel shows the recall performance following keyword and sentence context learning after five learning trials per item. As shown, the forgetting functions were now equally steep in both learning conditions, and overall there was a slight advantage of the keyword method. These data suggest that with more extended training the keyword method may be as effective as other methods in the long term, or, indeed, even more effective.

In conclusion, the studies by Wang and associates show that one particular combination of learning circumstances causes more forgetting following keyword learning than following rote and context learning: when immediate versus delayed recall is tested between participants rather than within participants and when at the same time the training phase involves relatively few learning trials per item. As noted by Gruneberg (1998), this combination of circumstances is rather rare in the foreign language classroom, where vocabulary learning typically involves repeated presentation of the new vocabulary as well as repeated testing, including testing immediately following training. Gruneberg therefore warns that the results of Wang and her collaborators should not be taken as a recommendation to foreign language teachers to dismiss the keyword method, obviously successful under more common circumstances. Instead, he suggests that for foreign words learned by means of the keyword method to become consolidated in memory, repeated presentation of the learning materials as well as repeated testing, including immediate testing, is advisable.

Experimenter-supplied versus participant-generated keywords and images

Some studies have addressed the question of whether the keyword method is more effective if the experimenter (or teacher) provides the keywords or the complete interactive images containing the referents of keyword and new word, or if instead the participants themselves generate them. This question is obviously important because a requirement that a keyword or interactive image is provided to the learner severely limits the method's applicability: Learners do not carry experimenters or teachers along when venturing out into foreign language worlds on their own. Possible reasons why self-generation might enhance learning are that it is a form of elaborative processing, which is known to promote long-term storage of the learning material, or that the keywords supplied by the experimenter may be idiosyncratic from the perspective of the learner and conflict with keywords the learner might have come up with. A reason why, instead, experimenter-supplied keywords might work best is that these may have been identified beforehand as the most effective on the basis of careful selection techniques. Furthermore, generating keywords on the spot may be rather demanding, especially for young learners (Levin, Pressley, McCormick, Miller, & Shriberg, 1979). Given the fact that there is no one to provide the learner with keywords outside the foreign language classroom, the most favorable outcome would be that self-generation is the most effective version of the method. Unfortunately a review of the literature (Campos, Amor, & González, 2002) concluded otherwise: Some studies have found equal efficacy of the experimenter-supplied and self-generated methods, a few studies have found that experimenter-supplied keywords are more effective, but no studies have obtained better results with self-generated keywords.

Campos, González, and Amor (2004) and Campos, Amor, and González (2004) combined the alleged advantages of experimenter-supplied and self-generated keywords by presenting one group of learners with keywords previously generated by people of the same age and socio-demographic characteristics as the participants. This procedure reduces the risk of providing keywords that are idiosyncratic. The participants supplied with these "peer-generated" keywords performed significantly better, both immediately after learning and after a delay, than both the participants in a self-generated group and in an experimenter-generated group. In a further experiment these authors added pictorial support during learning in the form of visual interactive images. This time, the advantage of the peer-generated keyword condition over the experimenter-generated keyword condition did not materialize, possibly because it was overruled by the extra advantage provided by the pictorial support. This interpretation was supported by the results of a third experiment, in which the interactive images in the keyword-supplied conditions were presented verbally and not as pictures. Once again the peer-generated keyword group showed the highest recall scores, on both an immediate and a delayed test.

We have seen that, as compared to rote-rehearsal learning, the keyword method may lead to relatively vulnerable memory representations as evidenced by relatively poor recall on a delayed test following keyword learning (Figure 3.3, upper panel). However, Thomas and Wang (1996) provided evidence to suggest that pictorial support during keyword learning increases the durability of the vocabulary learned by means of the keyword method. In one of a series of experiments a self-generated keyword condition and a rote-rehearsal condition were compared with a "keyword picture" condition, in which on each trial non-interactive pictures of the meanings of keyword and the new word to be learned were presented, as in the "separate picture" condition in Figure 3.1. The added picture increased the durability of the learned material: Long-term retention was better in the keyword picture condition than in the self-generated keyword condition, and the former was now equally as good as retention following rote-rehearsal learning. It thus seems that additional pictorial support increases the keyword method's efficacy.

Providing pictorial support appears especially advantageous for very young learners. In a study of English-American second- and sixth-grade children (of 7 and 11 years, respectively) learning Spanish, Pressley and Levin (1978) compared receptive cued recall in each of the five experimental conditions illustrated in Figure 3.1. The sixth graders showed considerably higher recall scores in all three keyword conditions ("interacting picture", "separate picture", and "separate word") than in two control conditions (the picture–word and word–word association conditions in Figure 3.1). Furthermore, the recall results in the keyword conditions did not differ between each other (71%, 67%, and 65% correct), nor did the results in the two control conditions (39% and 32% correct). In contrast, second graders performed best when provided with interacting pictures (62%), and better in the separate picture condition (45%) than in the separate word condition (where only the keyword but not a picture was provided; 23%). For these learners, the latter score did not differ statistically from those in the two control conditions (29% and 13.6%).

The authors explained these results in terms of a development of imagery-generation skills throughout the elementary school years, relating these to the information-processing demands of the three versions of the keyword method employed in this study. Of the three, the separate word condition is cognitively the most demanding, and the interacting picture condition is least demanding. In the interacting picture condition only the perception of the foreign word to be learned (*poisson*) and of the interacting picture is required. Instead, the separate word condition requires the perception of foreign word (*poisson*), its L1 translation (*fish*), and keyword (*poison*), followed by the generation of images of keyword and L1 word, which in turn is followed by the formation of an interacting image of the latter two. The separate picture condition is of intermediate difficulty. The data suggest the imagery-generation skill in second graders is not well enough developed yet to be exploited effectively in the more demanding of the three keyword conditions, whereas in sixth graders it is. In conclusion, when teaching foreign language vocabulary to young children using the keyword method, it is advisable to provide not only the keyword but pictorial support as well, preferably in the form of an interacting picture.

Conclusions

After this review of the research on foreign vocabulary learning by means of the keyword method and of how it compares to other methods, which method can we conclude is the most effective one? The answer is: it depends. More specifically, it depends on the quality of the keywords and/or the interacting images, the frequency with which the learning materials are presented (a higher frequency fostering the long-term efficacy of the keyword method), the moment recall is being tested (immediately after learning or delayed), the mode of testing (receptive or productive), and learner characteristics such as the age of the learners and whether or not the learners have substantial prior experience with foreign language learning (the experienced learners acquiring more vocabulary through rote-rehearsal learning than through keyword learning and the youngest learners acquiring most when interacting images are provided). Given the keyword method's complexity from the learner's point of view, maybe the most surprising outcome of all is that it fares so well under many circumstances, and sometimes better than other methods.

On second thoughts, however, the keyword method's success may be less surprising. I concluded an earlier section (p. 101) with the suggestion the reason the word–word association method is more conducive to learning than the keyword method in experienced language learners is that the former method allows them more freedom to exploit the rich stock of linguistic knowledge they have built up in the past. Yet the keyword method, and particularly the version that has the learners generate the keywords themselves, may be less of the straitjacket it appears at first sight. Recall that, in addition to using keywords to construct mental images, keywords can also exert their effects through "verbiage" (remember my *forbice* "scissors" example, where *forbice* was stored and remembered through the

Dutch translation of *Scissors are forbidden[verboden] for young children*). The suggestion is that imagery is not a prerequisite for the method to work. In all cases where the imagery component is skipped, the keyword method in fact resembles word–word association learning to a large extent, because both involve the presentation of a pair of translations on each single learning trial. For word–word association learning to become essentially the same as the verbiage version of the keyword method, the only component to add is that the learner searches memory for a keyword, a native language word similar in sound to the foreign word in the pair. This is exactly what many learners of a foreign language often seem to do spontaneously when trying to commit a new foreign word to memory. In other words, at least one version of the keyword method (no imagery; self-generation of keywords) is not so complex after all and may closely resemble a natural strategy of foreign vocabulary learning both outside the laboratory and during word–word association learning in the laboratory.

EASY AND DIFFICULT WORDS: EVIDENCE FROM PAIRED-ASSOCIATE LEARNING

Introduction

As mentioned before, the keyword method may not be optimally suited for learning abstract foreign language words and it is definitely unsuitable for learning cognates. In contrast, learning by means of the word–word version of the paired-associate learning paradigm is not constrained to subsets of a language's vocabulary. It can, for instance, be readily used to acquire both concrete and abstract words and cognates as well as non-cognates. Therefore, if the main purpose of an investigation is to find out what role these word variables play in foreign language vocabulary acquisition, word–word association learning is the natural choice of training method. The second paired-associate technique, picture–

word association, can also be used to study the acquisition of both cognates and non-cognates but is unsuitable to study abstract words for the obvious reason that these cannot easily be pictured.

The main goal of a series of foreign vocabulary learning studies run in our laboratory was to obtain detailed information on the effect of certain characteristics of the new foreign language (FL) vocabulary and the corresponding native language (L1) words on the learning process (the abbreviations FL and L1 will henceforth be used wherever the full terms would lead to cumbersome wording). Accordingly, we employed the word–word association technique as the learning method and manipulated characteristics of both the L1 and the FL terms in the translation pairs presented for learning. In addition, we manipulated the relationship between the lexical forms of the L1 and FL terms in the translation pairs. The stimulus variables that we manipulated across these studies were "cognate status" (whether or not the two terms in a translation pair share phonology and/or orthography), word concreteness (whether an L1 word—but thus also its translation—refers to a concrete entity or to an abstract concept), **word frequency** (whether the L1 word of a translation pair is commonly used in print and speech or occurs infrequently instead), and phonotactical typicality (a measure of the degree to which the phonotactical structure of the foreign word to be learned is akin to the sound structure of the learner's L1 words). The version of the word–word paired-associate technique that we used was uninstructed learning. In other words, the participants were allowed to choose their own learning strategy (and to switch strategies between trials whenever they felt like it).

The participants in these studies were all university undergraduates with Dutch as their native language and with considerable prior experience in learning foreign languages, chiefly gained in school. One of these studies (De Groot, 2006; De Groot & Van den Brink, 2008) also looked at the role of classical background music on learning, and a second study compared word–word learning with picture–word learning (Lotto & De

Groot, 1998). In two studies (De Groot, 2006; De Groot & Keijzer, 2000) the foreign "words" to be learned were in fact not words from an existing natural language but letter strings that we made up ourselves. Using such artificial words as the foreign vocabulary to be learned enables the systematic manipulation of some of the variables under study (cognate status; phonotactical typicality of the foreign words) and rules out effects of any specific prior knowledge of the new vocabulary that might otherwise exist. Across the studies, to assess the amount of learning that had taken place, both receptive and productive cued recall tests were administered. Two further characteristics of all these studies were that relatively large learning sets were presented to the learners, between 60 and 80 words, and that within each set a number of the present stimulus variables were orthogonally manipulated. Finally, all our studies consisted of multiple acquisition and testing sessions and included a retest about 1 week after acquisition in order to be able to determine the amount of forgetting that had taken place for the various types of words.

In the next sections I will concentrate on the stimulus manipulations in these studies, their effects, and how these can be accounted for. But first, some words on the effect of background music on learning are in order, as well as a few on a variable that we have never examined in our studies yet, but that has received considerable attention in memory research in recent years: the time interval between learning and sleep. To start with the former, an early review of the literature (Felix, 1993) had suggested that background music might be beneficial for learning, especially baroque, classical music. For this reason we chose one such piece in our study, a section of the Brandenburg Concerto of J. S. Bach. The recall scores were indeed larger in the music condition than when learning took place in a silent environment, but the difference was only statistically significant in the analysis by items, not by participants. This means that more of the new words were learned in the music condition than when these very same words were learned in silence, but that it could not be concluded that learners *generally* performed better with background

music. Apparently some do, but others are not affected by it. However, the efficacy of music was obvious from the fact that, not a single one excepted, in each of 32 different cells in the experiment music had a beneficial effect (see De Groot, 2006, and De Groot & Van den Brink, 2008, for details).

The absence of a statistically significant effect of music in the by-participants analysis indicated that a subset of the learners benefited from music whereas the remainder was not affected by it. This suggested that the sample of participants tested was not homogeneous but included individuals who differed on some critical variable, as yet unspecified. On the basis of an analysis of the literature we hypothesized that this variable might be extraversion: A number of studies have shown an interaction between this personality trait and a music manipulation, such that extraverts especially benefit from background music whereas introverts learn better in silence (Daoussis & McKelvie, 1986; Furnham & Allass, 1999; Furnham & Bradley, 1997). The reason why extraverts and introverts might respond differently to background music is that the neurological threshold of arousal differs between them: it is lower in introverts than in extraverts (Eysenck, 1967). As a consequence, optimal performance in introverts occurs at relatively low levels of stimulation (no music), whereas optimal performance in extraverts occurs at relatively high levels of stimulation (music; Furnham & Allass, 1999).

Further research that copies the conditions of our study but adds the personality trait extraversion or, more directly, brain arousal as an extra variable will have to reveal whether these hypotheses stand up to scrutiny. A first pilot study performed by a couple of students in our laboratory is promising. They split up the learners into a group of extraverts and a group of introverts (as assessed with questionnaires previously developed for that purpose). The recall scores for the extraverts did not differ between the music and silence conditions (61% and 60%, respectively), but the introverts performed considerably better in the silence condition (71%) than in the music condition (57%). Thus, as in the studies mentioned above, the variables extraversion and music interacted. But deviating from them, the learning by extraverts was not fostered by music but immune to it. In ongoing research we are looking directly at the learners' brain arousal and whether and how it is related to foreign vocabulary learning. Furthermore, we are currently examining the influence of type of background music on vocabulary learning and have so far identified one musical type that might hinder learning: vocal background music in a language that is mastered by the learners (similar vocal music sung in an unknown language did not affect learning performance). Plausibly, this detrimental effect results from the learners' attention being diverted away from the vocabulary-learning task to the content of the background songs. If these findings are supported by further studies, their applicability in natural foreign language learning settings is obvious.

A final current area of study to briefly mention here is research into the effect of sleep on retention of learned material, which has led to the important insight that the materials presented for learning have a better chance of becoming consolidated in memory if the learning episode is relatively soon followed by sleep rather than with a longer interval between learning and sleep. Studies that examined the effect of sleep on memory have primarily focused on procedural memory, but recently the beneficial effect of sleep on memory consolidation has also been demonstrated for foreign vocabulary learning by means of the present word–word paired-associate learning technique, a type of learning that leads to declarative memory representations: Gais, Lucas, and Born (2006) have shown that significantly more foreign words were retained when sleep followed relatively soon after learning than with more hours in between learning and recall, and that sleep deprivation affected recall aversely. These effects (observed in American high school students learning German) occurred while potentially confounding variables were controlled for such as at what time during the day learning took place (a variable that is correlated with different levels of brain arousal) and the amount of interference between learning and retention.

Studies examining the neural basis of the beneficial effects of sleep on memory consolidation have also started to appear (e.g., Davis, Di Betta, MacDonald, & Gaskell, 2008). The obvious recommendation that follows from these results is to not postpone a good night's rest too long after learning foreign vocabulary or whatever else it is that one would like to store in memory for good.

Word type effects on acquisition and retention

Acquisition

The studies that were briefly characterized above showed substantial effects of cognate status, concreteness (of the L1 words), and (phonotactical) typicality (of the foreign vocabulary) on learning, replicating similar results of earlier studies (e.g., cognate status: Granger, 1993; Kroll, Michael, & Sankaranarayanan, 1998; concreteness: Ellis & Beaton, 1993a, 1993b; Van Hell & Candia Mahn, 1997; typicality: Ellis & Beaton, 1993b; Service & Craik, 1993). Across our studies, the magnitude of the concreteness effects varied between 11% and 27%, meaning that the recall scores on the immediate tests were from 11% to 27% higher for concrete words than for abstract words. Similarly, immediate recall scores were between 15% and 19% higher for cognates than for non-cognates. The results of Kroll et al. (1998) suggest that even larger cognate effects may occur in less-experienced learners of a foreign language. Furthermore, the immediate tests showed 13.5% higher recall scores for foreign words with a typical phonotactical structure than for those with an atypical structure. Compared to these effects, the effect of word frequency (of the L1 words) was always rather small: It varied between 3% and 7%, and in two out of three studies (De Groot, 2006; De Groot & Keijzer, 2000) the effect did not generalize over all items. But whenever it occurred, it was in the same direction: Recall scores were higher when the new word forms had been paired with frequent L1 words during training than when paired with infrequent L1 words. These effects occurred both with receptive and productive cued recall and, consistent with the results of other studies (e.g., Ellis & Beaton, 1993a; see Figure 3.2) recall was considerably better (about 15%) with receptive cued recall than with productive cued recall.

In all of our studies the complete training session was split up in a number of sub-sessions (with mostly two learning trials per translation pair per sub-session) and a cued recall test (receptive or productive) was administered after each of them. The above description of the results concerned the effects averaged over all recall tests of a complete training session. Figure 3.4 illustrates

how the effects developed over training. It shows the development of the effects over three recall tests (T1, T2, T3), each of which was preceded by two learning trials per translation pair. The data shown are taken from De Groot (2006), the only study that included the typicality manipulation. In this study all testing had been done receptively, for the reason that, plausibly, atypical words are relatively hard to articulate for a learner unfamiliar with those forms, and the recall scores obtained in productive testing might therefore have conflated effects of typicality on memory storage (actual learning) and on pronunciation.

FIGURE 3.4

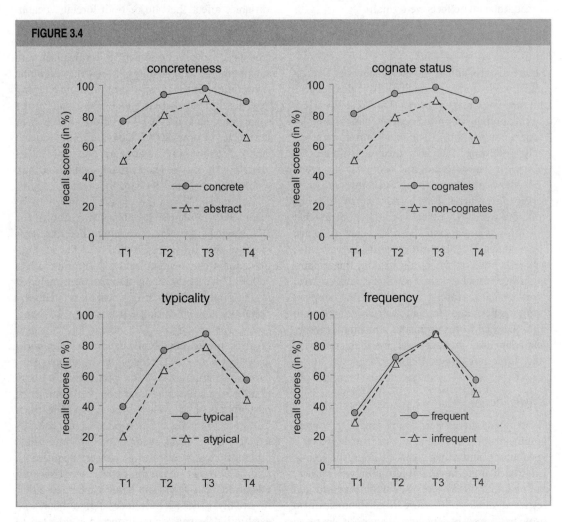

Recall scores as a function of item characteristics and test session. T1, T2, and T3 concern three test sessions during initial learning. T4 involves a delayed test 1 week after learning. Word–word association learning was used throughout. From De Groot and Keijzer (2006). Reprinted with permission from Wiley.

Zooming in on the concreteness effect (the difference between the recall scores for concrete and abstract words), it can be seen that it was especially large in the first recall test and that with additional training the learning of abstract vocabulary gradually caught up with the learning of concrete vocabulary. Overall, the data suggest that there is faster learning of foreign vocabulary if the corresponding L1 words are concrete than if the latter are abstract. As shown in Figure 3.4, exactly the same pattern was observed for the effects of cognate status, typicality of the foreign forms, and L1 frequency (although, as mentioned, the latter effects were small).

Retention

Figure 3.4 also shows the recall scores at a retest held 1 week after training (T4). No relearning of the new vocabulary prior to this retest occurred. Again zooming in on the concreteness manipulation, a comparison of the recall scores immediately following the last training sub-session (T3) with the corresponding scores at the retest (T4) shows that over the 1-week interval more forgetting occurred for abstract words than for concrete words. In other words, it appears that not only are concrete words easier to learn (learned faster) than abstract words, they are also less susceptible to forgetting. Again, the remaining three variables showed this same pattern: Non-cognates, foreign words with atypical phonotactics, and foreign words paired with infrequent L1 words during learning are forgotten relatively fast, as suggested by their relatively steep forgetting functions.

Recall latency

As pointed out earlier, fluent use of a foreign language not only requires that the language's vocabulary (and other forms of linguistic knowledge such as grammar and phonology) is known, but also that this knowledge can be accessed and retrieved rapidly. Therefore recall latencies also provide a measure of the degree of learning and of how learning develops over training. For this reason, in the above studies recall latency

was registered as well. Although the latency differences between conditions were not always as pronounced as the corresponding differences in recall scores, they always paralleled the recall scores: Relatively high recall scores were associated with shorter latencies than relatively low recall scores. Furthermore, these latency differences between, for instance, concrete and abstract learning materials, tended to be larger in the earlier stages of training than later on during training.

To summarize, in terms of both recall scores and recall latency, all four of the present stimulus variables affect the rate of both foreign vocabulary acquisition and retention, and the effects of three of these variables (cognate status, concreteness, and phonotactical typicality) are substantial. Unsurprisingly, words that combine two or more of the features that promote learning (e.g., foreign words that are cognates and, at the same time, have a typical structure) are learned best (De Groot, 2006; De Groot & Keijzer, 2000). Furthermore, it appears that words that are relatively easy to learn are retained better than words that are relatively hard to learn.

At first sight, this final finding appears to be inconsistent with the results of two studies (of L1 English speakers learning French) that manipulated the relative difficulty of the learning procedures (Schneider, Healy, & Bourne, 1998, 2002). Three such manipulations were included in these studies: blocking vocabulary items by semantic category during learning (e.g., *dos–back; bouche–mouth; figure–face; doigt–finger; yeux–eyes*) or presenting them mixed (e.g., *dos–back; avion–airplane; assiette–plate; jambon–ham; chemise–shirt*); receptive or productive learning and testing; pre-training or not pre-training the participants on the new vocabulary to be learned. The more difficult learning conditions generally led to lower recall scores on an immediate retention test, suggesting slower acquisition, than the easier learning conditions. However, relearning and retention 1 week later led either to equally good performance after difficult and easy initial learning conditions or even often to better performance following difficult learning conditions. In other words, hard initial training conditions can lead to a reduced loss of the learned material over time and vice versa. From these results the authors concluded that "any manipulation that increases the difficulty of a learning task may have different effects on initial and eventual performance" and that "variables that optimize training are not necessarily optimal for retention" (Schneider et al., 2002, p. 439). The beneficial effects of the keyword method as compared to, for instance, rote-rehearsal learning, when tested immediately after training but not when tested at a later point in time (pp. 101–103 and Figure 3.3, top and middle panels) provide independent support for the accuracy of this conclusion.

How can these findings be reconciled with the present result that words that are easy to learn are also better retained over time? A plausible solution is to distinguish between the difficulty of the *learning procedures* and the difficulty of the *materials to be learned*. It is the latter, not the former, that we manipulated in our studies. Combining the results of Schneider and her associates with ours it appears that easy words learned under difficult conditions will have the highest chance to consolidate in memory, and that difficult words learned under easy conditions will be most ephemeral. Of course, irrespective of the training method used, increasing the presentation frequency during training will counteract forgetting over time because it will increase the chance that permanent instead of temporary representations of the learned materials will be established in memory (see Atkinson, 1972, who explicitly makes this distinction). One of the keyword studies discussed above (Wang & Thomas, 1995a; Figure 3.3, lower panel) supports this claim: With five instead of two learning trials per item the keyword method resulted in memory representations that were equally well consolidated than those acquired with other training procedures. From this analysis two predictions concerning the effects of the present word type effects follow: (1) With a lower presentation frequency of the learning materials during training (that is, lower than used in our experiments), words that are easy and hard to learn will show equally steep forgetting functions because only

temporary representations will have been formed in memory for all words, easy and hard words alike. (2) With more extended practice, again the forgetting functions of easy and hard words will be equally steep, but this time because not only for easy words but also for difficult words (relatively) permanent representations will have been formed in memory. Current research in our laboratory aims to find out whether these predictions prove to be true.

Epilogue

The fact that the present four stimulus variables show similar patterns of results does not necessarily imply that the observed effects have one and the same source. Of the observed effects, those of cognate status and phonotactical typicality are intuitively the most obvious, because both concern aspects of the new forms to be learned: the orthographic (and phonological) form similarity between the foreign words and the corresponding L1 translations (cognate status), and whether or not the new forms have a sound structure that is familiar to the learner (typicality). It is more surprising that the concreteness and frequency of the L1 words exert any effect at all on learning. In these cases, the foreign word forms that are paired with concrete L1 words during learning do not systematically differ from those paired with abstract L1 words. Similarly the foreign word forms paired with frequent L1 forms during learning do not differ systematically from those paired with infrequent L1 forms. So whereas form aspects of the to-be-learned vocabulary plausibly underlie the effects of cognate status and typicality, the L1 words' knowledge structures that already exist in memory at the onset of foreign vocabulary learning must somehow cause the effects of L1 concreteness and L1 frequency.

Foreign vocabulary acquisition by means of paired-associate learning is essentially simply a process of labeling, of assigning a new name to an existing concept. In terms of this view, what exactly is it about the representation of a concrete L1 word that makes it relatively easy to attach a new name onto it? Similarly, what is it about the representation of an L1 word that is frequently used outside the laboratory that facilitates such a labeling process? (Note that the frequent L1 words in question are not more frequently used than the matched infrequent words in the actual paired-associate learning experiments.) I will address these questions in the next section, and thereafter theoretical accounts of the effects of phonotactical typicality and cognate status will be given. In so doing a number of more general views on the factors that determine vocabulary acquisition will be revealed. But first I will briefly pay attention to one further consistent result emerging from the data, but ignored so far: the fact that receptive cued recall leads to higher recall scores than productive cued recall.

Receptive versus productive testing

Figure 3.2 shows considerably larger recall scores with receptive testing than with productive testing. This finding consistently emerged in our studies as well and has been obtained many times before, for instance by Griffin and Harley (1996) and by Schneider et al. (2002). Several causes of the superior performance with receptive testing have been advanced. Horowitz and Gordon (1972) suggested the effect is due to a difference in availability between the L1 words, known prior to training, and the new L2 forms, availability being a measure of how readily an item comes to mind. According to these authors, paired-associate learning involves two independent components: associative learning and response learning. In their view, associative learning is symmetrical; that is, a link established between the words in a paired-associate pair is equally strong in both directions (but see Griffin & Harley, 1996). The reason that, nevertheless, it is relatively more difficult to retrieve the previously unknown form (the L2 word) upon the presentation of the previously known word (the L1 word) as the recall cue (productive testing) than vice versa (receptive testing) is that the new L2 form is less well established in memory, and therefore less available, than the previously known L1 form. On the basis of this analysis Horowitz and Gordon predicted that the difference between

receptive and productive testing should disappear if L1–L2 paired-associate learning is augmented by some separate procedure in which the learner is familiarized with the L2 word forms (for instance, by having the learners pronounce them a number of times prior to the actual training session). The researchers obtained support for this hypothesis in an English–Japanese study (but only when associative learning and response learning were intermingled and not when they were separated in time). Similarly, in one of their experimental conditions Schneider et al. (2002) pre-trained the L2 word forms and found that pre-training was especially beneficial for productive testing.

A different way of explaining the difference between productive and receptive recall is in terms of the inherent difference between production (or "encoding") and comprehension or recognition ("decoding") that it involves. Generally, comprehension tasks are easier than production tasks, perhaps because the former can be performed on the basis of memory traces that are less well consolidated or less complete than can production tasks (Griffin & Harley, 1996) or because of differences in neural activation thresholds required for the two types of tasks (e.g., Paradis, 2004; see pp. 292–294 for details). Or, according to Schneider et al. (2002): Production requires having full knowledge of the form of the word to be produced whereas comprehension only requires distinguishable but not necessarily complete knowledge. Receptive testing of newly learned words only requires the comprehension of the latter, whereas productive testing requires their production. Therefore the newly established memory representations for the foreign words may often be consolidated well enough (or contain sufficient information) to lead to successful performance in receptive testing but still too poorly to do so in productive testing.

Finally the different recall scores in productive and receptive testing may result from a difference in the interconnectedness of "old" L1 words and "new" L2 words in the mental lexicon (Ellis & Beaton, 1993a; see Griffin & Harley, 1996, for a similar view). The representation of an L1 word in lexical memory has many connections to (the representations of) other L1 words. In addition, it is connected to the representation of the new L2 word. In contrast, the representation of a newly learned L2 word is like a hermit in the mental lexicon, only being connected along one (still weak) tie to the corresponding L1 word. Consequently, the activation that is established in the representation of an L1 word upon its recognition will spread out over many links, one of them being the link connecting the L1 word with its newly learned L2 translation. In other words, recognition of the L1 word will only lead to a relatively small increase of activation in the associated L2 word's representation and will therefore only have a small effect on the latter's availability. In contrast, all activation that is established in the new L2 word's representation upon its presentation will move along this hermit's sole link towards the representation of its translation in L1, rendering the latter highly available. Given the fact that these accounts do not appear to be mutually exclusive, more than one of them (and possibly yet further ones, hitherto unidentified) may work in concert to produce the superior recall in receptive testing.

THE ROLE OF PRIOR KNOWLEDGE IN FOREIGN VOCABULARY LEARNING

It will be remembered that the paired-associate studies presented earlier (pp. 108–111) showed that it is easier to learn foreign language equivalents for concrete words than for abstract words. De Groot and Keijzer (2000) suggested two possible causes of this concreteness effect. As already mentioned, there is no reason to believe that the forms of the foreign words paired with abstract and concrete words differed somehow in complexity. For this reason, both suggested causes of the concreteness effects assume that the latter are due to differences between the stored meanings of concrete and abstract native language words in memory. Specifically, both accounts are based on the assumption that acquisition rate and retention depend on the amount of extant semantic

information in the memory representation of a foreign word's translation equivalent in L1: The more information stored in the L1 memory representation, the more opportunity the learner has to attach the to-be-learned foreign word form onto it. One account is in terms of dual-coding theory (Paivio, 1986; Paivio & Desrochers, 1980), the same theory as one of the two that served to explain the efficacy of the keyword method earlier (p. 96). Recall that dual-coding theory assumes the existence of both a verbal and an image system in memory. The theory furthermore assumes that concrete and abstract words are represented differently in this system: Concrete words (that are typically easy to imagine) are represented in both the verbal system and in the image system, whereas abstract words (usually hard to imagine) are only represented in the verbal system. In this set-up concrete L1 words provide two points of attachment for the foreign word whereas abstract L1 words provide just one. Note that this account assumes qualitatively different memory representation for concrete and abstract words: the presence of an image representation for the former but not the latter.

The second account of the concreteness effects only assumes a quantitative, not a qualitative, difference between the memory representations of concrete and abstract words: It hypothesizes an "amodal", monolithic, memory system in which all knowledge is stored in one and the same type of information elements that (unlike image representations) do not bear any resemblance to the input that led to their storage. That is, irrespective of whether the stored information was acquired through, for instance, perceiving an object or reading or hearing about it, the ensuing memory units all have the same format. And because all input is stored in a form that is neutral to the perceptual characteristics of the input, this approach does not distinguish between image and verbal representations. However, the number of such amodal information elements in memory is thought to differ between concrete and abstract words, the former containing more of them than the latter (De Groot, 1989; Kieras, 1978; Van Hell & De Groot, 1998a, 1998b). As a result, once again more points of attachment exist for concrete L2 words. A plausible cause for the larger number of stored information units for concrete words is that their **referents**, the objects, events, or entities they refer to, can be perceived by the senses (they are audible, tangible, palpable, visible) and that this leads to the storage of information (about the referents' form, color, smell, the sounds they make, etc.). This source of information is not available for abstract words.

The idea that the memory representations of concrete words do indeed contain more information than those of abstract words is supported by studies that have used the continued word-association task presented earlier (p. 92). In this task the participants are asked to give as many word associations as possible to each of a set of stimulus words in a certain time unit, say, 1 minute. The emerging scores are referred to as "m-scores ("m" for meaningfulness; Noble, 1952). Larger m-scores are obtained for concrete words than for abstract words (De Groot, 1989). The participants presumably perform this task by accessing the stimulus word's memory representation and then reading off the information that is stored there. The larger number of associative responses for concrete words thus indicates that more information is stored there.

There is independent evidence that seems to favor the second of these two accounts of the concreteness effect. A number of studies have shown that word concreteness is highly correlated with two other variables, **word imageability** and **context availability**. Word imageability is a measure of the ease with which the referent of a word evokes a mental image. Context availability is a measure of how easy it is (when the word is presented in isolation) to come up with a particular context or circumstance in which the word might occur. In fact, the concrete and abstract words presented in our studies were generally derived from word-imageability norms, not concreteness norms. The likely source of these correlations is one and the same underlying variable, namely the number of information elements in the underlying representations just mentioned: Concrete words, words that are easy to imagine, and words for which a context is readily available, have denser networks of infor-

mation elements than abstract words, words that are hard to imagine, and words for which it is hard to think up a context.

As mentioned, dual-coding theory assigns the effects of concreteness/imageability to an additional representation in an image system for concrete words as compared with abstract words. Because this additional representation will be there irrespective of whether a given word is presented in context or in isolation, the theory predicts the effect will not respond to manipulating contextual information. But contrary to prediction, this is exactly what happens (Schwanenflugel, 1991; Schwanenflugel, Harnishfeger, & Stowe, 1988; Van Hell & De Groot, 1998b, 2008). Between them, these studies have shown that concreteness/imageability effects disappear or become substantially smaller (in **lexical decision** in L1 and in L2, word translation from L1 to L2 and vice versa, and when reading sentences) when context is added to the words to be responded to or when concrete and abstract words (presented in isolation) are matched on context availability. Under the plausible assumption that matching words on context availability boils down to matching words on the number of (amodal) information elements in their representations, the second of the above accounts of the concreteness effect is perfectly compatible with these results: With equal numbers of information elements in the representations of concrete and abstract words the underlying source of the effect has ceased to exist. More importantly in the present context, a concreteness effect on foreign vocabulary acquisition should also disappear under these circumstances, and some evidence exists that indeed it does (Sjarbaini, 1998, in De Groot & Keijzer, 2000).

In fact, the continued word association study just mentioned (De Groot, 1989) not only showed larger scores for concrete words than for abstract words, but it also showed larger scores for frequent words than for infrequent words, although this difference was much smaller than the difference between **concrete** and **abstract words**. This finding suggests that the (small and unreliable) effects of L1 word frequency on foreign vocabulary learning (pp. 108–110) can be accounted for in the same way: Because the representations of frequent L1 words contain more information elements than those of less-frequent L1 words, the former provide more opportunities to fix the foreign word forms onto them.

But a second source of the L1 frequency effect must be considered. The reason a particular word is encountered relatively often in print and speech is that it expresses a familiar, common concept. In other words, word frequency is confounded with concept familiarity, and therefore concept familiarity may somehow underlie the observed effects of L1 word frequency. Arguably though, familiar concepts are represented in denser knowledge structures than unfamiliar concepts, so that ultimately again differential information density may cause the effects. Alternatively, equal amounts of information (numbers of knowledge units) may be stored for familiar and less-familiar concepts, but the information stored for the former may be more strongly rooted in memory. It is not unlikely that it is easier to fix new knowledge (in this case the new foreign words) onto well-consolidated memory structures than onto less-stable structures. According to both accounts then, just as the effects of word concreteness, the present frequency effects would result from (quantitative) differences in the **semantic memory** representations of different types of words.

The view advanced here, that information density of the L1 words affects the ease with which a new name can be hooked onto it, has been advanced before under a slightly different terminology. Reviewing the literature on foreign vocabulary learning, Service and Craik (1993) hypothesized that three factors play a crucial role. One of them is "the availability of semantic associations to link the new form to existing lexical items" (Service & Craik, 1993, p. 610). In their study on foreign vocabulary learning in relatively young and older adults, they manipulated this variable by *jointly* (rather than separately, as we did) varying L1 word imageability and frequency. "Easy" L1 words were at the same time frequent and easy to imagine; "difficult" L1 words were at the same time infrequent and hard to imagine. On the basis of the imagery

manipulation in these stimuli, the easy words were thought to have higher associative values than the difficult words. In agreement with the results presented above, learning scores were higher for foreign words paired with the former than for those paired with the latter, an effect that was equally large for both learner groups. This view, that the associative value of existing memory structures prior to learning affects the ease of learning, is also held responsible for the finding that paired-associate learning is more successful when both terms in the pairs are previously known than when (as in foreign vocabulary learning), only one is previously known: In the former situation, stored knowledge concerning both words can be exploited in the learning process (see also Papagno, Valentine, & Baddeley, 1991).

The important conclusion to draw from this discussion is that the learning of foreign vocabulary does not take place in a vacuum but exploits knowledge already stored in memory prior to the learning event. The data presented in this section thus constitute one of the many sources of evidence that during learning a new language, stored knowledge is used. We have come across another example suggestive of this before (pp. 98–101): The learners' amount of prior foreign language learning experience (read: the knowledge they accumulated in all of this prior learning) determined both the way they acquired new vocabulary best and how much of it they acquired (with the more experienced learners gaining most). Furthermore, the very fact that the keyword method is as effective as it has been shown to be across many studies testifies to the importance of exploiting stored knowledge during learning: A crucial aspect of the method is that it encourages the recruitment of prior knowledge in the form of keywords and imagery. As we shall see in the chapters to come, stored L1 knowledge is also implicated while using a later language in comprehension and production (instead of acquiring it), at both beginning and advanced levels. Furthermore, the effect of stored knowledge appears to work in both directions, not only from the first and native language to later languages, but also from the latter back to the first language.

PHONOLOGICAL SHORT- AND LONG-TERM MEMORY AND FOREIGN VOCABULARY LEARNING

As we have just seen, information structures that exist in *long-term* memory prior to the foreign language vocabulary learning episode can account for the effects of L1 word concreteness and frequency. Here I will turn to a well-known model of *working* memory, developed by Alan Baddeley and his colleagues (Baddeley, 1986, 2000; Baddeley & Hitch, 1974; Gathercole & Baddeley, 1993), to account for the effect of the foreign words' phonotactical typicality on their acquisition and, more generally, to illustrate how vocabulary acquisition comes about in terms of this model. The model is illustrated in Figure 3.5.

In its original form (Figure 3.5a) the model contained three components: a "central executive" and two "slave systems", called the "phonological loop", and the "visuospatial sketchpad". The central executive is an attention-control system that coordinates and organizes

activity within working memory, controls the transmission of information between other parts of the cognitive system, for instance, by retrieving information from long-term memory and storing information into it, and allocates resources to the two slave systems. Each of the two slave systems is specialized for processing and temporarily maintaining materials of a particular type. The phonological loop deals with verbal and acoustic material and the visuospatial sketchpad handles visual and spatial material. To be able to do its job, the phonological loop is equipped with two components: a phonological store and a rehearsal system. The former stores material in a phonological code that decays over time and the latter refreshes the decaying representations, maintaining them for the duration of the rehearsal process.

Because patients with clear short-term phonological deficits at first appeared to have an intact long-term memory, working memory and long-term memory were originally thought to be separate memory systems. More lately, these patients have been shown not only to experience problems with the short-term storage of verbal

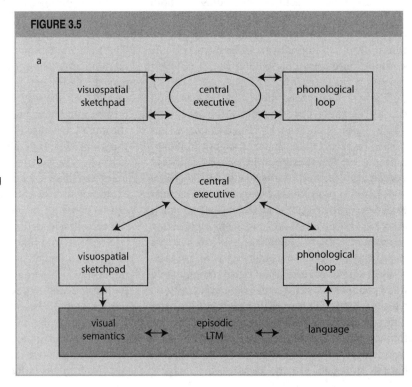

FIGURE 3.5

The original model of working memory proposed by Baddeley and Hitch (1974; Figure 3.5a) and a more recent version of the model (Figure 3.5b). In the newer model the phonological loop interacts with long-term memory and mediates the long-term learning of words. From Baddeley (2000). Copyright © 2000, with permission from Elsevier.

material but also to have specific deficits in long-term phonological learning (Baddeley, 2000). This has been one of the reasons for developing a new version of the working memory model, one that acknowledges that the phonological loop interacts with long-term memory and plays an important role in the long-term learning of the phonological forms of new words, both native and foreign. While the new phonological forms are kept in the phonological store during rehearsal, more permanent memory representations are being constructed (see Baddeley, Gathercole, & Papagno, 1998, and Gathercole & Thorn, 1998, for reviews). The new model is illustrated in Figure 3.5b. The shaded area represents long-term memory components that accumulate more and more knowledge over time. Non-shaded systems are "assumed to be 'fluid' capacities, such as attention and temporary storage, and are themselves unchanged by learning" (Baddeley, 2000, p. 418).

One source of evidence that the phonological loop or phonological short-term memory is an important vocabulary acquisition device comes from studies that examined vocabulary acquisition in young children. In some of these studies the children's ability to repeat spoken nonwords served as the signature of phonological short-term memory capacity. Gathercole and Baddeley (1989) found that small children who are good at repeating nativelike nonwords are better at learning new native vocabulary than children performing relatively poorly on the "nonword repetition task". Hu (2003) observed that young children who are good at repeating native language syllables are relatively good at learning words in a foreign language. Similarly, Gathercole and Baddeley (1990) found that language-disabled children with lower vocabulary scores than a control group performed relatively poorly on a nonword repetition task. The specific problem of the language-disabled children appeared to be an impaired capacity to represent unfamiliar phonological forms in short-term memory.

Service (1992) provided evidence that phonological short-term memory plays a crucial role in foreign language learning as well by showing that the ability of Finnish children to repeat spoken Englishlike nonwords before or at the start of an English foreign language course was a good predictor of their grades in English at the end of the course a couple of years later. She also discovered that performance on a task in which the children had to copy written nonwords was an equally good predictor of their English grades at the end of the course. Because it is assumed that printed material does not have automatic direct access to the phonological store, this finding suggests that printed material is automatically coded in a phonological form, which then gains access to the store (see pp. 183–188 for more evidence that printed letter strings are automatically coded in a phonological form). All these nonword repetition studies combined thus suggest that a large phonological short-term memory capacity supports the learning of unfamiliar language material, both native and foreign. (Incidentally, beneficial effects of short-term memory capacity on learning other aspects of language, such as grammar, have been observed as well, but this chapter being on vocabulary acquisition these will be ignored here; see e.g., French & O'Brien, 2008.)

The important role of phonological short-term memory in vocabulary learning is strengthened yet further by the results of a neuropsychological case study by Baddeley, Papagno, and Vallar (1988). These researchers found that a woman whose phonological memory was impaired as a consequence of having suffered a stroke was completely unable to learn nonwords that were paired with words in her native language, Italian. Yet further evidence that a relation exists between phonological short-term memory and the learning of unfamiliar phonological forms comes from studies that have studied the effect on learning of a number of experimental manipulations that are known to affect the workings of the phonological loop. One of these is "**articulatory suppression**" (see Baddeley et al., 1998, and Ellis & Sinclair, 1996, for other manipulations). Under circumstances of articulatory suppression the learners have to utter a sound (e.g., "bla") repeatedly during learning, an activity that disrupts the rehearsal of the learning materials.

Papagno et al. (1991) showed that the learning of L1–FL stimulus pairs in an articulatory suppression condition results in lower recall scores than learning in a control condition in which the learners performed a finger-tapping task while learning (conversely, encouraging rehearsal boosts the recall scores; Ellis & Sinclair, 1996). Interestingly, the disruptive effect of articulatory suppression did not materialize when associations between two native language words had to be learned, nor did it occur for L1–FL word pairs that allow for the creation of semantic associations between the native and foreign terms of the pair. This finding suggests that under certain circumstances long-term learning can bypass the route through phonological short-term memory, exploiting knowledge already stored in long-term memory.

If learning unfamiliar vocabulary requires the rehearsal of the new phonological forms, not only the learners' phonological memory capacity should predict learning success, but a relationship should also hold between the "pronounceability" of the learning materials and the recall scores: The phonological coding of new words that are easy to pronounce (and, thus, rehearse) should be easier than the phonological coding of new words that are hard to pronounce. Consequently, easy to pronounce new words should be easier to learn and retained better than hard to pronounce new words. (Note that the underlying assumption is that inner phonological coding of words involves the internal articulation of the material.) This is exactly what Ellis and Beaton (1993b) found in a study investigating L2 German vocabulary learning by L1 English undergraduate students. They observed a negative correlation between the recall scores of this group and the time taken by a second group of participants (drawn from the same population) to pronounce the German words presented for learning. In other words, short pronunciation times were associated with high recall scores and long pronunciation times with low recall scores.

Gathercole, Martin, and Hitch (in Gathercole & Thorn, 1998) and Service and Craik (1993) obtained similar findings. These authors varied the degree of "wordlikeness" or "phonological familiarity" of the new vocabulary learned by means of the paired-associate method. Wordlike familiar forms had a sound structure that resembled the sound structure of the learners' native language vocabulary, whereas unwordlike unfamiliar forms were alien to the learners. Recall scores were higher for the former than for the latter. Both studies thus suggest that the more readily new vocabulary can be pronounced, the more easily it will be learned. It is likely that this relationship also underlies the effect of phonological typicality reported earlier (pp. 108–110): Foreign words that are in accordance with the phonological system of the learners' native language (the "typical" foreign words in De Groot, 2006) are presumably easier to pronounce than words that do not accord with the L1 phonological rule system (the "atypical" foreign words). Hence the higher recall scores for the former type of foreign vocabulary.

But there is another reason why new words with a typical, wordlike sound structure may be relatively easy to learn. In addition to being easy to pronounce, typical new words also resemble the (L1) phonological structures already stored in long-term memory prior to the onset of learning. As discussed before (pp. 113–115), long-term learning may exploit information stored in long-term memory. This may be semantic information (as suggested there), but phonological information in long-term memory is likely to be used as well. A study by Cheung (1996) provided support for this hypothesis. The participants in this study were Cantonese-Chinese children who differed in their command of English as a second language. By implication, they also differed in the amount of English phonological knowledge in long-term memory. The participants' phonological short-term memory capacity was assessed with a nonword span test in which they had to repeat back sequences of Englishlike nonwords. In a subgroup of participants who were at a relatively early stage of English language development, nonword span predicted the number of trials required for learning new English vocabulary. For a more advanced subgroup of learners, nonword span was not a significant predictor of English vocabulary learning, plausibly because they exploited the extant long-term phonological knowledge of English during learning. These data suggest that phonological short- and long-term memory interact in foreign language vocabulary learning.

On the basis of this and related evidence, Baddeley and his colleagues have come to the conclusion that the phonological loop does not mediate long-term memory in a unidirectional manner but instead, "learning the sounds of new words appears to be mediated by both the phonological loop and long-term knowledge of the new language" (Baddeley et al., 1998, p. 161). In agreement with this view, Papagno and Vallar (1995) considered both differences in the capacity of phonological short-term memory and in the total number of vocabulary items stored in long-term memory as plausible sources of a difference in new word learning aptitude between polyglots and non-polyglot learners that they observed. Similarly, Service and Craik (1993, p. 610) claimed that both the "ease with which a phonological representation of the new form can be created and maintained in working memory" and "the phonological support from similar forms already in long-term memory" play crucial roles in acquiring foreign language words. At the same time, the present support for the view that phonological forms stored in long-term memory foster the learning of new words with similar forms constitutes a further source of evidence that prior knowledge is exploited during learning (see also pp. 98–101 and 113–115).

THE ROLE OF FORM SIMILARITY BETWEEN TRANSLATION PAIRS IN FOREIGN VOCABULARY LEARNING AND TEACHING

Introduction

Vocabulary acquisition is obviously not an all-or-none, instantaneous process, in which a learning trial either results in full learning of the new word or leads to no stored information on the new word whatsoever. Instead, every encounter with a word in speech or print is likely to leave some trace of new knowledge in memory, and there is experimental evidence to suggest that this process of gradual, incremental word learning holds for both the acquisition of word meaning and word form (and presumably for morpho-syntax as well). It is because word learning is incremental that scoring procedures may exploit both conservative and more liberal criteria for recall success and the fact that cued recall is generally higher with receptive testing than with productive testing (pp. 112–113) clearly points to the incremental nature of vocabulary acquisition: Still incomplete form knowledge will lead to recall failure in productive testing but may suffice for successful recall in receptive testing.

This incremental view of word form learning provides one of two plausible (not necessarily mutually exclusive) explanations of the substantial effects of cognate status presented earlier pp. 108–110): By definition, cognate translations share parts of their form whereas non-cognate translations have dissimilar forms. The implication is that the learning of cognates involves the learning of relatively few form components because much of the form is already in place prior to learning. Consequently, full form knowledge of a cognate translation is reached at an earlier moment in time, after fewer acquisition trials, than full form knowledge of a non-cognate translation.

A second explanation of the cognate effect locates the effect in the retrieval stage and not in the learning process itself. You may recall that foreign vocabulary learning by means of the keyword method involves the mediation of a keyword, a word in the learner's native language that sounds like the targeted foreign word. During recall, the phonological form of the keyword activates the similar phonological form of the targeted foreign word (or vice versa), thus leading to the response. Because, by definition, a cognate is phonologically similar to its very translation, it will evoke its translation directly during recall (and no mediation via a keyword is required).

A first indication to suggest that a cognate directly triggers its translation is that cognate words in a foreign language may be "known" by people totally naive with respect to this language. In a series of studies primarily designed to find out how bilinguals map word form onto word meaning (see pp. 129–144), Kroll and her colleagues needed both cognates and non-cognates as stimulus materials (e.g., Dufour & Kroll, 1995). In developing their cognate and non-cognate materials, these authors simply had monolingual English speakers guess the English translations of a set of foreign language words. The participants had no problems whatsoever carrying out this assignment and correctly guessed a large percentage of the cognate translations (the actual percentage correct obviously depending on the extent to which the language pair in question shares cognates; see Gibson & Hufeisen, 2003, discussed on p. 101, for similar findings).

Hall (2002) provided a further, albeit indirect, demonstration that cognates directly evoke their translations. He ran a study that addressed the question of whether learners automatically assume that similar forms across languages mean similar things. Spanish university students enrolled in an English language course were presented with **pseudocognates** (Englishlike nonwords that share form overlap with Spanish words), non-cognate nonwords, and true English words. Examples of pseudocognates are *stribe* and *campanary*, which resemble the Spanish words *tribo* ("stirrup") and *campanario* ("bell tower"), respectively, but that are not actual words; examples of non-cognate nonwords are *plude* and *thrimble*, with no form-similar words in Spanish. The participants were asked to indicate for each of the stimuli whether they thought they had seen it before and to write down what they thought the Spanish words closest in meaning to the English "word" could be. Even though none of the participants could ever have encountered any of the pseudocognates, in nearly 40% of the cases they reported having seen it before. The corresponding percentage for non-cognate nonwords was only 5%. This finding suggests that the pseudocognates contacted the similar Spanish words in memory and that this gave rise to a feeling of familiarity. An analysis of the provided translations showed that the learners indeed

thought that the pseudocognates were the English translations of the similar Spanish words.

De Groot and Comijs (1995) provided another demonstration of the fact that pseudocognates are readily mistaken for true cognates and that this even happens when the participants are fully aware that the pseudocognate is not the word it is taken for. In this study we presented Dutch–English bilinguals with a high level of proficiency in L2 English with Dutch–English word pairs and asked them to decide for each pair whether or not the words were translations of one another (this task is the translation recognition task introduced on p. 91). The great majority of the word pairs that required a "no" response consisted of dissimilar words; that is, words that do not share form overlap (e.g., *verf–table; verf* meaning "paint"). However, a small percentage consisted of "pseudocognates"; that is, words accidentally similar in form (e.g., *hout–house; hout* meaning "wood". Note the difference from Hall's use of the term "pseudocognate"; in his case the pseudocognates were not actual words). Translation recognition times for correct "no" responses to pseudocognate pairs were substantially longer than those to matched dissimilar non-translation pairs. Furthermore, considerably more errors (false positives) were made to pseudocognate pairs than to dissimilar non-translation pairs (26% and 3%, respectively).

The above evidence (Dufour & Kroll, 1995; Hall, 2002) that an unknown form triggers a similar known form and that the new form is automatically assigned the meaning of the similar old form (a process that Hall calls "the automatic cognate form assumption") illustrates a trap that foreign language learners frequently fall into, especially during the initial stages of learning: They assign an unfamiliar foreign language word the meaning of an L1 word with a similar form, even in cases where no meaning relation whatsoever holds between the two forms or when the two forms only share meaning in part and the sense currently assigned is contextually inappropriate. The occurrence of such "false cognate assumptions" may underlie the suspicious attitude toward cognates in many foreign language classrooms and in much research on foreign language learning, especially in applied linguistics. The fact that similar forms may share meaning completely, partially, or not at all, has also led to a plethora of terms to distinguish between the various forms of cognate relationship. Therefore, before discussing the various attitudes in research and teaching toward cognates and their reasons why, some words on the associated terminology are in order.

Defining cognates and non-cognates

The psycholinguistic literature on bilingual word processing (rather than L2 word acquisition) to be discussed in Chapter 4 has tried to unravel the effects of form similarity and meaning similarity between words in a bilingual's two languages on bilingual word recognition (e.g., Dijkstra, Grainger, & Van Heuven, 1999). In this line of research, L1–L2 translation pairs that share both form and meaning are called "cognates". The fact that degree of meaning overlap varies between cognate translation pairs is often ignored, perhaps as a consequence of the awareness that exact meaning equivalence of the two terms within a pair of translation "equivalents" may hardly ever hold anyway. L1–L2 translation pairs that share meaning but not form are called "non-cognates". L1–L2 word pairs that share form but not meaning are called **false friends** or pseudocognates as a class, but here more fine-grained distinctions are made that are reflected in the terminology. The subcategorization differentiates the type of form overlap (orthographic or phonological) and the degree of form overlap (complete or for the larger part). Forms with completely overlapping phonology or orthography (and with completely different meanings) are called **interlexical homophones** and **interlexical homographs**, respectively. Forms with largely overlapping phonology or orthography (and completely different meanings) are called interlexical homophonic **neighbors** and interlexical homographic neighbors, respectively (see p. 166 for examples of interlexical homographs).

Chapters 4 and 5 provide a substantial amount of evidence to suggest that word recognition and word production in bilinguals often involves the co-activation of a target word's false friends (*and* cognates) in the non-target language. The degree of co-activation depends on the bilingual's proficiency in the non-target language: The stronger the non-target language, the stronger a similar form in this language is co-activated when a word in the target language is encountered, and, consequently, the stronger its influence on processing the target word. In other words, a strong non-target language may noticeably affect processing a word in a weak target language, but the influence of a weak non-target language on a strong target language may be negligible or even non-existent. Because a foreign language is generally weaker than the native language, this means that the native language more often affects processing the foreign language than vice versa.

Although often ignored in these "processing" studies, the degree of *meaning* overlap of the two terms in a pair of cognates varies as well, in addition to degree of form overlap. This is where the linguistically oriented applied-linguistics literature has traditionally focused on and it is reflected in the terminology employed in this research area. In this approach, etymological relatedness has traditionally been assigned a crucial role in what counts as a cognate. For instance, on the basis of etymological relatedness Nash (1976, in Carroll, 1992) distinguished between "true cognates", "deceptive cognates", "**false cognates**", and "accidental cognates". True cognates (also called "good cognates"; Granger, 1993) are etymologically related and share meaning completely or almost completely (English *hotel* and Spanish *hotel*). Deceptive cognates are etymologically related but share only part of their meaning, for instance because one word splits into two or more translations in the other language (e.g., the French *experience* which translates to either *experience* or *experiment* in English). False cognates are etymologically related but no longer overlap in meaning between the languages; their meanings may be related, but also opposite (in English an *auditorium* is a place for a large gathering, whereas in Spanish an *auditorio* is an audience; *stretch* means "to extend" in English but *estretcher* in Spanish is "to make narrow"). Accidental cognates are not etymologically related but just happen to share form (English *juice* and Spanish *juicio*, "judge"; examples taken from Carroll, 1992, and Granger, 1993). These are the false friends or pseudocognates in the psycholinguistic literature described above. A further distinction has been made between "totally deceptive cognates" (French *actuel*, "current", "topical", and English *actual*) and "partially deceptive cognates" (the above *experience* example). In both cases a historical relation exists between the two terms in the cognate pairs. Finally, cognates are often distinguished from **loan words** and **borrowings**, where cognates share (besides form and meaning) one and the same historical root in a common ancestor language, whereas loan words and borrowings are imported from another language and, often, adapted to the phonological structure of the adopting ("host") language.

Attitudes toward cognates in research and teaching

Because all but the "good" or "true" cognates may mislead the learner, the attitude toward cognates in applied-linguistics research and foreign language teaching has often been to stress the potentially detrimental effect of cognates, to communicate the message that cognates are language elements to be mistrusted, or to ignore their existence altogether by not pointing out the systematic cognate relations that may hold between a native language and the target foreign language (see Granger, 1993, for a discussion). More recently, the awareness that under many circumstances cognates, also the "not-true" ones, may facilitate vocabulary learning has led to a much more positive attitude and even sometimes to an over-reliance on cognates.

To illustrate, Ringbom (1987) reasoned that the existence of cognates might be one reason why Swedes are generally better in English than Finns: English and Swedish are related languages, sharing many cognates, whereas English and Finnish are completely unrelated. The consequence is that a Finn will be at a complete loss when encountering an unknown English word, whereas in many cases a Swede may infer at least part of the

English cognate's meaning. It is plausible that explicitly pointing out to the foreign language learner that the native and targeted language share many cognates affects the way the learner approaches the vocabulary acquisition task, thus accelerating learning. Morrissey made the point that even deceptive or false cognates may be helpful because cognates "need not be suitable translation equivalents to function as decoding devices" (Morrissey, 1981, p. 67). For example, even though the English–French pair *treasure/trove–trouver* and the English–Spanish pair *auditorium–auditorio* are not translation-equivalent pairs, exploiting the known meanings of *treasure* and *auditorium* is likely to help the English learner of, respectively, French and Spanish in figuring out the meaning of French *trouver* ("to find") or Spanish *auditorio* ("audience"), *if* the formal resemblance is noticed at all. An anecdote related by Meara (1993, pp. 280–281) may serve as a final example of the accelerative effect that exploiting cognate relations may have on foreign vocabulary learning:

> There is, for instance, the well-known story of the Spanish soldier and the French soldier who met during the Napoleonic wars. The Spanish soldier asks the Frenchman to teach him French, and offers to pay one sou for every French word that he learns. The Frenchman agrees, tells the Spaniard that any Spanish word that ends in *-ación* can be turned into a French word ending in *-ation*, and requests his pupil to pay him 100 francs.

All these researchers advocate a "cognate approach" to L2 vocabulary acquisition, but a prudent one—one that points out the possible pitfalls as well. Describing four main patterns of "cognacy" relation that may hold between language pairs, Meara (1993) identifies one category of language pairs that may be particularly prone to pitfalls: pairs of languages that *do* share cognates, but where the use of cognates is restricted to one particular domain or register in one of the languages and is more general in the other; in other words, where a word in the one language and its cognate in the other language have a different distribution. For instance, Romance words in English are generally less broadly used than in the languages they originated from. Consequently, heavy reliance on cognates of, say, a French learner of English may often lead to an inappropriate, perhaps even ridiculous, word choice. For example, the French words *costume* and *chauffeur* are used more broadly in French than their English cognate terms in English: The former in French covers English (theatre) *costume* in addition to English (man's outfit) *suit*, and the latter covers both English (private) *chauffeur* and English (general) *driver* (examples taken from Granger, 1993). A French learner of English complimenting her English addressee with the elegant costume he is wearing would be exposed as a non-native speaker on the spot or, worse, judged to be a somewhat theatrical person. But despite the fact that such unfortunate uses of cognates do occur, many researchers now recommend a focus on cognate relations, considering it a means to accelerate foreign vocabulary acquisition, especially in the initial stages of learning. How reliance on cognates may be especially useful in the early stages of foreign vocabulary acquisition (see e.g., Kroll et al., 1998, and p. 136; further on) is illustrated by Banta (1981) with the metaphor of a crutch to put back in a corner after the first walking difficulties have been overcome: "Students will not run as long as they are dependent on it, but they will learn to walk more steadily and swiftly" (p. 136).

Carroll (1992) contributed to this discussion the important point that the attitude toward cognates in teaching has been misguided by the false assumption that learners should know about the etymology of words to benefit from cognates, or even that they come to the learning task equipped with this knowledge. However, from the viewpoint of both the foreign language learner and the bilingual language user, the fact that two words in a cognate pair share one and the same historical root is completely irrelevant and the language learner/user will generally not even be aware of this relation. As she puts it: "Words do not wear their historical origin on their sleeves" (Carroll, 1992, p. 102). If between-

language form similarity is noticed at all by the beginning learner he or she is likely to exploit it. This will promote learning in cases where the similar forms indeed share meaning but hinder learning if the form similarity is merely accidental. Learners at more advanced stages are less likely to exploit cognate relations *consciously*. Yet, as I have already pointed out above, also for them the difference between cognates and non-cognates is an essential one: During processing a word in the target language, representations of similar word forms in the non-target language (including those of cognates) are automatically co-activated (see Chapter 4, for evidence).

FROM FOCUSING ON FORM TO FOCUSING ON MEANING

Introduction

In the previous sections four word type effects that occur in foreign language vocabulary learning have been introduced and explained in terms of a number of general vocabulary-learning processes and mechanisms. Two of these effects (concreteness and frequency) involved characteristics of the L1 terms in the translation pairs. A third (phonotactical typicality) concerned an aspect of the new forms to be learned. The fourth (cognate status) concerned an aspect of the form relation between the two terms in a translation pair. These variables of the learning materials are by no means the only ones that affect the learning process. Laufer (1997) discussed the role of a couple of other potentially critical variables. One of these is what she calls "synformy", the accidental form similarity of two or more words in the target foreign language, such as the Hebrew words *halva'a* ("loan") and *halvaja* ("funeral"). Laufer illustrates the special problems these **synforms** (short for "similar lexical forms") may cause for the learner by recounting the unfortunate word choice of a university professor from the Unites States visiting Israel. In need of a loan, he addressed the local bank manager requesting a funeral instead.

Several studies have shown that these errors of synformy are especially common during the early stages of foreign language learning. The high incidence of these errors during the early stages of learning is consistent with a developmental view on vocabulary acquisition which holds that during the learning process the learner's attention shifts from a focus on form to a focus on meaning. This view has been proposed by several authors and constitutes one of the cornerstones of an influential model of bilingual memory organization, the revised hierarchical model of bilingual memory (Kroll & Stewart, 1994; see pp. 134–136). An important conclusion to be drawn from the pertinent studies is that this developmental course appears to hold for all of a person's languages, including the first. Consistent with this idea is that errors of synformy indeed appear to occur in native language use as well, especially when the targeted words are infrequent (and, hence, less well learnt than more frequently used words). However, the similarity seems often to go unnoticed, possibly because errors of this type made in native language use are not called synforms but **malapropisms** instead (after Mrs Malaprop, a character created by Sheridan who produced a great many of them). The phenomenon is often exploited in comedies, as when Archy Bunker said: "We need a few laughs to break up the monogamy" (intended word: *monotony*), a slip of the tongue that undoubtedly caused the burst of laughter he solicited for (the example is from Fay & Cutler, 1977).

Fay and Cutler (1977) listed the following six major characteristics of malapropisms: (1) the erroneous intrusion is a real word rather than a meaningless string of phonemes; (2) the targeted word and the error are unrelated in meaning; (3) there is a close relation between the pronunciations of target and error; (4) target and error are of the same grammatical class; (5) target and error frequently have the same number of syllables; (6) target and error almost always have the same stress pattern. Laufer (1988) performed a detailed analysis of synforms and found that these characteristics also hold for them. This similarity between malapropisms in L1 use and synforms in L2 use strengthens the hypothesis that they are manifestations of the same phenomenon and have the same cause or causes. One candidate cause may be incomplete knowledge of the precise form associated with a particular meaning. A second is that the relevant knowledge is fully in place but that the lexical retrieval process fails, so that in lexical memory a form similar to the targeted form is activated more and, as a result, inadvertently output. Plausibly, during the initial stages of learning incomplete knowledge is the major culprit, whereas in advanced learners and fluent native speakers of a language a malapropism/synform relatively often results from a processing failure.

With the above indications that malapropisms in native language use and errors of synformy in learning a second language have the same source and, therewith, that lexical development follows the same course in L1 and L2 learning, let us now turn to the relevant experimental evidence suggesting that the development of foreign word learning progresses from a focus on form to a focus on meaning.

Evidence

Early evidence that during the initial stages of foreign language learning similar forms in the targeted language are confused comes from an experimental classroom study by Cziko (1980). He had English learners of French at either an intermediate or an advanced level read French narrative texts aloud, and scored the type of reading errors they made. For comparison, a control group of native French speakers was also included. In analyzing the data two clusters of error types were distinguished, one that suggested the use of graphic information by the readers and a second suggesting the use of semantic and syntactic contextual information. For instance, when during reading the sentence *She took the piggy bank and out came some money, money* would be substituted by *many*, this would suggest the reader is relying on the graphic appearance of the word (note that in Laufer's, 1988, 1997, terminology *many* and *money* are synforms). In contrast, if *money* were substituted by *dime*, the reader apparently made use of the syntactic and semantic contextual information provided by the sentence (the example is Cziko's). Furthermore, if the reader relies heavily on graphic information, few parts of the written text should be deleted and few components should be added to the text. In other words, few deletion and insertion errors should be made. In contrast, sensitivity to contextual information would become manifest in relatively few errors that violate the syntactic and semantic constraints of the text material and relatively many substitution errors such as *dime* in the above example.

In agreement with earlier studies on the reading of English rather than French as a second language (Hatch, 1974; Oller, 1972), the data suggested that especially the intermediate learners of French were attentive to graphic information and relatively insensitive to contextual information: As compared to the advanced learners and French native speakers, they made relatively few deletion and insertion errors and relatively many graphical substitution errors (synforms). In addition, the intermediate learners made relatively many errors that violated the syntactic and semantic constraints of the context and relatively few that were in agreement with the contextual information. Overall, the data suggested that all reader groups drew on both graphic and contextual information (all types of errors occurred in all three groups, but in different proportions), but that during the initial stages of foreign language learning there was a relatively high reliance on graphic information and a relatively low sensitivity to contextual information, whereas with higher levels of fluency the sensitivity to contextual information increased. Interestingly, this is exactly the same developmental pattern as has been observed for the process of learning to read in a native language.

Other studies have provided converging evidence that graphically similar foreign language forms are confused in learners of the language concerned. For instance, in a word association study by Meara (in Laufer, 1997), form confusion seems to be the source of the response word *animal* to the stimulus word *béton* (meaning "concrete") provided by an English learner of French. Apparently, this learner mistook *béton*

for *bête* ("animal"). A study by Henning (1973) provided relevant insights into why these effects might occur, embedding them in a more general theory of memory advanced by Underwood (1969). I will start the next section providing an outline of Underwood's theory and then discuss how Henning took this theory as a starting point in trying to explain the error patterns that he observed when L2 learners at different proficiency levels performed a recognition memory test.

Underwood's attribute theory of memory

Underwood (1969) conceptualized what he calls a "memory" (that is, what is left in long-term memory after experiencing some event) as a set of different types of attributes. According to the theory, an event—say, the presentation of a word in a particular context—is stored in a memory trace that encompasses various aspects ("attributes") of the event; here, the word and the context it is presented in. Underwood hypothesized the existence of eleven such attributes, three of which are especially relevant in the present context: orthographic, acoustic, and "associative verbal". The orthographic and acoustic attributes concern the form aspects of words and have come to be stored as a result of attending to the form aspects of the word events. The associative verbal attribute concerns semantic information; more specifically, the type of information that in a word association test might be given as associative responses to the word in question. The associative verbal attribute might consist of, for instance, an antonym, a synonym, or a category name. This information has come to be stored in the memory trace as a consequence of semantic processing of the critical word during learning. In a nutshell, and applied to word learning, the core of the theory is the assumption that different aspects of a word to be learned are attended to and that what is attended to becomes part of the stored representation of the word.

Underwood underpins his theory by referring to the results of many studies. For instance, the well-known **tip-of-the-tongue phenomenon**

(Brown & McNeil, 1966) suggests that form aspects of words are attributes of memory. It is a phenomenon presumably all language users are familiar with. It involves the language user's failure to retrieve a particular (generally infrequent) word from memory, at the same time being convinced he or she knows the word and would manage to retrieve it if given sufficient time. Brown and McNeil demonstrated that in this "feeling-of-knowing" or "tip-of-the-tongue" state a number of aspects of the troublesome word could nevertheless be dug up, such as how many syllables it contained and what its first letter was. And *if* a word comes out at all, it is often a word that resembles the targeted word in form but not in meaning (that is, it is a synform or malapropism). A second example to illustrate the theory concerns an experience we are also all likely to have had: When trying to go back to a specific piece of information encountered earlier in a text, we often have a pretty good idea where-abouts in the text it occurred (e.g., on a left page toward the bottom). This suggests that spatial aspects of an event (its location) are encoded as well and, accordingly, one of the other attributes of memory assumed by Underwood was a spatial attribute (see Rothkopf, 1971, for experimental support).

Particularly relevant for the study of bilingual-ism is the inclusion of a language attribute or **language tag** in the set of memory attributes distinguished by Underwood (1969). Lambert, Ignatow, and Krauthammer (1968) were the first to propose such a tag, and in a review of the literature McCormack (1976) concluded that language is indeed coded on the memory trace of an encountered word. As we will see in later chapters (Chapters 4 through 6), the notion of a language tag has become widely accepted among the bilingual research community and in theories on language control by bilinguals the tag is often assigned a pivotal role.

An aspect of Underwood's theory that is especially important in the present context is the assumption that individual differences occur in the way the learning materials are coded. Con-sequently, the stored memories differ between individuals. Furthermore, he hypothesized the

occurrence of developmental changes in coding, both at the level of individual words and of indi-vidual language users. Specifically, Underwood assumed that in the stored memories of rare words one particular form attribute, the acoustic attribute (a physical/form aspect), dominates, whereas in the memories of common words associative verbal attributes (concerning mean-ing) are more dominant (Underwood, 1969). Similarly, he suggested that in young children, the acoustic attribute (form) is primordial, whereas with further learning the associative verbal attributes (meaning) become gradually more and more important. The meaningfulness of the learning material is assigned a crucial role in whether the acoustic or the associative verbal attribute is dominant: "Roughly, the greater the meaningfulness of the material being stored as a memory, the greater the dominance of the associative-verbal attribute; hence, the less prominent the role of the acoustic attribute" (Underwood, 1969, p. 567). Of course, for young children with relatively little language experience, words generally carry less meaning than for older children. Analogously, rare words, having been encountered relatively sparsely by the language user, will overall be less meaningful than common words, frequently encountered. These aspects of Underwood's attribute theory of memory are highly relevant for understanding foreign language vocabulary acquisition, as I hope to demonstrate below.

Bach and Underwood (1970) obtained evi-dence supporting the predicted development from dominance of acoustic attributes in the memories of younger children to a dominance of associative verbal (meaning) attributes in older children. Second and sixth graders were presented with a set of L1 words for learning. In a subsequent multiple choice recognition task, for each of the words in the training set four alternatives were presented, the correct word (e.g., *bad*) and three distracters: an associate of the correct word (*good*), a word that was acoustically similar to the correct word (*bag*), and a neutral word that did not share an acoustic or associative relationship with the correct word (*dot*). The task was to choose the correct word out of the four alternatives. The researchers were primarily interested in the type of errors made on the recognition test, predicting—on the basis of the attribute theory—that when the participant makes an error he or she is far more likely to choose an acoustic or associative distracter than the neutral distracter. Furthermore, they predicted that the number of acoustic errors would outnumber the associative errors for the younger participants, whereas the opposite pattern was predicted for the older participants.

The data confirmed both predictions, suggesting a dominance of acoustic attributes in the memory representations of the younger participants and of meaning attributes in those of the older participants. These findings, in turn, suggest a different focus of attention of younger and older participants during learning, with the former paying more attention to the surface (form) characteristics of the words to be learned, the latter more to their meaning. As already mentioned, the degree to which the learning materials are meaningful to the learners is ultimately held responsible for this pattern of results: The more meaningful a stimulus to the learner, the more it will foster meaningful encoding (including the activation of semantic associates).

A question that presents itself spontaneously in the context of this chapter on foreign vocabulary acquisition is whether the observed development is related to the learner's age or, instead, to the fact that stored word meanings gradually become richer the more often the corresponding words are encountered in speech or text (as the conclusion of the previous paragraph suggests). If the latter holds true, the same development from dominance of form to dominance of meaning should show up in learners of a foreign language at increasing proficiency levels, also when learning starts at a late age, and Underwood's theory would provide an account of such development as well. This is where Henning's (1973) study that I alluded to earlier comes in.

Adopting Underwood's theoretical framework, Henning set out answering the question of whether the development observed over age groups, as in the study by Bach and Underwood (1970), might also emerge across L2 learner groups of a similar age but with different levels of L2 proficiency. His terminology and approach is slightly different from the one used in the previous studies, focusing on different "clusters" or "families" of associated meanings and/or interrelated sounds that emerge in memory as a result of different encoding operations. This adds the interesting new viewpoint that different encoding operations not only lead to differential dominance of form and meaning attributes in individual word representations, but to different types of memory networks as well: form-based networks as a result of form coding; semantic networks as a consequence of encoding meaning.

Henning's participants were students from abroad studying English as a second language and English students studying Persian as a second language. For comparison with the learners of English and Persian, native speakers of these two languages participated as well. The participants were presented with a set of spoken L2 paragraphs, each about 30 seconds long, and narrated by a native speaker of the language (English or Persian). From these paragraphs a set of 60 words were later presented for recognition in a visual multiple choice test. In each case, the target word was presented among three distracters, all of which were either related in sound or in meaning to the target, or all were unrelated to the target. The results clearly suggested that, indeed, the same acoustic-to-semantic development occurs in late L2 learning as was observed in children developing their L1: The L2 learners at low levels of proficiency more often chose distracters acoustically related to the correct response word than distracters semantically related to the correct response or than distracters unrelated to the correct response. At higher levels of proficiency fewer acoustically related and more semantically related distracters were chosen; selection of semantic distracters was highest among the native speakers of the target languages. The relevant conclusion to draw from these results is that they suggest "that first and second language learning requires parallel cognitive developmental processes" (Henning, 1973, p. 186). In both cases the encoding strategies at the various proficiency levels appear to shift from form dominance to meaning dominance (see also Chapter 2 for a related development from form-to-meaning word learning in infants). A second important conclusion drawn by Henning is that instruction strategies should fit in with the encoding strategy adopted by the learner, focusing on form early on in teaching but on meaning at more advanced stages of proficiency.

THE REVISED HIERARCHICAL MODEL, ITS PRECURSORS, AND OTHER MODELS

Introduction

The studies discussed in the previous section have gone largely unnoticed in more recent psycholinguistic studies on L2 vocabulary development. Yet their results tie in nicely with some of the main findings of this later work and with the conclusions drawn from them. The conceptual similarity is especially salient when considering a laboratory study by Talamas, Kroll, and Dufour (1999). These researchers had more- and less-fluent English–Spanish bilinguals perform the translation recognition task: The participants were shown pairs of words in succession, one word in English, the other word in Spanish, and were asked to indicate whether the second word was the correct translation of the first. Two types of pairs that required a "no" response were of particular interest. The L2 Spanish word in these pairs was related either in form or in meaning to the correct translation of the L1 word (e.g., *man–hambre*, "hunger", instead of *man–hombre*, "man" versus *man–mujer*, "woman", instead of *man–hombre*).

The resemblance with the studies of Bach and Underwood (1970) and, especially, Henning (1973) is obvious. In all three cases the investigators used a recognition test and were primarily interested in the error patterns to distracters that were either form-related or meaning-related to a target word, assuming these error patterns would reveal a development from lower to higher proficiency levels in L1 (Bach & Underwood) or in L2 (Henning; Talamas et al.). A noteworthy difference was that in the two earlier studies memory of material presented just before the actual recognition test was tested, whereas the study by Talamas and her colleagues tested knowledge the participants were already equipped with the moment they entered the laboratory. Furthermore, Talamas and associates measured response times as well as error scores (false positives to distracters). Despite these differences in the exact procedures used, especially when considering the response time data of Talamas et al.'s study, the results were strikingly similar to Henning's observations: Both participant groups in the study by Talamas and her colleagues suffered interference from both form and meaning similarity between a Spanish "no-translation" word (*hambre*, *mujer*) and the actual Spanish translation (*hombre*), as indicated by the slower response times and larger percentage of errors obtained for these stimuli as compared to completely unrelated English–Spanish control pairs. The response time data of this study are presented in Table 3.2, collapsed across two presentation conditions (with the English word as the first word of each presented word pair and the Spanish word second, or vice versa).

As can be seen, in the less-fluent bilinguals interference was especially large when the Spanish word was related in form to the target Spanish word (*hambre* instead of *hombre*). In contrast, in the more-fluent bilinguals a relatively large interference effect was obtained when the Spanish

TABLE 3.2		
Translation recognition judgments		
Type of false translation pair	Less fluent	More fluent
Form related	972	903
Control	858	860
	114	43
Meaning related	898	967
Control	878	843
	20	124

Mean response times (in ms) for translation recognition judgments to false translation pairs as a function of type of false translation pair and level of fluency. Adapted from Talamas et al. (1999).

word was semantically related to the target word (*mujer* instead of *hombre*). The error data showed a less-pronounced pattern and the interaction between interference type and fluency level was not significant. Yet those data also suggested relatively large interference from form-related distracters in the less-fluent group.

Ferré, Sánchez-Casas, and Guasch (2006) extended these results in a Spanish–Catalan study by manipulating not only the L2 proficiency level of the participants but also the age at which L2 was first acquired. Three groups of bilinguals participated: early proficient bilinguals, late proficient bilinguals, and late non-proficient bilinguals. Again, level of L2 proficiency affected the pattern of results and, despite a number of differences between the two studies, the general pattern of results once more suggested that with increasing fluency in the L2 interference from form-related distracters decreases and interference from meaning-related distracters increases. L2 proficiency turned out to be a stronger determinant of performance than age of acquisition. This showed from the fact that the pattern of results was much more similar for the early and late proficient bilinguals than for the late non-proficient and late proficient bilinguals.

On the basis of these results the authors of both studies concluded that becoming more proficient in a foreign language involves a progression from a primary focus on form to a primary focus on meaning. The revised hierarchical model of lexical and conceptual representation in bilingual memory (e.g., Kroll, 1993; Kroll & Stewart, 1994) captures this development. The model was dubbed "hierarchical" because of the fact that it explicitly distinguishes between two representation levels in bilingual memory: a lexical and a conceptual level, the former containing the representations of the forms of words, the latter their meaning representations. (Note that the modifier "lexical" is used here in a narrow sense, referring to just one type of knowledge stored in the mental lexicon. In order not to get confused the reader should be aware of this ambiguity in terminology, which reflects common practice.) The lexical and conceptual levels are by no means the only levels into which bilingual

memory can be dissected (see De Groot, 2002, and Chapters 4 and 5 for models that make more fine-grained distinctions), but these are the two the revised hierarchical model focuses on. "Revised" refers to the fact that the model can be regarded a modified merger of two earlier such hierarchical models, the word association model and the concept mediation model, coined by Potter, So, Von Eckardt, and Feldman (1984).

In the next sections I will first present these earlier models, as well as a third one that, contrary to the remaining two, has somehow disappeared in the current literature on bilingual memory. Next, I will detail the revised hierarchical model and discuss the evidence in support of it and data that challenge it.

Precursors and other models

The precursors of the revised hierarchical model, the word association model and the concept mediation model (Potter et al., 1984), have been around under different names much longer. Over 50 years ago, Weinreich (1953) distinguished between three forms of bilingualism: **compound**, **subordinative**, and **coordinate bilingualism**. The upper panel of Figure 3.6 illustrates how a single word in L1 (its form; see above), its translation-equivalent form in L2, and the concept associated with these two words, are represented in bilingual memory according to each of these three models. The three differ from one another along two dimensions: the number of underlying conceptual systems that the bilingual possesses (one or two) and, in the case of a single conceptual system, the way in which this system is accessed when an L2 word is input: directly, or indirectly via the corresponding L1 word. The compound and subordinative system organizations (a and b, respectively) both assume a single conceptual system shared by both languages. The coordinate system organization (c) assumes two conceptual systems, one for each language. The compound and subordinative system organizations are in fact formally equivalent to the concept mediation model and the word association model, respectively, in the more current literature. The lower panel of Figure 3.6 presents these same three

FIGURE 3.6

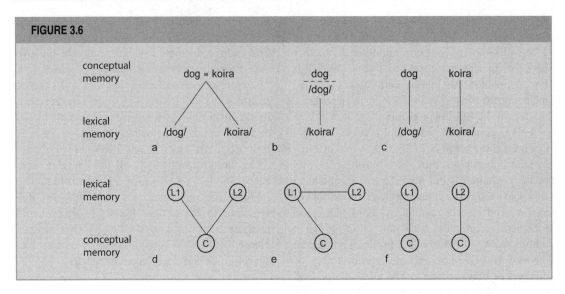

Upper panel: Three models of the organization of two types of vocabulary knowledge in bilingual memory as originally proposed by Weinreich: a = compound organization; b = subordinative organization; c = coordinate organization. Lower panel: These same models in one of their current forms: d = concept mediation model; e = word association model; f = coordinate model. Each circle (or "node") represents the form or meaning of a single word, in the lexical and conceptual representation layers, respectively. Adapted from Weinreich (1953) with permission from Degruyter and De Groot (2002).

models in the format that is common in more recent publications (e.g., De Groot, 1995, 2002).

A second way the concept mediation model and word association model are often visualized is by depicting both the L1 and L2 lexicon as a whole (rather than a single translation pair structure), each in the form of a box, and adding a box that represents conceptual memory. When this format is chosen, the boxes representing the L1 and L2 lexicons are usually drawn in different sizes—the L2 box the smaller of the two—to convey the fact that the L2 lexicon of most bilinguals contains fewer (and less-consolidated) words than their L1 lexicon. This set up is shown in Figure 3.7.

As is explicitly shown in Figure 3.6 (but also holds for Figure 3.7), in addition to separate lexical and conceptual levels, both the concept mediation model and the word association model (as well as the coordinate model) assume separate lexical representations for the L1 and L2 words of each translation pair. In other words, a pair of translations is represented in memory in (at least) three components (usually called "nodes"): two

lexical and one conceptual (see, e.g., Smith, 1997, for an analysis that substantiates the existence of such tripartite representation of translation pairs). However, the linkage patterns between the representations at the lexical and conceptual levels differ between the models and this is the reason why, when an L2 word is presented, the access route to conceptual memory differs between them.

In the research that first ensued from Weinreich's book, the focus has been on a hypothesized relation between each of the three types of bilingualism depicted by the models on the one hand and acquisition context on the other hand. More precisely, the three hypothesized types of bilingualism were thought to result from different acquisition contexts (Ervin & Osgood, 1954; Gekoski, 1980; Lambert, Havelka, & Crosby, 1958; see De Groot, 1993, 1995, for more detailed discussions). Specifically, compound bilingualism was thought to emerge from a common foreign language learning practice in school settings, in which foreign language words are paired with the corresponding words and their meanings in L1—that is, the paired-associate

FIGURE 3.7

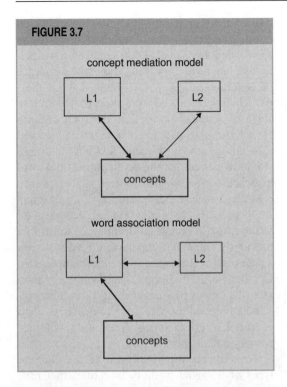

concept mediation model

word association model

Two models of cross-language connections between a bilingual's first (L1) and second (L2) language. L2 words are directly connected to conceptual representations (the concept mediation model) or via the L1 lexical representations (the word association model). Adapted from Potter et al. (1984); from Kroll and Tokowicz (2005) with permission from Oxford University Press.

technique discussed earlier (pp. 87–88). Furthermore, compound bilingualism was thought to emerge when a child grows up in a home where two languages are spoken interchangeably by the same people and in the same situations. In contrast, coordinate bilingualism was thought to ensue if a strict separation holds between the use of the two languages such that, for instance, language A is used exclusively at home and language B exclusively outside the home, in school, or at work. Alternatively, coordinate bilingualism might emerge when the bilingual's two languages are acquired in two distinct cultural settings, as in the case of emigration to another country.

Votaw (1992) entertained a somewhat different view on the relation between acquisition context and bilingual memory organization. She

suggested a critical determinant of the type of bilingualism to emerge is whether the bilingual lives among people who are monolingual or among people who share his or her two languages. Mixing languages among monolingual speakers would hinder communication dramatically. To prevent this, bilinguals in such a setting might develop a coordinate structure. Mixing languages among speakers of the same two languages who switch between their languages quite naturally might lead to (and at the same time reflect) a compound memory organization.

Interesting as these views might be, the evidence to support a direct relation between acquisition context and type of bilingualism has in fact generally been weak (but see Ji, Zhang, & Nisbett, 2004, for recent evidence that indeed suggests a relation between coordinate vs. compound bilingualism and acquisition context). One of the reasons may be that the underlying assumption that an individual bilingual's memory contains structures of one type only may be flawed. Instead, the compound–coordinate distinction should not be seen as dichotomous but as two idealized ends of a continuum, as Gekoski (1980) among others suggested. This view, but applied to the distinction between compound (concept mediation) and subordinative (word association) bilingualism, will be elaborated later (pp. 135–136), and was already considered as a possibility by Weinreich in his seminal publication: "It would appear offhand that a person's or group's bilingualism need not be entirely of the type A or B, since some signs of the languages may be compounded while others are not" (Weinreich, 1953, p. 10). He then continued to suggest the use of the word association technique (p. 92) across languages to find out the extent to which individual bilinguals store words in the various types of formats (on the assumption that coordinate bilingualism would lead to more different association patterns between a bilingual's two languages than the other forms of bilingualism). This suggestion has not fallen on deaf ears, because a number of later studies have indeed used the word association technique as a tool to study bilingual memory (Kolers, 1963; Taylor, 1976; Van Hell & De Groot, 1998a). The results of these studies suggest that, indeed, different types of structures may co-exist in an individual bilingual's memory.

In more recent work on bilingual memory representation the focus has been on the consequences for mapping word form onto word meaning, and vice versa, of the fact that the linkage patterns differ between the models. Given a word association structure, where direct connections from L2 word form representations onto conceptual memory are missing, understanding and speaking a second language must necessarily exploit the L1 word form representations. For instance, a visually presented L2 word must first access its L2 word form representation. The corresponding L1 word form representation is then accessed via the link connecting the two word form representations. Subsequently the L2 word form is assigned meaning via the connection between the L1 word form representation and the connected meaning representation. In other words, the L2 word is assigned the L1 word's meaning. Given a concept mediation structure, just as an L1 word, an L2 word can be assigned meaning directly via the connection from the L2 word form representation to the common conceptual representation. The word association model and the ensuing process of indirect mapping of form to meaning via the L1 lexical forms are assumed to be associated with relatively low levels of L2 proficiency. With higher levels of L2 proficiency, direct connections between the L2 form representations and conceptual memory have developed and the connections between the L1 and L2 word form representations are no longer used or are even dismantled.

After an earlier failed attempt to obtain support for such a development from word association processing to concept mediation (Potter et al., 1984), Kroll and Curley (1988) and Chen and Leung (1989) *did* obtain evidence to support it. The crucial difference between these studies was that the participants of low L2 proficiency in the studies by Kroll and Curley and Chen and Leung were at a lower stage of L2 development than the less-fluent participants tested by Potter and her colleagues. De Groot and Hoeks (1995) obtained support for the assumed development in a *trilingual* study with Dutch native speakers who had English as their strongest foreign language and French as a weaker foreign language. In a translation study evidence of concept mediation was obtained when these participants translated from their L1 Dutch into English, whereas translation from Dutch into French showed a pattern consistent with the word association model. Finally, a study by Chen (1990) suggested that the development from word association processing to concept mediation may occur extremely rapidly when a relatively small L2 vocabulary is learned in an experimental setting: Just 30 minutes of training 20 words in a previously unfamiliar language sufficed to obtain a data pattern consistent with concept mediation. In other words, it appears that already very soon after the onset of L2 acquisition, L2 comprehension and production start to become independent of the L1 lexical forms (see pp. 141–142 for converging evidence).

To complete this discussion of the different types of bilingual memory structures that have been proposed, one further type of model must be presented. It is a well-known fact that complete meaning equivalence of the two terms in a translation pair is a rare phenomenon. In addition to sharing a large part of their meanings, each member of a "translation equivalent" word pair has meaning nuances unique to the language to which it belongs. Furthermore, word meanings are not static entities but change over time, and differ between individuals (Pavlenko, 1999). Meaning elements may be added to or subtracted from a word's earlier meaning, and across individuals differences exist in the set of meaning aspects that, together, constitute a word's meaning. The models depicted in the lower panel of Figure 3.6, where a one-to-one mapping holds between word meaning on the one hand and representation structure on the other (that is, the complete meaning of a word is represented in a single memory node), do not do justice to these facts about bilingualism. Models of this type are called **localist** models. To remedy this neglect a further type of model has been suggested, one that can easily account for the different shades of meaning a word and its (closest) translation may

FIGURE 3.8

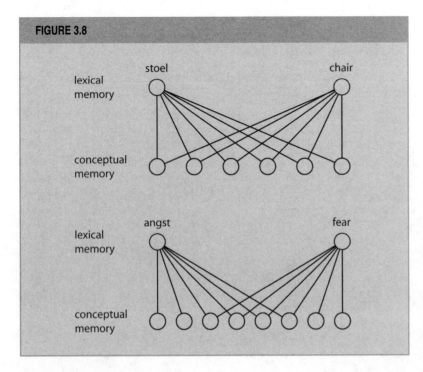

Distributed conceptual representations in bilingual memory. A word's meaning is spread out across a number of more elementary meaning units. *Angst* and *stoel* are Dutch for *fear* and *chair*. From De Groot (1992a, 1992b). Copyright © 1992 American Psychological Society.

have in a bilingual's two languages. At the same time it can account for changes in a word's meaning over time and differences between individuals in what exact meaning they assign to a word. The model in question assumes **distributed** meaning representations, in which a word's meaning is spread out over a number of more elementary meaning units that each stores one elementary part of a word's meaning (e.g., De Groot, 1992a, 1992b; Taylor, 1976). Figure 3.8 illustrates this idea. It shows two fictitious bilingual memory structures, one for a pair of translations that share meaning completely, a second for a pair of translations that each contains two language-specific meaning components. The fewer meaning components a pair of translations share, the closer the representation of the translation pair approaches the coordinate structure discussed earlier (Figure 3.6f).

The suitability of localist *word form* representations can be questioned for similar reasons: Word forms can be dissected into a set of more elementary components (letters or phonemes), some of which may be shared between a bilingual's two languages (as is the case with

cognate translations). For this reason, the bilingual memory structures with distributed meaning representations have subsequently been developed into structures in which the word form representations are also distributed over a number of more elementary features, this time form features (e.g., Kroll & De Groot, 1997; Van Hell & De Groot; 1998a).

A more recent modification to models of the distributed type was proposed by Finkbeiner, Forster, Nicol, and Nakamura (2004). Instead of focusing on the varying number of meaning and form elements different translation pairs may share, these authors focused on *clusters* of meaning elements that each constitute a word sense. They departed from the observation that each member of a pair of translations has language-specific senses in addition to the one or more senses that it shares with the other member of the translation pair. For example, in addition to the one common color-sense it shares with Japanese *kuroi*, English *black* has over 20 senses not shared with Japanese *kuroi* and, vice versa, Japanese *kuroi* has a number of senses that are alien to English *black*. This state of affairs is illustrated in

FIGURE 3.9

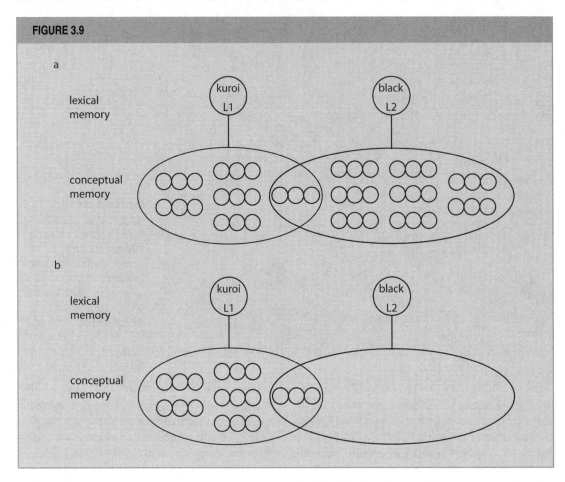

The sense model of bilingual memory representation. Each set of three circles represents one sense of Japanese *kuroi* or English *black*. *Kuroi* and *black* share one sense, the color sense. In addition, each has a number of language-specific senses. (a) The memory representation of *kuroi* and *black* in a Japanese–English bilingual with a high level of proficiency in both languages. (b) The memory representation of *kuroi* and *black* in a Japanese learner of English who has only acquired the color sense of English *black* and none of its English-specific senses. Adapted from Finkbeiner et al. (2004), with permission from Elsevier.

Figure 3.9a. Bilinguals who are all aware of the fact that a particular word pair, for instance *kuroi–black*, constitutes a translation pair may differ in the number of language-specific senses that they master (in both their L1 and L2) and, on average, fewer senses will be stored for the weaker language. In general, the less balanced their bilingualism, the larger the discrepancy between the number of senses mastered in their stronger and weaker language will be. For instance, a Japanese learner at a relatively early stage of learning English may only have acquired the color sense of English *black* and none of its English-specific senses (see Figure 3.9b). (Note that, in theory, it is also possible that a bilingual masters some language-specific senses of both words in a translation pair without being aware of the fact that the two have a shared sense as well—in other words, that they are translations of one another.)

The revised hierarchical model

The revised hierarchical model (e.g., Kroll, 1993; Kroll & Stewart, 1994) combines the word association model and concept mediation model presented above by assuming both direct links between the word form representations of a pair of translation equivalents as well as connections between each of the two form representations on the one hand and a shared conceptual representation on the other hand. Yet it is more than a mere fusion of the two earlier models because it assumes two, rather than just one, connections between the L1 and L2 lexical representations. In addition, it assumes directional differences in the strength of the various connections. It is these additions that can account for the developmental pattern in the studies discussed above (p. 128). Furthermore, they account for differences in the response patterns observed when bilinguals translate between their two languages from L1 to L2 or vice versa (see below). The model is illustrated in Figure 3.10.

In this figure, dashed and solid lines represent weak and stronger connections, respectively. The link between the common L1/L2 conceptual memory store and the L1 lexicon is stronger than the link between the former and the L2 lexicon as a result of the differential command of the two languages, L1 (generally) being the stronger language. Differential experience in the two languages is the source of this imbalance. The link from the L2 lexicon to the L1 lexicon ("lexicon"

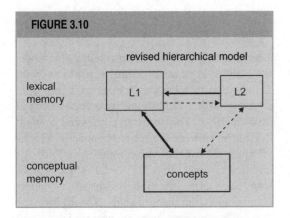

FIGURE 3.10

revised hierarchical model

lexical memory

conceptual memory

The revised hierarchical model of bilingual memory. L1 and L2 words are both directly connected to one another and indirectly, via conceptual memory. Solid lines reflect strong connections. Dashed lines reflect weak connections. Adapted from Kroll and Stewart (1994) and Kroll and Tokowicz (2005) with permission from OUP and Elsevier.

used in the narrow sense of referring to the forms of words) is assumed to be stronger than the link in the opposite direction, the reason being that— as assumed by the authors—during the initial stage of L2 learning the learner heavily relies on the L1 lexical elements, accessing the meaning of an L2 word indirectly, via its translation in L1. With increasing exposure to L2, the direct connection between the L2 lexical representation and the common meaning representation becomes stronger. Ultimately it is strong enough to enable direct meaning access from an activated L2 lexical representation (in comprehension) and direct retrieval of an L2 lexical representation following the conceptualization of a meaning to be expressed in L2 (in production). Several studies suggest that such "freeing" of an L2 lexical representation from the corresponding L1 lexical representation starts very early on in the learning process (see for evidence Altarriba & Mathis, 1997; Chen, 1990; Chen & Leung, 1989; De Groot & Poot, 1997; Kroll & Curley, 1988; Potter et al., 1984).

In the previous sentence I have deliberately avoided a statement like "freeing L2 from L1 comes about early on in the learning process", choosing a wording that focused on an individual pair of translations, *not* on the L1 and L2 language systems as a whole. The reason was that the wording "freeing L2 from L1" might suggest that during the process of learning an L2 a magical moment occurs at which the processing of all L2 words suddenly becomes independent of the corresponding L1 lexical representations (or even, that at that magical moment *all* types of linguistic knowledge in the bilingual system, not only lexical knowledge, become independent of L1). This, however, is extremely unlikely. Words differ from one another in many respects and, as we have seen before, (pp. 108–110), these differences affect their rate of acquisition. It is therefore much more likely that the development from reliance on L1 to L1-independent processing takes place at the level of individual words and that, consequently, an individual L2 learner is at different stages of learning for different words and word types.

In earlier publications (De Groot, 1992a,

1992b, 1993, 1995) I elaborated this idea, focusing on the logical consequence of such a view: that within a bilingual person's memory different types of memory representations co-exist. Frequently used words and words that, for various reasons are relatively easy to learn will reach L1 independence earlier than infrequently used and difficult words. Similarly—and making a connection with the above developmental model—fluent bilinguals (who have experienced the L2 words relatively frequently) will already have reached this state of L1-independent processing for relatively many L2 words, whereas less-fluent bilinguals will still exploit the L1 lexical representations relatively often. In terms of the concept mediation and word association memory structures hypothesized earlier, the memory of fluent bilinguals will contain relatively many concept mediation structures whereas the memory of less-fluent bilinguals will contain more word association structures. Dufour and Kroll put these same ideas the following way: ". . . individuals do not wake up one morning suddenly able to mediate their second language conceptually [. . .] direct concept mediation of L2 must be acquired gradually, occurring earlier for more familiar words and concepts" (Dufour & Kroll, 1995, p. 175).

This account can be extended to apply to the results of the Dutch–English–French trilingual study referred to above (De Groot & Hoeks, 1995): For English, the stronger foreign language of our native Dutch participants, L1-independent processing holds for relatively many words, whereas word processing in weaker French stills exploits the corresponding L1 word forms relatively often. So, depending on the various stages of development of each of the languages of a multilingual, different proportions of word association and concept mediation structures are likely to exist for any of these languages in relation to L1 (and to any of the other languages present).

Supporting evidence

Kroll and her colleagues collected various sources of evidence consistent with the revised hierarchical model. One of these concerned the translation recognition study by Talamas and colleagues (1999; Table 3.2) with which I started this section. It was shown there that less-fluent bilinguals are more slowed down by a distracter related in form to a word's actual translation (*man–hambre*, "hunger," instead of *man–hombre*, "man") than by a meaning-related distracter (*man–mujer*, "woman", instead of *man–hombre*), whereas the opposite held for more fluent bilinguals. This suggests a relatively large reliance on (or sensitivity to) form in the less-fluent bilinguals and a relatively large reliance on meaning in the more-fluent bilinguals (and was argued to reflect a development similar to developing L1 proficiency; Bach & Underwood, 1970). A second piece of supporting evidence is the finding that less-fluent bilinguals benefit more from a cognate relation between L1 words and their translations in L2 than do more-fluent bilinguals, both when L2 words have to be named and when L1 words are translated in L2 and vice versa (Kroll et al., 1998; Kroll, Michael, Tokowicz, & Dufour, 2002). Both these sources of evidence support the predictions of the model regarding the development of L2 fluency. The remaining evidence concerns the model's predictions that ensue from the assumed asymmetries in the strengths of the connections between the lexical and conceptual nodes within a single developmental stage. It is to this evidence that we will now turn.

Directional effects on translation latency

The data that first led to postulating the model were obtained in an experiment in which fluent Dutch–English bilinguals translated words from L1 Dutch to L2 English and vice versa (Kroll & Stewart, 1994). Due to the hypothesized strength differences between the various connections in the bilingual memory structures (see Figure 3.10), the authors assumed that L2 to L1 ("backward") translation primarily employs the strong direct connections from the L2 to the L1 word form (or "lexical") representations, whereas L1 to L2 ("forward") translation primarily exploits the indirect connections through the conceptual representation shared by L1 and L2. If true, L2-to-L1 translation follows a shorter translation route than L1-to-L2 translation. For this reason, the authors predicted shorter response times for L2-to-L1 translation than for translation in the reverse direction, a finding that had been reported before in the literature (e.g., Sánchez-Casas, Davis, & García-Albea, 1992; see Kroll, 1993, and Snodgrass, 1993, for reviews). The response time data confirmed this prediction (see also Miller & Kroll, 2002, and Tokowicz & Kroll, 2007; and see Francis & Gallard, 2005, for a trilingual demonstration of this asymmetry).

However, in a number of other translation studies the two translation directions produced equally long response times (De Groot, Dannenburg, & Van Hell, 1994, Experiment 1; the most fluent bilinguals in De Groot & Poot, 1997; La Heij, Hooglander, Kerling, & Van der Velden, 1996, Experiment 4; Van Hell & De Groot, 1998b) or even *shorter* response times in L1-to-L2 translation (De Groot et al., 1994, Experiment 2; Duyck & Brysbaert, 2004, Experiment 1; La Heij et al., 1996, Experiment 3; the *least* fluent bilinguals in De Groot & Poot, 1997). If indeed direction-dependent differences in translation time constitute an unequivocal signature of direction-dependent concept mediation versus word association translation, these latter findings especially would provide a challenge to the model. The former—equally long response times in both translation directions—could easily be accounted for in at least all those cases where rather fluent bilinguals were tested, because these may be expected to map not only L1 word forms but also L2 word forms straight onto meaning.

But, plausibly, translation time data do not provide the unambiguous evidence one would need to falsify or verify the revised hierarchical model, because there are more reasons why the latency difference between forward and backward translation predicted by Kroll and Stewart might occur. Snodgrass mentions three: ". . . faster access to a well-known than to a less well-known language, the difference between recognition and recall, and the well-known asymmetry between being able to understand a language and being able to speak it" (Snodgrass, 1993, p. 101). (Note that the latter two distinctions may in fact be two different ways to phrase one and the same distinction: Comprehension involves recognition

of the stimulus, whereas production involves its recall.) In agreement with the second of these possible accounts, the vocabulary-learning studies discussed before (see also Figure 3.2) consistently showed higher recall scores and faster recall for receptive cued recall than for productive cued recall. These test formats are essentially the same as L2-to-L1 translation and L1-to-L2 translation, respectively. The only difference between the format of the cued recall studies discussed earlier and of the present translation studies is that the knowledge tapped in the former had just been acquired in the learning episode immediately preceding the test episode, whereas in the translation studies it was acquired in the past.

The point to make here is that the relatively long response times when bilinguals translate from their L1 to their L2 rather than vice versa may result from the relatively demanding nature of producing instead of recognizing an L2 word (see also p. 112). Furthermore, the fact that it is harder to articulate words from the weaker L2 than from the stronger L1 after they have been retrieved successfully from memory (see De Groot, Borgwaldt, Bos, & Van den Eijnden, 2002, for evidence to support this claim) may also contribute to the longer translation latencies for L1-to-L2 translation, *if* this effect occurs at all. In other words, assuming qualitatively different translation routes for forward and backward translation is just one of multiple ways to account for directional differences in translation latency and the model is clearly in need for truly univocal support.

Directional effects of meaning variables

More compelling support for the revised hierarchical model comes from findings that suggest that meaning-related variables affect translation from L1 to L2 but not from L2 to L1, or the latter to a lesser extent than the former. Kroll and Stewart (1994) provided such evidence by demonstrating that either clustering the words to be translated into semantic categories (e.g., clothing, body parts, musical instruments) or presenting them in random order instead (e.g., a sequence *coat, suit, hand, flute, ear, piano, trousers . . .*), affected response times when L1 words were translated into L2 but not when translation was from L2 to L1: In forward translation, latencies were longer for words in the clustered lists than for words in the mixed lists; in backward translation no effect of clustering occurred (but see Salamoura & Williams, 1999, who in a Greek–English study obtained a clustering effect in backward translation, as manifested by *faster* translation of the clustered words). As the name indicates, semantic clustering involves a semantic manipulation. Therefore, the effect of this manipulation in L1-to-L2 translation but not in L2-to-L1 translation suggests the activation and exploitation of meaning representations in the former but not in the latter translation direction.

Sholl, Sankaranarayanan, and Kroll (1995) collected converging evidence using a transfer paradigm in which the effect of earlier picture naming on subsequent translation in English–Spanish bilinguals was determined. A number of the words to be translated had been presented as pictures and named just before the translation session started. Picture naming requires the retrieval of the concept associated with the depicted entity (see Chapter 5). Therefore, if word-translation times were affected by prior naming of the corresponding pictures, this would suggest that conceptual access had occurred during the translation process: The activation of a conceptual representation ensuing from concept retrieval on the critical picture-naming trial has not yet decayed completely the moment the corresponding word is presented for translation and the residual activation affects translation time (see, e.g., Durgunoğlu & Roediger, 1987, for a theoretical underpinning of this conclusion). As compared to words not presented as pictures before, words that had occurred as pictures in the picture-naming task were translated reliably faster in L1-to-L2 translation. In contrast, earlier picture naming had no effect on L2-to-L1 translation. This direction-dependent transfer from earlier picture naming or, more specifically, from earlier concept retrieval, to word translation, suggests that L1-to-L2 translation, but not L2-to-L1 translation, involves the activation of conceptual representations.

Finally, similar support for the model but in a strongly mitigated form emerged from a correlation study performed in our laboratory (De Groot et al., 1994). In this study a number of different semantic variables such as word imageability and word concreteness affected translation in both directions and often to the same degree. However, in a small subset of the analyses the semantic effects were slightly smaller in backward translation than in forward translation. We regarded these semantic effects as a signature of conceptual processing and, thus, of translation via conceptual memory. Accordingly, their presence in both translation directions led us to conclude that conceptual memory is involved in both forward and backward translation. In other words, the data refuted a strong version of the revised hierarchical model, which would claim that conceptual memory is never implicated in backward translation. But the fact that in a subset of the analyses the semantic effects were somewhat smaller in backward translation suggested that under some circumstances conceptual memory is involved less in backward than in forward translation. These findings thus support a weaker version of the model.

Directional effects of semantic priming and translation priming

Additional support for (a weaker version of) the model comes from the cross-language semantic priming studies introduced before (pp. 92–93). In priming studies a target stimulus to be responded to overtly is preceded by another stimulus, the "prime" that shares or does not share some relation with the target stimulus, and the effect of the earlier prime on target processing is determined. In *semantic* priming studies prime and target on the critical trials share a semantic relation to one another (e.g., prime: *ice*; target: *snow*) and target processing on these trials is compared to the processing of targets preceded by unrelated words (prime: *ace*; target: *snow*) or by some meaningless sequence of symbols (prime: ####; target: *snow*). In monolingual studies of this type the primes and targets are words from one and the same language. In bilingual semantic priming

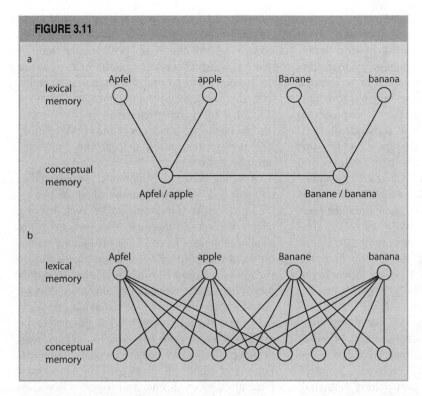

FIGURE 3.11

Two accounts of semantic priming from German *Apfel* to English *banana*: (a) in terms of localist conceptual memory nodes shared between German and English translation pairs and a connection between the two shared nodes Apfel/apple and Banane/banana; (b) in terms of distributed meaning representations in which German *Apfel* and English *banana* share a set of conceptual nodes. Adapted from De Groot (1992a).

studies, bilinguals serve as participants and the primes and targets may be taken from one and the same language (in the "within-language" condition) or the language of primes and targets differs (in the "between-language" condition).

The critical finding in these studies is the semantic priming effect, that is, the difference in response times (and error rates) to targets preceded by semantically related primes on the one hand and unrelated primes on the other hand. Assuming meaning representations of the localist type (see p. 132), these priming effects are often attributed to a process of activation spreading along the connections that exist in memory between the representations of related primes and targets. This process facilitates the access of the target words' representations through their pre-activation by the primes. Importantly, the locus within the memory system where these effects come about is *conceptual* memory; that is, the place where word meanings, not their forms, are stored. By implication, if semantic priming occurs, one may conclude that semantic access of the presented materials has taken place.

Within-language semantic priming reliably occurs, but between-language semantic priming has also been demonstrated many times (see Altarriba & Basnight-Brown, 2007, and Basnight-Brown & Altarriba, 2007, for recent reviews). These (as well as the within-language effects) can be explained by assuming shared meaning representations for translation pairs, a state of affairs that is illustrated in Figure 3.11a for a German–English bilingual: Given the German prime *Apfel* and the English target *banana*, the effect results from spreading activation between the shared conceptual node for German *Apfel* and English *apple* on the one hand and the shared conceptual node for German *Banane* and English *banana* on the other hand. An alternative account of within- and between-language semantic priming effects (De Groot, 1992a), shown in Figure 3.11b, assumes distributed meaning representations (see p. 133). According to this account, a semantic priming effect results from the fact that the prime's representation in lexical memory directly activates the elementary meaning nodes it shares with the target's representation in lexical memory. In this set-up, no connections between nodes within conceptual memory are required. In other words, the very moment the prime gains access to its (distributed) meaning representation in conceptual memory, the meaning of the target is also partially activated, causing the target to be processed relatively quickly when it is subsequently presented. As illustrated in Figure 3.11b, this account can also explain both the within- and between-language priming effects (the prime–target pair *Apfel* and *Banane* and the prime–target pair *Apfel* and *banana* share the same three nodes in conceptual memory).

As observed by Kroll and Sholl (1992), the semantic priming effects that occur in cross-language studies of this type are often asymmetrical: They are generally larger when the primes are in (the stronger) L1 and the targets in (the weaker) L2 than vice versa, especially when the duration between the onset of prime and target (the "stimulus onset asynchrony" or SOA) is relatively short. This result has been obtained both when the participants' bilingualism involved languages that employ the same script (e.g., English–Spanish; Schwanenflugel & Rey, 1986) and when the languages concerned employ different scripts (Chinese–English; Chen & Ng, 1989). In contrast, with relatively long SOAs the effect has at least twice been shown to be equally large with primes in L2 and targets in L1 as with primes in L1 and targets in L2 (Frenck & Pynte, 1987; Kirsner, Smith, Lockhart, King, & Jain, 1984). Recently, Basnight-Brown and Altarriba (2007) nuanced these findings by showing that the mentioned asymmetries hold when the L1 and L2 are the bilingual's dominant and non-dominant languages, respectively, but that they reverse when the L2 has become the stronger language, as often occurs over time (= L2 experience) in immigration settings.

As mentioned, the revised hierarchical model assumes that the connections between L1 word form memory and conceptual memory are stronger than those between L2 word form memory and conceptual memory (Figure 3.10). As a consequence, accessing conceptual representations from L1 form representations is easier

than from L2 form representations and conceptual access from an L2 representation may often fail. Kroll and Sholl (1992) argued that the relatively large effects of semantic priming when the primes are in L1 and the targets in L2 result from this privileged access to conceptual memory from L1 form representations: Because conceptual memory is the locus of the effect, priming will only occur if access to conceptual memory has indeed taken place.

A strong version of the model would predict null effects of semantic priming when the primes are in L2 and the targets in L1. Yet such priming effects do occur, although they are generally smaller than from L1 to L2. The combined results obtained with short SOAs thus support a weaker version of the model, which holds that L2 words may also access conceptual memory directly but do so less often (or less often quickly enough; see below) than L1 words. What has yet to be explained is why with longer SOAs symmetrical priming effects have sometimes been obtained. Kroll and Sholl (1992) suggested that a long interval between prime and target allows an L2 prime sufficient time to access conceptual memory indirectly, via the L1 word form representation. An alternative account of the combined data is to assume that L2 words also contact conceptual memory directly in all cases but that, due to the relatively weak links, the access process is too slow so that by the time the target is presented it has not yet been successfully completed.

Directional effects have also been observed for a second type of prime–target relation; namely, when the target is the translation of the prime word. As compared to targets that follow an unrelated prime, translation targets are often responded to more quickly. In fact, these **translation priming effects** are generally larger than semantic priming effects (see, e.g., Basnight-Brown & Altarriba, 1997; De Groot & Nas, 1991). Again, the effects are more robust when the primes are in (stronger) L1 and the targets in (weaker) L2 than vice versa, and especially when the primes are masked in such a way that they cannot be consciously perceived, weak effects or null effects have been reported from L2 primes to L1 targets (e.g., Jiang, 1999; Jiang & Forster, 2001).

A version of the revised hierarchical model which would stress the role of the direct connections between the translation pairs' lexical representations in the translation process must be rejected on the basis of these data. The reason is that it would predict especially strong translation priming effects from L2 to L1 as a consequence of the relatively strong lexical connections in this direction (see Figure 3.10). However, a version of the model that focuses on the differential strength of the links between the lexical and conceptual representations can account for these asymmetries. It can do so in the same way as it accounts for the asymmetrical semantic priming effects: They emerge from the privileged access to conceptual memory from L1 primes. Finkbeiner et al. (2004) suggested an alternative explanation of asymmetrical (semantic and translation) priming effects in terms of their sense-model of conceptual representation (see pp. 133–134 and Figure 3.9). They hypothesized that the magnitude of the priming effect depends on the proportion of the target word's senses that are activated by a prime. If, for instance, a bilingual has six senses for an L1 word but only one for its translation in L2 (see Figure 3.9b), an L1 prime will activate all senses (one) of its L2 equivalent. If instead its L2 translation serves as the prime it will only activate one sixth of the semantic representation of the L1 word. This asymmetry, the authors argued, underlies the asymmetry in the priming effects.

Counterevidence

The previous section presented evidence in support of the revised hierarchical model, as well as some apparent counterevidence that could be reconciled with the model by making some additional assumptions and accepting a weaker version of the model. However, the results of a series of further translation studies truly challenge the model and, particularly, the model's claim that L1 and L2 processing employ qualitatively different processing.

An early study that challenged the model, at any rate its strong version, employed a variant of the Stroop task (see p. 223). La Heij et al. (1990) examined the effect of L1 (Dutch) distracter words on L2 (English) to L1 translation. Shortly after its presentation, the English word to be translated (e.g., *spoon*) was replaced by a Dutch word (the distracter) semantically related (*vork*, "fork") or unrelated (*geit*, "goat") to the correct response word (*lepel*, "spoon"). Translation times turned out to be longer in the related condition than in the unrelated condition, a finding that would not have materialized had translation exclusively exploited the lexical route to the response. Because the study did not include an L1-to-L2 translation condition it is impossible to tell whether a translation asymmetry would have materialized; that is, a larger relatedness effect in L1-to-L2 translation. Such a finding would have supported a weaker version of the model. A follow-up study using a similar rationale but with non-verbal semantically related or unrelated stimuli as contextual distracters (e.g., pictures depicting a concept related or unrelated to the word to be translated) tested both directions of translation (La Heij et al., 1996). The results contradicted the predictions of the model in both its strong and weak form: Across four experiments, the relatedness effect was either equally large in both translation directions, or it was larger when translating from L2 to L1. The model predicts the opposite, smaller relatedness effects in L2-to-L1 translation.

In a word translation study by a former student and myself (De Groot & Poot, 1997) we obtained conceptually similar results, as did Duyck and Brysbaert (2004, 2008) in two number translation studies. Rik Poot and I looked at word translation performance of Dutch native speakers with different levels of proficiency in English L2. Concreteness effects on response times, error scores, and omission scores were obtained for both translation directions: Concrete words were translated faster, more often, and more often correctly, than abstract words. These effects suggest semantic processing and, therefore, the involvement of conceptual memory, in both translation directions. As with the analogous effects in La Heij et al.'s study (1996), these effects were either equally large in both translation directions or larger in backward translation. Perhaps most challenging for the revised hierarchical model was the fact that the concreteness effects tended to be largest in backward translation by participants at the earliest stage of L2 development, the group predicted by the model to rely on word-association translation most.

In a Dutch–French study, Duyck and Brysbaert (2004) wondered whether the so-called "number magnitude" effect might occur in the translation task, just as it had been shown to occur in a number of other tasks. The number magnitude effect is the phenomenon that magnitude information is activated more rapidly for small numbers (e.g., *two*) than for larger numbers (e.g., *eight*). Because a number's magnitude can be considered the core component of its meaning, whenever such an effect occurs it points at the involvement of conceptual memory during task performance. In the present context the critical questions thus are whether this effect occurs for both translations directions (Dutch to French and French to Dutch), and whether or not translation direction affects the size of the effect, if it occurs at all. All four experiments showed a number magnitude effect in both L1 (Dutch) to L2 (French) translation and in L2 to L1 translation: In both translation directions it took longer to translate number words representing large quantities (*acht* or *huit*, "eight") than number words representing small quantities (*twee* or *deux*, "two"). Furthermore, generally the size of the effect was not influenced by translation direction, suggesting that conceptual mediation is implicated to the same extent in both translation directions. A more recent Dutch–English–German trilingual extension of this study (Duyck & Brysbaert, 2008) *did* show an effect of translation direction, but contrary to the predictions of the revised hierarchical model, number magnitude effects were observed in backward translation, from both the L2 and the L3 into L1, but not in forward translation. These results are reminiscent of those of La Heij et al. (1996) and De Groot and Poot (1997; see above), who also showed larger semantic effects in backward translation.

A final set of studies that produced results that are difficult to reconcile with the predictions of the revised hierarchical model are the foreign vocabulary acquisition studies discussed earlier (pp. 108–110). These studies showed that from the earliest stages of learning, attaching a new label to a concrete concept is easier than attaching one to an abstract concept (see Figure 3.4). This was demonstrated by the learners' performance on productive and receptive cued recall tasks, which, as we have seen, are identical in format to the L1-to-L2 and L2-to-L1 translation tasks discussed here. This finding thus suggests that already during the very initial stages of foreign vocabulary acquisition, meaning is activated and exploited in the process. A similar result was obtained in Duyck and Brysbaert's (2004) study just discussed: These researchers also obtained the number magnitude effect, in both translation directions, when participants did not translate between two languages they already knew prior to the experiment, but between their L1 and a made-up language in which they had learned the number names only just before the translation task was administered.

An alternative view

In conclusion, there is a quite substantial body of evidence to suggest that both translation directions involve conceptual processing and that this holds true for learners at all stages of L2 development. As an alternative to the revised hierarchical model, La Heij et al. (1996; see also La Heij et al., 1990) therefore proposed a rather parsimonious view of how translation comes about—one that does not assume qualitatively different translation routes for forward and backward translation, nor for L2 learners at different proficiency levels (see Snodgrass, 1993, for a similar view). It is important to stress that this view embraces two of the central tenets of the revised hierarchical model; namely, (1) that concept activation is easier when the stimulus is an L1 word than when an L2 word serves as stimulus (assuming L1 is the stronger language), and (2) that an activated concept has easier access to the corresponding L1 word than to the corresponding L2 word. Both these assumptions derive from the differential strengths of the connections between L1 word forms and conceptual memory on the one hand and L2 word forms and conceptual memory on the other hand (see Figure 3.10), a difference that reflects differential past use of L1 and L2. The authors made no assumptions regarding the strength of the links between the word form representations of a translation pair, nor is it relevant for their argument whether or not such links exist at all.

La Heij and colleagues decomposed the translation process into two main components, one in which the meaning of the presented word is determined ("concept activation") and a second in which the response word is retrieved on the basis of the activated conceptual information ("word retrieval"). If a difference in dominance between L1 and L2 exists, L1 being the stronger language, the relative ease of these two component processes is likely to differ in the two translation directions: In L1 to L2 translation, Step 1, concept activation, is easy because it exploits a frequently trodden memory path (in L1 comprehension). The potentially problematic part of the translation process is Step 2, word retrieval, because it exploits a path that has been taken less often (in L2 production). The situation is reversed in L2 to L1 translation, where concept activation has been practiced less (in L2 comprehension) than has word retrieval (in L1 production). In other words, depending on the direction of translation, either concept activation or word retrieval is the time-consuming and vulnerable translation component. Of course, with balanced bilingualism, equally strong links are likely to exist between L1 and L2 word form representations and conceptual memory, and no direction-dependent asymmetries in the data are expected to occur.

Both La Heij and his colleagues (1996) and De Groot and Poot (1997) argued that their data could be accounted for in terms of this two-step view of the translation process. More recently, Francis and Gallard (2005) showed that their *trilingual* translation data could also be explained this way. These authors had English–Spanish–French participants translate in all six of the translation directions enabled by their trilingualism and showed that differences in comprehension

fluency (concept activation) and production fluency (word retrieval) between the three languages could explain all direction effects observed in this study. The point that all these authors made is that there do not appear to be qualitative differences between translating from the strong native language to a weaker second or third language and translating in the opposite direction. Instead they concluded that all translation is likely to be conceptually mediated. This conclusion, in fact, echoes the one that Potter et al. (1984) advanced in the very first study to test the word association and concept mediation views of bilingual memory that underlie much of the more recent work.

Conclusions

As mentioned, the view advanced above that translating words always involves the access of conceptual representations is consistent with two tenets of the revised hierarchical model, despite the fact that the model holds a crucially different view on word translation. The shared assumptions are that, in comprehension, concept activation is easier for words in a strong language than for words in a weaker language and that, in production, word retrieval is relatively easy in the stronger language. In addition, the translation recognition study by Talamas and colleagues (1999) with which I started this section had provided evidence that during foreign language learning there is a transition from reliance on form to a focus on meaning, a conclusion that tied in nicely with a similar developmental path hypothesized by researchers working in other research areas (pp. 126–128). The fact that learners at lower levels of L2 proficiency rely more on cognate relations between L1 and L2 than do learners at more advanced levels (Kroll et al., 2002) provided additional support for this contention. Apparently, a number of the model's main assumptions go unchallenged.

The model's aspect that obviously does not stand scrutiny is the assumption that backward translation occurs through tracing the link between the form representations of the words in a translation pair (the "word association" connection), bypassing conceptual memory. As a consequence, it also does not seem to be opportune to somehow attribute the relatively strong form reliance in the earliest stage of foreign language learning to the use of such links, as seems to be done. But why not simply regard this early form reliance as a phenomenon of interest in its own right, without trying to see it as evidence for the use of links directly connecting the new foreign word to its L1 translation? Given the fact that early on in the learning process (of late learners) it is the new word's form, not its meaning, that is the unknown element to be acquired, it is obvious that the learner at this stage is especially attentive to form. A corollary of paying an inordinate amount of attention to the unknown form is that meaning analysis is likely to be neglected. This is plausibly the reason why during initial stages of learning the learner is relatively insensitive to word meaning. In other words, it may be because the initial L2 learner has insufficient mental resources to attend to both the new word's form and its meaning that form analysis is privileged.

VOCABULARY ACQUISITION IN CONTEXT

Introduction

The previous sections all dealt with the very initial stages of foreign vocabulary acquisition and with the structure of the emerging memory representations. Second language words learned by means of the paired associate and keyword methods are just new labels assigned to concepts that already existed in memory prior to the learning episode; namely, the concepts associated with the new forms' L1 translations. Similarly, the bilingual memory structures discussed so far all assume that the form of a new L2 word inherits the meaning of its L1 translation. When this stage is successfully completed and, furthermore, the learner has managed to distinguish this specific form, associated with this specific meaning, from similar forms with a different meaning (the

"synforms" discussed earlier; p. 123), there is an awful lot more to do before he or she can enjoy the pleasures associated with the fluent use of a foreign vocabulary. For one thing, the size of the vocabulary (its "breadth") acquired by means of one or more of the direct methods presented so far, is likely to be too small for the learner not to run into the occasional deadlock when getting immersed in natural communication settings, in reading and speech. As pointed out earlier (p. 90), instruction time in the foreign language classroom is simply too limited to train more than just a basic foreign language vocabulary. Furthermore, the newly acquired vocabulary has no depth to speak of yet. As stated earlier, the new words' meanings are those of the corresponding words in the native language. Yet translation "equivalents" seldom share all aspects of their meaning so that adopting the L1 word's meaning as it is inevitably leads to a strong semantic "accent": The meaning aspects specific to the L1 word would be implied when using its L2 equivalent and, conversely, the meaning aspects specific to the L2 member of the translation pair would be missed out altogether. To become a proficient L2 user, the learner's L2 vocabulary has to become independent of the L1 vocabulary (it must become "autonomous") and the learner has to acquire the L2-specific meaning components; we have labeled these two processes "freeing" and "fine tuning" before (De Groot & Van Hell, 2005). Gaining the required level of depth involves the learning of the word's intensional and extensional meanings (Henriksen, 1999), processes that other authors have referred to as "network building" or "word web" formation and "packaging", respectively (Aitchison, 1987). (Recall that an L2 word's intensional meaning concerns the sense relations between this word and other words in the L2 vocabulary, such as its antonyms, synonyms, and hyponyms. Its extensional meaning involves its referential meaning; that is, knowledge concerning the entities or events in the external world to which it refers.)

A further thing to do is to strengthen the links between the words within the word web so that upon accessing one of them, those that it is connected with rapidly become available. Similarly, the lexical access process must speed up so that ultimately it can come about rapidly, effortlessly, and automatically. The moment this state is reached, the spared mental resources can be dedicated to the components of comprehension or production that will always be slow and effortful, that cannot be automated. One source of evidence that these developments take place comes from a number of studies that employed the semantic priming methodology (see pp. 92–93 and 138–140). For instance, Frenck-Mestre and Prince (1997) found that the within-L2 priming patterns that emerged for proficient non-native speakers were highly similar to those of native speakers, showing priming for various types of lexical relations. In a group of intermediate non-native speakers smaller priming effects were observed, suggesting weaker links between associated words in their L2 lexicon. A further experiment demonstrated that in the native and proficient non-native speakers both meanings of a lexically ambiguous prime word were activated, whereas in the intermediate non-native speakers only the dominant meaning was activated.

Similarly, Favreau and Segalowitz (1983) found that bilinguals who read in their L1 and L2 equally quickly (suggesting balanced bilingualism) exhibited the same pattern of semantic priming effects in both languages. The details of the observed patterns suggested that processing was highly automated in both languages. In contrast, bilinguals who read more slowly in their L2 than in their L1 (suggesting unbalanced bilingualism) showed different patterns of priming in their two languages, with the pattern emerging for the L2 suggesting a lower level of automaticity. As argued by Segalowitz and Segalowitz (1993) and Segalowitz, Segalowitz, and Wood (1998), developing automaticity of processing is not merely a matter of speeding up the various subcomponents of a task, in their case reading. Instead the development involves qualitative changes such as the elimination of slow task components that require conscious control.

So all of this additional learning and restructuring, as well as gaining fluency in exploiting the acquired knowledge, still has to take place after the foreign language learner has acquired a basic vocabulary in the classroom (or outside of it) through direct vocabulary-focused activities. It has therefore been concluded that most vocabulary is learned from context, especially from extensive reading in the target language (e.g., Krashen, 1989, 1993). How else can it be that foreign language learners, upon entering the university, already possess a receptive vocabulary of about 11,000 words (as assessed by Hazenberg & Hulstijn, 1996)? This same view has been advanced regarding vocabulary acquisition in L1. Educated native speakers of L1 may ultimately master, according to conservative estimates, between about 20,000 and 30,000 lexical items (Goulden, Nation, & Read, 1990; Nation, 1990), and even estimates of 100,000 lexical items occur (Sternberg, 1987). These numbers cannot possibly be covered with direct vocabulary instruction (including the "instruction" provided by parents, other caregivers, and peers).

This view of massive vocabulary acquisition through immersion, especially through reading, is often thought to imply the idea that vocabulary acquisition comes about incidentally, without the reader deliberately trying to commit individual words to memory. The idea is that even though a reader might read merely for recreation, specific word knowledge is acquired as a byproduct. Furthermore, some authors seem to assume these views imply that the learning of specific vocabulary in context is more effective than through direct methods that focus explicitly on vocabulary. This inference may however be unwarranted, as is suggested by the following quote (Sternberg, 1987, p. 89; italics added):

> Most vocabulary is learned from context [. . .]. What the claim does imply is that teaching people to learn better from context can be a highly effective way of enhancing vocabulary development. What the claim *does not imply* is that teaching *specific* vocabulary using context is the most effective, or even a relatively effective, way of teaching that vocabulary. Unfortunately, many believers in learning from context, as well as their detractors, have drawn the

second interference rather than the first. As a result, they are on the verge of throwing out a perfectly clean and healthy baby with its, admittedly, less than sparkling bath water.

In the next section I will discuss a number of studies that together have compared the efficacy of foreign vocabulary learning through reading texts with the efficacy of more direct vocabulary-learning methods and that cover both intentional and incidental learning instructions. To anticipate, their joint results indicate that intentional learning is more effective than incidental vocabulary learning and that, as already suggested by Sternberg, specific vocabulary is more effectively learned by means of direct methods than through reading texts. Still, the latter has an important role to play.

Evidence

Several studies suggest that reading texts simply for pleasure is not a very efficient way to learn *specific* foreign vocabulary. Hulstijn et al. (1996) had advanced learners of French read a French story consisting of 1306 words. The participants were told in advance they would have to answer comprehension questions after reading the story. This was done to promote incidental (and discourage intentional) vocabulary learning: "Students' attention was turned away from *particular unknown words* and directed towards an understanding of the *text as a whole*" (Hulstijn et al., 1996, p. 331, the authors' italics). The text contained eight target words unknown to the participants, printed in bold face. It was the learning of this specific vocabulary the researchers set out to test, in three conditions: In a control condition the participants were instructed to read the text and prepare to answer comprehension questions. In a "marginal glosses" condition, the L1 (Dutch) translations of the targeted unfamiliar words were given in the text's margin. Finally, in a "dictionary" condition the participants were free to use a dictionary whenever they felt like it. Two versions of the story were presented, to different participant groups. They differed from one another in the number of times the target words

were presented: just once or three times. Note that the control condition imitates a real-life incidental-learning situation most faithfully (although the bold face in which the target words were printed is rather unnatural, explicitly directing participants' attention to the target words and plausibly giving rise to intentional learning contrary to the authors' purpose).

Retention was tested in several ways, including a receptive test in which the participants were shown the target words among a set of words that had not appeared in the story, and had to indicate for each of these words whether it had appeared in the text and if so, what its meaning was (by writing down its Dutch translation equivalent). The left-hand part of Figure 3.12 shows the results of this test following the story version that included the critical words three times. The right-hand part shows the analogous results of a second test. In this test the target words were not presented in isolation but as part of a text fragment consisting of a few lines of the original text. In both cases the maximum score per condition would have been eight.

As shown, the condition that copied incidental learning under natural circumstances most faithfully (the control condition) produced rather poor results. In the out-of-context test condition, even after three occurrences of each of the critical words (printed in bold face) the meaning of less than one could be provided on average. Surprisingly, when context was added as an additional retrieval cue at test, performance remained low at slightly over one correct. The participants in the dictionary condition fared only slightly better, a finding the authors explained in terms of their observation that the participants had consulted the dictionary only occasionally (basically behaving as the participants in the control condition). The provision of glosses improved performance noticeably.

All in all, these data suggest that incidental learning in context does lead to some learning of words repeatedly presented in the text, but the learning outcome can by no means be called impressive. However, a related study by Rott (1999) showed that increasing the presentation frequency of the target vocabulary to six

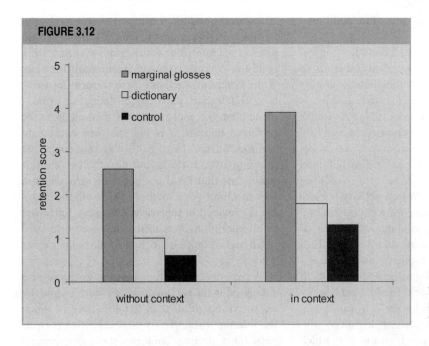

FIGURE 3.12

Retention scores as a function of reading condition and testing method. Data from Hulstijn et al. (1996).

presentations per word improved the learning scores considerably (to about 8 and 5 out of 12 in receptive and productive testing, respectively), although much of this gain was lost again 4 weeks after training. The results of Hulstijn and his colleagues furthermore suggest that a combination of reading and techniques that draw the learners' attention to specific vocabulary is more effective than mere reading.

A Hebrew–English/Arabic–English study by Laufer (2003b) strengthens the conclusion that just reading a text is a relatively ineffective way to learn specific vocabulary. In three experiments she compared recall in reading conditions similar to those of Hulstijn et al. (1996) with recall following one of three word-focused tasks that did not involve text reading. In the reading condition of each experiment, Hebrew or Arabic learners of English read an English short story containing 10 target words. The stories were either glossed in Hebrew (the two Hebrew–English studies), or bilingual dictionaries could be consulted during reading (the one Arabic–English study). The participants in both these reading conditions were led to believe that they would be tested for comprehension afterwards. It is likely that under these circumstances the

participants would focus their attention on the meaning of the text as a whole, not on individual words. The text contained 10 target words that, following the reading phase, were unexpectedly tested for recall in a cued recall task.

In the word-focused conditions the same 10 English words served as targets. In one of these conditions the participants were told the meanings of the words and were asked to create a sentence around each of them. In the second they were presented with the words and their meanings and asked to write a composition incorporating all 10 of them. In the third the researcher presented the participants with incomplete sentences and asked them to complete these partial sentences with the target words after looking up their meaning. Importantly, no reading context was provided in any of these three conditions and the participants' attention would thus be focused on the meanings of the target words. The results were straightforward: In all three experiments recall performance was considerably better following a word-focused task than following text reading. However, the reading condition also led to some learning, suggesting (as did the study by Hulstijn and his colleagues) that incidental learning through reading *does* occur (see Rott,

1999, for a review of studies providing additional evidence).

The combined results of these studies suggest that merely reading for comprehension leads to some growth in vocabulary, but that combining reading with a vocabulary-focused activity is more effective (Hulstijn et al., 1996). A similar finding but with the texts presented in auditory form in a multimedia environment was more recently obtained by Jones (2004). Furthermore, Laufer's study suggests that even *replacing* reading by a vocabulary-focused activity is more effective than merely reading for comprehension.

According to a definition of incidental vocabulary learning as involving all situations in which the participants are not explicitly asked to commit vocabulary to memory, all conditions in both Hulstijn and collaborators' study and in the Laufer study (including Laufer's word-focused activities) concerned incidental learning conditions. In a Dutch–French study, in which isolated sentences instead of complete texts served as context for the target vocabulary, Mondria (2003) posed the question of what the contribution of an intentional learning instruction to learning words in context might be. A further goal was to find out whether a "meaning-given" method might be equally effective as a "meaning-inferred" method.

In a meaning-given condition the learners were simply provided with the meanings of a set of unknown French words in the form of their Dutch translations and were instructed to memorize them. In one of three meaning-inferred conditions the learners first had to infer the words' meaning from context, to subsequently verify whether the inferred meaning was the targeted meaning, and, finally, to commit the correctly inferred meaning to memory. In the remaining two meaning-inferred conditions one or two steps from this procedure were skipped: In the "inferring" condition the participants were simply asked to infer the meaning of the target word from context. In the "inferring + verifying" condition they inferred the meaning and then checked whether their inference had been correct. The inferring and inferring + verifying conditions both concerned incidental learning because in

these conditions the participants were not asked to memorize the words. In contrast, the meaning-given and inferring + verifying + memorizing conditions both involved intentional learning. If the latter two methods were to turn out to be equally effective, it would be tempting to conclude that the meaning-given method is to be preferred because it is the less time-consuming method of the two. Note that not only the meaning-given method, but also the two context conditions that involve a verifying step are, in a way, meaning-given methods. After all, the meaning is provided in the verification step. Retention in all conditions was tested in a receptive cued recall task. Figure 3.13 shows the results of this study.

A first thing to note is that the instruction to simply infer the targeted French word's meaning led to poorer recall than the condition in which the inferred vocabulary was checked for correctness. This finding confirms the more general observation that language learners often make the wrong guesses on the basis of context (see Frantzen, 2003, and Huckin & Coady, 1999, for an overview of factors that determine guessing accuracy). The instruction to memorize the inferred and verified word improved performance substantially, suggesting a large effect of an intentional learning set on contextual learning. But most strikingly, the simple meaning-given method produced equally good results as the much more complex inferring + verifying + memorizing method. Accordingly, after establishing that, as expected, the former method indeed took relatively little time to apply, the author concluded the meaning-given method to be the preferred method. A further conclusion was that an explicit instruction to memorize target vocabulary boosts word learning in context dramatically.

Evaluation and conclusions

The studies discussed above focused on the learning of a *specific* set of words and all of them showed that incidental learning from context in its purest form (no glossing; no dictionary look-up) led to disappointingly low learning scores. There is, however, a further gain of incidental

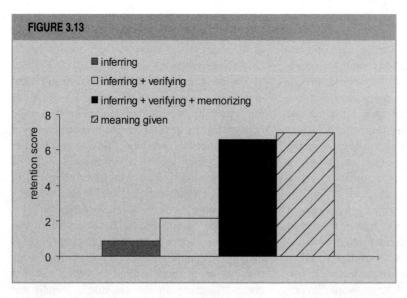

FIGURE 3.13

- ■ inferring
- □ inferring + verifying
- ■ inferring + verifying + memorizing
- ▨ meaning given

retention score

Retention scores as a function of learning condition. Data from Mondria (2003).

vocabulary learning through reading that is ignored in many of the pertinent studies, including those discussed above: If at least some learning of the vocabulary selected for testing has taken place, it is likely that some learning has also occurred for all the other words in the text. Imagine the situation where a reader reads a 500-word text that includes 10 unknown target words, each occurring once, and is subsequently tested on these 10 words in a receptive cued recall test. If the meaning of one of them can successfully be delivered during testing (e.g., in the form of its L1 translation), on average 1 out of every 10 of the remaining previously unknown (non-target) words in the text may be expected to also have been recalled successfully had they actually been tested. Furthermore, it is plausible that some learning of the selected 10 target words that were *not* successfully recalled at test has nevertheless occurred in the form of, for instance, some aspect of the word's form or a hunch of its meaning and perhaps some strengthening of the connection between form and meaning. However, the accrual that has taken place might have been too small to be detected in the cued recall test format. Similarly, all remaining unknown words in the text, those not selected for testing, may have left some trace of new knowledge in memory. This process of gradual acquisition was called "incremental" learning before.

In addition to the increments in knowledge regarding the previously unknown words, the memory representations of all previously *known* words may have undergone some change as a result of reading the text: They may have become more strongly established in memory so that on subsequent encounters they can be retrieved more quickly. They may also have become enriched with some new content; for instance, a previously unknown aspect of meaning or some new information on the linguistic environment in which the word can occur. In other words, some learning may have occurred for all of the words in the 500-word text, at least for all of those attended to (see, e.g., Huckin & Coady, 1999, for a discussion of the role of attention to individual words in learning vocabulary).

To summarize, many studies that have tried to establish the efficacy of vocabulary acquisition through reading seem to have ignored the fact that vocabulary acquisition proceeds incrementally, piecemeal, rather than instantaneously and completely from a single exposure (see also Bogaards, 2001, for an experiment that substantiates this claim). Furthermore, these studies have ignored the fact that not all tests are sufficiently sensitive to detect small gains in knowledge. As a consequence, the amount of vocabulary knowledge foreign language learners pick up from mere reading has arguably been highly underestimated.

However, this qualification of the efficacy of reading text to enhance foreign vocabulary knowledge should not be taken as a plea for the dismissal of the direct methods, such as paired-associate learning, the keyword method, or any other vocabulary-focused activity such as those discussed above. Even Sternberg, the fervent advocate of the view that most vocabulary is learned from context I quoted at the beginning of this section, acknowledges their crucial role in foreign language vocabulary acquisition. In so doing he stressed that direct methods exploit the fact that foreign language learners who are fluent in their native language already master the (larger part of the) *meanings* of many foreign words to be acquired (namely those of all words they know in their native language). When the learner is provided with an unknown foreign word directly paired with its L1 translation (as is done in paired-associate learning and the keyword method), the meaning of the former will become available instantaneously through its translation. This enables the learner to focus attention on the unknown parts of the foreign words to be learned: their forms and the knowledge of what meaning goes with each of them (that is, the link between form and meaning). Instead, during vocabulary learning from texts the learners must figure out the meanings of the unknown forms themselves, a process that detracts attention from learning the forms and that presumably takes a number of encounters with each unknown form, spread out across a number of texts and over an extended period of time. Obviously, this meaning-gathering process cannot be skipped because for a word to serve its referential function its form and meaning must be joined. And all the while this laborious meaning discovery process is taking place, the relevant meaning is just sitting there in memory! Hence Sternberg's conclusion: "If one has definitions available, then learning from context is not so efficient. Why waste a good definition?" (Sternberg, 1987, p. 95). Needless to say, the use of direct methods does not work for vocabulary not known in the L1. For adult native speakers this may hold for foreign concepts that are not lexicalized in L1 and for words that exist in L1 but are very infrequent. For child learners it

will be more common—the more common the younger the child. In these cases the provision of contextual information will obviously be conducive to learning.

But of course, even when the targeted meanings *are* known in advance, in many situations this knowledge cannot be exploited for the simple reason that the learner does not usually carry a bilingual dictionary around, nor is there a teacher around to help make the connection with the stored knowledge. This truism, combined with the fact that in the foreign language classroom the time available for direct vocabulary acquisition is limited, led Sternberg (1987) to his claim that most vocabulary is learned from context, through reading. A final point stressed by Sternberg—one that has often been ignored by others—is that context learning in the classroom should not equal having the students read texts extensively in class, but to teach them appropriate methods of how learners can learn most from context themselves; that is, to teach vocabulary-building skills.

To conclude, the little time available for vocabulary teaching in the foreign language classroom can best be spent on a combination of direct teaching of a base vocabulary that covers as large a percentage as possible of the words to be encountered in naturally occurring foreign language texts and discourse, augmented by the teaching of effective skills of how to build vocabulary from context. As mentioned in the introduction to this chapter, a basic vocabulary of the 3000 most frequent word families, covering about 5000 lexical items, suffices for a learner to comprehend the essence of many foreign texts because it covers about 95% of the texts' words (Laufer, 1992; Nation, 1993). When learners have reached this state and are furthermore equipped with a set of effective vocabulary-building skills, they can venture out successfully on their own on their path to advanced bilingual literacy.

Finally, what has been ignored fully in this section is how vocabulary is acquired from immersion in foreign language *speech*. Unlike in printed text, words are not contained as neat, discrete packages of information in the speech signal: Speech breaks often fall within words and are often lacking between words. Yet isolating the words' forms from the speech signal is a pre-requisite for aural vocabulary acquisition. In addition, unlike printed text the speech signal is transient and spoken words therefore cannot be lingered on to figure out what they might mean (except when they are rehearsed internally, but this happens at the cost of inattention to further input). Because of these facts, vocabulary learning from a speech context may be more effortful than from written text. But fortunately, though lacking reliable physical boundaries between words, the speech signal contains other cues to word boundaries; namely statistical information about the transitional probability of syllables and speech segments and prosodic cues such as the

words' stress patterns. Both infants (Saffran, 2001; Saffran et al., 1996a) and adults (Saffran, Newport, & Aslin, 1996b; Schön et al., 2008) use these sources of information successfully in isolating words from continuous speech. Possibly even, the prosodic information contained in speech but absent in print compensates for the lack of physical boundaries in speech, especially when prosody correlates with syllabic cues to segmentation (Schön et al.). In all then, the above conclusions regarding the best mix of direct vocabulary teaching and context learning (adapted to the aural modality, for instance by a focus on the aural forms of the words to teach directly) might also apply to the listener's perspective.

SUMMARY

- Learners reach a sufficient level of comprehension in a foreign language when their vocabulary covers 95% of the words in a text or discourse. A basic vocabulary of the 3000 most frequent word families, equaling 5000 lexical items, suffices to reach this state.
- Because instruction time in the foreign language classroom is too limited to teach more than a basic vocabulary through direct means, most vocabulary must be learned from context. Yet to acquire *specific* vocabulary, direct word-focused methods are more effective than context learning.
- Despite being a rather complex procedure for learning foreign vocabulary, the keyword method is effective across many different types of learners, languages, and learning environments. The method is also applicable to other learning materials than foreign vocabulary.
- The keyword method appears more effective with receptive testing of foreign vocabulary than with productive testing and it appears more effective for inexperienced foreign language learners than for experienced learners.
- After only a few learning trials per item the vocabulary learned by means of the keyword method is more prone to forgetting than the vocabulary learned by means of other methods (rote rehearsal; context learning). With more practice the various methods result in equal amounts of forgetting.
- Keywords provided by the experimenter or by the learners' peers seem more effective than self-generated keywords and pictorial support increases the efficacy of the keyword, especially in young learners. These findings limit the keyword method's efficacy outside the classroom and laboratory.
- Unlike the common imagery version of the keyword method, its verbiage version is arguably as suitable for experienced foreign language learners as are rote rehearsal and uninstructed learning.
- Foreign language learning gets easier the more experienced the learner is in learning foreign languages. The likely reason is that the learner exploits knowledge already stored in long-term memory.
- Word–word paired-associate learning is applicable to all types of words: concrete as well as abstract, cognates as well as non-cognates. The keyword method is unsuitable for learning abstract foreign words and for learning words that share a cognate relation with their L1 equivalent.

- Background music seems to affect foreign vocabulary learning in complicated ways, sometimes boosting learning and at other times impeding it, depending on the type of background music (e.g., vocal or instrumental) and learner characteristics (e.g., their level of baseline brain arousal).
- Foreign language equivalents of concrete L1 words are learned faster and remembered better than the foreign names of abstract words. Some evidence exists that learning the foreign names of words that occur frequently in L1 is easier than learning the foreign names of infrequent L1 words. The likely cause of the concreteness effect is that the representations of concrete L1 words in memory contain more information than those of abstract L1 words. Consequently it is relatively easy to attach the new foreign names to the representations of concrete L1 words. Arguably the effect of word frequency can be accounted for in a similar way.
- Foreign language words with typical phonotactical forms are acquired faster and retained better than foreign words with atypical forms. The cause of this effect is that learning the sounds of new words involves the operation of phonological short-term memory (the "phonological loop") and the exploitation of phonological information in long-term memory. The phonological loop operates smoothly on typical forms but is impeded when atypical forms are presented for learning. In addition, only typical sound forms can benefit from relevant phonological information in long-term memory.
- Foreign language words that share a cognate relation with the corresponding L1 words are easier to learn and are retained better than non-cognates. A reason is that the presentation of a word automatically activates similarly formed words in long-term memory, thus facilitating recall. An infelicitous effect of this process is that a word that shares form but not meaning with the input word can be mistaken for the latter's translation.
- Receptive cued recall leads to larger recall scores than productive cued recall. Reasons may be that the, previously known, L1 words are more available than the newly learned L2 words, that comprehension is easier than production, and/or that the L1 words are embedded in a large network of lexical connections whereas the new L2 word is only connected to its L1 translation.
- Encoding strategies during both first and second language learning shift from a predominant focus on the form aspects of the learning materials to a predominant focus on the meaning aspects. First and second language learning thus seem to involve a similar developmental route.
- The compound, coordinate, and subordinative models of bilingual memory organization differ from one another along two dimensions: the number of underlying conceptual systems that the bilingual possesses (one: compound and subordinative; two: coordinate) and, in the case of a single conceptual system, the way in which this system is accessed when an L2 word is input: directly (compound), or indirectly, via the corresponding L1 word (subordinative).
- It was once thought that compound, coordinate, and subordinative bilingualism result from different acquisition contexts and that any individual bilingual had memory representations of only one of these types. The evidence for these assumptions is weak and each bilingual may have memory structures of different types.
- The vast majority of translation "equivalent" word pairs consist of words that have language-specific meaning nuances and senses in addition to their shared meaning components. Also, word meaning changes over time and differs between individuals. These facts are better accounted for in terms of distributed models of bilingual memory than in terms of localist models.
- The revised hierarchical model assumes two direct links, of different strengths, between the two word form representations of a pair of translations, one from the L1 word to the L2 word and one in the reverse direction. In addition, it assumes a single conceptual representation shared by a pair of translations. This shared representation is connected with the L1 form representation by means of a strong link and with the L2 form representation along a weaker link.

- The revised hierarchical model was developed (1) to account for a gradual change from primary reliance on form to primary reliance on meaning with increasing L2 proficiency and (2) to explain differential amounts of meaning activation during processing L1 and L2.
- The revised hierarchical model assumes qualitatively different processes for translating words from L1 to L2 and from L2 to L1. A simpler view is that word translation always involves meaning access ("concept activation"), in addition to a second processing component, word retrieval, and that differential results obtained with L1-to-L2 and L2-to-L1 translation are due to differences in the relative ease with which these two processing components can be executed in each of these translation conditions.
- To reach a high level of proficiency in an L2 the learners' L2 vocabulary must become independent of their L1 vocabulary: L2-specific meaning nuances must be learned, L1-specific nuances must be lost, and knowledge regarding each L2 word's relations with other words in the L2 lexicon must be established. In addition, the access and retrieval of L2 lexical representations must be automated. These goals can never be met by classroom instruction alone but require extensive subsequent reading and/or oral communication in naturalistic L2 environments.
- An explicit instruction to memorize target vocabulary embedded in a larger linguistic context leads to the learning of far more foreign vocabulary than when no such instruction is given, but it is not more effective than simply presenting the foreign words to learn with their native language glosses with the instruction to memorize them. In general, contextual learning by reading texts is a less-effective way to learn *specific* vocabulary than out-of-context activities that focus explicitly on this vocabulary.
- The sparse time available for vocabulary teaching in the foreign language classroom can best be spent on a mix of direct teaching of a base vocabulary that covers as large a percentage as possible of the words to be encountered in naturally occurring foreign language texts and discourse, augmented by the teaching of effective skills for building vocabulary from context.

Comprehension Processes: Word Recognition and Sentence Processing

INTRODUCTION AND PREVIEW

Whereas Chapter 3 dealt with the acquisition of vocabulary, the major part of this chapter discusses how words, once learned, are recognized. When we hear or see a word, how does it make contact with its representation in the mental lexicon that contains the information which enables us to understand what it means? As mentioned before, word recognition is beyond doubt the most important constituent process of language comprehension and, therefore, to understand how language users can make sense of print and speech requires a detailed understanding of how word recognition comes about. One of the puzzles to solve is how it can be that it only takes fluent language users a quarter of a second or so to recognize a word despite the fact that they, even when they only master one language, have stored tens of thousands of words in their mental lexicon. A second mental process that plays an important role in language com-

prehension is **parsing**, the process of unraveling the grammatical structure of a sentence. Together with word recognition it enables the listener or reader to figure out the literal meaning of sentences. Parsing is dealt with in the final part of this chapter.

The term "word recognition" is used in both a narrow and a broad sense. When used in the narrow sense it refers to the moment a match occurs between a printed word and one (and just one) of the orthographic word-forms stored in the lexicon or between a spoken word and a single phonological word-form. Only after this match has taken place does all the information stored with this form, including the syntactical and morphological specifications of the word and, most importantly, its meaning, become available for further processing. The second stage in this two-step view of word processing is often called **"lexical access"**. Used in a broader sense the term word recognition includes both these processing steps, thus covering all mental activity from the perception of the word until all the knowledge stored with its lexical representation is available. To complicate matters further, the term "lexical access" is also used to refer to this complete process. In the ensuing discussion I will use the terms word recognition and lexical access interchangeably, referring to the complete process in both cases. In the next chapter, on speech production, in agreement with common practice I will use the term "lexical access" to refer to all the processing that occurs between the intention to produce a word (the "conceptualization" of a word) and the moment its lexical element is selected for production.

The present chapter and Chapter 5 are companion chapters that largely deal with one specific question regarding lexical access in bilinguals, addressing it from the perspective of word recognition (this chapter) or word production (Chapter 5). This chapter addresses the question of whether a spoken or written word encountered by a bilingual causes activation in both of the linguistic subsystems stored in bilingual memory or whether activation is restricted to the contextually appropriate subsystem, the one that contains the representation of the input word. Co-activation of information in the other subsystem is known as **language-nonselective lexical access**. Exclusive activation of information in the contextually appropriate system is known as **language-selective lexical access**. The analogous question regarding word production is whether or not during the process of generating a word output, from the moment its content is conceptualized to actually articulating it, co-activation occurs in the contextually inappropriate linguistic subsystem. If word production were to turn out to be language-nonselective, a next question presents itself: How then do bilinguals manage to separate their languages in production; that is, to produce relatively pure, monolingual, output whenever they intend to do so? This latter question will be touched upon here and there in Chapters 4 and 5 but will be more thoroughly covered in Chapter 6.

A sizable number of studies suggest that the presentation of a word to a bilingual often gives rise to parallel activation in both linguistic subsystems. In reviewing these studies either one of

two organizations could be chosen. One is to organize them around the types of *memory units* that are thought to be activated simultaneously in both subsystems upon the presentation of a word—for instance, units that represent phonology or units that store meaning. Another way is to organize the discussion around the types of *stimuli* that researchers have used to tackle the present question—for instance, cognates, or **interlexical homographs**. From a theoretical point of view the former approach is the most attractive, because it is the pattern of activation in the bilingual's memory system that these studies attempt to discover. Unfortunately, in cases where the data clearly suggest parallel activation in both subsystems, the identity of the co-activated linguistic units in the contextually inappropriate subsystem (henceforth also referred to as the non-target language) is not always clear. To illustrate, under many circumstances it takes bilinguals longer to recognize interlexical homographs (words that are ambiguous across languages, e.g., *coin*, meaning "corner" in French) than to recognize matched non-ambiguous control words. Because the only difference between the homographs and their controls is that only the former have two different meanings, it is tempting to conclude that the homograph effect indexes co-activation of the homograph's meaning in the other language. Yet, as we shall see, the effect has (among others) been explained in terms of a model of bilingual memory that does not even represent meaning. So either the assumption the effect is caused by co-activated meaning is wrong or the model is flawed. Because of this interpretative indeterminacy I have chosen a mixed organization of the experimental evidence, opting for the theoretically more interesting "memory-units" organization where it seems safe to do so (pp. 183–197 and adopting the theoretically more neutral "type-of-stimulus" organization in other sections (pp. 165–176 and 199–203).

All but the final section of this chapter deals with word recognition in bilinguals, visual word recognition as well as spoken word recognition, the stimulus words presented in word lists (often intermingled with meaningless strings of letters) and as part of complete sentences. The chapter concludes with a discussion of grammatical processing in bilinguals and specifically addresses the question of how bilinguals parse sentences in their two languages.

METHODS AND TASKS

Word recognition

The vast majority of studies on bilingual word recognition have used the lexical decision and word naming tasks, reflecting the immense popularity of these two tasks in monolingual studies on word processing. In the word naming task the participants simply read printed words aloud and response latencies and/or reading accuracy are registered. In (visual) lexical decision tasks the participants are presented with written letter sequences and have to decide for each of them whether it is a word or not. If it is, they must press a "yes" button; if it is not, they press a "no" button (occasionally an oral response is asked for). Again, response times and/or accuracy are registered. The nonword stimuli (those that invite a "no" response) are usually pseudowords; that is, letter strings that obey the orthography (and phonology) of the test language and that only differ from words in that they lack meaning. Using well-formed letter strings as nonwords is important because it increases the chance that the lexical decision response will be based on the outcome of the process of interest, lexical access, and not on the basis of a more shallow perceptual process that assesses whether the stimulus looks normal. The latter would be feasible for nonwords that violate the target language's orthography and phonology. Rubinstein, Lewis, and Rubinstein (1971) were the first to demonstrate such a "nonword legality" effect in the very same study that introduced the lexical decision task as a new research tool in the study of word recognition. Although the presence of nonwords is demanded by the task and it is imperative that they are constructed carefully, in most lexical decision studies they merely serve as fillers and the responses they invite are ignored in the analyses. But there is also

the occasional experiment in which nonwords are the focus of the researcher's attention or at least share this prominent role with words. A clear drawback of the lexical decision task—one that does not apply to word naming—is that it is rather unnatural because language users do not usually go about deciding whether the letter sequences they encounter in print are words or not.

An additional problem with both tasks is that neither of them provides a pure measure of lexical access. Lexical decision is essentially a discrimination task in which words and nonwords have to be distinguished from one another. The discrimination process is influenced by the extant experimental circumstances, the composition of the stimulus set, and specific characteristics of the stimuli. The response criteria set by the participants are not fixed but vary with these variables so that under different sets of circumstances different sources of lexical and non-lexical information (such as orthographic, phonologic, and semantic memory codes and the familiarity of the presented letter patterns) are exploited during response generation. A "word" decision may not even require complete word identification in all cases, even not when all nonwords are pseudowords, because a mere feeling of familiarity or of meaningfulness may suffice to tell actual words from nonwords (e.g., Balota & Chumbley, 1984; Grainger & Jacobs, 1996). Furthermore, the moment sufficient information has been assembled to conclude the stimulus is or is not a word, this assessment has to be translated into the correct response, "yes" or "no", and this response has to be executed. It is well known that the duration of this "post-lexical" response stage is not fixed but responds to the prevailing circumstances. In conclusion, whenever a particular effect is obtained in lexical decision, it is not always obvious that it is a marker of actual word recognition.

The word naming task has its own shortcomings. A clear disadvantage of this task is that in languages written in an alphabetic (or syllabic) script, and especially in alphabetic languages with regular grapheme–phoneme relations, responses can be assembled by merely applying the script-to-sound conversion rules, thus bypassing actual recognition (in the same way as pseudo-words can be read aloud despite the fact that they have no representation in the mental lexicon). There is evidence to suggest that this indeed sometimes happens: An important signature of lexical access is the occurrence of a frequency effect, the shorter response time that is generally obtained for frequent than for infrequent words. These frequency effects are often considerably smaller in naming than in lexical decision, and smaller in naming words in a language with a relatively regular orthography than in naming words in an irregular orthography (De Groot et al., 2002).

A second drawback of the naming task relates to the fact that performance in this task not only requires recognizing the word but also pronouncing it. As a consequence, any effect to be obtained may have its locus not in the recognition stage but in the production stage of the task; that is, at some point in time between recognition and the onset of vocalization. In an ingenious experiment Balota and Chumbley (1985) demonstrated that this is not an imaginary danger. They compared performance in a standard naming task (where the participants read aloud the words as quickly as possible from the moment they appear on the screen) with performance in a delayed naming task. In the latter task the words are not to be read aloud immediately upon their presentation, but only when a particular signal (in this particular study a pair of brackets surrounding each word) is presented. Interestingly, a frequency effect materialized despite the fact that the participants clearly had sufficient time to recognize the words, also the infrequent ones, before the response signal appeared. This finding led the authors to conclude that word frequency also affects the output stage of word naming. Frequency effects in delayed naming have since been obtained more often, including once in a study examining word naming in L2 English (De Groot et al., 2002). The conclusion to be drawn from this is that, as in the lexical-decision task, the locus of an effect in the naming task may be uncertain.

In conclusion, the two tasks that researchers use most often to examine lexical access both tap task-specific processes that have little to do with word recognition per se and that may conceal the task independent word recognition processes of interest. Grainger and Jacobs (1996) have visualized this state of the art with the Venn diagram presented in Figure 4.1.

The process of interest, word recognition, concerns the area where the circles representing lexical decision and naming overlap. Grainger and Jacobs call this the "functional overlap" between these two tasks. In addition to word naming and lexical decision, Figure 4.1 refers to a third category of tasks popular in studies on lexical access: **perceptual identification**. This is a class of tasks in which the stimulus word to be identified is presented in what is called a "data-limited" way, or "masked" or "degraded": It is presented too briefly or too vaguely to be clearly seen and the participants are asked to figure out what the stimulus might be. For instance, the word stimulus might be presented for, say, 40 milliseconds and preceded and followed by a pattern mask (called a "forward" and "backward" mask, respectively) consisting of a sequence of hash marks that impede a clear

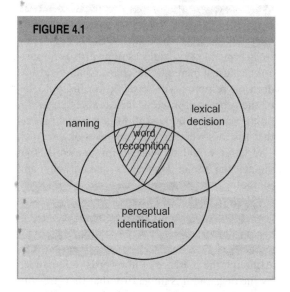

FIGURE 4.1

Venn diagram illustrating the concept of functional overlap. From Grainger and Jacobs (1996). Copyright © 1996 American Psychological Society.

view of the target stimulus. Certain word characteristics, such as word frequency, may then be manipulated and the researcher tries to find out which words are relatively easy to identify under these data-limited circumstances and which ones are hard to recognize. A related technique is to start out presenting the stimulus very briefly at the onset of experimentation and to subsequently increase the presentation duration incrementally up until the moment the participant can identify it.

In most of the bilingual studies to be discussed in the sections to follow the researchers had their participants perform one (version of one) of these three tasks, sometimes in combination with the **word priming technique** introduced before (pp. 92–93): A word target is preceded by an earlier stimulus, the prime, and the effect of the earlier prime on accessing the target's lexical representation is assessed. Across these priming studies, primes and targets can both be clearly visible, the targets may be clearly visible but the primes masked, or both primes and targets may be masked. Also, a **cross-modal priming** technique has been employed, in which the prime is presented aurally and the target visually.

Two versions of the lexical decision task have been developed specifically to study bilingual word recognition. These are **generalized lexical decision** (also called **language-neutral lexical decision**) and **language-specific lexical decision**. In generalized lexical decision a "yes" response is required if the presented letter sequence is a word in either of the participant's two languages; if not, a "no" response must be given. In language-specific lexical decision a "yes" response must only be given to letter strings that are words in the language specified by the experimenter prior to the onset of the experiment. Whenever a word in the other language is presented, a "no" response must be given, just as to real nonwords.

One version of the perceptual identification methodology applied in bilingual studies is **progressive demasking**, a task first used in a monolingual study by Grainger and Segui (1990). In this task the visual presentation of a target word alternates with that of a mask. During this alternation process, the presentation durations of target and mask gradually increase and decrease, respectively. The participant presses a button the moment target identification occurs and subsequently reveals the word's identity. In a second type of perceptual identification study the targets are presented for a fixed duration but too short to be easily identified. Because perceptual thresholds vary between individuals, these experiments often involve a preliminary session in which the presentation duration for that particular participant is determined. A perceptual identification technique used in the study of bilingual speech recognition is **gating**. In gating, increasingly larger fragments of spoken words ("gates") are presented to the participants, who are asked to guess the words from which the fragments are derived. For instance, they first hear the first 40 ms of English *pick*, then the first 80 ms, and so on, until the fragment is correctly recognized as the word *pick*. The task may thus be regarded an auditory variant of the progressive demasking task. The primary dependent variable is the "isolation point", the gate duration at which the target word is first guessed correctly and beyond which, at later gates, participants hold on to this identification. Other measures are how confident the participants are about the correctness of their guess, whether they might already have an idea about the language of the fragment before the corresponding word can actually be identified, and what the set of incorrect guesses prior to identification looks like.

In addition to the above three main categories of tasks, other tasks have been used but only occasionally. As lexical decision, a number of them are binary classification tasks in which on each trial one of two possible responses is required. But instead of categorizing letter strings as words or nonwords, a categorization on some other stimulus feature is required. The details of these tasks will be given along the way. For now it suffices to say that in evaluating the results obtained with these tasks the researcher should always be aware of the possibility that a particular effect might have its locus not in the process of interest but in the stage in which the outcome of the relevant process is translated into one of the two possible responses (the "post-lexical" stage referred to earlier). A similar warning is in order regarding a class of tasks, the so-called **go/no-go tasks**, that impel the participants to translate the outcome of the cognitive process of interest in an overt response on some trials ("go") but to withhold a response on other trials ("no-go"). An example is the **language go/no-go task**, in which bilingual participants have to produce an overt response whenever a stimulus is a word in their one language but to refrain from responding when it is a word in their other language.

Yet other studies infer the nature of cognitive processing involved during task performance from the participants' eye movements. **Eye-movement recording** is most often employed in reading studies, both monolingual and bilingual, in which participants read complete sentences or text, but the technique has also been exploited in studies on spoken word recognition: On each trial in a common application of the **eye-movement tracking paradigm** the participant hears the name of an object and has to identify the corresponding object among a larger set of objects on a visual display. The details of the pertinent studies and their rationale will be explained in due course and some more general features of the eye-movement recording methodology will be explicated in the next section, which deals with research methods used to study the processing of linguistic units larger than the word.

Sentence processing

Research that examines how language users process complete sentences makes use of a number of **off-line tasks** such as a grammaticality judgment task or a task that asks the participant to assign **thematic** (or "semantic") **roles** (e.g., agent or patient) to the noun phrases in a sentence. The goal of the latter type of studies is to find out what aspects of the surface form of sentences (e.g., word order or subject–verb agreement) play a role in determining the semantic relations between the words in a sentence. In addition to these off-line techniques, comprehension research exploits a number of rather sophisticated **on-line**

measuring techniques that are gaining popularity because they detect cognitive activity the very moment it takes place or only slightly after. One of these is **self-paced reading** combined with a **moving-window technique**: A text appears on the screen in successive segments (the "windows"). The participant summons each subsequent segment by pressing a key. This segment then appears in the position next to where the previous segment was. A trial starts with the presentation of groups of dashes separated by spaces, each group serving as a placeholder for a word in the text to be presented on that trial and each dash representing one letter. When the participant subsequently presses the key, the first segment appears, say the first two words, replacing the corresponding placeholders while the placeholders for the remaining words remain on the screen. Upon pressing the key next, the first two words are replaced by their placeholders again and the next segment appears, taking the position of the corresponding placeholders. This continues until the whole text has been read. The segments' size is determined by the researcher and depends on the specific question posed. The interval between two successive key presses is measured and is regarded the reading time for the current window.

In another version of the technique the window remains fixed in the same location on the screen and the successive segments all appear in this same place. In a third version the window does move, but the segments revealed in previous windows remain on the screen, a procedure that enables the reader to go back to earlier parts of the text. Finally, the **rapid serial visual presentation** (RSVP) technique presents segments (usually words) one by one at a fixed rate in the same location on the screen. The crucial difference between this technique and the three others just mentioned is that reading is not self-paced. Instead, the experimenter determines the presentation speed.

Self-paced reading techniques assume that the speed with which the participant progresses through the text reflects the speed of the comprehension processes involved and the mental processing load at every moment in time. A further assumption is that the moment a new segment appears, the participant immediately tries to integrate it in the representation of the previous text (this is the so called "immediacy" hypothesis). Furthermore it is assumed that at every moment in time the mind processes the word on which the eyes are currently fixating (this is called the eye–mind hypothesis; see Haberlandt, 1994, for a discussion).

Self-paced reading as studied by means of the moving-window (and fixed-window) technique provides a single measure of what might be going on mentally: the total, first-pass reading time for the current window. As cogently argued by a number of researchers (e.g., Frenck-Mestre, 2005a, 2005b; Rayner & Sereno, 1994), this performance measure is rather coarse-grained because of the many-faceted processing operations that may have taken place in between two successive button presses. The single total reading time measure collected for every single segment of text does not allow the researcher to determine which one(s) of these processing operations are reflected in the observed latency. The technique is also somewhat unnatural because under normal circumstances readers do not get to see a text in a piecemeal fashion and the reader, not the experimenter, determines the unit of reading.

A more natural and more sensitive on-line technique is "eye-movement recording" or "eye tracking", which registers the participants' eye movements and eye fixations while they read a text presented on a computer screen, documenting what the participants are looking at and for how long. Such recordings have shown that the eyes do not move smoothly through the text but jump from one region to the next with ballistic movements (called saccades), fixating for some time on the region where they land ("fixations"). Once in a while the eyes jump back to an earlier part of the text, a movement called a "regression". With this method, several measures are available. Consider the word *catastrophe* in the sentence *The islanders were struck by an unprecedented catastrophe that completely paralyzed them*. Now imagine that (after processing the earlier parts of the sentence) the eyes land on

catastrophe for the first time and specifically on its first syllable *ca* and then jump to the third syllable *stro* after a while. "First fixation duration" is the time between the moment the eyes first land in a particular region of interest (a word or larger fragment), here *ca*, and subsequently move elsewhere, to *stro* in the example. "Gaze duration" is the sum of first and all consecutive fixations within a region before the eyes move to another region (on either side of the critical region). This measure is the equivalent of the reading times obtained with the self-paced reading technique described above. In our example gaze duration is the sum of the fixations on *ca* and *stro*. If only one fixation is made to a particular word or fragment, first fixation duration and gaze duration are equivalent. "Total fixation duration" or "total gaze duration" on a particular region is the sum of the gaze duration on a region and the fixation time involved in later fixations on this same region (Rayner & Sereno, 1994). So after first having fixated on *ca* and *stro*, the eyes may regress to an earlier region, say to *den* in the adjective *unprecedented* that precedes *catastrophe*, and subsequently land somewhere on *catastrophe* again, say on *phe* this time. If after this moment the eyes never get back to *catastrophe* again, the total fixation duration for this word is the sum of the fixations on *ca* and *stro* and *phe*. Gaze duration (*ca* plus *stro*) is also referred to as "first-pass" reading time, whereas all later fixations in the same area (*phe*) are called "second-pass" reading time (the latter thus equaling total fixation time minus first-pass reading time; Frenck-Mestre, 2005b). A final measure is the "regression path duration": the time from first fixating a word until moving the eyes beyond that word, including the regression time. For example, if the eyes land on *ca*, *stro*, *den*, and *phe*, in that order, and then move on beyond *catastrophe* never to regress to this word again, the regression path duration equals the sum of the fixation durations of *ca*, *stro*, *den*, and *phe*. First fixation duration and gaze duration are assumed to reflect initial word recognition whereas regression path duration is thought to be a marker of higher-order reading processes such as semantic integration.

In addition to these measures of fixation time, measuring the length of the saccades and the pattern of regressions provides valuable further information on what is going on mentally during reading (see Frenck-Mestre, 2005b; Haberlandt, 1994; and Rayner & Sereno, 1994, for details). Contrary to the multidimensional nature of the data yielded by the eye-movement recording technique, the self-paced moving-window technique only provides the unidimensional gaze duration measure. To illustrate the resulting differential sensitivity of the two techniques, the recording of eye movements during reading can discriminate between initial parsing and later backtracking when the initial solution turns out to be wrong, whereas the self-paced moving-window technique cannot distinguish between these two processing components but merges them into a single measure.

A final technique for studying on-line comprehension processes concerns the registration of "event-related potentials" (ERPs). ERPs are small voltage changes in the electroencephalogram (EEG), measured with electrodes placed on the scalp, and induced by a particular stimulus, the eponymous "event". Such an event could, for instance, be one of the words in a visually or aurally presented sentence. One and the same stimulus may give rise to a number of different ERPs in the EEG, called "components", that may vary in polarity: They can be positive (indicated by P) or negative (indicated by N). It is common practice to plot negative components upwards and positive signals downwards. Components that differ in polarity are assumed to be generated by different groups of neurons. In addition to varying in polarity, the components vary in "latency", "amplitude", and scalp distribution or "topography". A component's latency is the time interval, expressed in milliseconds, between the onset of the critical event and the moment the voltage change is maximal. For instance, P600 refers to a positive-polarity ERP that is maximally strong 600 milliseconds after the onset of the critical event, and N400 refers to a negative-polarity ERP that is maximally strong 400 milliseconds after the event's onset. A component's amplitude is the degree of the voltage change relative to some baseline. A component's topography refers to where over the scalp's surface the electrical activity aroused by the stimulus is detected. Components are often named after their polarity and latency (as in N400 and P600) or after their topography and polarity (e.g., LAN, left anterior negativity). Alternatively, they are named after the assumed underlying functional process in combination with their polarity (e.g., MMN, for mismatch negativity, and SPS, for **syntactic positive shift**). This latter practice involves the danger that ultimately a different functional process than the one suggested by its name may turn out to underlie the component.

The component's qualitative features—that is, its topography and polarity—are assumed to reveal information on the neural structure and functional process involved (without identifying the exact locus of the neural structure in the brain; see pp. 407–411 for a more detailed description of the ERP technique). The quantitative features of a component, its amplitude and latency, are thought to reflect to what extent the underlying neural structure is involved and the time course of the functional process, respectively (see Hagoort & Ramsey, 2004, and Hahne & Friederici, 2001, for more details). The ERP methodology is especially well suited to provide information on *temporal* aspects of the various mental processes that go on during task performance, but provides a relatively imprecise measure of where exactly in the brain this processing takes place (because brain activity is detected at the scalp, not directly in the brain). In other words, the method is known to have a high temporal but low spatial resolution. As such, the ERP methodology complements two increasingly popular techniques of measuring brain activity during cognitive operations—**positron emission tomography (PET)** and **functional magnetic resonance imaging (fMRI)**. Both measure metabolic changes correlated with neural activity and reveal where in the brain this activity takes place but not exactly when. In other words, they have a high spatial but low temporal resolution. These techniques will be explained elsewhere (pp. 411–413). A particularly attractive feature of all three of these brain-imaging methods (ERP, PET, and fMRI) is that no overt behavioral response is required. By implication, no mental process that translates the process of interest (e.g., word recognition) into a behavioral response (e.g., a lexical decision and the associated manual or verbal motor response) is involved. Because such "nuisance" processes leave their own mark on the brain response, thus complicating its interpretation, doing without a behavioral response enables a (relatively) straightforward interpretation of the brain response in terms of the processes of interest. Still, many studies combine brain imaging with the registration of some overt behavioral response.

The ERP methodology is applied in many subdomains of study within the broad area of cognitive neuroscience and each of the associated cognitive functions studied—for instance, language, memory, visual perception, or attention—is characterized by a unique collection of relevant ERP components. Language comprehension has been shown to give rise to at least three ERP components, the presumably best known of which is the N400 already alluded to above. This component is elicited by any content (or "open-class") word and its amplitude is inversely related to the ease with which the word can be semantically related to its context. It is therefore thought to reflect semantic integration processes (Brown & Hagoort, 1993; Kutas & Van Petten, 1994). Kutas and Hillyard (1980) were the first to report the effect in a study that employed visual presentation of the materials but it has since been shown to occur with aural presentation as well. The two other ERP components that have been shown to occur during language comprehension appear to reflect the structural analysis of sentences. The first is named after its topography and polarity: LAN (left anterior negativity). It is manifest early on in the signal, mostly 300 to 500 milliseconds after the onset of the critical event, but sometimes even earlier, between 100 and 250 milliseconds after stimulus onset; in this case it is called ELAN (early left anterior negativity; e.g., Hahne & Friederici, 1999, 2001). The second is the P600 mentioned above, which occurs over centro-parietal electrodes (e.g., Neville, Nicol,

Barss, Forster, & Garrett, 1991; Osterhout & Holcomb, 1992). Friederici and her colleagues (Friederici & Kotz, 2003; Hahne & Friederici, 1999; Kotz & Friederici, 2003) have suggested that the ELAN and P600 are markers of two serial stages of syntactic analysis, an automatic structure-building stage occurring early, followed by one that is under the participant's attention control and that reflects syntactic integration processes.

THE PROCESSING OF INTERLEXICAL HOMOGRAPHS AND HOMOPHONES

Introduction

A much-debated question in the study of mono-lingual language comprehension is whether the linguistic context of a word exerts an influence on the way this word is recognized. Much of the pertinent research was inspired by Fodor's (1983) highly influential modularity of mind theory. Central in this theory is the concept of mental modules, information-processing devices that perform basic cognitive functions on incoming information, such as recognizing faces or words, and that are characterized by a number of characteristic features (not *defining* features, as they have often been taken to be; see Fodor, 1985, and Coltheart, 1999, for clarifications of the concept of a module). Some of these features are that modules tend to operate in a "domain-specific" way—which means that they only respond to input of a particular type, say faces or words— that they operate fast and mandatorily, and, most importantly in the theory, that they are "informationally encapsulated". This latter concept means that modules are impenetrable by information delivered by "higher" cognitive processes such as thinking, problem solving, or making inferences, and cannot exploit the background knowledge these higher cognitive processes make use of.

Given these features of mental modules, scientists have wondered whether the word recognition system of fluent language users might be considered a module as well: Word recognition in fluent readers and listeners is fast, mandatory (as is, for instance, shown by the occurrence of "Stroop effects"; see p. 255), and dedicated to the processing of one particular type of input. They have put this hypothesis to a test, focusing on the assumed information-encapsulation feature of modules. If the word recognition system is a module in Fodor's sense, neither the linguistic context of a word nor extra-linguistic contextual information should affect the way it is recognized.

A sizable number of studies have tackled this issue by looking at the way **lexical ambiguity** is resolved in sentence context. Lexically ambiguous words have two (or more) meanings that are unrelated. They are also called "intra-lexical homographs". An example is the English word *bug*, which can either refer to a type of insect or to a carefully concealed little microphone. The question posed in the ambiguity-resolution studies is whether all meanings of a word are initially activated or whether activation is restricted to the meaning that fits the context. Evidence of multiple, parallel activation irrespective of the nature of the contextual information, is regarded support for autonomy of word processing and, thus, for the notion that the mental lexicon operates as an informationally encapsulated module. In contrast, evidence that only the meaning compatible with the context is activated is seen as support for "interactive" word recognition; that is, the idea that the conceptual representation built from the linguistic context preceding the word permeates the lexicon with the effect that only the contextually appropriate meaning gets activated.

The majority of studies that attempted to resolve this issue employed a cross-modal sentence context version of the semantic priming methodology: The ambiguous word (e.g., *bug*) was presented in a sentence context and served as prime for a subsequently presented target. This target was either related to the contextually appropriate reading of the homograph (e.g., *ant*), to its contextually inappropriate reading (*spy*), or was unrelated to both readings (*sew*). Table 4.1 exemplifies the various conditions with materials employed by Swinney (1979) in one of the very first studies to use this methodology. In this specific study the cross-modal priming methodology was used: The context fragments, including the ambiguous word, were presented aurally and the targets were presented visually. A further important manipulation was the inter-stimulus interval (ISI) between prime and target; that is, the time interval between prime offset and target onset: The target was presented either immediately at the offset of the prime or a few syllables later. The results of this study supported the idea that initially multiple activation occurs and that only later is the contextually appropriate meaning selected on the basis of the contextual information: In the short ISI condition, targets related to both meanings of the ambiguous prime (both *ant* and *spy*) were processed faster than targets unrelated to either meaning (*sew*). In the long ISI condition, only the responses to targets related to the contextually appropriate meaning of the prime (*ant*) were facilitated as compared to the unrelated targets. These data suggest context-independent lexical activation and are thus in accordance with the view that

---

TABLE 4.1

The cross-modal priming methodology

Auditory context sentence	Rumor had it that for years the government building had been plagued with problems. The man was not surprised when he found several spiders, roaches, and other *bugs* in the corner _ of his room.		
Target word	contextually appropriate ANT	contextually inappropriate SPY	contextually unrelated SEW

The context sentence, including the critical ambiguous prime word (*bugs*), is presented aurally. The target word (ANT, SPY, or SEW, depending on the condition) is presented visually. The target is presented at prime offset (immediately following *bugs*) or a few syllables later (following *corner*). Example materials used by Swinney (1979).

word recognition is a modular process in Fodor's (1983) sense.

This same pattern of results has since been obtained more often (e.g., Onifer & Swinney, 1981; Tanenhaus, Leiman, & Seidenberg, 1979), providing additional support for what is called "multiple access". However, much evidence to support other views on ambiguity resolution has also been collected, including the opposite view that context constrains lexical activation at the very initial stage of lexical access so that only the contextually appropriate meaning becomes activated (e.g., Simpson, 1981). Yet other views are that not context but the relative frequencies of the homograph's meanings determine the order of access (Hogaboam & Perfetti, 1975), or that context and the relative frequency of the homograph's meanings interact to resolve the ambiguity (e.g., Tabossi, Colombo, & Job, 1987). In a comprehensive review of the literature, Simpson (1994) concluded that "the range of results obtained in ambiguity studies suggests clearly that the extreme views of the lexicon as either fully autonomous or promiscuously interactive are not tenable" and that "the truth must almost surely lie somewhere in between and must be highly dependent on characteristics of the context and on characteristics of the tasks required of the subject" (p. 372).

More recent studies have addressed the question of whether or not the word recognition system is a mental module in the sense defined above using newer and extremely sensitive paradigms. The evidence collected in these studies favors the conclusion that word recognition is *not* immune to contextual information. For instance, in an ingenious ERP study Nieuwland and Van Berkum (2006) showed that the **N400 effect** that is usually elicited by words that violate local lexical-semantic constraints (such as *clock* in the sentence *The girl comforted the clock*) disappears when the anomaly is in fact supported by the discourse context (e.g., a girl talking to a clock about his depression). More strikingly even, locally correct predicates (e.g., *salted* in *The peanut was salted*) showed an N400 effect if the prior discourse had set up a mental state in the

participants in which peanuts were considered animate beings (that, typically, are not salted). The prior context in question was a story about a peanut falling in love with an enchanting little almond. When the participants had been put in this state, the locally incorrect but globally correct *in love* in the sentence *The peanut was in love* failed to elicit an N400 effect. These and similar N400 findings (Van Berkum, Hagoort, & Brown, 1999; Van Berkum, Zwitserlood, Hagoort, & Brown, 2003) strongly suggest that the meaning representation of prior discourse has an *immediate* effect on word recognition (immediate, because the effect is already manifest 400 ms after the onset of the critical word). Dahan and Tanenhaus (2004) obtained converging support that context interacts with word recognition using the eye-tracking paradigm.

Bilingual studies

Bilingual studies on word processing have, in a modified form, adopted the rationale of the above monolingual studies on lexical ambiguity resolution. The general purpose of these bilingual studies is to find out whether lexical activation is encapsulated within a language (language-selective) or is not constrained by language (language-nonselective). In other words, if one and the same word means something different in a bilingual's two languages, are both meanings activated when it is encountered in the input or is only the word's meaning in the contextually appropriate language activated? In most cases, the cross-language ambiguous words tested were the interlexical homographs introduced earlier. As mentioned, these are words with the same orthographic form but different meanings in a bilingual's two languages. Examples are provided in Table 4.2. Occasionally **interlexical homophones** have served as the critical stimuli. These have an identical phonological form but different meanings in the two languages. (Note that, if the two languages are written in the same alphabetic script and largely share the same set of grapheme-to-phoneme correspondence rules, cross-language orthographic and phonological **homonymy** will be correlated.)

TABLE 4.2

Examples of English–German and English–Dutch interlexical homographs

English–German	English–Dutch
BAD ("bath")	BEER ("bear")
BALD ("soon")	BOOT ("boat")
BRAND ("fire")	BRIEF ("letter")
FAST ("almost")	DOOR ("through")
GIFT ("poison")	FEE ("fairy")
GRAB ("grave")	GLAD ("slippery")
GUT ("good")	KIND ("child")
NUN ("now")	ROOF ("robbery")
RAT ("advice")	STRAND ("beach")
STERN ("star")	WORST ("sausage")

The German and Dutch meanings of the homographs are in parentheses.

A noticeable difference between the monolingual and bilingual lexical ambiguity studies is that the large majority of the former have presented the critical words (the within-language **homonyms**) in a sentence context, whereas most of the latter have presented the analogous stimuli (the interlexical homonyms) in isolation. The presentation of sentence contexts in the monolingual studies directly follows from the main question motivating these studies: whether or not lexical access is encapsulated in the sense that it is not affected by a linguistic context. However, the specific question regarding encapsulation posed in the bilingual studies is a different one: Is lexical access in the one language encapsulated in the sense that the other language is not involved in the process? Given this different focus, it makes sense to start out looking for evidence of language encapsulation in out-of-context studies. If evidence of language-nonselective processing were to be found under those circumstances, the next logical step would be to look at the more constraining case, where sentence context points towards one of the (interlexical) homonym's meanings in particular. This is the research strategy that, without formulating it explicitly in advance, seems to have been taken, as may be concluded from the fact that all early studies have presented the homographs in isolation. Only just recently have studies on interlexical homonym

processing (and in particular homograph processing) in sentence context begun to emerge.

A second noticeable difference between the monolingual and bilingual studies is that the former explicitly focus on the processing of an ambiguous word's *meaning* because, as compared to unambiguous words, this appears to be the defining characteristic of an ambiguous word: that it has more than one meaning. Yet, as we will see, many bilingual studies on the processing of interlexical homographs seem not to have had this focus. This is most obvious from the fact that the model of bilingual word recognition that many researchers have turned to in explaining their effects, the bilingual interactive activation model (Dijkstra & Van Heuven, 1998), does not even include representations of word meaning (but can nevertheless account for much of the data). In the remainder of this section I will first summarize the data from out-of-context studies, explaining the methodological details along the way, and present a few of the relevant studies in more detail. Next, I will discuss the studies in which interlexical homonyms were presented in a sentence context, including some that have looked at how the brain responds to these stimuli (pp. 172–176). In a further section (pp. 177–181) I will present the models that have been developed to account for the assembled results.

Processing interlexical homographs and homophones out of context

Beauvillain and Grainger (1987) were the first to adopt the rationale of the monolingual ambiguity resolution studies and apply it to the study of bilingual lexical access by exploiting the dual-meaning characteristic of interlexical homographs (but studying the processing of such homographs out of context). The task they used was cross-language primed lexical decision: English–French bilinguals were presented with a set of stimulus pairs each consisting of a French prime word and an English target word (or nonword), the prime and target presented sequentially. They were instructed to read each prime and to then perform a lexical decision on the subsequent target. The vast majority of the primes were words in French only, but a number of them were French–English interlexical homographs such as *coin*. The question of interest was whether the interlexical homographs would facilitate the processing of subsequent English targets that were related to the homographs' English meaning (e.g., would *money* be responded to faster when it followed the "French" prime *coin* than when following an unrelated prime word). This turned out to be the case when the interval between prime and target was relatively short (150 ms). With a longer interval (750 ms) no such priming effect occurred. These findings suggest that, even though the majority of the primes were French only, both meanings of the interlexical-homograph primes were initially activated and that only at a later moment the contextually inappropriate meaning (the English meaning) was deactivated.

In retrospect, this evidence of language-nonselective processing seems hardly surprising because Beauvillain and Grainger's study involved the presentation of both French and English words. It has been suggested that in this situation both lexicons become automatically activated and the participants were thus performing the task in a "bilingual processing mode" (e.g., Grosjean, 1998; see pp. 288–291 for a detailed presentation of **language-mode theory**). A stronger test of language-nonselective word recognition would involve the presentation of words in one language exclusively to see whether also under those circumstances the non-target language permeates processing. This is the research strategy that some of the later studies have pursued by not employing the cross-language priming methodology (in which all primes are in the bilingual's one language and all targets are in the other language) and by not in any other way presenting language-mixed stimulus materials. Instead, they presented words in one language only (although some of them were interlexical homographs) and looked for evidence that, nevertheless, the experimentally absent language affected performance. However, as we will see, a number of the later studies, though not employing the cross-language priming method-

ology, have each in their own way and for their own reasons also included elements from the non-target language in the stimulus set, thus creating suboptimal conditions for testing the theoretical issue under study.

Given the fact that the most salient characteristic of an interlexical homograph is that it has different meanings in the bilingual's two languages, a noteworthy aspect of many of these later studies (De Groot, Delmaar, & Lupker, 2000; Dijkstra, De Bruijn, Schriefers, & Ten Brinke, 2000a; Dijkstra et al., 1999; Dijkstra, Timmermans, & Schriefers, 2000b; Dijkstra, Van Jaarsveld, & Ten Brinke, 1998; French & Ohnesorge, 1995; Gerard & Scarborough, 1989; Jared & Szucs, 2002; Kerkhofs, Dijkstra, Chwilla, & De Bruijn, 2006; Von Studnitz & Green, 2002a) is that they did not explicitly look for evidence that both of the homograph's *meaning* representations are temporarily activated upon its presentation. Instead, theoretically more neutral, they looked for evidence of co-activation in the non-target lexicon without making the a priori assumption that dual meaning activation would underlie such evidence. One of these studies (Kerkhofs et al., 2006) employed the semantic priming methodology, but now with primes and targets in the same language, and looking at both behavioral and brain responses (ERPs) to the critical stimuli. None of the other studies used the priming methodology. Instead, responses to (unprimed) interlexical homographs were compared with responses to (unprimed) unilingual control words; that is, words that exist in the target language only. The homographs and controls were matched on a number of variables that are known to affect processing difficulty, especially word frequency. The only difference between the two categories of words thus was the fact that only the homographs occur in both of the bilingual participants' two languages. Therefore, any difference in the responses to homographs and controls to be obtained is likely to result from this one difference and will, one way or the other, have to be explained accordingly. Co-activation of (yet to be specified) representation units in the non-target language is a plausible source of this effect.

In most of these studies the visual lexical decision task was used, either its language-generalized (language-neutral) or its language-specific form. These lexical decision studies have shown differences in response time and number of errors between homographs and controls in the majority of cases. Depending on the exact demands of the task (language neutral or language specific) and the composition of the stimulus set (the presence or absence of words from the non-target language among the "nonword" letter strings), response times to homographs were either longer or shorter than to their controls. This difference (in either direction) is called the **homograph effect**. The size of the effect depended on a number of variables, most notably on the relative frequency of the homograph in the two languages. It was generally especially large when the homograph was more frequent in the non-target language than in the target language and when, at the same time, the participants performed the language-specific version of the task. If language nonselectivity occurs under at least some circumstances, as these data suggest to be the case, these frequency effects are to be expected: A highly activated node in the lexicon of the non-target language (a node that represents a high-frequency word) will interfere more with responding than a less activated node in the non-target system (a unit representing a low-frequency word). In some cases, however, no homograph effect was obtained, suggesting the possibility of language-selective processing under at least some sets of circumstances.

That specific constellations of task demands and stimulus set characteristics can affect the direction of the homograph effects may be readily understood if we assume that the participants have at least some control over the way they execute the task and adapt task performance to the task's exact requirements. For instance, when the participants are instructed to perform language-specific lexical decision but no cost is incurred if, despite these instructions, they reconfigure the task and perform it in its language-neutral version (respond "yes" to any word, irrespective of language), they may in fact opt for this latter strategy. Such will be an option if no

"nonwords" are included that happen to be words in the non-target language. Under these circumstances, a lexical decision may be based on the homograph making contact with either one of two lexical representations, one for each language, and there is no need to check the language membership of the contacted representation. On average, this process will come to a conclusion at an earlier moment in time than when only one lexical representation matches the stimulus word, as is the case with non-homographic control words. This difference in completion time is reflected in relatively fast responses to homographs. In contrast, under circumstances where such task reconfiguration (performing the language-specific version of the task as if language-neutral decisions had been asked for) would punish the participants with a high error score (many false positives to words of the non-target language), they are likely to adopt the requested language-specific processing mode. Under these circumstances homographs will be responded to more slowly than their controls, especially when a homograph's meaning in the non-target language is more frequent than its meaning in the target language. The reason is that the representation of the more frequent non-target meaning will be accessed first, checked for language membership, and rejected, all of this causing a delay in processing the target meaning. But, importantly, in both cases, the fact that there is a difference between processing time for homographs and controls points to the activation of the non-target lexicon.

Analogous to the homograph effects, interlexical **homophone effects** have been obtained, for words that sound (approximately) the same in a bilingual's two languages but are orthographically different and have a different meaning in these languages. Dijkstra et al. (1999) separated the contributions of cross-language orthographic and phonological overlap in a study where Dutch–English bilinguals performed an English-specific lexical decision task to *visually* presented letter strings. Interestingly, the two types of cross-language similarity turned out to have opposite effects: Orthographic overlap produced a facilitating effect (as compared to only English control words), whereas phonological overlap produced an inhibitory effect. Doctor and Klein (1992) obtained similar results in an English–Afrikaans study, but in a more recent study (Haigh & Jared, 2007), French–English bilinguals responded *faster* to interlexical homophones than to control stimuli in an English lexical decision task.

Although it is not immediately clear why orthographic and phonological overlap occasionally produce opposite effects, both effects provide evidence of language-nonselective processing. Dijkstra and his colleagues hypothesized the reverse effects may explain why occasionally null effects of interlexical homography have been observed (e.g., De Groot et al., 2000, Experiment 2; Dijkstra et al., 1998, Experiment 1; Gerard & Scarborough, 1989): A facilitating effect of homography and an inhibitory effect of homophony might have cancelled one another. Alternatively, the experimental design may have been too insensitive to detect a real but small effect of homography. However, because of their ad hoc character these explanations of the occasional null effect are not really satisfactory.

A more satisfactory, because less ad hoc, approach would be to take these null effects at face value and assume that under specific circumstances bilingual word recognition is in fact language selective. An interlexical homograph study by Jared and Szucs (2002) provides support for this hypothesis. These authors tested French–English and English–French bilinguals in a word naming task in which visually presented English words had to be read aloud. In one condition the English target words were preceded by a block of French words, to be read aloud in French; in a second condition, they were not. The French–English bilinguals (with the target language English as their weaker L2) named the English homograph targets more slowly than non-homographic control words in both conditions, evidencing language-nonselective processing in both conditions. In contrast, the English–French bilinguals (for whom target English was the dominant language) named the English homographs more slowly than the control words when they were preceded by a French naming block but not when they were not preceded by a block of

French trials. These results suggest that under certain circumstances language-selective processing may occur. More precisely, they suggest that the stronger language can be immune to an influence from weaker L2. Furthermore, the pattern of results for the English–French participants demonstrates that under circumstances in which the activation of the non-target language is boosted somehow (here as a result of prior processing of a set of French words) the dominant language does not enjoy immunity. Converging evidence that language-selective processing may occur under some circumstances was obtained by Haigh and Jared (2007), who found support for language-nonselective processing when French–English bilinguals processed interlexical *homophones* in an English lexical decision task, but not when English–French bilinguals served as participants.

There is one more noteworthy outcome of Jared and Szucs' (2002) study that deserves mentioning here; namely the fact that these authors obtained an inhibitory effect of interlexical homographs, whereas Dijkstra et al. (1999) obtained faster responses for homographs than controls. Apparently, the exact task that is used, word naming or lexical decision, is a factor that determines the direction of the homograph effect. The inhibition in naming is plausibly due to the requirement of the naming task (but not the lexical decision task) that participants pronounce the target words. Homographs are typically pronounced differently in the two languages, and therefore the pronunciation process is likely to be frustrated by the co-activation of a different phonological form.

So far we have encountered two results that suggest that a participant adapts flexibly to the requirements of the task: Language-specific and language-neutral lexical decision appear to incite different processing strategies in the participants and the different direction of the homograph effects in lexical decision and naming suggests the same. To account for such flexible behavior, a number of theories on monolingual (e.g., Grainger & Jacobs, 1996) and bilingual word recognition (e.g., Dijkstra & Van Heuven, 2002; Green, 1998) have added some sort of task-setting component onto the word recognition system proper (see p. 180 for details). Performance in any given experiment is explained in terms of the joint operation of both of these components. Given the flexibility of task performance, in trying to resolve the dispute between the language-selective and language-nonselective processing views it is advisable to look for converging evidence from a number of different tasks that are all assumed to tap word recognition to at least some extent. If the effect of interest turns up in all of these tasks, this would strengthen the conclusion the effect is a real one, attributable to some feature of the actual word recognition process and not to some component specific to a particular task (see the notion of "functional overlap" introduced on p. 158 Grainger & Jacobs, 1996; Jacobs & Grainger, 1994).

Dijkstra and his colleagues (1999, 2000a, 2000b) have adopted this approach by looking at interlexical homograph processing in three other tasks: **language decision**, language go/no-go, and progressive demasking. As lexical decision, language decision is a binary classification task, where on each trial one of two possible responses is required: The bilingual participants are presented with words of both languages and have to decide for each word to which language it belongs (see also Grainger & Dijkstra, 1992). In general, in go/no-go tasks the participants only respond to one type of stimuli and are asked to let a stimulus pass without responding if it is of a different type. In the language go/no-go paradigm used by Dijkstra et al. (2000b) the bilingual participants only had to respond when a presented word belonged to one of their languages, specified by the experimenter. As in the lexical decision studies (and in Jared & Szucs', 2002, word naming study), in all cases, performance on interlexical homographs was compared to that on unilingual frequency-matched control words.

Figure 4.2 shows the data of the English (left) and Dutch (right) go/no-go conditions as obtained by Dijkstra et al. (2000b) in a study that tested Dutch–English bilinguals. The upper part presents the mean response times for homographs and controls; the lower part the corresponding percentages correct (hit rates). All data are split up over three groups of interlexical homographs: homographs with a high frequency of occurrence in English but a low frequency of occurrence in Dutch (HFE-LFD); homographs that occur frequently in Dutch but infrequently in English (LFE-HFD); and homographs with a low frequency of occurrence in both languages (LFE-LFD).

As shown, substantial differences between the homographs and controls occurred: Responding was faster and hit rates were higher for unilingual controls than for homographs. Furthermore, as in the lexical decision studies, the size of the homograph effects depended on the relative frequency of the homographs in the two languages: The effects were especially large when the task required a "go" response to a homograph that was more frequent in the non-target language than in the target language (LFE-HFD in the left panel; HFE-LFD in the right panel). This finding suggests that such a homograph activated its representation in the non-target language first, upon which the participants concluded they had to refrain from responding (an incorrect "no go"). Alternatively, this false start delayed correct responding, thus resulting in a long response time. Both language versions of the task thus suggest that the participants could not deactivate the non-target language, even though this would have improved performance dramatically. Not shown are the data of the progressive demasking and language decision tasks, but these also produced differences between homographs and controls.

Critics might object that under the particular circumstances of this study it would have been completely impossible *not* to process the "pass" stimuli (the words in the non-target language). Given that word recognition in fluent readers is an automatic process, how then could the participants have prevented these stimuli to access and activate the word recognition system? Should they have shut their eyes at the appropriate moments? But given that "go" and "pass" stimuli appeared at unpredictable moments, how would they have known what the appropriate moments were? The alternative assumption that the task set might work like some miraculous

FIGURE 4.2

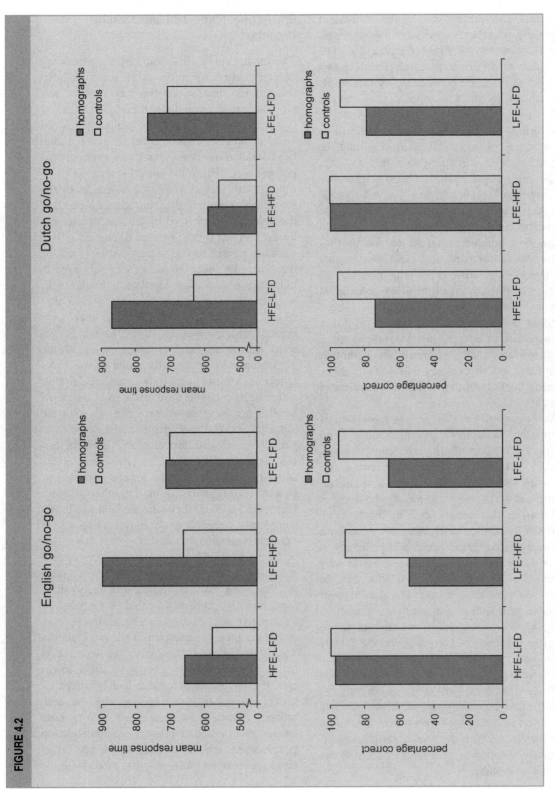

Mean response times (in ms) and percentages correct (top and bottom, respectively) for interlexical homographs and controls in the English (left) and Dutch (right) go/no-go conditions. Three groups of homographs were included: frequent in English but infrequent in Dutch (HFE-LFD); infrequent in English but frequent in Dutch (LFE-HFD); infrequent in both English and Dutch (LFE-LFD). Data from Dijkstra et al. (2000b).

drug that temporarily freezes the non-target language system (but not the target language system) into lethargy is equally implausible. The researchers might riposte that such considerations would miss the exact point made by this study: That, apparently, the non-target language cannot be deactivated or switched off at will. And yet, these critics have a point: The experiment is not unlike the hypothetical event of getting the instruction in the morning that this day you should only recognize your left-hand neighbors—the instructor trying to find out whether, if later that day you were to bump into Dolan Glowearth, your right-hand neighbor, he would indeed be a complete stranger to you. It thus seems that in this particular experiment—using the language go/no-go task—the question of whether or not co-activation of the non-target language can be prevented at all has been stretched ad absurdum. It is one thing for a language not to be activated mentally when it is not around in the environment; it is another thing for it not to be when it is actually there, imposing itself upon the viewer at unpredictable moments.

At the beginning of this section I raised doubts about the suitability of Beauvillain and Grainger's (1987) cross-language semantic priming study to investigate the present question, and it was for similar reasons: There too non-target language materials occurred among the stimulus materials, in that specific case in the form of primes to be read silently. Similarly, the above language-specific lexical decision experiments in which words from the non-target language were presented to be treated as nonwords, may be criticized for the same reason. The general point to make here is that the question of whether bilingual word recognition can or cannot be language selective can best be addressed in truly unilingual experiments because, given the automatic nature of word recognition (in literate language users fluent in that language), stimuli from the non-target language will always activate the associated language subsystem. Therefore experiments in which the non-target language is physically absent provide a more conclusive test of the issue at stake.

Processing interlexical homographs in context

Two further studies that examined the processing of interlexical homographs in bilinguals provided relevant information on the way context may modulate word recognition in bilinguals (Elston-Güttler, Gunter, & Kotz, 2005; Paulmann, Elston-Güttler, Gunter, & Kotz, 2006). In these studies behavioral responses as well as event-related potentials (ERPs) to the critical stimuli were collected. Both studies employed a version of the semantic priming paradigm introduced earlier and the task to be performed by the participants was lexical decision (in the ensuing discussion of this work, responses to the nonword stimuli will be ignored). In both studies, German–English bilinguals were shown interlexical homographs (e.g., the words *gift* or *bald*, meaning "poison" and "soon", respectively, in German) that were immediately followed by an L2 English target word expressing the German meaning of the homograph (e.g., the words *poison* or *soon*). An unrelated control condition was included in which English targets were preceded by unrelated English primes, matched on frequency with the homographs. The participants were instructed to perform L2 English lexical decisions on the targets. In one of these studies (Paulmann et al., 2006) the homograph primes were presented as isolated words, whereas in the other (Elston-Güttler et al., 2005) they were the final words of a complete L2 English sentence (see Table 4.3 for example materials).

In both studies, prior to the actual data collection phase of the study the participants watched one and the same originally silent film, now supplied with either a German or English narrative, each spoken by a native speaker of the language in question. This manipulation was intended to create what the researchers called a "global language context", which might bias the participants towards the language of the film fragment when performing the subsequent lexical decision task. We have encountered a similar context manipulation on p. 169, where a block of trials in the non-target language was or was not provided prior to

TABLE 4.3

Example materials used by Elston-Güttler et al. (2005)

Related	The woman gave her friend a pretty GIFT	*POISON*
Unrelated	The woman gave her friend a pretty SHELL	*POISON*
Related	Joan used scissors to remove the TAG	*DAY*
Unrelated	Joan used scissors to remove the LABEL	*DAY*
Related	His father's head was turning BALD	*SOON*
Unrelated	His father's head was turning TAN	*SOON*
Related	Jim had some problems with his GUT	*GOOD*
Unrelated	Jim had some problems with his AXE	*GOOD*

The sentence-final words (in capitals) serve as primes for the adjacent words, the targets (italized). In the related condition the targets are the English translations of the German meaning of the corresponding primes (thus, *Gift*, *Tag*, *Bald*, and *gut* mean "poison", "day", "soon", and "good", respectively, in German). In the unrelated condition the targets are unrelated to the corresponding primes.

data collection on the target materials (Jared & Szucs, 2002).

These two manipulations—the global language context manipulation and the comparison of a sentence context condition and an isolated word condition—are of particular interest because they have the potential to answer a question that may have bothered the reader up to this point: In the prototypical experiment discussed so far, the critical stimulus words, the interlexical homographs or homophones, were presented in isolation. But wouldn't it have been more natural to embed them in context, which is how we encounter these words in natural speech and print? This context generally supports only a single reading of the homograph. In contrast, when a homograph is presented in isolation, there is no context to constrain its meaning, a state of affairs that might foster language-nonselective activation. The more recent literature on within-language ambiguity resolution (p. 164 indeed suggests that context may constrain lexical activation to the contextually appropriate word. A

further variable that the investigators included was "block", comparing the priming effects in the first half (block) of the experiment with those in the second half. This was done to find out whether a language expectancy created by the film fragment might change over the course of the experiment: The participants in the conditions where the language of the film fragment and of the lexical decision part of the experiment differ may gradually become aware of this mismatch and this might affect their performance.

Of the experimental conditions included in these experiments, the one (in Elston-Güttler et al., 2005) in which the homographic primes were embedded in all-English sentences (see Table 4.3) that, in turn, were preceded by the film spoken in English, provided the strongest test of language-(non)selectivity: This all-English condition involves a strong bias towards the English meaning of the homograph and implements language use under natural circumstances rather faithfully, indeed much more faithfully than the isolated word experiments do. If, nevertheless, a homograph effect occurs, showing that the homograph's L1 (German) meaning was processed as well, this would provide a strong case that word recognition in naturalistic reading settings is language-nonselective.

As mentioned, in addition to behavioral responses, in these experiments ERPs were measured. The researchers focused on the N400 component in the ERP signal, time-locked to the target. The N400 to targets preceded by semantically related primes has been shown to be less negative than the N400 to targets following unrelated primes (e.g., Chwilla, Brown, & Hagoort, 1995). In agreement with the general interpretation of the N400 as reflecting semantic integration processes, it is thought that this difference in negativity (that is, the "N400 effect") reflects the difference in the ease with which the meanings of pairs of related words on the one hand and pairs of unrelated words on the other hand can be integrated. In the single word prime study (Paulmann et al., 2006), targets preceded by related homographic primes (prime: *gift*; target; *poison*) were responded to faster than targets unrelated to their primes (prime: *shell*; target:

poison). An N400 effect was also obtained: The N400 to related targets was significantly less negative than the N400 to unrelated targets. The language of the film fragment that preceded the lexical decision part of the experiment did not modulate these effects. As mentioned, Paulmann and colleagues also compared performance in the first and second halves of their experiment. The semantic priming effects, both on latency and the N400, turned out to be equally large in both parts of the study. These data suggest an influence of the non-target language (L1 German) on L2 English and, thus, language-nonselective processing.

However, when the primes constituted the final word in sentences (Elston-Güttler et al., 2005; Table 4.3), the results were crucially different from those reported above. In this study, only the German film context condition showed a pattern consistent with language-nonselectivity, and this only during the first half of the experiment. In the three remaining conditions (second half, German film; first half, English film; second half, English film), neither response latency nor the negativity of the N400 differed between related and unrelated targets. Figure 4.3 shows the ERPs for the German film condition, both for the first half of the experiment (Block 1; upper panel) and the second half (Block 2; lower panel).

The N400 priming effect is the area between the ERPs for related targets (solid lines) and unrelated targets (dashed lines) around 400 ms after target onset (that is, around position 0.4 on the x-axis). As can be seen, this effect only occurred in the first half of the experiment. In the second half the N400 amplitudes for related and unrelated targets did not differ from one another (the brain signals overlap). The data for the English film conditions (not shown) are similar to those of the German/second half condition, suggesting the absence of a priming effect by the homograph's German meaning and, therefore, indicating language-selective processing. In other words, in the experimental condition that mimicked natural language processing most faithfully (the condition that provided global language and sentence context information in the language of the target), only the contextually appropriate meaning of the homograph prime (the English

meaning) was activated. It thus appears that language-nonselective processing is not a ubiquitous phenomenon.

Two further investigations provided additional evidence to support this conclusion (Conklin & Mauner, 2003; Schwartz & Kroll, 2006). Whereas Elston-Güttler and her colleagues demonstrated that language context can restrict activation to the target language, these two studies both show that relative strength of the two languages is a further factor to constrain nonselective access. Conklin and Mauner's study closely resembled Elston-Güttler et al.'s (2005) investigation, the major difference being that it was run in both the participants' dominant language (English) and their weaker language (French). When the sentences and targets were in L2 French, a relatedness effect materialized, suggesting that the homographic prime's contextually inappropriate (L1) meaning was also activated. However, when the materials were presented in L1 English, the participants' dominant language, no relatedness effect occurred, which pointed to language-selective processing.

Schwartz and Kroll (2006) employed a different design and a different task, the read-aloud (naming) task. In this study, testing Spanish–English bilinguals, the homographs appeared somewhere in the middle in all-English sentences (rather than occurring in sentence-final position; see Table 4.4 for examples), and the homographs (and their controls) themselves were the targets to which the participants responded. The words in a sentence were presented word-by-word by means of the rapid serial visual presentation (RSVP) technique. The target word (homograph or control) occurred in red (bold in Table 4.4), and this was the signal for the participant to read it aloud. The words preceding and following the target were presented for 250 milliseconds each and did not require an overt response. The target words were embedded in two types of sentences. In "high constraint" sentences, the target's prior context strongly biased the homograph's intended meaning (its meaning in the language of the experiment, L2 English). In "low constraint" sentences there was no strong bias towards the homograph's appropriate meaning. (Note that

FIGURE 4.3

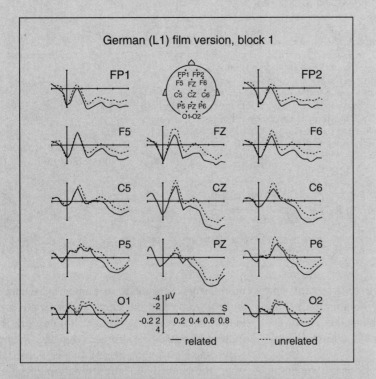

German (L1) film version, block 1

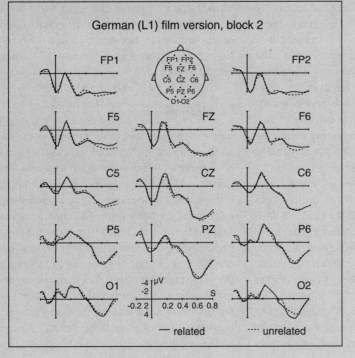

German (L1) film version, block 2

ERPs elicited by the critical targets. Solid and dashed lines represent the average voltage for related and unrelated targets, respectively, from 200 ms prior to target onset to 800 ms after target onset. The upper and lower panels show ERPs from the first and second half, respectively, of the experiment after viewing the German film version. Reprinted from Elston-Güttler et al. (2005). Copyright © 2005, with permission from Elsevier.

TABLE 4.4

Example materials used by Schwartz and Kroll (2006)

From the beach we could see the shark's **fin** pass through the water (H-HC)
We were a little nervous as we watched the **fin** of the shark go through the water (H-LC)
At the pond we could see a green **frog** jumping in and out of the water (C-HC)
The school children watched the **frog** jump from one rock to another (C-LC)
We vacuumed the rug and mopped the **floor** to help our parents (H-HC)
When we went inside we could see the **floor** was covered with dirt (H-LC)
We talked about the cows and chickens we saw when we visited the **farm** in New York state (C-HC)
During dinner our guest told us about the **farm** he was going to buy (C-LC)
I leave the bacon frying for a while in the **pan** to make it crisp (H-HC)
We went to the store to buy a **pan** for our kitchen (H-LC)
He gave me his number and I looked in my purse for a **pen** to write it down with (C-HC)
She left the house to buy a **pen** for her son (C-LC)
I sliced apples because I was going to bake a **pie** for my dinner guests (H-HC)
I rushed around because I was worried that the **pie** would not be ready in time (H-LC)
They did not tell the child that the delicious ham came from a **pig** because it was her favorite animal (C-HC)
They did not walk down the path because there was a **pig** blocking the way (C-LC)

Homographs (H) and control (C) words are printed in bold; HC = high-constraint sentence; LC = low-constraint sentence. Spanish *fin*, *floor*, *pan*, and *pie* mean "end", "flower", "bread", and "foot", respectively, in Spanish.

the experiment did not involve a bias towards one or the other meaning of the homograph.) Both balanced bilinguals and bilinguals with L1 Spanish clearly stronger than L2 English took part in the experiment.

If, while processing an interlexical homograph in context, its contextually inappropriate meaning (here, its Spanish meaning) is also temporarily active, this should result in slower processing of a homograph than of its control stimulus (the homograph effect). Such an inhibitory effect may be expected to be especially large in the low-constraint condition, in which the previous context does not strongly point at the targeted meaning. For balanced bilinguals, in neither condition was a homograph effect obtained: They responded equally fast, and made equally many errors, to homographs and controls in both the high- and low-constraint conditions. This same pattern held for the unbalanced bilinguals in the analyses with response time as the dependent variable. So far, the data suggest that context eliminates the homograph effect, even in the low-constraint condition, suggesting that the system processes homographs as if they were unambiguous words. However, the error analyses revealed a clear homograph effect in unbalanced bilinguals, which interacted with the sentence constraint manipulation: Considerably

more errors were made to homographs than to control words, and this effect was especially large in the low-constraint condition. It thus seems that in these bilinguals the stronger language, Spanish, was co-activated with weaker English, especially when the context did not strongly point at the homograph's targeted meaning. But what these results, just as those of the other studies discussed in this section, demonstrate more convincingly is that under certain circumstances language-selective processing occurs.

Conclusions

The studies discussed in the two previous sections show a mixed pattern of results from which, nevertheless, some general conclusions can be drawn. Many of them suggest language-nonselective processing of homographs (and, occasionally, homophones), and particularly many of those in which the homographs were presented in word lists. To draw from this the conclusion that bilinguals generally fail to block out the non-target language would, however, be premature because a number of studies have revealed factors that dampen the involvement of this language. One of them is the relative dominance of the two languages: If the non-target language is the weaker of a bilingual's two languages it is less likely to influence processing the target language than when it is the stronger of the two. Furthermore, immersing the participants in the non-target language prior to presenting the critical homograph stimuli—thereby plausibly increasing the activation level of the non-target language—increases the chance that this language permeates processing the target language. But most noteworthy, when the homographs were presented in circumstances that resembled natural language processing most faithfully—by embedding them in a sentence context and adding a global context in the same language as the sentence—the contextually inappropriate meaning of the homograph did not exert any effect whatsoever on processing its appropriate meaning. In later sections I will present converging evidence to suggest that there are limits to language-nonselective lexical processing. But first I will present two models of bilingual word recognition that were developed to account for the present interlexical homograph effects and for a number of other effects that suggest language-nonselective lexical access.

MODELS OF LANGUAGE-NONSELECTIVE LEXICAL ACCESS

The bilingual interactive activation model and its successors

The interlexical homograph effects obtained in a number of the isolated word studies presented above have been simulated successfully with the bilingual interactive activation (BIA) model developed by Dijkstra, Grainger, and Van Heuven (Dijkstra & Van Heuven, 1998; Grainger, 1993; Grainger & Dijkstra, 1992; Van Heuven, Dijkstra, & Grainger, 1998). It is a connectionist computational model of visual word recognition in bilinguals and concerns an extended version of McClelland and Rumelhart's (1981) interactive activation model (IA) of monolingual visual word recognition. The model can simulate the above homograph effects in certain conditions

despite the fact that in its original form it does not represent word meaning. This is surprising given the fact that the only obvious difference between interlexical homographs and unilingual control words is that the former but not the latter mean two different things across the bilingual's two languages. Apparently, the effect cannot be attributed exclusively to the processing of meaning. A number of other cross-language effects obtained in studies on visual lexical access in bilinguals (to be presented further on pp. 181–183) have also been successfully simulated with BIA. Furthermore, the model has simulated the monolingual behavioral data that McClelland and Rumelhart modeled in their IA model, suggesting that BIA can be regarded a true extension of IA. The left part of Figure 4.4 illustrates BIA's structure and processing assumptions.

The model contains four levels of representation units or "nodes", which represent visual letter features, letters, the orthographic forms of whole words, and language information, respectively. The bilingual's two languages share the feature and letter nodes, whereas the word nodes are organized in language subsets, which are fully connected between the languages (see below). The layer of language nodes contains just two nodes, one for each language. The model is "interactive" in the sense that representations at one particular level can activate and inhibit representations at adjacent higher and lower levels. Activation comes about via excitatory connections (visualized by means of an arrowhead); inhibition via inhibitory connections (visualized by means of a bullet head). In addition to the excitatory and inhibitory connections between representation levels, the model assumes inhibitory connections between all orthographic word form nodes. As a consequence of this interconnectedness of nodes within the word level, the word nodes mutually inhibit each other's activation. This is called "lateral inhibition". Importantly, inhibitory connections also exist between word nodes from different languages (e.g., Thomas & Van Heuven, 2005).

A visual word presented to the system first activates the feature nodes that correspond to the input. These, in turn, feed activation into the layer

FIGURE 4.4

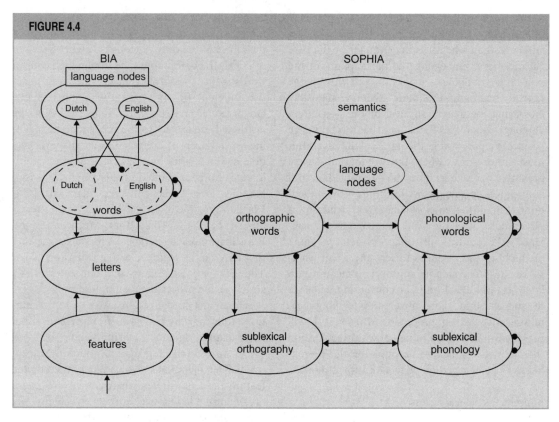

The bilingual interactive activation (BIA) model and the semantic, orthographic, and phonological interactive activation (SOPHIA) model of visual word recognition in bilinguals. Arrowheads represent excitatory connections. Bullet heads represent inhibitory connections. Adapted from Dijkstra and Van Heuven (1998) and Van Heuven and Dijkstra (2001).

of letter nodes, exciting the nodes for letters that contain the activated features and inhibiting the nodes for letters that do not contain these features. Similarly, activated letter nodes activate or inhibit word nodes, depending on the presence or absence of the corresponding letters (in the corresponding positions) in the words represented by the word nodes. For instance, when the English word *sand* is presented to the system, it will activate, via the feature level, the letter nodes *s*, *a*, *n*, and *d*, which in their turn will activate the word node corresponding to target *sand*, but also the nodes for similar words like *hand*, *sane*, and *sank*, which share most of their letters (in the same positions) with the actual stimulus. The word nodes for less similar words like *salt*, *wind*, and *sin* will also be excited by the activated

letter nodes they share with the input word *sand*, but this activation may be nullified by the inhibitory effect of the mismatching remaining letters. Importantly, activated letter nodes will activate word nodes corresponding to words in both languages. So in a Dutch–English bilingual, the letter nodes that are activated following the presentation of *sand* will also excite, among others, the word nodes for Dutch words like *zand* ("sand") and *mand* ("basket"), which also contain the majority of the activated letters. In their turn, activated word nodes transmit activation to the language node of the corresponding language, at which moment the latter starts to inhibit word nodes of the other language. All activated word nodes compete with one another in the recognition process, inhibiting each other through lateral inhibition, until the activation level in one of them will exceed a so-called "recognition threshold". In the case of the example, this will most likely be the node for *sand*. It is at that moment that the input *sand* will be recognized as the word *sand*.

If and when the activation level of a word node reaches the recognition threshold is not only determined by the match between stimulus and word node in terms of shared letters but by a number of other variables as well. One of them is the number of activated word nodes that compete with one another during the recognition process. A second is the level of activation in the word node when it is in its resting state. This "baseline" level of activation is not the same for all word nodes but differs as a function of when the corresponding word was last used ("recency") and—particularly important in the present context—the frequency with which it is used in natural language: Word nodes that represent frequent words are assumed to have a higher base-line level of activation in their resting state than the word nodes for infrequent words. As a consequence, when a frequent word is presented to the system, the recognition threshold of the corresponding word node will be reached at a relatively early moment in time. This account explains why we occasionally misread or mishear (and mispronounce) a less common word for a more common, similar word. But more to the point, it can also account for the fact that the size of the homograph effect depends on the relative frequency of a homograph's two readings, as reported above. How then are homograph effects explained in terms of BIA?

Dijkstra and Van Heuven (1998) assume two orthographic word node representations for inter-lexical homographs, one for each language. If a homograph is presented to the system, because of the perfect match of both its word nodes with the visual input, both of them will become highly activated. In contrast, when a non-homographic control word is presented there generally will be just one word node that reaches a high level of activation, namely the node that represents this control stimulus. The homograph effects obtained in the out-of-context studies are attributed to this

difference in the activation state of the recognition system upon the presentation of a homograph on the one hand and a control word on the other hand. The consistent effects of the relative frequency of a homograph's readings in the two languages are attributed to differences in the resting-level activation of the homograph's two word form nodes: Because of its higher resting level of activation, the word node associated with the homograph's higher-frequency reading has a head start in the recognition process and, therefore, its activation will reach the activation threshold relatively early, thus determining the response.

Dijkstra et al. (1999) considered a second interpretation of the homograph effect, now assuming that interlexical homographs are not represented in two separate word nodes but share one and the same word form node between the two languages, this node being connected differently to each of the two language nodes. They, however, regarded this set-up implausible because simulations of this model produced results that deviated from the corresponding behavioral data: Whereas, as we have seen, the behavioral data often show slower processing of interlexical homographs than controls, these simulations *always* resulted in faster processing of the former (Thomas & Van Heuven, 2005).

It thus appears that the model can deal with the out-of-context homograph effects. But what about the fact that sound (dis)similarity of a homograph's two readings (Dijkstra et al., 1999) has also shown to affect processing? The BIA model does not contain phonological (sound) representations and is therefore not equipped to explain these effects, nor can it explain the more substantial additional evidence (to be discussed on pp. 183–191) that during visual word recognition phonological memory nodes are activated as well. Similarly, what about the large likelihood that in more natural language use meaning plays a dominant role in the ambiguity resolution process? Yet, despite the truism that meaning assignment is the ultimate goal of any comprehension process, the BIA model does not include nodes that represent meaning. Finally, what about the fact that several experiments have shown that sentence context can nullify the homograph effect, suggesting that lexical access is not language-nonselective under all circumstances? To account for the effects of phonology and acknowledging the central role of meaning in language processing, the builders of the BIA model have subsequently proposed an extended model that, in addition to the various types of nodes that represent orthography and language, also includes nodes that represent phonology and semantics (Van Heuven & Dijkstra, 2001). The model is elegantly coined SOPHIA, to stress that semantics, orthography, and phonology are all included (the semantic, orthographic, and phonological interactive activation model). The right part of Figure 4.4 shows the model's components and general structure and the excitatory and inhibitory connections between the various types of representations.

Although not shown, the model represents orthography at a more detailed level than BIA does. Two additional layers are installed in between the original letter and word levels: a level of orthographic clusters and a level of orthographic syllables (the component "sublexical orthography" in Figure 4.4 thus summarizes three levels of units: one representing letters, a second representing letter clusters smaller than the syllable unit, and a third representing syllables). Phonology is represented in four analogous levels of nodes that represent phonological units of different sizes. The processing assumptions are to a large extent the same as those in BIA. Nodes at one particular level (e.g., orthographic syllables) can activate (via excitatory connections, indicated by arrowheads) and inhibit (via inhibitory connections, indicated by bullet heads) representations at adjacent levels (e.g., orthographic words and orthographic clusters). Representations within a particular orthographic or phonological component mutually inhibit one another via lateral inhibition. In contrast, orthographic units activate the corresponding phonological units and vice versa. For instance, if the written word *bird* has been presented to the system and has activated the orthographic word node for *bird*, the corresponding phonological form /burd/ will become activated as well.

SOPHIA is not merely an extended version of BIA, but differs crucially from BIA in one important respect: Whereas BIA contained both excitatory connections from each word node to the corresponding language node and inhibitory connections from a language node to all the word nodes of the other language, the latter connections have been removed in SOPHIA. Because these inhibitory connections served several important functions in the original model (see e.g., Dijkstra, 2005; Thomas & Van Heuven, 2005), their removal from the model demands alternative solutions to explain a number of the effects that have been simulated with BIA. An example is the **language-switching effect**; that is, the finding that words preceded by words of the same language are responded to faster than words preceded by words from the other language. This effect (and especially the analogous switching effect in speech production) will receive more attention in Chapter 6. For now it suffices to say that the solution that is presently explored, in a model called BIA+, is to add a task/decision system (a control system) to SOPHIA's word identification system (Dijkstra & Van Heuven, 2002). Importantly in the present context, this new system is also thought to be responsible for the fact that, as we have seen above, the interlexical homograph effect varies with the specific demands of the task (e.g., language-neutral versus language-specific lexical decision; lexical decision versus word naming) and with the composition of the stimulus set and changes therein during the course of the experiment. In general, Dijkstra and Van Heuven (2002) propose that the task/decision system is sensitive to extra-linguistic influences (such as participant expectancies) whereas the word-identification system is only affected by linguistic sources of information such as lexical, syntactic, and semantic information. The above finding that homograph effects may disappear in sentence context is attributed to processes operating within the word-identification system.

These proposed changes in the system's architecture may at first sight seem relatively minor ones but in fact involve no less than a landslide shift in the authors' views on what causes the homograph effects and their magnitude. Given that the original BIA model only encompasses a word identification component (a mental lexicon), the effects of interlexical homography were all attributed to processes of activation and inhibition in this lexicon and to its structural characteristics (threshold settings; facilitatory versus inhibitory connections between nodes; dual nodes for interlexical homographs). This is what is sometimes referred to as a "lexicon-internal" locus of control (e.g., Von Studnitz & Green, 1997, 2002a, 2002b). In BIA+, the effects are partly attributed to what Von Studnitz and Green have called "external control", that is, the ability of a lexicon-external task/ decision system to respond flexibly to a number of variables such as the specific requirements of the task. A similar external control system is a central component in a further influential model of how bilinguals' lexical performance is modified by the task context, namely, Green's (1998) inhibitory control model (see pp. 307–308 for details). This is no coincidence because in developing BIA+ its builders have been strongly influenced by Green's model, so much so that the two models now strongly resemble one another.

So far the evidence that lexical access is language-nonselective, at least in out-of-context studies, has come primarily from studies that examined how visually presented interlexical homographs are processed. The skeptical reader might therefore not be convinced. After all, interlexical homographs only exist for pairs of languages that employ the same alphabetic script and even within such language pairs the total number of interlexical homographs one can come up with is usually quite small. Is it maybe the case the BIA model has been developed to account for a rather idiosyncratic phenomenon, one that has little to do with how we recognize less exotic words? The homograph data are, however, not the only evidence to support the model. A second cornerstone of the model concerns the phenomenon that the memory representations of so called "neighbors" of the stimulus word are excited by the stimulus, irrespective of the language to which they belong. This is the main topic to be addressed in the next section. In a further

section I will present evidence that makes it clear the ultimate model of bilingual visual word recognition cannot do without a phonological component, a conclusion that has led to the development of SOPHIA.

Further support for the bilingual interactive activation model

According to the above description of BIA's functioning, complete form overlap between the presented input and the information specified in orthographic word nodes is not required for a word node to become activated upon the presentation of a word input: The stimulus *sand* not only activates the node <sand> but also the (same-language) nodes <hand> and <sank> as well as the (other-language) nodes <zand> and <mand>, among others. The relevant evidence has been gathered in studies that investigated the effect of a word's **neighborhood** characteristics on visual word recognition.

A word's neighborhood is defined as the set of words that share a substantial part of their (orthographic and/or phonological) form with the target word (where "substantial" in most studies has been taken to mean three letters out of four or four letters out of five). Monolingual neighborhood studies have shown that the time to recognize a visually presented word is influenced by the number and frequency of orthographically similar words, its "neighbors" (Andrews, 1989; Grainger, 1990; Grainger, O'Regan, Jacobs, & Segui, 1989; Grainger & Segui, 1990). This finding implies that word recognition does not take place independently from the rest of the lexical system but that a written word activates a whole set of orthographic word nodes in memory and not just its own representation. This conclusion and the associated methodology provided bilingual researchers with an additional means to address the question whether word recognition is language-nonselective. Specifically, they posed the question of whether neighborhood effects extend beyond the language of input: Does a visually presented word activate orthographically similar words in both of a bilingual's two languages? As we have seen, the BIA model assumes this to be the case. The results from a set of **cross-language neighborhood** studies provided the ground for this assumption. I will illustrate the logic of these studies in discussing two of them. The results of both have been successfully simulated with the BIA model (Dijkstra & Van Heuven, 1998), suggesting the model's architecture and processing assumptions are correct.

Grainger and Dijkstra (1992) had French–English bilinguals perform an English lexical decision task to three types of English target words (and to pseudowords), presented visually. The words in one of these groups, called "patriots", had many more neighbors in the target language English than in non-target French. A second group consisted of English words with many more French than English neighbors ("traitors"). The third group contained English words with approximately the same number of neighbors in both languages ("neutral"). Because word frequency is known to have a large effect on lexical decision time (see above for an explanation of why this is so), the three groups of English target words were matched on word frequency. The data, shown in Figure 4.5, demonstrated an influence of the relative number of neighbors in the two languages: Lexical decision times were longest in

the "traitor" condition, intermediate in the "neutral" condition, and shortest in the "patriot" condition. Van Heuven et al. (1998) obtained similar results and showed that the effect extends to other tasks, in their case, progressive demasking.

A further study made the important new point that a visually presented word does not have to be consciously perceived to trigger its word node and the nodes representing its within- and cross-language neighbors into activity. In a French–English study, Bijeljac-Babic, Biardeau, and Grainger (1997) used the masked priming methodology: Each word (or pseudoword) target was preceded by a word prime that was presented too briefly to be identified by the participants, and the participants' task was to make lexical decisions to the targets, which were clearly visible. The targets were all French words (or French-like pseudowords). The primes and targets were orthographically similar or dissimilar and the primes belonged to the same language as the targets or to the other language (e.g., French prime, French target: *soin–soif* vs. *huit–soif*; English prime, French target: *soil–soif* vs. *gray–soif*). Two groups of French–English bilinguals were tested, one group of balanced bilinguals and a second with L1 French stronger than

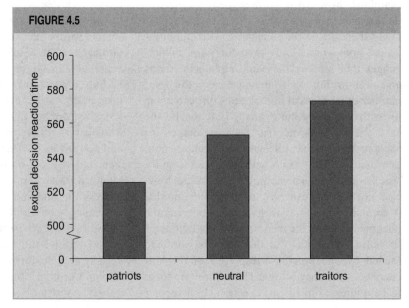

FIGURE 4.5

Mean lexical decision times (in ms) as a function of relative number of neighbors in the bilingual's two languages. Patriots are words that have more neighbors in the target language than in the non-target language. Neutral words have about equally many neighbors in both languages. Traitors have more neighbors in the non-target language. From Grainger and Dijkstra (1992). Copyright © 1992, with permission from Elsevier.

L2 English. In addition, a monolingual French control group was tested. Inclusion of this group enabled testing of the hypothesis that any effect of a prime in the non-target language to emerge would be due to co-activation of lexical representations in the non-target language and not merely to the orthographic similarity of prime and target supporting target processing in a more peripheral, non-lexical, stage of processing: If the effects were non-lexical, the between-language effects should also occur for the French monolinguals. However, if competition between lexical elements is the source of the effects, the monolingual French group should process targets following orthographically similar and orthographically dissimilar English primes equally fast. After all, these participants' mental lexicon does not contain any representations of English words to cause competition.

The results were clear-cut: In all three groups, when prime and target were words from the same language, French, targets preceded by orthographically similar masked primes were responded to more slowly than targets preceded by dissimilar primes. In contrast, when prime and target were from different languages, this inhibitory effect of orthographically similar primes only showed up in the bilinguals. This combination of results suggests that the source of the masked orthographic priming effect was indeed lexical. At the same time it suggests that, in bilinguals, lexical co-activation of neighbors extends to orthographically similar words in the non-target language. A further finding of interest was that the between-language effect was larger for the balanced bilinguals than for the group less proficient in L2 English (both groups performing the task in L1 French). This finding again suggests that the level of co-activation in a non-target language depends on the bilingual's degree of command over this language (see also pp. 174–176). Finally, these results demonstrate that even a masked prime can trigger the word identification system into activity, because this is the only way it can be explained that target processing is affected at all by the prior presentation of a prime. The effects can then be understood by assuming that in the case of orthographically similar primes and

targets there is extra fierce lexical competition that needs to be resolved, delaying the response.

PARALLEL PHONOLOGICAL ACTIVATION IN TWO LANGUAGES

Evidence from same-alphabet bilingualism

Many studies have provided evidence of simultaneous activation of phonology in a bilingual's two languages. They have done so in various ways and, between them, they show that parallel phonological activation not only occurs in same-alphabet bilingualism but also in forms of bilingualism involving languages that use different alphabets. I will first discuss the evidence from same-alphabet bilingualism (this section) and proceed with a discussion of the cross-alphabet studies. Many of these studies were inspired by a number of monolingual studies that have shown that the moment a printed word hits the visual word recognition system, its phonological form is assembled automatically by applying the language's spelling-to-sound (or **grapheme** to phoneme) conversion rules (e.g., Frost, 1998; Jared, Levy, & Rayner, 1999; Van Orden, 1987; Van Orden, Johnston, & Hale, 1988). Interestingly, also when reading non-alphabetic scripts such as syllabic Japanese and even ideographic Chinese, the written words automatically activate a sound code (Erickson, Mattingly, & Turvey, 1977; Perfetti, Liu, & Tan, 2005; Perfetti & Zhang, 1995; Tzeng, Hung, & Wang, 1977) despite the fact that these scripts are not based on grapheme–phoneme associations. As with alphabetic scripts, syllabic scripts reflect the associated languages' sound system: Their written symbols correspond to syllables, which are units of speech. The fact that these scripts also manifest automatic activation of phonology is therefore not so surprising. However, the relation between the printed characters of ideographic Chinese and phonology is, albeit not totally absent, much more opaque. The finding that in that case the printed symbols also activate phonological codes thus suggests that phonological activation plays a central role in written language processing in general (see Frost & Katz, 1992, for a complete volume dedicated to the relation between orthography and phonology in various scripts). But more to the point in the present context is that, in bilinguals, one and the same visually presented word may lead to parallel spelling-to-sound coding in both languages, as the ensuing discussion will illustrate.

Employing the lexical decision task, Nas (1983) obtained early evidence that during visual recognition of L2 words bilinguals assemble these words' phonological forms just as native speakers of this language do. Although he was primarily interested in how bilinguals process *words* in their L2, part of the critical evidence was based on an analysis of how they process nonwords. It is these data that I will present here. The participants were Dutch–English bilinguals who were presented with L2 English stimulus materials. The nonwords were all letter sequences that obeyed the phonological rules of English and looked like common English words. Half of them were so-called "cross-language pseudo-homophones": When pronounced according to the grapheme–phoneme conversion rules of L2 English, they sounded like real L1 *Dutch* words (e.g., the pseudohomophones *snay* and *roak* sound like the Dutch words *snee* and *rook*, meaning "incision" and "smoke", respectively). The remaining nonwords were non-homophonic controls (e.g., *prusk* or *floon*). Correct "no" decisions to cross-language pseudohomophones took longer than to non-homophonic nonwords, and more errors were made to the former. These findings suggest that the participants generated the phonological forms of the presented nonwords, applying the L2 English grapheme–phoneme conversion rules, and that the phonological forms of the pseudohomophones thus generated contacted those of the similar-sounding Dutch words. This apparently created a tendency to respond "yes" (mistaking the nonword for a word), which was either suppressed, slowing down the response, or was given in to, resulting in an error. Of course, if the nonwords are phonologically coded, the words will be

as well, because up until the moment of lexical access there is nothing that distinguishes the type of nonwords used (obeying the phonological rules of English) from words. In other words, these nonword data inform L2 *word* processing and show that non-native speakers of English use the English sound-to-spelling rules to generate phonological codes for English written words.

— Jared and Kroll (2001) took this research an important step further by posing the question of whether bilinguals apply spelling-to-sound conversion rules in both of their languages in parallel or whether, instead, only the set of spelling–sound correspondences of the target language is activated upon stimulus presentation. They examined this question using the word naming task, testing English–French and French–English bilinguals. Three types of English stimulus words were presented visually, the types differing from one another with respect to their neighborhood characteristics. One type of words contained a "word body" (that is, the medial vowel plus final consonants) that is always pronounced in the same way in English. Examples are the words *drip*, *gulp*, and *gosh*, containing the bodies *-ip*, *-ulp*, and *-osh*. These words are said to have English "friends" only. The words of the second type had inconsistently pronounced bodies: bodies that, in English, are pronounced in more than one way. These words are said to have English "enemies". Examples are *steak* and *bead*, where *–eak* and *–ead* can also be pronounced differently in English, as in *beak* and *head*. Studies on English word naming have generally obtained longer naming latencies for words with spelling patterns that are inconsistently pronounced in English than for consistent words (Glushko, 1979; Jared, McRae, & Seidenberg, 1990), suggesting that the different pronunciations compete during the naming process. The third type of words had *French* enemies, containing bodies pronounced differently (from the English pronunciations) in French (*-ait* as in the English *bait* versus *-ait* as in the French *fait*). This type was included to find out whether longer naming latencies would also be obtained for English words with French enemies. Such a result would suggest that also words from the non-target language take part in the naming competition, thus revealing that parallel application of both the English and French spelling-to-sound conversion rules takes place.

Jared and Kroll (2001) included a couple of variables that might modulate the involvement of the French competitors. For instance, they presented a block of French filler words, to be named in French, in between two blocks of English naming trials. The question addressed with this manipulation was whether for competition by French enemies to occur in English word naming, French should have been recently activated. Jared and Szucs' (2002) homograph study discussed before (see p. 169) shows that such "warming up" of the non-target language can indeed increase the overall competition in the bilingual language system. Another variable they manipulated was the participants' relative fluency in the two languages.

In agreement with the earlier monolingual neighborhood studies (e.g., Jared et al., 1999), longer latencies and more errors occurred for English words with English enemies than for English words containing spelling bodies that are always pronounced the same way in English, but the cross-language effects were more mixed. The data showed especially strong interference effects of French enemies when English naming followed

the French naming session. The effects were generally modest, and, in fact, most of the time non-existent, when English naming preceded French naming. Figure 4.6 illustrates this effect of French and English block order, collapsing over a group of participants more fluent in French and a group more fluent in English (only response time data are shown). The corresponding data of the English enemies condition are shown for comparison.

As shown, when the English words with French enemies were named before the block of French words, their response times were equally long as those for English words that do not have French enemies. However, the naming of English words with French enemies was slowed down considerably when it followed a session of French naming. This suggests that recent activation of the other language system is a prerequisite for language-nonselective, parallel spelling-to-sound coding to occur. The relative fluency of English and French also modulated the effect of French enemies: The non-target language especially interfered with naming (demonstrating parallel sound-to-spelling coding) if it was the stronger language of the two. This finding converges with similar results presented above. Jared and Kroll (2001) concluded that spelling-to-sound conversion rules of a bilingual's two languages can

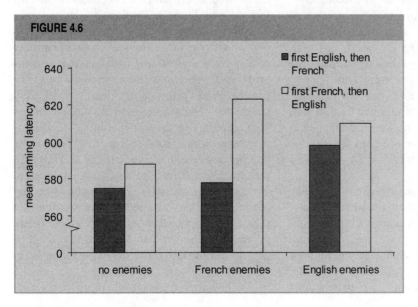

FIGURE 4.6

first English, then French

first French, then English

mean naming latency

640
620
600
580
560
0

no enemies   French enemies   English enemies

Mean naming times (in ms) for English words as a function of word type and presentation order: before or after a block of French trials (see text for details). Data from Jared and Kroll (2001).

be activated simultaneously, but not under all circumstances.

A related study by Van Leerdam, Bosman, and De Groot (2009), testing Dutch–English bilinguals, provided converging evidence of parallel phonological coding in a bilingual's two languages. These authors used a new task, the "bimodal matching task", in which on every trial a printed word was displayed while at the same time a speech segment, consisting of a vowel followed by a consonant, was presented aurally. The printed word was always a word in the participants' L2 English (e.g., *mood*). The speech segment was or was not the correct pronunciation of the printed word's body and the participants' task was to decide whether or not the speech segment matched the printed word's body by pressing either a "yes" or a "no" button. The critical comparison was between two types of "no" trials. In one of these types of trials (the "catch" trials) the speech segment was derived from a Dutch enemy of the printed English word; that is, from a Dutch word with the same printed word body as the English word but pronounced differently in Dutch. For instance, the English word *mood* might be accompanied by the spoken body of Dutch *lood*, which (just as the spoken bodies of other Dutch neighbors of this word, such as *dood, rood*, and *brood*) is pronounced as the spoken body in English *road*. The second type of "no" trials were control trials in which the English printed word had no such enemy neighbors in Dutch. A huge effect of type of "no" trial was observed, the catch trials leading to extremely high numbers of false positives. This finding suggests that the printed English words gave rise to parallel phonological activation in English and Dutch, in other words, that phonological coding of printed L2 words is language-nonselective (the analogous experiment with printed L1 words was not performed).

In a series of studies, Brysbaert and his colleagues approached the question whether language-nonselective phonological activation occurs from a different angle, using the masked priming technique. In these studies, briefly presented visual targets were preceded by briefly presented visual primes and the participants were asked to identify the targets. To decrease the legibility of the primes and targets, they were interspersed between two masking signals (the "forward" and the "backward" mask). The participants were not aware that primes were presented and thought they were participating in experiments aimed at discovering how briefly presented words (the targets) are recognized.

Using this methodology, Brysbaert, Van Dyck, and Van de Poel (1999) asked monolingual French speakers and Dutch–French bilinguals to identify French targets that were preceded by either Dutch or French primes. In a "homophonic" Dutch–French condition, the primes were Dutch words or Dutch-like nonwords that, if pronounced according to the L1 Dutch letter–sound conversion rules, were homophonic to the French (L2) target words. Examples are the prime–target pair *voet–voute* (where *voet* is Dutch for "foot" and *voute* is French for "vault"), and the pair *soer–sourd* (where *soer* is a Dutch-like nonword and *sourd* is French for "deaf"). Performance in this condition was compared with a "graphemic control" condition, where, on average, the prime (again a Dutch word or a Dutch-like nonword) shared as many letters with the target as the corresponding homophonic prime did, but without sharing phonology (e.g., *volk–voute*, where *volk* is Dutch for "people", and *siard–sourd*, where *siard* is a Dutch-like nonword). In the French–French condition the primes were French-like nonwords that were either homophonic with the target (*fain–faim*), graphemically similar to it (*faic–faim*), or unrelated controls (*fint–faim*). The dependent variable was the percentage of correct target identifications. Any difference in performance to the targets in the homophonic and graphemic control conditions to emerge would have to be attributed to the homophony relation between prime and target in the former condition and would, by implication, suggest that automatic spelling-to-sound coding of the primes had occurred. The conclusion that this coding procedure occurred *automatically* follows from the fact that the primes could not be perceived consciously. The results are presented in Figure 4.7.

As shown, even though the participants were

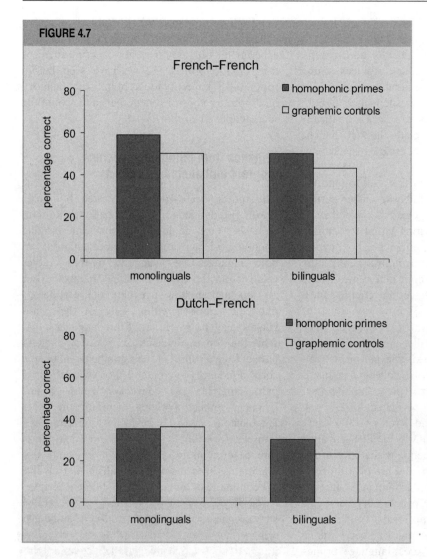

FIGURE 4.7

Probability of correct target word identification as a function of prime type (homophonic vs. graphemic), participant group (monolinguals vs. bilinguals), and prime language (French and Dutch in conditions French–French and Dutch–French, respectively). Data from Brysbaert et al. (1999).

unaware of the primes, in the French–French condition identification performance was better for targets preceded by homophonic primes than for targets preceded by homographic control primes. This "phonological priming effect" was equally large in monolinguals and bilinguals, indicating that L2 speakers exhibit automatic phonological coding to the same extent as L1 speakers. Of particular interest, bilinguals also showed the effect in the Dutch–French condition, and it was statistically as large as in the French–French condition. Duyck, Diependaele, Drieghe, and Brysbaert (2004) replicated the Dutch–French part of this study and extended it by including two groups that differed in their level of fluency in L2 French. Again all targets were in L2 French. The phonological priming effect materialized once more and turned out to be equally large for a group of nearly balanced Dutch–French bilinguals and a group of Dutch–French bilinguals less proficient in French. Finally, Van Wijnendaele and Brysbaert (2002) wondered whether the effect would also materialize if the primes were words from L2 and the targets were L1 words. Now testing both Dutch–French and French–Dutch bilinguals, they obtained the effect for both groups in an experiment with Dutch primes and French targets (that is, with targets in L2 for the Dutch–French group but in L1 for the French–Dutch group). In fact, the effect was equally large for both groups. All in all, this set of studies provides strong evidence that upon the presentation of a printed word the spelling–sound correspondences of both of a bilingual's languages can be automatically activated in parallel. Especially the fact that the primes were not perceived consciously makes this conclusion hard to avoid.

The studies discussed in this section (and the interlexical homophone studies discussed earlier; e.g., Haigh & Jared, 2007) lead to the following three conclusions: (1) During visual recognition of L2 words bilinguals assemble the phonological forms of these words just as native speakers do; (2) This process comes about automatically and unconsciously; (3) Under certain circumstances the grapheme-to-phoneme conversion rules of both languages are activated in parallel. Such parallel activation seemed a universal phenomenon in the visual masking experiments performed by Brysbaert and his colleagues but was modulated by context (the "block-order" manipulation) and the participants' L2 proficiency level in Jared and Kroll's (2001) study. What remains is to explain why parallel activation was a less robust phenomenon in the latter study. A possible reason may be the use of a different methodology: the identification of masked targets following masked primes (Brysbaert and his colleagues) versus unprimed naming (Jared and Kroll). The results of the Brysbaert studies clearly showed that the cross-language primes, though not consciously perceived, accessed and activated the non-target language system. These primes may thus have acted as a warm-up of the elements in the non-target language, just as a prior block of non-target language trials (the French block) in Jared and Kroll's study appeared to have done. That Jared and Kroll obtained evidence of parallel phonological activation in this very condition supports this analysis. Alternatively, the different results may be due to the participants in Jared and Kroll's study having somehow adapted themselves to the specific experimental condition (e.g., expecting French target words following a block of French

words but not otherwise). Similar adaptive behavior was not possible in the masked-priming experiments because it requires conscious perception of the primes. As we have seen before (pp. 180–181), recent models of bilingual memory incorporate a control system that can account for such adaptive behavior.

Evidence from bilingualism across different alphabets and dialects

All studies discussed so far tested bilinguals whose two languages share the same, Roman, alphabet. One could argue that the parallel phonological activation of representations in both languages that is suggested by these studies results from this use of a shared alphabet. After all, no matter how irregular the grapheme–phoneme relations within some of these languages may be (as in English), languages that share the Roman alphabetic script are all likely to have at least a subset of their grapheme–phoneme correspondences in common. For such language pairs, applying the conversion rules of one language implies applying them for the other language as well. The evidence for language-nonselective phonological activation would therefore be even more convincing if it would also materialize in forms of bilingualism that involve the command of languages with different scripts.

Thierry and Wu (2004) cleverly demonstrated the occurrence of parallel activation of languages written in different scripts, in so doing providing indirect support that this parallel activation also involves phonological memory representations. In this study English monolinguals and Chinese–English bilinguals performed a semantic decision task: They were presented with pairs of English words and had to decide for each pair whether or not it consisted of related words (e.g., post–mailbox: "yes"; novel–violin: "no"). Unknown to the participants, the stimulus materials were manipulated on a hidden variable: The Chinese translations of the words in half of the semantically related and unrelated word pairs shared a logographic character. The Chinese translations of the words in the remaining half of the stimulus pairs did not share any form resemblance. The four experimental conditions emerging from the semantic relatedness and form similarity manipulations are illustrated in Table 4.5.

As expected, the monolingual English participants were not affected by the hidden form similarity factor but only exhibited an effect of the semantic manipulation. The bilingual participants were similarly affected by the semantic factor. In addition, they showed a different pattern of responses for the shared character word pairs on the one hand and the non-shared character pairs on the other, both on behavioral measures (response times and error rates) and on ERPs recorded during task performance. This finding suggests that the stimulus words' Chinese translations were activated during English task performance. Although it is not absolutely certain that this co-activation involved the phonological forms of the Chinese translations in addition to their orthographic forms (the logographic characters), the interconnectedness assumed between orthographic and phonological codes in memory (see Figure 4.4) suggests that in this experiment the Chinese co-activation implicated phonological co-activation. The fact that the participants were totally oblivious of the hidden form manipulation furthermore suggests that co-activation of non-target Chinese orthography and phonology was automatic. A couple of other studies provide more direct evidence of automatic phonological coding in a non-target language when the target and non-target languages are written in different scripts. These (and some related studies) will be discussed in the remainder of this section.

One of the pertinent studies, by Gollan, Forster, and Frost (1997) tested Hebrew–English and English–Hebrew bilinguals using a priming paradigm. Hebrew and English use completely different alphabets (they contain completely different sets of letters, differ in the number of letters, and the Hebrew alphabet consists entirely of consonants). The primes were masked such that they could not be perceived consciously and the targets were clearly visible letter strings to be categorized by the participants as words or nonwords (lexical decision). On the trials wherein both prime and target were words, they could either both be words from the same one of the participants' languages (both Hebrew or both English) or the language of prime and target differed (the "between-language" condition). I will focus my discussion on the results of the latter condition.

The primes and targets in the between-language condition were either translations of one another or they were unrelated words. Some of the primes in the translation stimuli shared a cognate relation with their targets, whereas others did not. Because Hebrew and English are written in alphabetic scripts that bear no orthographic resemblance to one another, in this particular study cognate relatedness meant that prime and target had similar *phonological* forms. A reliable **translation priming effect** (the difference in response times for translation stimuli on the one hand and matched, unrelated prime–target stimuli on the other hand) occurred, but only with primes in the stronger L1 and targets in the weaker L2 (see also p. 140). But especially

---

TABLE 4.5

Experimental conditions in Thierry and Wu (2004)

	Semantically related	Semantically unrelated
Partly shared forms	post–mailbox you jū–you xiang	novel–violin xiao shuo–xiao tiqin
Completely different forms	bath–shower xi zao–ling yu	rabbit–desk tu zi–ke zhuo

The participants performed a semantic decision task in English: They decided whether pairs of English words consisted of semantically related or unrelated words. Unknown to the participants, half of the related and unrelated pairs shared a Chinese character; the other half consisted of two words with completely different visual forms.

important in the present context was that these effects from L1 on L2 were larger when primes and targets were cognates than when they were non-cognates. The enhanced translation priming effect for cognate translations, which (in addition to meaning) share phonology but no orthography, once again suggests that under certain circumstances bilinguals may automatically activate and apply spelling–sound correspondences in the non-target language (here, the language of the prime). The reason why the activation must have occurred *automatically* is that the primes could not be consciously identified.

Employing a completely different paradigm, Tzelgov, Henik, Sneg, and Baruch (1996) provided converging evidence that phonological activation in a non-target language may occur in different-alphabet bilingualism. The researchers employed the Stroop color-naming task (or, simply, the **Stroop task**) and, as Gollan and her colleagues, they tested Hebrew–English bilinguals. In Stroop experiments the participants are presented with color words printed in different colors and are asked to name the color of the words and ignore their names. When the color word stimulus and the color it is printed in mismatch (e.g., the word *red* printed in green ink), the color naming response is substantially slower than when they match. This difference is the **Stroop effect**. Tzelgov and his colleagues observed a Stroop effect for stimuli that they coined "cross-script homophones": nonsensical letter strings written in the Roman alphabet that, when pronounced according to the English spelling-to-sound conversion rules, sound like Hebrew color words. For instance, if the English pronunciation rules are applied to the nonwords *kahol* and *adom*, they sound just like the Hebrew words for blue and red, respectively. When the color of the printed stimuli had to be named in Hebrew, such cross-script homophones were responded to slower when their English pronunciations mismatched the color name to be produced than when they matched with the color response. This Stroop effect suggests that the nonsensical strings were automatically coded according to the English sound–spelling rules, causing interference in the case of a mismatch between the emerging phonological code and the requested Hebrew response.

Whereas the studies by Gollan et al. (1997) and Tzelgov et al. (1996) demonstrated that automatic phonological activation of a non-target language occurs in different-alphabet bilingualism, a further bi-alphabetic study indicated that one and the same letter string can give rise to the simultaneous activation of the phonological rule systems of both alphabets. Lukatela, Savić, Gligorijević, Ognjenović, and Turvey (1978) demonstrated this phenomenon to occur in Serbo-Croatian, a Slavic Indo-European language written in two different alphabets, the Roman and the Cyrillic. Some of the letters of the Serbo-Croatian writing system appear in both alphabets but sound differently in each of them. The researchers presented letter strings to their (monolingual, bi-"scriptal") participants for lexical decision. In the critical condition a letter string was a word if pronounced according to the letter-to-sound conversion rules of the one alphabet but a nonword if pronounced according to the rule system of the other alphabet. If phonological coding occurs simultaneously according to the rule systems of both alphabets, the stimuli in this condition should give rise to response conflict and, thus, slow down responding. This is exactly what the researchers found.

As mentioned earlier, automatic phonological activation has also been shown to occur in languages that use scripts that are not sound-based, such as ideographic Chinese (e.g., Tzeng et al., 1977). An interesting feature of Chinese is that its one written script is pronounced differently in the various dialects of Chinese so that bi-dialectal Chinese speakers have two different phonological representations stored in memory for one and the same written character. This state of affairs gives rise to the question whether word recognition in bi-dialectic Chinese speakers involves the simultaneous computation of two pronunciations of one and the same character, just as the Serbo-Croatian study has shown simultaneous phonological coding of one and the same letter string according to the rule system of two alphabetic languages.

Lam, Perfetti, and Bell (1991) addressed this question in a study that is conceptually similar to the Thierry and Wu (2004) study with which I started this section. They compared the performance of bi-dialectal Chinese speakers with Cantonese as their native and strongest dialect and Mandarin as their weaker dialect with the performance of Mandarin mono-dialectal Chinese speakers on a same–different decision task: The participants were presented with pairs of Chinese characters and had to decide for each pair whether, *within* a given dialect, the two had the same pronunciation. The bi-dialectal speakers received the materials in two blocks, one with Cantonese as the target dialect, the second with Mandarin as the target dialect, and were instructed to focus on the target dialect exclusively. Obviously, the mono-dialectal group only performed the task in Mandarin. Four groups of materials were tested.

In Group 1 (DD) the two characters presented on a trial had different pronunciations in both Cantonese and Mandarin; in Group 2 their pronunciations were the same within both dialects (SS); in Group 3 their pronunciations were the same in Cantonese but differed in Mandarin (SD); finally, in Group 4 they were different in Cantonese but the same in Mandarin (DS). If pronunciations are computed simultaneously in the two dialects, so the authors reasoned, character pairs of the SD and DS types should lead to conflict in the bi-dialectal speakers because the computation according to one dialect will lead to a "same" response whereas computation according to the other dialect will lead to a "different" response. This response conflict will have to be resolved and, therefore, lead to a relatively slow response, as compared to the *same* target response ("same" or "different") in the corresponding non-conflict condition (SS or DD). In addition, the response conflict might lead to relatively many errors. In contrast, because such a response conflict would not exist for the Mandarin mono-dialectal speakers, their responses to SD and DD stimuli (in both cases "different" is the correct response) should not differ from each other in terms of response times and errors. Similarly, their responses to the SS

and DS stimuli ("same" in both cases) should not differ from each other.

These predictions were all borne out by the data and the authors concluded that a Chinese character simultaneously activates the two associated phonological forms in bi-dialectal speakers. The similarity with the bilingual case is striking and warrants an explanation of the analogous bilingual and bi-dialectal effects within one and the same theoretical framework. Attributing all of these effects to one and the same source is even more compelling considering a final result that Lam and his colleagues obtained: An asymmetry was observed in the bi-dialectal speakers such that the interfering effects of non-target Cantonese (the stronger dialect) on target Mandarin were considerably larger than the interfering effects of non-target Mandarin (the weaker dialect) on target Cantonese. This finding will remind the attentive reader that the analogous asymmetry has repeatedly been obtained in bilingual studies. Considering the evidence assembled from the variety of sources so far it seems safe to conclude that a stronger language invades a weaker language more radically than a weaker language penetrates the stronger and that the same holds for a pair of dialects of different strengths.

To summarize, the studies discussed in this section point out that reading by different-alphabet bilinguals and bi-dialectal language users involves the same automatic phonological activation across languages as observed in same-alphabet bilingualism.

Language-nonselective phonological activation in spoken language comprehension

In all studies on parallel phonological activation in two languages discussed so far, printed stimulus materials were used, reflecting the dominance of visual over auditory stimulus presentation in research on word recognition, both monolingual and bilingual. Yet the primary focus of these studies was on phonological activation in the bilingual's mental lexicon upon the presentation of a word and not on the pattern of activation established in memory units that represent orthography. The pattern of phonological activation in the lexicon was thus established indirectly, via automatic phonological coding of orthographic input. In addition to the evidence of language-nonselective phonological activation thus gathered, converging evidence has been obtained from a set of studies on spoken language comprehension, in which activation of phonological memory units was established directly by a speech input.

A sizable number of these studies have used the **eye-movement tracking paradigm** that was first used by Tanenhaus, Spivey-Knowlton, Eberhard, and Sedivy (1995) to study the process of on-line spoken language comprehension. In experiments employing this methodology the participants are presented with aural instructions to manipulate real objects on a visual display. For example, they might be asked to "touch the starred yellow square" when the display holds a number of blocks differing in marking, color, and shape, or they might be given the instruction to "put the five of hearts that is below the eight of clubs above the three of diamonds" when the display is composed of seven miniature playing cards including two fives of hearts. The participants wear a head-band with equipment that tracks their eye movements while they carry out the instructions. Using this technique Tanenhaus and his colleagues gathered fine-grained temporal information about the process of spoken language comprehension on a millisecond time scale. They found, for instance, that visual context affects the resolution of temporary syntactic and lexical ambiguities. As an illustration of the latter situation, consider the situation wherein the visual display contained both a candy and a candle and the participants were asked to "pick up the candy and put it above the fork". The mean time to initiate an eye movement to the target candy turned out to be longer in this case than when the display did not contain a distracter object whose name shared initial phonology with the target (*candle*), thus suggesting that the visual context can influence the process of word recognition. Furthermore, the example suggests that, just as a printed word initially gives rise to activation

of a set of orthographic word representations in the mental lexicon that all share orthography with the target word (pp. 181–182), a spoken word initially activates a set of phonologically similar word candidates in memory. In studies on spoken word recognition this set of activated representations is often called the "**cohort**", Marslen-Wilson's cohort model of auditory word recognition (1987) being the eponym of the activated set.

Marian and Spivey employed the eye-movement tracking paradigm in three bilingual studies to see whether the activated cohort also includes phonological representations of words in the non-target language (Marian & Spivey, 2003a, 2003b; Spivey & Marian, 1999). The participants in these studies all had Russian as (stronger) L1 and English as (weaker) L2 and were residents of an English-speaking country. They sat in front of a board with four objects on it, among them, for instance, a stamp. They received spoken instructions such as (in the L1 Russian condition) the Russian equivalent of *put the stamp below the cross: poloji marku nije krestika* (where *marku* is an inflected form of *marka*, which is Russian for *stamp*). In a corresponding L2 English condition the instructions were in English. In a between-language competitor condition, in addition to a stamp, the board carried an object whose name in the non-target language shares word-initial phonology with the target word. For instance, with Russian *marku* as the critical stimulus word, one of the distracter objects was a marker. The names of the remaining two (filler) objects on the board were dissimilar from both the Russian and English names of the target object. This situation is visualized in Figure 4.8.

In a control condition, none of the three non-target objects' names was similar to the name of the target object in either language. Marian and Spivey (2003a, 2003b) also included a within-language competitor condition, with the target word and its competitor in one and the same language (as in Tanenhaus et al.'s, 1995, original experiment; e.g., target: *marker*; within-language competitor: *marble*, in an L2 English condition). The dependent variable was always the proportion of trials on which eye movements were made to the competitor object in comparison to

FIGURE 4.8

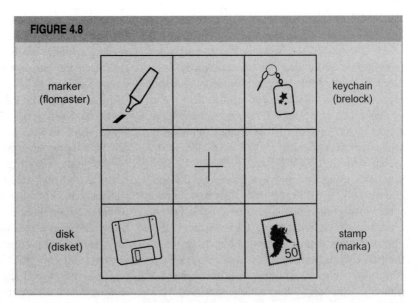

Example display presented to Russian–English bilinguals in an eye-movement tracking study. On this trial the participants receive the spoken instruction *poloji marku nije krestika* (*put the stamp below the cross*). Russian *marku* ("stamp") is the target stimulus, which is similar to English *marker*, the between-language competitor. Adapted from Marian and Spivey (2003a) with permission from Wiley-Blackwell.

a filler object. Such eye movements suggest co-activation of this object's name during the word recognition process.

The three studies differed from one another with respect to the care that was taken to prevent the participants becoming aware they participated in a bilingual experiment. In Spivey and Marian (1999) and Marian and Spivey (2003a) the same bilingual participants took part in both a Russian L1 and an English L2 condition, in two separate sessions. Therefore it is plausible they suspected their bilingualism was being studied. As especially Grosjean (e.g., 1997a, 1998; see pp. 288–291 for details) has argued, this might increase the level of activation of the non-target language and, thus, the chance that this language causes interference. Therefore, to be able to conclude that the recognition of spoken words is generally language-nonselective, evidence of cross-language competitor activation should ideally be collected under testing circumstances in which the participants have no idea they are participating in a bilingual experiment; that is, when the participants are in a **monolingual mode**. Marian and Spivey (2003b) installed such a condition by testing different groups of participants, drawn from the same population, in an English L2 and a Russian L1 experiment.

In all three studies, the bilinguals showed both within-language and between-language competitor effects: They made more eye movements to within- and between-language competitors than to filler objects. Control groups of monolingual English speakers showed competitor effects in the within-language competitor condition only, ruling out the possibility that the between-language effects in the bilinguals might have been an artifact of poor stimulus selection. The within-language effects converged with Tanenhaus et al.'s (1995) results and with other evidence that during speech recognition a word input activates not only its own lexical representation but also a whole set of lexical items similar to the presented word (e.g., Marslen-Wilson, 1987). The between-language effects demonstrated that the cohort of activated lexical representations included elements of both the target language and the non-target language. This finding indicates that, as visual word recognition, spoken word recognition can be language-nonselective.

However, the between-language effects varied between studies. Whereas Marian and Spivey (2003a) and Spivey and Marian (1999) observed them in both languages, in the monolingual-mode condition (Marian & Spivey, 2003b) they only materialized when the task was carried out in L2 English. In other words, competitor interference was obtained from the stronger L1 onto the weaker L2, but not from weaker L2 onto stronger L1, an asymmetry that we have also encountered when discussing the evidence for language-nonselective processing of written words (e.g., Jared & Kroll, 2001; see pp. 184–185). That this asymmetry is a robust phenomenon, also when speech input is processed, is suggested by the results of a couple of further studies that closely replicated Marian and Spivey's (2003b) study. Weber and Cutler (2004) tested Dutch–English bilinguals using the same eye-tracking paradigm and also taking care the participants had no reason to suspect their bilingualism was being tested. Under these circumstances, these authors also obtained cross-language competitor effects when the participants performed the task in weaker L2 (English), but not when testing was in stronger L1 (Dutch). Similarly, Blumenfeld and Marian (2007), obtained a cross-language competitor effect when German–English bilinguals (with German the stronger language of the two) performed the task in L2 English but not when English–German bilinguals (with German the weaker language of the two) performed it in L1 English. It thus appears that speech perception in the stronger L1 may be immune to an influence of a weaker L2 but not vice versa, and that this asymmetry especially holds when the participants have no reason to believe their bilingualism is being tested. Interestingly, in Blumenfeld and Marian's study, immunity of the strong L1 only held for L1 English targets that have non-cognate translations in weaker L2 German. L1 English targets with cognate translations in L2 German *did* show a cross-language competitor effect (in the condition with L2 English targets both cognates and non-cognates manifested the effect). This finding suggests that the presentation of a cognate boosts the activation of a relatively weak non-target language to a sufficiently high level for it to interfere with target processing.

Earlier in this chapter (p. 170) I briefly explained why it is desirable that a particular theoretical issue, here whether the recognition of spoken words is language-selective or language-nonselective, is investigated by means of a "converging evidence" approach in which evidence is collected using more than one experimental task.

The studies discussed in this section so far all employed the eye-tracking paradigm, but converging evidence has been obtained in two studies that used the gating technique. Grosjean (1988) employed it in a French–English study, testing the participants in L2 English only. Schulpen, Dijkstra, Schriefers, and Hasper (2003) tested Dutch–English bilinguals in both language conditions, mixing the languages during presentation of the materials (thus having the participants perform the task under **bilingual mode** circumstances). In both studies, gating performance to interlexical homophones and matched non-homophonic controls was compared (see p. 159). Grosjean's homophones and controls were verbs presented in an all English sentence context, whereas the stimuli used by Schulpen and colleagues were all nouns presented in isolation. Despite the differences between these two studies, their results converged: In both of them successful identification of interlexical homophones required a longer fragment to be presented on a gating trial than successful identification of non-homophonic control words. Furthermore, the participants were less confident in their identification of homophones. Schulpen and collaborators obtained these effects in both language conditions. Grosjean's findings indicate that a homophone's reading in the stronger non-target language was co-activated with its reading in the weaker target language and that this impeded the target's identification. Schulpen et al.'s results point out that in their study the reverse also held: that a homophone's reading in the weaker non-target language was co-activated with its reading in the stronger target language and interfered with recognition. At first sight this finding seems not to be in agreement with the data obtained in the above eye-tracking studies, which had only shown competitor interference from stronger L1 onto weaker L2. A plausible reason for this deviant result is that in this study the L1 and L2 stimulus words were presented mixed. This procedure may have put the participants in a bilingual mode, boosting the activation of the weaker language to a sufficiently high level for it to interfere with processing the words from the stronger language.

All in all, the results of the above studies converge on the conclusion that spoken L2 words (when L2 is the weaker language) give rise to language-nonselective phonological activation in bilingual lexical memory. The eye-tracking data suggest that the opposite does not hold; that is, that spoken L1 words (with L1 the stronger language) do not activate the phonological representations of similarly sounding L2 words. Finally, the gating data are not altogether conclusive due to a procedural infelicity contained in one of the pertinent studies. Nevertheless it seems legitimate to conclude that their results are compatible with those obtained by means of the eye-tracking methodology.

Spurious activation in non-native listening

To conclude this section, one related further line of research deserves to be discussed here. It demonstrates that there is more lexical competition in the bilingual system than in the monolingual system from a different angle than the studies reviewed above. The studies in question (e.g., Broersma, 2002, 2005, 2006; Escudero, 2007; Weber & Cutler, 2004) build on the observation that non-native listeners of a language often experience problems perceiving the speech sounds of this language accurately and confuse non-native sounds that are not distinctive in their native language. Probably the best-known example is the confusability of /r/ and /l/ by native speakers of Chinese and Japanese with the effect that they cannot tell the difference between, for instance, English *wrist* and *list*. A plausible cause of these perceptual problems is that the information stored in the associated non-native phoneme categories in memory is imprecise or incomplete, or perhaps that the two sounds of a confusable pair are not represented in separate phoneme categories in memory but fused into a single category. What is more, the one phoneme category onto which both non-native sounds are mapped does not even have to be a non-native-specific category but can be an extant native category that represents native speech sounds similar to both elements of the confusable non-native pair. This possibility follows from models

of non-native speech learning which assume that non-native sounds that are similar to native sounds are assimilated to the latter's phoneme categories. This idea is advanced both in the perceptual assimilation model of Best and her colleagues (Best, 1994; Best et al., 1988) and in the speech learning model of Flege and collaborators (e.g., Flege 2002; Flege, Schirru, & MacKay, 2003; see also pp. 22–23 and 271–274).

Because phoneme identification is a waystation en route to word recognition in the aural modality (see Figure 4.9, to be discussed later), such deficiencies in the representations of non-native speech sounds and the assimilation of non-native sounds to native phoneme categories may be expected to affect the way non-native speakers recognize words. And indeed they do, as has been demonstrated in a variety of ways. Specifically, they have been shown to result in an excessive amount of spurious lexical activation in the non-native lexicon. The experimental materials in the relevant studies were always based on sound contrasts that are hard to distinguish by non-native speakers. An example is the contrast between /æ/ (as in *accident* and *flash*) and /ɛ/ (as in *execute* and *flesh*), which are not represented separately in Dutch phonetic space. In one experiment (Broersma, 2002, 2005) native and non-native speakers of English (the non-native speakers being Dutch–English bilinguals highly fluent in English) listened to monosyllabic English words and nonwords and had to make a lexical decision to each of them. All words contained one vowel or one word-final consonant known to be confusable with one particular other vowel or consonant, respectively, by Dutch native speakers (e.g., it contained /æ/ or /ɛ/). The nonwords were all "near-words", constructed from the real words by replacing the critical vowel or consonant by its confusable counterpart. The results were clear: As compared to native speakers, non-native listeners mistook relatively many of the near-words for words, suggesting that the near-words activated the representations of the corresponding actual words beyond their recognition threshold.

Two further studies (Escudero, 2007; Weber & Cutler, 2004), both testing highly proficient Dutch–English bilinguals in their non-native

English, employed the eye-tracking paradigm discussed above. On each trial in the Weber and Cutler study the participants heard a word that they had to match to the corresponding picture, presented together with a set of distracter pictures. While performing this task, the participants fixated their eyes longer and more often on pictures whose names only differed from the targeted pictures' names in that they contained a confusable sound (e.g., target: a picture of cattle; competitor: a picture of a kettle) than on pictures with less confusable names (e.g., a picture of a beetle). Native English speakers did not show this effect of distracter type. Escudero (2007) extended these findings to the recognition of previously unknown non-native words. She first had her participants learn the meanings of a set of nonsense English words such as /tɛnzə/, /tændək/, and /tunzər/ by pairing them with pictures of nonsense objects. This training phase was followed by an eye-tracking phase: On each trial the participants heard one of the newly learned words (e.g., /tɛnzə/) and their eye fixations to the corresponding picture (the picture of the object called /tɛnzə/ before) and to distracter pictures (the pictures showing the objects called /tændək/ and /tunzər/) were registered. Again the pictures with confusable names (/tændək/) were fixated on relatively often. Both these findings suggest that non-native listeners easily confuse spoken words that only differ in one, confusable, sound (in word-initial position).

In a final experiment (Broersma, 2005, 2006), fluent but non-native (Dutch) and native speakers of English performed a lexical decision task on visually presented trisyllabic words (and nonwords) that were all preceded by an auditory prime. During the construction of the materials each critical trisyllabic word was paired with a second one with which it shared first-syllable stress. Furthermore, up to and including the vowel of the second syllable the sounds of the two words in a pair were identical except that the first vowel of one was /æ/ whereas in the other it was /ɛ/ (e.g., accident versus execute). For each word pair a phonologically and semantically unrelated trisyllabic word was also selected, which was to serve as target in a control con-

dition. The aural primes were subsequently constructed by, first, recording all of the selected words as spoken by a male native speaker of British English and, next, excising the first part of each recorded word up to and including the vowel of the second syllable. (In addition, filler word-target materials as well as nonword-target materials were constructed, to be ignored in the ensuing discussion.) During data gathering, each critical target could be preceded by an Identity prime, a Mismatch prime, or a Control prime. An Identity prime was the sound segment excised from the target itself (e.g., prime: acci, from accident; target: accident). A Mismatch prime was the sound segment excised from the word the target had been paired with (e.g., prime: exe, from execute; target: accident). A Control prime was a sound segment excised from an unrelated word (e.g., prime: pove, from poverty; target: accident).

The author hypothesized that a Mismatch prime (exe) would activate the subsequent target (accident) more in non-native speakers than in native speakers, thereby facilitating target recognition to a relatively large extent. An Identity prime was hypothesized to facilitate target recognition equally in both groups. These predictions were borne out by the data: As compared to the unrelated control condition (and with proportion correct serving as the dependent variable), the non-native speakers showed a clear priming effect of Mismatch primes, whereas the native speakers showed no such effect. Furthermore, the priming effect of Mismatch primes in the non-native listeners was equally large as the priming effect of Identity primes in both listener groups. These data thus suggest that non-native speech input causes a relatively large amount of spurious activation in the non-native lexicon: In non-native listeners the cohort of lexical representations activated by a speech fragment is larger than the cohort that is activated by this same speech fragment in native speakers (here, for instance, the speech fragment exe activated both the representations of words starting with exe and acci in non-native listeners but only those of words starting with exe in native listeners). Cutler (2005) and Broersma (2006) argued that already this one ambiguity of /æ/ and /ɛ/ in Dutch non-native speakers of English may increase the number of (English only) competitors during the lexical selection process by tens, maybe even hundreds, on average. Given the fact that more than one of these ambiguities may exist within a particular non-native language, it becomes clear that "the increase of lexical activation may be very large in non-native listening" (Broersma, 2006, p. 1522). Because, as we have seen in the first part of this section, the lexical cohorts formed during non-native listening also include lexical representations belonging to the other language, the cohort sizes during L2 processing may be truly impressive.

But by far the most noteworthy—because counterintuitive—conclusion to draw from the present work is that, apparently, despite the fact that the non-native lexicon contains fewer lexical elements overall than the native lexicon, more lexical elements compete for selection in non-native than in native listening. (Incidentally, the same might hold for non-native language production, as the following anecdotal evidence suggests: While working on this book, a zillion times writing errors such as "... *this hypothesis was threatened* [instead of *strengthened*]" and "... *greater then* [for *than*]" miraculously emerged on the screen.)

Explaining language-nonselective phonological activation effects

The combined studies reviewed in this section so far provide a substantial amount of evidence that, when presented with a *written* word, under many circumstances (but not always) bilinguals apply the spelling-to-sound conversion rules of both languages in parallel; that the phonological codes generated via one of these sets of rules contact similar sounding representations in the other language; and that generating such phonological codes may occur automatically in the non-target language (as in the target language) even under circumstances in which the participants are led to believe it is a monolingual study they are participating in. Furthermore, the data show that the presentation of a *spoken* word activates a cohort

of lexical items that all share phonology with this spoken word and that, if the presented word is from weaker L2, the activated cohort includes words from both of the bilingual's two languages. If the presented word is from stronger L1 the same only holds under specific circumstances or for a specific type of stimulus materials (cognates).

Earlier on I introduced SOPHIA (Figure 4.4), the extended version of the bilingual interactive activation model that includes phonological representations of different sublexical word units (phonetic features, phonemes, phoneme clusters) and of whole words (phonological words). Upon the presentation of visual word input, the corresponding orthographic representations of both languages are activated first. These then transmit activation not only upwards to the next level of orthographic representations but also laterally to the phonological nodes they are connected with and further upwards (as well as downwards again) until the lexical competition process has been resolved and the input word is recognized. Conversely, when auditory input is presented, the corresponding phonological representations of both languages are first activated. These then transmit activation laterally to the orthographic representations as well as further up to the next level of phonological nodes. The model has not yet been tested against bilingual behavioral data. Nevertheless, given the components that it contains and the way these are interconnected, it has the potential to successfully account for both the evidence of orthographic and phonological language-nonselective activation. The biggest challenge will be to also accurately model the circumstances under which language-nonselectivity does *not* hold, such as has been shown often to be the case when the target stimuli are words from stronger L1.

A second model that may ultimately successfully account for parallel phonological activation in a bilingual's two languages is BIMOLA, the bilingual interactive model of lexical access (Grosjean, 1997a; Léwy & Grosjean, 1996; see Figure 4.9). Whereas BIA (Figure 4.4) was originally developed as a computational model of written word recognition, BIMOLA was

FIGURE 4.9

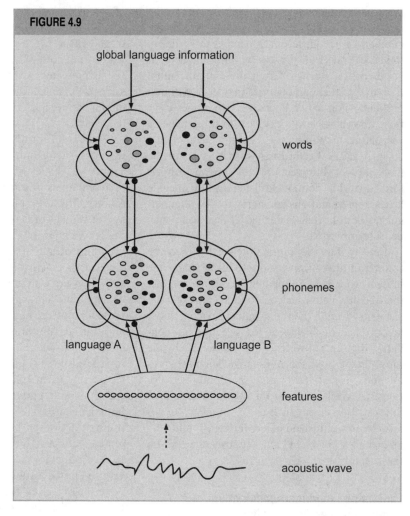

global language information

words

phonemes

language A   language B

features

acoustic wave

The bilingual interactive model of lexical access (BIMOLA), a model of spoken word recognition in bilinguals. Arrowheads represent excitatory connections. Bullet heads represent inhibitory connections. From Léwy and Grosjean (1996). Adapted from Grosjean (1997b). With kind permission by John Benjamins Publishing Company, Amsterdam/Philadelphia. www.benjamins.com

developed to account for spoken word recognition from the outset. Whereas BIA extended an earlier monolingual model of *visual* word recognition (the interactive activation model of McClelland & Rumelhart, 1981), BIMOLA was modeled on TRACE, a computational model of monolingual *spoken* word recognition (McClelland & Elman, 1986).

BIMOLA represents the auditory features, phonemes and the spoken forms of words in three layers of nodes. The feature-level nodes are shared between the two languages, whereas the nodes representing phonemes and word forms are organized in separate language subsets that are both part of a larger system (e.g., Paradis, 2004). A comparison of Figure 4.4 and Figure 4.9

shows many similarities between BIA (and SOPHIA) and BIMOLA, such as the core assumption of interactivity: Activated nodes at different levels can activate (via the excitatory connections) and inhibit (via the inhibitory connections) nodes at neighboring levels. Furthermore, within-level lateral inhibition occurs in both models. But there are also crucial differences between the models. For instance, whereas in BIA and SOPHIA the lateral inhibition exerted by a word affects words from the same and the other language, BIMOLA restricts lateral inhibition to units (phonemes, words) of the other language (between subsets). Maybe more importantly, BIMOLA does not assume language nodes on the grounds that "There is no empirical evidence such a node exists, nor do we know how this node is created when a new language is learned" (Léwy & Grosjean, 1996). An important function of the language nodes in BIA (but not in SOPHIA, nor in BIA+; Dijkstra & Van Heuven, 2002) was to suppress the activation of the non-target language. BIMOLA assumes other ways to see to it that the targeted language is activated most: The two word subsets receive a different amount of top-down pre-activation, based on external information that specifies what the **base language** is (see pp. 289–290 for details). Furthermore, once a word or a phoneme in a subset becomes activated it sends a small positive signal to the other words and phonemes, respectively, in the same subset. This way the subsets corresponding to the target language will be activated relatively highly.

Given this set up, an auditory word input will give rise to activation of phonological representations in both languages, first at the language-independent level of the phonetic features and from there higher up in the system. Two of the effects the model has successfully simulated so far suggest that it can indeed account for language-nonselective phonological activation: the "unit similarity effect" and the "base language homophone effect" (Grosjean, 1988; Léwy & Grosjean, 1996). The unit similarity effect is the phenomenon that a unit, for instance a phoneme, presented in one language and sharing properties with a unit in the other language, will co-activate the latter. The base language homophone effect is the phenomenon that words from the other language (the **guest language**; see pp. 289–290) that have close homophones in the base language are more difficult to process than other guest language words.

To conclude, both SOPHIA and BIMOLA may ultimately be able to account for the present evidence of language-nonselective phonological activation. Because of its interconnectedness with the visual word recognition system and, hence, its potential to explain more phenomena, SOPHIA appears to be the more attractive of the two models. Nevertheless, because it was specifically developed as a model for spoken word recognition, BIMOLA seems the most natural candidate to explain language-nonselective phonological

effects. What is furthermore in favor of BIMOLA is that it can do without language nodes, which one cannot help thinking of as being rather artificial constructs.

THE PROCESSING OF COGNATES

Bilingual studies

The studies on parallel activation in bilingual memory that I discussed in the previous sections all focused on the effect of various types of between-language word *form* similarity on processing. Pairs of interlexical homographs share their complete orthographic form between languages. Interlexical orthographic neighbors share most, but not all, of their orthographic form with their counterparts in the other language. Interlexical homophones and homophonic neighbors share phonology between languages. If the two languages in question use the same alphabetic script, interlexical homophones and homophonic neighbors also share orthography (and are, by implication, interlexical orthographic neighbors at the same time). The words in none of these types of cross-language word pairs share any meaning between the languages.

A further type of between-language word relation is the cognate relation, where a pair of L1 and L2 words share both form and meaning. In other words, a pair of cognates constitutes a pair of translations with identical or similar orthography and/or phonology. I have already treated cognates at length in Chapter 3 (pp. 119–120), discussing the finding that foreign words sharing a cognate relation with the corresponding L1 words are easier to learn than non-cognate foreign words. Some related findings regarding cognates were also discussed there, such as the phenomenon that an unknown form that resembles the form of an L1 word automatically triggers the latter. It may be obvious that the process underlying this phenomenon is the same as the one underlying the above effects of interlexical neighbors, homographs and homophones: In all cases the effect is due to the stimulus exciting (the representations of) a set of similar forms in the mental lexicon. It will therefore not come as a surprise that cognates have also been used to study word recognition in bilinguals. In this section I will review some of the pertinent studies. Processing differences between cognates and non-cognates have also been the object of study in word production research that employed tasks like word association, word translation, and picture naming. These will be reviewed in Chapter 5.

We have already seen (p. 168) that the direction of interlexical homograph effects (that is, whether interlexical homographs are processed faster or slower than their non-homographic controls) varies with the specific demands of the task the participants must perform. The word recognition studies that have compared the processing of cognates and non-cognates suggest that this also holds for the "cognate effect", the difference in processing time (and error percentages) for cognates on the one hand and non-cognates on the other hand. The far majority of these studies have shown a facilitating effect of cognates; namely, that bilinguals respond faster to cognates than to matched non-cognates (matched on, for instance, word frequency, concreteness, and length). Across these studies a number of different tasks have been used such as primed or unprimed lexical decision (Caramazza & Brones, 1979; De Groot et al., 2002; De Groot & Nas, 1991; Gollan et al., 1997), progressive demasking (Dijkstra et al., 1999), and semantic categorization (Sánchez-Casas et al., 1992). However, at least one study, an English–Spanish word naming study by Schwartz, Kroll, and Diaz (2007), has shown *longer* latency times for cognates than for non-cognates. How can this deviant result be understood?

The answer to this question is likely to be found in the specific requirement of the naming task to pronounce the target word, a requirement that does not hold for the other tasks. The previous section has provided much evidence that phonological activation of visually presented words is language-nonselective. As a consequence of its cross-language orthographic similarity, a visually presented cognate stimulus will give rise to strong activation of the orthographic word

nodes representing both terms in a cognate pair and each of these nodes will transmit activation to the corresponding phonological nodes. When the two terms in a cognate pair are phonologically dissimilar, the activated phonological node corresponding to the non-target element of the pair, preparing a response that mismatches the response solicited for, will act as a nuisance competitor in the naming process. The consequence is a delayed naming response.

This analysis can also explain similar inhibitory effects in two further word naming studies that were presented in previous sections: Jared and Szucs (2002) obtained longer naming latencies for interlexical homographs than for non-homographic controls (p. 169), and Jared and Kroll (2001) obtained longer naming latencies for target words that had an enemy neighbor in the non-target language (e.g. the English word *bait* having French *fait* as an enemy because the word body –*ait* is pronounced differently in the two languages see pp. 184–185) than for control words. By definition, the phonological form of (the word body of) an enemy neighbor in the non-target language (*fait*) differs from that of the corresponding word in the target language (*bait*) and also interlexical homographs will usually be pronounced differently across languages. The co-activated homograph's or neighbor's phonology in the non-target language will therefore interfere with processing and slow down the naming response. Only in cases where the homograph's two pronunciations would happen to be identical in the two languages, might a *facilitating* effect of interlexical homography be expected to occur.

If this analysis of cognate inhibition in word naming is correct, one might expect naming performance to improve if the competitor's phonology is more similar to the phonology of the target. Possibly even, if the two words in a cognate pair are pronounced exactly the same, naming cognates might be faster than naming matched controls. The former prediction was borne out in Schwartz et al.'s (2007) English–Spanish study, in which the cognate effects were examined in much more detail than suggested above, the authors attempting to unravel the effects of degree of orthographic and phonological resemblance of cognates. The study included (in addition to non-cognates) four types of cognates, namely cognates with: identical orthography and nearly identical phonology; identical orthography but more dissimilar phonology; relatively dissimilar orthography and nearly identical phonology; and both relatively dissimilar orthography and phonology. Note that these differences between the four cognate groups in terms of orthographic and phonologic similarity concerned differences in the *degree* of between-language resemblance. Because Spanish and English are both Roman-alphabetic languages, cognate pairs that share orthography but at the same time have completely dissimilar phonology are unlikely to exist. A clear effect of degree of phonological similarity occurred: Naming orthographically identical cognates with nearly identical phonological forms was faster and much more accurate, both in L1 and L2, than naming orthographically identical cognates with more dissimilar phonology.

After discussing interlexical homograph effects earlier (p. 168) and suggesting why the direction of these effects might differ between studies, I concluded with the statement that the very occurrence of such an effect, irrespective of its direction, constitutes evidence of language-nonselective word recognition. Similarly, the present facilitating and inhibitory cognate effects have all been interpreted to reflect language-nonselective bilingual word recognition or, in other words, co-activation of elements in the nontarget language. Later on (pp. 203–205) an alternative account of cognate effects will be presented. But first some words are in order on the effect of sentence context on cognate effects and, in a separate section, on cognate processing in trilinguals.

Earlier on we have seen that interlexical-homograph effects can disappear if the homographs and their controls are presented in a sentence context (Elston-Güttler et al., 2005; Schwartz & Kroll, 2006), suggesting that sentence context prevents the activation of the homograph's representation in the contextually inappropriate language subsystem. Schwartz and Kroll also looked at the effect of sentence context on the processing of cognates and non-cognates.

In the high-constraint condition of that study (see Table 4.4) cognates and non-cognate controls were named equally fast, suggesting language-selective processing. In contrast, in the low-constraint condition cognates were named faster than their non-cognate controls, a finding that suggests language-nonselective processing. The joint homograph and cognate data suggest that the modulating effect of context on homograph processing is more pervasive than on cognate processing: With naming time as the dependent variable, the homograph effect disappeared in both highly and weakly constraining contexts, but the cognate effect only disappeared in the highly constraining contexts but remained in the weakly constraining condition. Recently, Van Hell and De Groot (2008) replicated Schwartz and Kroll's cognate results in an experiment in which Dutch–English bilinguals performed a lexical decision task instead of word naming. As in Schwartz and Kroll's investigation, the stimulus materials were presented in L2 English. Cognates processed in isolation and in a low-constraint sentence context were responded to faster than matched non-cognates. In a high-constraint context condition the cognate effect disappeared.

In a further Dutch–English study, Duyck, Van Assche, Drieghe, and Hartsuiker (2007) similarly obtained a cognate effect when cognates and non-cognate controls were presented in isolation or in a low-constraint sentence context and the participants had to provide lexical decision responses to the (L2 English) target stimuli (no high-constraint sentence condition was included). These authors split up their cognate materials into a group of identical cognates (e.g., *lip–lip*) and a group of non-identical cognates (e.g., *ship–schip*) and obtained a cognate advantage for both groups, but it was relatively large for the identical cognates. A further Dutch–English experiment suggested there may be a limit to the cognate effect in low-constraint sentence contexts and, thus, to language-nonselective activation. This experiment, with again L2 words as test stimuli, employed the eye-tracking methodology. This technique allows relatively natural reading on the part of the participants and does not require any secondary task such as lexical decision that possibly interferes with the normal reading process. An analysis of first fixation duration, gaze duration, and regression path duration (see p. 161) showed a robust cognate effect for identical cognates but none for non-identical cognates. Apparently, degree of between-language cognate similarity is a factor to be taken into account. This conclusion is strengthened by the results of a subsequent study (Van Assche, Duyck, Hartsuiker, & Diependaele, 2009) in which the researchers again studied the processing of cognates and non-cognates in low-constraint sentence contexts employing the eye-tracking technique, but this time the test was done in (stronger) L1 Dutch. Even under these circumstances a cognate effect materialized, suggesting also that the more dominant language is not immune to an influence from the other language under all circumstances. The data furthermore showed that first fixation duration, gaze duration, and regression path duration all decreased with an increasing cross-language overlap of the two terms in the cognate pairs, thus once again pointing at a role for degree of between-language cognate similarity. However, in a near replication of this study (Van Assche, 2009), now including both a high-constraint and a low-constraint sentence context condition, none of the reading measures showed a cognate effect, also not in the low-constraint condition. Contrary to Van Assche et al. (2009), this finding suggests that the dominant native language is processed in a language-selective way.

To summarize, although the evidence is somewhat mixed, the general picture that emerges from the sentence context studies with interlexical homographs or cognates as the critical stimuli is that both highly and weakly constraining sentence context prevents co-activation of an interlexical homograph's representation in the non-target language but that only highly constraining contextual information prevents co-activation of a cognate's representation in the non-target language. Generally, a weakly constraining sentence context does not nullify the cognate effect, although it does seem to do so under special circumstances. It is tempting to regard the relatively persistent cognate

effects in low-constraint sentence contexts as evidence of language-nonselective word processing. However, the differential results for interlexical homographs on the one hand and cognates on the other hand may also be due to possible representational differences between interlexical homographs and cognates. These will be discussed further on, following a discussion of a few trilingual studies to which I will now turn.

Trilingual studies

In one sense, the modifier "bilingual" concerns an imprecise qualification of the studies that we have considered so far in this chapter. The suggestion is that the participants in these studies had a command over exactly two languages, no more and no less. However, many of them may have possessed at least some knowledge of more languages than just the two *under study* and actually use it in communication. Although it is in agreement with common practice, with hindsight this labeling convention is somewhat unfortunate, especially now that a study by Lemhöfer, Dijkstra, and Michel (2004) has shown that multiple non-target languages may have additive effects on processing the target. These researchers tested Dutch–English–German trilinguals in a German (L3, the weakest language) lexical decision study. Two groups of cognate stimuli were presented. One group consisted of German words that shared orthography with both Dutch and English ("triple" cognates); a second group consisted of German words that only shared orthography with their Dutch translation equivalents ("double" cognates). The double cognates were responded to faster than a group of matched German non-cognate control words. In their turn, the triple cognates were processed faster than the double cognates. Apparently, during L3 word recognition both L1 and L2 were co-activated with L3 and each of these two sources of co-activation contributed separately to the cognate effect. In terms of the authors' vivid metaphor: Upon the presentation of a cognate word, the three languages together provide one "echo" (as the authors called the phenomenon) which speeds up the response. It thus appears that all languages known join forces in generating a response, just as all languages known have earlier been shown to be exploited in acquiring foreign vocabulary (pp. 98–101).

A second trilingual lexical decision study, by Van Hell and Dijkstra (2002), makes the—by now familiar—point that level of proficiency in a non-target language determines whether or not and to what extent the latter exerts an effect on processing the target language. The participants were Dutch–English–French trilinguals with L1 Dutch as their strongest language, English as their strongest foreign language, and French as a weaker foreign language. Across two experiments, the participants' proficiency in L1 Dutch and L2 English was kept constant, but L3 French pro-ficiency differed between experiments. A further noteworthy aspect of this study was that the authors took great care to let the participants believe they were taking part in a monolingual experiment. Dutch words that have an English cognate translation were consistently responded to faster than matched Dutch words with a non-cognate English translation. In contrast, the analogous cognate effect of L3 French only materialized when the participants' fluency in French was beyond some minimal level. The combined results show that also a weaker lan-guage may influence the processing of a dominant L1, but only if some minimal level of proficiency in it has been attained. These effects occurred despite the fact the participants were not aware their trilingualism was being tested and thus have no reason whatsoever to consciously activate the non-target languages.

Explaining cognate effects: An alternative account

Up until this point, just like the effects of inter-lexical homographs and interlexical neighbors, cognate effects were attributed to co-activation of memory nodes representing elements of the non-target language during target processing. Depending on the exact nature of the materials, the co-activated nodes may represent orthog-raphy, phonology, or meaning, or a combination

of these. The implicit assumption was that cognate and non-cognate pairs are represented in bilingual memory in similar types of represen-tational structures, with each element of both a cognate translation pair and a non-cognate translation pair being represented in a separate set of memory nodes (together representing orthography, phonology, and meaning). However, several authors have suggested an alternative to this account of the cognate effects in terms of co-activation of representational units in the non-target language. This alternative is that cognate effects result from qualitatively different repre-sentations for cognate and non-cognate pairs. An important reason to consider such an account is that in one important respect cognates differ from interlexical homographs and interlexical neighbors: They share both form *and* meaning between a bilingual's two languages. Two versions of this alternative view have in fact been proposed.

From the different patterns of cross-language semantic priming effects occurring for cognates and non-cognates, De Groot and Nas (1991) suggested that cognates and non-cognates might be represented differently at the conceptual (meaning) level of representation. Van Hell and De Groot (1998a) drew a similar conclusion from an experiment that compared bilingual word association behavior within a language and between languages. To account for the results of these studies, two possibilities were considered, one in terms of localist representation models and a second in terms of distributed representa-tion models. According to the localist view, a word meaning is represented in a single node in memory. According to the distributed view the meaning of a word is spread out over a number of nodes, each of them representing one aspect of the word's meaning (cf. Figures 3.6 and 3.8, and Figures 3.11a and 3.11b; see pp. 132–133 and 139–140 for further details). In terms of the local-ist view, a pair of cognates may share a single conceptual representation in bilingual memory whereas the two members of a pair of non-cognates might each have a separate conceptual representation. In terms of the distributed view, both cognates and non-cognates share a number of conceptual nodes, but cognates share more of them than non-cognates do.

The Spanish–English and Catalan–Spanish work of Sánchez-Casas, García-Albea and their colleagues has provided maybe the most compelling support for the idea that cognates and non-cognates are represented in qualitatively different representations in bilingual memory and that this difference may underlie the above cognate effects (e.g., García-Albea, Sánchez-Casas, & Igoa, 1998; Sánchez-Casas et al., 1992; Sánchez-Casas & García-Albea, 2005). These researchers set up a detailed research program in which they tried to pin down the separate contributions of form and meaning similarity between primes and targets to the masked priming effects that are reliably obtained when a target stimulus is preceded by its, masked, cognate translation (e.g., masked prime: *rich*; target: *rico*). This work suggested that neither form nor meaning similarity on its own suffices for the priming effect to occur. Interestingly, it also demonstrated that the effects obtained for cognate translations strongly resemble those obtained in masked priming studies in which morphologically related words from one and the same language are presented as prime and target. These combined findings led the authors to conclude that morphology determines the way words are stored in both monolingual and bilingual memory. More specifically, they concluded, in line with other authors before them (Cristoffanini, Kirsner, & Milech, 1986; Kirsner, Lalor, & Hird, 1993), that cognate translations share a morphological representation in bilingual memory whereas each member of a pair of non-cognate translations has a separate morphological representation in bilingual memory.

Unlike in models of monolingual word recognition (see e.g., Taft, 1994; Taft & Forster, 1975; Taft, Hambly, & Kinoshita, 1986), in models of bilingual word recognition morphology is typically the Cinderella among the various types of linguistic domains that are distinguished. In the models discussed in the previous sections so far, morphology is blatantly absent, possibly because the computational modeling of bilingual word recognition has been based on words con-

sisting of a single morpheme only. Sánchez-Casas and García-Albea (2005) attempted to rectify this neglect by hypothesizing various possible loci for an extra, morphological, representational level in some of the existing models. They proposed to insert the extra morphological layer in between the levels of word nodes and language nodes in BIA (Figure 4.4, left), or in between the levels of orthographic/phonological words and semantics in SOPHIA (Figure 4.4, right). These proposals still await computational modeling.

That ultimately special attention will have to be paid to morphology in models of bilingual word recognition is dictated by the results of two empirical studies that looked at the influence of morphological complexity of words in lexical decision by monolinguals and bilinguals: Lehtonen and Laine (2003) found that Finnish–Swedish bilinguals decomposed many more morphologically complex Finnish words into their constituents during recognition than Finnish monolinguals did. Lehtonen, Niska, Wande, Niemi, and Laine (2006) observed a similar tendency when comparing the performance of Swedish monolinguals and Swedish–Finnish bilinguals on a Swedish lexical decision task, but here the difference between bilinguals and monolinguals was relatively small. Furthermore, the performance of the monolinguals differed between the two languages: Finnish monolinguals decomposed more words than Swedish monolinguals did.

These differences between the two studies are plausibly due to a difference between these two languages in morphological richness: In Finnish a noun can have up to 2000 different inflectional forms, whereas Swedish is a morphologically relatively limited language. Degree of morphological richness has consequences for the way words are stored in the mental lexicon and processed: If a word has many different inflected forms (such as is the case for Finnish) the chance that each single one of them has developed a separate representation in the mental lexicon is considerably smaller than if a word has relatively few different inflected forms. Without such a "full-form" representation in memory for a specific word, recognition will involve a decomposition process in which the word is first analyzed into its constituents, which can then be recognized. Full-form representations develop over word recognition practice. Because the, fewer, morphological inflections per Swedish word have each been encountered far more often than each of the much larger number of Finnish inflected forms, Swedish monolinguals will have relatively many full forms stored in the mental lexicon; hence the difference in frequency of decomposition between Swedish and Finnish monolinguals. The difference between the Finnish monolinguals and Finnish–Swedish bilinguals performing in Finnish can be understood by realizing that the monolinguals, with a large amount of practice in just one language, Finnish, have had more opportunity to develop full-form representations of morphologically complex words than the Finnish–Swedish bilinguals. The analogous, although smaller, difference between Swedish monolinguals and Swedish–Finnish bilinguals performing in Swedish can be explained in the same way. The reason it is relatively small plausibly is that Swedish, because it is morphologically limited, has also given the bilinguals the opportunity to develop many full-form representations.

But let us return to the cognate effects in relation to representational structure that started this discussion: Whatever the exact locus of qualitatively different cognate and non-cognate representations in bilingual memory—a yet to be included morphological layer in the system, a semantic level, or any other level yet unspecified—the important message to bear in mind is that *representational* differences between cognates and non-cognates may underlie the apparent manifestations of language-nonselective processing. The notion of language-nonselective processing implies the co-activation of one or more *separate* language-specific memory nodes belonging to the non-target language while processing a target language stimulus. The crucial message to be communicated here is that, plausibly, when a cognate is processed, no such co-activation is involved because the assumed two, separate, language-specific representations of the two terms in the implicated cognate translation pair in fact do not exist. Alternatively,

such separate representations may exist but may not be the (sole) source of the cognate effect. As we shall see in Chapter 5, cognate effects in speech production tasks are equivocal for similar reasons.

Summary and conclusions

The above discussion of cognate effects in bilingual word recognition concludes this review of studies addressing the question of whether bilingual lexical access is language-nonselective or language-selective. And what, from a bird's eye view, can we conclude on the basis of the assembled evidence? As we have seen, in the majority of studies the experimental materials consisted of lists of critical words intermingled with control words. The joint evidence collected in these out-of-context studies clearly points to an influence of the non-target language on target word processing, suggesting co-activation of elements of the non-target language and, thus, language-nonselective processing. The evidence also suggests that the effect of the non-target language is modulated by the relative strength of the bilingual's two languages: The influence of the non-target language was especially strong when it was the stronger language of the two. When the non-target language was the weaker language, smaller effects or even null effects on target processing materialized. Boosting the activation of the non-target language, for instance, by presenting a block of words from this language before a critical block of test materials, increased its influence on processing the target language. Under those circumstances even the stronger language turned out not to be immune against an influence from a weaker non-target language. All in all it appears legitimate to conclude that the vast majority of the out-of-context studies suggest language-nonselective word processing. In fact, even the apparent counterevidence, the observed null effects of a relatively weak non-target language, does not challenge this conclusion because these null effects do not necessarily indicate that in these cases no elements in the non-target language were activated at all. An alternative account is that there was co-activation in this language subsystem but that it was simply too weak to affect processing the stronger target language.

In contrast to the out-of-context studies, in the few studies that embedded the critical materials in context and in which the language of context and critical materials was the same one, no influence of the non-target language occurred except in some of the cognate studies that, as we have seen, must be regarded with caution. This result is especially important because these context studies resemble natural language processing more closely than the out-of-context studies do. Up until this point in the discussion an influence of the non-target language on target language processing was assumed to result from co-activation in the non-target language subsystem and, therefore, to index language-nonselective language processing. Analogously, the most natural interpretation of a non-influence of the non-target language in the context studies is that the latter is not activated during target processing and, thus, that this null effect indexes true language-selective processing. Yet, as we have just seen, the interpretation of null effects may be equivocal and we must therefore keep our minds open for the possibility that this null effect also does not index language-selective processing. An alternative interpretation may be that, just like words presented out of context, words presented in context activate representations in both of the bilingual's language subsystems but that the activation in the non-target language's subsystem is somehow ignored by an attention system that supervises task performance. The effect is that target processing is not hampered by this co-activation. This suggestion may seem completely ad hoc at this point, but in Chapter 5 I will present the results of a couple of studies on bilingual word production that can only be understood if we accept the conclusion that this is in fact what happens in at least some bilinguals some of the time. Furthermore, it is consistent with the recent addition of a control system to models of word recognition that I introduced earlier (pp. 180–181) and to which I will return in later chapters.

SENTENCE PROCESSING

Introduction

The studies discussed so far in this chapter all focused on word recognition in bilinguals. The few studies in which sentence materials instead of isolated words were presented to the participants also had this focus on word recognition rather than on the way whole sentences are processed: Their goal was to find out how contextual information affects word recognition in bilinguals. In this section I will present a set of studies that were designed to provide information on the way bilinguals process sentences, and especially on how they parse them. Parsing is the technical name for uncovering the grammatical structure of a sentence, identifying its constituent parts as subject, verb, object, and so on. As mentioned before, word recognition and parsing together enable the language user to come up with the literal meaning of a sentence.

As was the case for the above studies on bilingual lexical access, the experimental methods used in the bilingual parsing studies have been adopted from the research on monolingual language comprehension. In this particular case, the bilingual research community took on the common practice of studying parsing by looking at the way syntactically ambiguous or syntactically and/or semantically anomalous sentences are processed. Across these studies sentence processing has been measured with a varied set of techniques, such as eye-movement recording during self-paced reading (Frenck-Mestre, 2002, 2005b; Frenck-Mestre & Pynte, 1997), the moving-window technique (Dussias, 2006; Dussias & Cramer, 2006; Dussias & Cramer Scaltz, 2008), and ERP recording (e.g., Hahne & Friederici, 2001; see pp. 160–162 for a description of these techniques). In addition to these on-line measures, off-line techniques have been used, such as having participants indicate which one of the nouns in simple noun-verb-noun sentences fulfills the role of subject (McDonald, 1987; McDonald & Heilenman,

1992) or having them make grammaticality judgments on legitimate and illegitimate sentences (Mack, 1986).

In reviews of the literature, Frenck-Mestre (2005a) and Kroll and Dussias (2004) presented the various parsing models that have been proposed and the evidence for each of them. Serial **syntax-first models** (e.g., Frazier & Rayner, 1982) assume that the parser initially ignores syntax-external sources of information such as contextual-semantic information, lexical information, or information on the relative frequency of occurrence of particular sentence constructions. These models assume that the parser initially automatically applies a universal parsing strategy that assigns the encountered sentence the simplest structure possible on the basis of syntactical information only (where degree of complexity of the emerging structure is determined by the number of "nodes" required to describe the sentence—the fewer, the simpler the structure). Only later, if and when this strategy encounters a deadlock, other sources of information may be implicated in a reanalysis of the sentence.

To illustrate, consider the sentence-initial fragment *The student graded. . . .* According to syntax-first models, when *graded* is first encountered it is interpreted as the main verb of the sentence and, accordingly, the parser would expect to encounter a direct object next, because this analysis produces the simplest structure. The consequence of this privileged analysis is that the reader should experience a problem when the sentence continues with . . . *by the professor received an A*, in which *graded* turns out not to be the main verb but the verb of a reduced relative clause (example taken from Frenck-Mestre, 2005a). As compared to unambiguous control sentences, such temporarily ambiguous reduced relative-clause constructions have shown to cause problems to readers (e.g., Ferreira & Clifton, 1986), as indicated by, for instance, relatively long reading times or eye fixations in the disambiguating area (*by the professor*). The processing delay is likely to be due to a repair process that needs to take place when the initial analysis turns out to be incorrect.

A second type of syntactically ambiguous construction with which the syntax-first principle can be illustrated is when the main verb permits both a direct-object complement and a sentence complement, as does the main verb *admitted* in the following pair of sentences, borrowed from Dussias (2006) and Dussias and Cramer (2006, 2008):

1a. *The ticket agent admitted the mistake might not have been caught* (sentence complement)

1b. *The ticket agent admitted the mistake when he got caught* (direct object).

The information what types of constructions are enabled by a particular verb is known as the verb's subcategorization frame and is assumed to be stored in the verb's lexical representation. Importantly, according to the syntax-first account, Sentence 1b should be easier to process than Sentence 1a because its resolution involves the simpler syntactic structure.

Earlier on in this chapter (p. 164) *lexical* ambiguity effects were discussed in terms of Fodor's (1983) modularity of mind theory. The present syntax-first account of *syntactic* ambiguity resolution agrees with this theory because it assumes that initial syntactic analysis is impenetrable by other sources of information than syntactical information. In modularity of mind theory, this feature of "information encapsulation" is regarded the main characteristic of a modular process.

This modular syntax-first view is challenged by monolingual studies suggesting that parsing *is* permeable by other sources of information, such as semantic information provided by the sentence fragment preceding the ambiguity or by the subcategorization information stored in a main verb's lexical representation. To illustrate, consider the following three sentences, one of which (2a) was already introduced above.

2a. *The student graded by the professor received an A.*

2b. *The paper graded by the professor received an A.*

2c. *The student graded the professor with an A.*

Sentences 2a and 2b have an identical structure and, except for one lexical element, are identical to one another in all respects. Because of their identical structure, syntax-first models predict that they are equally hard to process. Furthermore, according to syntax-first models, both should be more difficult than Sentence 2c, where *graded* is the sentence's main verb. But contrary to these predictions the evidence shows that Sentence 2a is more difficult than Sentence 2b (Frenck-Mestre, 2005a). The source of this difference must lie in the use of the lexical item *student* in Sentence 2a versus *paper* in Sentence 2b, since this is the only difference between the two sentences. The suggestion thus is that semantic lexical information is implicated in the parsing process. More precisely, the [-animacy] feature of the lexical element *paper* seems to have reduced the likelihood that readers treat this noun as the subject of *graded*. This renders a main-clause interpretation (favored by syntax-first models but only appropriate in Sentence 2c) less likely in Sentence 2b than in Sentence 2a. Apparently, the semantic information provided by a lexical element that precedes the syntactic ambiguity can help resolve the ambiguity (Frenck-Mestre, 2005a).

Other evidence to suggest that lexical information interacts with syntactic information during sentence parsing comes from studies that have used the ambiguity exemplified in Sentences 1a and 1b above, where the main verb allows both a direct-object complement and a sentence complement. The specific type of lexical information to be exploited in this case concerns a bias provided by the main verb towards one or the other type of complement. The preferred subcategorization frame of the verb *admitted* is the sentence complement, honored in Sentence 1a but violated in Sentence 2a. In contrast, other verbs, such as the verb *confirm*, prefer a direct-object complement to a sentence complement. This presumably is the reason why Sentence 3 is harder to process than Sentence 1a, despite the fact that the two sentences have exactly the same structure (see Dussias & Cramer, 2006, for a discussion of the pertinent monolingual studies).

3. *The CIA director confirmed the rumor could mean a security leak*

The important point to make is that this effect suggests that lexical information associated with the main verb is implicated in syntactic analysis, a conclusion that defies the syntax-first view. The reason why different verbs favor different structural analyses presumably is that verbs differ from one another in terms of the structures in which they are preferentially used: In naturally occurring English, *admit* is more often followed by a sentence complement than by a direct object and the opposite holds for *confirm*. In other words, the bias information in the verb's lexical representation is based on linguistic experience.

Still further sources of extra-syntactical information, to be ignored here, have been shown to affect sentence parsing (see Frenck-Mestre, 2005a, for a review). These data from monolingual studies all suggest that sentence parsing is an interactive, non-modular, process in which syntactic and other sources of information operate in concert to come up with the proper analysis of the sentence. Adherents of the syntax-first models have parried this conclusion by pointing out that these non-syntactic sources of information might not come into play until after an unsuccessful first parse, during a second, repair, stage. Evidence that under certain circumstances syntactically simpler constructions are more difficult to process than syntactically more complex constructions would perhaps more seriously challenge syntax-first models. Such a result has in fact been obtained in a monolingual study in which direct-object constructions were more difficult to process than sentence-complement structures despite the fact that the former concern the syntactically simpler structures (see Dussias & Cramer, 2006, for a discussion). Subsequent bilingual studies have produced similar results. It is to a discussion of some of the bilingual studies on sentence parsing that I will now turn.

The resolution of syntactically ambiguous sentences

A small number of bilingual studies on sentence parsing have contributed to solving the above theoretical controversy between syntax-first and interactive-parsing models by trying to discover how bilinguals resolve syntactic ambiguities. As dependent variables they have generally used behavioral measures obtained on-line by means of the moving-window technique or eye-movement registration. In addition to informing the above controversy, the purpose of these studies was to find out whether L2 speakers and native speakers use similar parsing strategies, what the effects of L2 proficiency and the relationship between L1 and L2 on L2 parsing might be, and whether preferred parsing strategies in a bilingual's one language might modify the preferred strategies associated with the other language. A second group of bilingual studies employed a popular off-line technique to determine how L2 speakers assign function (e.g., subject, object) to the various noun phrases in a sentence and, especially, whether the function-assignment procedures they execute in their L1 transfer to L2. The focus in the current section will be on the former class of studies, but I will also present some representative results from the second class.

In a Spanish–English study, Dussias and Cramer (2006; Dussias, 2006) employed the self-paced moving-window technique (see p. 160). The ambiguous constructions they studied were those exemplified in Sentences 1a, 1b, and 3 above, in which the main verb allows both a direct-object complement and a sentence complement but contains a bias towards one of these (cf. *confirmed* versus *admitted*). The time between the moment the disambiguating information (e.g., *might not* in Sentence 1a and *could mean* in Sentence 3) appeared on the screen and the participant pressed the space bar for the next window served as dependent variable. The test materials were all in the participants' L2 English. The critical data of this experiment are presented in Figure 4.10.

As shown, verb bias interacted with sentence construction type: When the main verb preferred

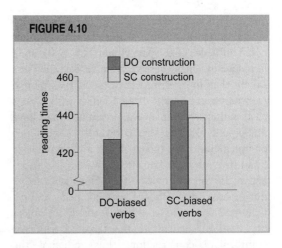

FIGURE 4.10

Mean reading times for syntactically ambiguous verbs (in ms) as a function of verb bias and sentence construction type. For DO-biased verbs the direct-object complement is the preferred construction. For SC-biased verbs the preferred construction contains a sentence complement. Reprinted from Dussias and Cramer (2006) and Dussias and Cramer Scaltz (2008), Copyright (2008), with permission from Elsevier.

a direct-object construction, latencies were shorter when the sentence indeed continued with a direct object than when it proceeded with a sentence complement, and the opposite pattern held for verbs that prefer a sentence complement. This interaction was statistically significant. These data suggest that a syntactically simpler structure (the direct-object construction) is not necessarily easier to parse than a more complex structure (the sentence-complement structure), a finding that challenges the syntax-first models. The data also show that, as native speakers, L2 speakers can exploit lexical verb-bias knowledge during parsing. As we shall see next, this result does not imply that it is exclusively L2 lexical knowledge that they exploit while processing L2 sentences.

Although the above interaction between verb bias and sentence construction type was statistically significant, subsequent analyses showed that the difference between the two conditions with sentence-complement biased verbs (the two right-hand bars in Figure 4.10) was not. Dussias and Cramer (2006) wondered why these verbs had not shown a clearer effect of sentence construction type and hypothesized the reason might be an influence of the participants' L1, Spanish, a language in which these verb biases are much less salient than in English. For instance, the Spanish translation equivalent of an English verb with a clear sentence complement preference may have an equally strong bias towards a sentence complement and a direct-object complement. If Spanish verb-bias knowledge was in fact co-activated with English verb-bias knowledge during task performance, co-activated Spanish will once in a while have primed the direct-object construction instead of the targeted sentence complement construction, thus reducing the difference between the two construction-type conditions. A subsequent study with improved materials (Dussias, 2006; see also Dussias & Cramer Scaltz, 2008) supported this interpretation and, in so doing, provided indirect evidence that when bilinguals parse L2 sentences, L1 verb knowledge is co-activated and influences processing.

As we have seen in the earlier parts of this chapter, not only does L1 influence L2 word recognition under many circumstances, but occasionally the opposite—an influence of L2 on L1 word recognition—has been shown to occur as well. Dussias (2006) showed that an influence of L2 on L1 parsing can also occur (and see Dussias & Sagarra, 2007, for a further demonstration of this phenomenon). Two groups of Spanish–English bilinguals were included, one group that was immersed in an English (L2) environment and a second that was immersed in a Spanish (L1) environment. The participants read L1 Spanish sentences while their eye movements were being recorded. The performance of these two groups of bilinguals was compared to that of Spanish monolinguals. The critical sentences contained a relative clause ambiguity for which the favored solution differs between Spanish and English. The construction in question is illustrated in the following example:

4. *Alguien disparó contra el hijo de la actriz que estaba en el balcón (Someone shot the son of the actress who was on the balcony).*

In this sentence either the head of the complex noun phrase (*el hijo*; "the son") or the second noun phrase in this phrase (*la actriz*; "the actress") can be the subject of the relative clause. Spanish favors the former ("N1 attachment", "high-attachment", or "non-local attachment") analysis (Cuetos & Mitchell, 1988), whereas English favors the latter ("N2 attachment", "low-attachment", or "local attachment") analysis (Frazier, 1987). In other words, Spanish readers of Sentence 4 would typically regard *el hijo* as the subject of the relative clause whereas English readers of the English translation of this sentence would usually take *the actress* to be the subject of the relative clause. An earlier study examining how Spanish–English bilinguals and English–Spanish bilinguals parse this type of structure in both languages had shown that both participant groups generally favored low attachment over high attachment, also when they processed Spanish sentences (Dussias, 2003). All testing in that study was done in a predominantly English-speaking environment in the United States. The critical finding in the present study—which only tested L1 Spanish sentences—was that the participants immersed in L1 Spanish behaved like the Spanish control participants, showing shorter total fixation times for sentences in which the correct solution involved high attachment. In contrast, the participants immersed in L2 English showed shorter total fixation times for sentences whose correct solution involved low attachment, thus behaving like English monolinguals. This second result demonstrates an influence of L2 on L1 parsing. In addition, the fact that the English and Spanish immersion environments produced different results suggests that extensive current experience with one language in particular affects parsing solutions. It is therefore plausible that, similarly, the dominant low-attachment preference in the 2003 study had been caused by the fact that all (L1 Spanish) participants were tested in an (L2) English-speaking environment. In other words, contextual linguistic and cultural information appears to influence parsing. It may be obvious that this constitutes an additional challenge for the syntax-first models of parsing.

In two further studies, Frenck-Mestre (2002,

2005b) tested the same type of ambiguous structures as illustrated in Sentence 4 (this time in L2 French) but looking at the effect of level of L2 proficiency on L2 parsing and using the eye-movement recording methodology. Across these studies L2 proficiency was manipulated by comparing the performance of three groups of late learners of French: beginning Spanish–French bilinguals, beginning English–French bilinguals, and proficient English–French bilinguals. A control group of French native speakers was also included and first-pass gaze duration on the disambiguating region (see p. 161) served as the dependent variable. As mentioned above, English favors low attachment. French, however, favors high attachment and we have seen this also holds for Spanish. So the three groups of learners differed on two dimensions: L2 proficiency and whether or not their L1 and L2 share the same attachment preference.

Consistent with the preferred solution in French, the native speakers' first-pass gaze duration in the disambiguating area was significantly shorter for the sentences in which high attachment provided the correct solution than in sentences where low attachment was correct. The group of beginning Spanish–French bilinguals manifested this same preference. Unfortunately, the cause of this finding is indeterminate: These participants may show this pattern because they exploited the same strategy as native French speakers do and independent of their L1, but they may also have used the preferred L1 parsing strategy, a strategy that happens to be the same as the one favored for L2 French. The pattern obtained for the beginning English–French bilinguals is more informative and, in fact, suggests that less-advanced L2 learners apply the analysis preferred in their L1 when reading these ambiguous constructions in L2: Unlike the native French speakers (and the beginning Spanish–French learners) they showed shorter first-pass gaze durations for low-attachment constructions. In contrast, the proficient English–French bilinguals were faster at reading high-attachment constructions, thus showing the same preference as native French speakers. Clearly then, if a learner's L1 and L2 favor different parsing

solutions for a given structure, L2 parsing strategies may change with increasing L2 proficiency: Initially the learner analyzes the L2 structure in the way he or she analyzes similar structures in his L1. At a more advanced level the learner analyzes it in the same way as native speakers do.

A corollary of this conclusion is that data that do not clearly point towards one preferred parsing strategy—a "native-language" or a "second-language" strategy—may be due to the learner being in a transitional stage in between L1 preference and L2 preference. This is how Frenck-Mestre (2005b) explained the fact that in a similar study with German–English and Greek–English bilinguals (Felser, Roberts, Gross, & Marinis, 2003) no clear preference for either strategy was observed. Alternatively, a parsing pattern that does not clearly point towards the use of one preferred strategy may reflect the use of a special strategy by L2 learners. For instance, while processing a structural ambiguity, learners may rely more on lexical information and less on structurally based parsing strategies than native speakers do, as Papadopoulou and Clahsen (2003) proposed on the basis of the results of a study with learners of L2 Greek.

Converging evidence that degree of L2 proficiency determines whether an L1-preferred or an L2-preferred parsing strategy is applied to L2 sentences, or some mixture of both, has been obtained in off-line experiments studying the way bilinguals assign functions or "thematic roles" to the various noun phrases in L2 sentences. In a typical experiment of this type the participants read or listen to simple, transitive sentences—both grammatical and ungrammatical ones—containing two concrete nouns and an action verb and are asked to choose the noun in each sentence that performs the action specified by the verb. The sentences vary on a number of features (called "cues") that language users are known to exploit in figuring out such "form–function" relations in natural language comprehension. Across languages, common such cues are word order, subject–verb agreement in person and number, case, and whether or not a noun refers to a living entity ("animacy"). Individual languages differ from one another in the cues they rely on most in assigning function, as has been demonstrated in a bevy of studies performed in many languages (see Table 7.3, p. 366, for examples of the various types of sentences used in these studies). This work provided the cornerstone of a well-known model of sentence comprehension called the competition model (e.g., MacWhinney, 1997; MacWhinney, Bates, & Kliegl, 1984; "competition" refers to the competition between conflicting cues in the resolution process). Native speakers of English, for instance, make especially strong use of word order. For example, given a noun-verb-noun, NVN, sequence, the first noun is assigned the role of actor in the far majority of cases. Instead, for native speakers of Japanese, animacy is an especially strong cue: If one out of the two nouns in an NVN sequence refers to a living being and the other to an inanimate being, the former is assigned the subject role; in English, word order may overrule this, semantically plausible, solution. For native French speakers noun–verb agreement is the strongest cue.

The above methodology was subsequently adopted in studies on bilingual sentence comprehension (e.g., MacWhinney, 1987; Vaid & Chengappa, 1988). A major question addressed in the bilingual studies is what cues—those dominant in L1, those dominant in L2, or maybe a mixture of both—L2 learners primarily rely on when processing L2 sentences (see Cook, Iarossi, Stellakis, & Tokumaru, 2003, for a study that tried to determine what cues bilinguals use when processing their L1). McDonald and Heilenman (1992) posed this question in a cross-sectional study of late L1 English learners of French at four different levels of French proficiency. The researchers found that when performing the agent-assignment task to French (L2) sentences, the learners' dependence on word order and noun–verb agreement gradually moved towards the pattern typical of French native speakers: Word order became less important and noun–verb agreement became more important. So apparently, the way bilinguals process sentences in their L2 gradually changes from an L1 strategy towards one that resembles L2 processing more (see Su, 2001, for converging evidence from a Chinese–English study). The results thus mimic those obtained by Frenck-Mestre (2002, 2005b) in the on-line sentence parsing studies presented above.

Summary and conclusions

The joint results of the studies discussed above suggest that with increasing L2 practice the parsing strategies of L2 learners come to resemble those of native speakers and that, just as native speakers, L2 learners exploit extra-syntactic sources of information during L2 parsing. Furthermore, the present results warrant the conclusion that during early stages of L2 learning, parsing strategies the learner prefers to use in his or her L1 transfer to the parsing of L2 sentences. But perhaps most remarkable is the finding that the opposite situation—an L2 parsing strategy applied to L1 sentences—may occur as well (Dussias, 2003, 2006; Dussias & Sagarra, 2007). This finding reminds of the effects of L2 on L1 word recognition reported in the earlier sections of this chapter (see pp. 365–367 for more evidence). As we have seen, the effects of L1 on L2 word recognition and vice versa are usually attributed to co-activation of the memory representations of words from the non-target language during target language processing. Similarly, the present manifestations of transfer from L1 to L2 parsing strategies and vice versa suggest language-nonselective activation of parsing procedures.

This evidence of language-nonselective grammatical processing in bilinguals suggests a qualification of the conclusion drawn above that with increasing L2 proficiency L2 speakers' parsing strategies come to resemble the parsing strategies of native speakers. Although this may be true, L2 parsing by proficient L2 speakers may never become truly indistinguishable, under all circumstances, from native monolingual speakers' parsing. If L1 parsing can be shown not to be immune from an L2 influence under all circumstances it is rather unlikely that the reverse situation, L2 immunity, would always hold for proficient L2 users: The co-activation of the generally stronger L1 parsing procedures will affect the procedures applied to L2 sentences. Clahsen and Felser (2006a, 2006b) have indeed revealed subtle differences between sentence parsing procedures in highly proficient L2 speakers and native speakers (although they propose a different explanation for these differences than the one advanced here; namely one in terms of the depth of the syntactic representations that learners and L1 speakers compute during sentence processing).

A final remark is in order here; namely that to be able to detect a reciprocal influence of a bilingual's L1 and L2 parsing strategies at all, the two languages' preferred parsing solutions for a particular sentence construction must differ (as was indeed the case in the above studies). The reason is that if the two languages share the same parsing preference for this type of construction one can never tell whether the L2 speaker used a native language or a second language parsing strategy. In retrospect, the point seems too obvious to be worth musing on, but it can easily be overlooked in designing experiments aimed at informing the present dispute.

The processing of semantic and syntactic anomalies

A further set of studies has examined the way bilinguals process semantically and/or syntactically anomalous sentences using the ERP methodology (see pp. 162–163). A couple of these will be discussed here (see Kotz, 2009, for a more complete review). They have shown that several aspects of sentence processing may be delayed in bilinguals as compared with monolinguals. They furthermore suggest that nativelike semantic analysis of L2 sentences is in place before nativelike syntactic analysis, although also with respect to semantic analysis differences may remain between native speakers and even relatively fluent L2 speakers. A few other studies have looked at syntactic processing in bilinguals employing the fMRI methodology. The primary question addressed in these studies was whether the two languages of a bilingual are processed by the same or different brain areas. (Recall that fMRI is especially well suited to find out where in the

brain a particular cognitive process takes place.) This "localization" question will be addressed in Chapter 8 and, accordingly, it is there that I will discuss the fMRI studies.

Ardal, Donald, Meuter, Muldrew, and Luce (1990) provided early evidence of delayed semantic analysis in sentence processing by bilinguals and showed that the delay holds for both of a bilingual's languages. These researchers recorded event-related potentials while early and late English–French and French–English bilinguals read sentences in their L1 and L2. A group of matched English monolinguals was also included, obviously only to be tested in English. The critical sentences contained a semantic anomaly, always in sentence-final position (e.g., *I generally like menthol bottles*). The primary dependent variable was the N400 elicited by the anomalous words in the critical sentences (and by sentence-final words in non-anomalous control sentences). The results showed that the N400 elicited by anomalous words was delayed in bilinguals as compared with monolinguals, and that it was delayed in the bilinguals' L2 as compared with their L1. In other words, monolinguals seem to be faster at detecting semantic anomalies than bilinguals, and bilinguals detect anomalies faster in their L1 than in their L2. Age of L2 acquisition did not modulate these effects. The authors attributed these effects to more highly automated language processing in monolinguals than in bilinguals and to more highly automated L1 than L2 processing in bilinguals. A further finding of interest was that in bilinguals the amplitude of the N400 to anomalous words was somewhat smaller in L2 than in L1, especially in the least-fluent bilinguals. A subgroup of monolinguals with a relatively low L1 fluency showed this same reduction of the N400 in their L1 as compared to more-fluent L1 users. Apparently, so the authors concluded, the amplitude of the N400 somehow reflects level of language fluency.

Weber-Fox and Neville (1996) obtained partly similar results in a study that tested proficient Chinese–English bilinguals varying in the age at which they first started to acquire English. The participants performed acceptability judgments on English sentences that were either correct or semantically or syntactically anomalous. All age groups showed an N400 effect (that is, a difference in the amplitude of the N400 for semantically anomalous sentences on the one hand and semantically correct sentences on the other hand). Furthermore, for the participants who had acquired L2 English after 11 years of age, but not for those with younger acquisition ages, the effect was delayed as compared with an English monolingual control group. These results thus suggest that at least for relatively late learners semantic processing in L2 is relatively slow. It remains unclear why an effect of acquisition age materialized whereas Ardal and his colleagues (1990) had shown similar results for early and late learners. Importantly though, in both studies an N400 occurred for bilinguals as well as monolinguals. This finding legitimates the conclusion that semantic processing is qualitatively the same in bilinguals as in monolinguals.

In their analysis of the ERP signal, Weber-Fox and Neville (1996) also looked for the occurrence of ELAN and P600, the two components that are assumed to index syntactic processing (see p. 163) and in a more recent Japanese–German study Hahne and Friederici (2001) also focused on all three components. The results of both studies suggest that syntactic analysis may be qualitatively different in bilinguals and monolinguals. Furthermore, and contrary to the above conclusion, the latter study suggests that also semantic processing may, in one respect, differ qualitatively between monolinguals and bilinguals. To get some idea of how semantic and syntactic processing was manipulated in these studies, consider sentences 5a–5d below, which exemplify the four types of German passive sentences that Hahne and Friederici presented to their participants (English translations are given in parentheses). The participants in this study were late Japanese learners of German who were clearly dominant in Japanese and the sentences were presented aurally (instead of visually, as in Weber-Fox & Neville, 1996).

5a syntactically correct   *Das Brot wurde*
   semantically correct   *gegessen (The*
   (no violation)   *bread was eaten)*

5b syntactically correct   *Der Vulkan wurde*
   semantically incorrect   *gegessen*
   (semantic violation   *(The volcano was*
   only)   *eaten)*
5c syntactically incorrect   *Das Eis wurde im*
   semantically correct   *gegessen*
   (syntactic violation   *(The ice cream*
   only)   *was in-the eaten)*
5d syntactically incorrect   *Das Türschloss*
   semantically incorrect   *wurde im gegessen*
   (semantic and   *(The door lock*
   syntactic violation)   *was in-the eaten)*

As these sentences illustrate, both semantic and syntactic congruency were manipulated. The sentences could be incongruent (anomalous) on one or both of these dimensions or they were congruent on both. The ERP responses were measured time-locked to the final word of each sentence, which was always a participle. In their analysis of the ERP signal the authors focused on the difference between the ERP responses to (the final words of) correct sentences on the one hand and to each of the three types of incorrect sentences on the other hand (these differences being the ERP effects). The brain responses of the German L2 speakers were compared to those of native German speakers who had been presented with exactly the same materials in an earlier study. The pattern of results obtained for the L2 listeners differed from that shown by the native listeners in a number of respects. In the ensuing discussion, I will first deal with the N400 effect, the marker of semantic processing, and will then continue with a discussion of ELAN and the P600, the components that are thought to reflect syntactic processing. The focus will be on how a semantic and/or syntactic violation affects these components.

In the bilingual participants the incorrect sentences that only involved a semantic violation (5b) significantly modulated the N400 over centro-parietal electrodes as compared to the correct sentences and this N400 effect did not differ statistically from the analogous effect in the native-speaker group (see pp. 408–409 for information about the locus of these electrodes on the skull). This finding converges with the results obtained by Ardal et al. (1990) and Weber-Fox and Neville (1996). Unlike in these two earlier studies, and even though the participants were late bilinguals, this effect was not delayed as compared to the corresponding effect in native speakers. It lasted longer in the bilingual group, however, suggesting that bilinguals' semantic integration processes take relatively long. From these results one might once again be inclined to conclude that semantic processing is qualitatively the same in native speakers and L2 speakers (albeit slower). Yet this conclusion would be premature, because both conditions that involved a semantic anomaly (5b and 5d) showed an effect in bilinguals that was not observed for native speakers: a late right anterior-central negativity around 700–1100 ms following the critical sentence-final word in incorrect sentences as compared with correct sentences.

To account for this pattern of results, the authors suggested that two types of semantic processing must be distinguished: the processing of lexical semantic knowledge and of more general conceptual semantic knowledge that is also implicated in non-verbal semantic tasks. The data can then be accounted for by assuming that lexical-semantic processing, tapped by the N400 component, is the same in native and L2 speakers of a language, whereas only bilinguals exploit conceptual-semantic information while processing verbal materials in their L2. The assumed distinction between lexical semantics and language-independent conceptual knowledge that underlies this analysis has been made by other researchers as well (e.g., Paradis 2004; see pp. 234–236 for a discussion).

Further differences between native and L2 speakers of German were observed when the processing of correct sentences was compared with the processing of sentences that included syntactic violations (5c and 5d). The pattern of results resembled those of the analogous conditions in the reading study by Weber-Fox and Neville (1996): Whereas in native speakers syntactic violations modulated the early left anterior negativity (ELAN) as compared to correct sentences, this effect was not evident in L2 speakers. The ELAN component is thought

to reflect an automatic first-pass parsing process stage in which the parser "assigns the initial syntactic structure on the basis of word category information only" (Hahne & Friederici, 1999, p. 195). Therefore, the absence of the ELAN effect in bilinguals suggests this process has not been automated yet in L2 learners. The second marker of syntactic processing, the P600, also showed a difference between native and L2 speakers: Whereas in native speakers a syntactic violation modulated this component, in the L2 speakers the P600 did not differ between correct and incorrect sentences. Because this component is thought to reflect controlled syntactic repair and re-analysis processes, Hahne and Friederici (2001) suggested this result indicates that L2 speakers do not engage in these repair processes.

To summarize, in both L1 and L2 sentence processing, bilinguals show N400 effects similar to those observed for monolinguals, suggesting that semantic integration processes are qualitatively (largely; see below) the same in monolinguals and bilinguals. There is some evidence that semantic integration is delayed in bilinguals as compared to monolinguals and that the delay is relatively large when bilinguals process their weaker language. Other evidence suggests the delay only occurs in late bilinguals. Yet a further set of experimental results suggests that the N400 lasts longer in bilinguals than in monolinguals, indicating that bilinguals' semantic integration processes take relatively long to complete. Finally, one of the above studies showed a second negativity, occurring later than the N400, in bilinguals but not in monolinguals. This may indicate that in one respect semantic integration processes are different in bilinguals than in monolinguals after all. The authors hypothesized this ERP component indexes the use of conceptual-semantic information by bilinguals but not monolinguals during semantic integration. In contrast, the N400, common to monolinguals and bilinguals, may reflect the use of lexical-semantic information. Finally, the data suggest that syntactic analysis differs qualitatively between native and L2 speakers. This showed, first, from the presence of a differential ELAN to syntactically correct and incorrect sentences in native speakers but the absence of this ELAN effect in L2 speakers. It furthermore showed from the fact that a syntactic violation modulated the P600 in native speakers but not in L2 speakers. The first of these findings indicates that initial first-pass parsing differs between native speakers and L2 speakers; the second may mean that, unlike native speakers, L2 speakers are not involved in second-pass re-analysis yet.

One factor that affects the ERP patterns in L2 learners while they process anomalous and normal sentences was underexposed in the above discussion; namely, the level of proficiency the bilinguals have attained in their L2. Yet, a growing number of studies show that L2 proficiency is a more important determinant of the ERP patterns to be observed in L2 speakers processing their L2 than L2 acquisition age and that the same holds for the patterns of brain activation as observed in fMRI research (see e.g., Abutalebi et al., 2005, and Kotz, 2009, for reviews; see also Chapter 2, pp. 73–74). To illustrate the important role that level of L2 proficiency plays in the way sentence anomalies are processed (as reflected in the ERP patterns) let us look at a study by Ojima et al. (2005) that resembled Hahne and Friederici's (2001) study

but included a proficiency manipulation: Two groups of late Japanese learners of L2 English were included, one at an intermediate level of English proficiency, the second at a high level of English proficiency. A control group of English native speakers was also included. At variance with the results of the studies discussed above, this study demonstrated that not only semantic processing but also syntactic processing in L2 speakers may resemble that of native speakers: The ERPs to semantic anomalies in English sentences read by both the intermediate- and high-level learners of English resembled those of the native English speakers. In contrast, syntactic anomalies evoked a similar pattern of ERP responses in the high-proficiency learner group and the English native speakers but a different one in the learner group of intermediate proficiency. Plausibly then, the fact that the above studies had shown qualitatively different syntactic analysis processes in L2 learners and native speakers was due to the L2 learners' relatively low level of L2 proficiency. Ojima and his colleagues concluded that a late, post-childhood, start of L2 learning per se is no impediment to attaining nativelike performance in both grammar and semantics, underscoring the current view that L2 proficiency level is what matters most.

SUMMARY

- Unilingual studies on the resolution of lexical ambiguities using behavioral measures have produced mixed results, suggesting that word recognition is neither fully autonomous nor fully interactive under all circumstances but that the specifics of task and context determine how the ambiguities are resolved. Instead, recent studies employing the ERP methodology, with its high temporal resolution, suggest that word recognition is a highly interactive process, thus providing evidence against a modular view of word recognition.

- In many but not all studies that examined the processing of interlexical homographs and homophones in isolation a homograph/homophone effect was obtained. This indicates that even when words are processed in isolation bilingual word recognition is not always language-nonselective. Specifically, word recognition in the stronger language appears to be language-selective if the activation in the weaker language is not boosted by some experimental manipulation.

- A strong test of language-nonselective bilingual word recognition requires the presentation of exclusively unilingual language materials. Apparent evidence of language-nonselective word recognition in experiments that also present words from the non-target language is inconclusive because these words, however few, will boost the activation level of all representations in the lexicon of the non-target language, thus increasing their availability.

- Language-nonselective lexical access is constrained by the relative dominance of a bilingual's two languages and by context: (1) If the non-target language is the stronger of a bilingual's two languages, lexical access tends to be language-nonselective; if the non-target language is the weaker language of the two, lexical access tends to be language-selective; (2) Immersing the bilingual participants in the non-target language prior to having them perform a word recognition test increases the degree of activation in the non-target language's memory system and, consequently, of language-nonselective lexical access. Similarly, immersing them in the target language prior to having them perform a word recognition test increases the degree of activation in the target language's memory system and, consequently, of language-selective lexical access.
- The bilingual interactive activation (BIA) model of bilingual lexical access contains four levels of representation units that represent visual letter features, letters, orthographic word forms, and language information, respectively. Representations at one level can activate and inhibit representations at adjacent levels via excitatory and inhibitory connections. The model assumes language-nonselective lexical access: Activated letter nodes activate word nodes in both of a bilingual's languages.
- BIA explains the interlexical homograph effects by assuming two word node representations for interlexical homographs, one for each language, but just one for non-homographic control words. When a homograph is presented to the system both of its word nodes will become activated but when a control word is presented, only its one word node will be activated. The homograph effects are attributed to this difference in the activation state of the recognition system following the presentation of the two types of words.
- In lexical decision experiments, when interlexical homographs are presented in isolation the size of the homograph effect is especially large when the homograph is more frequent in the non-target language than in the target language. BIA explains this effect by assuming that the memory representations of frequent words have higher baseline levels of activation than those of infrequent words. As a consequence, the memory representations of frequent words have a head start in the recognition process.
- A word stimulus activates both its within-language neighbors and its cross-language neighbors. This result follows directly from BIA's assumption that lexical access is language-nonselective.
- In BIA+ a task/decision system is added onto the word identification system. This system can explain why the interlexical homograph effect varies across different tasks and with different compositions of the stimulus materials. Whereas the word identification system is only affected by linguistic sources of information, the task/decision system is sensitive to extra-linguistic influences such as participant expectancies.
- Studies that examined phonological activation in same-alphabet bilingualism have shown that during visual recognition of L2 words bilinguals assemble the phonological forms of these words just as native speakers do, that this process comes about automatically and unconsciously, and that under certain circumstances the grapheme–phoneme conversion rules of both languages are activated in parallel. The few studies that tested different-alphabet bilinguals and bi-dialectal language users suggest these conclusions also apply to these forms of bilingualism.
- Studies that examined the recognition of spoken words using the eye-tracking methodology have shown that the words of weaker L2, but not those of stronger L1, give rise to language-nonselective phonological activation in bilingual lexical memory. Though not totally univocal, the results of gating studies are compatible with these conclusions.
- Generally, the non-native (L2) lexicon contains fewer lexical elements than the native lexicon. Nevertheless, a spoken non-native word input causes more spurious activation in a bilingual's non-native lexicon than the spurious lexical activation caused by this same word if presented to a native speaker.

- Two models of word recognition, SOPHIA and BIMOLA, may ultimately be suitable to explain language-nonselective phonological activation. One salient difference between the two models is that in SOPHIA the lateral inhibition exerted by a word affects words from the same and the other language, whereas BIMOLA restricts lateral inhibition to units (phonemes, words) of the other language. Another difference is that SOPHIA but not BIMOLA assumes two language nodes, one for each language.

- Whereas in many tasks cognates are processed faster than matched non-cognates, in word naming they are often responded to more slowly. The likely reason cognates are processed relatively slowly in word naming is that in this task the stimulus must be named aloud. The activated phonological representation of the cognate's translation in the non-target language triggers a response that mismatches the correct response. This pending response will act as a nuisance competitor in the naming process. The consequence is a delayed naming response.

- There is some evidence that in both high-constraint and low-constraint sentence contexts interlexical homograph effects disappear. This suggests that both types of sentence context block co-activation of an interlexical homograph's representation in the non-target language.

- In high-constraint sentence contexts but generally not in low-constraint sentence contexts cognate effects disappear. This suggests that only highly constraining sentence context blocks co-activation of a cognate's representation in the non-target language.

- In general, the modulating effects of sentence context on interlexical homograph effects and cognate effects indicate that context constrains language-nonselective processing in bilinguals.

- The source of cognate effects on word recognition is equivocal: They may either be due to co-activation of a cognate's translation equivalent in the non-target language, to some representational difference between cognates and non-cognates, or to both.

- The most natural interpretation of the observed null effects of the non-target language in the context studies is that when words are presented in a larger linguistic context the non-target language is deactivated. An alternative interpretation is that words presented in a larger linguistic context also activate lexical representations in both of a bilingual's linguistic subsystems but that the activation in the non-target language's subsystem is ignored by an attention system that supervises performance. This idea is consistent with the recent addition of a control system to models of word recognition.

- When parsing syntactically ambiguous sentences both native speakers and L2 speakers make use of lexical knowledge to resolve the ambiguity. Furthermore, the language the bilingual has recently been exposed to most determines which parsing strategy he or she adopts in resolving a syntactic ambiguity. Both findings challenge the modular syntax-first model of parsing.

- If an L2 learner's L1 and L2 favor different parsing solutions for a given type of grammatical structure, with increasing L2 proficiency the strategy the learner employs to parse L2 sentences may change from the strategy he or she prefers to use while parsing sentences in L1 to one used preferably by native speakers of L2.

- When L1 sentences are parsed in an L2 immersion setting, L2-specific parsing strategies may dominate L1 parsing. When bilinguals parse L2 sentences, L1 lexical knowledge influences the parsing solution that is chosen. Both findings suggest the occurrence of language-nonselective activation of parsing procedures.

- Studies that examined how native speakers and L2 speakers process semantically anomalous sentences indicate that semantic integration processes are largely similar in native speakers and L2 speakers although they may be delayed and last longer in L2 speakers.

- Studies that examined how native speakers and L2 speakers process syntactically anomalous sentences indicate that syntactic analysis differs qualitatively between native speakers and L2 speakers. Specifically these studies suggest that initial first-pass parsing is automated in native speakers but not in L2 speakers and that only native speakers execute a repair or re-analysis on a second pass.
- Recent studies on the processing of semantically and syntactically anomalous sentences by native and L2 speakers indicate that the above conclusions apply in particular to L2 speakers who have not attained a high level of L2 proficiency. In contrast, proficient L2 speakers may process these sentences in the same way as native speakers do.

5

Word Production and
Speech Accents

INTRODUCTION AND PREVIEW

While learning about research on bilingual language comprehension in Chapter 4 you have probably noticed that much of that work was built on the study of monolingual language comprehension: Similar questions were posed and they were tackled using the same tasks and methods, adapted to the bilingual case. This situation also holds for studies on bilingual language production, which have gratefully taken advantage of the large body of knowledge acquired in earlier research on monolingual language production: They pose similar questions about the content and structure of the knowledge base underlying language production, the processing mechanisms involved, the nature of the processes through which stored knowledge is accessed and exploited during language production and the order in which these processes are executed. Furthermore, they often use the same research methods, thereby endorsing their rationale.

Chapter 4 largely dealt with the question of whether, when, and to what extent bilinguals can deactivate or switch off the contextually inappropriate ("non-selected", "non-target") language during language comprehension. A central question examined in work on bilingual language production is the analogous one: In the intermediate stages between conceptualizing and delivering a message in the selected language, does co-activation occur of memory nodes in the non-selected language or is the non-selected language totally deactivated? Reflecting the broad interest in this topic, studies that have addressed this question will be covered extensively in this chapter, providing relevant evidence from both picture naming and Stroop studies. One specific set of picture-naming studies, those that employed the so-called "language-switching" methodology, will not be covered in this chapter but in Chapter 6 instead, which takes a different point of view: After having established, in Chapters 4 and 5, that in both bilingual language comprehension and production the bilingual's two language systems are often activated in parallel, how then can it be ensured that (most of the time) the targeted element is ultimately selected?

Before presenting the bilingual studies, the models and methods developed in the research field of monolingual speech production that provided the groundwork for the bilingual work will be introduced, paying special attention to two central stages of the speech production process: **lemma selection** and **phonological encoding**. The way these two stages are sequenced—strictly serial or partly in parallel—concerns one of two core questions in a lively debate about the architecture of the speech production system. The second core question in this debate is whether these two stages proceed strictly unidirectionally or interact with one another. In addition to presenting the monolingual base work, these two sections will also present the proposals of bilingual researchers on how to adapt the monolingual models to bilingualism.

A further section reviews studies that employed the word translation task. A salient feature of this task is that it involves both a comprehension component and a production component. Another salient feature is that, by definition, it always implicates the use of both languages. Unlike picture naming and the Stroop task, which at least in theory can be performed with the non-target (or "non-response") language completely at rest, word translation is only possible when both languages are activated, either simultaneously or in rapid alternation: Its comprehension component requires one language (the "source" language) to be active and its production component requires that the other language (the "target" language) is on the alert. The word translation task has already been introduced in Chapter 3 in a discussion of how bilinguals map word form onto word meaning (pp. 136–137). In the present chapter I will focus on its resemblance with other word production tasks and the experimental results obtained using the word translation task will be related to those gathered by means of these other tasks. In Chapter 6 the translation task will reappear (pp. 314–336). But whereas the present chapter treats the translation of separate words, there I will primarily deal with the much more complex task of translating larger linguistic units and, especially, with simultaneous interpreting, con-

ceivably the most complex of all forms of linguistic behavior.

Dealing with a task that involves both comprehension and production spontaneously calls up the question of whether these two types of processing exploit the same or different underlying representations and cognitive machinery. This issue is briefly addressed in a further section. The chapter concludes with a discussion of one particular characteristic of the output that emerges from the bilingual speech production process: The speech accents that are noticeable in the L2 speech of the majority of late L2 learners and that can often be detected in early learners as well. (In Chapter 7 bilinguals' less noticeable, yet detectable, accents in their L1 speech will be discussed.) The final part of this section will review studies that examined the comprehensibility of accented L2 speech. But first of all I will present the most popular research methods employed in speech production research. I will do so with a bird's eye view in the Methods and Tasks section, detailing the picture–word naming and Stroop tasks in the course of the later sections.

METHODS AND TASKS

Many studies on speech production, both monolingual and bilingual, have focused on one specific part of the full speech production process—word production. Word production consists of several processing stages from (and including) the conceptualization of the lexical concept the speaker intends to verbalize to articulating the associated word. To get the word production process going, the concept to be verbalized must first be established in the experimental participant's mind, preferably by means of a stimulus that is non-verbal because in veridical speech production the process also starts off with a non-verbal mental representation. The most popular way do this is by presenting the participant with a picture depicting the targeted word, with the instruction to name it as rapidly as possible. While generating the naming response the participant passes through various mental stages, starting with the visual analysis of the picture. This first stage is of no particular interest to the speech production researcher but it is a necessary prerequisite for triggering the stages of interest because it loads the concept to name in the production system. Then follow the stages of interest.

Different versions of this **picture-naming task** have been used. In addition to the "simple" (but, in cognitive terms, still rather complex) picture-naming task, in which the participants simply name the pictures in the specified language and no potentially distracting information is presented with it, the **picture–word interference task** has been used. In this version of the task the picture is accompanied by a word and the relation between picture and word is systematically varied. This word can have an interfering or a facilitative effect on picture naming and the exact conditions under which such effects occur and the direction of the effects (facilitative or inhibitory) tell us something about the word production process (see pp. 237–246). In yet another version of the picture-naming task the picture does not have to be named explicitly but a response must be based on its internally generated name. The instruction may, for instance, be to determine whether the depicted object's name contains a specific phoneme. Alternatively, a particular grammatical judgment must be based on the picture's name, generated tacitly. The exact task to be performed by the participants might, for instance, be a go/no-go task in which the participants have to respond overtly on only a subset of trials. For example, they may be asked to respond if the picture's name starts with a consonant but to refrain from responding if it starts with a vowel. The primary question of interest in bilingual picture-naming studies is whether a particular component of the depicted object's lexical representation in the non-target language affects responding. If it does, this would suggest that bilingual word production is language-nonselective.

A further popular speech production task is the Stroop color-naming task, which we have already briefly encountered in Chapter 4 (p. 190): The participants are presented with color words printed in different colors and are asked to name the *colors* of the words, not the words themselves. Alternatively, they are presented with color patches, each patch being accompanied by a color word. In this version of the task the participants have to name the color of the patch and to ignore the word. Both versions of the Stroop task are conceptually very similar to the picture–word interference version of the picture-naming task. Whereas in picture naming the production system is loaded with a concept by means of the presentation of a picture, in the Stroop task a (color) concept is established in the production system by means of the color patch or the color word's color. The word component of the Stroop stimulus serves as distracter in the naming process. The original unilingual version of the task (with word input and response in the same language) has been adapted to the bilingual case and the task's bilingual version provides a means to study the involvement of the non-target language during task performance. In the bilingual version the colors have to be named in the participants' one language whereas the distracters are words in their other language. A problematic aspect of both the picture–word interference task and the Stroop color-naming task is that in both cases the process of interest, word production, is executed in parallel to a word recognition process that interacts with the production process. Because the precise nature of this interaction is not fully known, the fact that it occurs severely complicates the interpretation of the results. Furthermore, a constraint of both tasks (and the picture-naming task in general) is that they can only be applied to the study of a limited set of words, concrete words and color words, respectively. In addition to presenting a picture or a color, a third way to establish a lexical concept in the speech production system is by presenting the participants with a definition. An advantage of this procedure is that it can be used for concrete as well as abstract words but a disadvantage is that the word production process is set in motion by verbal instead of non-verbal information.

As we shall see, the picture-naming task can be used to study the cross-language activation of all sorts of lexical information: meaning, phonology, and grammar. The question of whether the activation of grammatical knowledge is language-selective or language-nonselective has also been studied with the "sentence completion (or sentence generation) paradigm", in which the participants are presented with sentence fragments to complete into full sentences. As with the translation task, it involves both a comprehension and a production component. In monolingual research on language production the paradigm has been used to elicit a particular class of grammatical mistakes—errors in subject–verb number agreement (e.g., Bock & Miller, 1991). In experiments using this methodology the participants are given complex noun phrases such as *The key to the cabinets*. Their task is to complete the phrases into full sentences (by adding, for instance, *is lost*). The two nouns in the complex noun phrase may differ in number (as in the example) or may have the same number (*The key to the cabinet*). The former situation leads to more agreement errors during completion (as in *The key to the cabinets . . . are lost*) than the latter. This finding is attributed to the fact that the two nouns prime completions with differential numbers. This creates a response conflict, which may lead to an error. This paradigm has been adapted to the study of bilingual speech production by exploiting the fact that noun number does not always converge across a bilingual's two languages. For instance, *scissors* and *trousers* are plural in English but their Greek equivalents are singular whereas, conversely, *hair* and *money* are singular in English but plural in Greek (Hatzidaki, 2007). If in a unilingual condition bilinguals are affected by this incongruence while performing the sentence completion task, as compared to a condition where noun number is the same in the two languages, this would suggest language-nonselective grammatical processing. A similar technique, both in a monolingual (e.g., Bock, 1995) and a bilingual version (see p. 252), has been used to study pronoun–antecedent number agreement.

This overview of ways to study speech production is by no means exhaustive. Most notably missing are the common observational methods used to analyze speech dysfluencies, such as

hesitations and pauses, and errors in spontaneous speech (see Bock, 1996, for a review). Both methods have been applied to monolingual and bilingual speech production alike. The reason for confining myself here to the above experimental methods is that these are the ones that were used in the selection of studies to be discussed below.

MODELS OF MONOLINGUAL AND BILINGUAL SPEECH PRODUCTION

Levelt's model of monolingual speech production

A major part of the research on monolingual speech production has been inspired by Levelt's (1989) theory of the speech process as illustrated in Figure 5.1. It covers the whole trajectory from the conceptualization of a message to be expressed to actual articulation, and describes the various types of knowledge structures that are accessed and retrieved en route and their temporal order. Boxes in the figure represent processing components; the circle and ellipse represent knowledge stores.

The first steps in the production process involve the conception of the intention to express a particular thought in words, the selection of the required information from the relevant memory stores, and the ordering of this information for expression. This aggregate of activities is called **conceptualizing**, and the system involved is called the "conceptualizer". The output of the conceptualizer is a conceptual structure called the **preverbal message**. This output possibly takes the form of a collection of activated memory nodes, each representing a particular conceptual component, an element of meaning. Speakers are known to monitor their own speech. This activity is also taken care of by the conceptualizer. The ellipse that is connected with the conceptualizer in the figure and from which the conceptualizer draws the information required for expressing its intention, represents a database of declarative knowledge. It includes all the factual ("encyclopedic") knowledge stored in the speaker's

FIGURE 5.1

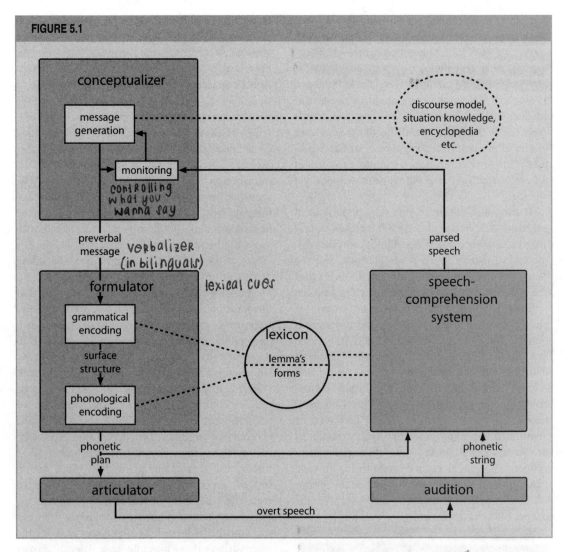

Levelt's (1989) model of the speech process. Boxes represent processing components. Circle and ellipse represent knowledge stores. From Levelt (1989), © 1989 Massachusetts Institute of Technology, by permission of The MIT Press.

long-term memory as well as knowledge on the present discourse situation (e.g., who the interlocutors are, what their goals are, what everybody has said so far).

The preverbal message constitutes the input for the second processing component, the **formulator**, which translates the preverbal message into a linguistic structure. It does so in two steps: **grammatical encoding** and **phonological encoding**. These two processes are taken care of by the "grammatical encoder" and the "phonological encoder", respectively. The grammatical encoder consists of procedures to access entries in the mental lexicon (the knowledge store represented by the circle in Figure 5.1) and to build syntactic constructions. Lexical items (or "entries") are composed of two parts that, together, contain four types of information: the word's meaning, its syntactical characteristics, its morphological characteristics, and its phonological form (because the model deals with speaking, the fact that, in literate language users, lexical entries also contain orthographical information is ignored). An entry's part that specifies its meaning and syntax is called its **lemma**, whereas the part that specifies its morphological and phonological properties is called **lexeme** (Kempen & Huijbers, 1983). It is the lemma component of the lexical entries that is contacted by the procedures executed by the grammatical encoder. The output of the grammatical encoder is a "surface structure": an ordered string of lemmas grouped in phrases or sub-phrases whose sound is not yet specified.

During the next processing step, phonological encoding, a phonetic plan is built for each lemma and the utterance as a whole. During this process, the lexical entries' lexemes are accessed and the elements in the grammatical encoder's output are morphologically and phonologically adapted to their linguistic environment. The output of phonological encoding is an internal representation of how the planned utterance should be articulated. It is variously called the "phonetic plan" or "internal speech".

The next step is articulating; that is, the execution of the phonetic plan. This process is taken care of by the "articulator". As already mentioned, speakers monitor their speech, a process that exploits the speech comprehension system. The model assumes monitoring to take place on both internal speech—that is, the output of the formulator—and on overt speech, the output of the articulator.

Levelt (1989) hypothesized the different processing components to be dedicated specialists: He assumed that each of them serves one (and just one) function, for instance to translate a preverbal message into a surface structure, that it can, in principle, only operate on one type of input, and that it works autonomously. This latter characteristic means that it is not affected by processing activity elsewhere in the system. In terms of Fodor's (1983) modularity of mind theory presented earlier (p. 163), the processing components in Levelt's model are "informationally encapsulated" modules.

A further processing assumption of the model is that the operations of the formulator are "lexically driven". This means that grammatical encoding and phonological encoding are mediated by the information that becomes available when lexical entries are activated by the preverbal message. Figure 5.1 does not show a direct connection from the preverbal message to the lexicon. Yet it is the preverbal message that "triggers lexical items into activity" (Levelt, 1989, p. 181). More specifically, the meaning component of a lexical item's lemma becomes activated automatically when it matches the information in the preverbal message. The moment this happens, the associated syntactical information also becomes available (e.g., that the item is a female noun, which is pluralized with an -s or that it is an intransitive verb), and this information drives the grammatical encoding process.

A final hypothesis reflected in the model is that the information flow is top-down, with no feedback from processors that start operating at a later point in time (e.g., the formulator) back to those that start earlier (e.g., the conceptualizer). But even when first presenting his model, Levelt (1989) considered the possibility there might be one exception; namely, that the outcome of phonological encoding might feed back to the process of grammatical encoding and, especially, to the lemma selection part of that process. The reason for this qualification was that several sets of experimental results appeared hard to reconcile with a strict top-down serial view of processing. One such source of counterevidence is the so-called "lexical bias" effect; that is, the observation that phonological speech errors constitute real words more often than would be expected on the basis of chance (Baars, Motley, & MacKay, 1975; Dell & Reich, 1981; and see Costa, Roelstraete, & Hartsuiker, 2006, for a bilingual lexical bias effect across languages). If grammatical and phonological encoding take place in two serial and independent steps, errors that occur during the second stage should result in words and nonwords equally often. A second source of counterevidence is the occurrence of "mixed" errors, errors that resemble the targeted lexical item both in form and meaning (such as *oyster* for *lobster*). These errors were found to occur more often than would be expected on the basis of a chance estimate (e.g., Dell & Reich, 1981). These findings have led several authors (most notoriously Dell, 1986) to assume feedback from the phonological encoding stage back to the grammatical encoding stage (see, e.g., Levelt & Maassen, 1981; Levelt et al., 1991; Schriefers, Meyer, & Levelt, 1990, for more complete discussions, including suggestions of how to reconcile this apparent counterevidence with serial production models).

The primary goal of much of the monolingual speech production research to date has been to answer this very question, whether grammatical encoding and phonological encoding occur strictly top-down ("forward") or whether there is feedback from the phonological level back to the level of grammatical encoding. However, the terminology has changed somewhat over the years, presumably because of the fact that the lexicalization component of the complete production model has become the main focus of attention in studies on speech production (see pp. 229–234). Current terminology distinguishes between the stages of "lemma selection" and phonological encoding, and both processes are conceived of as the spreading of activation in a lexical network. In addition to a distinction between forward-only processing and forward-and-backward ("interactive") processing, a second distinction is made in current theories of speech production. It is commonly assumed that a particular conceptual content (the preverbal message) activates not one lemma but a set of lemmas, each of them sharing a part of its semantic content with the conceptualized content (this set of activated lemmas is known as the "semantic cohort"). Ultimately only one of the activated lemmas must be selected for production. The second distinction referred to here concerns the view that only the selected lemma is phonologically encoded, versus the view that shortly after their activation, and prior to one of them being selected, the phonology of all activated lemmas becomes temporarily activated.

In practice, the above two theoretical distinctions have led to three types of speech production models: "discrete two-stage processing models" (e.g., Levelt et al., 1991; Schriefers et al., 1990),

"unidirectional cascaded-processing models" (e.g., Humphreys, Riddock, & Quinlan, 1988; Peterson & Savoy, 1998), and "interactive activation models" (e.g., Dell, 1986). These models all distinguish between three levels of representation in the speech production system: a prelexical conceptual level and two lexical levels, one of the latter storing the lexical items' lemmas and the second storing their lexemes; that is, their phonological forms. However, they differ in their assumptions regarding the way activation flows between these representational levels and, especially, between the two lexical levels.

Discrete two-stage models assume that activation can only flow in a forward direction from the lemma level to the lexeme (or phonological) level. In addition they assume that activation is not transmitted from the lemma level to the lexeme level until after processing at the lemma level has been completed; that is, after one lemma has been selected from the initially activated set of lemmas (the semantic cohort). Unidirectional cascade models also hold that activation only flows forward, but contrary to the discrete two-stage models they assume that this activation flow does not await the completion of processing at the lemma stage. The moment a lemma becomes activated by the preverbal message it starts sending activation down to the lexeme level. The consequence of this combination of processing assumptions is that all elements in the semantic cohort are temporarily phonologically encoded. Finally, as with the unidirectional cascade models, the interactive activation models assume that all initially activated lemmas immediately pass on their activation to the corresponding lexemes. But unlike the unidirectional cascade models, these models assume that activation may also flow back from activated lexemes to lemma representations.

As mentioned, a conceptual structure activates all lemmas that share content with the conceptualized structure. Although translation "equivalent" words typically do not share meaning completely between the two languages in question, their meanings generally overlap to a large extent, maybe even more so than the meanings of within-language synonyms (Hermans,

Bongaerts, De Bot, & Schreuder, 1998). Unless languages can be fully sealed off from one another (which we have seen not to be the case), this prompts the question of whether, when bilinguals intend to utter a word, the associated conceptual content will activate not only lemmas in the target language but also the lemma of the targeted word's translation in the non-target language (and maybe other lemmas in the non-target language as well). Such an outcome would constitute evidence of language-nonselective speech production. This is one of the main questions addressed in the bilingual speech production research to be reviewed below. If the semantic cohort indeed contains lemmas from both languages, a further question is whether all lemmas in the semantic cohort, irrespective of language, are phonologically encoded or just one; namely the one that emerges as the winner in the stage where lemmas compete for selection. Accordingly, a second main question posed in the bilingual speech production research is whether the lemmas of both terms in a translation pair transmit their activation to the corresponding phonological forms, the lexemes, or whether phonological form activation is restricted to the target-language lemma. Before presenting the relevant evidence I will first discuss the earliest attempts to apply Levelt's (1989) model to bilingual speech production, and next zoom in on the lexicalization process in some more detail.

Levelt's model applied to bilingualism

De Bot (1992) and De Bot and Schreuder (1993) were the first to extend the insights obtained in monolingual speech production research to bilingualism, building on Levelt's (1989) model. One of the facts about language that a bilingual production model should deal with is that languages differ in the way they lexicalize the conceptual information in the preverbal message. A particular subset of the preverbal message's conceptual components may be expressed in a single word in one language but may require a whole phrase to be expressed in another language. This is one of the issues De Bot and Schreuder (1993) attempted to solve. Their solution involved an extension of Levelt's model with an extra component, the "verbalizer", which receives input from the preverbal message (the "conceptual structure") and carves it up in such a way that it matches the semantic information in the targeted lemmas. If the information in the conceptual structure is indeed lexicalized differently in a bilingual's two languages, this process results in different sets of information chunks, depending on the language currently spoken. Subsequently, the constructed chunks are output by the verbalizer and trigger the lemmas into action. (Note the difference with Levelt's model, in which lemmas are accessed directly by the information in the preverbal message.)

As acknowledged by the authors, this is all easier said than done, because chunking the conceptual information such that it matches the lemmas' meaning components implies that the verbalizer knows in advance what semantic information it can expect to find in the lemmas. On what other grounds could it carve up the conceptual structure into chunks that the lexicon can handle? In this respect the original model in which lemma triggering requires no fore-knowledge of knowledge structures that are only accessed later in the production process, seems preferable. But the point made by De Bot and Schreuder—that languages differ in the way they carve up conceptual space in their vocabulary—is an important one and will have to be addressed in any model of bilingual language production that strives for completeness.

A second issue these authors addressed was how language selection comes about: How do bilinguals manage to produce speech according to their choice—that is, to produce (relatively) pure monolingual speech in either of their two languages—or to code-switch freely between the two, depending on their current intentions? What adjustment to the monolingual production system could account for this flexible behavior of the bilingual speaker? The authors' solution to guarantee monolingual output was to assume that the decision about what language to speak is determined by the conceptualizer, because only this component of the production system has access to the knowledge relevant for making a language choice (e.g., knowledge regarding the present discourse and what languages the interlocutors master). The information representing this choice is one component of the conceptualizer's output—that is, of the (language-nonspecific) preverbal message—it is called the **language cue**. In addition the authors assumed that the semantic information within each lemma includes the knowledge of what language the lemma belongs to (this piece of information is often called the "language tag"). With this set-up, the match between the preverbal message and the semantic information in the lemma of the target language will generally be larger than between the former and the semantic information in the translation-equivalent lemma in the non-target language. As a result, the targeted lemma will generally become more highly activated than the lemma of its translation equivalent so that the words that exit the production system will generally be words of the selected language.

But what about a situation in which language mixing does not impede communication or is even considered natural and desirable, for instance because the addressee is fluent in the same two languages as the speaker and both share the same bilingual social background? De Bot (1992) adopted the earlier idea (Green, 1986) that bilinguals generate two speech plans simultaneously, one for the selected language and one for the other language, which is also active. Because this way the language not currently in use is always present "in the background", foregrounding this language with a language switch can occur rapidly and effortlessly. De Bot and Schreuder (1993) proposed a different solution, namely that the language cue in the preverbal message may be assigned a different weight in different situations: If switching languages would incur the risk of a communicative breakdown, the language cue may be assigned a high value, thus ensuring it will increase the activation level of the targeted lemma. In a context where language switching is quite common, would not hinder communication, and would be experienced as quite natural, the language cue may receive a low value, thus allowing mixed output to occur.

Two of the theoretical constructs in this

seminal work—the language cue as part of the conceptual structure (the preverbal message) and some piece of information specifying the language membership of a lexical item (the language tag)—have since become more generally accepted in models of bilingual speech production. A number of the studies that imply these constructs will be discussed further on in this chapter. Chapter 6, which is exclusively dedicated to the way bilinguals select and control their two languages, covers studies that incorporate these concepts more explicitly. In addition to the present view of language selection in terms of a language cue, other views on how language selection comes about will be reviewed there as well.

THE CORE OF SPEECH PRODUCTION MODELS: LEXICALIZATION

As mentioned, much research on speech production has focused on the lexicalization component of the complete production process and specifically on lemma selection and phonological encoding. Because of this focus, visual illustrations of the speech production process usually zoom in on the lexicon, ignoring the broader context of the complete process. An illustration of how this is done in reports of bilingual speech production studies is presented in Figure 5.2, which I have borrowed, in adapted form, from Kroll, Sumutka, and Schwartz (2005). The figure depicts one possible pattern of activation that may be established in bilingual memory when Dutch–English bilingual participants are asked to name pictures in one of their languages, here English. In addition to the picture to be named, it shows the three levels of representations commonly assumed in speech production models: the prelexical conceptual level and the lexical lemma and phonological form (lexeme) levels.

Picture naming is the task used most frequently in word production research because the outcome of the picture analysis process is regarded similar to the output of the mental conceptualization process in natural speech

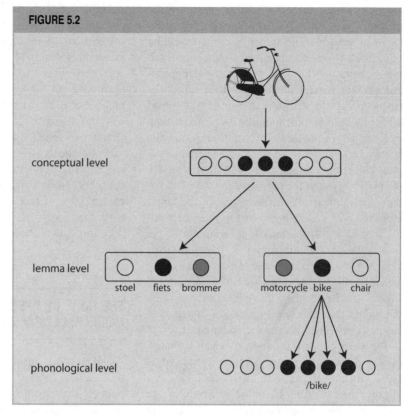

FIGURE 5.2

A model of picture naming in bilinguals. The (Dutch–English) participants' task is to name the picture in English (*stoel = chair; fiets = bike; brommer = motorcycle*). In this example model lemma activation is language-nonselective and phonological activation is language-selective. Circles represent memory nodes. Black nodes are highly activated; grey nodes are weakly activated; unfilled nodes are totally deactivated. Adapted from Kroll et al. (2005).

production, and this output is thought to set off the remainder of the production process in the same way in picture naming and common speech production. In brief, the full picture-naming process is assumed to consist of the following chain of operations: The computation of the visual percept, the activation of an appropriate lexical concept, the selection of the target word from the mental lexicon, phonological encoding, phonetic encoding, and the initiation of articulation (Levelt, Praamsma, Meyer, Helenius, & Salmelin, 1998). In the sections to follow, these steps, and especially those in between visual percept computation and phonetic encoding, will be fleshed out in more detail.

Just as conceptualizing a word to speak out loud, the first stage of the picture-naming process as sketched in Figure 5.2, the perceptual analysis of the picture, results in the activation of a subset of conceptual memory units usually called "nodes" (the filled circles are the activated nodes). Each of the activated nodes specifies one meaning

aspect (or "conceptual component" or "conceptual feature") of the targeted word (e.g., –animate or +artifact). In terms of Levelt's (1989) model, together with the language cue hypothesized by De Bot (1992), De Bot and Schreuder (1993) and others (e.g., Poulisse, 1997; Poulisse & Bongaerts, 1994), these activated conceptual components constitute the preverbal message. This type of representation, where a word's meaning is spread out over a number of more elementary meaning units, is called "distributed" or "componential", or "decomposed" (see p. 133 and Figures 3.8 and 3.11b, Chapter 3, for a similar model),

The activated components at the conceptual level feed their activation down to the lemma level, along unidirectional links. In this specific model, at the lemma level each word is represented in a single, "non-decomposed" unit (see, e.g., the monolingual models of Jescheniak & Levelt, 1994, and Roelofs, 1992, 1997, and the bilingual model of Poulisse, 1997, and Poulisse &

Bongaerts, 1994). Such type of representation, for which a one-to-one mapping holds between a linguistic entity to be represented (here, a lemma) and the representing memory structure, is often called a "localist" representation (see also p. 132). Figure 5.2 depicts a situation in which lemmas for words semantically related to the targeted word are also activated, but to a lesser degree than the target word's lemma. Furthermore, activation is not restricted to the targeted language (the one the participants are asked to use while naming the pictures) but lemmas in the non-target language are activated as well. In other words, lemma activation is hypothesized to be language-nonselective. From the lemma level activation spreads further down, again along unidirectional links, to the phonological level, where a word's phonological word form is represented in a pattern of activation over a number of nodes each representing a part of its sound, for instance, one phoneme. Figure 5.2 depicts the situation where this only happens for the most highly activated lemma in the target language and for none of the activated lemmas in the non-target language. In other words, in the depicted model phonological encoding is language-selective and it exemplifies the discrete two-stage models introduced earlier.

The mixture of representation and processing assumptions assumed in Figure 5.2 is just one of a larger number of possible sets of assumptions. For instance, as we have seen, instead of activation only spreading forward along uni-directional links, some monolingual models assume forward as well as backward spreading of activation, a state of affairs that presupposes bidirectional links between the units in adjacent representation levels (Dell, 1986). Roelofs' (1997) WEAVER model assumes a mixture of bidirectional and unidirectional connections, and similar proposals have been made for bilingual production models (e.g., Costa, Santesteban, & Caño, 2005).

Furthermore, instead of non-decomposed representations at the lemma level, some authors (e.g., Bierwisch & Schreuder, 1992; Butterworth, 1989; Dell, 1986) assumed that the meaning part of a lexical entry's lemma is "componential" or "decomposed". As mentioned, this means that it

consists of a set of semantic components, each of them representing one aspect of the word's meaning. Recall that Levelt's (1989) original model assumed that a preverbal message, consisting of a set of activated conceptual elements, triggered lemmas whose meaning specification matched this set into activity. The componential view of lexical semantics provides a natural explanation of this triggering process, because the activated (prelexical) conceptual elements may map directly onto the lexical-semantic components. It also provides a ready explanation of the fact that not one lemma but a set of semantically related lemmas are triggered, because the (componential) meaning part of semantically related lemmas will all share a subset of their meaning components with the information content of the preverbal message. Consequently, they will all be directly triggered by the preverbal message. The degree to which each of them is activated depends on the degree of overlap between preverbal message and the lexical-semantic content of the lemma.

In models that assume the lemmas' meaning representations to be non-decomposed, multiple activation of semantically related lemmas is more readily explained in terms of spreading activation in a lexical-semantic network in which the lemmas of semantically related words are connected to one another: The activated conceptual elements in the preverbal message trigger one lemma into activity and from this lemma, activation spreads through the network to those of semantically related lemmas. According to this account, the lemmas of words semantically related to the target word are thus not directly activated by the preverbal message, but indirectly, following prior activation of the target word's lemma (see Levelt, 1999, for a more complete discussion of the contrast between decomposed and non-decomposed lexical semantics).

However, assuming both the existence of prelexical conceptual elements as well as lexical-semantic conceptual elements, the latter being part of a lexical entry's lemma, seems to involve an unattractive doubling of memory components. This may be the reason why in more recent work, instead of containing both the lexical item's semantic and syntactic information (as in Levelt,

1989), the lemma consists of the associated word's syntactic information only (see e.g., Bock & Levelt, 1994; Levelt, 1999, Levelt, Roelofs, & Meyer, 1999; Roelofs, 1992, 1997). In these models the upper layer in the visualized models (e.g., the conceptual level in Figure 5.2) no longer depicts a prelexical representation level but lexical semantics instead, and all processing between the perceptual processing of the picture and lexical-semantic activation remains unspecified (*if* further intermediate processing occurs at all). Figure 5.3 shows a (monolingual English) version of this type of model, with non-decomposed meaning representations organized in a semantic network and spreading activation between them. Because the concepts semantically related to the targeted concept are only indirectly activated, through spreading activation, and, therefore, relatively weakly activated, the corresponding lemmas are also activated less than the targeted lemma. A core assumption in these

models is that the access of a word's phonological form is mediated by the access of the word's lemma and the associated syntactic features: Activation from the conceptual level spreads to the lemma level where syntax is specified, and from there to the lexeme level (the phonological level), where the phonological form is specified. Caramazza (1997) called this assumption the "syntactic mediation hypothesis".

Caramazza (1997) proposed a model, the independent network model, which is radically different from those reviewed so far. In this model, not only do lemmas no longer contain semantic information, but they are dismissed altogether (see Starreveld & La Heij, 1995, for a similar proposal). His main reason to get rid of lemmas is that the results of a diverse set of cognitive-neuropsychological studies point towards the conclusion that access to a word's phonology is independent from access to syntactic information, thus falsifying the syntactic

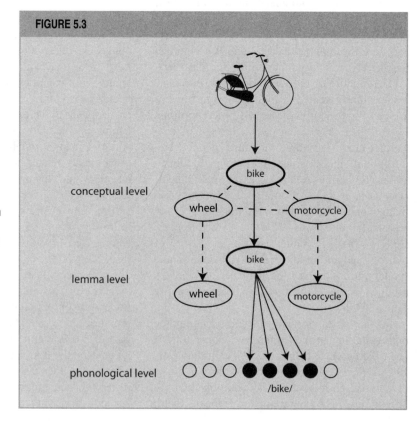

FIGURE 5.3

A model of picture naming in monolinguals. The (English) participants' task is to name the picture in English. The lexical conceptual representations are non-componental and organized in a semantic network. Concepts semantically related to the targeted concept are indirectly activated through spreading activation in the semantic network.

conceptual level

lemma level

phonological level

/bike/

mediation hypothesis. In other words, a word's syntactic make-up is not prepared prior to, but independent from, specifying its phonology. Caramazza then argues that the original motivation to postulate a separate lemma level was the assumed dependence of lexeme activation on the representations that specify syntax; that is, the lemmas. If this dependence does not hold and, at the same time, lemmas are devoid of meaning, why then would lemma representations exist in the first place? The only role a lemma would continue to play is to serve as a "way station to syntactic and phonological representations" and "the lemma node would have been rendered superfluous" (Caramazza, 1997, p. 188).

The alternative proposed by Caramazza is a production process in which activation from a lexical-semantic network flows on directly to both phonological (and orthographic) lexemes and to a network of syntactic features, and from the phonological lexemes on to segmental phonological information (e.g., units that represent phonemes). In addition, direct connections

exist between the phonological (and orthographic) lexemes and the syntactic features network. This set-up, illustrated in Figure 5.4 is called "independent" because the activation of the lexemes is no longer mediated by syntax. (Note that the orthographic component of the model and its connections with other parts of the system are not shown.) As can be seen, the model assumes componential instead of localist word meanings. How these lexical meaning components are activated as a result of prior conceptual processing remains unspecified, as was also the case for the "lemma-dependent" models that only assign syntax, not meaning, to the lemmas.

Considering these more recent views, there appears to be a second possible reading of Figure 5.2, one that is crucially different from the one advanced above: Also here, the conceptual level may represent lexical semantics instead of, as assumed before, a set of activated elements in a (non-linguistic) conceptual system which activates the lemma's meaning part (the latter no

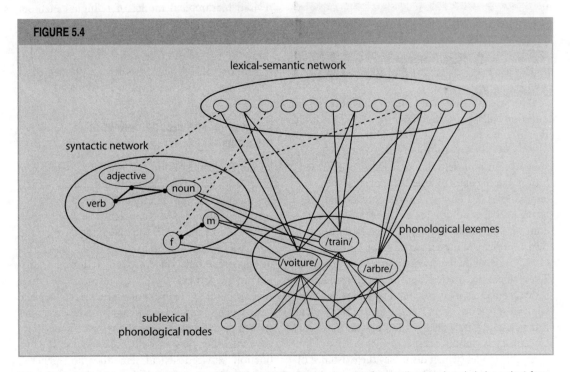

FIGURE 5.4

The independent network model of lexical access illustrated for French. Access of a word's phonology is independent from syntactic access and no lemma representations are assumed. Adapted from Caramazza (1997).

longer being stored in the lemma). In other words, the units at the conceptual level may either represent prelexical conceptual knowledge or lexical-semantic knowledge. Phrased in yet a different manner, the three visualized representation levels may represent lexical knowledge solely (meaning, syntax, and phonology) or a mixture of prelexical and lexical knowledge.

In reports of monolingual and bilingual speech production research the exact assumptions regarding representation and processing are often not explicated but taken for granted. This does not just involve the risk of uncertainty about how to interpret a particular illustration of the production process (as in Figure 5.2). A further risk is that two similar-looking illustrations, in fact representing two different views on representation and processing in word production, may mistakenly be interpreted as representing one and the same type of model. To illustrate this point, Figure 5.5 depicts the representation and processing assumptions that Costa, Caramazza, and Sebastián-Gallés (2000) hypothesized to hold for picture naming by bilinguals, in this specific case Spanish–Catalan bilinguals. This figure illustrates the production process hypothesized for words that have a cognate- or a non-cognate translation equivalent in the other language (upper and lower panels, respectively).

The research designed to test the hypotheses in question will be discussed later (p. 246). The point to make here is that, at first sight, these figures look very similar to Figure 5.2 and therefore suggest they represent the same levels of representation but labeled differently. For instance, the lemma level in Figure 5.2 appears to be the same as the lexical nodes level in Figure 5.5. But, on the contrary, the models depicted in the latter illustration represent bilingual versions of Caramazza's (1997) independent network model (Figure 5.4): The semantic nodes represent Caramazza's lexical-semantic network and the lexical and sublexical nodes represent the phonological lexemes and sublexical phonological nodes in Caramazza's model, respectively. As we have seen, this model (which dismisses the existence of lemmas) is radically different from the majority of the models discussed above. The first impres-

sion of close similarity to another model thus carries a serious risk of biasing a reader towards a completely wrong interpretation of a model and the data that led to it.

On the other hand, the opposite may occur as well: Visual illustrations of models that look rather different at first sight do not necessarily imply radically different assumptions regarding representation and processing. For instance, the number of representation layers shown is often not an indicator of the number of processing steps assumed by the modeler, but simply a way to focus the reader's attention on the steps that are the object of study in a particular investigation. To give one example, because in many bilingual studies the way word meaning maps onto word form has been the main object of study, visual renderings of the underlying representation and processing assumptions often only display two representational levels, one representing word meaning and a second representing the word's complete form. A number of these models were presented in Chapter 3, when discussing the revised hierarchical model of bilingual memory and its precursors (see pp. 129–135). It is only because these models do not pretend to have anything to say about the representation of, say, syntax or sublexical units such as phonemes or letters, that no further levels are visualized.

Conceptual knowledge and word meaning

To conclude this section, a brief discussion is in order on a research dispute that arguably underlies much of this ambiguity and especially the two possible readings of the conceptual level of representation in Figure 5.2: the one in terms of lexical semantics (word meaning) versus the one in terms of the preverbal conceptual structure. The dispute in question is whether or not word meanings exist separately from more general conceptual knowledge. Levelt's original model assumes such to be the case, and other researchers have advanced this view as well. For instance, the distinction between lexical semantics and general, non-linguistic, conceptual knowledge forms the basis of the three-store hypothesis of Paradis

FIGURE 5.5

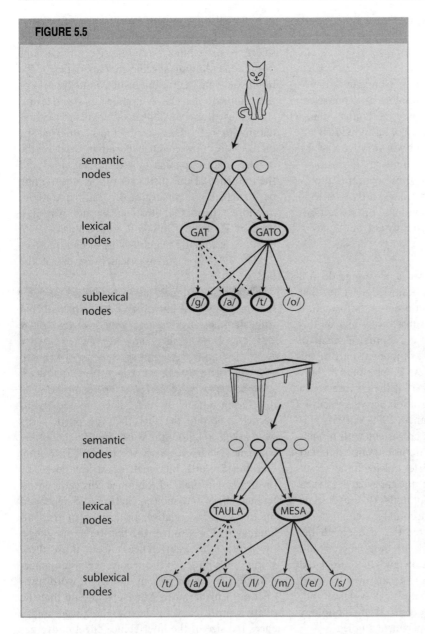

semantic nodes

lexical nodes

sublexical nodes

semantic nodes

lexical nodes

sublexical nodes

A model of picture naming in bilinguals. The (Catalan–Spanish) participants' task is to name the pictures in Spanish. The upper and lower panels illustrate the memory representations of the Catalan–Spanish cognate pair *gat–gato* ("cat") and non-cognate pair *taula–mesa* ("table"), respectively. Lexical and sublexical activation are both language-nonselective. Lexical nodes represent phonological lexemes. From Costa et al. (2000). Copyright © 2000 American Psychological Society.

(e.g., Paradis, 2004), and, as we have seen, De Bot and Schreuder (1993) also distinguished between the two (and see also Pavlenko, 1999). In terms of the above discussion, all theorists who assume (1) that lemmas contain meaning and (2) that lemmas are triggered by some match between prelexical conceptual information and the lemmas' meaning components appear to hold this view. An argument in favor of the validity of the distinction between lexical semantics and non-linguistic conceptual knowledge is that concepts exist that are not lexicalized.

Francis (1999, 2005) advanced the following parsimonious view of the relationship between general conceptual knowledge and lexical-semantic concepts: All humans possess a (non-linguistic) conceptual system consisting of a large set of conceptual elements. Semantics comes into play in the way this conceptual system maps onto language or, more precisely, instantiates language (Francis, 2005, p. 252):

> Any of the concepts a person can know ought to have the potential to be expressed in any human language. Of course, the concepts actually realized in an individual's language input or output will vary with systematic patterns across languages. Semantic representations may be those concepts that are referred to by particular words or sentences [. . .]. Word meanings, or semantic representations of words, would be a particular type of concept.

According to this view, word meanings do not exist separately from a knowledge store that contains non-linguistic conceptual information but are represented by subsets of units in this store. One and the same conceptual element in this store may serve as a component part of the meaning of many words. As Francis puts it: "any word meaning is identified with a subset or a particular pattern of activation across the entire [conceptual] system" (Francis, 1999, p. 195). This view appears to be most consistent with models of word production that do not assume different levels of conceptual and lexical-semantic representations but it remains unclear what it is then that activates the subsets of nodes that instantiate word meanings in the conceptual system.

Having thus familiarized the reader with the general outline of models of monolingual and bilingual speech production and the associated concepts and terminology, I can now proceed with a discussion of the empirical evidence and, first, the details of the general methodology employed in many of the pertinent studies.

PICTURE NAMING

Introduction

As mentioned, just as in the study of bilingual comprehension, research on language production in bilinguals has pursued the question of whether bilingual language production is language-selective or language-nonselective or perhaps both, depending on specific characteristics of the linguistic and extra-linguistic context and/or the bilingual speaker. A number of the relevant studies used one version or other of the picture-naming task. Of these, a subset has employed the picture–word interference paradigm, where the picture is accompanied by a distracter word and the influence of this distracter on picture-naming performance is determined. This paradigm developed from the Stroop task and was first used by Rosinski, Golinkoff, and Kukish (1975) to study automatic reading skills of children (see Levelt, 1999, for an historical overview of the task's roots).

In an early bilingual study using the distracter methodology Ehri and Ryan (1980) showed that English–Spanish bilinguals named pictures more slowly, in both of their languages, when a word from the non-target language was superimposed over the picture than when a neutral distracter stimulus (a series of Xs) was superimposed. The interfering effect of the superimposed word occurred despite the fact that the participants were asked to ignore the word. In a further study Mägiste (1984b; see also Mägiste, 1985), testing German–Swedish bilinguals at various levels of proficiency in their L2, obtained this same interference effect and showed that its size depended on the learners' relative proficiency in the two languages: The stronger the non-target language, the larger the interference effect. Both these studies thus hinted at the occurrence of language-nonselective activation in bilingual word production. Furthermore, Mägiste's finding that the relative proficiency in the two languages influences the size of the interference effect converges with similar results in the comprehension studies discussed in Chapter 4: The stronger the non-target language, the larger the chance it will permeate in processing the target language. However, not having been specifically designed to do so, these studies did not provide any information on the exact level or levels in the bilingual production system where co-activation of the non-target language occurred. Specifically, they did not state whether it stopped at the lemma level or proceeded on to the phonological level.

More recent bilingual picture-naming studies, using both the distracter methodology (Costa & Caramazza, 1999; Costa, Miozzo, & Caramazza, 1999; Hermans et al., 1998) and versions of the task in which pictures are presented without distracters (Colomé, 2001; Costa et al., 2000; Gollan & Acenas, 2004; Kroll, Dijkstra, Janssen, & Schriefers, 2000; Rodriguez-Fornells et al., 2005), focused on various aspects of the theoretical contrasts introduced earlier. For example, they examined whether both the lemma and phonological form of words from the non-response language are activated or whether or not backward spreading of activation between the different types of representations occurs. The distracter studies among this set were closely modeled on a number of highly influential monolingual production studies that used a sophisticated methodology trying to answer the analogous questions regarding monolingual processing. In the next sections I will first describe this methodology and I will then continue with a review of the bilingual studies.

The picture–word interference task

Methodology

The monolingual picture–word interference studies alluded to above investigated the processes of lemma selection and phonological encoding by manipulating both the type of distracter words presented with the picture and the time interval between the presentation of distracter and picture. Distracter and picture were presented simultaneously (a "stimulus onset asynchrony", SOA, of 0 ms), the distracter preceded the picture (a negative SOA) or followed the picture (a positive SOA). Across the various studies both visual and auditory distracters have been used. The main dependent variable in most of these studies (as well as in their bilingual counterparts) was picture-naming latency: the time duration between the onset of picture presentation and the onset of the participant's naming response. Five

types of distracter words have been used (not necessarily all of them in one and the same study). Table 5.1 shows example materials used by Levelt et al. (1991) in a monolingual Dutch study: The distracter word is identical to the picture's name (Identical), semantically related to the picture's name (Semantic), phonologically related to the picture's name (Phonological), phonologically related to a word that is semantically related to the picture's name (Phonological-Semantic; e.g., in Table 5.1 *stoep* is phonologically related to *stoel*), or unrelated to the picture's name (Unrelated).

In comparison to neutral or unrelated distracters, semantic distracters (e.g. a picture of a desk accompanied by the distracter word *chair*) have been shown to slow down the picture-naming response (e.g., Bajo, Puerta-Melguizo, & Macizo, 2003; Levelt et al., 1999; Roelofs, 1992; Schriefers et al., 1990; Starreveld & La Heij, 1995, 1996). In production models that assume the existence of lemma representations this effect is attributed to a competition between the lemmas of picture and distracter, which are both activated upon presentation of the picture (see, e.g., Figure 5.3). The occurrence of this effect depends on the time relation between picture and distracter: Schriefers et al. (1990; a study in which the distracters were presented aurally) obtained the effect only when the semantic distracter preceded the picture (i.e., with a negative SOA), but not when they coincided or when the picture was presented first.

Interestingly, this same study showed completely different results for phonological distracters. First, the effect of these distracters was facilitative rather than inhibitory: they speeded up the picture-naming response. Second, these facilitative effects occurred when picture and distracter coincided and when the picture was presented first; that is, with SOAs that had shown null effects of semantic distracters. Conversely, no such effect was observed when the phonological distracter preceded the picture. Again, this result is opposite to the one observed with semantic distracters. The combined data thus suggest early semantic inhibition of semantic distracters and later phonological facilitation of phonological

---

TABLE 5.1

Example materials used by Levelt et al. (1991)

Picture's name	Identical distracters	Semantic distracters	Phonological distracters	Phonological-Semantic distracters	Unrelated distracters
bureau ("desk")	bureau ("desk")	stoel ("chair")	buurman ("neighbor")	stoep ("pavement")	muts ("cap")
cactus ("cactus")	cactus ("cactus")	stekel ("sting")	kakkerlak ("cockroach")	steno ("shorthand")	tas ("bag")
geweer ("rifle")	geweer ("rifle")	oorlog ("war")	gewei ("antlers")	oorzaak ("cause")	koets ("coach")
vinger ("finger")	vinger ("finger")	ring ("ring")	vink ("finch")	rits ("zipper")	kwast ("brush")
radio ("radio")	radio ("radio")	muziek ("music")	radar ("radar")	museum ("museum")	kerk ("church")

Example materials used by Levelt et al. (1991) in a monolingual Dutch picture–word interference study. The meanings of the Dutch words are in parentheses.

---

distracters. The authors attributed the facilitative effect of phonological distracters to boosted activation of the phonological segments that need to be selected in the final stage of picture naming: The phonological analysis of, say, the auditory distracter *buurman* (Table 5.1) activates a subset of the same phonemic segments that must be retrieved to name the target picture (this name being the phonologically similar *bureau*). This additional activation of the targeted phonological elements from a second source speeds up the picture-naming process.

The interaction between SOA and type of distracter, semantic or phonological, can be understood if we consider the various processing stages, and their order, in the two processes that operate in parallel in the picture–word interference task: naming the picture and processing the distracter. These two processes operate in opposite directions, top-down and bottom-up: Following a perceptual analysis of the picture, picture naming begins with the activation of a set of nodes in the conceptual level of representation. From there activation floods downward to the phonological level, activating the elements in the intermediate level (or levels) en route. Distracter processing starts off at the phonological level and works upward from there. At some point in the system the two processes will meet and affect each other. What this meeting point is and, consequently, what the nature of the interference will be, is likely

to depend on the time relation between picture and distracter. This is illustrated in Figure 5.6, in terms of simplified processing models that distinguish between lexical semantics (meaning) and phonology only.

As shown, depending on the SOA, either the meaning activation stage or the phonology activation stage of picture naming and distracter processing coincide. For the phonological components to coincide, the distracter must be presented relatively late because phonological activation is the final step in picture naming but the first step in distracter processing (if the distracter is presented aurally). In contrast, because conceptual activation is an early processing stage in picture naming but a late step in distracter processing, for this processing component to coincide in picture and word processing the distracter must be presented earlier. Note that this analysis assumes that semantic interference and phonological facilitation result from coinciding conceptual and phonological processing, respectively.

From the fact that semantic and phonological distracters are effective at different SOAs, Schriefers et al. (1990) concluded, contrary to interactive activation models of lexical access (see p. 227), that lexicalization in word production is composed of two unidirectional successive stages, one of meaning activation and a second of phonological activation. Levelt et al. (1991) and

FIGURE 5.6

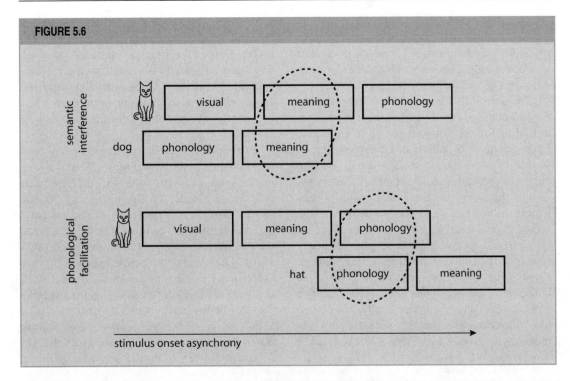

The dependency of the semantic interference and phonological facilitation effects in the picture–word interference task on the stimulus onset asynchrony between word distracter and picture.

Jescheniak and Schriefers (1998) built on this study by posing the question of whether phonological activation only occurs for the lemma that emerges as the winner from the cohort of initially activated lexical candidates (the semantic cohort) or also for the other members of the semantic cohort. The latter is the position taken by the cascaded-processing models presented earlier p. 227). (This question can be studied with the phonological-semantic distracters; see Table 5.1.) A difference between these two studies was that the semantic distracters in Levelt et al.'s study were (non-synonymous) members of the same semantic category as the picture's name (e.g., picture's name: *sofa*; semantic distracter: *chair*), whereas Jescheniak and Schriefers also used semantic distracters that were near-synonyms of the picture's name (e.g., picture's name: *sofa*; semantic distracter: *couch*). The combined results of these two studies suggest that phonological activation does not occur exclusively for the targeted word (the picture's name) but that near-

synonyms of this word are also phonologically activated (see Peterson & Savoy, 1998, for additional evidence). However, phonological activation does not appear to occur for words that are less-strongly semantically related to the target.

Bilingual studies

Hermans and his collaborators (1998) were the first to use the above distracter methodology to examine whether bilingual word production is language-nonselective. More precisely, they posed the question of whether, when bilinguals are asked to name pictures in their L2, the representations of the corresponding translations in L1 are also activated. If this were to turn out to be the case, they furthermore wanted to know whether this activation stops at the translation's lemma representation or is transmitted further down to the phonological level so that both words in a translation pair are phonologically encoded. The above results of Jescheniak and Schriefers

(1998) and Peterson and Savoy (1998) in particular suggested the latter might be the case because, plausibly, translation equivalents share at least as much meaning between one another as near-synonyms of one and the same language do.

The participants in this study were Dutch–English bilinguals with a high level of proficiency in L2 English, yet clearly dominant in L1 Dutch. Each picture to be named in L2 English (e.g., a picture of a mountain) was presented with an aural distracter, which could be of four types. Two of the types were the semantic and phonological distracters presented above (semantic: *valley*; phonological: *mouth*). A further type of distracters concerned words phonologically similar to the Dutch translations of the pictures' names (e.g., *bench* for *berg*, where *berg* is the Dutch translation of *mountain*). Note that this type of distracter is conceptually similar to the "phonological-semantic" distracters in the monolingual studies (see Table 5.1). After all, a word's translation is semantically closely similar

to the word it translates. I will refer to these as "phonological translation" distracters. The fourth group of distracters consisted of words that were completely unrelated to the pictures' names (e.g., *present*). These unrelated distracters again provided a baseline condition from which the effects of the other distracters could be assessed.

Two experiments were run and in both of them the stimulus onset asynchrony (SOA) between picture and distracter was varied. Distracters preceded the onset of the picture by 300 ms (SOA –300) or 150 ms (SOA –150), coincided with the onset of the picture (SOA 0), or followed the picture 150 ms after the latter's onset (SOA +150). The crucial difference between the two experiments was that in one of them the distracters were all English words (as in the examples above), whereas in the second the distracters were Dutch words. Table 5.2 shows some example materials from both experiments. Note that the semantic distracters in the second experiment

---

TABLE 5.2

Example materials used by Hermans et al. (1998)

Picture's name	Semantic distracters	Phonological distracters	Phonological translation distracters	Unrelated distracters
mountain (berg)	valley	mouth	bench	present
peacock (pauw)	chicken	people	power	blanket
belt (riem)	leather	belly	reef	jaw
snail (slak)	beetle	snare	slack	bag
pin (speld)	button	pig	span	bill
mountain (berg)	dal ("valley")	mouw ("sleeve")	berm ("roadside")	kaars ("candle")
peacock (pauw)	kip ("chicken")	piste ("ring")	paus ("pope")	verf ("paint")
belt (riem)	leer ("leather")	berk ("birch")	riet ("reed")	park ("park")
snail (slak)	kever ("beetle")	sneeuw ("snow")	slag ("blow")	kroon ("crown")
pin (speld)	knoop ("button")	pint ("pint")	spek ("bacon")	koek ("biscuit")

Example materials used by Hermans et al. (1998) in a bilingual picture–word interference study in which Dutch–English bilinguals named pictures in L2 English. Top half: English distracters; bottom half: Dutch distracters. The Dutch names of the pictures and the meanings of the Dutch distracters are presented in parentheses.

allow a test of the hypothesis that the semantic cohort activated by the picture includes not only the lemma of the Dutch translation equivalent of the English target (*berg*), but also lemmas of words semantically related to the target's translation (*dal*, "valley").

The results of these two experiments are presented in Table 5.3, in terms of the difference scores between the unrelated control condition on the one hand and all three experimental conditions on the other hand.

The experiment with English distracters showed a facilitation effect of phonological distracters (*mouth*) in all four SOA conditions, suggesting (contrary to Schriefers et al., 1990) that phonological coding of the picture's name already starts during an early stage of lexical access. Furthermore, it showed an inhibitory effect of semantic distracters (*valley*), except in the condition where the distracter followed the picture (SOA +150). As with the analogous effect in the monolingual studies, this finding was attributed to the occurrence of co-activation of semantic competitors during lemma selection. Finally, phonological translation distracters (*bench*) slowed down picture naming, but only reliably so when the presentation of the distracter

when does phonology play a role

and picture coincided (SOA 0). This finding was interpreted as evidence of co-activation of the pictures' L1 names.

The authors suggested this evidence of language-nonselective word production might not have been more robust (occurring in more SOA conditions) because, due to differences in the pronunciation of corresponding phonemes in English and Dutch, the phonological overlap between the English phonological translation distracters (*bench*) and the Dutch names of the pictures (*berg*) may in fact have been rather small. This is why they ran their second experiment, assuming that Dutch phonological translation distracters (e.g., *berm*) share more phonology with the Dutch name of the pictures. With this set-up, the phonological translation distracters exerted an inhibitory effect on English picture naming in all but one of the SOA conditions, condition SOA +150 being the exception. However, this time the effects of the phonological distracters disappeared in three of the SOA conditions. The reason may be that now the overlap between the (Dutch) phonological distracters (*mouw*) and the target picture's English name (*mountain*) may have been too small to cause an effect. Interestingly, in this experiment too the semantic distracters caused an effect (although it was only significant in Condition SOA –150), providing some evidence that the semantic cohort activated by the picture also includes lemmas of words semantically related to the target's translation (*dal*, "valley").

Hermans and his coworkers discussed these results in terms of the three types of production models introduced earlier: the discrete two-stage models, the unidirectional cascade models, and the interactive activation models (p. 227). They concluded the evidence to be equivocal on this point because the time course of the various effects, as assessed with the different SOAs, did not fit the predictions of any model. Importantly though, the results—and especially the strong phonological translation effects in their second experiment—*did* indicate that at some point during picture naming in the weaker L2 the picture's translation in L1 is also activated. In other words, they suggested that bilingual word production

TABLE 5.3 When they hear the distraction

Hermans et al.'s (1998) results

	SOA –300 ms	SOA –150 ms	SOA 0 ms	SOA +150 ms
English distracters helps				
Phonological	19*	24*	31*	64*
Semantic	–44*	–19*	–31*	10
Phonological-translation	–14	–5	–28*	–5
Dutch distracters				
Phonological	–8	–5	–10	35*
Semantic	–17	–37*	–19	–13
Phonological-translation	–30*	–38*	–35*	–7

Differences (in ms) between the mean latencies for the unrelated condition on the one hand and the phonological, semantic, and phonological-translation conditions on the other hand at each Stimulus Onset Asynchrony (SOA). Differences that are significant are marked with *. Adapted from Hermans et al. (1998).

is language-nonselective. However, the evidence does not indicate whether only lemma selection or also phonological encoding is language-nonselective.

What has remained somewhat implicit in the above discussion is the common assumption that response selection in word production tasks is directly related to the amount of nuisance activation in the language system. Regarding the bilingual studies this means that activated lexical nodes in the non-target language (e.g., the lemma of Dutch *berg*) compete with lexical nodes from the target language during the selection process (e.g., of *mountain*). In a series of experimental and theoretical articles, Costa and his colleagues considered an alternative—that there may be activation in the non-targeted language system that does not compete with elements of the target language during the selection process but is ignored instead. One of the pertinent papers (Costa, Colomé, Gómez, & Sebastián-Gallés, 2003) is a replication of Hermans et al. (1998) with nearly balanced, early Spanish–Catalan bilinguals. The phonological translation effect again materialized in some of the conditions (as did the effects of the other types of related distracters). However, in their theoretical analysis of this result Costa et al. (2003) argued this effect is also compatible with the view that the selection process is language-selective, meaning that only activated words from the target language compete for selection. This alternative view was first introduced by Costa et al. (1999) and Costa and Caramazza (1999) and encompasses the theoretically important distinction between language-nonselective versus language-selective *activation* on the one hand and language-nonselective versus language-selective *selection* on the other hand. The crucial point these authors make is that during word production lexical elements in both of the bilingual's lexicons may be activated simultaneously, but that from this it does not imperatively follow that the activated elements in both languages are considered during the actual selection process. An alternative to language-nonselective (or "language-nonspecific") selection is that the selection mechanism ignores the activation in the non-

target language. In the next section I will present the data that led them to propose this alternative account.

Lexical activation versus lexical selection

The type of production model Costa and his colleagues take as a starting point in their studies does not assume lemma representations but distinguishes between semantic nodes, lexical nodes, and sublexical nodes (see Figure 5.5). Each lexical node represents a word's complete phonological form and each sublexical node represents a component part of a word's phonology, for instance, one phoneme. As in Caramazza's (1997) model (Figure 5.4) activation at the semantic level flows directly to the (phonological) lexical nodes (which Caramazza, 1997, called "phonological lexemes").

Within the theoretical context of such a processing system, Costa et al. (1999) carried out a study employing the distracter methodology. The participants in this study were highly proficient, balanced, Catalan–Spanish bilinguals, who named pictures in their L1 (Catalan). Contrary to Hermans et al. (1998) and Costa et al. (2003), the distracters were now presented visually rather than aurally. This difference is not a trivial one because the modality of the distracter determines the exact order in which the various types of memory representations will become activated. Specifically, when an aural distracter is presented, it will immediately activate the corresponding phonological sublexical nodes, and this prior to access of the corresponding phonological lexical node and, finally, word meaning (see also Chapter 4, Figure 4.9, BIMOLA, a model of auditory word recognition). In contrast, a visual distracter will activate phonology only indirectly, via activated orthographic sublexical and lexical nodes (see Chapter 4, Figure 4.4, SOPHIA). As a consequence of this difference, the SOA range suitable to test the above theoretical distinction between discrete two-stage and unidirectional cascade models of speech production should differ between studies that present visual distracters and those that present auditory distracters (see Starreveld, 2000, for a similar line of reasoning).

However, the most important new feature of this study was that it added a new distracter condition, the so-called "identity" condition. In this condition the distracter was the name of the picture in the target language or in the non-target language. For instance, a picture of a table to be named in L1 Catalan (*taula*) was accompanied by the visual word *taula* or by its L2 Spanish translation *mesa*. I will confine my discussion to the rationale of including this condition and the related results.

The authors started out questioning the common assumptions in studies on monolingual word production that the most highly activated lexical node is selected from the set of activated lexical nodes and that the ease with which a target is selected depends on the level of activation of the non-target competitors: The higher one or more non-target competitors are activated, the harder target selection is. In other words, ease of selection in monolingual word production is thought to be a function of the amount and fierceness of co-activation in the system. Costa and his associates hypothesized that this imperative relation between activation and selection might not hold for the bilingual case: Activation at the semantic level of representation may activate lexical nodes in both languages simultaneously, but only the activated lexical nodes of the target language may be considered for selection (and those of the non-target language ignored). The authors thus divided the question of whether bilingual word production is language-selective or language-nonselective into two sub-questions: (1) Do or do not activated semantic nodes transmit their activation to lexical nodes in both languages, and if they do, (2) do the activated lexical nodes of both languages compete for selection or does the selection process only consider the activated lexical nodes of the target language? In other words, if *activation* is language-nonselective, *selection* may still be language-selective.

The identity condition, and especially its cross-language version (in which the picture, to be named in Catalan, was accompanied by its name in Spanish; e.g., a picture of a table, *taula* in Catalan, accompanied by *mesa*, its Spanish name) provided the means to answer both these

questions. First, if the participants can switch off the non-target language completely, no effect of presenting a distracter in the non-target language should emerge. This state of affairs would receive support if picture-naming time in the identity condition and in an unrelated control condition (with, e.g., the Spanish distracter *jamon*, "ham") were the same. In contrast, a difference in picture-naming latency between these two conditions would suggest co-activation of the lexical node in the non-target language. Second, if such a difference indeed occurs, the *direction* of the effect would reveal the nature of the selection process: The language-nonspecific (or language-nonselective) selection hypothesis predicts *longer* latencies (that is, inhibition) in the cross-language identity condition than in the unrelated condition, whereas the language-specific (or language-selective) selection hypothesis predicts *shorter* latencies (facilitation) in the identity condition.

The grounds for these predictions are illustrated in Figure 5.7 (note that the level of sublexical nodes is not shown). If lexical node *activation* is *language-selective*, a picture of a table will first activate the corresponding semantic nodes and from there the lexical node representing Catalan *taula* but not the lexical node representing Spanish *mesa*. In a language-selective activation account the cross-language identity distracter *mesa* may activate the corresponding semantic nodes (indirectly, via its orthographic lexical node in an orthographic lexicon, as shown in Figure 5.7) but this activation is not transmitted down to the (phonological) lexical node level. Alternatively, and in line with a strong version of language selectivity, the processing of a cross-language identity distracter is blocked altogether so that it also does not activate the corresponding semantic nodes. If, instead lexical node *activation* is *language-nonselective*, both the picture and the cross-language identity distracter *mesa* will first activate the corresponding semantic nodes; from there, the lexical nodes representing *taula* and *mesa* will both be activated, and both relatively highly because the level of activation in the activation-sending semantic nodes, coming from two sources, is relatively high.

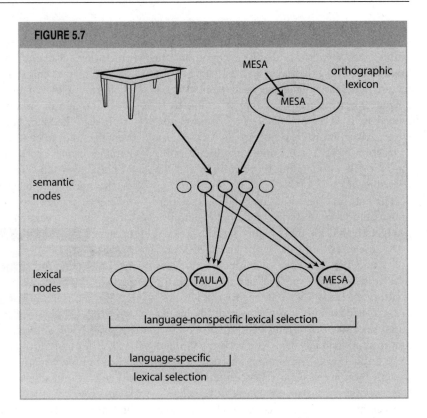

FIGURE 5.7

Picture naming with visual word distracters in Catalan–Spanish bilinguals. The picture must be named in L1 Catalan. Language-nonspecific lexical selection means that the highly activated lexical nodes representing Catalan *taula* and Spanish *mesa* compete for selection. Language-specific lexical selection means that the highly activated *mesa* node does not compete with the *taula* node during selection because it is ignored by the selection mechanism. Adapted from Costa et al. (1999).

If the *selection* process is *language-nonselective*, both these highly activated nodes are considered for selection. Non-target *mesa* will act as a strong competitor in the selection process (as compared with the lexical node representing an unrelated control distracter, which is only activated by the distracter word and not by the picture) and slow down the picture-naming response. In contrast, if the *selection* mechanism is *language-selective*, only considering activated lexical nodes in target Catalan, it will not suffer from the fact that Spanish *mesa* is also highly activated. At the same time the fact that, as compared to an unrelated distracter, the Spanish distracter *mesa* has increased the level of activation in the *taula* lexical node (via the activated semantic nodes), selection of this node should be *faster* in the cross-language identity condition than in the unrelated control condition.

The data agreed with a processing model that assumes language-nonspecific activation followed by language-selective selection: Picture-naming latency was shorter in the cross-language identity condition than in the unrelated control condition. The fact that no null effect of distracter type (identical vs. control) was obtained suggests that lexical *activation* is language-nonselective. The fact that the observed effect was facilitative, not inhibitory, is consistent with the idea that lexical *selection* is language-selective: Even a strongly activated lexical node in the non-target language does not slow down processing. Apparently, only the activated lexical nodes in the target language are considered for selection.

In a follow-up study, Costa and Caramazza (1999) obtained exactly the same pattern of results, now testing proficient but non-balanced Spanish–English and English–Spanish bilinguals naming pictures in L1 Spanish (the Spanish–English group) or L2 Spanish (the English–Spanish group), and with the distracters printed in English. The data pattern consistent with language-selective lexical selection occurred not only when the pictures were named in the participants' dominant language but also when naming was in the weaker L2. This suggests that even lexical node activation in the stronger L1 can be ignored during the selection process. As noted by the authors, it remains to be seen at what stage during second language acquisition the mechanism involved in language-specific selection becomes functional (assuming it is not functional right from the onset). But whatever the answer to that question, the results of this second study demonstrate that balanced bilingualism is not a prerequisite for the mechanism to be functional. Yet it remains possible that during earlier stages of acquisition selection is language-nonselective (as *inhibition* caused by a cross-language identity prime would demonstrate).

Evaluation

As the reader may have experienced, the picture–word interference task is a complex paradigm and, consequently, the interpretation of the data emerging from the relevant studies is complex as well and equivocal at times. As pointed out by Kroll et al. (2005), a likely cause of this data ambiguity is the simultaneity (or temporal proximity) of two stimuli: the picture and the aural or visual distracter. As a consequence of this simultaneity, two processes proceed in parallel and, initially, in opposite directions: An encoding process works from the conceptualized picture down to the actual naming response and a second, decoding, process works upward, from a phonological or orthographical analysis of the distracter word to the activation of a conceptual representation. At some point these two processes meet and influence one another. Sophisticated experimental procedures are required to determine with certainty the exact point of interaction, procedures that may contain elements based on inaccurate assumptions. These aspects of the task complicate the interpretation of what is going on and may lead to inaccurate conclusions.

It is for similar reasons that Starreveld (2000) concluded that, in order to understand the origin of distracter effects in picture-naming studies, a theory of how the distracter is perceived and processed is as indispensable as a theory of how the picture is perceived and processed. According to him, both such a theory of perception and of

production specify an interval in which the distracter manipulation is potentially effective. He then concludes that: "It is only when these two intervals overlap that a specific context effect [= distracter effect] can be found" (Starreveld, 2000, p. 521). A particular null effect (e.g., of a phonological distracter with a negative SOA) may therefore be due to a failure to catch this critical point of interaction rather than indexing a theoretically important feature of the speech production process (e.g., discrete serial processing of meaning and phonology). For similar reasons, Bock (1996), in a review of methods used in speech production research, made a plea for a more analytic consideration of these methods. She generalized this statement to tasks used in research domains other than speech production such as word recognition, where the reverse sometimes happens: Here the actual process of interest, recognition, is sometimes confounded by a production component of the task, as is the case in word naming (see Chapter 4). Just as a theory of speech production based on the distracter methodology cannot do without a theory of recognition, so a theory of recognition based on word naming cannot do without a theory of production, she argues.

So where does all this leave us now? Can we build our theory of bilingual speech production on evidence collected by means of a methodology that is surrounded with uncertainty? As the reader may recall, this state of affairs is not at all uncommon in experimental research and is caused by the fact that many tasks, in addition to reflecting the theoretically important cognitive process of interest, pick up additional nuisance processes that are hard or impossible to avoid. In Chapter 4 (p. 170) I have presented a common solution to this problem; namely, to look for converging evidence from other tasks. If a particular finding emerges across a number of tasks that arguably all capture the core of the process of interest, this effect is likely to reflect this process (see also Figure 4.1). In fact, converging evidence of language-nonselective activation in speech production has already been gathered. It has, for instance, been obtained in studies that have employed versions of the picture-naming task that do not involve two simultaneous processes that during their initial stages work in opposite directions through the lexical system. It is to these studies that I will turn to next.

Simple picture naming

Evidence of language-nonselective phonological encoding

The main theoretical issue addressed in the simple picture-naming studies to be presented here is whether phonological encoding occurs for the translation of the picture's name in the non-response language. (The qualification "simple" refers to the fact that in this version of the task the picture is presented on its own, unaccompanied by a distracter; in other respects this task too may require rather complex processing.) Such a finding would support (the bilingual version of) word production models that assume (unidirectional or interactive) cascaded processing. In contrast, results suggesting otherwise would support the discrete two-stage models of word production. Part of the relevant evidence was provided by Costa et al. (2000). In choosing their stimulus materials they were guided by Jescheniak and Schriefers (1998) and Peterson and Savoy (1998), who had examined the occurrence of phonological encoding (henceforth also "phonological coding" or "phonological activation") of non-target items in monolingual picture naming (see p. 239). These authors obtained evidence of phonological activation of near-synonyms of the target but not of words less-strongly related to the target. This suggested that nearly complete semantic overlap with the target is a prerequisite for phonological encoding of a non-target to occur. Because translation equivalents share most of their meaning between languages, *if* phonological encoding of non-target lexical nodes occurs at all it should at any rate occur for the picture's name in the non-target language.

To demonstrate such phonological coding, Costa et al. (2000) exploited the fact that translation pairs may or may not share phonology. The former are known as "cognates", the latter as "non-cognates". The authors compared the naming of pictures that lexicalize in cognate translations in the participants' two languages with the naming of pictures that lexicalize in non-cognates. Figure 5.5 illustrates the word production processes assumed for Catalan–Spanish cognate and non-cognate words, respectively. The representations of Catalan *gat* and Spanish *gato* share a large part of their constituent sublexical nodes (/g/, /a/, and /t/), whereas there is little overlap between the sublexical phonological representations of Catalan *taula* and Spanish *mesa* (/a/). If activated lexical nodes in the non-target language indeed send activation down to the phonological level, picture naming should be faster for cognates than for non-cognates because in the case of cognates the sublexical phonological representations of the targets to be produced receive activation from two sources: from the target's lexical node, but also from the lexical node of its translation. If, however, a single lexical node (the one representing the target word) is first selected from the set of activated lexical nodes and only this node sends down its activation to the phonological sublexical nodes, then picture naming should be equally fast for pictures with cognate and non-cognate names. The results were clearcut: Picture naming in L2 (Spanish) by Catalan–Spanish bilinguals was faster for cognate pictures than for non-cognate pictures. More recent studies have shown this same effect to occur in picture naming by Dutch–English bilinguals (Christoffels, De Groot, & Kroll, 2006; Christoffels, De Groot, & Waldorp, 2003; Kroll et al., 2000) and Spanish–English bilinguals (Hoshino & Kroll, 2007). Interestingly, these latter authors have shown that the effect also emerges in different-script bilingualism: A cognate effect was observed for Japanese–English bilinguals as well, and it was as large as the effect obtained for the Spanish–English bilinguals. This suggests that the additional orthographic similarity of same-script cognates does not contribute to the effect.

In a further experiment Costa and his colleagues tested the hypothesis that the amount of activation sent down to the phonological sublexical level is proportional to the lexical node's activation level. If true, a relatively large cognate effect should be observed when the non-response language is the participant's dominant language. The ground for this hypothesis is that under those circumstances a cognate target's sublexical representation should receive relatively much activation from the lexical node of its translation (for instance because for words in the dominant language the connections between the various layers of nodes in the system are relatively strong). The data confirmed this prediction: Larger cognate effects were obtained when pictures were named in the weaker language than in the stronger language. These experiments thus suggest that the picture's names in both languages are phonologically encoded. This finding rules out discrete two-stage models of bilingual word production and supports cascaded models. Both the unidirectional and interactive versions of cascaded models are compatible with the results (Figure 5.5 illustrates the unidirectional cascaded models). In a later study that examined the lexical bias effect (see p. 226) in bilingual speech production, Costa, Santesteban, and Ivanova (2006) opted for the interactive models.

The present interpretation of the cognate effect in picture naming is primarily one in terms of processing, not representation: It is attributed to a process of language-nonselective phonological coding that differentially affects cognates and non-cognates. In Chapter 4 (pp. 203–205) it was suggested that the cognate effects obtained in bilingual word recognition studies might originate from representation differences between cognates and non-cognates. If such differences exist, the possibility should be considered that these also underlie the above cognate effects in picture naming. Aware of this possibility, Costa et al. (2005) considered two options: shared morphological representations for cognates but not for non-cognates (e.g., Sánchez-Casas & García-Albea, 2005) and shared semantic representations for cognates but not for non-cognates (e.g., Van Hell & De Groot, 1998a). However, they regarded neither of these options as plausible. They wondered how, if cognates share one and the same morphological stem, ultimately two different phonological forms can be realized in speech, one for each language. Their main reason for not

embracing the idea that cognates and non-cognates have different semantic representations was that they found it hard to see how degree of *form* similarity between a pair of translations could affect the representation of *meaning*.

However, a reason why the meanings of cognates and non-cognates might be represented differently in bilingual memory is that L2 learners are likely to notice the form similarity between cognate translations and may assume that when translations have similar forms they are likely to have more similar meanings than when they have different forms. As a consequence they may exploit different learning strategies when learning cognate and non-cognate translations and different meaning representations may ensue. Evidence that the cognate status of translation pairs affects L2 vocabulary acquisition has been presented in Chapter 3 (pp. 108–110 and 119–121). Furthermore, direct evidence that the meaning representations of cognates and non-cognate pairs do indeed differ from one another does in fact exist (e.g., Taylor, 1976; Van Hell & De Groot, 1998a). Rejecting differential meaning representation as a possible source of the cognate effect in picture naming thus seems premature. In conclusion, the form similarity of cognate translations may have become reflected in one or more representational differences between cognates and non-cognates that may underlie the cognate effect in picture naming and other tasks.

Further evidence

The possibility that representational differences between cognates and non-cognates are a source of the cognate effects forces us to conclude that the data are equivocal: The cognate effects observed in the simple picture-naming task might not index language-nonselective phonological encoding after all. However, the authors of a couple of other studies that did not rely on the distinction between cognate and non-cognate translations seem to have a very strong case indeed when arguing that phonological encoding is language-nonselective. Particularly noteworthy about one of these studies (Colomé, 2001) is that the participants were kept completely ignorant about the bilingual nature of the experiment and that the non-response language was in no way physically present. From the discussion of the recognition studies presented in Chapter 4 the reader may recall that a common weakness of many studies in this research area is that the non-target language is actually physically present in the form of stimulus materials from that language or implied by the general context of the experiment. It is not surprising that under those circumstances the non-target language is also activated. Unequivocal evidence of language-nonselective processing demands complete ignorance on the part of the participants that their bilingualism is being tested, as well as an experimental set-up and stimulus set that do not trigger the non-target language into activity, *if* complete deactivation is an option at all (this being the debated issue). Colomé's study meets these requirements. In contrast, the bilingual picture–word interference studies discussed before did not do so because the non-target language was physically present in the distracters.

Colomé (2001) used a version of the "phoneme-monitoring task", which was first used to study monolingual speech *perception*. In the original version of this task participants are presented with series of sentences or words and are asked to monitor each of these stimuli for the presence of a particular phoneme, specified prior to the onset of each trial (Blank, 1980). Colomé adapted this task such that it became a component of a picture-naming task. Her participants, Catalan–Spanish bilinguals, were presented with pictures, but instead of being asked to name each picture aloud they had to generate its name tacitly and to then monitor the internally generated name for the presence of a particular pre-specified sound. In a first experiment the participants first saw a letter on a screen and were asked to transpose it mentally into its sound. Subsequently, the letter was removed from the screen and a picture appeared, to be named tacitly. The participants' task was to indicate as rapidly as possible whether or not the presented letter's sound occurred in the picture's name in L1 Catalan. In two further experiments the presentation of the picture preceded the letter. As mentioned, care was taken that the participants had

no reason to believe their bilingualism was being tested and non-target Spanish was in no way present in the experiment.

In addition to trials that required a "yes" response, there were two types of trials that each required a "no" response: trials in which neither the Catalan nor the Spanish name of the picture contained the specified phoneme, and trials in which the picture's Catalan name (e.g., *taula*, "table") did not contain the specified sound (e.g., /m/) but whose name in Spanish *did* contain this sound (*mesa*). If the picture's name is encoded phonologically in both languages, trials of the latter type would be relatively hard to reject. The reason is that the specified phoneme would be activated and cause interference because the participant might be inclined to respond "yes", an inclination that must subsequently be suppressed. In agreement with this prediction, in all three experiments response times were longer for this latter type of trial, providing evidence of language-nonselective phonological encoding.

Also looking for evidence of phonological activation of the picture's name in the non-target language, Rodriguez-Fornells et al. (2005) modified this clever paradigm: Spanish–German bilinguals and monolingual German speakers were presented with pictures and asked to perform a go/no-go task: When the picture's name in the target language started with a vowel they had to push a button and when it started with a consonant they had to let it pass without responding. Alternatively, they had to push the button when the picture's name in the target language started with a consonant and had to withhold a response when it started with a vowel. To be able to perform this task the phonological representation of the picture's name needs to be mentally inspected. For bilinguals, the target language switched between blocks of trials (which is why in this study the bilingual participants presumably suspected their bilingualism was being studied; furthermore, both languages were physically present). Obviously, the German monolinguals only performed the task in German. Across a number of experiments behavioral responses (response times and errors), electrophysiological (ERP) brain responses, and fMRI data were gathered.

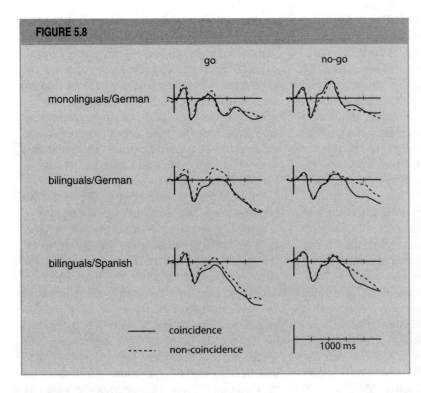

FIGURE 5.8

go   no-go

monolinguals/German

bilinguals/German

bilinguals/Spanish

——— coincidence

- - - - - non-coincidence

1000 ms

ERPs elicited at a right fronto-lateral recording site by two types of pictures. In the "coincidence" condition (solid lines) the pictures' names in German and Spanish either both begin with a vowel or they both begin with a consonant. In the "non-coincidence" condition (dashed lines) they begin with a vowel in German and a consonant in Spanish, or vice versa. For German monolinguals no coincidence effect occurs. The bilinguals show an enhanced negativity for non-coincidence trials, between 300 and 600 ms following target onset in the go trials and from 600 ms onward in the no-go trials. From Rodriguez-Fornells et al. (2005), © 2005 Massachusetts Institute of Technology, by permission of MIT Press Journals.

The pictures were selected such that on half of the trials (constituting the "coincidence" condition) the names in both languages would lead to the same response (either go or no-go) because they both started with a vowel or both with a consonant (e.g., *Esel–asno*, "donkey"; *Kerze–vela*, "candle"). On the other half of the trials (constituting the "non-coincidence" condition) the two languages invited different responses because the picture's name in one language started with a vowel whereas its name in the other language started with a consonant (e.g., *Trichter–embudo*, "funnel"; *Eidechse–lagarto*, "lizard"). An effect of the coincidence/non-coincidence manipulation would suggest that the phonology of the picture's name in both languages would be activated and thus provide evidence of language-nonselective phonological encoding. Of course, null effects of this manipulation should be obtained for monolinguals, because they only have one name for each picture.

Both the behavioral and the brain data sug-gested phonological activation of the non-response language: For bilinguals, but not for monolinguals, the percentage of correct responses was lower in the non-coincidence condition than in the coincidence condition and, overall, bilinguals made more errors and responded more slowly than monolinguals. This finding indicates that the picture's name in the non-target language was also retrieved at least some of the time, caus-ing interference on the trials where it invited a response that deviated from the targeted response. Part of the electrophysiological evidence is pre-sented in Figure 5.8. It shows the ERPs, recorded at right fronto-lateral electrode sites, for monolin-guals and bilinguals on go trials and no-go trials and in both the coincidence and non-coincidence condition.

As can be seen, on both go and no-go trials, the ERPs in the bilingual group showed an increased negativity for non-coincidence trials as compared to coincidence trials (recall the convention to plot negative signals upwards and positive signals downward). This coincidence effect emerged between 300 and 600 ms in the go trials and between 600 and 800 ms in the no-go trials (see the original report for an explanation of this latency difference). In agreement with expectation, the monolingual German group did not show a coincidence effect. Again, this pattern of results suggests interference from the picture's name in the non-target language, thus at the same time suggesting that language-nonselective processing occurs all the way down to the level of phonology.

The fMRI data showed a differential effect of the coincidence manipulation for monolinguals and bilinguals in three brain regions: the left prefrontal cortex, the supplementary motor area (SMA), and the anterior cingulate cortex (ACC; see Chapter 8 for a localization of these brain areas). The activation in these areas was larger in bilinguals than in monolinguals. The left prefrontal cortex has also been shown to be involved when bilinguals have to switch between their two languages on command during overt picture naming (Hernandez, Dapretto, Mazziotta, & Bookheimer, 2001; Hernandez, Martinez, & Kohnert, 2000; see also pp. 440–441): Furthermore, in monolingual studies the involvement of the left prefrontal cortex has been demonstrated in tasks that require executive functioning, such as choosing between response alternatives, switching between tasks, and inhibiting irrelevant stimuli. Rodriguez-Fornells and his colleagues therefore concluded that to inhibit responses based on activation in the non-target language, bilinguals recruit brain areas that are typically involved in executive functioning. The ACC has earlier been shown to be involved in, among others, conflict tasks such as the Stroop task. It has been suggested that its role is to monitor performance in conflict situations. I will present some of this evidence in Chapter 8, including a set of monolingual studies (e.g., Carter et al., 2000; MacDonald, Cohen, Stenger, & Carter, 2000) that suggest a control system in which (part of) the prefrontal cortex and the ACC fulfill complementary goals to ensure control when conflict looms: The ACC, monitoring performance, signals to the prefrontal cortex when control must be more strongly

engaged; the prefrontal cortex responds to this with increased brain activation. The relevant point to make here is that it seems that bilinguals recruit these same two brain areas to prevent the contextually inappropriate language overtaking responding in the present go/no-go task. In other words, it appears that language control in bilinguals exploits more general processes and mechanisms of cognitive control. This important issue will be addressed more explicitly in Chapters 7 (pp. 393–401) and 8 (pp. 435–446).

In conclusion, both of the above "covert naming" studies suggest that word production in bilinguals is language-nonselective all the way down to the stage of phonological encoding. Of the two, Colomé's (2001) study provides the strongest evidence because the participants in her study were kept completely ignorant about the bilingual nature of the experiment and the non-target language was in no way implied by the general context of the experiment. The special merit of Rodriguez-Fornells et al.'s (2005) investigation is that it provides information on the temporal aspects of the interference caused by activation in the non-response language. Furthermore, it identifies the brain areas involved and, in so doing, suggests that when coping with cross-language interference bilinguals exploit mechanisms that are also used to control other forms of behavior.

Evidence of language-nonselective grammatical encoding

If phonological encoding is language-nonselective one might expect grammatical encoding also to be language-nonselective. This prediction follows most naturally from serial word production models that assume the existence of lemmas that (1) specify the associated words' syntactic information and that (2) imperatively mediate between the conceptual and phonological levels in the production system (see p. 232): It is hard to see how language-nonselectivity could apply to a later stage in the production process (phonological encoding) but not to an earlier stage (grammatical encoding) that provides input for the later phonological stage. It is easier to accommodate evidence of language-selective grammatical encoding on the one hand and of language-nonselective phonological encoding on the other hand in terms of (a bilingual version of) Caramazza's independent network model (1997; p. 233, Figure 5.4). As we have seen, this model denies the existence of lemma representations and posits that a word's syntactic make-up is prepared independent of and in parallel with its phonology. Yet, also in terms of this model, there is no compelling reason why the activation spreading down from the semantic representations to representation units that specify syntax should be confined to the response language. A couple of studies have addressed this issue, with mixed results.

Rodriguez-Fornells, Lutz, and Münte (2010; see also Rodriguez-Fornells, De Diego Balaguer, & Münte, 2006), Costa, Kovacic, Franck, and Caramazza (2003), and Lemhöfer, Spalek, and Schriefers (2008) examined whether the assignment of grammatical gender to a word in the response language is influenced by the gender of its translation equivalent in the other language. All three studies exploited the fact that grammatical gender can match or mismatch between a bilingual's two languages. Rodriguez-Fornells and his collaborators had German–Spanish bilinguals and German monolinguals perform a go/no-go task similar to the one used in Rodriguez-Fornells et al. (2005; see above). This time however the go/no-go response involved a decision regarding the gender of the tacitly named word: The participants had to push a button when the grammatical gender of the picture's name in the response language was masculine and had to let it pass without responding when it was feminine (or vice versa). The pictures were selected such that on half the trials the picture's name in German and Spanish had the same gender (e.g., der Speer—el dardo, "dart"; both masculine). On the remaining half of the trials the picture's name in the two languages had a different gender (e.g., die Rakete—el cohete, "rocket"; feminine and masculine, respectively). An effect of this manipulation in bilinguals would suggest an influence of the picture name's gender in the non-response language and, hence,

that syntactic encoding is language-nonselective. Both behavioral measures and ERPs served as dependent variables. Costa and his collaborators employed the more common overt picture-naming task (without distracters), asking the participants to respond with a noun phrase consisting of both a noun and the corresponding definite article. They tested bilinguals whose two languages have similar grammatical gender systems (Catalan–Spanish; Italian–French; all of these languages have only two gender values, feminine and masculine) as well as bilinguals whose two languages have more dissimilar gender systems (Croatian–Italian; Croatian also has neutral gender). Also in this study the grammatical gender of the two names of a picture could be the same or different in the two languages, and monolingual control groups were included. Finally, Lemhöfer and her colleagues used the same procedure as Costa and his collaborators, testing German–Dutch bilinguals in L2 Dutch picture naming and including both pictures with names that were German–Dutch cognates as well as "non-cognate" pictures; that is, pictures with totally dissimilar names in German and Dutch.

Despite their common characteristics the three studies produced disparate results. The bilinguals in Rodriguez-Fornells et al.'s study responded more slowly and made more errors on trials with a gender difference between the two languages than on same-gender trials. These findings suggest an interfering influence from the non-response language and, thus, language-nonselective grammatical encoding. The effect could not be attributed to inappropriately matched stimulus materials in the same-gender and different-gender conditions because the monolinguals performed equally well in both conditions. Analogous effects were obtained in the ERP data: Monolinguals did not show an effect of gender coincidence but in bilinguals different-gender trials elicited a large negativity when compared with same-gender trials, just as the vowel-consonant go/no-go task of Rodriguez-Fornells et al. (2005) had shown a relatively large negativity on non-coincidence trials. In contrast, in none of the five experiments performed by

Costa and his colleagues was a difference obtained between the same-gender and different-gender conditions, not even when the bilinguals' two languages had very similar gender systems, and in all cases the performance of bilinguals equaled that of monolinguals. Accordingly, the authors concluded that the two gender systems of a bilingual are functionally autonomous. Apparently, variations in the experimental procedure and/or the stimulus materials can have a major influence on the data and therefore lead to completely different conclusions. Lemhöfer et al.'s study revealed that the cognate status of the stimulus materials is one variable that affects the results: As with Rodriguez-Fornells and his colleagues, these authors obtained clear effects of cross-language gender compatibility versus incompatibility, but these effects were larger for cognates than for non-cognates and in a further experiment in which the picture-naming task was preceded by a period of pre-training the gender identity of the L2 test materials the effect of gender (in)compatibility occurred for cognates only. The authors suggested that the high percentage of cognates (50%) in their experiments had probably boosted the activation of non-target L1 German, including this language's gender information.

Hatzidaki (2007) employed a very different paradigm to study the question of whether grammatical encoding is language-selective or language-nonselective; namely, the bilingual version of the sentence completion paradigm introduced earlier (p. 224). She compared the performance of English–Greek and Greek–English bilinguals in a "divergent" and a "convergent" condition. In the divergent condition one of the elements in a pair of Greek–English translation-equivalent nouns was plural and the other was singular (e.g., the plural *scissors* and *trousers* are both singular in Greek and the singular *hair* and *money* are both plural in Greek). In the convergent condition the nouns of a translation pair were either both singular or both plural. The dependent variable was the number of subject–verb number-agreement errors that were made in these two conditions in a task that required the participants to complete simple

noun phrases (such as *the hair* or *the trousers*) into complete sentences (e.g., *the hair . . . is short*; *the trousers . . . are black*).

Hatzidaki observed more subject–verb number-agreement errors on divergent nouns (e.g., a participant might complete *the hair* with *are short*) than on convergent nouns, suggesting that the number of a noun's translation in the non-response language was also activated and interfered with processing. This effect consistently materialized across a series of experiments that manipulated the relative strength of the participants' two languages, and whether or not the presented noun and the invited completion were in the same language or switched between languages. In the "non-switch" (monolingual) conditions the effects were larger when the test language was the participants' weaker language than when it was their stronger language. This finding converges with a similar asymmetry demonstrated in research on bilingual language comprehension (see Chapter 4) and shows that the stronger language is relatively immune to influences from the weaker language. Furthermore, the effects were larger in the switch conditions than in the monolingual conditions, a finding that is not so surprising given the fact that task performance in the switch condition necessarily requires that the participants keep both linguistic subsystems activated.

This evidence of language-nonselective grammatical encoding was strengthened by the results of a second, conceptually related, technique which focused on pronoun–antecedent number agreement. It used the same convergent and divergent nouns as used in the subject–verb number-agreement experiments but this time the participants were presented with complete sentences including the critical noun and a predicate, and were asked to complete it with a "tag" question (e.g., stimulus: *The scissors in the drawer got stolen*; possible completions: *didn't it* or *didn't they*). The critical dependent variable was the number of times a pronoun agreement error occurred in the tag question (*it* instead of *they* in the example, where *scissors* is the antecedent of the pronoun *it/they*). These errors occurred more frequently in the divergent-noun condition than in the convergent-noun condition. This suggests that the contextually inappropriate language was also activated during performance.

To summarize, the few studies that examined whether grammatical encoding in bilingual speech production is language-selective or language-nonselective do not all converge on a consistent set of outcomes. Nevertheless they warrant the conclusion that under certain circumstances grammatical encoding is language-nonselective, just as phonological encoding has been shown to be.

Summary and conclusions

The evidence presented in this section warrants the conclusion that under many circumstances word production in bilinguals, as assessed by means of the picture-naming task, is language-nonselective, irrespective of whether L1 or L2 is the response language. That this evidence has been assembled in studies that exploited different versions of the task is important, because two task versions used in the studies discussed above bring along potential interpretation problems: The evidence collected with the simple picture-naming task that compared cognate and non-cognate naming is equivocal because representational differences between cognates and non-cognates might underlie the apparent support for language-nonselective phonological encoding. The evidence collected with the picture–word interference task is difficult to interpret because it is not entirely clear how the decoding process aroused by the distracter word interacts with the encoding process incited by the picture. In addition, the suitability of this task can be questioned because the non-response language is physically present in the distracter words. This likely boosts the level of activation of the non-target language and, therewith, its potential to influence target processing. In view of these considerations, it may be concluded that of the task versions presented above, the one used by Colomé (2001) and Rodriguez-Fornells et al. (2005) is best suited to address the question of (non)selectivity of word production. (Recall that the participants in these studies did not name the picture overtly but had to give some response to its internally generated name.) This version of the task does not require the non-response language to be physically present at all (although it was in Rodriguez-Fornells et al.'s study) nor does the critical evidence have to be derived from a cognate manipulation. The behavioral and brain evidence collected in these two studies strongly suggests that during word production the response word's translation in the non-response language is co-activated with the target all the way down to the level of sublexical nodes.

The studies that focused on grammatical processing produced more mixed results: The data patterns of three of them (one actually employing a task different from picture naming and therefore somewhat improperly included in this section; Hatzidaki, 2007) suggested language-nonselective grammatical encoding whereas the fourth pointed at language-selective grammatical encoding. As argued above (p. 251), a bilingual version of Caramazza's (1997) independent network model (which assumes that grammatical knowledge and lexical-phonological knowledge are stored independently from one another) could in principle account for evidence of both language-selective and language-nonselective grammatical processing. Therefore the present set of data seems to fit this model best, although it would still need to be explained what caused the different results across the above three studies.

The evidence of language-nonselective word production in the majority of the studies discussed above converges with the analogous evidence assembled in the "out of context" word-recognition studies reviewed in Chapter 4. In that chapter, in addition to the out of context studies, a couple of experiments were discussed that examined the recognition of words presented in a sentence context. As you may recall, in those studies a much weaker influence of the language not in use was detected and in some conditions none whatsoever. Studies that examine bilingual word production in sentence context are strikingly absent in the literature and, indeed, in all picture-naming studies reviewed above single words were produced out of context. It therefore remains to be seen whether an influence of the non-response language will again materialize when pictures have to be named in a sentence context. Given the effect of context on bilingual word recognition it would not come as a surprise if those experiments also failed to show an influence of the non-response language under certain circumstances. As noted in Chapter 4 (p. 206), the most natural and parsimonious interpretation of such null effects would be that the language not in use is deactivated. Nevertheless, as also pointed out there, a second possibility must be considered; namely, that elements of the non-response language are activated after all but that such activation is ignored during selection and therefore does not hamper processing. That this is a feasible option is suggested by the studies by Costa et al. (1999) and Costa and Caramazza (1999; see pp. 242–244), in which strongly activated lexical nodes in the non-target language did not slow down word production.

COLOR NAMING WITH DISTRACTERS: THE STROOP TASK

Introduction

The previous section discussed evidence of language-nonselective bilingual word production as gathered in experiments using the picture-naming task. The methodology of one of the task versions that were described there, the picture–word interference task, is very similar to that of the so-called Stroop task and, in fact, the picture–word interference task was introduced by Rosinski et al. (1975) as a transformed version of the original Stroop task. The Stroop task has been an important piece of equipment in the cognitive psychologists' tool kit since 1935, when the eponymous author J. Ridley Stroop published the results of a study in which he first introduced it. In his original study Stroop had participants either name the color of color words printed in a conflicting color (e.g., say "red" to the word *green* printed in red) or read the words (e.g., say "green" to this word). So in the color-naming condition

the participants had to ignore the words and in the word-reading condition they had to ignore the colors in which they were printed. Performance in these two conflict conditions was compared to performance in two corresponding non-conflict (or neutral) conditions: reading color words printed in black and naming the color of colored patches in the form of squares. (Ironically, in a further experiment, and with World War II looming, colored swastikas instead of squares served as non-conflict stimuli in the color-naming condition!)

With this methodology Stroop introduced an alternative to the methods used at the time to study the effect of response conflict or interference. The standard technique had been to have participants learn pairs of stimuli of the type *a–b* (e.g., the pair of nonsense syllables *pluk–malk*) in a paired-associate learning experiment (see pp. 87–89) until an associative bond has been formed between the two elements of the pair such that when the *a* term is presented *b* is readily given as the response. Subsequently, the *a* terms of the learned pairs are paired with new *b* terms (e.g., *pluk–krek*), a procedure that causes strong response interference when subsequently the original *b* terms have to be given as responses to the *a* terms again. The reason is that a conflict is created between two responses, the two different *b* terms *malk* and *krek*. The important new aspect of Stroop's methodology is that the response conflict exists in one and the same stimulus where two inherent aspects of the stimulus potentially compete with one another, the color and the name. Furthermore, the task does not require an experimental training phase to create the competition because the stimulus has already become associated with both possible responses through past practice (naming colors and reading words). Stroop observed that a mismatching color only caused a small interfering effect on word reading but that the interference of a conflicting word on color naming was substantial. He attributed this differential effect to a stronger associative bond formed in the past—due to more extensive practice—between a word and its name than between a color and its name. In contemporary terminology, the differential effect for color naming and word reading may be due to the fact that word reading is a more highly automated process than color naming.

It can readily be seen that the word component within these compounded Stroop stimuli (word and color integrated within one and the same stimulus) is comparable to the distracter in the picture–word interference experiments discussed above and that the printed words' color is comparable to the picture. The resemblance with the picture–word interference task is even larger for a later version of the Stroop task in which color and word are not two different dimensions of one and the same stimulus but are separated, as when a white or black color word is printed on a colored background. With such versions of the task, as in the picture–word interference paradigm, the temporal relation between word and color can be systematically varied and the time course of the interference can be tracked (e.g., Glaser & Glaser, 1982). In accordance with this analysis that the two tasks involve very similar processes, similar effects of distracters have been obtained in both tasks: As we have seen, semantically related distracters inhibit picture-naming performance whereas phonologically related distracters facilitate responding. These same effects have been obtained in Stroop color-naming studies.

The Stroop methodology has been adopted in countless studies on, especially, the development of automaticity and attention control (see MacLeod, 1991 for a review). In this line of research new conditions have been added to the studies' design: In addition to a conflict (or "incongruent") condition and a neutral condition, a "congruent" condition is often included, in which color and word match. Dependent on the exact conditions included, the Stroop effect is the difference in response time either between the congruent and incongruent conditions or between the neutral and incongruent conditions. The inclusion of all three conditions makes it possible to decompose the Stroop effect into a facilitation component (for color words printed in the matching color) and an inhibitory component (for color words printed in a conflicting color).

Bilingual studies

The bilingual research community has embraced the Stroop methodology, transformed into its bilingual counterpart, the **bilingual Stroop task**, to see whether color naming is also hindered if the "carrier" of the color to be named is a conflicting color word in the non-response language. For instance, if a Spanish–English bilingual is to name the color of printed words in English, will the response be relatively slow if the Spanish word *azul* ("blue") is printed in green (and the invited response thus is English *green*)? A positive answer to this question would suggest that the non-target language cannot be switched off while producing the color-naming response, thus providing evidence of language-nonselective processing.

The earliest of these studies (Dyer, 1971; Fang, Tzeng, & Alva, 1981; Kiyak, 1982; Obler & Albert, 1978; Preston & Lambert, 1969) compared performance in a neutral condition (with, for instance, color patches or colored nonsensical strings of letters as the stimuli) with two incongruent experimental conditions, one "intralingual", the other "interlingual". In the intralingual incongruent condition the language of the color words and the invited responses was one and the same (e.g., the Spanish word *azul*, "blue", printed in green and requiring a color response in Spanish: *verde*). In the "interlingual" incongruent condition the language of color words and responses differed (*azul*, "blue", printed in green, to be responded to with English *green*). Across these studies, different language combinations were examined: Chinese–English; Japanese–English; Spanish–English; Turkish–English; French–English; Hungarian–English; German–English; and Hebrew–English. Some of these language combinations involved one and the same writing system (e.g., German–English, both alphabetic languages), whereas others involved two different writing systems (e.g., Chinese–English, involving an idiographic and an alphabetic language).

A major theoretical issue tackled by the majority of these early studies was whether in bilingual memory the two languages are stored in a single integrated system, with connections both between words of the same language and between words from different languages (the "interdependent storage" or "shared storage" view), or in two separate systems, one for each language (the "independent storage" or "separate storage" view), with no connections between words of different languages. The occurrence of an **interlingual Stroop effect** was seen as support for interdependent storage; the absence of such effects was thought to imply separate storage. *Smaller* interlingual than intralingual effects were interpreted as a mixture between these two: Words from the bilingual's two languages are connected with one another, but the connections involved are weaker, and/or there are fewer of them, than those between words of one and the same language. These studies also looked at the role of interlingual form similarity of the color words. For instance, would German *braun* interfere more in an incongruent English color-naming condition because of its form resemblance with English *brown* than would Spanish *azul*, which does not share form with the English word *blue*? Furthermore, these studies looked at the role of language similarity as a whole (rather than at the level of individual color–word translation pairs): Would the interlingual Stroop effects be larger when the bilingual participants' two languages share the same alphabet than when they use a different alphabet? Would they be larger when the participants' languages share the same type of script (e.g., both alphabetic scripts) than when they are written in different scripts (e.g., an alphabetic script and a logographic script)?

Interlingual Stroop effects consistently occurred, and generally (but not always; see below) they tended to be smaller than the analogous intralingual effects. Reviewing the literature, Fang et al. (1981) observed that the difference between the magnitude of the interference effects in the intra- and interlanguage conditions decreases as the similarity between the bilingual's two languages increases. For instance, with the orthographically similar languages German and English the interlingual interference effect was only 36 ms smaller than the intralanguage effect.

In contrast, with the idiographic–alphabetic combination Chinese–English, the interlanguage interference effect was 213 ms smaller than the intralanguage effect. Fang and his colleagues hypothesized that different writing systems employ different processing mechanisms whereas similar writing systems compete for the use of the same processing mechanism. They then argued that both the size of the interference effects and the difference in size of the interference effects in the intra- and interlingual conditions depend on whether or not one and the same processing mechanism is involved during task performance. In contrast, most other authors interpreted the pattern of results in terms of the degree of within- and between-language interconnectedness in bilingual memory: Within bilingual memory the representations of color words from the two languages are connected but the between-language interconnectivity is not as strong as the within-language interconnectivity, and the more dissimilar the languages, the smaller the between-language interconnectivity.

However, a couple of more recent studies have shown *larger* interlanguage than intralanguage effects (e.g., Gerhand, Deregowski, & McAllister, 1995; see Brauer, 1998, for a review). This finding is inconsistent with both an account in terms of shared versus separate processing mechanisms and one in terms of differences in degree of interconnectedness between a bilingual's two languages and suggests that, in addition to language distance, other variables may play a role. What might these additional variables be? An interlingual Stroop study by Mägiste (1984b; see also Obler & Albert, 1978) suggested that the relative proficiency in the two languages might be one of them. She manipulated this variable in a German–Swedish study and showed that the relative size of the intra- and interlanguage Stroop effects depended on it: If the response language was the dominant language, the intralingual interference effect (with printed words in this same dominant language) was larger than the interlingual interference effect (with printed words in the weaker language). In contrast, if the response language was the weaker language of the two, more interlingual (from the stronger language of the printed word to the weaker response language) than intralingual interference (from weak to weak) was obtained. Notice that these findings converge with results from various word recognition studies reported in Chapter 4 and from a number of picture-naming studies reported earlier in the present chapter, which had all shown that the stronger language interferes with processing the weaker language more than vice versa.

Although the important role of relative language strength has not been challenged since, three later bilingual Stroop studies qualified Mägiste's (1984b) conclusion. Chen and Ho (1986), testing Chinese–English bilinguals at different levels of proficiency in L2 English, replicated Mägiste's results when L1 Chinese, the stronger language, was the response language: At all proficiency levels Chinese words produced larger interference effects than English words (in other words, in all cases the intralingual interference was larger than the interlingual interference). However, when L2 English was the response language, words of the stronger L1 (Chinese) only produced more interference than words of the weaker L2 during the initial stages of acquiring L2 English. In participants with an English proficiency beyond these initial stages, L2 words produced more interference than L1 words despite the fact that L1 was still the stronger language of the two. In other words, in all conditions except when beginning learners had to respond in their weak L2, the intralingual interference effects were larger than the interlingual effects. Tzelgov, Henik, and Leiser (1990) replicated these results in an Arabic–Hebrew study. Notice that in both these studies (and unlike in Mägiste, 1984b) the participants' two languages are written in dissimilar scripts: different alphabets (Arabic and Hebrew), and different writing systems (Chinese and English).

More recently, Brauer (1998) extended these results: In English–German and English–Greek bilinguals with relatively low levels of L2 proficiency, words from the stronger L1 produced more interference than words from the weaker L2, regardless of response language and language similarity. In contrast, in high-proficiency bilinguals, language similarity did play a role: English–German and German–English bilinguals (similar languages) showed equally large interlanguage and intralanguage effects, but for English–Greek and Greek–English bilinguals (dissimilar languages) the intralanguage effects were larger than the interlanguage effects. In other words, across all studies the pattern was the same for low-proficiency bilinguals, the largest interference caused by words of strong L1 irrespective of the response language. With high levels of proficiency, depending on language similarity, the intralanguage effects were either larger than (dissimilar languages) or equally large as (similar languages) the interlanguage effects.

The pattern of results, though complex, appears to be consistent (but see Lee, Wee, Tzeng, & Hung, 1992). But how should it be explained? Like the investigators in the earliest bilingual Stroop studies (e.g., Dyer, 1971; Kiyak, 1982), Chen and Ho (1986) interpreted their results in terms of interconnectedness of the two languages in bilingual memory. However, they were more specific about the types of memory connections they had in mind and also added a processing account: They explained their results in terms of the word association model and concept mediation model of bilingual memory presented in Chapter 3 (see pp. 129–131 and Figure 3.7). They suggested that during the initial stages of foreign language acquisition learners always access the meaning of L2 words indirectly, via the lexical representations of their translation equivalents in dominant L1 (access through "word association"). In contrast, more proficient L2 learners were thought to access the meaning of L2 words directly, without L1 lexical mediation (access through "concept mediation"). Tzelgov et al. (1990) and Brauer (1998) followed Chen and Ho (1986) in their interpretation of the effects, except that Brauer added the hypothesis that proficient bilinguals with very similar languages access the meaning of L2 words both directly and indirectly (via their L1 translation), and that these two routes are exploited simultaneously (he calls this the "multiple-access" strategy).

Because these studies typically do not detail the various mental processing stages in the Stroop task and where along the route the printed word comes in, it is often quite hard to see how exactly the observed pattern of results fits the authors' views on L2 word processing at different L2 proficiency levels and the associated differences in the underlying memory representations. Of the latter three studies, the one by Brauer (1998) is most explicit in this respect. He attributes smaller effects to longer routes in the underlying systems so that the activation caused by the distracter word arrives in some critical memory representation too late to still cause an effect. To give one example, the smaller interference with weak L2 words than with strong L1 words in low-proficiency bilinguals was attributed to the larger number of mental processing steps in the former case: Because a weak L2 word has to pass through the corresponding L1 lexical representation before accessing conceptual memory (see Chapter 3, Figure 3.7, the word association model), its interfering effect is relatively small. The implicit additional assumptions apparently are that by the time it gets there, in relatively many cases (and more often than with a strong L1 distracter word) (1) the conceptual analysis of the color has already taken place (the color has been recognized), (2) the result of this analysis—activation in a layer of conceptual nodes—has already been transmitted to the corresponding lexical representation of the response language, (3) the phonology corresponding to this targeted representation has also been accessed, and (4) the targeted word has been articulated. In other words, the activation induced by the weak L2 word arrives in the relevant place (conceptual memory) too late to still affect the response.

The reason that in the above studies the processing stages in the Stroop task were not described in great detail presumably is that their primary goal was to become informed on bilingual lexical *representation*, the task just serving as the tool to reach this goal. Other studies have used the bilingual Stroop task to address other questions, such as whether or not orthographically different and similar languages pose the same demands on one and the same central processor (see the study by Fang et al., 1981, reviewed above, and Lee et al., 1992, for a

discussion). It is only natural that the way a particular set of experimental results is presented and explained varies with the exact topic under study. The last bilingual Stroop study to be discussed here, a Hebrew–English study by Tzelgov et al. (1996; see also p. 190), had yet a different focus and, as a consequence of its specific focus, provided detailed information on how the distracter stimulus is processed.

Tzelgov and his collaborators used a modified version of the bilingual Stroop task in which, in addition to words, "cross-script homophones" were used as distracters: nonwords written in the letters of the *non-response* language but that, if pronounced in this language, sound like a color name in the *response* language. Examples are the Englishlike nonwords *kahol* and *adom* that, if pronounced according to the spelling-to-sound correspondence rules of English, sound just like the Hebrew words for blue and red, respectively. The main question these investigators addressed was whether a written word makes direct contact with its lexical representation or whether, instead, the word's phonological form is first automatically generated via the application of grapheme–phoneme conversion rules, after which the generated code makes contact with the word's lexical representation. If the latter holds and the non-response language cannot be blocked off, cross-script homophones might also produce an interference effect.

Englishlike cross-script homophones like *kahol* and *adom* (English being the participants' L2, the weaker language) indeed produced a reliable Stroop effect when Hebrew was the response language. This finding indicates that the participants automatically applied the English (L2) spelling-to-sound conversion rules when performing the task in Hebrew. However, this effect was not always as large as the corresponding intralingual effect (when, e.g., the Hebrew word for blue was printed in red and Hebrew was the response language again). This replicates the common finding that generally (but not always; see above) the intralingual effects are larger than the interlingual effects.

To summarize, bilingual Stroop studies have reliably produced both intra- and interlingual

Stroop effects and the size of these effects depended on the participants' relative proficiency in their two languages and on the degree of similarity of the languages. The effects have usually been explained in terms of the degree of within- and between-language interconnectedness of the linguistic elements in bilingual memory. Only occasionally have the exact processing steps involved been described explicitly.

Conclusions

An account of performance in any task includes implicit or explicit hypotheses about representation structures, processing operations, and the interdependence between the two. Considering this truism, it may have struck the reader that, despite the procedural and conceptual similarities between the bilingual picture–word interference task and the bilingual Stroop task, different aspects of the full processing account are highlighted in these two research lines. The bilingual picture–word interference studies (pp. 239–242) focused more on processing than on representation. In contrast, most of the bilingual Stroop tasks stressed aspects of representation, focusing especially on the type and degree of interconnectedness of meaning and form representations between the bilingual's two language systems. This difference in theoretical focus involves the risk that the tasks' commonalities are obscured. It is therefore instructive to take one of the processing models tested in the picture-naming studies as a starting point and see how Stroop effects can be explained in terms of this model.

In terms of Figure 5.2, analogous to the bike in this figure, the color of the printed word in the Stroop task would be the conceptual content to be verbalized. Let us take as an example the Spanish word *azul*, "blue", printed in green and an English–Spanish bilingual serving as participant in a bilingual Stroop experiment following an instruction to name the colors in English. Just like an object concept (e.g., "bike"), a color concept ("green") activates a set of conceptual features that, in their turn, activate a number of lemmas. The lemma set activated by the color green includes lemmas for color words in both the

response language (here English) and the non-response language (Spanish). All these lemmas (e.g., the lemmas for *green*, *blue*, *verde*, and *azul*) compete for selection (according to the standard view, but see pp. 242–244). Among the competitors is the lemma that corresponds to *azul*. This lemma has also received activation from a bottom-up process triggered by the word *azul* (cf. the activation sequence incited by the distracter *mesa* in Figure 5.7). As a result, this lemma becomes a strong competitor of the color name to be produced, *green*, causing the inhibitory Stroop effect. One can also see how *verde* ("green") printed in green would implement the between-language identity condition which Costa et al. (1999; see p. 244) have shown to produce facilitation in the picture–word interference paradigm.

Looking at bilingual Stroop effects in terms of bilingual word production models this way is not meant to radically dismiss the above accounts of these effects in terms of, for instance, differences in strength between the representations of related words within and between languages or in terms of a development from indirect to direct mapping of L2 words onto meaning. Instead, the exercise is simply meant to highlight the similarities between the Stroop task and the picture–word interference task (as some other authors have done; La Heij et al., 1990). An understanding of their shared features will no doubt facilitate the interpretation of the data collected in studies that exploit either task, an interpretation that, as the reader may have experienced, can be quite challenging at times. Ultimately, a complete understanding of the effects observed with both tasks will have to take both the processes involved and the knowledge structures exploited by these processes into consideration.

WORD TRANSLATION

Word translation as word production

In the previous section the similarities between the bilingual picture–word interference task and the bilingual Stroop task were highlighted. There is still a third bilingual task that has been likened to these two tasks—word translation. The word translation task has a long history in the cognitive study of bilingualism, but it has been used primarily to study the question of how L2 word-forms are mapped onto meaning (e.g., De Groot, 1992b; Kroll & Curley, 1988; Kroll & Stewart, 1994; Potter et al., 1984; see Chapter 3, pp. 136–137 for a discussion of this work), or simply to find out what aspects of words make them hard or easy to translate. On the assumption that word translation is conceptually mediated (this in fact being a debated issue in the form-to-meaning mapping studies), a quick glance at, for instance, Figure 5.7 shows how it implicitly comprises the word translation process: Ignore the picture of a table and read *mesa* as the word to be translated; translation then is the process of getting from *mesa* to *taula*.

Noticing the cross-task similarities, La Heij et al. (1990) were the first to wonder whether word translation is similarly influenced by distracter words as are picture naming and the traditional Stroop tasks. They addressed this question in a study in which Dutch–English bilinguals translated L2 English printed words into L1 Dutch. Each stimulus word was paired with a printed Dutch distracter word, which could be of three types: It could be orthographically related, semantically related, or unrelated to the Dutch translation of the stimulus. For instance, the stimulus *yellow* (*geel*, in Dutch) could be paired with the orthographic distracter *geest* ("spirit"), the semantic distracter *bruin* ("brown") or the unrelated distracter *muts* ("cap"). Notice that the distracters appeared in the *language of output*, the language the participants translated into (also notice that orthographic distracters were at the same time phonological distracters because they also shared a phonological relation with the targeted response). When the stimulus words preceded the distracters by 140 milliseconds, translation was faster in the orthographic distracter condition than in the unrelated distracter condition, just as this type of distracter (but called a phonological distracter) has been shown to facilitate performance in the picture-naming task. Conversely, it

was slower in the semantic distracter condition than in the unrelated control condition, again, just as this type of distracter inhibits picture naming.

Miller and Kroll (2002) replicated these results in an English–Spanish study and showed that the effects also occurred when the participants had to translate in the reverse direction, from their L1 into their L2. Importantly, these authors also included a condition in which the distracters appeared in the same language as the stimulus input. For example, *yellow* could be accompanied by the semantic distracter *brown* or the unrelated distracter *cap*. Under these circumstances, the orthographic and semantic distracters did not noticeably affect translation performance.

What could have caused this effect of distracter language, and especially, why do not distracters in *both* languages affect responding, as they do in picture naming (see p. 240)? In their analysis the authors point to an important difference between translation and picture naming: The former but not the latter provides relevant information about the language of output in the form of the language information present in the stimulus. If, say, *silla* ("chair") is presented to a Spanish–English bilingual, the language identity of the stimulus is known as well. In contrast, in picture naming no such language information is incorporated in the stimulus. The authors suggest this early language information available in translation has the effect that the participants can constrain the selection process to the language of production. In other words, in word translation, when the distracter words are elements of the production language, they compete for selection, but when they do not belong to the production language (but to the language of input) they do not compete for selection. In contrast, because no language information is encompassed in a picture to be named, distracter words in both languages compete for selection with the targeted word in picture naming.

Two recent studies (Bloem & La Heij, 2003; Bloem, Van den Boogaard, & La Heij, 2004) have examined the effects of distracter words in word translation in greater detail, comparing them with the effects of distracter pictures on word translation and manipulating the time interval (stimulus onset asynchrony; SOA) between the presentation of the distracter and the word to be translated. The most interesting new findings were that semantic distracter pictures quickened rather than slowed down the translation process and that the semantic interference caused by semantic distracter words was reversed into semantic facilitation when the distracters preceded the stimulus word by 400 ms instead of being presented in close temporal proximity to the target. The authors accounted for these results in terms of a new model of word production, the conceptual selection model (CSM), that localizes semantic facilitation at the conceptual representational level and semantic interference at the lexical level and that, in addition, assumes that activation in lexical nodes decays faster than activation in conceptual nodes. A crucial assumption in this model is that not all concepts that are activated by an input automatically activate their lexical representations. Instead, it is assumed that at the conceptual level one concept is selected and that only this concept is lexicalized. This is the model's feature from which it derives its name. At the same time, the selected concept also spreads activation to the lexical representations of semantically related words so that CSM also assumes a "semantic cohort" of activated lexical representations, as do the production models discussed earlier in this chapter.

So far, the details of the full translation process remained implicit, as did a salient difference between word translation and picture naming (or Stroop color naming, for that matter); namely, that processing starts off at different points in these two tasks: After a first structural analysis of the visual information, picture naming involves the immediate access of conceptual memory. In contrast, in translation, following a perceptual analysis, the target word first accesses the orthographic lexicon (or the phonological lexicon, if words are aurally presented for translation) and only then conceptual memory (see Figure 5.7). In the next section I will describe the various processing stages and representational structures involved in word translation in more detail

and explain how the emerging view of word translation can account for a couple of common findings obtained when participants perform this task. Unlike in the studies just reviewed, the studies in question have not used the distracter methodology but simple word translation instead.

Explaining cognate and concreteness effects in word translation

The cognate effect

A robust finding in simple word translation studies is that cognates are translated faster than non-cognates (Christoffels et al., 2006; De Groot, 1992b; De Groot et al., 1994). Earlier on in this chapter (p. 246) I have already discussed the similar finding of Costa et al. (2000) that in simple picture naming (without distracters) pictures that depict cognate words are named faster than pictures that depict non-cognates. Because in simple picture naming neither of the cognate terms of a translation pair is physically present, the effect cannot be due to early perceptual processing somehow favoring cognates. Accordingly, Costa and his colleagues localized the effect in a later processing stage (see Figure 5.5, p. 235): As a consequence of language-nonselective phonological encoding, many of the sublexical phonological nodes that together represent a cognate's name receive activation from two sources: from the target's lexical node and the lexical node representing its translation. In contrast, the sublexical phonological nodes that represent the name of a non-cognate receive activation from the target's lexical node only. The boosted activation in the former set of sublexical nodes facilitates name retrieval.

Given the present analysis that the final stages of word translation, downward from the conceptual (or semantic) level, are similar to those in picture naming, this account can also serve to explain the cognate effects in word translation. But this is unlikely to be the complete story. Earlier on (p. 247) I have already discussed the possibility that representational differences may exist between cognates and non-cognates. For instance, cognates may share more semantic nodes between languages than do non-cognates (e.g., De Groot, 1992a; Taylor, 1976; Van Hell & De Groot, 1998a). Furthermore, they may share a morphological representation in memory whereas non-cognates do not (e.g., Sánchez-Casas & García-Albea, 2005; see Chapter 4, p. 204). Support for the former of these hypotheses comes from word association studies that have compared within- and between-language word associations in bilinguals (e.g., within-language: stimulus *boy*, response *girl*; between-language: stimulus *boy*, response *fille*, "girl", in an English–French bilingual). The studies in question have shown that within- and between-language associations to cognate stimuli are more often translations of one another (as is the case in the example) than those to non-cognates. Several authors (Taylor, 1976; Van Hell & De Groot, 1998a) have accounted for this effect in terms of distributed representations in semantic memory that are partly shared between a pair of translations augmented by the hypothesis that the amount of sharing is larger for cognate translations than for non-cognate translations (see Van Hell & De Groot, 1998a, for details).

In word translation there is a further possible source of the cognate effects. If the two languages involved in a translation act share one and the same alphabetic script, a cognate translation pair will consist of two words that share orthography (in addition to phonology). If word recognition is language-nonselective, as we have seen it is under many circumstances (see Chapter 4), a visually presented cognate word will automatically trigger (via activation of the orthographic sublexical nodes) the orthographic lexical representations of *both* terms in a translation pair (see pp. 199–202) and both of these then feed activation to the same set of semantic nodes. The likely consequence is that these semantic nodes will be activated relatively highly as compared to the situation where a non-cognate is presented for translation (which does not activate the orthographic lexical representation of its translation equivalent or only very weakly so). Figures 5.9a and 5.9b visualize this state of affairs, building on and extending Figure 5.5. The effect of the

increased activation of the semantic nodes representing cognates is that the nodes at later levels in the translation production process, those representing the phonological lexical representations and sublexical phonology, will also be activated relatively highly and the cognates' names will be relatively easy to retrieve.

To summarize, three sources of the cognate effect in word translation can be identified: facilitated name retrieval due to language-nonselective phonological encoding that favors cognates over non-cognates; representational differences between cognates and non-cognates at the semantic-representational level and/or a morphological level (not shown); relatively strong activation of the associated semantic nodes when a cognate is presented for translation. In translation production, these various sources may all join forces in privileging the processing of cognates over non-cognates.

Given the fact that the activated semantic nodes feed activation to the phonological lexical nodes of both elements in the translation pair, not just to the lexical node that corresponds to the targeted response, what remains is to explain why, satisfying the instructions, the input word is indeed generally translated, not repeated. (Notice that the accounts of picture naming advanced in this chapter give rise to the analogous question of why the picture is generally named in the target language.) To account for this it may be assumed that some general control mechanism, external to the language system proper, translates the exact task requirements in a set-up of the language system in which the phonological lexical representations of the output language are more highly activated than those of the input language. This idea will briefly return later in this section and will be elaborated in more detail in Chapter 6. Alternatively, we may resort to the language-specific lexical selection mechanism that Costa and his colleagues (1999) introduced to account for their picture naming data (pp. 243–245). Only the activated lexical nodes of the target language are considered for selection; activation in non-target language nodes is ignored. Arguably, this process of selective attention also demands the involvement of a control

FIGURE 5.9

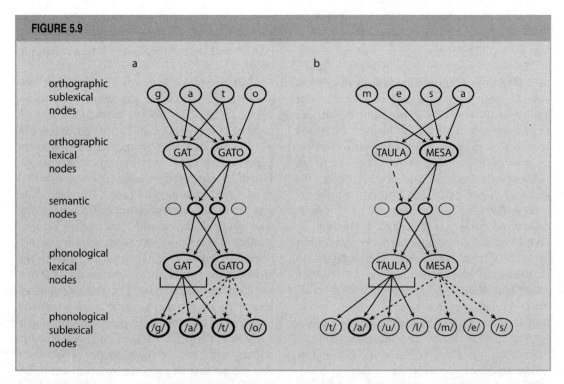

A model of translating cognates (a) and non-cognates (b). The Catalan–Spanish participants' task is to translate Spanish *gato* and *mesa* into Catalan *gat* and *taula*. Spanish *gato* strongly activates the orthographic lexical nodes of both *gato* and *gat*. As a consequence, the semantic nodes that represent the meaning of this translation pair are activated relatively strongly, as compared to the semantic nodes that represent the meaning of the non-cognate pair *mesa–taula*.

system of the type just suggested. In Figure 5.9 this idea of language-specific lexical selection is illustrated by means of the bracket underneath the phonological lexical node of the response language.

The concreteness effect

A second variable that affects word translation is word concreteness: Concrete words are translated faster than abstract words (De Groot, 1992b; De Groot et al., 1994; De Groot & Poot, 1997; Van Hell & De Groot, 1998b). Because this effect holds for non-cognates and cognates alike, neither the convergence of activation in the relevant set of phonological sublexical nodes from two phonological lexical nodes nor differential activation of the relevant set of semantic nodes caused by the convergence of activation from two

activated orthographic lexical nodes can account for these effects. After all, if the concrete and abstract words presented for translation are non-cognates, these two sources of the effect cease to exist. Out of the three sources of differential translation performance for cognates versus non-cognates that were considered above, only one remains to account for the concreteness effect: a difference between the semantic representations of concrete and abstract words in the sense that the former share more semantic nodes between languages than the latter Again, some evidence comes from word association studies: Within- and between-language word associations to concrete words are more often translations of one another than those to abstract words (Kolers, 1963; Van Hell & De Groot, 1998a). Another source of evidence is the finding that bilinguals rate the words in concrete translation pairs as more semantically similar to one another than the words in abstract translation pairs (Tokowicz, Kroll, De Groot, & Van Hell, 2002).

However, a complete account of the concreteness effect in word translation is likely to be more complex than just suggested, because concrete and abstract words differ on more dimensions than concreteness alone. To mention three: the meaning components of concrete words tend to be more correlated than those of abstract words (McRae, De Sa, & Seidenberg, 1997), the meanings of abstract and concrete words are represented in a qualitatively different way in conceptual memory (e.g., Crutch & Warrington, 2005), and concrete words have fewer translations on average in the language to be translated into than abstract words (Schönpflug, 1997; Prior, MacWhinney, & Kroll, 2007; Tokowicz & Kroll, 2007), perhaps because concrete words tend to have a relatively small number of fixed meanings whereas abstract words have more, but context-dependent, meanings (Crutch & Warrington, 2005). Tokowicz and Kroll, in an English–Spanish study, have shown that the speed advantage of concrete words over abstract words disappears when the stimuli presented for translation have only one translation in the other language. In contrast, words with multiple translations showed the common advantage for concrete words.

A further finding obtained by Tokowicz and Kroll (2007) was that words with multiple translations were translated more slowly than words with just one translation. Laxén and Lavaur (2010) replicated this finding in a French–English study, employing the translation recognition task (see p. 91). The reason a particular word has more than one translation usually is that it is ambiguous or has a close synonym in the language of input. As a consequence, words with multiple translations (e.g., French *femme*, meaning both "woman" and "wife" in English) are likely to activate more semantic nodes than words with just a single translation, especially when they are translated out of context (as in the present type of experiments). The joint set of activated semantic nodes then transmit their activation onto more than one phonological lexical node in the output language (e.g., both the English lexical

nodes for *woman* and *wife*), and these will compete for selection, causing the delay in responding (the example is borrowed from Laxén & Lavaur, 2010).

If ambiguity or synonymy in the input language indeed underlies the number of translations effect, the above interaction between number of translations and word concreteness in word translation is in actual fact an interaction between number of meanings and concreteness. If true, a similar interaction may be expected to occur in monolingual tasks. This prediction was confirmed by Tokowicz and Kroll (2007), who obtained the expected interaction between number of meanings and concreteness in a monolingual lexical decision task. As concluded by the authors, the similarity of the results for the bilingual translation task and the monolingual lexical decision task suggests that a general property of the language processing system is likely to underlie both sets of data, one that has nothing to do with bilingualism per se. Whatever this general system property may turn out to be, these data point out that number of meanings of the stimuli presented for translation is a factor to take into account when interpreting concreteness effects in word translation.

In addition to cognate status, word concreteness, and number of meanings, there are other word characteristics that affect word translation, maybe most notoriously word frequency (see e.g., De Groot, 1992b; De Groot et al., 1994). I will refrain from detailing all of these in terms of the view of word translation developed in this section. Instead, I will conclude with an analysis of how this view can account for one further specific feature of translation performance—that translation errors are often words semantically related to the stimulus word, but in the language of output (e.g., stimulus: Dutch *cirkel*, "circle", response: *square*; stimulus: Dutch *kaars*, "candle", response: *flame*; stimulus: Dutch *handdoek*, "towel", response: *blanket*). These translation errors are similar to speech production errors in unilingual settings where, instead of the targeted word, a semantically related word is accidentally output by the system. The similarity of this error type in translation and unilingual word production suggests a common underlying cause (thereby constituting independent evidence for the main tenet of the present section: that word translation and monolingual and bilingual word production can be accounted for in terms of one and the same set of processes and associated system architecture). Specifically, the likely source of this type of error (see also De Groot, 1992a) is the fact that a set of activated semantic nodes activates more lexical representations than just the two focused on in Figures 5.9a and 5.9b. As we have seen in earlier parts of this chapter (see, e.g., Figure 5.2) the lexical representations of semantically related words, in both languages, are also activated, and one of these may accidentally be selected.

How then, if performance in such a varied collection of tasks exploits the same set of memory nodes at various levels in the system, does the response required by a specific task and not one required by an alternative task generally emerge from the system? A solution to this problem was already suggested above, when accounting for the fact that in word translation it seldom occurs that the input word is inadvertently repeated as output. The suggested solution was to assume the existence of some general control system in addition to the language system proper, as some have done (e.g., Dijkstra & Van Heuven, 2002; Green, 1998; Roelofs, 1992). Depending on the task's demands, a specific system configuration is chosen that suppresses or ignores task-irrelevant activation and/or fosters task-relevant activation. This control system may fail at times, perhaps due to a lapse of attention or to system overload. At such a moment an error will occur; for instance, a semantic error in translation or a switch to another task or language. Plausibly, the language-specific selection process proposed by Costa et al. (1999) is a manifestation of the workings of a control system of the type outlined here. In Chapters 6 and 8 I will provide further details on how such a system might work and on the brain mechanisms that appear to be involved.

To conclude, it seems that performance in a large number of word production tasks such as monolingual and bilingual picture naming, monolingual and bilingual Stroop color naming,

and word translation is based on activation patterns in one and the same underlying, layered, memory system augmented by a general control system that, one way or the other, sees to it that the current goal is met (for instance, by boosting the activation in task-relevant memory nodes and/or suppressing the activation in task-irrelevant memory nodes and/or by ignoring task-irrelevant activation).

COMPREHENSION AND PRODUCTION: MAKING A CONNECTION

In the preceding section a model of word translation was presented which regarded it as a form of word production in which the content to be expressed in speech is established in the layer of conceptual nodes through an initial word recognition process. As with every visual illustration of a mental process that intends to highlight the component structures and processes involved, ignoring others, the model's illustration involves the risk of seeding a misunderstanding: Figure 5.9 may be worth a thousand words but the story it tells so pointedly may give rise to the unintentional and presumably false inference that activated nodes representing sublexical orthography do not directly spread their activation to the corresponding sublexical phonological nodes. Instead it suggests that semantic nodes and orthographic and phonological lexical nodes mediate between the transmission of activation from orthographic to phonological sublexical nodes. To draw such a conclusion would not do justice to the results of myriad[1] studies, particularly in the domain of research on word reading, that suggest otherwise. Some of this evidence was presented in Chapter 4 (pp. 184–186), where I discussed a number of studies which showed that orthographic sublexical nodes automatically activate the corresponding phonological sublexical nodes, suggesting direct connections between these two types of nodes. Also models of speech production assume the existence of these connections, sometimes implicitly, at other times explicitly (e.g., Roelofs,

Meyer, & Levelt, 1996). Similarly, through past reading, the complete orthographic forms of words are likely to have become connected with their phonological counterparts. As a result, the activation of an orthographic lexical node will activate its phonological counterpart directly.

Figure 5.10a presents the same types of memory nodes as Figure 5.9 but in a format different from the hierarchically layered one that is conventionally used in production studies and without differentiating between sublexical and lexical nodes. But contrary to Figure 5.9 it explicitly acknowledges the fact that orthographic nodes not only feed activation to phonological nodes indirectly, via semantic nodes, but also directly. In a word translation task where the words to be translated are presented in printed form, the input word first activates the orthographic nodes and from, there activation spreads to both semantic and phonological nodes. In a word production task such as picture naming, the semantic nodes are activated first.

This alternative presentation illustrates the imaginative power a visual illustration of a mental process can have: This new layout immediately suggests the hypothesis that it may represent, in an admittedly very sketchy way, language processing in general, encompassing both language comprehension (both reading and understanding spoken input) and language production. This hypothesis is rendered more explicit in Figure 5.10b, which includes bidirectional instead of

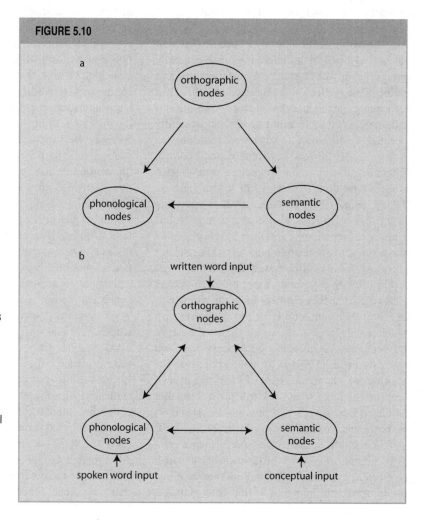

FIGURE 5.10

(a) A language-processing system that assumes unidirectional spreading of activation from orthographic to phonological nodes, both indirectly via semantic nodes as well as directly. (b) The same system but now including bidirectional connections between the various types of nodes. It suggests that word production from a conceptual input and the recognition of spoken and written words exploit one and the same underlying processing architecture.

unidirectional connections between the different types of nodes in the system. In other words, Figure 5.10b expresses the hypothesis that word production, visual word recognition, and auditory word recognition exploit one and the same underlying processing system instead of there being separate systems dedicated to each one of these processes. It is based on visual illustrations of a model of monolingual reading and spelling (e.g., Van Orden, Pennington, & Stone, 1990; Bosman & Van Orden, 1997), the phonological coherence model, and also bears a striking resemblance to SOPHIA (see Figure 4.4), a model of bilingual word recognition.

Although attractive because of its parsimony, Figure 5.10b does not enjoy the status of a truism but summarizes a multifaceted hypothesis of which each component must be validated empirically. Whether or not comprehension and production share representational structure needs to be settled empirically for each of the representation domains that we have distinguished: word meaning, word form (both orthographic and phonological), and sublexical (again, both orthographic and phonological). Shared representation may hold for some domains but not for others. Furthermore, if the data point out that for a particular domain separate representations for comprehension and production exist, these representations may or may not be connected. In view of the topic of the present chapter, speech production, learning to know the exact relationship between comprehension and production is particularly important because speakers are known to monitor their own speech, employing their comprehension apparatus in doing so (see Figure 5.1). If comprehension and production share one and the same set of underlying representations, this means that this one set is exploited simultaneously (or maybe in rapid alternation) during the production and monitoring of speech. Similarly, revealing the relation between comprehension and production is likely to inform our understanding of simultaneous interpreting, which involves the simultaneous use of these two processes most of the time (or, again, their use in rapid alternation; see Chapter 6, pp. 316–319).

In fact, the relation between comprehension and production and the underlying architecture of the language system have been studied thoroughly since the second half of the last century. For instance, the motor theory of speech perception (e.g., Liberman & Mattingly, 1985) assumes that we perceive phonetic elements in terms of the motor commands in the brain that drive the muscles used when we produce these sounds in speech. A further example concerns the possibility of grammatical encoding and grammatical decoding being "entangled" processes rather than operating independently from one another, as they are most often thought to do (Kempen, Olsthoorn, & Sprenger, 2009). Allport, MacKay, Prinz, and Scheerer (1987) dedicated a complete volume to the relation between comprehension and production. In one of the contributions to this volume, Monsell (1987) considered six possible models for the relationship between speech comprehension and speech production, and reviewed the evidence in support of each of them. All of these models shared the assumption that the conceptual representations are common to speech comprehension and production. They differed from one another in terms of the degree of interconnectedness between, and the sharing of, the other types of representations that he distinguished: phonological word nodes, sublexical phonological nodes, acoustic representations and articulatory representations.

To be able to choose between the alternative models, Monsell considered evidence from three sources of experimental data: cross-modal repetition priming studies, dual-task studies, and neuropsychological studies. In the relevant cross-modal studies the participants first had to perform some "priming" task that involved the production of words (e.g., speak the word out loud) and, subsequently, some task that involved the auditory comprehension of the words produced earlier (e.g., perform an auditory lexical decision). In the latter task, called the "probe" task, also words occurred that had not been produced before. The question of interest was whether probe words that had been produced before would be responded to faster than those not produced before. Such priming effects would suggest that phonological word nodes are shared between comprehension and production. Alternatively they could be accounted for in terms of models that assume separate phonological word nodes for production and comprehension that are, however, connected in two directions via the sublexical nodes. In contrast, the absence of a priming effect of earlier production on later comprehension would suggest the existence of separate phonological word nodes for comprehension and production and, *at the same time*, the non-existence of the above indirect connection between them via the sublexical nodes. Priming from earlier production to later comprehension of the same words occurred under many circumstances, ruling out the latter type of model (see Monsell, 1987, for details).

The dual-task studies in question (e.g., Shallice, McLeod, & Lewis, 1985) compared a dual-task condition where participants have to simultaneously perform a speech comprehension task (e.g., detect words belonging to a prespecified semantic class in a series of aurally presented words) and a speech production task (e.g., read aloud visually presented words) with a control condition in which participants only performed one task. If performance in both tasks exploits a single set of phonological word representations, a performance decrement in the dual-task condition as compared to the control condition should occur. Contrary to this prediction (and contrary to the above results obtained in cross-modal priming studies), the decrement in performance in the dual-task condition as compared to the single-task condition was negligibly small, suggesting that separate phonological word nodes for speech comprehension and speech production exist. Neuropsychological evidence supports this conclusion: Both cases of impaired auditory word comprehension with preserved word production and cases of impaired word production but preserved word comprehension have been reported. Weighing the combined evidence from these three lines of research, Monsell (1987) opted for a model that contains both separate phonological word nodes and separate phonological sublexical nodes for speech comprehen-

sion and speech production, but with connections in both directions between the phonological sublexical input nodes and the phonological sublexical output nodes. In addition, he assumed that the acoustic and articulatory representations are connected in both directions. These conclusions tally with those drawn by speech production researchers (Levelt et al., 1991; Roelofs et al., 1996). However they seem to be at variance with the way speech accents in bilinguals are explained. These accents, and especially the accent in bilinguals' L2 speech, are the theme of the final part of this chapter. To anticipate, the relevant work suggests that phonological sublexical representations are shared between speech comprehension and speech production.

SPEECH ACCENTS IN NON-NATIVE SPEAKERS

Introduction

So far this chapter has dealt with the mental processing that takes place in the mind of (monolinguals and) bilinguals while they produce words, ignoring the physical characteristics of the speech signal that emerges from this mental work. In this section I will remedy this neglect by focusing on one particular characteristic of this signal; namely the fact that it often accented. This is true of the speech of the majority of non-native speakers and even bilinguals with a high level of fluency in their L2 are more often than not recognized as non-native speakers just from the way their speech sounds. However, the degree of "accentedness" varies greatly between individual L2 speakers and in a small minority of them not a hint of an accent can be detected. These facts raise a number of questions, such as what causes the accent and what aspects of speech are affected (e.g., particular phonemes or suprasegmental prosodic features). To what extent does the accuracy in pronouncing L2 speech sounds depend on the accuracy with which these sounds can be perceived? Does an accent affect the comprehensibility of an L2 utterance and the time taken by a perceiver to process it and, if so, to what degree? Does familiarity of a native listener with the non-native speaker's L1 affect the perceived accentedness and/or the comprehensibility of this speaker's L2? In this section I will present a selection of studies that have tackled one or more of these questions. I will first review a number of studies that were primarily concerned with identifying causes of the non-native accent and will conclude with a discussion of studies that focused on the relation between accent and comprehensibility.

Causes

A factor that has consistently been shown to affect the degree of accentedness of L2 speech is the age at which the speaker began to learn this language: The younger the learner was at the time, the less accented L2 speech is. Global accent differences between young and older L2 learners can easily be detected by having native speakers perform a general accentedness rating of the L2 speech (e.g., Flege, Munro, & MacKay, 1995a; Flege et al., 1999). Experiments in which L2 speakers and native speakers are asked to produce individual vowels and consonants provide the data for a more fine-grained analysis of the accent differences between native and non-native speech (e.g., Flege, Munro, & MacKay, 1995b). A similar age of acquisition effect occurs in perception: Early L2 learners outperform late learners in the identification of L2 speech sounds (e.g., Broersma, 2005; MacKay, Meador, & Flege, 2001; Weber & Cutler, 2004; see also Chapter 4, pp. 195–197, and see Chapter 2, pp. 47–77 for age of acquisition effects on L2 grammar). Whereas the reliability of these effects is beyond doubt, there is an ongoing debate on what causes them.

The explanation that has inspired a substantial amount of work in this research area, and that, due to its appeal, seems to have assumed the status of uncontestable truth among the general public, is that there is some critical period for the acquisition of language (be it the L1 or any further language) early in life. Penfield (1963) and

Lenneberg (1967) were the first to posit this view, which has come to be known as the "critical period hypothesis" (CPH). They attributed the loss of the facility to learn a language after this period—which they thought to end around puberty—to a loss of neural plasticity. If language acquisition coincides with the critical period a nativelike pronunciation (as well as nativelike performance in other subdomains of language; see Chapter 2) will be attained. If language acquisition only coincides with part of this critical period or starts after its offset, complete L2 mastery can no longer be attained and L2 speech will remain accented. Whereas Lenneberg hypothesized that the acquisition of language in general is constrained by the critical period, others have proposed that especially the capacity to acquire a nativelike pronunciation is constrained by it (e.g., Scovel, 1988). A large part of Chapter 2 dealt with the hypothesis that L2 grammar learning is determined by a critical period. The present section discusses the critical period hypothesis in relation to L2 speech accents.

Birdsong (2005) evaluated a couple of predictions that can be derived from the critical period hypothesis. One of them is that no L2 speaker who started learning this language after the closure of the critical period can attain nativelike performance. The existence of just a single late learner whose L2 speech is indistinguishable from native speech would constitute irrefutable counterevidence. Such evidence has, however, been obtained repeatedly, just as late L2 learners have been identified with nativelike L2 grammatical ability (Chapter 2). For instance, Bongaerts (1999) asked native English speakers to rate English speech samples spoken by advanced L1 Dutch learners of English on a 5-point scale ranging from 1 (very strong accent, definitely non-native) to 5 (no foreign accent at all, definitely native). All learners had started their English training relatively late in life, around the age of 12. Nevertheless, the judges mistook the speech of about half of these advanced learners (five out of eleven) as being spoken by native speakers of English. This result suggests that starting to learn a second language relatively late in life is not an insuperable impediment for acquiring an authentic pronunciation.

Dutch and English are both Germanic languages and have similar sound systems. The support for the possibility of successful late speech learning would be even more convincing if it could also be shown for learners of an L2 typologically more distant to the L1. In a second study Bongaerts (1999) addressed this issue by replicating the Dutch–English study with advanced Dutch L1 learners of French (French being a Romance language). This time fewer of the advanced learners were judged to be native-like, but still there were three (out of nine) who passed the "native" test. Abu-Rabia and Kehat (2004) have since obtained a similar result for late learners of Hebrew who differed in L1 background. The findings of all three studies (and see also Bongaerts, Van Summeren, Planken, & Schils, 1997) thus indicate that an early start is not a mandatory requirement for acquiring an unaccented pronunciation. As hypothesized by Bongaerts, it is a combination of factors—intensive training in perceiving and producing the L2 speech sounds, massive L2 input, and a high motivation to sound nativelike—that leads to unaccented L2 speech.

If at some point early in life, at the offset of the critical period around puberty, a special ability for speech learning is lost, the degree of L2 speech accent must be linearly related to the age of acquisition for L2 speakers first exposed to the L2 before the offset point (recall that "age of acquisition" refers to the age the learner first starts learning the L2): The longer before the closure point of the critical period the learner began learning the L2 and, thus, the longer the learner has taken advantage of the special language learning ability, the less accented his or her L2 speech should be. In contrast, the degree of accent in L2 speakers who started learning the L2 beyond the offset point should not be systematically related to age of acquisition (see Chapter 2 for a thorough discussion of these predictions). In other words, the CPH predicts that, across the whole age of acquisition spectrum covering both the years before and after the assumed offset point of the critical period, age of

acquisition on the one hand and degree of L2 accent on the other hand should be related non-linearly. Specifically, a discontinuity in the age (of acquisition)–accentedness function should be observed at an onset age of about 15 years. Various studies have shown that such discontinuity does not occur but that the relation between onset of learning and degree of accent is linear across the whole age spectrum.

Figure 5.11 presents the results of a cross-sectional study by Flege et al. (1999; see also Birdsong, 2005, and Flege, 1999). These authors had a group of American-English native speakers rate a set of English sentences spoken by 240 native Koreans (and by 24 native English speakers) for overall degree of foreign accent. The Korean participants had all immigrated to the United States between the ages of 1 and 23 and had lived there for at least 8, and on average 15, years at the time the rating was done. As shown, not even a hint of a discontinuity can be observed in the age–accent function, neither at an arrival age of 15 years, nor at any other arrival age (note that onset of L2 learning was equated with the age of arrival in the L2-speaking country; this is common practice in this research area). Instead, degree of L2 accent was linearly related to arrival age: the later the Koreans had arrived in the United States, the stronger their L2 accents. This same pattern had also been obtained in an earlier study, in which the accentedness of native Italians' L2 English was rated (Flege et al., 1995a). These data thus suggest that there is no *age-bounded* period of time in which humans are especially well equipped to learn (the phonology of a) language. In addition, they *do* show that the age at which L2 learning starts is an important predictor of degree of accent.

Age of acquisition is not the only variable to affect the degree of L2 accent. In a series of studies Flege and his colleagues have identified amount of continued L1 use after immigration to the L2-speaking country as a further relevant variable (e.g., Flege, Frieda, & Nozawa, 1997; Piske, MacKay, & Flege, 2001). In one of the pertinent studies (Flege et al., 1997) the researchers had native English speakers rate the accentedness of English sentences spoken by both native

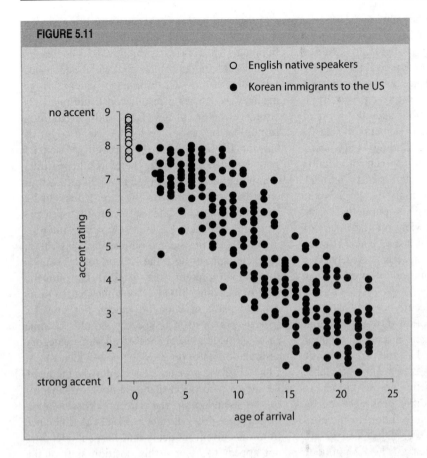

FIGURE 5.11

Degree of accent in L2 English in Korean immigrants in the United States as a function of age of arrival. The accent ratings were produced by native speakers of English. The rated accents for a control group of native English speakers are shown for comparison. Reprinted from Flege et al. (1999), Copyright 1999, with permission from Elsevier.

English speakers and native Italian speakers who had immigrated to an English-speaking area in Canada at a young age (5.7 years on average). The raters' task was to judge the language background, English or Italian, of each speaker. Ratings were done on a 4-point scale: definitely Italian; probably Italian; probably English; definitely English. The native Italians consisted of two groups that were matched on age of arrival but that differed according to self-reported use of Italian in their daily lives (36% in the "high-use" group versus 3% in the "low-use" group).

The data showed a clear effect of amount of L1 use: The Italians who still spoke Italian relatively often were perceived to have significantly stronger accents than the Italians who still spoke Italian only occasionally. A further finding of interest was that, despite their early arrival in Canada, both L1 Italian groups had detectible foreign accents. This finding challenges the

critical period hypothesis because it suggests that an early onset of L2 acquisition is by no means a guarantee that nativelike L2 speech is attained.

To account for the effect of amount of L1 use on L2 speech accent, Flege and his collaborators developed a new model of L2 speech learning, the "speech learning model" (e.g., Flege et al., 1997). The model assumes a common system that holds both the phonetic elements (also "phonetic categories", "phonemic categories", or "phoneme categories") of the L1 and the L2. (These phonetic elements can be likened to the phonological sublexical nodes in the speech-production models presented earlier in this chapter.) The L1 and L2 elements in this common system influence one another, in both directions, during production. The strength and directionality of this cross-language influence is thought to vary as a function of a number of factors; among others, relative language dominance and the present (related) variable, amount of L1 and L2 use. In this view, the stronger accent of the L2 speech of the high-L1-use participants is caused by the L1 phonetic elements influencing the targeted L2 sounds more in high-L1-use participants than in low-L1-use participants. It is plausible that the interaction takes the form of co-activation of L1 phonetic elements during L2 production. If true, these findings once again show that during bilingual speech production both language systems are activated in parallel, and this all the way down to the level where the speech output takes its phonetic shape. Importantly, the present view on the cause of speech accents also predicts a speech accent when bilinguals produce L1 speech. Evidence in support of this prediction will be presented in Chapter 7 (pp. 363–365).

In addition to the occurrence of such co-activation of the language not in use, Flege and his colleagues hypothesized a second type of interaction between the L1 and L2 phonetic elements (Flege et al., 2003; see also Flege, 2002), one that leads to phonetic representations in bilingual memory that differ from the corresponding representations in the phonetic memory system of native speakers. The authors suggested that during the development of the L2 phonetic system, the degree of similarity between the L1 phonetic categories stored in memory and the new L2 categories to learn determines whether or not separate new categories for the L2 sounds are established in memory: The greater the perceived dissimilarity between an L2 sound and the most similar L1 category, the larger the chance that a new category will be formed for the L2 sound. If the new L2 sound is very close to an extant L1 category, and is therefore perceived as an instance of this category (even though slight differences between the L2 and L1 sounds may be detected), the former is "attracted" by the latter and the two merge into a single phonetic representation in memory. This process is called **phonetic category assimilation**. During this process of merging, the attracting L1 category is assumed not to remain fixed in phonemic space but to shift somewhat to a position that reflects the acoustic characteristics of the L2 sound that it absorbs.

Flege and his co-workers assume this assimilation process to take place more often in late bilinguals than in early bilinguals. The reason is that late bilinguals have already established relatively strong L1 phoneme categories in memory, which, as a result, constitute relatively strong attractors of new L2 sounds. In addition to number of years of prior L1 use, amount of current L1 use affects the strength of the L1 phoneme categories and, therefore, their attraction potential. These merged representations thus contribute importantly to the accentedness of L2 speech of, especially, late learners and L2 speakers who still use their L1 relatively often. Interestingly, because the merged representations contain characteristics of both the L1 and the L2 sounds that they represent (the original L1 phonetic category having shifted away somewhat from its original place in phonetic space), not only L2 speech but also L1 speech should become accented as a consequence of phonetic category assimilation (see pp. 363–365 for evidence). In Chapters 2 and 4 we have encountered a model of L2 speech perception that assumes a similar process of assimilation, the perceptual assimilation model (Best, 1994; Best et al., 1988). A difference from the current model is that Best's model does not appear to assume this position shift of the attracting category. This difference can perhaps be traced back to the different phenomena the two models primarily address, Best trying to account for perceptual discrimination problems that non-native listeners often experience and Flege attempting to explain the ubiquitous speech accents in non-native speakers.

In addition to phonetic category assimilation, Flege and his colleagues assumed a process of **phonetic category dissimilation**. This process becomes operative when an L2 sound to be acquired differs relatively much from the closest L1 sound. Under these circumstances a separate L2 phonetic representation is established in memory. But in order to obtain maximal distinctiveness between the new L2 sound and the closest L1 sound, the two adopt slightly exaggerated values on the phonetic characteristics that distinguish them. For instance, English /eʹ/ is characterized by more tongue movement than Italian /e/.

The Italian learner of English, noticing this difference, might establish a new category in memory for English /e'/ that exaggerates the English–Italian contrast with the effect that English /e'/ spoken by this native Italian is produced with *more* tongue movement than this /e'/ uttered by native speakers of English. Just as category assimilation, category dissimilation is thus a source of accented speech. Flege et al. (2003) obtained experimental support for the occurrence of both category assimilation and dissimilation, showing that early Italian–English bilinguals who use L2 infrequently exaggerated tongue movement in the production of English /e'/ (suggesting dissimilation), whereas late Italian–English bilinguals demonstrated less tongue movement than L1 native speakers would (suggesting assimilation).

Figure 5.12 illustrates these processes of assimilation and dissimilation (adapted from Flege, 2005). Figure 5.12a depicts the position of each L1 vowel in a (hypothetical) phonetic vowel space at the onset of L2 acquisition. The vowel space is delineated by the vowels' first two formants (the concentrations of acoustic energy in particular frequency ranges in the speech signal). In Figure 5.12b the L2 vowel system to be learned is superimposed on the L1 vowel system. Finally, Figure 5.12c illustrates the processes of assimilation and dissimilation that occur during the process of L2 speech learning. As can be seen, both processes result in the vowels of both L1 and L2 taking slightly different positions in the vowel space as compared to those taken by the vowels in monolingual speakers of the two languages. The result of this is accented speech in both languages.

To summarize, Flege and his colleagues suggested that the effects of age of L2 acquisition and amount of current L1 use on L2 speech accents *and* L1 speech accents result from two forms of interaction among the L1 and L2 phonemic categories in a phonemic space shared by both. In other words, there is no longer a reason to attribute the age of acquisition effects to the existence of a circumscribed period in life in which humans are especially well equipped to acquire speech (and language in general). Accordingly, Flege and his collaborators assume

that the capacity for speech learning remains intact over a lifetime, an assumption that is supported by the fact that many cases have been documented of late L2 learners without detectable L2 speech accents (e.g., Bongaerts, 1999). However, it requires effort as well as an optimal L2 learning environment to be able to counteract the effects of the above two types of interaction in bilingual phonetic memory: extensive training in perceiving and producing the L2 (and the motivation to sound nativelike that goes with it) and massive L2 input. In terms of Flege's speech learning model, the effect of this extensive L2 exposure and drill should be that in the shared vowel space the L2 vowels ultimately occupy the same positions as they do in native speakers' phonetic memory. In other words, the effects of the processes of assimilation and dissimilation should be undone or the processes themselves must be prevented from occurring. The speech learning model assumes a close relation between the production and perception of speech sounds: The accents in L2 production arise from phonemic categories, either shared by L1 and L2 or unique to the L2, which came into being as a result of perceptual processes. Finally, perhaps the most interesting aspect of the model is that it predicts speech accents not only in bilinguals' L2 but also in their L1. More evidence to support this prediction will be presented in Chapter 7 (pp. 363–365).

The comprehensibility of accented L2 speech

Given the fact that speech accents abound in the L2 speech of many bilinguals and that traces of an accent may even be detectable in the L2 speech of highly fluent bilinguals, a question that presents itself is whether and to what extent an accent hampers listeners' comprehension, causing comprehension failures, delays in comprehension, or perhaps both. Munro and Derwing addressed this question in a series of studies in which English was always the bilinguals' L2 (Derwing & Munro, 1997; Munro & Derwing, 1994, 1995, 1999). In these studies degree of accent was determined by having native speakers of English

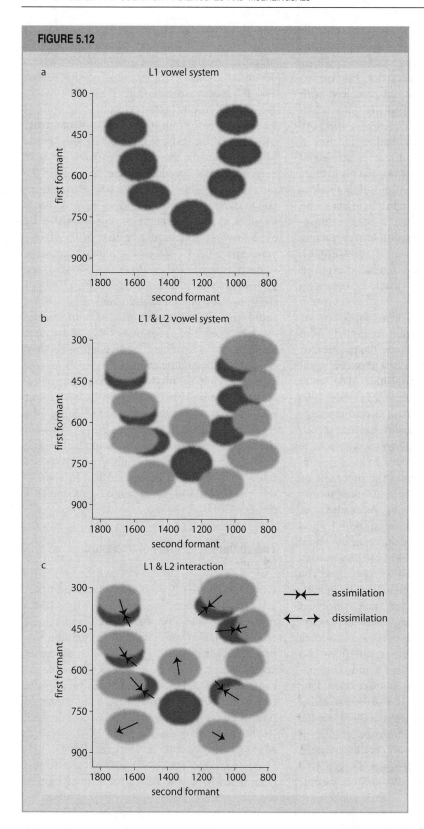

(a) An L2 learner's L1 vowel system at the onset of L2 acquisition. (b) The targeted L2 vowel system added onto the L1 vowel system. (c) The processes of assimilation and dissimilation that occur during L2 speech learning. Adapted from Flege (2005).

rate the speech of L2 English speakers on a 9-point scale. The scale varied between 1 (no foreign accent) to 9 (very strong foreign accent). Degree of comprehension was measured in two ways, by means of "comprehensibility" ratings and "intelligibility" scores of the L2 speech. The first of these concerned listeners' judgments on a 9-point scale varying between 1 (extremely easy to understand) and 9 (extremely difficult to understand). The second was a more objective measure which had been introduced earlier by Gass and Varonis (1984). It was based on the listeners' transcriptions of the L2 speakers' speech following an instruction to the listeners to do so as carefully and completely as possible. The intelligibility scores were derived from the deviations between the transcripts thus obtained and the intended utterances.

The L2 English speakers in these studies were from different language backgrounds: Mandarin, Cantonese, Japanese, Polish, and Spanish. Their task was either to describe the events depicted in a series of cartoons presented to them (Derwing & Munro, 1997; Munro & Derwing, 1999) or to read aloud a set of sentences that were either true (e.g., *Elephants are big animals*) or false (e.g., *Most people wear hats on their feet*; Munro & Derwing, 1995). Regarding the latter test, in addition to judging the degree of accent and comprehensibility, the listeners judged each sentence to be either true or false, and the time to perform this judgment was measured. These data were compared to the listeners' responses to the same set of sentences but spoken by native English speakers. In a fourth study (Munro & Derwing, 1994) the researchers had L2 speakers first perform the cartoon description task and, subsequently, had them read aloud the transcriptions of their own utterances. This was done to find out whether there are differences in accentedness between extemporaneous speech and read materials. No such differences were observed and I will therefore ignore this study in the ensuing discussion. A final question the researchers addressed was whether listeners can select the specific language background of an L2 speaker when given several options to choose from.

The most noteworthy result of these studies is that the accent ratings were generally considerably harsher than the comprehensibility ratings: Although accent did affect comprehensibility, in many cases material that was judged to be highly accented received a low score on the comprehensibility scale (indicating that the accent did not cause a comprehension problem). The discrepancy between the accent ratings and the intelligibility scores was even larger: Despite the fact that relatively few of the speakers' utterances were rated to be without an accent, in the far majority of cases the listeners' transcription of the speakers' utterances closely matched the targeted utterances, suggesting that most words were perfectly well understood. This pattern held for both proficient (Munro & Derwing, 1999) and intermediate (Derwing & Munro, 1997) L2 speakers. The study comparing the L1 English listeners' performance on the true–false sentence judgment task (Munro & Derwing, 1995) showed that the L1 English speakers' utterances were slightly more often verified correctly (98% correct) than the L2 speakers' utterances (93%). Furthermore, the former were verified somewhat faster than the latter.

These findings suggest that a foreign accent does incur a cost on the part of the listeners, both in terms of comprehensibility and in terms of processing time. These costs may be the source of the irritation that an L2 accent has been reported to cause in native speakers of the language (Munro & Derwing, 1995). However, the data also show that the adverse effects of accent on comprehensibility are generally quite small, and that many L2 speakers' utterances, despite being accented, are perfectly intelligible and do not hamper communication noticeably. Irritation therefore seems a rather disproportional reaction to the minor inconvenience an accent causes for the listener.

A final noticeable finding is that listeners performed well above chance in identifying the L2 speakers' L1 background in a forced choice task. Not surprisingly, the languages that are typologically relatively close to one another were mistaken for each other more often than typologically more distant languages: The two

Asian languages Cantonese and Japanese and the two Indo-European languages Spanish and Polish were more often confused with one another than the other language pairs that can be formed from this set of four languages (Derwing & Munro, 1997). These findings point towards the following two conclusions: (1) Even though it may appear that we, hearing a foreign language, are completely ignorant of the language, we must at least have picked up some knowledge about its phonology through past experience. How else could it be that the listeners in these experiments could often successfully detect an L2 speaker's L1 language background? (2) A bilingual's L1 phonetic system leaves its mark on L2 speech. This latter conclusion, of course, repeats the main conclusion drawn above, that L2 speech accents are caused by an interaction between the L1 and L2 phonetic systems, resulting in L2 phonemic categories that deviate from the corresponding categories in monolingual speakers.

SUMMARY

- Models of speech production can be classified in three categories: discrete two-stage models, unidirectional cascade models, and interactive activation models. Discrete two-stage models assume that activation can only flow in a forward direction from the lemma level to the lexeme level and that activation is not transmitted from the former to the latter until after one lemma has been selected from the initially activated set of lemmas, the "semantic cohort". Unidirectional cascade models also assume that activation only flows forward. In addition they assume that the moment a lemma becomes activated it immediately starts sending activation down to the lexeme level. As a result, all elements in the semantic cohort are temporarily phonologically encoded. Finally, like the unidirectional cascade models, the interactive activation models assume that all initially activated lemmas immediately pass on their activation to the corresponding lexemes. But unlike the unidirectional cascade models they assume that activation may also flow back from activated lexemes to the corresponding lemmas.

- Any bilingual speech production model should deal with the fact that languages differ in the way they lexicalize the conceptual information in the preverbal message: A particular subset of the preverbal message's conceptual components may be expressed in a single word in one language but may require a whole phrase to be expressed in another language. One solution that has been proposed is to add a so-called "verbalizer" to the model, a processing component that receives input from the preverbal message and carves it up in such a way that it matches the semantic information in the targeted lemmas.

- A second issue to explain by any model of bilingual speech production is how the selection of the currently intended language comes about. One way it can do this is by including a piece of information that specifies this intention (a "language cue") in the preverbal message and to include in each lemma a piece of semantic information that specifies to what language it belongs (a "language tag").

- Monolingual and bilingual models of speech production often zoom in on the lexicalization component of the full process; that is, on lexical access. These models usually include three levels of representations, representing preverbal concepts, lemmas, and the words' phonological forms ("lexemes"), respectively. Lemma and lexeme representations can be represented in a single memory node (that is, they can be of the "localist" type) or the information they contain can be spread out over multiple memory nodes ("distributed" or "componential" representations). Multiple lemma activation in models that assume localist lemma representations can be accounted for in terms of spreading activation in a lexical-semantic network.

- Recent speech production models no longer assume that lemma representations contain both semantic and syntactic information, but syntactic information only. According to most models of this type, activation in the phonological level is mediated by the syntactic information in the lemma. Caramazza's independent network model dismisses lemmas altogether.
- Monolingual picture–word interference experiments have shown that the aural presentation of semantic distracters slows down picture naming but only when the distracter coincides with the picture or precedes it. In addition these studies have shown that aural phonological distracters speed up picture naming but only when the picture is presented first. These semantic interference and phonological facilitation effects are attributed to the convergence of, respectively, semantic and phonological activation in the two types of processes involved in the picture–word interference task: top-down picture naming and bottom-up word processing.
- Bilingual studies using the picture–word interference task have suggested that at some point during picture naming in the weaker L2, the picture's translation in L1 is also activated. This finding indicates that word production in bilinguals is language-nonselective. It is however not clear whether only lemma selection or both lemma selection and phonological encoding are language-nonselective.
- According to a common view of language-nonselective lexical access in bilingual speech production, strongly activated lexical representations in the non-response language should hinder production. A couple of bilingual picture–word interference experiments proved this assumption wrong and led to a model of bilingual lexical access in which a stage of language-nonselective activation is followed by a stage of language-specific lexical selection.
- In picture naming by bilinguals a cognate facilitation effect is observed. This effect suggests that phonological encoding is language-nonselective, thus supporting cascaded models of bilingual speech production. The effect may however also result from representational differences between cognates and non-cognates.
- Conclusive evidence in support of language-nonselective lexical access in bilinguals requires that the participants in an experiment do not suspect that their bilingualism is being tested and that the stimulus materials are exclusively unilingual. Experiments that employed the bilingual version of the picture–word interference task do not fulfill these requirements.
- Whereas the picture-naming studies legitimate the conclusion that both lexeme activation and phonological encoding are language-nonselective, it is too early to tell whether grammatical processing is also language-nonselective.
- Bilingual Stroop studies have reliably produced both intra- and interlingual Stroop effects, and the size of these effects depended on the participants' relative proficiency in their two languages and on the degree of similarity of the languages. The effects are usually explained in terms of the degree of within- and between-language interconnectedness of the linguistic elements in bilingual memory.
- Careful task analysis reveals that word translation, Stroop color naming, and picture naming share many processing components.
- The cognate effect in word translation may be caused by (1) facilitated name retrieval due to language-nonselective phonological encoding that favors cognates over non-cognates, (2) representational differences between cognates and non-cognates, (3) relatively strong activation of the associated semantic nodes when a cognate is presented for translation.
- Performance in a large number of word production tasks such as monolingual and bilingual picture naming, monolingual and bilingual Stroop color naming, and word translation is based on activation patterns in one and the same underlying, layered, memory system augmented by a general control system that sees to it that the current goal is met (that is, that the requested task and not another one is performed).

- Word production, visual word recognition, and auditory word recognition may exploit one and the same underlying processing system with components that are either fully shared or highly interconnected between production and recognition and between the aural and visual modality.
- Onset age of L2 acquisition ("age of acquisition") and degree of L2 accentedness are linearly related: The younger the L2 speaker was when first starting to learn the L2, the more nativelike his or her L2 sounds. Despite popular wisdom, for various reasons this age of acquisition effect cannot be explained in terms of the existence of a critical period for language learning early in life. A further variable that determines degree of L2 accentedness is the extent to which the L2 speaker still speaks the L1.
- L2 speech accents can partly be explained in terms of the merger of L2 phonetic categories with extant L1 phonetic categories in a phonetic memory system shared by the L1 and L2: L2 sounds that closely resemble an L1 phonetic category in this system assimilate with this L1 category. A second cause of the L2 accent is a process of dissimilation, which applies to L2 sounds that differ strongly from all L1 sounds: They take a position in phonetic memory which exaggerates the actual physical distance between the new L2 sound and its closest L1 sound.
- The stronger the L1 phonetic categories in memory, the stronger their assimilative and dissimilative effects during L2 speech learning and, consequently, the stronger the L2 accent. The strength of the L1 phonetic categories depends on amount of previous L1 use. Therefore, the older the L2 speakers were when they first started learning the L2 and the more often they still use the L1, the stronger the L2 accent.
- Accented speech does affect its comprehensibility but this adverse effect is small, even in cases where the accent is a strong one.
- Listeners can detect the L1 background of L2 speakers. This is independent evidence of the influence of L1 phonetic categories on the L2 categories.

Language Control

INTRODUCTION AND PREVIEW

In the previous chapters we have seen that when bilinguals are conversing with their interlocutors in one of their languages the mental system that stores the other language is not completely at rest. In general a picture emerged of a bilingual linguistic system that is noisier than the language system of monolingual language users because, during both language comprehension and language production, linguistic elements of both linguistic subsystems are activated. Yet, when witnessing bilinguals partaking in conversations that are intended to be unilingual, it is obvious that they are quite successful at coping with this extra fierce mental rivalry. Generally, if a bilingual has selected one language for current use, his or her speech contains few intrusions of the non-selected language, and misunderstandings arising from mistaking an input for a word in the other language are rare. Apparently, some efficient mental control mechanism is at work that prevents such infelicities from hampering the conversation flow, a mechanism that enables the bilingual to mentally control the language of input and output. In addition to generally

guaranteeing language-pure comprehension and production in such "monolingual" circumstances (where a single language is selected for use), the mechanism involved must also enable language control in translation situations, where there is input in one language (usually called the **source language**) while output in the other language (the **target language**) must be produced. Here switching off one linguistic subsystem (if such were possible at all) is not a feasible option because the translation act requires the parallel involvement of both languages. Alternatively, rapid mental switching between the two linguistic subsystems must take place. In this chapter I will present a number of views on language control in bilinguals; that is, on how they manage to adapt their language use to the specific requirements of the current communicative context, selecting one of their two languages or using both languages in translation.

A prerequisite for language control is that language membership of individual lexical items (and of other types of linguistic knowledge structures) is built into the bilingual's language system. The system must somehow specify which ones of the stored units belong to the one linguistic subsystem and which ones belong to the other. A number of proposals as to how this is done have been advanced. According to one of them, the elements of each language are embedded in a separate network of strongly interconnected elements within bilingual memory, called a "subset". The connections between the units within a subset are formed by their co-occurrence in the environment and possibly by mental contiguity; that is, by their co-occurrence in thought. In other words, the representations of the linguistic units belonging to one particular language become strongly interconnected in bilingual memory because they co-occur in linguistic expressions and are encountered as such by the language user. A unit's embedding within one of these networks determines its language membership. The subset concept may be applied to a complete language system (e.g., Paradis, 1981, 2004) or to sub-components of the system such as a component that stores phonemes or one that stores the phonological forms of complete words (e.g., Grosjean, 1997a). A second proposal regarding the structural implementation of language membership posits the existence of two so-called "language nodes" within the memory system of a bilingual, one for each language (e.g., Dijkstra & Van Heuven, 1998, 2002). The form representations of all L1 words are connected to the L1 language node. The form representations of all L2 words are connected to the L2 language node. Language membership is determined by these connections between word form representations on the one hand and language nodes on the other. A third proposal (e.g., Green, 1998; Poulisse, 1997) is that the lemma representation of each word contains a "language tag", a piece of information that specifies that this particular lemma belongs to L1 or L2. These three proposals are not mutually exclusive, but more than one of them may be assumed within one and the same view on bilingual control.

The various views on bilingual language control that have been proposed can be distinguished from one another along four inter-related theoretical dimensions. The first of these concerns the *scope* of control; that is, whether control is exerted globally or locally. Global control means that all elements of one or both languages are affected by the control process at work. For instance, some control process may simultaneously activate all units of the targeted (selected) language and at the same time deactivate or inhibit all elements in the non-targeted (non-selected) language. Contrary to global control, local control exerts its effect on specific elements within the language system. The second dimension of control concerns the *direction* in which it operates, proactively or reactively. Proactive control (also called "early" control) is involved when, for instance, the intention to speak one language and not the other results in a preparatory setting of the system that increases the availability of the elements of the selected language through pre-activation, while perhaps at the same time decreasing the availability of the non-selected language, through deactivation or inhibition/suppression. This preparatory setting of the system subsequently influences performance on the language task to be executed. In contrast, reactive control (or "late" control) means that the control process operates on the imminent outputs of the language system, preventing elements of the non-response language from emerging in speech (in production) or preventing an input element from being assigned a meaning in the non-target language (in comprehension). The third dimension concerns the *locus* of control; that is, whether the control process exerts its effect on the language system proper or on the output of the language system. Finally, the fourth dimension concerns its *source*, internal ("endogenous") or external ("exogenous"): The control process may be set in motion by a stimulus presented to the system (exogenously), or it may result from the intention to speak one language and not the other or to perform some other language task such as translation. Different forms of control may cooperate to secure smooth processing so, for instance, control may at the same time be exerted globally by some proactive control process and locally by some reactive control process.

Following the usual Methods and Tasks section, this chapter presents a number of different views on bilingual language control in unilingual settings. Although not always using the above terminology, each of these views incorporates a specific set of assumptions regarding the above four dimensions of control. To avoid the risk of misrepresenting the original authors' views I will generally refrain from molding them in the present terminological framework. Nevertheless, to get a good grasp of the differences between the various theoretical stances, it helps to bear these four dimensions of control in mind while getting acquainted with these views. Following the sections dealing with control in unilingual settings, the final section of this chapter is dedicated entirely to language control in translation and, especially, simultaneous interpreting.

METHODS AND TASKS

Probably the most popular techniques for studying language control in bilinguals are the picture–word interference paradigm, the bilingual Stroop task, and the "language-switching paradigm". The former two have already been dealt with in Chapter 5. In the current chapter I will primarily focus on the **language-switching paradigm**. In studies using this paradigm the bilingual participants have to switch between their two languages, mostly at odd moments but sometimes in a regular pattern, the researcher trying to find out what happens in their minds during both non-switch and switch trials. The technique has been employed in both comprehension and production studies and in a number of different forms, the production studies often encompassing simple picture naming as the task to be performed by the participants. In the earliest language-switching studies (Kolers, 1966; Macnamara, 1967; Macnamara, Krauthammer, & Bolgar, 1968; Macnamara & Kushnir, 1971) a "blocked" design was used: Non-switch blocks in the comprehension studies showed materials in one of the participant's two languages only and non-switch blocks in production studies invited speech in just one language. In contrast, in the switch blocks of the comprehension studies mixed language materials were presented: With one of the languages often serving as base language, some of the words or phrases within a sentence or a text were in the other language. Similarly, in the switch blocks of the production studies participants had to switch between the languages on request. What language to use on a particular trial was signaled by a cue; for instance, a circle presented prior to a picture to name cued the use of one language and a triangle cued the use of the other language.

The blocked design is still being used occasionally, but in the majority of the more recent studies the switch and non-switch conditions were embedded within one and the same series of stimuli presented to the participants. Within comprehension studies of this type (e.g., Grainger & Beauvillain, 1987) two successive words from the same language constitute a non-switch trial and two successive words from different languages constitute a switch trial. Similarly in production studies (e.g., Meuter & Allport, 1999), two successive trials in a series may be cued for a response in the same language (non-switch) or for responses in different languages (switch). In the earliest comprehension studies (Kolers, 1966; Macnamara, 1967) the participants were presented with complete (unilingual and code-switched) sentences. Instead, the experimental materials in the later studies were generally smaller stimuli presented "out of context". In the comprehension studies these were often words and nonwords presented one by one, each requiring a lexical decision response. In the production studies they were usually sequences of digits or pictures to be named one after the other.

The critical dependent variable in all these studies was the time it took to switch between languages, the so-called "switch cost". In the seminal studies by Kolers and Macnamara and his colleagues the cost per switch was measured globally by, first, calculating the difference in overall response time for a mixed block on the one hand and a unilingual block on the other hand and, second, dividing this difference by the number of language switches in the mixed block. In the more recent studies (where the switch and non-switch conditions were encompassed within one and the same series of trials) the switch costs were measured locally, at the very point where the switches occurred. An advantage of measuring switch costs locally is that it enables a comparison of the costs incurred by a switch to L1 on the one hand and to L2 on the other hand. As we will see, a number of studies have shown that these switching costs are not equally large, and the observed directional difference in their size is one of the cornerstones of one of the theories of bilingual control to be reviewed in this chapter (pp. 307–313).

A problematic aspect of measuring switch costs is that they are confounded with "mixing costs": Studies on task switching—say between color naming or word reading in the classical color Stroop task—have shown that it not only takes longer to respond on a switch trial than on a non-switch trial (the switch cost) but that response times are also generally longer, even on non-switch trials when responding alternates between different tasks, than when the participants only perform one task. This effect is called the "mixing cost". A plausible reason is that in the mixing condition the participants must keep two tasks ready in working memory (Monsell, 2003). Especially because a substantial amount of evidence suggests that language switching is a specific form of task switching, exploiting the same cognitive machinery (see pp. 393–401 and 435–446), the occurrence of mixing costs is something to keep in mind when designing language-switching studies. A further experimental procedure, the "alternating-runs paradigm", has been used to avoid a possible confound between switching and mixing costs. In this paradigm the tasks alternate in a constant and predictable pattern every N trials (Monsell, 2003).

In a number of respects the language-switching studies characterized above do not constitute a veridical imitation of language switching in natural discourse. One obvious reason is the fact that most of these studies have examined language switching out of context; that is, on sequences of words that would never join together in naturalistic linguistic structures. Another reason is that the moment a language switch occurred, and the type of linguistic unit involved, were both determined by the researcher. Instead, in naturalistic bilingual speech production the bilingual speakers themselves—though

likely at least partly driven by the particularities of the communication setting—determine when to switch languages, and in naturalistic bilingual speech comprehension their interlocutors determine when to switch the input language (where "determines" should not be taken to mean that language switching always involves a conscious choice on the part of the speaker). The loci of experimenter-imposed and naturally occurring switches may not coincide, and an experimenter-imposed switch may involve a linguistic unit that under more natural circumstances might never involve a language switch. A switch imposed by the experimenter may impede processing—as the switch costs observed under those conditions show they do—whereas a switch that occurs naturally may not hamper the conversational flow or may even enhance conversational fluency.

For these reasons, some researchers (and especially François Grosjean; see pp. 288–291) have studied language switching in experimental settings that had the participants themselves determine when to switch languages. In these studies the frequency of occurrence of such participant-motivated switches was manipulated by varying the information the participants received regarding their (imaginary) addressees or by varying the context in which a conversation took place; for instance, formal versus informal. More detailed information on these studies, including their rationale, will be presented in due course, but a final note to make here is that naturally occurring switches may be of two types, intentional and non-intentional, the latter being inadvertent lapses into the other language. It has been suggested that non-intentional switches occur especially frequently at points where the two languages "meet" because of the use of a similar linguistic structure; for instance a grammatical structure shared by the two languages or a word with a cognate translation in the other language (e.g., Broersma & De Bot, 2006; Clyne, 1967).

Simultaneous interpreting, the main theme of the final section of this chapter, has primarily been tackled experimentally by identifying one or more components of the full task and then comparing the performance of professional interpreters on the one hand and ordinary bilinguals on the other hand on the component tasks (e.g., word retrieval, working memory, or input comprehension). Alternatively, the performance of ordinary bilinguals and professional interpreters on one or more component tasks is correlated with these same individuals' performance on the full task. Although other methods to study simultaneous interpreting are available (see Christoffels & De Groot, 2005, for a review), my focus will be on this componential approach. The underlying assumption is that mental control while performing this extremely complex task can be maximally secured when as many of its component parts as possible run automatically. The interpreter's limited conscious mental resources can then all be allocated to the task's components that defy automation, including a monitoring process that oversees performance and intervenes whenever a performance failure looms.

Common dependent variables in studies on simultaneous interpreting are reaction time measurements that reflect the speed with which knowledge is retrieved from memory, error scores, quality-of-performance measures, measures that reflect the participants' working memory capacity, and the so-called **ear–voice span** (EVS). The EVS is the time lag between the moment a source-language fragment is spoken by the speaker and the moment the equivalent of this fragment emerges in the interpreter's aural rendition of the source language. It is measured as the number of words or seconds between input and corresponding output and varies as a function of local interpreting difficulty and specific relationships that hold between the source and target language. For instance, sentences in the source language may typically have a subject-object-verb structure (as in German and Japanese) whereas sentences in the target language may generally have a subject-verb-object structure (as in English). Given this state of affairs the interpreter will often be forced to interrupt his or her rendition of the source language until the speaker has output the verb, in the meantime keeping the corresponding object phrase in working memory (e.g., Crystal, 1987;

Goldman-Eisler, 1972). These forced delays increase processing load and lengthen the EVS.

In recent research on language control in bilinguals the important new insight has emerged that this form of control is a manifestation of cognitive control in general, and that bilingual language control and other forms of cognitive control such as inhibiting contextually inappropriate actions or ignoring goal-irrelevant activation in the cognitive system are effected by the same cognitive equipment. What is more, the evidence suggests that bilinguals are often better than monolinguals on tasks that require these other forms of mental control. This evidence will be discussed in Chapter 7 (pp. 393–396) and information on the brain structures involved will be provided in Chapter 8 (pp. 435–446).

LANGUAGE CONTROL AS SWITCHING BETWEEN LANGUAGE SUBSETS

Introduction

The theoretical starting point of the earliest language-switching studies (Kolers, 1966; Macnamara, 1967; Macnamara et al., 1968; Macnamara & Kushnir, 1971) was the idea that bilinguals form stronger associations among the words within each of their languages, than between words across their languages, and that this is why they can keep their languages functionally separate or, in terms of Macnamara (1967), how they secure "linguistic independence". These authors thus adhere to the subset notion introduced earlier, and it is this notion that they set out to test by means of the language-switching methodology. Bilinguals in the switch conditions were assumed to go in and out of their language subsets upon each language change in linguistic input or output, selecting one language subset to process the current linguistic input or to produce the current output. Retreating from one language subset and accessing the other was assumed to require extra effort beyond the effort involved when no mental switch of language subset is required. From this, the authors predicted slower performance on switch trials than on non-switch trials. Two separate mental switching devices were assumed: an input switch and an output switch. The input and output switch were assumed to govern the selection of the appropriate language subset in speech comprehension and speech production, respectively.

Whereas going out of one language and entering the other was thought to require effort and thus extra processing time, subsequently staying in a language once switched to, was thought to be automatic and effort-free. Macnamara et al. (1968, p. 213) used the following vivid analogy to illustrate this point:

> Indeed, the whole study of bilingualism gives one the distinct impression that the bilingual's linguistic performance is similar to that of the musician who observes the notation for key at the beginning of a piece of music and then forgets about it though in his playing he performs the actions appropriate to the key. Similarly, the bilingual once started in one language can forget about which language he is speaking and yet obey the rules of that language.

As we shall see, some of the more recent related work appears to take a different stance, assuming that some control mechanism is incessantly monitoring the imminent output of the language system to see whether it might contain elements of the contextually inappropriate language and, if so, suppressing them. A further view expressed and put to a test in this early work was that the hypothesized input switch operates automatically whereas the hypothesized output switch was thought to be subject to voluntary control (Macnamara & Kushnir, 1971; Macnamara et al., 1968). This assumed difference between input switch and output switch was motivated by the fact that bilinguals can deliberately choose to speak one language rather than the other but have no control over the language of input. Recently, in a different theoretical framework, Costa and Santesteban (2004a) have made this very same point.

Other authors (e.g., Grainger, 1993; Grainger & Beauvillain, 1987) have subsequently interpreted Macnamara et al.'s view of language switching as going in and out of language subsets to imply that the language currently accessed is "switched on" (activated) and that the language not in use is "switched off" (deactivated). This implication is not stated explicitly in the original reports of Macnamara and his colleagues, although these authors do mention that other researchers before them *seem* to have proposed the switching device works by somehow switching one language off and the other on: "Penfield and Roberts (1959) described this device as a 'curiously effective automatic switch' which they seem to visualize as having the effect of when one language is on, the other is necessarily off" (Macnamara et al., 1968). There is, however, no a priori reason to assume that the "in-out" account of language switching implies that the elements of the language currently not accessed are "off", deactivated. Indeed, the latter assumption would be hard to reconcile with the plethora of studies, discussed in Chapters 4 and 5, demonstrating that the non-selected language is often co-activated with the language currently in use.

Another possibility, fully consistent with the in-out view of Macnamara and his colleagues, is that the elements of the language not in use can be activated but that this activation is ignored and may even go unnoticed. Such a state of affairs would be consistent with one of the views on bilingual control that has emerged in the recent literature (e.g., Costa et al., 1999; Costa & Santesteban, 2004b; see pp. 242–245 and 310–312). On that account, the device that Macnamara and his colleagues metaphorically called a "language switch" might well be some mental control mechanism that sees to it that whatever goes on in the non-targeted language subsystem is neglected. Viewed from this perspective, the studies of Macnamara and his co-workers appear surprisingly modern, both with respect to the methodology they used and the results they obtained. It is to a more detailed description of these studies that I will now turn.

Evidence

Macnamara (1967) and Macnamara et al. (1968) intended to examine output switching but because of the nature of the stimulus materials used in the first of these studies (triads of words) it was uncertain whether the switching mechanism at work had indeed been the hypothesized output switch, not the input switch, or both of them. The 1968 study prevented this possible confound by presenting language-neutral stimuli to the participants; namely, digits instead of words. For this reason I will confine myself to a discussion of this second study. It is also the most comprehensive study of the two, including a manipulation that allows for a test of the authors' hypothesis that output switching is subject to voluntary control. Furthermore it included a comparison between language switching and switching between two tasks that both involved the use of one and the same language. It is especially this latter comparison that gives Macnamara's work its modern flavor, because presumably the most topical question addressed in current research on bilingual control is whether or not the mechanism involved in language switching differs at all from the control mechanism involved in switching between other pairs of tasks that do not involve a language switch.

Macnamara et al. (1968) used a digit-naming task that in modified form has been adopted in more recent work on language switching (e.g., Finkbeiner, Almeida, Janssen, & Caramazza, 2006; Meuter & Allport, 1999). French–English participants named blocks of digits in their one language, in their other language, or switched between languages within a block of trials. In some of the mixed-language blocks the switches occurred on a regular basis and could therefore be anticipated. In other mixed blocks the switch patterns were irregular. If output switching is under voluntary control, switching costs should be relatively small in the former condition, so the authors reasoned, because a regular switching pattern makes it possible for the participants to predict a language switch. A null effect of this manipulation would suggest that the output

switch operates automatically. As mentioned, the authors also looked at the effect of switching between a pair of tasks performed in one and the same language. In this part of the study the participants either named all digits within a block (in one and the same language), added 1 to all digits presented within a block (e.g., if 2 appeared, the participant was to say 3; all responses again in the same language), or they switched, within one and the same block, between naming the presented digit or adding 1 onto it (again in one and the same language). This "digit-switching" condition was included to see whether there is something special about language switching or, in other words, to see whether such a thing as a language switch exists at all.

The data showed a longer average response time per digit-naming trial in the language-mixed blocks than in the unilingual blocks, thus confirming the prediction that switching languages takes time and, according to the authors, supporting the subset organization of bilingual memory. When the switch patterns were regular, average response time per trial was .21 seconds longer in language-mixed blocks. With irregular switch patterns, the difference between unilingual and mixed conditions was .39 seconds per switch trial. This difference between the regular and irregular language-switching conditions confirmed the authors' hypothesis that output switching is under deliberate control. Furthermore, the digit-switching condition produced costs that were surprisingly similar to the costs obtained with language switching: respectively .22 seconds and .39 seconds per switch in the regular and irregular conditions. The authors concluded that language switching "seems to require no psychological skill peculiar to bilingualism, but rather a skill which is equally applicable in a larger number of operations in which persons are asked to switch modes of response rapidly" (Macnamara et al., 1968, pp. 213–214). The authors refrain from elaborating on the wider theoretical implications of this result. If going out of one language subset and accessing the other is the source of the language-switching cost, as they assume, what equivalent explanation could account for the data in the digit-switching condition? What pair of memory subsets does the participant switch between in this particular case? And if the results are not specific to language control, exactly how do they inform the more general process of control involved? Whatever the answers to these questions, some related later work, performed in a different theoretical context, has also noted the similarity between language switching and switching between other pairs of tasks (e.g., Green, 1998; Hernandez et al., 2001; Meuter & Allport, 1999). This work as well as the theoretical implications of this observation will be discussed later on in this chapter and in Chapter 8.

Contrary to Macnamara et al. (1968), Macnamara and Kushnir (1971) studied the input switch, once again testing French–English bilinguals. Having verified that a cost of language switching also occurs in comprehension tasks (silent reading of unilingual or language-mixed texts and sentences) in two preliminary experiments, in two further experiments the authors set out to test their hypothesis that the input switch operates automatically. In one of these experiments the participants silently read blocks of sentences in which unilingual English sentences alternated with language-mixed sentences, and were asked to judge the truth or falsehood of each of the sentences (e.g., unilingual true: *turnips are vegetables*, language-mixed true: *turnips sont vegetables* versus unilingual false: *horses smoke potatoes*, language-mixed false: *horses smoke pommes de terre*). The crucial manipulation here was the pattern in which the unilingual English and mixed sentences alternated: fixed (English sentence, mixed sentence, English sentence, mixed sentence, etc.) or in random order. If the input switch operates automatically, no effect of this manipulation should occur and language switches in the language-mixed sentences should take equally long in the fixed and random conditions. The second experiment was a replication, except that the participants were now presented with spoken sentences. The authors reasoned that this modified procedure ensured that *input* switching was indeed being tested because in silent reading the possibility remains that the participants say

the words out loud to themselves. If so, the output switch might be implicated. They considered this much less likely with auditory presentation of the materials.

Once again, language switching took an observable amount of time in all experiments. In most cases language switching took around .20 to .30 seconds per switch, irrespective of whether the presentation was visual or aural. There was one clear exception: The fixed alternation condition resulted in a *longer* switch time (.43 seconds) than the random alternation condition (.33 seconds). If input switching were under voluntary control, the opposite pattern, a smaller switch cost in the fixed-alternation condition, should have been obtained. It is for this reason the authors interpreted their results as support for their view that input switching occurs automatically, perhaps brushing aside too lightly the curious result that no null effect but a reversed effect of the fixed–random alternation manipulation was obtained.

Further studies and evaluation

That switching the language of input or output incurs a cost has been replicated many times since the switching paradigm was first introduced by Macnamara and Kolers. That the effect is robust is therefore beyond all doubt, but what causes it has been disputed ever since these early studies were rediscovered and the questions they addressed were picked up again. In two studies on input switching, Grainger and Beauvillain (1987) and Soares and Grosjean (1984) were the first to challenge the interpretation of the switch cost in terms of a language switch. Grainger and Beauvillain, in a French–English study, used the visual lexical decision task introduced in Chapter 4 (p. 157). Soares and Grosjean presented unilingual or mixed spoken sentences to their Portuguese–English participants. The majority of the words in the mixed sentences belonged to the participants' one language (the "base" language) but some of them belonged to their other language (the "guest" language). The task used by the researchers was the "phoneme-triggered lexical decision task": On each trial the participants were presented with a sentence preceded by a particular phoneme and had to detect the stimulus (word or nonword) that began with this phoneme. Upon locating this stimulus in the speech input, they had to indicate as quickly as possible whether it was a word or a nonword. In both studies the switch cost was measured locally.

Thus employing different tasks, these researchers replicated the main finding of the early studies; namely, that language switching incurs a cost. As we have seen, this finding is consistent with the notion of some device that switches between language subsets. At first sight, a further finding of Grainger and Beauvillain (1987) seems problematic for this account of the switch cost: Unlike words with a language-nonspecific spelling pattern (that is, words that are orthographically legal in both languages), words with a language-specific spelling pattern (orthographically legal in one language only; for instance, English words containing the letter clusters *wh*, ck, or *ght*, or French words containing the letter sequences *eau*, *oie*, or *oux*) did not show the expected switch cost. According to the in-out account of language switching, a switch to the other language should *always* incur a cost, irrespective of the orthographic characteristics of the word presented on a switch trial. However, in a later study Thomas and Allport (2000) attributed this null effect to a missing control condition. With the missing condition reinstated, they obtained a switch cost for words with language-specific and language-nonspecific spelling patterns alike. The results of both studies thus appear to be consistent with the concept of a language switch, so why is it that these later authors rejected it? Grosjean appeared to be doing so because of the inconclusiveness of the origin of the switching cost: "It is not because bilinguals may, at times, process code switches more slowly than base-language words that researchers can conclude there is a language switch [. . .] involved in the processing; the delay could be due to numerous other factors" (Grosjean, 1997a, p. 250; see also Grosjean, 1988). The main reason for Grainger and Beauvillain (1987) to reject the

concept of a language switch is their assumption that it implies the language not in use is switched off, deactivated, or—in terms of the terminology used in Chapters 4 and 5—that bilingual word recognition is language-selective. But, as I pointed out above, this is not the essence of Macnamara's account of the switching cost, nor does it follow from it logically: The language not in use, whatever its state of activation, may be ignored one way or the other.

In later reports (Grainger, 1993; Grainger & Dijkstra, 1992), Grainger provided an account of the pattern of switch costs obtained in the 1987 study in terms of two models of bilingual word recognition that both assume that processing is initially language-nonselective. One of these is the BIA model introduced in Chapter 4 (pp. 177–181). Exactly how this model (and its successor BIA+) may account for the cost of language switching will be detailed later in this chapter. The second model, the bilingual activation verification model (BAV), assumes the existence of two lexicons, one for each language, with word representations in both of them responding to a word input. Following this initial activation, the activated nodes in one of the lexicons are first searched for a match with the input (in a so-called "verification" stage). If no match is obtained, the activated nodes in the other lexicon are searched through. The lexicon that resulted in a correct match on the previous trial is the one searched first, and this is the source of the switch cost: If the language of the current trial differs from the language of the previous trial, the search starts out in the wrong lexicon, resulting in a relatively slow response.

Soares and Grosjean (1984) chose a serial search explanation of their data similar to the one assumed in BAV but one embedded in language-mode theory to be presented in the next section. Language-mode theory distinguishes between a base language and a guest language. The base language is the contextually most appropriate language and, therefore, the currently most activated language. Whereas according to BAV the language of the previous trial determines which lexicon is searched first, Soares and Grosjean assumed that the base language lexicon is always consulted first. Only if this search fails to produce a match with the input, is the other language, the guest language, searched. The language switches that they examined in their mixed condition always concerned guest language words and the delay in recognition observed for these words were seen as support for this serial search view. Notice, however, that a stringent test of this particular serial search view requires that response times associated with switches from the guest language words back to the base language should also be measured. Soares and Grosjean's explanation of the switch costs predicts that in these cases no cost occurs.

It is noteworthy that both these accounts, in terms of BAV and language-mode theory, assume the existence of lexical subsets in bilingual memory, one for each language. These appear to be similar to, if not the same as, the language subsets that Macnamara and his colleagues hypothesized to exist and set out to test by means of the language-switching paradigm. Perhaps even more noteworthy is the earlier-mentioned conclusion drawn by Macnamara et al. (1968) that language switching does not require a special psychological skill but a skill that is also deployed in other situations where people have to switch between tasks. It thus seems that they never looked upon the language switch as some mental device developed through bilingualism and dedicated exclusively to language control in bilinguals. Yet it is as if the above (and present-day) critics of the language-switch concept have assigned it the more narrow meaning of such a specialized device. As the next sections will show, 40 years later both the subset view and the view of language switching as an instance of task switching in general feature prominently in theories on bilingual language control. A further central issue in contemporary theories on control is whether and to what extent the level of activation within the language subsets can be affected by sources external to the language system, such as the intention to speak one language and not the other. That language-external sources have this power is a central tenet in language-mode theory, the theory of language control in bilinguals to which I will now turn.

ACTIVATION AND DEACTIVATION OF THE LANGUAGE SUBSYSTEMS: THE BILINGUAL'S LANGUAGE MODES

Language-mode theory

Language users may find themselves in many different communicative settings. To name just a few: they may talk to a child, their partner, a friend, or to some official; they may take part in a formal or an informal conversation, comment upon the weather or discuss the opacity of a country's tax system. All these different settings invite the choice of a specific "register"; that is, the use of the specific vocabulary and grammatical constructions that fit the communicative context. For monolinguals the language of discourse in this multitude of communicative worlds will always be the one language they have mastered. But for bilinguals, especially those who are reasonably fluent in both of their languages, language is yet another source of variability. The specific characteristics of the communicative setting determine what language is being spoken, just as they determine the registers used by monolinguals. In addition, the properties of the communicative context appear to determine the incidence of code switches and the fluency of the bilingual's speech. François Grosjean launched the concept of the bilingual's "language modes" to account for the apparently systematic way the bilingual's speech responds to the environment and to changes therein. More specifically, and especially in his later work, he describes the various states of activation of the bilingual's language system that result from the prevailing circumstances and that, in their turn, command the language of output and affect the way speech and text is recognized (e.g., Grosjean, 1988, 1989, 1997a, 1997b, 2001; Soares & Grosjean, 1984). An important underlying assumption in his theory is that the bilingual's language system is organized in two subsets, one for each language, and that these subsets can be activated or deactivated as a whole and independently from one another.

In his early publications, Grosjean (1989, 1994, 1995) describes how bilinguals "find themselves at various points along a *situational* continuum" (Grosjean, 1994, p. 1657) (italics added) and how these different points induce different language modes (occasionally called "speech modes"). When talking to monolingual speakers of their one or other language, they inevitably restrict themselves to speaking this one language exclusively. This monolingual behavior is enabled by the "monolingual mode" they are in. At the other end of the situational continuum they are communicating with bilinguals with whom they share their two languages, happily mixing the two languages frequently. When this behavioral pattern occurs, the bilingual is said to be in a "bilingual mode". These two conditions are considered the end points of a continuum of modes, which also covers intermediate states.

In cognitive terms, the bilingual's monolingual behavior is enabled by a mental state, the monolingual mode, in which the language in use is maximally activated and the other language is deactivated as best as possible but, as stressed by Grosjean in various publications, with presumably always some residual activation remaining. In contrast, the bilingual mode concerns a mental state in which both languages are highly activated, but still to different levels. The reason the two are differentially active is that bilinguals always "choose" one of their two languages as the main language of the interaction. The choice of this language results in enhanced activation of the language subsystem in question. The currently chosen language is called the "base" (or "matrix", or "host") language or Language A. The other language is called the "guest" language or Language B. The behavioral effect of a monolingual-mode setting is the occurrence of relatively few switches to the other language, as well as relatively many hesitations at moments when the selected language lacks the means to express a particular conceptualized message easily. The behavioral effect of a bilingual-mode setting is more language mixing and more fluent speech.

The correlation between degree of language mixing and speech fluency just suggested (more switches and more fluent language use when

bilinguals operate in a bilingual mode) may strike the reader as inconsistent with the evidence presented earlier (pp. 285–287), where a language switch was always associated with a slowing down of processing. A way to resolve this apparent conflict is to consider the fact that Grosjean's theory primarily deals with language switching under natural circumstances, whereas the switches in the studies discussed earlier were produced in experimental situations that were a far cry from natural language use. In natural bilingual speech the speaker himself may govern language switching, presumably exploiting this option at points where the other language expresses the targeted concept most faithfully and when at the same time a switch to the other language does not involve the risk of a communicative breakdown (because the interlocutor is fluent in this other language as well); *not* to switch languages at that point (for instance, because it is not an option since the interlocutor is a monolingual) might actually slow down processing. Conversely, in the switching experiments discussed earlier the switches were experimenter-imposed and were arguably often enforced in unnatural places where there was no reason to switch in the first place. This might cause the slowing down of performance at the switch point, possibly through a system reset that is required at that point.

In Grosjean's later work (e.g., Grosjean, 1997a, 1997b, 1998, 2001) the focus shifted from the *situational* continuum that induces different mental language modes to a continuum of language modes itself and the correlated patterns of activation of the two language subsystems. In this later work Grosjean also emphasized that the language-mode concept encompasses two factors: (1) which of the two language repertoires is chosen as the base language, the language to use, in a particular setting, and (2) what the state of activation of each of the two languages is at a particular moment in time. Figure 6.1 represents these two dimensions of the concept on the vertical and horizontal axes, respectively. Three states are depicted. In all of them Language A is the base language, activated the most. The three states differ in the level of activation of Language B, the guest language. The latter is deactivated as

The language-mode continuum. The level of activation of Language A (the base language) and Language B (the guest language) is represented by the degree of darkness of the squares (black = maximally activated; white = inactive). The horizontal dimension represents the state of activation of a bilingual's two languages at a particular moment in time, the activation of Language B varying between nearly inactive and reasonably highly activated (but less so than Language A). From Grosjean (1997b). With kind permission by John Benjamins Publishing Company, Amsterdam/ Philadelphia.

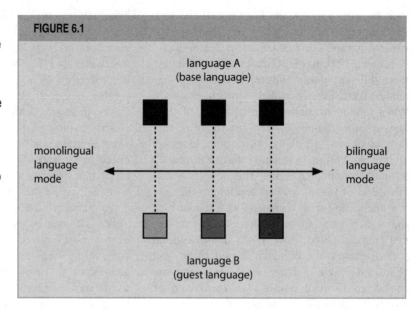

FIGURE 6.1

language A
(base language)

monolingual
language
mode

bilingual
language
mode

language B
(guest language)

best as possible on the monolingual side of the continuum and is gradually activated more when moving towards the bilingual side. In this later work some suggestions are also made as to how the language-mode concept could be extended to account for language use in speakers of more than two languages such as trilinguals (Grosjean, 2001) and in simultaneous interpreting (Grosjean, 1997b; see pp. 323–324). A final point to note here is that the choice of the base language (or the "intention" to speak one language and not the other) and taking position on the language-mode continuum presumably often do not involve deliberate, conscious decisions on the part of the interlocutors. Instead, they emerge automatically from the current circumstances, the interlocutors' knowledge thereof, and the nature of the input the interlocutors receive. Similarly, because language switching and how frequently it occurs is a consequence of the state of the mental system, it is quite plausible that language switching will more often come about automatically, rather than resulting from a conscious choice to switch. In other words, non-intentional switches plausibly outnumber intentional switches.

Earlier in this chapter I introduced four contrasts according to which theories on bilingual control can be distinguished from one another: proactive versus reactive control, global versus local control, internal (endogenous) versus external (exogenous) control, and whether the language system proper or the output from the language system is affected by the control process. Language-mode theory assumes that a base language is chosen prior to the onset of a discourse—a choice that determines the activation setting of the language system. This implies that bilinguals are assumed to control the use of their languages proactively. But in addition the theory states that during ongoing discourse the activation levels of the two language subsets are not rigidly fixed but fluctuate, depending on, for instance, the nature of the input or changed goals. So control is not exclusively governed by a proactive setting of the system, but "goes with the flow" as well. Regarding the second distinction, it is obvious the notion of global control is adhered to: The mode setting affects the level of activation of all elements within both language subsystems at the same time. With respect to the third contrast, it appears the theory assumes the occurrence of both external and internal control, because both the intention to speak a particular language (internal) and the type of input the system receives (external) exert an influence on the activation levels of the two language subsystems. Finally, the control processes exert their effect on the level of activation of the entities stored within the language system proper and not on the output from the system.

Although, as we will see, language-mode theory can account for the situational dependency of the number of code switches in, and the fluency of, bilingual speech, a problematic feature of the theory is that it contains some circularity in the reasoning on how relative activation of the language subsystems relates to the speech data: The bilingual, responding to the specifics of the communicative context, adopts a language mode that becomes reflected in the different activation states of the two language subsystems. This pattern of mental activation then leads to a particular speech pattern characterized by the degree of language switching that occurs and the degree of speech fluency. Finally, it is this speech pattern that then leads to the conclusion as to what mode the speaker is in; that is, what the relative level of activation of the two language subsystems is.

Evidence

In an experiment that copies natural communication rather veraciously, Grosjean (1997a) presented a convincing demonstration of the ability of bilinguals to adapt their speech to the specifics of the communicative setting. He presented French–English bilinguals, fluent in both languages, with stories in French and instructed them to summarize them in spoken French. One of the variables in this study was the (imaginary) person addressed. In one condition (French) the participants were told the person to address had just arrived in the United States, spoke only French at home, and, although he could read and write English, still had difficulties speaking it. In the second condition (Bilingual A) they were told the person addressed had lived in the United States for 7 years, worked for a French government agency teaching French, and only spoke French at home.

Finally, in a third condition (Bilingual B) they were informed the person to address had lived in the United States for 7 years working for a local firm, had French and American friends, and spoke both languages at home.

The second variable was the topic described by the French stories: They either concerned situations found in France or typical American activities. The stories in the latter condition (called "bilingual" stories) contained a number of code switches into American at places where a **code switch** might naturally occur (because guest language English but not base language French has a word that exactly expressed the concept to be verbalized). The dependent variables were the number of French and English syllables that were uttered in the summaries the participants came up with, and the number of hesitations they contained. Figure 6.2 shows, for the bilingual stories, the numbers for each of these three variables in the three different addressee conditions.

The participants clearly adjusted themselves to the addressee profiles provided by the experimenter. When they imagined addressing the "French" interlocutor, more French and fewer English syllables were uttered and more hesitations occurred than when Bilingual B was spoken to. Speaking to Bilingual A produced an intermediate pattern of results. These data suggest that the instructions had led the participants to believe that the French addressee was not yet fluent enough in English not to be impeded by their code switching into English, that Bilingual A was probably fluent in English but was a purist who didn't appreciate language switching, and that Bilingual B, also fluent in English, didn't mind code switching and presumably code switched a lot himself. Apparently, to maximize the communicative effect, the participants had adapted their speech to the bilingual profile of the person spoken to.

The differences between the addressees can also explain the variation in the number of hesitations across the conditions. As mentioned, the stories presented to the participants contained a number of English words because French was less suited to express the associated concepts. But apparently, bearing in mind the addressees' profiles, the participants in condition French, and

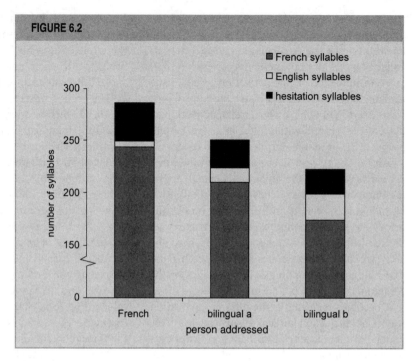

FIGURE 6.2

Number of French, English, and hesitation syllables as a function of the (imaginary) person addressed. The addressees in conditions French, Bilingual A, and Bilingual B differ in their command of French. From Grosjean (1997a).

to a lesser extent in condition Bilingual A, nevertheless attempted to express them in French. This caused the relatively large numbers of hesitations in these conditions as compared to condition Bilingual B, but presumably also the large variation in the number of French syllables across the conditions: Retelling the English code switches in French required rather elaborate, long-winded expressions. As a consequence, the overall number of French syllables was larger in condition French than in condition Bilingual A, and larger in the latter than in condition Bilingual B.

In terms of the language-mode continuum illustrated in Figure 6.1 these data suggest that when talking to the addressees French and Bilingual B the participants positioned themselves towards the monolingual and bilingual end of the continuum, respectively. When talking to Bilingual A they took an intermediate position on the continuum. The second manipulation (topic) provided additional support for this adaptability of bilingual speakers by showing that the bilingual stories produced about 10 times as many English syllables as the monolingual stories.

Similar results were obtained in a Turkish–German study by Treffers-Daller (1998) and a Dutch–French–English study by Dewaele (2001). Both studies involved a manipulation of the addressee and again showed that this variable affects the number of code switches and speech fluency. Dewaele (2001) added formality of the setting to the set of variables that bilingual/multilingual speakers adapt to in their speech. He tested Dutch L1 speakers who were learners of both French and English in a formal and an informal interview setting where French was the base language of the interviews. The informal setting involved a relaxed conversation between interviewer and participants about their hobbies, studies, and politics. The participants were told that the content of their speech was more important than the form. The formal condition concerned an oral exam that was to assess the participants' proficiency in French. Here it was stressed that the evaluation of the test depended on both speech content and speech form. The formality of the interview setting had a large impact on the number of code switches. On average, in the informal setting 9% of the utterances were mixed, whereas in the formal setting the number of mixed utterances dropped to 3%. These results are consistent with the language-mode hypothesis, suggesting that the participants in the formal interview setting operated more towards the monolingual end of the continuum than those in the informal setting.

Evaluation: An alternative account?

On the face of it all three studies discussed above provide convincing support for language-mode theory. Yet a remark by Dewaele (2001) triggers an alternative interpretation of the observed fluctuations in the number of code switches and hesitations, one that may turn out to provide a real challenge for the theory. Dewaele noted that a bilingual in a bilingual mode—where, according to the theory, both language subsystems are highly activated—might nevertheless produce few mixed utterances because a conscious output-monitoring process may prevent imminent language switches from actually emerging in the output. As we have seen in Chapter 5 (p. 224), a similar monitor (and plausibly the very same monitor) is also assumed to operate on internal speech during monolingual speech production thus preventing speech errors from popping out of the system (e.g., Levelt, 1989). But given the fact that the incidence of language switches is a major marker of the bilingual's current language mode, how can it be justified that this time this important marker is ignored and overruled; that this time the few switches that occur are not taken to indicate what they seem to indicate—that the person is operating in a monolingual mode? Whatever the answer to this question, introducing a monitor in a model of the bilingual speaker may be problematic for the theory as it is, because, instead of the relative activation levels of the base and guest languages, flexible behavior of the monitor may underlie the different numbers of code switches across conditions: Base and target language may, in theory, always be equally activated, but the monitor may operate in a strict or a more lenient way, depending on the characteristics of addressee and setting (see also De Groot, 2002). If this account were true, it would rip the heart out of language-mode theory in its present form. The claim that bilinguals respond to the specific characteristics of the communicative setting would not be challenged. However,

the view that the different speech patterns across settings are mediated by differential activation of the two language subsystems would lose ground. Further on (pp. 307–308) I will present a theory of bilingual control (e.g., Green, 1986, 1998) that encompasses a control mechanism that supervises processing and acts upon the imminent output of the bilingual language system, and which thus appears to bear more than a superficial resemblance to the monitor introduced here.

In fairness to language-mode theory, this data ambiguity—the fact that one and the same data set can be explained in more than one way—is by no means a unique feature of the work discussed here but is omnipresent in much of the related work and beyond. Indeed, the studies on language switching reviewed earlier in this chapter also produced data patterns consistent with more than one theoretical interpretation, and the sections to come will add yet further explanations of the switch data. This data equivocality partly reflects the limitations of the tasks and procedures available to the researcher. Regarding language-mode theory, the strongest evidence to support it would arguably involve first finding a means to locate the language subsets in the brain, and next finding out whether and how the activation in these brain areas would respond to manipulations of the type presented above. Unfortunately, even though over the past 20 years the tool kit of the neurocognition researcher has become enriched with impressive new techniques to spot and measure brain activation, these techniques may turn out to be unsuitable for the present purpose. The reason is that evidence is accumulating that the bilingual's two languages are stored in exactly the same brain areas (e.g., Fabbro, 1999; Hernandez et al., 2000; Klein, Milner, Zatorre, Meyer, & Evans, 1995; Paradis, 1990, 1997, 2000) so that identifying the activation levels associated with the different languages may not be possible. Evidence suggesting otherwise—namely, that the left hemisphere is the home of the native language whereas later languages are subserved, at least partly, by the right hemisphere (e.g., Kim, Relkin, Lee, & Hirsch, 1997)—can be accommodated with this view by assuming that the right hemisphere is primarily involved in coping strategies when a language is still underdeveloped. In other words, activation patterns in the brain that at first sight suggest distinct cortical localization of native and later languages may in fact result from the participants' unbalanced bilingualism and the need to use compensatory strategies while using the weaker language (e.g., Paradis, 1997; see also Chapter 8, pp. 427–435).

To summarize, various sources of evidence suggest that a bilingual adapts to the specific characteristics of the current communicative context such as its formality and the person being talked to. However it remains to be seen whether this adaptability concerns fluctuations in the degree of activation of the bilingual's two language subsets or fluctuations in the attentiveness of a mental monitor that watches over the output of the language system.

A NEUROLINGUISTIC THEORY OF BILINGUAL CONTROL

As we have seen, the central idea of language-mode theory is that bilinguals exert control by balancing the activation levels of the two language subsystems in such a way that they meet the goal of the current communicative setting. The activation levels of the two language subsystems can be set proactively and globally, simultaneously affecting all elements within both language subsets. Despite a difference in terminology, these ideas are very similar to those encompassed by a comprehensive neurolinguistic theory of bilingualism (and language processing in general) that Michel Paradis has developed over many years (e.g., 1994, 1997, 2001, 2004). As language-mode theory, Paradis's theory assumes language control in bilinguals to result from differential activation of the bilingual's two language subsystems that is triggered by the intention to speak one language and not the other. But in the presentation of their ideas, these scholars employ somewhat different emphases: Paradis is more explicit about the neural mechanisms involved in the differential setting of the subsystems and focuses more on what the consequence of language choice is for the activation level of individual lexical items rather than on the subsets as wholes. Grosjean's focus, instead, is on the way contextual factors affect the activation levels of the linguistic subsystems.

A central assumption in Paradis's theory is that a memory item (e.g., a stored word) becomes available for further processing when a sufficient number of positive neural impulses have reached its neural substrate. The amount of impulses that is required to reach this point constitutes the item's "activation threshold" (Paradis, 2004). It is assumed that activation thresholds vary with the frequency and recency of the item's use and, consequently, differ between items: Frequently used items have lower thresholds than infrequently used items, and recently used items have lower thresholds than items used longer ago. In other words, frequent items and recently used items require fewer neural impulses to reach their activation thresholds than infrequent items and items used further back in time. This proposal is functionally equivalent to a view on word recognition that we have already encountered in Chapter 4 pp. 177–181; e.g., Dijkstra & Van Heuven, 1998). There, fixed activation thresholds but different baseline levels of activation for frequent and infrequent words were assumed as well as a temporary increase in a word's baseline activation level after it has just been recognized. An item is selected if its activation exceeds the activation of all possible competitors. This is ensured not only by activating the target item with neural impulses but also by concurrently raising the activation thresholds of competing items, thus inhibiting them. A further assumption is that language production requires lower threshold settings than language comprehension. The reason is that in production the neural impulses to activate the relevant memory items must be generated within the system, whereas in comprehension they are excited by an external source; namely, the input that impinges on the eyes or ears. Generating the neural impulses within the system is thought to be a mentally more demanding process than having them aroused by external stimulation.

Like Grosjean, Paradis assumes that the

bilingual language system is organized in two subsets, networks of strongly interconnected elements. Additional assumptions are that both are part of a larger neurofunctional language system which is independent from a further system, a neurofunctional cognitive system. The two language subsets and the cognitive system combined are known as the "three-store" model. Each language subsystem stores the grammar of that language as well as the language's vocabulary and each individual lexical item is assumed to contain the word's lexical meaning, its syntactic constraints, its morphological characteristics, and its orthographic and phonologic forms. The conceptual system stores concepts in a language-independent way as a set of conceptual features onto which the words' lexical meaning map. These views on the content of lexical items and the existence of a separate language-independent cognitive system are similar to those advanced in Levelt's (1989) model of the monolingual speaker, in which a word's lexical meaning and syntactical specifications together constitute its lemma and its morphological and phonological properties constitute the word's lexeme (see pp. 224–226 for a more detailed account).

Paradis rejects the idea that language identity of a word is explicitly represented in the bilingual system by means of language tags (e.g., Green, 1998; Poulisse, 1997; Costa et al., 1999) or language nodes (e.g., Dijkstra & Van Heuven, 1998, 2002), considering such entities totally redundant. According to him, a word's position in one of the linguistic subsets and the unique mapping within this subset of the word's form to its lexical meaning, as well as the unique mapping of the latter to a subset of the conceptual features in the conceptual system, enable successful recognition and production, irrespective of the language identity of the word. These mappings are the product of past language experience. The fact that bilinguals can tell to what language each of the words in their vocabulary belongs is—so Paradis claims—a form of metalinguistic knowledge that is not represented in the language system proper.

The language subsets can be activated and inhibited independently of one another, globally and proactively, and this process is set into motion the moment one of the languages is selected for use. When a bilingual intends to use one of her languages, neural impulses are fed to the targeted language subset and, at the same time, the activation thresholds of all elements in the other subset are automatically raised, thus preventing interference from this language in production (although it may still be possible to comprehend input from the non-selected language, as a consequence of the relative ease to excite the neural substrate from external stimulation; see above). Paradis likens this process to the activation and inhibition of different sets of muscles when one raises one's arm, and claims the processes involved are a general property of all cerebral systems and subsystems (Paradis, 2004, p. 211). The intention to use one language and not the other—which triggers these processes of differential activation and threshold raising—is part of the conceptualized message in the non-linguistic cognitive system. Paradis's model shares this assumption with many other views on bilingual speech production (De Bot & Schreuder, 1993; La Heij, 2005; Poulisse & Bongaerts, 1994).

A special attraction of the activation threshold hypothesis (and of its sibling, language-mode theory) is that it, if complemented with a control mechanism, can explain a number of symptoms/recovery patterns of **bilingual aphasia** (Paradis, 1997, 2001, 2004; see also Green, 1986, 2002): **blending, selective recovery, sequential recovery,** and **differential recovery**. Blending (the inability to avoid switching between the languages; e.g., Fabbro, Skrap & Aglioti, 2000; Meuter, Humphreys, & Rumiati, 2002; Perecman, 1984) may be due to a control mechanism failing to keep the activation thresholds of the elements in the non-selected language high enough for these elements not to be selected inadvertently. Selective recovery (where there are lasting aphasic symptoms in one language) may result from permanent inhibition (too-high threshold settings) of one of the languages. Sequential recovery (where one language only begins to reappear after the other one has been restored) suggests temporary inhibition of one of the languages. Finally, differential recovery (where both languages are recovered in parallel but at different speeds) suggests greater inhibition of the one than the other language during the recovery process. In other words, all four types of aphasia may result from the corrupted workings of some control mechanism responsible for regulating the setting of activation thresholds, rather than to the content of one or both language subsystems being damaged. This idea that control failure rather than damaged linguistic knowledge may at times cause the bilingual aphasia is strengthened by the fact that the speech errors produced by non-aphasic people under stressful circumstances are similar to the errors produced in language pathology (Dornic, 1978): The stressful circumstances may deplete the available mental resources leaving too few of them to secure the impeccable operation of the control system. Similarly, non-aphasic bilinguals operating in a bilingual mode may at times exhibit the excessive language-mixing characteristic of the above "blending" type of bilingual aphasia (Grosjean, 1985).

As argued by Green (1986), a fifth type of bilingual aphasia first reported by Paradis, Goldblum, and Abidi (1982), "alternate antagonism" combined with "paradoxical translation", can also be accounted for in terms of a failing control system operating on a possibly intact language system. The Arabic–French aphasic patients in question manifested a rather bizarre form of linguistic behavior in which the availability of the two languages seemed to take turns. These patients alternated between relatively unobstructed spontaneous production of one of their languages accompanied by an inability to spontaneously produce the other, and the exact reverse pattern at some later point in time, say the next day or later the same day, while comprehension was always good in both languages. More curiously even, the language available for spontaneous production could not be translated into, whereas the language unavailable for spontaneous production could: When, say, French was available for spontaneous production, translation from French into Arabic was possible but translation from Arabic into French was not. Conversely, when Arabic was available for spontaneous production, Arabic could be translated

into French but translation from French into Arabic failed. An interpretation in terms of a damaged language system is implausible, because how then could each language be available at least some of the time? Green (1986) explained this puzzling linguistic behavior in terms of a control mechanism that fails to generate sufficient resources to activate relevant parts of the language system the moment they are needed and to simultaneously inhibit other parts.

In conclusion, the hypothesis that permanent or ephemeral failures of a language-independent control system underlie various forms of linguistic failure is a productive one that can account for pathological and non-pathological linguistic behavior alike.

THE EMERGENCE OF LANGUAGE SUBSETS

It should be clear by now that many theorists adhere to the notion of language subsets to account for the fact that bilinguals are rather successful in keeping their languages separate. The subset/subsystem notion is a core concept in the views on bilingual control presented in this chapter so far. In a number of places I have briefly hinted at how these subsets may come into being: by co-occurrence in past linguistic experience of the elements of one and the same language such as the contiguity between different words in the sentences we encounter, between word forms and their meanings, between lexical meanings and the conceptual information in a language-neutral conceptual system onto which the lexical meanings map (if such difference between lexical and conceptual meaning exists at all; see pp. 234–236). The consequence of co-occurrence is interconnectedness of the memory units ("nodes") that represent the co-occurring entities. The more frequently they occur together, the stronger the connections. And because, of course, the language units of one and the same language are encountered in contiguity more frequently than language units that belong to different languages (which may co-occur at code switch points and during translation), the within-language memory connections get stronger than the between-language connections and the two languages become insulated from one another, encapsulated.

The underlying process that creates these bonds between memory nodes is their co-activation, a process that Hernandez, Li, and MacWhinney (2005) call **resonance**: According to a learning principle called **Hebbian learning**, co-activated memory nodes get linked up with one another (what "fires together, wires together", as the maxim goes; see Murre, 2005, for an overview of this and other learning principles that may drive first and second language acquisition, as it drives learning in other domains), and the more often nodes fire together, the stronger the bond between them becomes. When a link between nodes has first been established by co-occurrence, further strengthening occurs when an input corresponding to one of these nodes is presented to the system: As a consequence of spreading activation along the links that connect the activated node with other nodes, the latter are also activated, all resonating with the activation-sending node and all getting more strongly connected with the former and each other as a consequence of this. The ultimate result of frequent co-activation of the nodes representing the elements of one language is widespread resonance within a language system once it has been selected for use. As a result of this state the language user is "caught" within the language, a state that Hernandez and his colleagues call "entrenchment". Because in this state the elements (e.g., words, phonemes, meanings) of the language in use are much more activated than those of the non-selected language, the former are much more available and, therefore, other-language intrusions only occur infrequently.

On p. 284 I cited Macnamara et al. (1968), who likened the bilingual to a musician who, after observing the notation for a key at the beginning of a piece of music, performs the piece in the appropriate key effortlessly and automatically, completely forgetting about the key the piece is meant to be played in. It appears the analogous case of the bilingual who has no trouble staying in one language once having accessed it is enabled by this process of entrenchment through wide-spread resonance in the language subsystem. The corollary of being stuck within one language is a cost when external circumstances enforce a switch into another language, as happens when an experimenter imposes one. It should be obvious by now that entrenchment does not imply the non-selected language subsystem is totally deactivated, but that whatever activation is going on over there does not cause any serious trouble because it is outweighed by the much larger activation of the selected language, or because activation in the non-selected subsystem is ignored.

Hernandez and his associates (2005) explain why early simultaneous bilinguals in particular are likely to develop a strong firewall between the two language subsets in this way, without denying that late bilinguals may also develop a state of functional language independence not only for their L1 but also their L2. A hint of evidence supporting this suggestion was provided by Linck, Kroll, and Sunderman (2009) in a study that at the same time indicates that immersion learning promotes the emergence of L2 language independence. These researchers compared two groups of American-English learners of Spanish on their performance on a language fluency task. The groups had had between four and six semesters of training in Spanish and were matched as closely as possible on self-rated proficiency in Spanish and a number of other variables. The crucial difference between them was that one group had acquired Spanish in a Spanish immersion environment and was tested in this environment, whereas the other group had acquired it in a classroom setting and was tested in the L1 English environment.

In the fluency task the participants were presented with a series of category names (e.g., *clothing, furniture*) and were asked to generate as many exemplars as possible to each category name within 30 seconds (e.g., *dress, skirt, trousers, sock . . .*). Both an L1 English and an L2 Spanish condition were included. The finding of special interest here was that in the L2 Spanish condition the immersed learners generated more exemplar names within this same unit time than the classroom learners did, whereas the opposite result emerged when L1 English was invited. The higher scores for the immersion participants performing in L2 suggest that they had developed, likely through resonance, stronger links between L2 words than the classroom participants. Linck and her colleagues suggested the smaller scores when performing in their L1 were due to them inhibiting their L1 in the immersion context. An alternative explanation is that there was no active inhibition of the L1 but that it was simply less available as a result of its less-frequent current use and the consequence this has for the average L1 word's most recent use (that is, it might be a recency effect). In fact, this account receives support from the further finding that, returned to their L1 environment a couple of months later, the immersed group's fluency in L2 Spanish remained superior to that of the classroom group while their L1 English fluency was equally as good as the classroom learners' L1 fluency.

More anecdotally, while I spent a week in France recently I was appalled to discover that the country's national language with which I was once reasonably familiar was completely unavailable to me, while at the same time I was aware I had not lost it (see pp. 347–351). What appeared to be happening was that I was kept hostage by my rather weak Italian, a language I had been immersed in not long before for a couple of months while working on this book. Whenever a foreign language escaped from my mouth, it was always Italian not French, and even attempts at mediation by my native Dutch could not set me free. It was as if my Italian immersion experience had created the beginning of a functional subset that, once caught in it, frustrated my attempts to access French. That it was Italian—not my native Dutch or any other of the languages I have some knowledge of—that I was entrenched in may be a manifestation of both the foreign language effect and the typological distance effect to be discussed in Chapter 7 (pp. 343–346). What the experience also illustrates is the importance of maintaining a language for it to remain available for use.

But there is also more formal evidence to support the existence of language subsets and how they come into being, in the form of two connectionist learning models that have both shown that language subsets develop from bilingual language input: the bilingual simple recurrent network (BSRN; French, 1998; French & Jacquet, 2004) and SOMBIP, the self-organizing model of bilingual processing (Li & Farkas, 2002). In Chapter 4 two other connectionist models were presented, one that accounts for visual word recognition in bilinguals (BIA) and a second that models the recognition of spoken words in bilinguals (BIMOLA). Both of these models are "localist" connectionist models in which the represented entities such as words and phonemes are each represented by a single processing node in the network (see p. 132 for details) and neither model was designed to explain how learning comes about. Instead, they represent a fixed state of a hypothetical bilingual at one particular level of L2 proficiency. In modeling this state, all the representations ("nodes") in the system, their baseline activation levels and activation thresholds, and the inhibitory and excitatory connections between them, must be set by hand. Modeling two different levels of proficiency would require performing this handiwork twice, once for each level of proficiency.

In contrast to these stationary models, connectionist learning models simulate the emergence of the representations and their subsequent evolution with increased language experience. Both BSRN and SOMBIP learn by computing statistical regularities in input sentences. BSRN received as input simple artificial French and English noun-verb-noun sequences that were generated by a "language generator". SOMBIP was presented with realistic child-directed speech produced by an English-speaking father and a Cantonese-speaking mother who followed the one-parent/one-language principle when addressing their child.

BSRN's architecture is based on Elman's (1990) simple recurrent (SRN) model, which concerns a "distributed" connectionist network; that is, a network in which the represented entities such as words and phonemes are each stored not in a single processing node (as in "localist" models) but distributed across many different

FIGURE 6.3

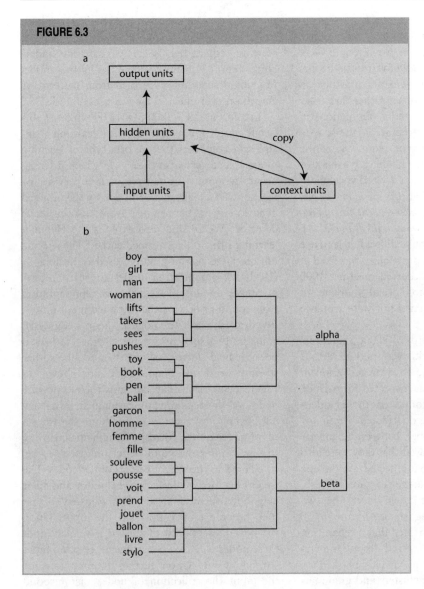

(a) A simple recurrent network (SRN) model consisting of three layers of nodes and a set of context nodes. The latter enable the model to retain a previous internal state of the model. (b) The clustering by language and grammatical class that emerged after the model was fed with a large number of French and English three-word sentences that were constructed from one French and one English mini-lexicon. Each mini-lexicon consisted of four subject nouns, four verbs, and four object nouns. Reprinted from French and Jacquet (2004), Copyright 2004, with permission from Elsevier.

processing nodes (see Chapter 3, p. 133 and Figures 3.8 and 3.11b). Figure 6.3a provides an illustration of the structure of the network.

The system consists of three layers of nodes: a layer of input nodes (24 in all), a layer of hidden nodes (32 in all), and a layer of output nodes (24 in all). In addition there is a set of context nodes (in SRN called a "buffer"), the inclusion of which allows these models to retain a previous internal state of the model. Memorizing a prior state is a prerequisite for regularities in the input presented to the model to be detected and, thus,

a prerequisite for learning simple grammar (see e.g., Murre, 2005, for details). Retention of the prior material is effectuated by copying the state of activation in the hidden nodes into the buffer after each learning cycle. BSRN processes a continuous stream of sentences one word at the time and its task is to predict every next word. The input sentences were all constructed from 24 words: 12 French words and their 12 English translations. Each mini-lexicon consisted of four subject nouns (English: *boy, girl, man, woman*; French: *garçon, fille, homme, femme*), four verbs

(English: *lifts, takes, sees, pushes*; French: *souleve, prend, voit, pousse*), and four object nouns (English: *toy, ball, book, pen*; French: *jouet, ballon, livre, stylo*). French (1998) stressed the fact that these words carried no semantic information and that he could have chosen other, arbitrary symbols for the purposes of his simulation (in other words, the ensuing structure of the lexicon to be discussed next did not require semantic input to be built). The language generator combined elements from this 24-word vocabulary into legal sentences (e.g., *boy lifts toy man sees pen man takes book femme souleve stylo fille prend stylo femme pousse ballon woman takes book . . .*). Language switching was only allowed at sentence boundaries and switching probability was fixed at 0.001; that is, switching occurred once per 1000 sentences. There were no special markers to indicate a switch of languages nor were sentence boundaries marked.

A total of 300,000 words (100,000 sentences) were fed into the model this way, and at various points during training the state of activation in the hidden-layer nodes was inspected for each of the words. French (1998) found that these hidden-layer representations were distributed over many nodes and highly overlapped between languages. But a cluster analysis showed that they were also clustered into clear sets that reflected, on the one hand, the grammatical categories subject, verb, and object, and, on the other hand, the two languages French and English (see Figure 6.3b). The latter finding demonstrated that a separation in language subsets had emerged despite the fact that the input had not been explicitly marked for language. These language clusters and grammatical clusters were already stable after the presentation of 60,000 words (20,000 sentences). This pattern of results was replicated in a further study wherein the lexicons contained 768 words each (instead of 12) and the number of nodes in the layers of input, hidden, and output nodes was increased (to 48, 100, and 48, respectively). After the presentation of 30,000 sentences the languages separated out again. These simulations with BSRN thus support the view, propagated by Paradis and Grosjean, that no language tags or language nodes are required for language

separation to be successful. A further point to stress here is that language separation does not seem to require the use of two separate underlying neural substrates, because in the model functional separation emerged from patterns of activation over one and the same set of nodes.

Li and Farkas' (2002) SOMBIP exploits a different architecture and different learning principles. It combines the use of a type of learning model called "unsupervised"—in which learning occurs without an analogue of a supervisor or teacher who provides information on the targeted behavior—with the use of a word co-occurrence detector (WCD) and also exploits the Hebbian learning principle mentioned earlier. The specific unsupervised learning model used is Kohonen's (1982) self-organization model (SOM) that self-organizes an input, extracting a representation from it and projecting the extracted input onto a two-dimensional topological map. SOMBIP contains two such maps, one storing the lexical phonological forms of words and the other storing word meanings. They are shown in Figure 6.4a. Each map contains a collection of nodes. At the beginning of learning, an input, say a lexical phonological form, randomly activates a set of nodes on the corresponding map according to how similar the input pattern happens to be, by chance, to the weight vectors of the nodes. The weight vectors of the activated nodes and their neighbors on the map are then adjusted so that they become more similar to the input. Upon the next presentation of this or a similar input these nodes will, as a consequence, respond more strongly to it. Upon further presentations of the input the collection of nodes that respond will gradually become smaller up until the moment the input gives rise to a very high level of activation in just a few neighboring units. This set is the ultimate representation of the input stimulus.

The phonological forms that were fed into the lexical phonological map were the lexical phonological forms of the 400 most frequent words in the Chinese–English child corpus mentioned above, consisting of 184 Chinese words and 216 English words, together covering 56% of all word tokens in the corpus. The corresponding meanings

FIGURE 6.4

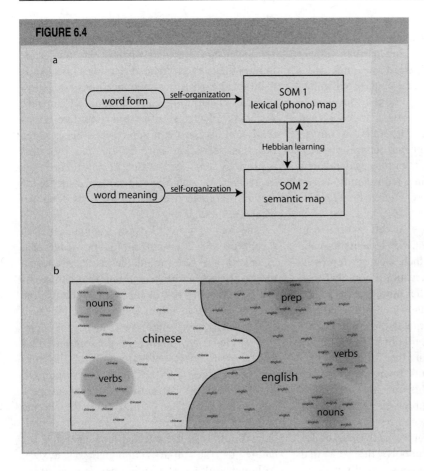

(a) Two self-organizing maps, storing the lexical phonological forms of words (SOM 1) and word meanings (SOM 2), respectively. The stored representations are extracted from phonological word forms and word meanings presented during training. (b) The organization in SOM 2 after training. Chinese and English representations are clustered in different areas on the map. Similarly, words of different grammatical classes are clustered in different areas. Adapted from Li and Farkas (2002), Copyright Elsevier 2002.

that were fed into the semantic map were not readily available but had to be derived first by running the whole corpus through the WCD one by one. For each word, the WCD computed with which other words it co-occurred and how often, only considering the 400 target words and ignoring all other words. The result of this computation for each word was regarded as the word's meaning (notice that this amounts to a definition of what constitutes a word's meaning that may not be shared by everyone). Finally, when WCD had done its job of extracting word meanings for the 400-item vocabulary, the process of self-organization on the phonological and semantic maps could start. Hebbian associative learning ("what fires together, wires together") was ensured by presenting each phonological form and its associated meaning to the corresponding maps simultaneously.

Figure 6.4b shows the organization in SOM 2, the semantic map, after the network had been trained on the 400-word vocabulary. As can be seen, the Chinese and English representations on the map were not randomly intermingled but are clustered in different areas on the map. In other words, despite the fact that the material that was fed into the WCD and the self-organizing maps did not contain any explicit information about the language every single word belonged to, two language subsets had emerged (but see Thomas & Van Heuven, 2005, who argue that explicit language membership information was provided to the system after all). Furthermore, the words within the separate lexicons were clustered in grammatical categories, and (not shown) within a grammatical category words with similar meanings also tended to be grouped together. These results all suggest that categories may emerge from statistical learning (see Chapter 2 for evidence from infant studies). A final note to make here is that Li and Farkas adhere to the view that lexical word meaning exists separately from more general conceptual knowledge (see Chapter 5, p. 234) and that the clusters that emerged on the semantic map concerned lexical-semantic meaning. This offers a way to reconcile the clear language separation that emerged in this map with the rather general view that in bilinguals meaning representations are largely (but not exclusively) shared between the two languages.

To summarize, language subsets emerge from the co-occurrence of linguistic elements and the ensuing co-activation of their memory representations, the co-activation creating a bond between these representations. The more frequent the co-occurrence of particular linguistic elements and, hence, the more frequent the co-activation of their memory representations, the stronger the connections between the latter become. Connectionist models of bilingual language acquisition that exploit this learning mechanism have shown language subsets to emerge even though the words and sentences that were fed into these models were not explicitly marked for language. This finding supports the view that the bilingual language system can do without language tags or language nodes or any other piece of information that explicitly states the language identity of a linguistic entity.

LANGUAGE CONTROL IN A LANGUAGE-NONSELECTIVE ACTIVATION FRAMEWORK

Introduction

So far, three views on bilingual language control have been presented and in all of them the notion of language subsets played a crucial role. The early language-switching work of Macnamara and colleagues (pp. 283–286) assumed that bilinguals go in and out of their language subsystems upon each language switch. Later authors have taken this account to imply that

bilinguals can switch their languages on and off, and that an "in" state implies the elements in the subsystem are activated whereas an "out" state implies they are deactivated. However, as already mentioned earlier, this inference does not follow imperatively from the in-out account of language switching: Elements in the subsystem that is currently not accessed can nevertheless be activated but this activation may be ignored by some control system. An in-out account can thus be reconciled with the substantial evidence of language-nonselective activation reviewed in Chapters 4 and 5.

The second view, Grosjean's language-mode theory (pp. 288–291), explicitly acknowledges that there is always some minimal level of activation in the non-selected subsystem but that bilinguals can nevertheless control the output because the level of activation differs between the two subsystems: The more highly activated subsystem, the selected one, dominates the output. This difference in degree of activation of the subsystems emerges from both top-down (internal, endogenous) and bottom-up (external, exogenous) sources; in other words, from the specific intention of the speaker (e.g., to produce unilingual output in the selected language) and the nature of the input (unilingual or mixed). Although a different terminology is used, these views are very similar to those assumed by Paradis in his neurolinguistic theory of bilingual control (pp. 294–296). In that theory language choice results in differential activation-threshold settings within the two language subsets, a process that is functionally equivalent to activating one subsystem while at the same time deactivating or inhibiting the other.

Whereas the most central idea in Grosjean's and Paradis's conceptions of language control is that language choice induces, proactively and globally, differential levels of activation in the two linguistic subsets, the two views on control that I will present here both stress that bilingual language processing is basically language-nonselective. This means that the representations in both language systems may be highly activated, at least during the initial stages of processing. One of these views accounts for language control in visual word recognition, the other for control in word production. The subset notion is not a central concept in either of these two views although, as we shall see, in one of them it appears to slip in after all, but in disguise. It concerns the bilingual interactive activation model introduced earlier in another context (Dijkstra & Van Heuven, 1998; Grainger, 1993; Grainger & Dijkstra, 1992). To account for language control, the model assumes the existence of two language nodes, one for each language. The second of the two views to be presented here assumes that language control in word production can be secured if the conceptualized message contains a language cue. As a result, the words that are output by the system will generally be ones belonging to the targeted language.

Language control in bilingual visual word recognition

In Chapter 4 (pp. 177–179) I described the details of BIA's architecture and the way the model processes a visual word that is presented to it (see also Figure 4.4). I will not repeat that exercise here. It suffices to say that a word stimulus activates, via two levels of feature and letter nodes, orthographic word nodes that represent words of both languages. How then, with all this language-nonselective activation going on in the word recognition system, is the input word ultimately recognized correctly and, specifically, how does the model account for the processing cost caused by experimenter-imposed language switches? It is here that the language nodes are brought into play. These two nodes, one for each language, are connected by means of an excitatory link to each of the orthographic word nodes of the corresponding language. Furthermore, each of them is connected by means of an inhibitory link to all orthographic word nodes of the other language (see Figure 4.4). It was mentioned above that BIA encompasses a language subset organization in disguise. It is this language-specific linkage between orthographic word nodes on the one hand and language nodes on the other hand that provided the ground for that claim.

As a result of this interconnectedness between word nodes and language nodes the latter operate as "language filters" that modulate activity of the word nodes in the word recognition system, as follows: An activated word node sends on activation to the corresponding language node, boosting the latter's activation. In turn, this language node will then send inhibitory feedback to all the word nodes of the other language, deactivating the latter. Therefore, if the language of the word presented on the current trial is different from the language of the previous word, the level of activation in the word node representing the current word is relatively low and this slows down its recognition. This accounts for the cost of language switching. Conversely, if the language of previous and current word is the same one, the word node representing the currently presented word is on average more highly activated than any competing word nodes in the non-target language and this secures language control.

In addition to this bottom-up, stimulus-driven language node activation, Dijkstra and Van Heuven (1998) assumed that the activation of the language nodes can also be influenced top-down by non-linguistic contextual sources of information from outside the word recognition system such as, in an experimental setting, the specific instructions given to the participants or, in a natural context, specific knowledge about the interlocutors. This top-down modulation of language node excitation then again affects the activation of nodes within the word recognition system. In this respect BIA resembles the views on control encompassed in Grosjean's language-mode theory and in Paradis's neurolinguistic theory, where language choice resulted in a differential setting of the activation levels of the representations in the selected and non-selected language. What is new is the assumption that this differential setting is mediated by language nodes, constructs that do not exist in Grosjean's language-mode theory or in Paradis' activation threshold hypothesis. The implication of allowing language node activation and, as a consequence, activation of nodes within the word recognition system, to be influenced by top-down processes is that word recognition according to BIA is not rigorously language-nonselective after all.

Whereas the above account attributes the cost of language switching to a process of inhibition within the word recognition system, more recently several authors have put forward the view that the switching costs arise from processes *outside* the mental lexicon (Green, 1998; Thomas & Allport, 2000; Von Studnitz & Green, 1997, 2002a, 2002b). To perform a particular task, a control structure (also called a "task schema") has to be set up that links outputs from a system, here the word recognition system, with the response required by the task. These task schemas may either be retrieved from long-term memory or set up anew the moment they are needed. Two such schemas are the so-called "language task schemas", each of which is operative when material in the language in question is processed. In this scenario the switch cost does not result from inhibition of the targeted representation within the lexicon, but from the inhibition of the language task schema that is currently called for. In other words, the switch cost reflects the time it takes for the currently appropriate task schema to be recovered from inhibition (Thomas & Allport, 2000).

The adherents of this alternative view come up with various sources of evidence, direct and indirect, to suggest that switch costs indeed arise from inhibition of a specific task schema and not from inhibition of a specific node within the word recognition system. One is the finding that switch costs do not reliably occur in all situations where one would predict them to emerge if the within-lexicon account were true. For instance, Caramazza and Brones (1979) did not obtain a switch cost in a semantic categorization task in which Spanish–English participants were presented with word pairs each consisting of a category name and the name of an exemplar of this or another category. Their task was to decide as quickly as possible for each pair whether or not the instance belonged to the category. Categorization took equally long when the words in a pair belonged to the same language or to different languages. Lexical access is a prerequisite for meaning assignment, and meaning assignment is a prerequisite for performance in the semantic categorization task. For this reason, the absence of a cost of language switching cannot easily be reconciled (if at all) with a view that assumes the lexicon is the locus of the switch costs: Delayed lexical access on the switch trial should have resulted in delayed meaning assignment and, therefore, in delayed semantic categorization. Other evidence is that the magnitude of the costs varies with the specific requirements of the task (e.g., Von Studnitz & Green, 1997) and that test circumstances can be created in which language switching incurs a benefit rather than a cost (Thomas & Allport, 2000; Von Studnitz & Green, 2002b).

Dijkstra and Van Heuven (2002) developed a successor of BIA, BIA+, which acknowledges that language switch costs have a lexicon-external locus. This version of the model still contains the language nodes, but the inhibitory connections from the language nodes to the word nodes of the other language have been removed. As a consequence, language nodes no longer suppress activation in word nodes of the other language and, therefore, word recognition is now strictly language-nonselective initially. The only remaining function of the language nodes is that they serve as language tags. To account for the language switch costs and a number of other effects, such as the fact that the direction of interlexical homograph effects varies with the specific demands of the task (see Chapter 4, p. 168) and the effects of non-linguistic contextual information and participant strategies, Dijkstra and Van Heuven added a task/decision system onto the original BIA word identification system. As a result, BIA+ has come to strongly resemble Green's (1986, 1998) model of "inhibitory control", the model of bilingual control that I will turn to further on.

Language control in bilingual word production

La Heij (2005) presented a view on language control in bilingual word production that builds on earlier work by De Bot and Schreuder (1993) and De Bot (1992; see p. 228) and on extensions of that work by Poulisse (1997) and Poulisse and Bongaerts (1994). In developing his ideas he took as starting point the common assumption that the word corresponding to the most highly activated lexical representation will ultimately be selected and output by the system. In his specific solution of the control problem La Heij drew an analogy between, on the one hand, the state of mind monolinguals are in when they have more than one lexical option available to them to label a particular conceptual content and, on the other hand, the bilinguals' common state of mind of having two words (one in each language) for one and the same concept. In the monolingual case, for instance, synonyms may exist that express one and the same concept, a concept may be expressed with its category name (e.g., *dog*) or with the name of a specific exemplar of the category (*terrier*, or *poodle*), or a concept may be expressed in both a formal and a slang term.

If more than one lexical item matches the content of the preverbal message that is output by the conceptualizer (the component of the speech production system that builds the conceptual structure to be expressed in speech; e.g., Levelt, 1989; see Chapter 5, p. 224 for details), how then is the intended lexical element selected from this set of possible candidates and output by the system? In the monolingual literature this multiple mapping of conceptual content onto lexical items and the problem it creates for language production is known as the "convergence problem" and has led to much debate as to how the monolingual speaker solves it (e.g., Levelt, 1989; Roelofs, 1992). One of the solutions has been to assume some sort of lexicon-external checking mechanism, a monitor that before the selected item is being output determines whether it is in fact the intended item. If it is not, the selected item is withheld, another one is selected from the set of alternatives, and the checking process starts anew. La Heij characterizes this process as "simple access, complex selection". The "simple access" part of this qualification refers to a "sufficing" conceptualizer, one that is sloppier than could be.

La Heij proposed a selection process that presupposes a straightforward relation between the amount of conceptual information specified in the preverbal message on the one hand and the number of lexical elements that compete for selection on the other hand: The more elaborate the information in the preverbal message, the fewer lexical items provide a satisfactory match with this information and, consequently, the larger the chance the intended item is output by the system. The reason is that, first, lexical items are activated proportionally to the amount of overlap between the information contained by the preverbal message and the information specified in the lexical items, and, second, the most highly activated element is output by the system. In the monolingual case, if the preverbal message contains the specification that, for instance, slang should be used, it is likely that the lexical item containing this specification will be more highly activated than a more formal "equivalent". Consequently, it will be the slang word that emerges in the output. La Heij characterizes this process as "complex access, simple selection": If the process of conceptualization is so elaborate (complex) that its output contains all the essential information the speaker wants to express, the intended word falls naturally out of the process in the far majority of cases. As he puts it, under those circumstances "[. . .] there is no convergence problem to be solved" (La Heij, 2005, p. 294).

Notice that this view presupposes that perfect synonyms do not exist. In principle, two different words mean different things, if only because they are used in different contexts (this being meaningful). A slang word is not the meaning equivalent of its more formal counterpart, synonyms like *thin* and *slim* mean different things, and, more obviously, so also do *dog* and *poodle*. Levelt (1989) also adhered to this view that synonymy within a language does not exist, instead embracing the "principle of contrast" (Clark, 1987, 1988), which states that all forms in a language contrast in meaning. This principle is considered to be an important driving force in language acquisition (when you encounter a new form, assume its referent is different from the referents of forms you already know and try to figure out what it is).

The analogous solution for the bilingual case is to assume that, just as the intention to use formal language or slang, or a category name or a sub-ordinate term, the intention to speak in one language and not the other is part of the information contained in the preverbal message. In other words, no theoretical distinction has to be made between, for instance, the information about which register to use and the information about which language to use, a view that has been expressed by many other researchers in the field (De Bot & Schreuder, 1993; Paradis, 1997, 2001). Following Poulisse and Bongaerts (1994) and Poulisse (1997), La Heij proposed that the language information in the preverbal message takes the form of a "language cue". It is furthermore assumed that each lexical item contains a "language tag" that specifies its language membership. The language cue and the rest of the conceptual information in the preverbal message cooperate in activating lexical items, a process that will generally result in the highest activation for the targeted item and, as a consequence, in its selection. Take as an example the English–French bilingual who intends to express the concept "boy" in French. Among the conceptual information in the preverbal message is the language cue +French. If lexical items indeed contain language tags, French *garçon*, containing the French language tag, will become more highly activated than English *boy*, which contains the English tag. As a consequence, *garçon* will be selected and output.

When comparing this model of language control in word production with the other proposals discussed so far, a distinguishing feature is that it does not require the proactive control assumed in Grosjean's language-mode theory and Paradis' activation threshold hypothesis. Elements in the non-target language do not have to be deactivated, however slightly. The language cue sees to it that a word in the intended language is output by enabling the activation in the corresponding lexical entry to exceed that of its equivalent in the non-target language. The model also does not require the reactive suppression of the non-target language, to be discussed below. A further noteworthy feature of the model is that it assumes control operates locally, on specific lexical items, and not globally, by activating and/ or deactivating a whole language subsystem. Finally, a view of control in terms of a language cue as part of the conceptualized content to be expressed suggests how fluent language mixing can come about in situations where such is allowed or even desirable: The speaker can refrain from choosing a language, with the effect that the preverbal message does not contain a language cue. A slightly different version of this account has already been presented on p. 229. There it was suggested that the language cue can be assigned different weights in different situations.

LANGUAGE CONTROL THROUGH REACTIVE SUPPRESSION

Introduction

When glancing over the figures that illustrate performance in language comprehension and production tasks in Chapters 4 and 5 it may be noticed that they all sketch various components of the language system and how these connect to one another, but none of them includes a control mechanism that guides and regulates performance in specific language tasks. Yet the language system is always used, both in natural situations and in the laboratory, with a specific purpose, and depending on the specific goal it will be used differently each time. I have already implicitly introduced this issue in Chapter 5, where I showed how one and the same part of the underlying language system may be implicated in naming pictures in L1 or in L2, in translating words from L1 to L2 or vice versa, and plausibly in a number of other word generation tasks as well. The implication is that an account of linguistic performance is never complete when it ignores a control system that enables the language system to be used as requested (in the laboratory) or intended (in a natural context). Perhaps the most appealing evidence to support this claim is found in the bilingual aphasia literature, where some forms of pathological language behavior can only be understood by assuming an intact language system that is operated on by a failing control system (see p. 295). One researcher who has consistently stressed the importance of efficient and unobstructed control operations in fluent language use and of sufficient resources to "fuel" these processes is David Green (Green, 1986, 1993, 1998, 2005; Green & Price, 2001; Price, Green, & Von Studnitz, 1999; Von Studnitz & Green, 1997, 2002a, 2002b). He and his colleagues have played a major role in introducing these insights in research on bilingualism.

The insight that control plays an important role in language behavior has also paved the way to the awareness that bilingual language control and the systems involved may resemble, or even be the same as, the control processes and control structures required in other situations where multiple responses compete for selection. Accordingly, a number of authors have embedded their views on bilingual control within a more general theory of the control of action. Some of them envision bilingual language control as a process whereby the inadvertent selection of a competitor in the contextually inappropriate language is prevented by a process of "reactive inhibition" or "reactive suppression" of the competitor. It is especially this view that is advanced in Green's work to be presented here, but the idea is also central in the influential work of Ellen Bialystok to be presented in the next chapter, on the cognitive consequences of bilingualism (pp. 393–396). Here, I will first present Green's inhibitory control model, including a discussion of a study by Meuter and Allport (1999) that had a major impact in this field of study for two reasons: In this study the language switching paradigm that Macnamara and his colleagues first used to study bilingual language control (pp. 281–283) was revitalized and the paradigm was modified in such a way that it encompassed what has come to be regarded the litmus test of the phenomenon of reactive suppression. I will then proceed by discussing a number of studies that included Meuter and Allport's critical test of suppression and produced results suggesting that control is not secured through reactive suppression in all cases.

The inhibitory control model

A central construct in Green's (1998) inhibitory control model of bilingual language control is a supervisory attentional system (SAS), which he adopted from Norman and Shallice's (1986) theory on the control of behavior. In this theory SAS is a resource-limited control structure that is involved in the planning, regulation, and verification of non-routine voluntary actions and that is assumed to reside in the prefrontal regions of the brain. SAS is a subsystem of a larger control system in which simple, well-learned actions are carried out automatically by ready-made memory structures that specify action sequences, called "schemas". The SAS supervises the routine running of the schemas and intervenes when necessary (e.g., to prevent action slips). It does so by altering the activation levels of the running schemas. Unlike Norman and Shallice, Green applies the term schema not only to the above-mentioned ready-made structures in long-term memory that have resulted from past experiences and that underlie automatic, routine behavior, but also to "mental devices or networks that individuals may construct or adapt on the spot in order to achieve a specific task" (Green, 1998, p. 69). In his view a task schema thus appears to be the equivalent of an understanding of the task instructions by the participants; that is, their mental representation of the instructions, complemented with a setting of the system that enables them to perform the task as requested. Task schemas for tasks that have been previously performed (e.g., reading words aloud) can be retrieved from memory as such or adapted, if necessary, and schemas for tasks that are novel (e.g., lexical decision) have to be constructed on the spot. In Green's model, which is illustrated in Figure 6.5, this process of schema retrieval, adaptation, and construction is commanded by the SAS.

In the model, the "conceptualizer" is a non-linguistic system that builds conceptual representations from information in long-term memory. In doing so it is driven by a goal to achieve some effect through the use of language. The intention to produce a word in a specific language

The inhibitory control model of bilingual language control. The bilingual lexico-semantic system stores the bilingual's word knowledge. The SAS (supervisory attentional system) is a general control system that regulates language behavior by constructing, or retrieving from memory, so-called "language task schemas" that see to it that the bilingual language user performs the targeted task. From Green (1998) with permission from Cambridge University Press.

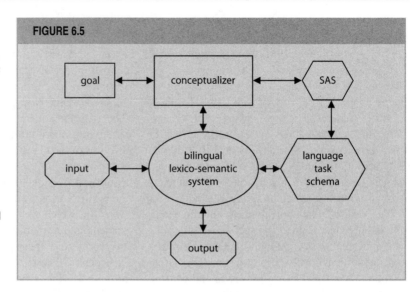

FIGURE 6.5

is part of the conceptual representations (cf. the language cue in, e.g., La Heij, 2005). The "bilingual lexico-semantic system" is part of the actual language system and stores the bilingual's word knowledge; for instance, knowledge regarding the words' forms and meanings. Especially central in Green's model is a word's lemma, which specifies its syntactic properties such as its gender and is assumed to be used in both production and comprehension tasks. Each lemma contains a language tag specifying the word's language membership. During, for instance, word production, conceptual information from the conceptualizer activates lemmas in the lexico-semantic system proportional to the degree of information shared between the conceptual representations and the lemmas in the lexico-semantic system. So far Green's model is very similar to the views of, among others, La Heij (2005) presented above. But two of its characteristics set the model apart from the other theories on language control presented so far. The first concerns the feature already introduced above—the (explicit) inclusion of a control mechanism (SAS) that regulates language behavior by retrieving or setting up task schemas that specify in what way the language system must be used to perform the requested task. Its second unique feature is a process of reactive, local suppression of contextually inappropriate lexical elements.

When the goal is to perform a particular task, the SAS installs the relevant language task schema. This schema then controls behavior (i.e., regulates the output of the lexico-semantic system) in two ways: by altering the activation levels of the lemmas within the lexico-semantic system and by inhibiting pending outputs from that system (Green, 1998, p. 69). When, for instance, the bilingual is asked to name pictures in L2, the relevant schema (presumably one that exists as such in memory because the task is a rather natural one) is activated and enables task performance by increasing the activation level of lemmas with an L2 language tag in the lexico-semantic system, decreasing the activation of L1-tagged lemmas in the system, and by reactively inhibiting imminent L1 outputs from the system. If, instead, the task is picture naming in L1, the opposite pattern of control is established by the SAS. When the task is translating L1 words into L2, the SAS installs a schema that specifies L1 as the input language, inhibits the schema for naming the input in L1, and activates a schema for producing L2 as the output. The degree of reactive inhibition is proportional to the level of activation of the non-target language's lexical items: the more active a lemma in the non-response language, the more it will be inhibited. Therefore suppression will generally be stronger in circumstances where L2, often the weaker language, is the language of output (and stronger L1 has to be suppressed) than when L1 is to be output. (This is so because the memory representations of the linguistic elements belonging to the weaker language will generally have lower activation levels than those belonging to the stronger language.)

From this description of the workings of the model it may be inferred that Green assumes control can be exerted, on the hand, proactively and globally, by adapting the activation levels of all lemmas in both language subsets before task performance starts and, on the other hand, reactively and locally, by suppressing the activation in the lemmas of words from the non-response language that still threaten to slip through. In theory, the model could do without proactive, global control altogether: Even if the ultimately most highly activated element in the bilingual's lexicon were to correspond to a word in the currently inappropriate language, selection of this word could be prevented through late suppression.

As mentioned, Meuter and Allport (1999) provided a result that has been regarded as the litmus test of reactive suppression because the result in question indeed seems to suggest that reactive suppression is proportional to the level of activation of the to-be-suppressed lemmas. Meuter and Allport used an adapted version of the numeral-naming task of Macnamara et al. (1968; see p. 285) in which unbalanced bilingual participants named the Arabic numerals 1 to 9 in either their L1 or L2. The numerals were presented in lists of various lengths in which switch and non-switch trials occurred in an unpredictable order within one and the same list. The language to use on a particular trial was indicated by the color of the numeral's background, blue or yellow. A crucial aspect of this study was that, unlike in Macnamara et al.'s study, response times were registered for every single trial, switch and non-switch. This way the authors could test their "relative strength hypothesis", which states that the size of the switching costs depends on the relative strength of the bilingual's two languages: The switching cost was (paradoxically) expected to be *larger* for a switch

into the stronger language L1 than for a switch into the weaker language L2.

Meuter and Allport (1999) derived this prediction from similar asymmetries that have been observed when participants have to switch between an easy, behaviorally relatively dominant task (e.g., word reading by well-practiced readers) and a more difficult, behaviorally weaker task (e.g., color naming). The cost that accompanies a switch between tasks is typically larger when the participant has to switch from the weaker (color naming) to the more dominant (easier, more practiced) task (word reading) than with a switch in the reverse direction, from dominant to weak. This counterintuitive effect is explained in terms of differences in the required level of suppression of the non-target task, in combination with a phenomenon called "task set inertia": To enable task performance, the non-target task must be actively suppressed and the target task must be activated. The stronger the non-target task, the more it has to be suppressed in order not to interfere with target task performance. Task set inertia is the phenomenon that the task set of the previous trial carries over into the current trial. In other words, with a switch from color naming to word reading, the relatively strong suppression of the dominant word-reading task on the previous trial lingers on to the subsequent trial, causing a relatively large delay in producing the word-reading response now required (Allport, Styles, & Hsieh, 1994). Meuter and Allport (1999) hypothesized that the language-switching task implements this general paradigm of switching between a well-practiced and a less-practiced task, and, therefore, predicted a similar asymmetry in the data. The data are presented in Figure 6.6.

As shown, language switching into both languages incurred a cost, a finding that replicated a similar result in Macnamara et al.'s (1968) seminal study and that has since been replicated by many other researchers (e.g., Costa & Santesteban, 2004b; Hernandez et al., 2000; Jackson, Swainson, Cunnington, & Jackson, 2001; Kroll et al., 2000). But presently of more interest, the predicted language-switching asymmetry occurred as well: The cost of switching was larger for switches into the dominant L1 (143 ms)

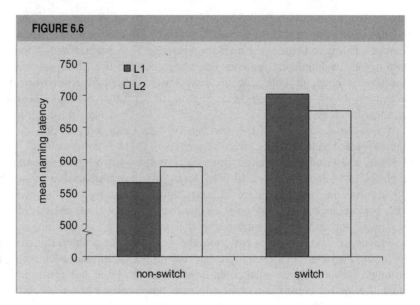

FIGURE 6.6

Mean numeral naming time (in ms) as a function of response language and trial type. On non-switch trials naming in L1 is faster than in L2. On switch trials naming is faster in L2. Data from Meuter and Allport (1999).

than for switches into the weaker L2 (85 ms), with the effect that on a switch trial a response in stronger L1 took longer than in weaker L2 (which is why the effect is sometimes called "para-doxical"). The fact that the response pattern was similar to the one obtained with other task pairs consisting of a dominant and a weaker task supports the authors' theoretical starting point that language switching is just a special case of this more general methodology and that one and the same interpretation, suppression combined with task set inertia, may account for this specific data pattern in all these cases.

As mentioned earlier (p. 281), Macnamara et al. (1968) did not measure the cost of language switching locally, at the very point where it occurred, but by subtracting the overall response time for complete blocks of non-switch trials from the overall response time for complete blocks of switch trials. For that reason they could never have detected the asymmetry in the switch costs that is critical to be able to assign it the present interpretation: that it results from unequal suppression of a stronger and a weaker task (or "task schema", in Green's terminology). Nevertheless, as we have seen, one of the main conclusions these early authors drew from their data is remarkably similar to Meuter and Allport's account of the language switch data

collected 30 years later—that there is nothing special about language switching but that it concerns a manifestation of task-switching behavior in general. To repeat the relevant quote: "language switching [. . .] seems to require no psychological skill peculiar to bilingualism, but rather a skill which is equally applicable in a larger number of operations in which persons are asked to switch modes of response rapidly" (Macnamara et al., 1968, pp. 213–214). What is more, Macnamara and his colleagues already provided direct evidence to support their claim by showing that the language-switching task produced exactly the same switching costs as a condition where participants switched between two non-language tasks. It is for these reasons that I characterized Macnamara's work as having a modern flavor to it.

Data that qualify the inhibitory control model

If an asymmetry in the required level of suppression due to an uneven command of the two languages indeed underlies the asymmetrical switch costs, then the smaller the proficiency difference between the two languages, the smaller the asymmetry in the size of the switch costs should be. In balanced bilinguals, where both languages are equally strong, the asymmetry in the switch costs should even disappear altogether. Meuter and Allport (1999) performed a number of post-hoc analyses on their data that suggest this to be the case. Costa and Santesteban (2004b) subsequently tested this prediction in a series of five experiments, using a picture-naming task instead of a numeral-naming task. In a first experiment, using this new task they replicated Meuter and Allport's finding, testing unbalanced Spanish–Catalan and Korean–Spanish bilinguals. For both groups an asymmetrical switch cost was obtained, with switching into the dominant language producing the largest switch cost. More interestingly, in three experiments in which balanced Spanish–Catalan bilinguals highly proficient in both languages were tested, the asymmetry did indeed disappear.

So far the results are consistent with the predictions of the inhibitory control model, suggesting that in both balanced and unbalanced bilinguals language control requires reactive suppression of the non-target language; in unbalanced bilinguals the degree of suppression is especially large when weaker L2 is the response language and stronger L1 the language to be suppressed, whereas in balanced bilinguals the degree of reactive suppression is always the same. But Costa and Santesteban (2004b) considered an alternative interpretation of the absence of an asymmetry in the switch costs shown by balanced bilinguals. What if they exploit a qualitatively different sort of selection mechanism, one that does not require reactive inhibition of the non-response language at all, as had been suggested by earlier studies of this research group that had exploited the picture-naming interference task (see Chapter 5, pp. 242–245)? To answer this question, they looked at the switching behavior of early balanced, proficient Spanish–Catalan bilinguals who were learners of yet another language (L3) in a switching task involving L1 and L3. The reactive suppression account predicts that under these circumstances the asymmetrical switch cost should re-emerge. However, contrary to this prediction the switch costs were equally large when switching into the L1 and the L3, as was the case when these bilinguals switched

between their equally strong L1 and L2. The researchers concluded (see also Costa, 2005) that language selection in participants highly proficient in at least two languages might not come about through a process of reactive inhibition of the non-response language. Instead they suggested that in the process of developing a high proficiency in two languages, bilinguals may develop a control mechanism that somehow only takes lexical elements of the response language into consideration in the selection process, ignoring activated lexical elements in the non-response language.

A further study that delved yet deeper into this issue (Costa et al., 2006) extended and qualified these conclusions. One of the questions the authors posed was whether such a language-specific selection mechanism perhaps only develops in participants of the type tested by Costa and Santesteban (2004b); namely, *early* bilinguals speaking two *similar* languages. The data of this new study suggested that neither age of acquisition of the L2 nor language similarity plays a critical role: Symmetrical switching costs also showed up when bilinguals who were highly proficient in two dissimilar languages (Spanish and Basque) switched between these languages. Furthermore, symmetrical switching costs turned up in a group of Spanish–English bilinguals who had grown up in a monolingual Spanish environment and had started to acquire English later in life but were quite fluent in it at the time of testing. Yet a further experiment showed that for the symmetrical switching cost to occur it was no prerequisite that a strong L1 was one of the test languages: Whereas Costa and Santesteban (2004b) had shown a symmetrical switching cost between strong L1 and weak L3, the present study showed the same result when participants highly proficient in both L1 Spanish and L2 Catalan switched between their strong L2 Catalan and weak L3 English.

So far it appeared that bilinguals and trilinguals who are highly proficient in at least two languages, irrespective of the age at which they had started to acquire their L2 and the similarity of their L1 and L2, have developed a language-specific selection mechanism that does not involve inhibitory reactive control and that they can apply generally when switching between any two of the languages they know to at least some extent. Two further experiments, however, proved this latter conclusion to be wrong and showed that there are limits to the exploitation of this non-inhibitory selection mechanism: The asymmetrical switch cost (with, again, a larger cost when switching into the stronger language) reappeared when Spanish–Catalan–English–French quadrilinguals, highly proficient in L1 Spanish and L2 Catalan but with a much weaker command of L3 English and a very feeble command of L4 French, were tested in English and French. This finding suggests that for the language-specific selection mechanism to be operative at least a high command of one of the test languages is required. A final experiment suggested that this is a necessary but not a sufficient requirement, because an asymmetrical switch cost was also obtained when a further group of participants switched between strong L1 and a small vocabulary they had acquired just before the actual picture-naming study.

To account for the complex pattern of data gathered in their studies, Costa and his colleagues tentatively hypothesized that a prerequisite for the language-specific selection mechanism to be functional is that words are solidly established in language-specific lexicons. If this requirement is not met, all participants, even those highly proficient in two non-test languages, have to resort to the inhibitory control strategy that—so the asymmetrical switch costs suggest—is the only strategy available to unbalanced bilinguals (but see below). What remains to be explained under this account is why switch costs occur under all circumstances, even when selection does not exploit the reactive suppression mechanism but a language-specific selection mechanism and the costs are symmetrical. The most plausible explanation of these costs is that they index the resetting that is needed (i.e., the installment of a new language task schema) when a new stimulus–response association is required.

All studies discussed in this section so far examined the effects of language switching under circumstances where the switches were experi-

menter imposed. As mentioned before, in natural language use bilinguals themselves determine which language to use, and language switching does not always slow down processing but may even increase speech fluency (pp. 288–289). In an English–Spanish study Gollan and Ferreirra (2009) obtained evidence to suggest that the asymmetrical switch costs typically observed in unbalanced bilinguals result from the fact that in the pertinent studies they were not free to choose the response language. In addition to an English-only and a Spanish-only condition in which all pictures had to be named in the same language, a voluntary switching condition was included in which the participants were told they could either name a picture in English or Spanish ("just say whichever name comes to mind most quickly"; p. 643). The participants were divided into two groups, one consisting of balanced bilinguals and a second consisting of unbalanced bilinguals dominant in English. One finding of interest was that most of the participants in the voluntary switching condition indeed switched voluntarily between the languages even though switching generally involved a cost in time. This finding testifies to the robustness of the switch costs. But of special interest in the present context was the finding that the switch costs observed in this condition were symmetrical in the balanced and unbalanced bilinguals alike. In other words, when language switching is voluntary the response pattern observed for unbalanced bilinguals resembles that of balanced bilinguals, and neither pattern suggests that control is secured by means of a reactive inhibition.

The studies by Albert Costa and his group and by Gollan and Ferreira (2009) narrowed down the circumstances under which bilingual control might be exerted by means of a reactive inhibitory control mechanism. Finkbeiner, Gollan, and Caramazza (2006) went a step further, producing a set of data which, according to them, indicates that language control might never come about by means of reactive suppression of the non-response language, and that evidence suggesting otherwise may be due to a specific feature of the stimuli typically used in these studies: They are usually "bivalent", meaning that each of them can take two values, its name in L1 and its name in L2. The experiment in question involved series of numeral-naming and picture-naming trials. The pictures all had to be named in L1 (they were "univalent"), whereas the numerals had to be named either in L1 or in L2 (they were "bivalent"). The participants were all unbalanced bilinguals with English as their L1 and an L2 that varied between them; that is, they were the type of participants that in the experiments by Costa and his associates always seemed to use the inhibitory control mechanism. The numeral-naming data once again showed a pattern consistent with a reactive inhibition account of language control: Responses were slower on language switch trials than on non-switch trials and the switch cost was relatively large when switching was from L2 into L1. But contrary to prediction, picture naming (always in L1) was not slower when the preceding numeral was named in L2 than when it was named in L1. Accordingly the authors rejected an account of language control in terms of reactive inhibition of the non-response language.

Finally, two studies by Philipp and collaborators (Philipp, Gade, & Koch, 2007; Philipp & Koch, 2009) contributed to the present debate by introducing a new language-switching paradigm that enables a direct measurement of the reactive inhibition assumed by the inhibitory control model. In these studies German–English–French trilinguals named visual stimuli (numerals and colors) in all three languages, a cue indicating which language to use in naming the current stimulus. Two types of stimulus triads were included, so-called "n-2 repetition sequences" and "n-2 non-repetition sequences". Presented with the last stimulus of an n-2 repetition sequence, the participants had to switch back to the language used to name the first stimulus of the triad (ABA; e.g., naming in German followed by naming in English, followed by naming in German). In contrast, n-2 non-repetition sequences required responses in three different languages (CBA; e.g., French, English, German). Responding to the third stimulus took longer in sequences of the ABA type than in CBA sequences, a finding the authors attributed to

persisting inhibition of language A in ABA sequences, in which the switch from A to B had involved reactive inhibition of A. In other words, and contrary to Finkbeiner et al.'s (2006) conclusion, the data from these studies support the inhibitory control model.

Summary and conclusions

The occurrence of asymmetrical switch costs in the majority of conditions testing unbalanced bilinguals suggests that an account of language control in terms of reactive suppression of elements of the non-response language as assumed by the inhibitory control model at least applies to bilinguals of this type when they are forced to switch between the languages. Using a different paradigm, the studies by Philipp and her colleagues (Philipp et al., 2007; Philipp & Koch, 2009) provided converging support for the model. But the joint data also indicate that balanced bilinguals might secure language control by means of the language-specific selection mechanism proposed by Costa and his colleagues. It remains to be seen whether and under what circumstances the third control process discussed in the preceding sections—differential proactive activation of elements in the two language subsets resulting from the intention to use one language and not the other—contributes to language control.

Whereas the evidence in support of the inhibitory control model's assumption of reactive suppression is somewhat mixed, the model's core assumption that language control is effected by a control system external to the language system proper has by now become widely accepted. The language system can be used in a multitude of different ways and the number of different options is especially large in the case of bilingual and multilingual language users. Exhibiting the linguistic behavior that is desired under specific circumstances (e.g., speaking in L1, naming an object in L2, counting in L3, translating from L1 to L2) requires the involvement of a control system which exploits the language system in accordance with the language user's current goals, monitors performance, and keeps it on track. Another important assumption of the inhibitory control model is that the control system involved is not dedicated exclusively to language processing but is implicated in the control of behavior in general. The fact that asymmetrical switch costs have also been observed in experiments where the participants switched between pairs of tasks involving one and the same language (e.g., between color naming and word naming) supports this hypothesis, as does the fact that, just as in studies on language switching, in these task-switching studies the asymmetrical switch cost does not always occur (Monsell, 2003).

Further evidence that a more general control system takes care of language control comes from studies showing that bilinguals outperform monolinguals on a number of non-linguistic tasks that demand a high level of cognitive control. The hypothesis that motivated these studies was that bilinguals have become experts in cognitive control in general because their bilingualism requires that they incessantly control their language output. This line of work will be presented in Chapter 7 (pp. 393–396). A final source of evidence comes from brain research showing that the brain regions activated during tasks that require the control of language are the same as those activated in tasks that require control in other cognitive domains. In both cases specific regions in the frontal lobe appear to be implicated (see Chapter 8, pp. 435–446).

Particularly important in the context of the present chapter (which primarily accounts for language-switching effects) is that assuming a language-external control system that enables the language system to be used according to the current goals provides a simple explanation for the ubiquitous language-switching costs in both comprehension (pp. 286–288; and see Jackson, Swainson, Mullin, Cunnington, & Jackson, 2004, for a more recent study on receptive language switching) and production (the present section): Language switches in both input and output necessitate a reset of the control system so that the task to be performed on the previous trial can be interrupted and the currently requested one installed. This resetting of the system takes time

and slows down the response on a switch trial. For similar reasons, a switch between pairs of tasks involving one and the same language will delay responding. Once the system has been reset to accommodate the current task requirements, relatively little control may be required to maintain the existing state of control. This idea was already expressed in an earlier quote taken from Macnamara et al. (1968), to be repeated in abbreviated form here: "... the bilingual once started in one language can forget about which language he is speaking and yet obey the rules of that language" (see p. 284 for the full quote).

To conclude, it appears that language switching is in fact a type of task switching that is taken care of by a general control system that regulates both language processing and other forms of cognitive processing. Another way of putting this is to claim that there is no such thing as a mental language switch.

CONTROL IN SIMULTANEOUS INTERPRETING

A characterization of translation and simultaneous interpreting

One specific form of language switching has been neglected in this chapter so far—one that is practiced by most bilinguals some of the time in naturalistic communicative settings. It concerns "translation", a term that refers to any act of rephrasing a message in one language, the "source" language, in another language, the "target" language, while maintaining semantic equivalence. Word translation, where the source language input is a single word, has already been dealt with in earlier chapters (pp. 136–137 and 261–265). In this section I will primarily deal with the translation of larger linguistic segments, focusing on issues of control. Translating is practiced in different ways (see Table 6.1). They differ from one another with respect to the modalities of input and output (writing, speech, sign language, and combinations of these) and the timing of the input and output relative to one another. For instance, in **consecutive interpreting** the

TABLE 6.1

Forms of translation

Translation (used in a broad sense): All tasks where a message expressed in SL is transposed in TL.

Translation (used in a narrow sense): Converting written SL into written TL. This form is also called *text-to-text translation*.

Simultaneous interpreting: Converting spoken SL into spoken TL. In doing so the interpreter listens and speaks at the same time most of the time, trying to keep the "ear–voice span" (the lag between an input segment and the corresponding output) as short as possible.

Consecutive interpreting: As in simultaneous interpreting SL and TL are both spoken, but listening and speaking occur in succession: The interpreter only starts to speak after the speaker has finished speaking.

Semi-consecutive interpreting: As consecutive interpreting, but listening and speaking alternate: The speaker interrupts his or her speech once in a while, at which points the interpreter takes over to translate the prior spoken fragment.

Sight translation: There is no speaker delivering a speech but a written SL text, which the interpreter translates orally into TL.

Simultaneous interpreting with text: A speaker reads his or her text aloud from paper while the interpreter reads a copy of this text and produces an oral rendition simultaneously.

Spoken-language translation: Converting one spoken language into another spoken language (simultaneously, consecutively, or semi-consecutively).

Sign-language translation: Converting spoken SL input into a sign language (simultaneously, consecutively, or semi-consecutively).

Machine translation: Using a computer to translate between natural languages. Typically interactive systems are used, in which human beings pre-edit or post-edit the text that is input into or output by the computer.

Transliteration: The conversion of written names of people, places, and institutions from one script into another script, as when Russian СПУТНИК becomes SPUTNIK in English.*

Transcription: The conversion of the sound of names of people, places, and institutions between languages written in different scripts, a process that often results in different spellings for one and the same name (Tchaikovsky, Tsjaikowskij, Csajkovszkij).*

The term "translation" is used to refer to any act of converting a message in one language (the "source language"; SL) into another language (the "target language"; TL), while maintaining semantic equivalence.

Based on Crystal (1987), De Groot (1997), and Gile (1997).

* Examples taken from Crystal (1987).

---

speaker and interpreter take turns, never speaking at the same time, whereas in **simultaneous interpreting** the speaker's speech and the interpreter's rendition of it overlap approximately 70% of the time (Chernov, 1994).

Each type of translation task is characterized by a unique set of processing and storage requirements and, therefore, each requires its own unique set of skills to be performed optimally. For instance, a simultaneous interpreter must constantly divide attention between at least three task components: comprehending input, producing output, and memorizing parts of the analyzed input that must await expression in the output because of sequencing differences between the source language and the target language. To illustrate the memory component, consider the difference between SOV languages (in which sentences typically have a subject-object-verb

structure, e.g., Japanese) and SVO languages (e.g., English). When presented with an SOV source language sentence to be translated into an SVO target language sentence the interpreter cannot start his or her rendition of the object structure before the speaker has output, and the interpreter has translated, the verb structure. In the meantime, the interpreter must memorize the input's object structure. The amount of attention to be devoted to comprehension, production, and memorizing fluctuates with the continuously changing demands posed by the input (due to variations in, e.g., its rate, clarity of diction, grammatical complexity, information density, and information complexity), the output (e.g., whether or not it contains tongue-twisters; whether or not the concepts to express are lexicalized in the target language), and the amount of information to be temporarily retained (see

Christoffels & De Groot, 2005, for a review). This necessitates the constant regulation of the exact portion of attention that must be allocated to each of the ongoing activities and this orchestration, the "coordination component", is regarded as a fourth attention-demanding component of simultaneous interpreting (Gile, 1995, 1997). Finally, there is an ongoing debate about whether a complete model of simultaneous interpreting should also encompass a separate translation component (e.g., Anderson, 1994; see the "transcoding" view of interpreting presented in the next section). So, in all, simultaneous interpreting appears to challenge working memory excessively. In contrast, the mental bottleneck in consecutive interpreting is the relatively long time interval between input and output, which creates the problem that parts of the analyzed input may have dissipated from memory the moment the interpreter must take the floor. To compensate for such memory loss the consecutive interpreter often jots down notes while the speaker is delivering his or her speech. These can later help to reconstruct any lost information.

To substantiate the present claim that different versions of the translation task are enabled by different sets of skills, let us consider a study by Gerver, Longley, Long, and Lambert (1984). These authors provided a detailed analysis of consecutive and simultaneous interpreting, focusing on what it takes to be able to rapidly grasp and convey the essence of the speaker's input. Based on this analysis they developed a battery of tests, 12 in all, that were administered to students selected for a graduate course on consecutive and simultaneous interpreting. The performance of the participants on all these tests was correlated with the ratings they received in their final interpreting examinations. Two observations suggested that each of these tests assessed an ability that is relevant for skillful interpreting: First, all participants who passed the examinations scored higher on all tests than all participants who failed the examinations and, second, all test scores were positively correlated with the examination ratings. But of special interest here was the finding that, as shown by a factor analysis, simultaneous interpreting and con-

secutive interpreting were related to different sets of skills: The tests that reflected an ability to reconstruct information from memory and the examination ratings on consecutive interpreting loaded highly on one factor; tests that all required speed and accuracy of perceptual and productive linguistic processes and the examination ratings on simultaneous loaded highly on a second factor.

The (im)possibility of simultaneity

The characteristic of simultaneous interpreting that is likely to contribute most to its complexity is its eponymous component: the simultaneity of a number of processing components, including comprehension and production. The simultaneity of these two task components per se is not a unique characteristic of simultaneous interpreting because in monolingual speech production speakers are known to monitor their own speech. In doing so they exploit their comprehension system (see Chapter 5, p. 224 and Figure 5.1). What *is*, however, unique to simultaneous interpreting in this respect is that interpreters have to comprehend *somebody else's* speech—speech that they have not conceptualized themselves. There is evidence to suggest that at the same time they still monitor their own speech to some degree (e.g., Gerver, 1976; Isham, 2000), although they fail to detect errors more often than regular speakers do (Moser, 1978). This relative insensitivity to errors may be due to a conscious strategy of interpreters to pay as little attention as possible to their own output in order to be able to concentrate more on the incoming message (Fabbro & Darò, 1995; Moser-Mercer, Frauenfelder, Casado, & Künzli, 2000).

Christoffels and De Groot (2004) provided support for the present suggestion that the simultaneity requirement of the task contributes importantly to the task's complexity. They studied the effect of simultaneity of comprehension and production in an extremely simplified version of the task: The participants, reasonably fluent Dutch–English bilinguals without any professional interpreting experience, were asked to interpret simple short sentences in two conditions. In the simultaneous condition they were instructed to start translating on-line; that is, as soon as possible after the onset of the input sentence; in a delayed (off-line, consecutive) condition they were asked to start delivering their translation after completion of the input sentence. Even in this low-demand substitute for the real task, performance deteriorated as a result of the simultaneity requirement: The quality of the output was worse, fewer words were output, and less of the input material was recalled in the simultaneous condition than in the consecutive condition. That the adverse effects of simultaneity remain after task training was demonstrated by Darò and Fabbro (1994) and Lambert (1989). These authors compared the memory performance of advanced interpreting students following listening and simultaneous interpreting. Despite the fact that simple materials were used (short stories built from simple words and syntax), presented at a modest input rate, the results showed poorer recall in the interpreting condition than in the listening condition. Similarly, Gerver (1974) had interpreting students answer comprehension questions following, among other things, just listening to stories or after simultaneously interpreting them. In the interpreting condition fewer questions were answered correctly than in the listening condition. In all four of these studies the participants interpreted from a spoken language to a second spoken language. Interestingly, in a study in which the target language was signed instead of spoken, recall following interpreting (by professional sign-language interpreters) equaled recall following listening (Isham, 2000; Isham & Lane, 1993). This suggests that the relatively poor performance following spoken-language interpreting is somehow caused by the requirement of concurrent listening and speaking.

An important note regarding the task's simultaneity is in order here; namely, that it is not at all clear in what sense it is actually simultaneous. We *do* know that in simultaneous interpreting the speaker and interpreter produce speech simultaneously most of the time, so in this sense the task is obviously simultaneous. The implication is that the interpreter executes at least some subcomponents of comprehension and production simultaneously. What we do not know, though, is exactly which ones this concerns. Both speech comprehension and speech production involve automatic subcomponents (e.g., perceptual analysis and articulation) as well as attention-demanding subcomponents (e.g., conceptualization of input and output). By definition, automatic processes—if executed by different processing mechanisms—can be performed simultaneously effortlessly. Similarly, automatic processes are often thought not to interfere with ongoing attention-consuming processes. A processing bottleneck typically only occurs when more than one of a task's subcomponents draws on our limited attention resources and when, at the same time, together they require more resources than actually available. The question of present interest is therefore whether interpreters can truly perform a number of the *attention-demanding* subcomponents of comprehension and production simultaneously or whether, instead, at any moment in time they manage to somehow interweave one of the attention-demanding comprehension components with one or more of the automatic production components (or, vice versa, one or more of the automatic comprehension components with one of the attention-demanding production components).

This question concerning the possibility of "divided" attention has been a main area of research since the middle of the twentieth century. The typical studies addressing this question are dual-task or multiple-task studies. In these studies, as in simultaneous interpreting, participants have to perform two or more tasks concurrently and performance under dual- or multiple-task conditions is compared with performance in a single-task control condition. Two early influential studies of this type (Hirst, Spelke, Reaves, Caharack, & Neisser, 1980; Spelke, Hirst, & Neisser, 1976) tackled the question of whether attention can be divided over several attention-demanding processing operations simultaneously in an experimental set-up that, intuitively, seems to be equally as demanding as, or even more demanding than, simultaneous interpreting. A small number of participants were trained in reading stories while concurrently writing to dictation sentences unrelated to the stories. (This dual-task setting is plausibly more demanding than simultaneous interpreting because it involves the processing of two unrelated contents; in simultaneous interpreting it is one and the same content that must be understood and rephrased in the other language.) After massive practice in which the task demands were gradually increased, it appeared that one or two participants managed to perform both tasks with comprehension while their reading speed was as fast as when they read without concurrent writing. Because both reading for comprehension and writing sentences to dictation require attention resources, the authors concluded that simultaneity of more than one attention-demanding activity appears possible, at least for some individuals after massive training. Yet the possibility could not be definitely ruled out that, in fact, these participants had alternated rapidly between the reading and writing-to-dictation tasks and that this was what they had learned to do through extensive practice.

Similarly, in simultaneous interpreting the interpreter may rapidly alternate mentally between the attention-demanding components of the task. Alternation from comprehension to production would be a safe option at points where elements in the source text can be predicted on the basis of prior context, background knowledge, and information redundancy. Studies on monolingual discourse processing have shown that language users do indeed exploit such sources of knowledge to anticipate upcoming words. For instance, Van Berkum, Brown, Zwitserlood, Kooijman, and Hagoort (2005) and Otten, Nieuwland, and Van Berkum (2007) found that words inconsistent with a specific prediction based on prior discourse evoke an ERP response different from the ERP elicited by prediction-consistent words, and this prior to the moment the critical word appears in the input. The ability to anticipate specific words in simultaneous interpreting enables the interpreter to ignore parts of the input so that more attention can be devoted to other task components such as production or memorizing. Especially prepared, well-structured

texts enable anticipation (Adamowicz, 1989). Consistent with the present suggestion that anticipation facilitates interpreting, Gerver and his colleagues (1984) have shown that the interpreting performance of student interpreters is correlated with their performance on a "cloze test", a test that required them to restore materials that had been deleted from connected discourse. One of the skills this test indexes is the ability to engage in anticipatory processes: to predict what is yet to come on the basis of an understanding of the prior discourse.

Kempen et al. (2009) provided indirect, monolingual evidence to suggest that whatever goes on in parallel in simultaneous interpreting it is not the grammatical decoding and encoding components of source language comprehension and target language production. They had their participants perform either one of two tasks: reading with correction, and reading and paraphrasing. In both cases visually presented sentences appeared on the screen phrase by phrase. In the reading with correction task sentences with a direct-speech construction had to be read aloud and, if they contained an error, corrected on line. Part of these sentences contained a reflexive pronoun that agreed with the corresponding subject (*The headmaster complained: "I have seen a nasty cartoon of myself in the hallway"*) whereas others contained a mismatching reflexive pronoun (*The headmaster complained: "I have seen a nasty cartoon of himself in the hallway"*). (The experiment was run in Dutch with Dutch participants; the example sentences thus concern translations of the materials actually presented.) The response time between the reflexive in the input and in the output served as the dependent variable. In the reading and paraphrasing task, the above two types of sentences had to be paraphrased on line into their indirect-speech counterparts and the participants had to correct any error they might come across. The invited output sentence in reply to both of the above two example input sentences thus was: *The headmaster complained that he had seen a nasty cartoon of himself in the hallway.* Even though these two tasks are monolingual ones, their resemblance with simultaneous interpreting will be obvious: Also in simultaneous interpreting input sentences have to be transposed into output sentences on line. In particular, the paraphrasing task bears a close resemblance with simultaneous interpreting. In both cases an input message has to be understood and an output message has to be produced with the same meaning but a different wording, the only clear difference between the two tasks being that only one of them involves a language switch from input to output. Because of this similarity, in the translation literature within-language paraphrasing has been referred to as "unilingual translation" or "intralingual translation" (e.g., Anderson, 1994), and the task is often used as exercise during the training of translators and interpreters (see e.g., Moser-Mercer, 1994).

In the reading with correction task, when the input sentence contained a mismatching reflexive (*himself*) the response time was relatively long (*myself*: 460 ms; *himself*: 502 ms). The delay at the mismatching point is plausibly due to the decoder being taken by surprise when it encounters a mismatch between the decoded structure so far and the input encountered at the mismatch point. In contrast, in the reading and paraphrasing task, the response time to the correct *myself* input sentences was *longer* than to the incorrect *himself* input sentences (*myself*: 507; *himself*: 461). This finding suggests that the encoded structure has completely overwritten the input structure, as if only one of them can be available at any one moment in time. This, in turn, suggests that decoding an input structure and encoding an output structure cannot proceed in parallel but occur in rapid alternation instead. The longer response time in the reading and paraphrasing task when the input contains *myself* as the reflexive form can be attributed to the mismatch with encoded *himself*, the encoder being taken by surprise when it encounters *myself* instead.

To conclude, even though these results were obtained in a monolingual study, there is no obvious reason why the conclusion that grammatical decoding and encoding cannot occur simultaneously could not be generalized to simultaneous interpreting as well. Lacking a language switch, the reading and paraphrasing task appears to be cognitively less demanding than simultaneous interpreting. Furthermore, the materials concerned separate sentences instead of longer text, thus arguably posing relatively few demands on memory as compared with simultaneous interpreting. If simultaneous decoding and encoding were possible at all, one would have expected to obtain support for it in this relatively easy task.

Following the above characterization of simultaneous interpreting, the larger part of the remainder of this chapter will be dedicated to two questions, each dealing with a different aspect of control in simultaneous interpreting. The first concerns language control: Given the fact that simultaneous interpretation always involves the use of two languages, how can it be secured that the source language intrudes into the target language output as little as possible? The second, to be called "processing control", deals with control in a more general sense. As we have seen, simultaneous interpreting is an extremely complex skill, involving several attention-demanding components as well as their coordination and rapid sequencing. How then do (some) people come to master this skill and the obviously extremely complex control operations it involves? Both aspects of control are plausibly effectuated by a language-external control system of the type sketched earlier (p. 314). In later sections I will address each of these two questions in turn. But first I will explain the notions of **conceptually mediated translation** versus **transcoding**, as well as the phenomenon of **natural translation**. Without an account of these concepts, a general characterization of translation processes, and especially simultaneous interpreting, would be wanting.

Conceptually mediated translation, transcoding, and natural translation

The term "conceptually mediated" (or "vertical") translation refers to a form of translating that is hypothesized to exploit the same comprehension and production apparatus as used in monolingual language tasks. According to this view, the task involves, first, the processing of a speech input upward through the source language system, from a peripheral analysis of the input up to the point where the input is assigned a non-verbal conceptual representation and, next, a downward process that sets off with this conceptualized representation and concludes with the articulation of speech or with the writing down of text (in written translation). In theory then, any individual who can communicate both receptively and productively in two languages separately can translate between them, even when knowledge regarding translation-equivalent structures across these languages is completely lacking and no specialized translation strategies have been developed.

In contrast to conceptually mediated translation, the second hypothesized translation procedure, "transcoding" (or "horizontal" translation), assumes that source language input structures, be they words, common phrases, or idiomatic expressions, are directly replaced by the corresponding target language structures. Earlier in this chapter (p. 297) I described the process by which the memory representations of entities that co-occur in the environment become connected through a process of joint activation ("what fires together, wires together"). This learning mechanism is also likely to underlie transcoding: During each translation act, translation-equivalent structures in memory will be activated in close temporal proximity, even when translation comes about via the vertical route, and as a consequence they will be linked up with one another. The more often the same two translation-equivalent structures are co-activated through translation, the stronger the link between them will become and the more easily available one term of the pair will become given the other term. The consequence is that especially experienced translators and interpreters will possess a large stock of memory structures that enable transcoding. Paired-associate learning (see Chapter 3) is an additional means to form and strengthen such links between translation-equivalent memory structures. The present two hypothesized translation strategies are visualized in Figure 6.7.

A phenomenon called "natural translation" suggests that conceptually mediated translation is a general translation strategy that is already used by young children. The term refers to the translating that is done in everyday circumstances by bilinguals without any special training in translating. As shown by several authors (e.g., Harris & Sherwood, 1978; Malakoff, 1992), any individual with a certain degree of competence in two languages can communicate between the two and, thus, act as a translator for monolingual speakers of each language. This form of translation behavior can already be observed in very young bilingual children, starting soon after the onset of their first linguistic utterances (Harris, 1980). This suggests that translation ability is concomitant with bilingualism, an emergent property of bilingualism that exploits the language-processing machinery and knowledge structures that are already in place and used in monolingual settings. Furthermore, the fact that even young children manifest this behavior shows that already at a young age bilinguals have functionally separated their languages, because only when the knowledge of what language individual linguistic items belong to is in place, is translation possible. (This, incidentally, also suggests that a once-popular view of code switching in young bilingual children as resulting from linguistic confusion must be wrong.) Finally, the phenomenon indicates the existence of **metalinguistic awareness** (defined as "the ability to reflect on and manipulate the structural features of language independent of meaning"; Bruck & Genesee, 1995, p. 307) in very young bilinguals. This conclusion follows from the fact that translation is only possible by stepping back "from the comprehension and production of an utterance in order to consider the linguistic form and structure underlying the meaning of the utterance" (Malakoff & Hakuta, 1991, p. 147).

This evidence that bilinguals without appreciable translation experience dispose of a natural translation ability obviously does not imply that they translate in the same manner as professional translators. In addition to evident quantitative differences between "natural" translators and professionals in translation speed and accuracy,

FIGURE 6.7

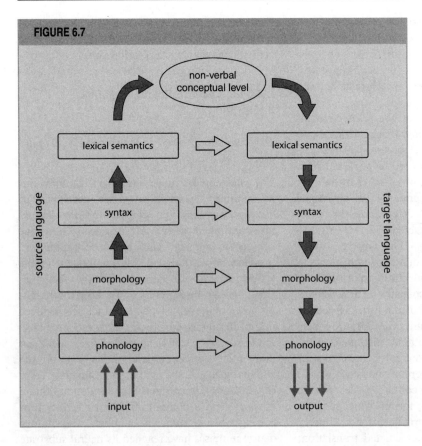

Two translation strategies (based on Paradis, 1994). The grey arrows depict conceptually mediated translation: The input is fully analyzed by the source language system in a bottom-up fashion. Next, the emerging conceptual representation is processed top-down by the target language system. The white arrows depict the transcoding process in which source language structures are directly transformed into their equivalents in the target language. Adapted from Christoffels and De Groot (2005) by permission of Oxford University Press, Inc.

qualitative differences are likely to exist between them because processionals may use special strategies and skills that they developed on the job. One possible difference concerns the degree of transcoding exhibited by lay translators and professionals: Because professionals possess a relatively large stock of well-established translation structures in memory (see above), they plausibly rely on transcoding more than non-professionals do (Paradis, 1994). Yet this is a source of dispute in the literature. Whereas Paradis regards the frequent use of transcoding a signature of professionalism and as beneficial for translation and interpreting performance, according to other scholars (e.g., Seleskovitch, 1976) it indicates a lack of expertise and hinders performance.

As is often the case when opposing views are held, there may be a kernel of truth in both of them. Because many words have more than one

meaning and, therefore, translate into more than one word in another language, one can easily see how the automatic triggering of one particular target language word by a source language word (by activation spreading along the direct link between the corresponding memory structures) may lead the translator up the garden path. Because of the relatively strong memory connections between a source language word and its frequent translation(s), this danger is especially large when the currently targeted meaning is a relatively infrequent one. But it is also easy to see how the swift availability of translation-equivalent structures along transcoding connections in memory can help to reduce processing load, freeing mental resources for non-automatic task components. As long as some resources are spared for a monitoring process that oversees performance and intercepts incorrect translations delivered by a transcoding structure, the beneficial effects of transcoding presumably outweigh the risks involved. For such monitoring to take place no special mechanism needs to be postulated because, as mentioned earlier, interpreters are known to monitor their speech (e.g., Gerver, 1976; Isham, 2000).

Whatever the attitude of the research community towards transcoding, there is evidence to suggest that it does in fact occur, also in translation and interpreting by professionals. Isham (1994) and De Bot (2000) observed that the form of recently encountered grammatical structures in the source language determines the exact choice of grammatical target language structures, and many studies (e.g., De Groot, 1992b; Christoffels et al., 2003) found cognate effects in translation; that is, differential performance for cognates and non-cognates. These effects demonstrate an influence of the form aspects of the source language input on translation performance. Yet in conceptually mediated translation the downward production process sets off from a non-verbal conceptual message which, by definition, does not contain traces of the source language's input forms. This suggests that the above effects originate from another process than conceptually mediated translation; and transcoding—enabled by ready-made transcoding structures in memory—is a plausible candidate (but see pp. 261–263 for alternative accounts). Furthermore, a study by Fabbro, Gran, and Gran (1991) suggested that both professional and student interpreters exploit a mixture of transcoding and conceptually mediated interpreting, but with the professionals relying more on the latter than the students. When the interpreter is particularly stressed or tired, the use of form-based interpreting strategies increases, presumably because it requires less mental resources than conceptually mediated interpreting (Darò & Fabbro, 1994). In other words, for professional interpreters transcoding may be a convenient backup strategy to resort to during circumstances of excessive mental load. It thus appears that Seleskovitch (1976) was right in positing that the excessive reliance on transcoding reflects a lack of expertise. But having this strategy in reserve benefits

performance the moment mental load during interpreting exceeds some critical level and conceptually mediated interpreting fails.

Language control in simultaneous interpreting

Differential activation of language subsets and processing components

The views on language control in simultaneous interpreting are built on those developed to account for language control in monolingual tasks and again assign crucial roles to language subsets, a language cue in the conceptualized message, and a language-tag component in the lexical lemma. To account for the fact that simultaneous interpreters must keep both languages simultaneously active and yet produce output in only one of them, the target language, Paradis (1994, 2004) extended his views on differential activation and inhibition of the two language subsets in monolingual tasks (pp. 294–296). Recall that Paradis assumes that a memory item becomes available for further processing when a sufficient number of excitatory neural impulses have reached its neural substrate and that the amount of impulses required to reach this point was called the item's "activation threshold". He furthermore assumes that thresholds are not fixed but can be adapted to the language user's current goals, for instance, to use one language or the other. Regarding simultaneous interpreting he suggested that the thresholds of all the elements in both subsets are clearly set well below a level that would frustrate source language comprehension, target language production, or both, but that at the same time the thresholds of the elements belonging to the source language are set higher than those of the target language elements.

One might wonder whether a relatively high threshold setting of the source language elements would involve the risk that their comprehension is impeded. But as we have seen, Paradis's views include the idea that relatively high threshold settings still enable comprehension because of the relative ease with which input from an external source brings about the neural impulses that activate the targeted memory items. So even if the thresholds are set at a relatively high level, sufficient neural impulses will be incited by the input for the comprehension thresholds to be reached. Instead, for production to be possible at all, lower thresholds are required because the arousal of the neural impulses to activate the targeted memory items, now coming from internal sources, is more demanding. Therefore, the number of impulses exciting the relevant memory items will be relatively small and production is only possible if the associated thresholds are relatively low. The implication of this state of the language system for simultaneous interpreting is clear: Even if during simultaneous interpreting the thresholds of the elements belonging to the source language subsystem are raised towards relatively high levels, comprehension is still possible. At the same time, these relatively high thresholds prevent output in the source language. In fact, the only difference between this account of language control in simultaneous interpreting and the account of language control in monolingual production tasks presented earlier is that the latter allow for an even larger difference in the threshold settings for the two languages, with, specifically, the thresholds of memory elements in the non-response language raised to maximally high levels.

Still, there may be situations in which Paradis's (1994) solution to set the thresholds of the source language elements at a relatively high level involves the risk of suboptimal comprehension and subsequent breakdown. This situation may arise when the current comprehension requirements are taxing due to, for instance, poor quality of the speaker's diction. Adapting to these circumstances by lowering the thresholds of the source language elements might solve this problem but would create a new one because the lower settings might render source language elements available for production, thus leading to language-mixed output. Because of the comprehension problem this would cause for the (monolingual) listeners, this situation must be avoided under all circumstances. In fact, the risk of mixed output was what motivated the dif-

ferential threshold setting of source and target language in the first place.

Grosjean (1997b, 2001) proposed a different solution that circumvents this problem. It is illustrated in Figure 6.8. Just like Paradis he split up the language system into two linguistic subsystems, viewing these as knowledge stores. Onto each subset he added two processing mechanisms, an input mechanism (or "component") and an output mechanism. According to Grosjean, as the language subsystems proper (the knowledge stores), these processing mechanisms can be activated to different degrees. He assumed that in simultaneous interpreting the source and target language subsystems are both highly activated and to equal degrees (the interpreter is in a "bilingual mode"; see pp. 288–291). In addition, to allow for accurate comprehension of the source language, this language's input component is highly activated. Instead, to prevent source language elements from emerging in the output, the output component of the source language is completely deactivated. In addition, both the input and output components of the target language are activated: The output component of the target language must obviously be activated highly to enable production in this language, and this language's input component must be activated so that interpreters can monitor their output. Because of the relative ease of comprehension as compared to production, a relatively low level of activation of the target language's input component (which is the equivalent of a high threshold setting in Paradis's model) would suffice. However, because this component is a different one from the analogous source language input component and is exclusively dedicated to comprehension anyway, there is no reason why it should be activated less than the corresponding output component.

Grosjean's view on simultaneous interpreting thus explicitly distinguished between two knowledge stores (the language subsets) on the one hand and four processing mechanisms on the other hand. The exact content of the knowledge stores is not explicated. Presumably lexical knowledge such as morphological, grammatical, and form information regarding words is implied.

A view on language control in simultaneous interpreting. The language system contains two language-specific knowledge stores (the black squares) and two language-specific input-processing and output-processing mechanisms each (the circles). During simultaneous interpreting both knowledge stores are highly activated, as are the two input-processing mechanisms and the output-processing mechanism of the target language. The output-processing mechanism of the source language is deactivated. Adapted from Grosjean (2001). Copyright © 2001. Reproduced with permission of Blackwell Publishing Ltd.

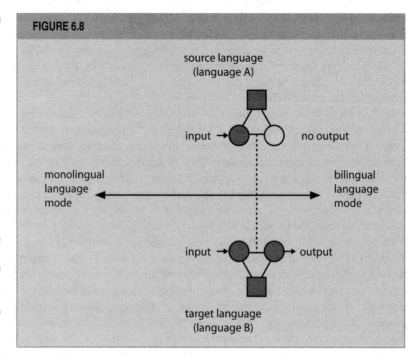

FIGURE 6.8

But form aspects of lexical entries are plausibly represented separately for comprehension and production, an assumption that in the literature emerges in the proposal of separate input and output lexicons. Extending this possibility to the bilingual case implies the existence of (at least) four lexical knowledge components: an "input lexicon" that consists of two subsets, one for each language, and an "output lexicon" again containing two subsets. Christoffels and De Groot (2005) suggested an account of language control in simultaneous interpreting in terms of such a four-component view of the lexicon, incorporating the common notion of differential activation of language subsets. This set-up is illustrated in Figure 6.9.

We hypothesized that these four subsystems of the bilingual language system can be activated independently from one another. Because in simultaneous interpreting the source language must be understood and the target language produced, the input lexicon of the former and the output lexicon of the latter must be highly activated. In addition, to allow for monitoring of the target language's output, the target language's

input lexicon must be activated. Finally, to prevent words from the source language emerging in the output, the source language's output lexicon must be deactivated as much as possible.

So whereas Grosjean proposed a solution in terms of two equally highly activated language subsets augmented by a total of four differentially activated input and output processing mechanisms, each dedicated to one language only, the present proposal distinguishes between four differentially activated knowledge stores and remains implicit about the processing mechanisms that operate on these knowledge stores. Comparing the present view with Paradis's account of language control in simultaneous interpreting, the only essential difference is the splitting up of Paradis's source and target language subsystems in a part that contains elements dedicated to comprehension and one with elements exclusively used for production. This seemingly minor change may be crucial, however, because it does not run the risk of comprehension failure as a consequence of too low an activation level (or, in Paradis's terminology, too high a threshold setting) of the source language's

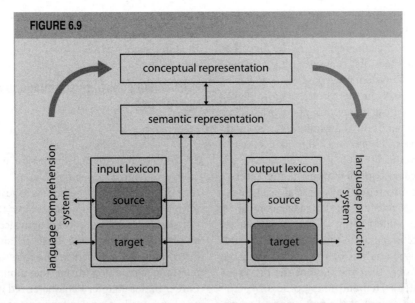

FIGURE 6.9

A view on language control in simultaneous interpreting. Conceptually mediated translation takes the route via the conceptual representation level. Lexical transcoding takes the shortcut via the lexical-semantic representations. Separate input and output lexicons are assumed for each language subsystem. The source language's input lexicon and the target language's output lexicon are highly activated to enable source language comprehension and target language production. The target language's input lexicon is also activated to some extent so that the output can be monitored. The source language's output lexicon is completely deactivated. From Christoffels and De Groot (2005) by permission of Oxford University Press, Inc.

subsystem in Paradis's account. In the present model, the activation of the source language's input lexicon can safely be set at a maximum level without running the risk that the source language intrudes in the output. The reason is that the elements in the input lexicon are specialized for comprehension and are alien to the production process.

A language cue in the preverbal message

The common element in all three views of language control in simultaneous interpreting presented so far is the assumption of differential activation of complete language subsets, subcomponents thereof, or language-processing mechanisms. The plausibility of these views ultimately depends on evidence suggesting the existence of each of the hypothesized separate components of the language system and of a control system that can perform the obviously

delicate maneuvers required to differentially set the activation levels of all of them, proactively and globally. Especially in the latter respect a further proposal, based on La Heij's (2005) view of language control in monolingual word production presented earlier (pp. 304–306; see also De Bot, 2000), is more parsimonious. As described there, this author advanced a "complex access, simple selection" view of lexical selection that consists of two steps. First, an elaborate ("complex") conceptualization process delivers a detailed output (the "preverbal message") that contains all the information a speaker wants to communicate, including his or her goal to use slang or to express the conceptualized content in, say, the L2. The conceptual information specifying the targeted language is called the "language cue". Second, a "simple" selection process subsequently takes place in which the lexical entries that are maximally activated by the preverbal message are selected for production, generally one per lexical concept in the preverbal message. If a bilingual's intention is to speak in L2, the inclusion of the L2 language cue in the preverbal message guarantees that generally L2 speech will emerge from the system because the lexical entries for L2 words will on the whole be more highly activated than those representing L1 words.

On the assumption that simultaneous interpreting comes about via the conceptually mediated ("vertical") route presented earlier, this view on language control in monolingual settings does not seem to require any special adjustment to be able to account for language control in simultaneous interpreting. The deverbalized conceptual representation that is the end product of the linguistic analysis of the source language input is plausibly the equivalent of the preverbal message that La Heij and many others hypothesize to be the output of the first (conceptualization) step of speech production (see Chapter 5). This conceptual representation must subsequently be expressed into target language speech. As long as the interpreter adds the intention to produce speech in the target language to this conceptual structure in the form of the appropriate language cue, the output will generally be in the targeted language because the words in this language will be activated relatively highly by the conceptual structure. In other words, just as the language cue guarantees that the targeted language will be output in unilingual conversational settings, it also sees to it that output in the target language emerges during interpreting. Furthermore, just as the monitoring system intercepts speech errors on their way out in common monolingual speech production, in simultaneous interpreting it will intercept the odd word in the source language on its way out. The only clear difference between the two situations is that the conceptual content that sets off production is the end product of decoding the source language input in interpreting, but comes from within the cognitive system in common monolingual language production. Unlike the above views, this account of language control in simultaneous interpreting does not require the proactive setting of the activation level of various mental subsystems. As long as the interpreter keeps in mind his goal to produce output in the target language, he will satisfy his audience, at least in this respect.

Processing control in simultaneous interpreting

Introduction

So far the focus of the discussion has been on *language* control in simultaneous interpreting; that is, on how interpreters manage to produce output in the target language despite the fact that both language subsystems are activated. But there is obviously more to control in simultaneous interpreting than merely seeing to it that the output language differs from the input language. Earlier in this chapter I characterized interpreting as an extremely complex task that taxes working memory inordinately because it encompasses several components that all consume attention and must be executed under speed stress and interwoven within the same unit time. A consideration of the task's requirements will easily convince anyone that the task is excruciating, and can only succeed under the confident guidance of an unrelentingly alert control system with a large capacity and that can rely on a large database of swiftly available knowledge. How then is interpreting possible at all, at least for some dedicated and perhaps gifted individuals? To what extent does it exploit, on the one hand, the knowledge structures and linguistic skills that come with a high level of proficiency in the two languages concerned and, on the other hand, specialized knowledge, skills, and strategies that are not concomitant with fluent bilingualism? And if the latter contribute to successful performance, do they reflect an innate aptitude or do they result from task-relevant training (are interpreters born or bred)? Knowing what knowledge and skills come with fluent bilingualism and which ones require specialized training (or are innate) is not only of theoretical interest but has practical implications as well: It informs both the development of interpreter training programs and the assessment procedures that admit students to the program.

In the next sections I will present the results of a number of studies that have addressed one or more of the above questions. As we will see, rather than probing the participants' performance on the full simultaneous interpreting task, many of the relevant studies tackle these questions by focusing on one or more of the hypothesized task components, such as working memory, comprehension, or a sub-skill of these. The underlying assumption of this componential approach—common in the study of complex tasks—is that performance on the full task is related to the degree of mastery of its components. This approach does not imply the assumption that full-task performance is a direct function of the performance on the component tasks. Instead, there is the understanding that the requirement to execute all of the constituent parts in concert and under severe time pressure may modulate the way each of them is executed in isolation, independent from the others. The components of the interpreting task that I will focus on are comprehension of the source language, word retrieval, and working memory.

Comprehension processes

One set of studies examined comprehension processes in interpreting and other tasks by comparing the performance of expert interpreters/ translators and non-experts. McDonald and Carpenter (1981) had experts and amateur German–English translators perform a task, "simultaneous translation", which involved a mixture of simultaneous interpreting and written text-to-text translation. The participants were presented with written text fragments that they had to translate orally as quickly as possible while reading them. Their translation behavior was inferred from the eye movements that were registered while they performed the task (see p. 161 for details). The data showed that the patterns of eye movements for both participant groups, the experts and amateurs alike, were similar to those that characterize normal reading processes: The participants tended to assign meaning and reference to each word as soon as possible, as readers typically do (this strategy is

known as the "immediacy strategy"). Furthermore, as readers do, they used syntactic and semantic cues in the input to chunk the reading materials into meaning units consisting of several lexical elements. These findings suggest that at least in some respects expert and non-expert translators use similar comprehension processes during translation and that the comprehension processes used in translation build on those used in common unilingual reading situations. As we shall see later, the latter conclusion does not imply that comprehension processes during translation are identical in all respects to those employed in monolingual language processing.

A study by Dillinger (1994) similarly indicated that expert and non-expert simultaneous interpreters use similar comprehension strategies. In this study interpreters and fluent bilinguals without any interpreting experience were asked to interpret English materials into French. Dillinger's unit of analysis was the "proposition", which in linguistic theory refers to a basic meaning unit consisting of something or someone being talked about (called an "argument") and an assertion made about this argument (the "predicate"). With the number of processed text propositions serving as the dependent variable, the two groups responded the same way to a number of syntactic and semantic text manipulations such as the density of syntactic clauses, whether a clause concerned a main or a subordinate clause, and the density of propositions. The differences between the two groups that did emerge were primarily quantitative: Unsurprisingly, the accuracy of interpreting was better for the experienced interpreters.

Other quantitative differences between the comprehension processes in professional interpreters and non-interpreters were identified by Bajo, Padilla, and Padilla (1999) in a study where the participants did not perform any full translation task but simply read text for comprehension. One group of non-interpreters consisted of students in a translation and interpreting program who had finished their training in text translation but had not yet been trained in simultaneous interpreting. A second group of non-professionals consisted of highly proficient balanced bilinguals who had never participated in such a training program. The participants read through texts presented on the screen word-by-word by means of one version of the self-paced reading technique (see p. 160 for details): Each time the participant pressed a button the next word appeared on the screen. In experiments using this technique the time duration between two successive button presses is considered the reading time for the word presented last. The reading time per word turned out to be significantly shorter for the professional interpreters than for the control group of proficient balanced bilinguals, whereas those for the group of translation students were in between those of the other two groups. The depth of text comprehension did not differ between the groups. In a further test the participants were presented with exemplar–category word pairs (e.g., *finch–bird* or *finch–clothing*) and were asked to decide for each of them whether the first word referred to an exemplar of the category named by the second word. The response times in this task, which presumably reflect the speed with which meaning is assigned to words, were shorter for the professional interpreters than for the other two groups. These joint findings thus suggest that interpreters excel in word recognition, one of the sub-skills of text comprehension. As stressed by the investigators, the finding that the professional interpreters outperformed the balanced bilinguals is of special interest, because it suggests that the faster word recognition and meaning assignment of the interpreters did not merely result from a high level of proficiency in both languages but from specific training. This hypothesis was confirmed in a retest taken about 10 months later. During the intervening months the student group but not the non-student control group had practiced all sorts of exercises aimed at improving rapid word recognition and semantic access. The student group demonstrated shorter reading and categorization time on the retest, thus demonstrating the efficacy of skill-relevant training. In contrast, the non-student group had not become any faster on either task.

A further set of studies examined whether the requirement to simultaneously comprehend and translate the input materials in translation influences the comprehension processes by directly comparing the participants' performance on a simple comprehension task and a translation task. Gerver (1974) had interpreting students either listen to spoken stories or simultaneously interpret them, after which they had to answer comprehension questions. In the interpreting condition fewer questions were answered correctly than in the listening condition. This finding suggests that the requirement to simultaneously perform other mental operations in addition to comprehending the aural input has an adverse effect on comprehension. In a second study, Macizo and Bajo (2004) had fluent Spanish–English bilinguals who were experienced translators/interpreters either read and repeat a set of "object relative" sentences or read and translate them, in two separate blocks each preceded by block-appropriate instructions. In object relative sentences the noun that refers to the agent of the main verb must be assigned the role of patient in an embedded relative clause (e.g., *The judge who the reporter interviewed dismissed the charge at the end of the hearing*, in which *judge* is the agent of the main verb *dismissed* but the patient of *interviewed*). Sentences of this type are known to require more processing resources than their "subject relative" counterparts (*The judge who interviewed the reporter dismissed the charge at the end of the hearing*, in which *judge* is the agent of both the main and relative verb). The reading materials appeared word-by-word in the center of the screen and the presentation rate was self-paced, each next word appearing upon a key press by the participant. The time between two successive key presses was registered as the reading time per word. Repeating or translating started after the final word of the sentence had been read and a message (either the word *repeat* or the word *translate*) appeared on the screen (but note that the participants always knew in advance whether the sentence to be presented was to be repeated or translated).

The investigators argued that, if comprehension processes are the same in normal reading and in reading for translation, reading time per word should be the same in the read-then-repeat and the read-then-translate conditions. Contrary to this prediction, reading times were longer when the participants read for subsequent translation than when they read for subsequent repetition. This finding suggests that comprehension processes vary depending on the specific goal of reading. The reading time difference between the two conditions was especially large in the sentence area where computation demands were highest (around *interviewed* in the above sentence, which is the place where readers have to figure out the thematic role of *reporter*). Level of comprehension was the same in the two conditions. The researchers attributed the reading time difference between the two conditions to additional processing in the reading phase of the read-then-translate condition. They hypothesized that this extra processing concerned the transcoding operation discussed earlier.

Converging evidence was obtained in two further studies by the same research group (Macizo & Bajo, 2006; Ruiz, Paredes, Macizo, & Bajo, 2008) in which professional Spanish–English translators/interpreters were presented with two blocks of L1 Spanish sentences. As in Macizo and Bajo (2004) they were instructed to read then repeat one block of sentences and to read then translate (in L2 English) those of the second block. Macizo and Bajo (2006) manipulated the cognate status of the words in sentence-initial and sentence-final position. The results showed that when the participants were asked to read and translate the sentences the reading times for cognates were faster than those for non-cognate control words, especially in sentence-final position. However, when the participants were instructed to read and repeat the sentences this cognate effect did not materialize. The authors concluded that when professional translators/interpreters process linguistic materials with the purpose of translating them, lexical elements of the target language are also activated while target language activation does not occur when they merely process the input for comprehension. It may be remembered that cognate effects do not constitute unequivocal evidence of parallel activation in the target language (see pp. 203–205 and 247). Aware of this fact, Ruiz

et al. (2008) ran a further study in which they manipulated the syntactic congruency between the source language sentences and the corresponding target language sentences and the frequency of some of the target language words (while the frequency of the corresponding source language words did not vary). In the read-then-translate condition, but not in the read-then-repeat condition, the reading times were affected by both these manipulations, a finding that again indicates co-activation of structures in the target language's linguistic system in the former but not the latter condition. Once again the authors attributed these effects to transcoding operations during comprehension in the read-then-translate conditions. In other words, the results of all three studies suggest that the requirement to translate modulates the comprehension processes as executed in unilingual reading.

To summarize, the joint results of the above studies suggest that in some ways the comprehension processes of professional translators and amateurs involved in a translation task resemble the comprehension strategies that readers normally use in common unilingual reading. Comprehension processes in translation thus seem to build on those used in normal reading. In addition, the above results revealed a number of quantitative differences between the comprehension processes of professional and amateur translators, including faster word recognition and faster meaning assignment in professionals. Finally, they showed that reading for translation in professional translators modifies normal unilingual comprehension processes. Whether this also holds for amateur translation is undetermined because, to my knowledge, the relevant experiment has not been performed yet.

Word retrieval and working memory

In one of the studies reviewed above (Bajo et al., 1999) it was found that professional translators/interpreters recognize and assign meaning to words faster than proficient bilinguals inexperienced in translating and interpreting. A couple of other studies have shown that interpreters possess other special abilities as well, while at the same time suggesting that some of the sub-skills required for interpreting can be developed by other means than interpreting experience. Christoffels et al. (2006) compared the performance of two groups of Dutch–English bilinguals without any professional interpreting experience and a group of professional interpreters on a number of simple tasks that were all assumed to reflect a basic cognitive sub-skill of simultaneous interpreting. The two groups of inexperienced interpreters differed from one another in L2 English proficiency (and amount of L2 language training): One consisted of unbalanced bilinguals, all university undergraduates, with stronger L1 Dutch and weaker (but still relatively strong) L2 English. The second concerned balanced bilinguals with Dutch as their L1 who, just like the interpreters, had a university degree in English, and were all teachers of English and, as such, practiced English professionally on a daily basis, again just as the interpreters did.

One set of tests assessed the participants' fluency in retrieving words from memory: picture naming in L1 and L2 and word translation in both directions. The importance of rapid and automatic word retrieval for interpreting is evident because any conscious effort required to retrieve the appropriate target language word for a concept to be expressed reduces the mental resources available for other non-automated processing operations. Indeed, Carroll (1978) assumed "verbal fluency" (as the swift availability of linguistic knowledge, and especially vocabulary knowledge, is often called) to be one of the most important requirements for a successful career as a simultaneous interpreter. In agreement with this view, word retrieval fluency has been shown to be positively correlated with performance on a simultaneous interpreting task in bilinguals without any prior task training (Christoffels et al., 2003).

Two further tests that we administered are commonly thought to reflect both the storage and processing functions of working memory. One of these was the oft-used "reading span test" (Daneman & Carpenter, 1980): The participants are presented with increasingly large sets of

written sentences and asked to read them with understanding and to concurrently try to remember the final word of each sentence. Following each set the participant is asked to reproduce the final word of all sentences presented in the set. The presentation procedure stops the moment the participant fails to recall all sentence-final words of the immediately preceding set. The dependent variable is the participant's reading span score; that is, the largest sentence-set size for which the participant exhibited perfect recall. Alternatively, the dependent variable is the total number of sentence-final words of all previous sentence sets successfully recalled up until the moment of failure to reproduce all sentence-final words of the just-presented set. To make sure that the participants do indeed read with understanding and do not just try to memorize the sentence-final words, at random moments the participants must answer questions regarding the previous sentence's meaning. Our second test concerned the "speaking span test" (Daneman & Green, 1986): Participants are presented with sets of words of increasing size and asked to construct sentences that contain all the words of a set. This test is thought to assess the ability to produce sentences and remember words simultaneously. The speaking span score is the largest number of words for which participants successfully create a sentence (or the total number of words successfully embedded in sentences up until the moment of failure to construct a sentence around the word-set just presented). Notice that the demands of these two memory span tests mimic the requirement in interpreting to concurrently comprehend and memorize linguistic material on the one hand, and to concurrently produce and memorize linguistic material on the other hand.

Performance on the reading span test is known to correlate positively with reading comprehension (Daneman & Carpenter, 1980). The likely reason is that many processes that must be carried out to get a good grasp of the message communicated by a text—such as finding the antecedents of anaphors, resolving syntactic ambiguities, and making inferences—require that earlier parts of the text are kept in working memory. In other words, good comprehension requires the concurrent storage and processing of information, and it is exactly this ability that the reading span test assesses. The demands on working memory during interpreting are much larger than during reading comprehension: Not only does good comprehension of the source language necessitate the concurrent processing and storage of the input, thus already taxing working memory, but the sequencing differences between the source and target language, and the temporary retention of parts of the input this requires, also demands additional capacity. Furthermore, a part of the working memory resources must be allocated to the production of an earlier input fragment and to coordinating the various task components. Given these demands of the interpreting task, performance on the reading span test may be expected to be relatively good for interpreters. Similarly, interpreters may be expected to excel on the speaking span test because, as mentioned, it reflects the ability, required in interpreting, to concurrently maintain information in memory and construct output that expresses this information.

The upper and lower parts of Figure 6.10 summarize the main results of the working memory and word retrieval tasks, respectively. A quick glance at these four graphs immediately reveals that on the word retrieval tasks (picture naming and word translation) the interpreters and teachers performed at similar levels, and that both groups outperformed the student group (except on the task that indexes a skill that all groups may be expected to be equally experienced in: picture naming in L1). In contrast, on the working memory tasks the interpreters clearly outperformed both other groups, which did not differ from one another statistically. These joint findings strongly support two conclusions: First, one of the component skills of professional interpreting, swift word retrieval in L2, appears to emerge from extensive practice in the L2, suggesting that it is concomitant with proficient bilingualism. (To what extent teacher training contributed to the high word retrieval fluency of the teachers is not clear. It would require a control group of balanced bilinguals without any teacher training to find out.) Second, a further prerequisite for professional interpreting, a large

working memory capacity, is not a side-effect of proficient bilingualism but appears to emerge from extensive on-the-job interpreting practice.

However, a second possible cause of the differential span scores of interpreters on the one hand and non-interpreters on the other hand should be considered: It might be that the high scores of interpreters reflect a large innate working memory capacity, and that the interpreting profession appeals to individuals with this special ability (that is, they may self-select for the job). However, studies by Bajo et al. (1999) and Padilla, Bajo, Cañas, and Padilla (1995) suggested that it is not good working memory genes but, indeed, extensive task practice that underlies the large working memory capacity of interpreters. Like Christoffels et al. (2006), these researchers had professional interpreters and different groups of control participants perform a number of tasks, including the reading span test. Among the controls was a group of students in a translation and interpreting training program who had finished their training program in text-to-text translation but had not yet been trained in simultaneous interpreting. A further control group consisted of participants who had finished their undergraduate studies in other fields and, aiming at other careers, had not had any training in translation and interpreting. The results of both studies showed larger reading spans in the interpreters than in the other groups of participants, who did not differ between them. The finding that the translation and interpreting students did not perform any better than the other control group points at interpreting practice as the source of the superior working memory of interpreters.

In the foregoing, a number of skills have been identified that characterize the professional interpreter and that are all likely to be prerequisites for performing the task at a professional level: rapid word retrieval given a concept to express, a large working memory capacity, rapid word recognition and meaning assignment during reading. In addition to these special abilities of interpreters, a further one has been identified: Interpreters not only have a relatively large working memory capacity, they also appear to exploit working memory differently from

FIGURE 6.10

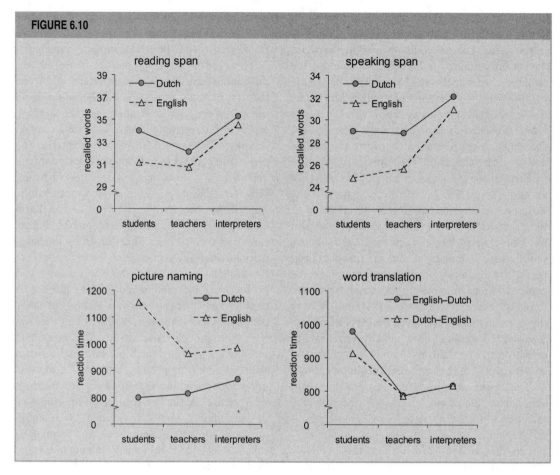

Mean number of recalled words on the reading span and speaking span tasks per group, and mean reaction times (in ms) on the picture-naming and word translation tasks per group. Adapted from Christoffels et al. (2006) Copyright 2006, with permission from Elsevier.

non-interpreters. The critical evidence comes from studies that exploited the articulatory suppression technique introduced earlier in the context of the working memory model of Allan Baddeley and his colleagues (e.g., Baddeley, 1986; Gathercole & Baddeley, 1993; see Chapter 3, pp. 116–119). In addition to a "central executive", this model contains a "phonological loop", a subsystem specialized for processing and temporarily maintaining verbal material. To be able to maintain verbal material, the phonological loop is equipped with a rehearsal system. When a task must be performed that requires the involvement of the phonological loop, the proper working of the loop can be frustrated by articulatory suppression; that is, by getting the participants to perform a secondary task that engages their articulation apparatus so that it is no longer available for the rehearsal required by the primary task. This secondary nuisance task often involves the concurrent and repeated uttering by the participants of some nonsense sound (e.g., the nonsense syllable *bla*). The consequence of occupying the loop this way is deteriorated performance on the primary task as compared with performance in a condition where the articulation apparatus is not kept busy by a secondary task (e.g., Papagno et al., 1991).

As we have seen above, comprehension requires the temporary retention of the input materials, and to fulfill this requirement the phonological loop's rehearsal system must be deployed. In simultaneous interpreting, however, the requirement to produce vocal output in the target language while making sense of the input equals an articulatory suppression condition. How then is comprehension possible at all? Bajo et al. (1999) and Padilla et al. (1995) hypothesized that the answer may be that interpreters use their working memory differently from non-interpreters. They set out to test this hypothesis by studying word learning with and without articulatory suppression. Lists of words were *visually* presented to professional interpreters, student interpreters, and non-interpreter controls who were asked to read and memorize the words. In the articulatory suppression condition, but not in the control condition, the participants were asked to repeat the syllable *bla* during learning. Following the presentation of each word list, recall was tested. The results showed that the professional interpreters were not adversely affected by the concurrent articulation requirement: They recalled equally as many words in the suppression condition as in the non-suppression condition. In contrast, the other groups of participants showed the typical adverse effect of concurrent articulation and to an equal degree. These findings thus confirm the researchers' hypothesis that interpreters use their working memory differently from non-interpreters, including interpreting students with relatively little experience on the task. Specifically they suggest that the working memory of professional interpreters does not (always) need the support of the phonological loop to operate effectively. What remains is to explain why and under what circumstances this is and, specifically, why interpreters were not affected by concurrent articulation in the experiments described above. Additional research by Padilla, Bajo, and Macizo (2005) ruled out several options, including the possibility that interpreters are *generally* good at combining tasks even with tasks they have not practiced in combination before. The results suggested that only when the words to learn were highly familiar to them did concurrent articulation not impede performance. The authors

concluded that the interpreters' ability to simultaneously comprehend and produce speech is somehow related to their ability to use word knowledge efficiently.

The above articulatory suppression experiments can tell us something about how simultaneous interpreting is done because, as in simultaneous interpreting, vocal output is produced while at the same time an input has to be processed. Yet in a number of respects the articulatory suppression condition in these experiments deviates from veridical simultaneous interpreting. First, the source language input in true-to-life interpreting differs greatly from the analogous test materials in the above word-learning tasks and plausibly poses different processing demands. Second, in common simultaneous interpreting the input material is spoken, not written, as in the above studies. (Alternatively, the input material is signed, in the case of interpreting from a sign language to a spoken language; see below.) In these respects, two further studies using articulatory suppression mimicked simultaneous interpreting more closely by presenting the input materials aurally. In one of them (Isham, 2000), monolingual under-graduate students listened to pre-recorded short stories that were interrupted by a tone from time to time. Upon hearing this tone they had to write down as much as they could recall from the story so far. One condition involved just listening to the story. In a second condition the participants had to repeat the word "double" while listening to the stories. To guarantee that the participants would process the meaning of the stories, after listening to each of them true/false questions were posed regarding the stories' content. The results showed both poorer recall and poorer comprehension in the concurrent articulation condition than in the just listening condition. These results converge with the above evidence of an adverse effect of concurrent articulation with visual word input in the non-interpreter group (Bajo et al., 1999; Padilla et al., 1995).

Because Isham (2000) did not test interpreters it is impossible to tell whether they would be similarly affected by concurrent articulation or whether, as in the above studies with visual input, they would again show immunity to articulatory suppression. The results of a second study, by Darò and Fabbro (1994), indicate that prior interpreting experience does not counteract an adverse effect of concurrent articulation when the input is aural instead of visual. These authors had advanced Italian–English student interpreters first learn and then recall series of spoken digits in three conditions. In a listening condition the digit series to be learned were presented binaurally over headphones and the participants were asked to reproduce as many of them as possible after each series. In an articulatory suppression condition the participants were asked to continuously utter two nonsense syllables during learning. Finally, in a simultaneous interpreting condition the participants had to translate the digits in the other language during learning. The interpreting condition led to poorer recall than the other two conditions and the suppression condition showed poorer recall than the just listening condition. The results of this experiment thus suggest that the requirement to listen and speak at the same time has a negative effect on memory even in participants trained in interpreting. They furthermore point out that the additional requirement to translate has a separate adverse effect on memory.

The results of a second experiment in Darò and Fabbro's (1994) study, which included a veridical simultaneous interpreting condition, confirmed these conclusions. In this experiment the same participants as tested in the above digit recall experiment listened to one story in one condition and had to simultaneously interpret another story in the second condition. Right after listening to or interpreting the story, a recall test was administered in which they had to reproduce the story verbatim. The interpreting condition led to lower recall scores than the listening condition. Because of a missing articulatory suppression condition that does not at the same time involve translation, it is impossible to tell to what extent concurrent articulation and translation contributed to the decreased recall separately. Nevertheless, these results indicate that the requirement of concurrent listening and speaking frustrates the memory performance of advanced student interpreters. A couple of studies reviewed by Isham (2000) strengthen this conclusion and suggest it can legitimately be generalized to professional interpreters. In one of these studies it was found that professional interpreters also perform worse on a verbatim recall test after interpreting short stories than after just listening to them (Isham, 1994). However, when the target language was signed instead of spoken, recall performance was equally good after listening and interpreting (Isham & Lane, 1993). These findings thus suggest that it is indeed the simultaneity of *listening* and *speaking* that affects recall and that even professional interpreters are affected by it. Furthermore, the equivalence of recall following listening and sign-language interpreting indicates that, unlike in advanced student interpreters (Darò & Fabbro, 1994), the requirement to translate has no separate detrimental effect on the memory performance of professional interpreters.

Summary and conclusions

In the preceding sections I have presented a set of findings that typify professional interpreters. As compared with other bilinguals, they are relatively fast at executing a number of tasks that tap basic sub-skills of the full interpreting task: retrieving the name for a concept to express, recognizing words, and assigning meaning to them. They furthermore possess a relatively large working memory capacity and exploit this capacity in a way different from non-interpreters. This latter characteristic of professional interpreters was revealed in experiments looking at the adverse effects of articulatory suppression on recall in a task that involved the learning of series of visually presented words: Whereas both non-interpreters and interpreting students were hampered by the concurrent articulation task, professional interpreters were not. This suggests that professional interpreters can do without working memory's phonological loop when they process written language material. However, this null effect of articulatory suppression does not warrant the conclusion that they can also do without the phonological loop when processing spoken source language input, because related experiments with aural input *do* show detrimental effects of concurrent articulation on memory.

Earlier in this chapter the question was posed as to how simultaneous interpreting is possible at all. At least part of the answer to this question must lie in the above special skills that professional interpreters have developed. A processing characteristic that is known to be correlated with processing speed is "automaticity". By definition, an automated mental process does not require attention and can be performed in parallel to both other automatic processes and processes that require attention. To the extent that fast processing indeed signals that the process in question has become automated, the above finding that professional interpreters are relatively fast at all sorts of sub-skills thus suggests they have automated these sub-skills to a higher level than other language users have. As a consequence, they have more mental resources to spend on the components of the full interpreting task that defy automation, such as resolving textual ambiguities or working out the meaning of conceptually difficult materials. In other words, it is plausible that the relatively large working memory capacity of professional interpreters follows directly from their fast and, presumably, automatic word recognition and word retrieval skills.

The studies discussed above all point towards the conclusion that professional interpreters are not endowed with the above special abilities by nature. Instead they indicate that these abilities result from the training of task-relevant linguistic sub-skills in translation and interpreting programs and from extensive on the job practice. In addition, one study has shown that at least one of the required sub-skills, fluent word retrieval, may not require any specific training but comes with a high level of proficiency in both languages.

The special abilities of interpreters that I focused on in the preceding sections—that is, fast word-retrieval and word-recognition skills and a large working-memory capacity—by no means constitute the complete set of skills that interpreters need to develop to successfully practice their profession. Earlier I presented the requirement to concurrently listen and speak as a major stumbling block in simultaneous interpreting. Although it is unclear whether this ability can ever become fully automated, this skill can also be improved with practice. Before practicing it on the full task, in interpreting-training programs it is often first exercised with the so-called "shadowing" task (repeating a spoken input verbatim) and the paraphrasing task, which both share with simultaneous interpreting the requirement to concurrently listen and speak. Nevertheless they are considered to be easier, because neither paraphrasing nor shadowing requires the involvement of two languages and, in addition, shadowing does not involve rephrasing the input. Practicing paraphrasing also increases the fluency in rephrasing an input in a different way while remaining faithful to the input's content. This is yet another skill that simultaneous interpreters must acquire (e.g., Gerver et al., 1984; Moser-Mercer, 1994). It is also trained by having the students generate synonyms for words.

A further ability to develop concerns the task's coordination requirement, which Gile (1995, 1997) identified as a separate component skill of simultaneous interpreting (see p. 316). As mentioned, this component takes care of regulating the exact portion of attention that at each moment in time must be assigned to each of the various ongoing activities. Research on the acquisition of complex skills in general (in which the present coordination component is usually referred to as "control of attention" or "attention management") has shown that training this component skill separately from training the full complex skill improves performance on the full task (Gopher, 1992; Gopher, Weil, & Siegel, 1989). Interestingly, this work has also shown that coordination skills acquired in a particular context can transfer between complex tasks; for instance, from gaming to air traffic control. Plausibly then, to come to master the coordination skill involved in interpreting also does not require it to be practiced with the full, awesome task.

A final ability to develop (if the interpreter-to-be is not naturally endowed with it) is immunity to speed stress. It is required for interpreting because of the speaker-based nature of simultaneous interpreting: It is the speaker, not the interpreter, who determines the speed of interpreting and the speaker is unlikely to have much consideration for the fact that the interpreter is concurrently involved in many more activities than just figuring out the message the speaker is communicating.

In conclusion, to master simultaneous interpreting takes at least fast and automated sub-skills that unburden the interpreter's limited attention capacity, thus freeing resources for the task's components that invariably defy automation. For any task-relevant sub-skill that requires attention but can become more highly or fully automated with practice, specific exercises should be developed to be included in interpreting-training programs, excepting the occasional sub-skill that does not need specific training but is concomitant with a high level of fluency in both languages. Of the abilities reviewed above, arguably especially the skills of simultaneous listening and speaking and of coordinating the task's major components are unlikely to develop without specific practice. Exercises that involve these skills are therefore good candidates for inclusion in the program. Still, we have seen that more ordinary language skills such as word recognition and semantic access also get faster by specific exercises in an interpreter-training program.

SUMMARY

- Theories on language control in bilinguals can be distinguished from one another on four interrelated dimensions: the scope of the control process (whether it operates globally, affecting all elements in bilingual memory, or locally, affecting specific elements), the direction in which it operates (proactively or reactively), the locus where it exerts its effect (within the language system or on the output of this system), and the source of the control process (internal or external).
- An experimenter-imposed language switch generally delays processing. One account of this effect assumes two language subsets of which at each moment in time only one is in use. The moment a language switch occurs or is commanded some mental language-switching device sees to it that the mind retreats from one language subset and accesses the other. This operation takes time to execute, thus producing the slowed response.
- It has sometimes been assumed that the above "in-out" account of the cost of language switching implies that the linguistic elements in the currently accessed subset are activated whereas those in the subset not in use are deactivated. This assumption does not follow imperatively from the in-out account.
- Language-mode theory is a theory of bilingual language control which assumes that in any communicative context one language is chosen as the base language and that this language is always highly activated. The degree of activation of the other language, the guest language, depends on situational factors such as the person being talked to and the formality and topic of the conversation. The more highly activated the guest language, the more language mixing occurs.
- Various sources of evidence suggest that a bilingual adapts flexibly to the specific characteristics of the current communicative context. In agreement with language-mode theory this evidence of adaptability can be explained in terms of fluctuations in the degree of activation of the bilingual's two language subsets, but it may also index fluctuations in the attentiveness of a mental monitor that watches over the output of the language system.
- In Paradis's neurolinguistic model of bilingual language processing, language control is secured by activating the targeted items with neural impulses while at the same time raising the activation thresholds of competing items, thereby inhibiting them. This model can account for various forms of bilingual aphasia by assuming that they result from the failure of a control system to set and maintain the activation thresholds of the lexical items in both languages at the appropriate levels while at the same time the language system proper is undamaged.

- Language subsets emerge from the co-occurrence of linguistic elements and the ensuing co-activation of their memory representations, the co-activation creating a bond between these representations. Connectionist models of bilingual language acquisition that exploit this learning mechanism have shown language subsets to emerge even though the input presented to the models was not explicitly marked for language. This suggests that the language membership of linguistic units does not have to be stored in memory explicitly.

- According to the bilingual interactive activation model a word input activates lexical representations of words from both languages. Language control is secured by two language nodes, one for each language, that are activated by input from the corresponding language and then suppress the activation in memory units representing linguistic elements of the other language.

- One way to secure language control in speech production is to add a language cue to the preverbal message and a language tag to the information contained in the lexical entry. This way the preverbal message will activate the representations of words in the targeted response language more highly than those in the other language.

- In the inhibitory control model language control is effected, on the one hand, proactively and globally by adapting the activation levels of all lemmas in both language subsets in agreement with the specific language task to perform and, on the other hand, reactively and locally by suppressing the activation in lemmas of words in the non-target language that still threaten to slip through.

- A characteristic effect of reactive suppression is the asymmetrical switch cost: A larger cost when the switch is from a weaker into a stronger language than when it is from a stronger language into a weaker language. However, when trilinguals highly proficient in two languages but less proficient in a third language switch between one of their strong languages and the weaker language, the switch costs are symmetrical. This and related findings have led to the suggestion that under certain circumstances bilingual language control exploits a language-specific selection mechanism instead of a reactive inhibitory mechanism.

- Similar results in studies on language switching on the one hand and task switching on the other hand suggest that language switching is a form of task switching and that the cost of language switching is caused by a resetting operation executed by a general control system.

- Simultaneous interpreting can be decomposed into at least four task components: comprehension, memorizing, production, and coordinating. Presumably the attention-demanding subcomponents of comprehension and production do not take place truly simultaneously but in rapid alternation.

- During simultaneous interpreting a mixture of two strategies is used: conceptually mediated translation and transcoding. Professional interpreters rely more on the former strategy than student interpreters. Because it involves the automatic triggering of translation-equivalent structures, the transcoding strategy is a useful backup strategy under circumstances of excessive mental load.

- Views on language control in simultaneous interpreting are derived from those that account for language control in unilingual tasks. Control can be effected either by the differential proactive activation of language subsets, subcomponents of these subsets, language-processing mechanisms, or combinations of these, or by adding a language cue to the conceptual structure that emerges from the linguistic analysis of the source language input.

- In some ways the comprehension processes of professional translators and amateurs involved in a translation task resemble the comprehension strategies that readers normally use in common unilingual reading. Comprehension processes in translation thus seem to build on those used in normal reading. Still, reading for translation in professional translators modifies normal unilingual comprehension processes.

- As compared with other bilinguals, professional interpreters are relatively fast at executing a number of tasks that tap basic sub-skills of the full interpreting task: retrieving the names for the concepts to express, recognizing words, and assigning meaning to them. In addition, they possess a relatively large working memory capacity. The evidence suggests that these special abilities result from the training of task-relevant linguistic sub-skills in translation and interpreting programs and from extensive on-the-job practice.
- Professional interpreters exploit their relatively large working memory capacity differently from non-interpreters, as evidenced by their immunity to articulatory suppression on tasks that require them to learn visually presented words. This suggests that professional interpreters can do without working memory's phonological loop when they process written language material. Because related experiments with aural input *do* show detrimental effects of concurrent articulation on memory, this null effect of articulatory suppression does not warrant the conclusion that interpreters can also do without the phonological loop when processing spoken source language input.
- The relatively large working memory capacity of professional interpreters is a direct consequence of their fast and, presumably, automatic word recognition and word retrieval skills, because the more sub-skills run automatically the more mental resources are available for the components of the full interpreting task that defy automation.

Cognitive Consequences of Bilingualism and Multilingualism

INTRODUCTION AND PREVIEW

In the early 1920s the *British Journal of Psychology* published two articles on the relation between bilingualism on the one hand and mental development (Smith, 1923) and intelligence (Saer, 1923) on the other hand. Since then the questions of whether and how bilingualism and multilingualism impact on cognitive functioning, in the domain of language and beyond, continue to engage policy makers, educators, language and cognition researchers, and parents of children growing up bilingually. It is easy to see why this topic draws the attention of such diverse groups of people. Cognitive functioning obviously affects academic achievement and, related to this, social and economic success in life and well-being in general. A detailed understanding of the relationship between bilingualism and cognitive functioning informs, for instance, policy makers and educators on what language policy to pursue regarding the instruction of immigrants, and parents with a different language background on what language(s) to use in their homes. On the basis of the insights gained from careful research that addresses these questions, professionals and parents may create the circumstances that foster the beneficial effects of bilingualism and multilingualism, and frustrate their potentially harmful effects.

This chapter discusses studies in this area of research, addressing both the effects of bilingualism and multilingualism on language functioning and on cognitive domains other than language. In the preceding chapters we have already encountered many sources of evidence to suggest that bilingualism and multilingualism impact on language functioning: Many studies discussed earlier have shown that bilinguals and multilinguals have not mentally compartmentalized their languages in neatly separated sections, with solid firewalls between them, but that all of the languages known interact with one another, both during acquisition and use. The speech accents (pp. 268–273) and code switches (pp. 291–293) that characterize the L2 speech of most foreign language speakers are presumably the clearest evidence to substantiate these claims, but so far we have witnessed other evidence as well. For instance, a number of studies discussed in Chapter 3 suggested that new languages do not develop in a vacuum, independently of those already acquired, but that prior vocabulary knowledge about other languages is exploited during, and accelerates, the acquisition of vocabulary in a new language. Similarly, myriad studies reviewed in Chapters 4 through 6 pointed out that bilinguals cannot switch off a non-selected language at will. Instead they demonstrated that concurrent activation in the non-targeted language(s) is common under many circumstances and influences the way the targeted language is processed. All these instances of **cross-linguistic** (or cross-language) **influence** or "transfer" are equally many demonstrations of the fact that linguistic expressions of bilinguals and multilinguals differ from those of monolinguals, thus underscoring the above claim that bilingualism and multilingualism affect language functioning.

In the study of transfer effects in language acquisition and use the far majority of researchers have focused of the influence of the first language on later languages. Cross-linguistic influences in the reverse direction, from later languages onto the first, have received relatively little attention. Laufer (2003a) suggested two possible reasons for this neglect. The first relates to the fact that many researchers in the field of applied linguistics have been primarily interested in the early stage of learning a second language. Cross-linguistic influence during this non-advanced stage is almost entirely from the L1 to the L2. The second reason may be that much of the work on second language acquisition was motivated by the question of how members of immigrant communities could come to master the dominant language of the host country as soon as possible. As a consequence, researchers focused on how this new language was acquired and not on its effect on the immigrants' L1.

A further reason for the focus on influences from L1 on later languages is plausibly that unlike the L2 and other non-native languages, the L1 is considered a stable, independent system that is not affected by knowledge of other languages. But, contrary to this view, evidence is accumulating that transfer occurs not only from the L1 to

the L2 and yet later languages, but also in the reverse direction, and between each pair of non-native languages, again in both directions (see Cook, 2003a, an edited volume that is dedicated entirely to the effects of a second and later languages on the first; see also Pavlenko, 2000, a comprehensive review of studies that, together, show pervasive influences of L2 on L1 in all domains of language: phonology, morphosyntax, the lexicon, conceptual representation, and pragmatics). The general picture that is gradually emerging is one of a highly dynamic multilingual language system with much cross-talk between the various language subsystems.

The inevitable consequence of a multilingual language system of the type sketched here must be that the linguistic utterances of bilinguals and multilinguals differ from those of monolingual speakers of the languages in question. For this reason several researchers have criticized the practice, common at one time, of regarding the expressions of monolinguals as the norm against which the language of bilinguals and multilinguals should be evaluated, a comparison that in the past has often led to the harsh verdict that the language use of bilinguals and multilinguals, and especially their use of non-native languages, is inferior to monolinguals' language use.

Annoyed about this unfair practice—because shouldn't we applaud people who, for whatever reason, have come to master more than one language?—Grosjean raised a warning finger against those who looked upon bilinguals' language performance this way: "[. . .] beware! The bilingual is not two monolinguals in one person" (Grosjean, 1989, p. 3). He fervently rejected this "fractional" view of bilingualism, advancing a holistic view instead, which states that the frequent use of two languages produces a specific speaker-hearer and that the L2 user is a person in his or her own right. In making his point Grosjean (1989, p. 6) resorted to the analogy of the hurdler who blends two skills, those of jumping and sprinting:

When compared individually with the sprinter or the high jumper, the hurdler meets neither level of competence, and yet when taken as a whole the hurdler is an athlete in his or her own right [. . .]. A high hurdler is an integrated whole, a unique and specific athlete; he or she can attain the highest levels of world competition in the same way that the sprinter and the high jumper can.

Similarly, Cook (1991, 2003b) introduced the term "multi-competence" to refer to the special competence of a bilingual speaker-listener, different from the competence of a monolingual speaker-listener but by no means inferior to it, and Jessner (1999) embraced this same view of multilingualism when stating that "multilingualism is no multiple monolingualism" (p. 201).

A couple of sections in this chapter provide further evidence that the various languages in the bilingual and multilingual language system all interact with one another and that the overall language system is in a continuous state of flux. Following the usual Methods and Tasks section I will zoom in on a hitherto underexposed issue, the use of a (still weak) third language, revealing a number of variables that affect the pattern of transfer from the earlier languages onto the third. The type of transfer focused on is code-switching from the earlier languages into the L3 and the regularities observed therein. The next section departs from the assumption that language loss following an extended period of disuse of the language in question can be viewed as a form of language change, one that is plausibly caused by cross-linguistic interference from the language(s) currently used to the neglected language. In this section both L2 loss and L1 loss will be covered. The subsection on L1 loss highlights the extreme case of the relatively rare individuals who from the one moment to the next are completely isolated from their L1 because of their adoption into families and communities that are completely ignorant of it. The results of these studies suggest the possibility of true and irrevocable loss. In contrast, the studies on L2 loss after a long period of disuse, to be treated in a second subsection, suggest that a language apparently lost can be reactivated,

thus pointing at an interference account of forgetting.

Following the discussion of language loss, a further section presents evidence of L1–L2 interaction in different domains of language—phonology, grammar, and semantics—in circumstances where both languages are still being used, albeit in different proportions and not necessarily both in all social settings. This situation holds, for instance, for many immigrant communities. Although either language influences the other, the focus will be on effects of the L2 on the L1. Earlier studies of this type highlight the corrosion or "loss" of the L1 language system in immigrants (e.g., Ammerlaan, 1997; Weltens, De Bot, & Van Els, 1986). Accepting the above notion of multi-competence, the studies discussed here focus more on the *changes* in L1 as a consequence of its contact with a later language, without qualifying them as loss.

Whereas up until this point effects of bilingualism (and multilingualism) on language functioning have been dealt with, the next section highlights its effects on non-verbal cognition. It discusses the consequences of cross-language linguistic variation for the way bilinguals think about and perceive the world. Specifically, it deals with the question of whether the thought and perceptual processes of bilinguals change when they switch from their one language to the other and whether they differ from those of unilingual speakers of the languages concerned. In studies that address this question the bilingual participants' two languages are known to differ in one particular aspect, say, their grammatical tense system, and it is examined whether this specific contrast causes language-dependent thought and/ or language-dependent perception in a specific conceptual domain (e.g., the concept of time). Finally, the last part of this chapter looks at the effect of bilingualism per se on cognition, not at the way a particular linguistic contrast might lead to language-specific thought processes in speakers of the pair of languages in question. The effect of bilingualism on one specific aspect of cognitive functioning will dominate this discussion—its effect on "cognitive control" (also called "attention control" or "executive control").

METHODS AND TASKS

The most salient methodological characteristic of the majority of studies dealing with the above questions is that the performance of bilinguals on one or more tasks is compared to that of (near) monolinguals. This methodology is generally used to assess an influence of L2 on L1 (pp. 361–371), to study language-specific thought processes in bilinguals (pp. 371–385), and to study the effect of bilingualism per se on verbal and non-verbal cognitive functioning (pp. 385–401). In the ideal experiment the monolingual comparison group consists of pure monolinguals lacking any knowledge of any language other than their native language and who do not differ from the bilinguals in other respects such as socioeconomic status, educational level, cultural background, age, and intelligence. It may be obvious that it is next to impossible to satisfy all these constraints. As noted by Cook (2003b), the widespread use of second languages alone is already a reason why pure monolinguals are hard to find, and those that may eventually be hunted down are likely to be unsuitable as controls because they presumably differ from the bilingual participants to be tested in other respects, for instance, a non-standard or unfinished education. Add to the widespread immigration and study of foreign languages in school the rapidly increasing globalization in many areas of modern society and it is clear that pure monolinguals are a species likely to become extinct in no time.

Given the lack of pure monolinguals, the typical study includes "monolinguals" with a negligibly small amount of L2 knowledge or, at the most, L2 learners at a much less advanced stage than the participants that constitute the bilingual group. In studies that try to reveal an influence of a specific L2 on a specific L1, it might not always be problematic if the control participants master an additional language aside from the L1 at a more advanced level, as long as this language is not the L2 under study. Yet one should be aware that the acquisition of *any* language next to the L1 boosts the language user's metalinguistic awareness and this, in turn, may affect L1 processing (Cook, 2003b). Furthermore, in studies that try to find out whether a specific linguistic contrast between L2 and L1 affects L1 processing, the researcher must ascertain how any additional language compares to the L1 in this respect. Without this knowledge neither a reliable effect nor a null effect of the target L2 on L1 can be properly interpreted because this further language may have contributed to the effect. This same point applies to studies examining whether a specific linguistic contrast between two languages induces language-specific thought processes in bilingual speakers of this language pair or perhaps thought processes that result from some merger of the contrasting structures. Of course, in studies whose goal is to find out whether bilingualism per se affects cognitive functioning, irrespective of the language pair involved, the control participants are not allowed to master any other language than their L1 beyond some negligibly low level.

The choice of the bilingual participants also requires precision. As we shall see further on (pp. 385–388), misguided procedures in selecting the bilingual sample led the investigators of many early studies to conclude that bilingualism has an adverse effect on cognitive development. The bilingual and monolingual groups in these early studies were not properly matched on a number of background variables, most notoriously socioeconomic status (SES), sex, and age. Furthermore, the bilingual sample included children with unequal levels of competence in their two languages. Many later studies that controlled for these background variables and that selected balanced bilingual children have generally shown bilingualism to be beneficial for cognitive development. As observed by Cummins (1976), the participants in many of these later studies were from families with a relatively high SES whereas the bilingual participants in many of the earlier studies were from low-SES families. High SES is typically associated with a form of bilingualism called **additive bilingualism**, whereas low SES is associated with **subtractive bilingualism** (see p. 387 for details; alternative labels for these two forms of bilingualism are "elitist" and "folk" bilingualism, respectively; e.g., Cummins 1976). The societal and personal circumstances that constitute additive bilingualism are believed to have positive cognitive consequences whereas those that constitute subtractive bilingualism appear to have negative effects on cognition.

The tasks, testing instruments, and paradigms used in the various lines of research presented in this chapter are too numerous to describe here and many of them have in fact already been introduced in the preceding chapters. The ones not encountered before will be explained in the course of this chapter in the context of the theoretical issue they are thought to address.

CROSS-LANGUAGE INFLUENCES ON THIRD LANGUAGE USE

Introduction

A relatively recent new research area is the study of third language (L3) acquisition and especially the influence of L1 and L2 on L3 acquisition and use. The abbreviation "L3" in these studies usually refers to language number three in order of acquisition, after L1 and L2. But somewhat confusingly, "L3" may also refer to the language *currently* acquired, even though the learner has already acquired more than one foreign language after the L1 (e.g., Hammarberg, 2001). The presence of two or more prior languages is likely to cause more complex interactions between the extant languages than pure bilingualism does. In the case of bilingualism, a cross-linguistic influence on a target language can only be due to the one non-target language present, whereas in trilingualism or in multilingualism any of the non-target languages, or more than one of them at the same time, may be responsible for the cross-linguistic influence. An important goal of the trilingual studies is to reveal regularities in the patterns of transfer observed in the L3 output and to identify the underlying causes.

Such regularities have indeed been observed

and several relevant factors have been identified. One of them is the **typological distance** or, more plausibly, the *perceived* typological distance between a prior language and the L3: A language that is typologically relatively close and, therefore, similar to the L3 influences L3 acquisition and use more than a typologically more distant language (e.g., Ahukanna, Lund, & Gentile, 1981; Cenoz, 2001; Kellerman, 1977, 1983; Ringbom, 1987). Thus, when acquiring an Indo-European language such as German, a native speaker of a non-Indo-European language such as Hindi or Chinese may exploit her knowledge of L2 English, as German is an Indo-European language, more than her L1 knowledge. A second factor has variously been referred to as the **foreign language effect**, the effect of "L2 status" (Cenoz, 2001; Hammarberg, 2001), or the "L2 effect" (Murphy, 2003). It concerns the phenomenon that the learners' L2 (or other languages acquired after the L1, but *not* their L1) is the source of cross-language influence on L3 (e.g., Clyne, 1997; Williams & Hammarberg, 1998), even when L1 is more dominant than L2. Williams and Hammarberg suggested two possible causes of this effect. First, different acquisition mechanisms may underlie L1 and L2 acquisition, and the L2 acquisition mechanism may be reactivated when learning further new languages. Second, during L3 acquisition the learner may attempt to suppress L1 because it is non-foreign, and rely on a prior foreign language, hence L2, as a strategy to tackle the L3. A third factor that has been suggested to affect cross-linguistic influence is whether or not a language learned previously is still used by the L3 learner: A language still in use is activated more easily than a language that is no longer used, and the former is therefore more likely to exert an influence on the new language. A fourth factor is the specific context in which the communication takes place. This context is thought to create a specific language mode in the trilingual speaker; that is, a particular state of relative activation levels of the three languages. The more highly activated a non-target language, the larger its influence on the targeted language will be (e.g., Grosjean, 2001; pp. 288–291).

Contrasting the roles of typological distance and L2 status

One of the relevant insights to emerge from this area of research is that the different prior languages, L1 and L2, might serve different functions in L3 acquisition and processing. One of the pertinent studies is Hammarberg's (2001; see also Williams & Hammarberg, 1998) longitudinal single-case study of a polyglot learner of Swedish (Sarah Williams, one of the researchers; SW) who had English as L1 and a high command of German (and a weaker command of two further foreign languages, Italian and French). The case study was based on a large corpus of audio-taped conversations between SW and one and the same interlocutor (Hammarberg, the second researcher) that took place over a period of 2 years and in which Swedish (the current "L3") was the target language. SW started the project without any prior knowledge of Swedish. Conversation was enabled by the fact that the two conversational partners shared knowledge of English, German, and French and, consequently, resorted to frequent language switching.

Hammerberg (2001) categorized all of SW's switches from target Swedish into any of the other languages into seven categories. The switches within six of these categories all had a specific pragmatic purpose such as posing a question or providing some comment. A general characteristic of all these types of switches was that SW clearly did not attempt to use L3 Swedish during these interaction moments in a conversation. A seventh type of switches, labeled WIPP (without identified pragmatic purpose) by the author, was of a different type: The speaker lapsed into one of her other languages than targeted Swedish, apparently without intending to do so. Other authors have referred to this type of switches as "non-intentional" language switches (Poulisse & Bongaerts, 1994). These switches were typically short, concerned function words (e.g., pronouns, prepositions, and conjunctions) more often than content words, and were often followed directly by a self-repair. When considering the language SW switched to,

TABLE 7.1

Intentional and non-intentional switches

	L1 English	L2 German
Intentional 1	70	29
Intentional 2	100	0
Intentional 3	100	0
Intentional 4	89	11
Intentional 5	73	24
Intentional 6	68	29
Non-intentional	4	92

Percentages of non-intentional switches and six types of intentional switches into L1 English and L2 German of a trilingual trying to speak in L3 Swedish. Adapted from Hammarberg (2001).

a strikingly consistent pattern occurred. It is illustrated in Table 7.1, in which I refer to Hammarberg's pragmatics-based and WIPP switches as intentional and non-intentional switches, respectively. In order to highlight the consistency of the switch pattern, I have presented the data for each type of intentional switches separately (Intentional 1–6). The reader is referred to the original publication for details about the exact type of switches included in each of these six categories.

As shown, SW nearly always switched to either L1 English or L2 German. But more interestingly, all categories of intentional switches predominantly involved a switch to L1 English, whereas the vast majority of the non-intentional switches concerned a lapse into L2 German. On the basis of these data Hammarberg (2001) concluded that both L1 and L2 were co-activated to a considerable degree during L3 processing but that they clearly had different roles to play: L1 English was "chosen" (but maybe unconsciously so) as the language of the interaction with the interlocutor at moments when there was no intention to speak L3. During these moments in the conversation L1 was apparently more highly activated than L2 (presumably as a consequence of the intention to momentarily speak in L1). In contrast, during intentional L3 production, apparently L2 German was the most highly co-activated non-target language. Looking for the cause of L2 German's prominent role when L3 was targeted, Hammarberg examined whether the typological distances between L1 English and L2 German on the one hand and L3 Swedish on the other hand might have been the source of this effect. After concluding that English and German are about equally close to Swedish, he rejected an account in terms of German L2 being more similar to Swedish and opted for an explanation in terms of German's L2 status instead. In other words, the large number of intrusions from L2 German during L3 Swedish speech production may be an instantiation of the foreign language effect introduced above.

However, a closely related study by Cenoz (2003) qualified the latter conclusion. Whereas the L1 and L2 in Hammarberg's study were about equally close to the L3, Cenoz studied a combination of three languages where the target L3 (English) was more closely related to the L1 (Spanish) than to the L2 (Basque). Whereas both Spanish and English are Indo-European languages (the former of the Romance branch, the latter of the Germanic branch), Basque is a non-Indo-European language of unknown origin. This combination of languages thus enabled the researcher to find out whether typological distance matters at all and to evaluate Hammarberg's conclusion that the foreign language effect caused the large number of transfer lapses into L2 during L3 processing. Importantly, Cenoz's study was not a single-case study but included a whole group of English learners, all primary school students. Any systematic transfer effect to emerge could therefore not be attributed to some form of idiosyncratic learner behavior (which may underlie the outcome of any single-case study).

The participants were presented with two "picture stories", each consisting of a series of pictures that together formed a story, and were asked to tell the story in L3 English. The (audio-taped) stories were subsequently transcribed and the researcher looked for language switches similar to the intentional and non-intentional switches identified by Hammarberg (2001). On average, about 85% of the total number of utterances were in target L3 and about 15% of the utterances concerned a switch into another language. Contrary to Hammerberg (2001), the intentional switches (concerning interactions with the experimenter) were predominantly in L2 Basque (89%) and only a very small proportion of these were in L1 Spanish (2.6%). The remaining intentional switches concerned blends of Basque and Spanish. In contrast, and again opposite to Hammerberg's results, the non-intentional switches (called "transfer lapses") were predominantly in L1 Spanish (78.6%) and far less often in L2 Basque (19%). In other words, once again L1 and L2 appeared to play different roles, but their roles were opposite to those observed by Hammarberg.

How can this reversal of the roles of L1 and L2 be explained? Cenoz noted that the language commonly used in school in interactions between the teachers and children was L2 Basque. He therefore suggested that the children adopted this same language in interactions with the experimenter when performing the story-telling task. Consequently, the majority of the intentional switches in the experimental setting were in L2 Basque. Similarly, the common language of interaction between Hammarberg and his participant SW outside of the experimental setting was L1 English. Again, this common mode of interaction was adopted as well in the interactive moments of the experimental setting when the participants switched intentionally to a non-target language.

What remains is to explain why L1 (Spanish) was the predominant language of the transfer lapses in Cenoz's study, whereas L2 (German) had assumed that role in Hammarberg's study. As Cenoz pointed out, the most plausible interpretation is one in terms of typological distance: The language typologically closest to target L3 is the main source of the transfer lapses. In his study L1 Spanish, relatively close to L3 English, assumed that role. This interpretation can be reconciled with Hammarberg's results by assuming that, in the absence of a clear difference between L1 and L2 in terms of their relative distance to L3, the L2 is the primary source for non-intentional switches. In terms of differential levels of activation, under these circumstances the L2 is more highly activated than the L1 and is, therefore, the main source of cross-linguistic influence.

A tentative conclusion to draw from all of this is that the foreign language effect becomes manifest when the non-target languages are about equally close to the target language. However, when L1 and L2 differ in their distance from L3, distance to the L3 determines which language is the source of the cross-linguistic effect. Another way of putting this is that "linguistic distance is a stronger predictor of cross-linguistic influence than L2 status", as Cenoz did in an earlier study (2001, p. 18; see De Angelis, 2005, for a further demonstration of the role of typological distance in third language speech).

A study by Dewaele (1998) suggested that yet a third factor—the order in which the target language was acquired, as L2 or L3—affects the pattern of cross-linguistic influence. As in Hammarberg (2001), the two non-target languages (Dutch and English) were about equally close to the target language (French), so it is unlikely that any difference between the cross-language effects of the two non-target languages to emerge would be attributable to differences in distance from target French. Dewaele's critical data were the participants' "lexical inventions" (neologisms), wordlike units that deviate from the targeted form (such as *capitral* for *capital* or *chujet* for *sujet*). The data were collected in discussions in which the learners participated and in formal and informal interviews held with them. For the participants in this study, target French was either their L2 (with Dutch as L1 and English as L3) or their L3 (with Dutch as L1 and English as L2).

Interestingly, the pattern of intralingual (a French-based intrusion in target French) and interlingual intrusions (from either English or Dutch into target French) differed between these two groups of participants. The L2 French group showed a larger percentage of intralingual intrusions than the L3 French group, suggesting that French was more highly activated in the French L2 speakers than in the French L3 speakers. But more interestingly for our present purposes was the pattern observed for the interlingual intrusions: L2 English was the main source of these intrusions in the group with French as L3 (suggesting that English was the most activated of the non-target languages), whereas L1 Dutch was the main source of intrusions in the group with French as L2 (suggesting that non-target Dutch was more activated than non-target English). The relatively large influence of L2 English on L3 French replicates Hammarberg (2001), thus providing additional evidence for the view that, if the two non-target languages are equally close to target L3, it is the *foreign* non-target language that dominates cross-linguistic transfer. The relatively large influence of non-target L1 Dutch when target French was acquired second in order suggests that order of acquisition of the non-target languages is a further factor that governs cross-linguistic influence.

So far I have discussed three factors that determine the pattern of cross-linguistic influence when multilinguals have selected one of their languages for current use: typological distance between the non-target languages and the target language, foreign language status of the non-target languages, and order of acquisition of target and non-target languages. These three are by no means the only variables to affect the nature of cross-linguistic influences in the speech of multilingual language users. Some others have already been briefly mentioned before (language mode and whether the non-target language is still being used regularly; see Murphy, 2003, for a comprehensive overview of the relevant factors identified so far). Not mentioned yet is the level of proficiency in the selected language: The higher the proficiency in this language, the smaller the cross-language influence of the other languages (e.g., Poulisse & Bongaerts, 1994). In other words, it appears that increases in proficiency lead to increased autonomy of the language in question, as if, with practice, it gradually becomes more encapsulated and immune to external influences (cf. the emergence of language subsets discussed on pp. 296–302). A further relevant factor is the relative strength of the non-target languages: the stronger one is more likely to intrude into the selected language than the weaker one. To be able to determine what role each of these factors plays in cross-language transfer, all of the other ones need to be taken into account as well.

LOSS OF A FORMER LANGUAGE

Second language loss after years of disuse

Introduction

All of us are familiar with the phenomenon that skills get rusty when they have been out of practice for a long time, to the point that they seem to be lost altogether. This holds for language as for any other skill. There must be legions of adults who at some point beyond their younger years experience the frustration of noticing that a language they once learned at school has effectively dissipated from their minds. But is it indeed irrevocably lost or just buried away in memory's undercrofts, patiently awaiting the moment to be revitalized? Is loss perhaps selective, affecting some domains of language more than others, or part of a domain but not all of it? And if true loss indeed occurs, what are the factors that determine forgetting? In two pioneering studies Bahrick posed a number of these questions with respect to L1 English speakers' knowledge of L2 Spanish acquired up to 50 years (Bahrick, 1984) or 8 years (Bahrick & Phelps, 1987) prior to testing. These two studies have since inspired many studies on the life span of earlier acquired but not properly maintained linguistic knowledge; in other words, studies that examine "language loss" or "language attrition" (see De Bot & Weltens, 1995, for a review).

Bahrick's studies focused on L2 attrition over a period of disuse, but the same questions can be, and have been, posed with regard to L1, which may be vulnerable to forgetting as a consequence of massive and exclusive exposure to an L2 (e.g., Isurin, 2000; Isurin & McDonald, 2001). It is as if the language one is currently exposed to gradually replaces a prior one under circumstances wherein the latter is no longer used. Accordingly, in this field of research the old, "attriting", language and the language currently used are often labeled LA and LR (for the "attriting" and "replacing" languages, respectively). In this section I will confine myself to a discussion of a few studies

dealing with L2 attrition over time, including Bahrick's seminal studies. The phenomenon of L1 loss will be treated later (pp. 353–359). As we shall see, the question of whether or not the attriting L1 merely becomes inaccessible or can, under certain extreme circumstances, truly disappear from memory over an extended period of disuse remains unsettled. Accordingly, whenever the word *replace* is used in the following sections, suggesting true loss, it should not be taken literally but to also cover the notion of inaccessibility.

In a cross-sectional study, Bahrick (1984) focused on the effects of the originally acquired level of proficiency in L2 Spanish and the number of years between learning and testing on the degree of loss. The participants had previously learned Spanish in their school years, and were tested on recall and recognition of vocabulary, reading comprehension and grammar, 10 tests in all. To assess the originally acquired level of L2 Spanish, a questionnaire was administered to determine their original level of training (number of Spanish courses taken) and what grades they had received. The questionnaire also probed the extent to which the participants had rehearsed Spanish in the intervening years. Generally, the use of Spanish during this interval was limited, too limited to reveal any effect of rehearsal in the data or to contaminate the effects of prior proficiency and elapsed time. Both variables strongly affected performance. The left parts of Figure 7.1 shows the effects of training level (= proficiency) on retention (collapsed over the various time intervals between learning and testing). The right part of Figure 7.1 shows the effects of elapsed time (collapsed over all proficiency levels).

Even a cursory glance at these figures reveals clear relations between proficiency and elapsed time on the one hand and retention on the other hand: The higher the original level of training, the more Spanish was retained over the years; the more time had passed since training, the more of the originally acquired knowledge was lost. But more surprisingly, even as long as 50 years after acquisition, and with limited intervening rehearsal, a substantial amount of the original

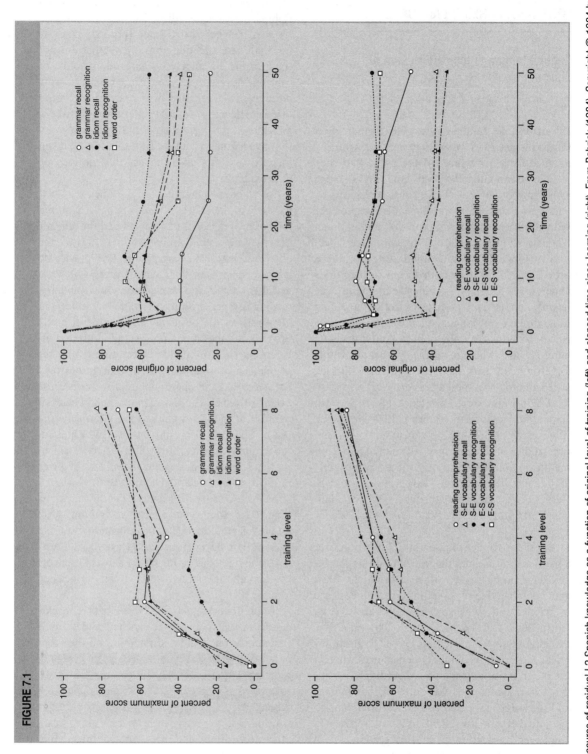

FIGURE 7.1

Measures of residual L2 Spanish knowledge as a function of original level of training (left) and elapsed time since learning (right). From Bahrick (1984). Copyright © 1984 by the American Psychological Association. Reproduced with permission.

knowledge was still maintained. However, inter-actions between the two variables (not shown) suggested that this latter finding did not apply to the participants with the lowest levels of originally acquired L2 proficiency. For these participants loss appeared to be complete after an extended period of disuse, as if language know-ledge acquired in the past must have reached some minimal threshold at the time for it to become resistant to loss. This possibility has indeed been advanced by some authors (see, e.g., De Bot, 1998) and it is also consistent with the notion (Atkinson, 1972) that a vocabulary item can be in one of three states after training: P, for "permanent", T, for "temporary", and U, for "unknown". An item in state P is known and this knowledge is relatively permanent and not affected by the later learning of new items. In con-trast, an item in state T is only known temporarily because items learned later interfere with it, thus causing it to be forgotten (or become inaccess-ible). In terms of a threshold account, an item in state T has not been learned to threshold yet and is therefore susceptible to loss.

A further result that speaks from Figure 7.1 is that the retention functions have similar shapes for all language components tested, suggesting that vocabulary and grammar are equally sus-ceptible, or equally immune, to loss. Finally, and especially noteworthy, the retention functions do not have a constant slope, indicating that prior language knowledge is not lost with a constant speed per unit elapsed time since learning. Instead, during the first years after learning relatively much of the acquired knowledge gets lost but following this period relatively little additional forgetting occurs and, later still, retention appears to stabilize. Bahrick coined the word "permastore" to refer to the memory con-tent with a life span of 25 years or longer. A final result that can be observed in Figure 7.1 is that, as usual (but excepting part of the idiom data) rec-ognition scores are higher than recall scores (see also pp. 95 and 112–113).

Bahrick (1984) thus identified two variables that affect the amount of forgetting: the level of proficiency acquired during initial training and the time passed since training. In a later study

Bahrick and Phelps (1987) suggested a role of one further determinant of L2 loss: the length of the interval between the separate training sessions during initial acquisition (and see Hansen, 2001, for still further critical variables). This study also showed that individual words differ from one another in terms of forgetting rate. The study concerned a follow-up on a laboratory experi-ment conducted about 8 years earlier. In this earlier experiment native English college students had had to learn and relearn 50 English–Spanish translation pairs in successive training sessions, with intervals of a few seconds to a month between the separate sessions. Testing was done by means of the receptive cued recall test (p. 86). Each training session consisted of a number of alternating presentation and test rounds and the presentation of each single translation pair during training was discontinued the moment it had led to a correct cued recall response on the immediately preceding test (this procedure is called the "dropout" procedure). The next training session—held either immediately after the previous session or 1 or 30 days later—first started with a round of testing and continued with the above dropout procedure. As a con-sequence of this training procedure, it was pos-sible for an item to be presented just once (namely, in the first presentation round of the first session), but the average number of presentations varied substantially between items.

Both the number of presentations of an English–Spanish pair (and, by implication, the ease with which the Spanish word in the pair was acquired) and the intersession interval during training affected the retention scores substan-tially: The fewer presentations during training, the larger the retention scores, and the longer the interval between training sessions, the larger the retention scores. The first of these results con-verges with the finding, discussed on pp. 108–110, that words that are easy to learn—as suggested here by the fact that they led to correct recall after a relatively small number of presentation trials—are hard to forget. (In terms of Atkinson's, 1972, terminology, this finding indicates that easily learnable words reach a P state relatively quickly.) Whereas Bahrick and Phelps (1987) did not elaborate on the specific properties of individual words that make them easy to learn and hard to forget or, conversely, hard to learn and easy to forget, some of the relevant word features were identified in this earlier section (the frequency and concreteness of the L1 word in a translation pair; whether or not the L2 word is a cognate of its L1 translation; whether or not the L2 word sounds like L1 words). The beneficial effect of a large interval between the training sessions is consistent with earlier reports on the positive effects of such "distributed" (as opposed to "massed") training (see e.g., Underwood & Ekstrand, 1967).

The savings paradigm

Impressive as they may be, the recall and recognition scores obtained by Bahrick (1984) plausibly underestimate the amount of L2 knowledge that is actually still retained. Even though a non-response on a recall or recognition test might suggest the linguistic element in question has been lost completely, traces of knowledge may still exist but they may be too weak to base the required response on (this state of extant but inaccessible knowledge is sometimes called "dormant"; e.g., Green, 1986). Support for such residues of knowledge apparently lost has been obtained with the "savings paradigm", which was first applied during the early days of experimental psychology. Ebbinghaus (1885) found that the relearning of material previously known ("old") but subsequently seemingly lost was much easier than the learning of material never encountered before ("new"). One convincing demonstration of this phenomenon (although lacking a "new" control condition) was presented earlier in Chapter 3 (p. 95), where it was described how it took someone just 1.5 hours of relearning to regain a 350-word Italian vocabulary acquired with the keyword method 10 years earlier and not rehearsed since. The advantage of old materials over new materials can only be understood if the old material is in fact still at least partly intact. Nelson (1978) developed a sophisticated version of the savings method for general application in memory research, a method that De Bot and Stoessel (2000) subsequently first introduced in

the study of L2 vocabulary loss. Table 7.2 presents the various steps of the paradigm as applied in these studies.

The first step in the savings method as applied in studies of L2 loss consists of the compilation of a set of L2 materials, typically vocabulary, that the participants have (almost certainly) known in the past. The receptive cued recall test is subsequently used to assess which ones of these previously known words are retained and which ones are "lost": All of the selected words are presented to the participants for translation into L1. The words that are successfully translated (and thus retained) are subsequently removed from the set and a subset of those the participants fail to translate serve as the "old" (but seemingly lost) words. To these old words a set of new words is added; that is, L2 words the participants (almost certainly) had not acquired in the past. Next, the selected old and new L2 words are presented for learning using the paired-associate paradigm, an L2 word being presented with its L1 translation

TABLE 7.2

The savings method as applied in the study of second language loss

Step 1: Compile a set of L2 words the participants have almost certainly known in the past

Step 2: Use the receptive cued recall test to assess which words of this set are still known: Present each L2 word for translation in L1

Step 3: Remove the words that are still known from the original set

Step 4: Select a subset of the unknown words. These words constitute the experimental group of "old" words

Step 5: Compile a set of L2 words the participants have almost certainly not known in the past. This set constitutes the experimental group of "new" words

Step 6: Present each of the old and new experimental words together with its L1 translation in a training session employing the paired-associate paradigm

Step 7: Distract the participants by having them perform some distraction task

Step 8: Present each of the trained old and new words as cue in a cued recall task to be translated into L1

The "savings effect" is the difference between the recall scores for the old and new words. It reflects the amount of retained vocabulary.

on each separate learning trial. Presentation frequency of each learning trial varies between studies but is typically small. This training session is followed by a distraction task. Finally, in a "savings" session, the trained old and new L2 words are presented as recall cue in a receptive cued recall task and the participants are asked to come up with their translation in L1. The relevant dependent variable is the "savings effect"; that is, the difference in recall performance for old and new words.

Savings effects have generally been observed, irrespective of whether the L2 was originally acquired in a natural setting (e.g., De Bot & Stoessel, 2000; Hansen et al., 2002) or in the classroom (e.g., De Bot, Martens, & Stoessel, 2004), whether the participants had been exposed to the L2 at a very young age (e.g., De Bot & Stoessel) or as young adults (e.g., Hansen et al.), or whether the "lost" L2 was typologically relatively close to the L1 (e.g., De Bot & Stoessel) or rather distant from the L1 (Hansen et al.). The size of the effect differed between studies, but was spectacularly large at times. To illustrate, consider the results of Hansen and colleagues' study, in which the savings method was used to determine the residual L2 knowledge of L1 American-English speakers who, as young adults, had spent between 1.5 and 3 years in Japan or Korea as missionaries and had at the time become quite fluent in Japanese and Korean, respectively. In this study the researchers focused on the effects of the size of the retained L2 vocabulary at the time of testing (as assessed in Step 2 of the savings paradigm; see Table 7.2) and the duration of elapsed time since L2 learning on the savings effects. The results for the Japanese group (which are representative of the Korean group as well) as obtained in Step 8 of the procedure are shown in Figure 7.2 (in percentages; 100% = 16 words) as a function of elapsed time (upper panel) and retained L2 vocabulary (lower panel).

As can be seen, generally strikingly large savings effects occurred. The savings effects (the differences between "old" and "new" L2 words) tended to become smaller with amount of elapsed time (upper panel), but even between 36 and 45 years after learning the effect was still substantial.

Especially noteworthy is the fact that the retention function does not show the relatively rapid decline during the first years of L2 disuse which was evident in Bahrick (1984; see Figure 7.1). The authors suggested that Bahrick's retention function may not apply when the originally acquired level of proficiency was relatively high, as was the case in their study. This is consistent with the above-mentioned idea that knowledge that has surpassed a critical threshold is relatively impervious to forgetting, or, in other words, has reached a stable state in memory (Atkinson's, 1972, "P state"). Finally, the lower panel of Figure 7.2 shows that the amount of retained L2 vocabulary at the onset of retraining also affected performance: The more L2 words a participant still knew (as assessed in Step 2 of the procedure), the larger the savings effect for the "old" words (words selected in Step 1 as likely known in the past but *not* recalled in Step 2 of the procedure and selected as experimental items in Step 4). Interestingly, not only the L2 words presumably known in the past, but also the new words (selected in Step 5) depended somewhat on the amount of retained vocabulary: Participants with a relatively large retained L2 vocabulary were not only relatively successful in relearning vocabulary known before, but they also tended to learn more of the completely new L2 vocabulary. This is a further demonstration of the "rich-get-richer" phenomenon (the "Matthew effect") of which we have seen various other manifestations in earlier sections of this book (e.g., on p. 100).

Summary

A persistent question in memory research is whether prior knowledge that cannot be retrieved is truly lost or merely inaccessible, perhaps because it is overwritten by information that has entered memory more recently (a phenomenon known as **retroactive interference**). The studies discussed above strongly suggest that much prior knowledge (if not all) has not vanished from memory but needs some trigger to become available again. In the present case of seemingly lost L2 vocabulary a brief renewed contact with the language concerned, or more precisely, with

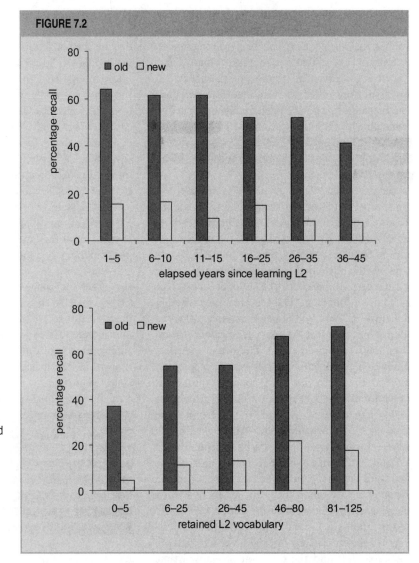

FIGURE 7.2

Percentage cued recall after training by means of the savings paradigm for old and new Japanese words as a function of elapsed years since L2 learning and retained L2 vocabulary. Adapted from Hansen et al. (2002). Reprinted with permission from Wiley-Blackwell.

the specific L2 words apparently lost, appears to serve as a most effective igniter to reactivate L2 words that had become dormant due to protracted disuse.

At a more fine-grained level of analysis the above studies have identified a number of variables that affect the degree of L2 forgetting: (1) The more time has elapsed between first acquiring an L2 word and a later attempt to retrieve it again, the larger the chance that it can no longer be successfully retrieved. Plausibly, the amount of elapsed time itself is not the crucial variable here but the correlated amount of exposure to the L1, and other languages, in the years between first learning the L2 and digging it up again. The more intervening years, the more retroactive interference from the more recent and current languages. (2) The higher the originally acquired level of L2 proficiency, the more immune to forgetting the originally mastered L2 memory structures have become. Furthermore, it appears that some minimal level of L2 proficiency must have been acquired originally for knowledge to have any chance at all to become permanently stored in memory. (3) Relatively long intervals between the separate training sessions lead to more permanent L2 knowledge structures than relatively short training intervals do. (4) The acquisition and forgetting rates differ for different (types of) L2 words. Other studies on vocabulary learning and forgetting reported earlier in this book, testing retention 1 week instead of years after learning, had shown four word variables to determine the rate of acquisition and degree of forgetting: the frequency and concreteness of the L1 word in a translation pair; whether or not the L2 word is a cognate of its L1 translation; whether or not the L2 word sounds like L1 words (pp. 108–111). It may well be that some or all of these variables also underlie the variability in the forgetting rates of individual L2 words observed in the studies reviewed above.

First language loss after adoption

Production tasks

One might wonder whether, unlike a language acquired later in life, the first and native language is relatively immune to forgetting, especially in cases where L1 acquisition is well under way or even completed at the onset of L2 acquisition. That the L1 might enjoy such a privileged status accords with the conventional wisdom that early in life our brain machinery is optimally suited for language acquisition (pp. 47–48). In this section I will discuss a few studies that looked at the durability of unused L1 knowledge. The evidence suggests that the L1 is as susceptible to loss (or inaccessibility) as an L2. What is more, it suggests that under certain circumstances the degree of L1 loss may be far more dramatic than the loss observed in the L2 studies discussed above, where many of the apparently lost vocabulary items could be reactivated by just a brush of a reminder. A unique, and possibly critical, characteristic of these studies is that they tested participants who were adopted in childhood and, from the one moment to the next, ceased to receive any further input in their first language. Such a context may lead to a different pattern of L1 loss than one where the native language is still regularly used, as is often the case in immigrant communities immersed in an L2-dominant environment.

Among the latter populations substantial corrosion of the L1 occurs, but when the participants are allowed sufficient retrieval time much of the prior knowledge can still be dug up from memory (e.g., Ammerlaan, 1997).

In a single-case longitudinal study Isurin (2000) tracked the process of L1 loss in a Russian orphan (S) who was adopted by an English-speaking American family when she was 9 years old. After her arrival in the USA she no longer received any L1 Russian input because her adoption parents did not speak any Russian, nor was there a Russian-speaking community in the city where she came to live. S's L1 performance was monitored in eight test sessions administered at regular intervals, from 1 month after she arrived in the USA until about a year later. A special feature of this study was that not only the process of L1 loss was monitored, but also S's parallel gains in L2. The reason for doing so was the investigator's assumption that first language forgetting is directly related to second language acquisition or, more generally, that any change in the language system as a whole affects the rest of the system. This is also a central tenet in a "dynamic systems" approach to second and multilingual language acquisition and attrition that has recently been advanced (e.g., De Bot, Lowie, & Verspoor, 2007; Jessner, 1999, 2003).

The type of linguistic knowledge studied by Isurin (2000) was vocabulary, and the tasks used to assess it were three versions of the picture-naming task (see p. 223 for details). In one version of the task, called the "standard version", S was asked to name a set of pictures, block-wise, in either L1 Russian or L2 English, as specified by the investigator prior to each block. In a second version, for every picture presented to her S was free to name it in either Russian or English. In a third version, called a "blocking task" by the researcher but more commonly known as the "picture–word interference task" (see p. 237), the pictures all had to be named in L1 Russian but they were accompanied by their names in English, to be ignored. The pictures' L2 names were hypothesized to block the L1 Russian names, rendering them less available than when only a picture was presented. The pictures depicted objects and actions, to be named with nouns and verbs respectively. Both percentage correct scores and response latencies served as dependent variables. Note that these tasks are all instances of production tasks and, as such, more demanding than the receptive cued recall test used in the above studies on L2 loss that exploited the savings paradigm. The evidence of L1 loss obtained in the present study may thus overestimate the actual degree of loss. Figure 7.3a presents the percentage correct scores and response times obtained with the standard version of the task (administered in seven of the eight test sessions), collapsed over the noun and verb pictures.

The percentage correct scores show that L1 retention decreased gradually while L2 acquisition increased steeply over the first four test sessions and that both remained stable over later sessions, suggesting that L1 forgetting is slower than L2 acquisition. The response time data indicated that the retrieval of L1 words gradually became harder from the beginning of L2 immersion. These findings show that already a couple of months after being separated from the L1 environment, in which S had been immersed for no fewer than 9 years, her L1 vocabulary had started to corrode, as evidenced both by failures to come up with the picture's Russian name and the increased retrieval time on successful naming trials. The free-naming task (not shown) provided converging evidence by showing that already at the first test session about 45% of the pictures were named in L2 English, and that before the end of S's first year in the L2 environment L2 had become the preferred language of naming. A similar follow-up study conducted 1 year after the final test session—and only 2 years after S arrived in the USA—manifested a truly dramatic loss of L1 vocabulary: About 60% of the L1 vocabulary items could no longer be retrieved and the 40% that could took an extremely long time to dig up from memory (over 10 seconds). A more fine-grained analysis that focused on the individual vocabulary items showed a straightforward relation between L1 forgetting and L2 acquisition: The sooner a particular L2 name for a concept had been acquired, the sooner its L1 equivalent became difficult to access, as if

the new L2 word replaced the corresponding L1 word. This suggests that the loss (or inaccessibility) of the L1 vocabulary was caused, at least in part, by retroactive interference from the newly acquired L2 words. Direct support for this suggestion was obtained in a follow-up study by Isurin and McDonald (2001). In this study the researchers attempted to mimic the retroactive interference occurring under naturalistic circumstances in a carefully controlled laboratory study. Monolingual English-speaking students first learned a list (List 1) consisting of either Russian or Hebrew words by means of the picture–word association technique. Next, their recall of List 1 was tested. This test stage was followed by a second learning phase in which a list in the other language was presented for learning (List 2). After studying List 2 its retention was tested. Finally, a retest followed of the words on List 1. For half of the participants List 2 consisted of translation equivalents of words on List 1 whereas for the remaining participants it only contained new words. The critical finding was that the participants who had been presented with translation equivalents instead of new words on List 2 showed a relatively large retroactive interference effect. As concluded by the authors, this finding suggests that the acquisition of a translation equivalent of a word known before has the effect of rendering the earlier word for the same concept less available, up to the point that it cannot be retrieved again when it is not re-used once in a while.

The critical reader might be reluctant to generalize this conclusion to the more natural circumstances of L1 loss witnessed over a period of prolonged disuse, as in Isurin (2000) and in the studies to be discussed below. For one thing, in the laboratory study of Isurin and McDonald (2001) not the participants' actual L1 (English) but a totally new language (e.g., List 1 Russian) took the role of the L1 in naturalistic studies on L1 loss, whereas yet a further new language (List 2 Hebrew), took the role of the L2 in naturalistic studies. It thus ignored the possibly special status of a true L1 in language acquisition. Furthermore, the time between first learning an "L1" (the List 1 words) and then an "L2" (the List 2 words)

FIGURE 7.3

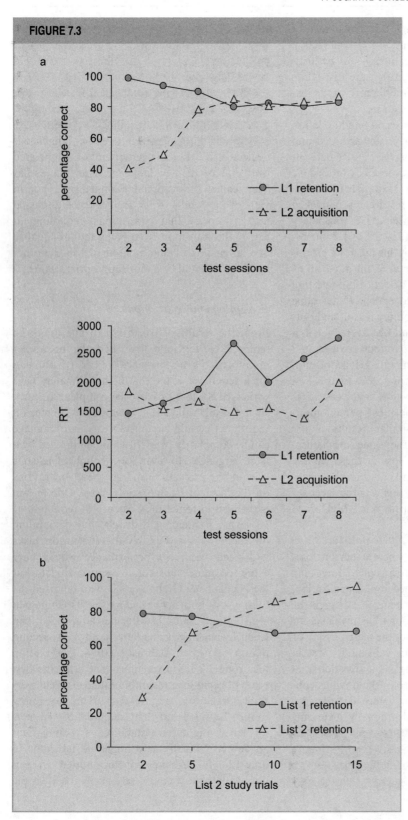

(a) Percentage correctly named pictures in L1 Russian and L2 English and corresponding picture-naming times (in ms) in a number of test sessions spanning about 1 year following S's adoption. From Isurin (2000). Reproduced with permission from the author and Cambridge University Press. (b) List 1 and List 2 retention as a function of number of List 2 study trials. The List 1 and List 2 retention functions are assumed to mimic L1 vocabulary loss and L2 vocabulary acquisition, respectively, over time. From Isurin and McDonald (2001) with permission from the Psychonomic Society.

spanned no more than a single experiment instead of an extended period of time, as in Isurin (2000). Because of these differences it may not be justified to extend the conclusion that the List 1 loss was caused by retroactive interference to the loss of L1 in naturalistic circumstances.

However, the results of a second manipulation suggested that this concern is unwarranted and that L1 vocabulary loss observed under naturalistic circumstances is indeed caused by retroactive interference by the newly acquired L2 translations of L1 words. The researchers mimicked increasing exposure to specific L2 vocabulary over time in naturalistic situations of L2 immersion and L1 deprivation by having four groups of participants each receive different numbers of List 2 study trials (2, 5, 10, or 15) before retesting them on the List 1 learned earlier. If the same mechanism underlies vocabulary loss in and outside the laboratory, List 1 and List 2 retention as a function of number of List 2 study trials should resemble the L1 retention and L2 acquisition functions obtained by Isurin (2000; Figure 7.3a upper panel). This turned out to be the case, as is shown in Figure 7.3b. The most parsimonious interpretation of these similar results across studies is that one and the same mechanism caused the L1 and List 1 loss in these studies. Retroactive interference is likely to be the mechanism in question because this was the mechanism manipulated by Isurin and McDonald (2001).

As concluded by Isurin (2000, p. 164): "... in a pure attrition situation, where a person loses any contact with L1, the process of L1 forgetting might be directly determined by L2 acquisition, and accessibility of lexical items in L1 might be affected by the acquisition of L2 equivalents for the same concepts". Whether the mere passing of time is an additional factor causing L1 loss in naturalistic attrition settings is a question that cannot be answered because of the obvious confound between elapsing time since L1 interruption on the one hand and gradually increasing L2 input on the other. Yet the resemblance of the pattern of loss obtained under those circumstances and the one obtained in the laboratory, in which the pattern was replicated within the span of a single experiment, suggests the passing of time itself is no cause of memory loss. A further conclusion to draw from the above results is that true bilingualism or multilingualism, in which the different translation equivalent words for one and the same concept all remain accessible, requires that all languages, including the L1, are maintained permanently. If an earlier language is neglected it will be overwritten or suppressed over time by the new language. This process has been called "transitional bilingualism", but in view of the results of the studies to be discussed next it appears that "transitional monolingualism"—the transition from being monolingual in one language to being monolingual in the other language—would be a more appropriate name.

Perception and recognition tasks

From the results of Isurin (2000) one might be tempted to conclude that, had the researcher monitored S's performance in her L1 Russian for a few more years, she might ultimately have witnessed S's loss of L1 to be complete. In turn, such a result would lead towards the conclusion that under certain circumstances a first language can be completely overwritten or suppressed by a later language. However, for a couple of reasons it would be premature to draw these conclusions on the basis of Isurin's study alone. One reason is that Isurin tested the existence of remnants of L1 in her participant with relatively demanding production tasks. Possibly, if recognition tasks had been used, S's performance would have exhibited more substantial residues of L1 (but see Nicoladis & Grabois, 2002, who reported the total loss of both active *and* passive L1 Chinese in a girl about 2 months after her adoption by an English-speaking Canadian family.) A second reason relates to Bahrick's (1984) observation regarding L2 loss over time: that after the first years of rapid loss, retention settled at a relatively stable level (see Figure 7.1). The possibility cannot be ruled out that, similarly, S's L1 performance might have stabilized at some point above zero. Finally, one might be reluctant to draw the far-reaching conclusion that L1 can ultimately be lost completely on the basis of the single case of a child suddenly deprived of her L1. In these respects, two further studies on L1 loss in adopted children provided more convincing evidence that a second language may replace a first if L2 learners are suddenly completely cut off from their native language.

In a brain-imaging study, Pallier et al. (2003) examined whether the neural circuits that subserve language learning become less plastic as they become attuned to the native language. Such loss of plasticity (or "crystallization", as the authors call this phenomenon) has been advanced (e.g., Lenneberg, 1967) as a possible cause for the fact that children are better at learning (some aspects of) language than older learners and to the related hypothesis that there is a circumscribed period early in life wherein a human being is particularly sensitive to language stimulation (see pp. 47–78 for an extensive discussion of this "critical period hypothesis" and of age of acquisition effects in language learning). Pallier and his collaborators aimed to test the prediction of the crystallization hypothesis that exposure to the first language leaves permanent traces in the neural circuits involved in language processing and investigated this issue by means of event-related functional magnetic response imaging (fMRI; see pp. 412–413). Their participants were 16 adults, 8 of whom were born in Korea and adopted by French families when they were between 3 and 8 years old. Just like the participant in Isurin's (2000) study, from the moment of adoption they were completely cut off from their L1. At the time of testing they were fluent in their L2 French and reported having completely lost their L1 Korean. The remaining eight subjects were all native monolingual speakers of French none of whom had any knowledge of Korean.

The Korean participants' claim that they had completely lost their L1 was confirmed by their behavioral responses in three tests that all assessed relatively low-level aspects of L1 perception and comprehension. In one test they listened to sentences in each of five languages and spoken by native speakers of those languages: Korean, Japanese, Polish, Swedish, and Wolof (the latter being a tonal language spoken in Senegal, Gambia, and Mauritania). All of these languages were unknown to the control participants and the latter four were unknown to the L1 Korean participants. Whether Korean was also completely unknown to the Korean participants was, of course, the issue under study. The task was to indicate for each sentence, on a scale of 1 to 7, their degree of confidence that the sentence was in Korean. The second test involved the auditory presentation of a set of French, Korean, Japanese, and Polish sentences. Each sentence was followed by a 400-ms speech fragment and the participants were to decide whether or not this fragment had occurred in the preceding sentence, notifying their decision by pushing one of two buttons. Each trial in the third test consisted of the presentation of a printed French word, followed by the aural presentation of two Korean words. The participants had to indicate which one of the two Korean words was the correct translation of the French word. Brain images were collected during the second of these three tests. The behavioral results of all three tests are depicted in Figure 7.4.

The first test (Figure 7.4a) showed that for none of the languages did the ratings (is the sentence in Korean?) differ between the L1 Korean participants and the French controls and that the ratings for Korean and Japanese sentences were higher than for the three remaining languages. These data suggest that all participants, including the French controls, could tell the difference between Asian languages and the other languages but that none of them, not even the Korean L1 speakers, could tell the difference between Japanese and Korean. Similarly, the French and Korean L1 participants performed comparably on the speech-fragment detection task, performing better when French sentences were presented than when Korean, Japanese, or Polish sentences were presented and showing equal performance for the latter three languages (Figure 7.4b). Finally, both the Korean L1 and the French group performed at chance level on the third test, where they were asked to select the Korean translation equivalent of a French word from two Korean words (Figure 7.4c).

The behavioral data obtained in these three

FIGURE 7.4

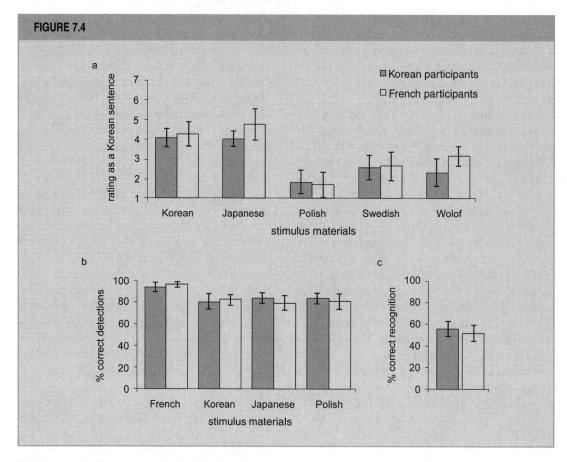

Performance of native Korean and native French participants on three tests (see text for details). Adapted from Pallier et al. (2003) by permission of Oxford University Press.

tests thus suggest that L1 loss can ultimately be complete and that this holds not only for production (as tested by Isurin, 2000) but also for perception and word recognition. Furthermore, the fact that these findings were obtained for a whole group of participants suggests that this phenomenon is common under circumstances of complete isolation from further L1 input instead of only inflicting the occasional atypical person. A follow-up study by Ventureyra, Pallier, and Yoo (2004), aimed to find out whether phonemic contrasts that exist in Korean but not in French might be less susceptible to forgetting, provided converging evidence: 18 L1 Korean participants drawn from the same population as tested by Pallier and his colleagues (2003) did not perform any better than French native speakers on a task

that required them to discriminate between pairs of sounds that represented different phonemes in Korean but not in French.

In view of the primary goal of Pallier and his collaborators (2003), to find out whether early exposure to L1 leaves permanent traces in the brain, two results revealed by the fMRI data (collected in the second test) were particularly interesting. The first was that the brain images of the adopted L1 Korean speakers did not show any specific activation to Korean sentences as compared to Polish and Japanese sentences, as if Korean was equally as unknown to them as Polish and Japanese. Second, in the adopted Koreans and the L1 French speakers the same brain regions responded more to the known language French than to the unknown languages Polish and Japanese. The only difference between the two participant groups was that, when listening to French sentences, the activated brain regions were more extended in the L1 French speakers than in the L1 Korean speakers.

As concluded by the authors, these data provide evidence against the crystallization hypothesis, which predicts a pattern of activation specific for the Korean group when listening to Korean as well as differences between the activated brain regions in the French and Korean groups when listening to French. The data suggest that the native language can be completely lost and replaced by a second language when at a relatively young age a language learner is suddenly completely cut off from further native language input. Because the adoption age had varied between 3 and 8 years, these results in their turn suggest that brain plasticity at age 8 is still sufficiently great to enable complete learning of a new language. This evidence of continued plasticity of the brain after early childhood is supported by an increasing number of studies in an increasing number of functional domains, including at least one that demonstrated the phenomenon for second language learners (Mechelli et al., 2004). Finally, the above data point out that an L2 settles in the same brain areas as the native language does (see also, e.g., Perani et al., 1998, and pp. 427–435 for an extensive discussion).

To conclude, the form of dramatic L1 loss witnessed by Pallier et al. (2003) and Ventureyra et al. (2004) has been called "catastrophic forgetting" in computational modeling of neural networks, and has been shown to emerge under circumstances that resemble those of the Korean participants immediately after their adoption. As discussed by Ellis and Lambon Ralph (2000), the critical feature of computer simulations showing catastrophic forgetting is that they employed a learning scheme in which the presentation of a first set of patterns to learn was suddenly and completely discontinued the moment a new set of patterns was introduced. With this learning scheme the set of patterns learned first was gradually lost and fully replaced by the second set. Instead, when the learning

scheme was "cumulative" and "interleaved", meaning that the second set of patterns did not fully replace the first set but the presentation of the early items continued following the introduction of the second set, the items first acquired were not only retained but, in fact, retained better than the second set of items (that is, the typical age of acquisition effect was obtained; see Chapter 2). This presentation scheme resembles the situation of L2 learners who continue to use their L1 regularly after immersion in an L2 environment, as holds for most immigrants.

An evaluation of the conflicting results

The studies on L1 and L2 loss discussed above seem to point towards the conclusion that L1, acquired early in life, is more susceptible to forgetting than an L2, acquired later in life. Is this a conclusion that can legitimately be drawn from the reported evidence or can differences be pointed out between the two sets of studies that may have contaminated the results and that compel a reconsideration of this conclusion? One possible difference to consider is differential exposure to the corroded language in between first acquiring it and testing its remains at some later point in time: It may be that the above studies on L2 loss have accidentally tested participants who, albeit not having used their L2 actively in the intervening period, might still have been passively exposed to it. Ventureyra et al. (2004) brought up the potential importance of this factor when trying to accommodate their data with a seemingly conflicting result. As mentioned, their participants, adult Koreans adopted by French families when they were between 3 and 8 years old, showed no sign of residual phonological knowledge of Korean. In contrast, two other studies have shown that adults who had been regularly exposed to a *non-native* language during the first years of their life just by overhearing it were better at learning the phonological system of this language than adult learners who had lacked such early overhearing experience (Au, Knightly, Jun, & Oh, 2002; Oh, Jun, Knightly, & Au, 2003). This finding clearly suggests that under certain circumstances just overhearing a language during early childhood may leave permanent traces of its phonology in memory. The importance of continued exposure to prevent loss is also suggested by Ellis and Lambon Ralph's (2000) study that completed the previous section.

A second potentially crucial difference between the different groups of studies on language loss reviewed above is that they focused on different types of linguistic units. Different linguistic domains may differ in their vulnerability to loss, and it may be that the L2 studies happened to concentrate more on the less-vulnerable linguistic domains. What speaks against this hypothesis is that vocabulary has been found to be the first component of the language system to attrite (see Isurin, 2000, for a discussion) and that especially phonology is relatively immune to loss. Yet the above studies on L2 loss have shown impressive savings despite the fact that vocabulary was the domain of study. Conversely, the studies by Pallier and his colleagues (Pallier et al., 2003; Ventureyra et al., 2004) focused primarily on phonology and yet showed massive loss.

A third potential confound might be that the originally acquired level of L2 proficiency of the participants in the above studies on L2 attrition was higher than the original level of L1 proficiency in the reviewed studies on L1 loss. As suggested by Hansen et al. (2002), a high level of initial proficiency may lead to memory structures that are relatively impervious to forgetting, and Bahrick (1984) obtained evidence that supported this suggestion (see p. 349). But contrary to this suggestion, the participants in the above studies on L1 loss had, on average, been immersed in their L1 for a longer period of time before being isolated from it than, for instance, the participants in the study by Hansen and colleagues had been immersed in their L2 Japanese and Korean. (Note, however, that the participants in Hansen et al. were late L2 learners and, consequently, started the learning process with a relatively large body of semantic, conceptual, and metalinguistic knowledge that is likely to facilitate the learning process and may thus compensate for a short duration of learning.)

A fourth potentially relevant factor is a difference in the test methods used across studies. As mentioned, some have used relatively demanding production tasks, whereas others have used less-demanding perception and recognition tasks that are probably more suitable to detect residual linguistic knowledge. Furthermore, in some studies (those on L2 loss) the savings paradigm was used, involving a session of retraining the language apparently lost, whereas other studies (those on L1 loss) did not encompass any retraining. The latter have plausibly underestimated the amount of retention because residual knowledge, present but dormant, may require external stimulation in order to become available again. As it stands, the first of these two differences cannot explain why the above studies on L1 loss showed the most dramatic loss because two of them (Pallier et al., 2003; Ventureyra et al., 2004) used perception and recognition tasks exclusively, and nevertheless detected no hint of retained L1 knowledge, not even in phonology, the linguistic domain considered to be relatively immune to loss. A recent study indicates that the second difference between the various studies—that is, the absence or presence of a period of relearning the apparently lost language—might indeed contribute to the disparate results. Hyltenstam, Bylund, Abrahamsson, and Park (2009) used an experimental method that conceptually resembles the savings paradigm (encompassing a retraining component) and detected L1 phonetic remnants in some adopted persons. In this study two groups of adult learners of Korean were tested on a phonetic discrimination task. One group consisted of L1 Koreans who had been adopted by Swedish families while they were between 0.3 and 10.5 years old. The second group consisted of native speakers of Swedish. A subset of the group of L1 Korean adoptees (7 out of 21) performed better on this task than all individuals in the control group of native Swedish speakers. This was the case even though the L1 Swedish participants had spent more years studying Korean than the L1 Koreans had. These savings effects suggest that at least some adoptees retain some traces of L1 phonology but that it takes a period of relearning the L1 for this knowledge to become accessible again.

A final possibly critical difference between the above studies is the age at which the attrited language was first learned, L1 by definition being learned earlier than L2. Differences in the age of first learning a language may be correlated with differences in the way the learner approaches the learning task. For instance, language learning in adults may exploit conscious strategies and metalinguistic knowledge not available to young learners yet (see, for instance, Bley-Vroman's, 1988, fundamental difference hypothesis discussed in Chapter 2, p. 66) and these may result in relatively stable knowledge. Furthermore, older language learners possess a larger stock of conceptual knowledge to exploit, including the meanings of many words of the new language to be learned. In other words, faced with the task of learning a new language, in at least one way an older learner has less to learn than a child. This frees attention to be allocated to the unknown language components. A final difference between younger and older language learners is the degree of plasticity of their brains. Even though recent studies have shown that the brain keeps its plasticity beyond early childhood, neural plasticity does decrease with age, as evidenced by the study of Mechelli et al. (2004) mentioned above. These authors showed that the density of **gray matter** in the left inferior parietal cortex (see pp. 415–418) of bilinguals—gray-matter density reflecting the degree of the brain's plasticity—is larger the younger the bilingual was when he started to acquire his second language. Plausibly, the more plastic the brain, the more drastically older knowledge is replaced by new.

To summarize, at this point it would be premature to conclude that the L1 is more prone to forgetting than languages learned later in life, because the pertinent evidence was obtained in studies that differ from one another in a number of arguably critical ways: the amount of continued active use and/or passive exposure to the corroded language in between initial learning and later testing; the types of linguistic knowledge that were examined during testing; the originally acquired level of fluency in the attrited language;

the test methods used to assess the degree of loss; the age at which the attrited language was first learned. These differences must all be taken into account in designing new studies to settle the question whether an L1 is more susceptible to loss than an L2.

THE INTERACTING LANGUAGES OF BILINGUALS AND MULTILINGUALS: EFFECTS ON THE FIRST LANGUAGE

Introduction

The previous section focused on what happens with a previously known language when it is no longer used actively and passively. Instead, the present section highlights some consequences of "active" bilingualism and multilingualism on the use of the separate languages involved. As we shall see, an influence of the active but not currently selected language(s) is omnipresent and appears to affect all domains of language. The consequence is "accented" language not only with respect to phonology—the language domain with which the word *accent* is usually associated—but also with respect to grammar and semantics, and not only in L2 but also in L1. The focus in this section will be on the latter. Two possible sources of these accents will be considered: competition between activated representations of linguistic elements in the multiple language subsystems of bilinguals (and multilinguals), and differences between the memory representations of linguistic units between monolinguals and bilinguals. The former source of accents concerns a difference in processing or "performance", between monolinguals and bilinguals; the latter a difference in structural knowledge or "competence".

A couple of decades ago Edith Mägiste had already collected a substantial amount of evidence that the active use of more than one language affects the processing of all of the languages concerned, including the L1, and that competition between activated memory representations may be the source of the ensuing cross-language effects. Such effects consistently emerged across a series of studies that together employed a diverse set of comprehension and production tasks such as word reading and picture naming (see Mägiste, 1986, for a review). One of these studies (Mägiste, 1979) compared the performance of German and Swedish monolinguals, German–Swedish bilinguals, and trilinguals with a third language in addition to German and Swedish, on a number of tasks. All participants were high-school students in Sweden and the bilingual and trilingual participants had lived in Sweden for on average 5 years and used each of their languages daily. Figure 7.5 shows the results of all groups of participants on three of the tasks, word reading, number naming, and object naming, and with both German (the L1 of the bilingual and trilingual groups) and Swedish as the test language.

That bilingualism and trilingualism affects performance shows from the fact that on all three tasks the German and Swedish monolinguals were faster than the bilinguals and trilinguals. This held when the bilinguals and trilinguals performed the tasks in both non-native Swedish and in native German, a finding that indicates that the L1 is also not immune to cross-language influences. A similar result was obtained when a color-word Stroop task (see p. 223) was employed (Mägiste, 1984a). Also noteworthy is the fact that the decelerating effect of mastering one or more additional languages beyond the test language was additive, the trilinguals responding more slowly than the bilinguals. We have already come across a similar finding before (p. 202), where Dutch–English–German trilinguals produced *faster* lexical decision responses to German–Dutch cognates than to non-cognate controls and yet faster responses to words that were cognates across all three languages (called "triple" cognates; Lemhöfer et al., 2004). Mägiste attributed the longer latencies for bilinguals and the yet longer ones for trilinguals to co-activation of memory representations in the non-selected languages during task performance. Similarly, Lemhöfer and colleagues assumed that co-activation in the non-targeted languages underlies

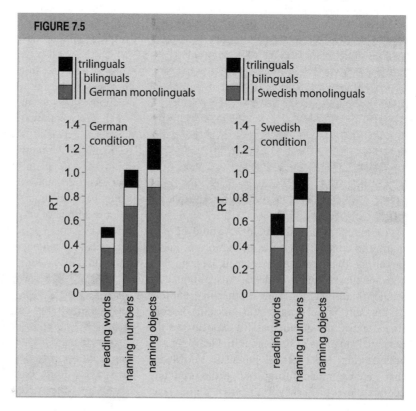

FIGURE 7.5

Mean response times (in seconds) for three tasks performed in German and Swedish by monolinguals, bilinguals, and trilinguals. Adapted from Mägiste (1979) with permission from Elsevier.

the beneficial effect of cognate status they obtained. That the direction of the cross-language influence differed between these studies is likely due to the differences in task demands and stimulus materials between studies (see p. 168 for similar results and a discussion).

Mägiste's work and similar recent studies (e.g., the picture-naming studies of Ivanova & Costa, 2008, and Gollan, Montoya, Fennema-Notestine, & Morris, 2005) demonstrate convincingly that additional languages influence the way the selected language is processed and that this even happens when the selected language is the dominant and first language. What they do not do, though, is identify the exact linguistic elements in the non-selected language(s) that cause the cross-language effect (although in a task like naming a pictured object, a good guess at what causes the effect is easy to make: the object's name in the other language). Similarly, relatively coarse measures of cross-language influence have been used in the study of other domains of language, such as the ratings of L2 phonological speech accents discussed in Chapter 5 (pp. 268–273). In the studies presented there native speakers simply rated sentences spoken by L2 speakers on a scale of, say, 1 to 9 on degree of phonological "accentedness". This method has also been used to find out whether bilinguals have a detectable speech accent in their L1, as compared to monolingual speakers of that language, and evidence that such is indeed the case has been reported (e.g., Flege et al., 1999; see also Flege, 2002). Although informative, such a procedure does not reveal exactly which aspects of speech—for instance, particular phonemes or prosodic features such as intonation or stress pattern—caused the accent. The goal of other studies has been to pinpoint the exact source of a particular cross-language effect by means of a careful contrastive analysis of how a particular knowledge structure is represented and processed in the bilingual's or multilingual's different languages. As a result these studies can not only tell which domain of language is involved in the effect, for instance grammar or phonology, but also which specific linguistic structure in a non-selected language is likely to cause it. The rest of this section will be devoted to a couple of studies that exemplify this approach.

Accents in first language phonology

In the domain of phonology the so-called "voice onset time" (VOT) has repeatedly been exploited to pinpoint the source of a speech accent. The VOT is the time between the release of the air and the moment the vocal cords start to vibrate when a speaker produces a consonant. Languages differ from one another in the way particular consonants are realized in speech, with shorter or longer VOTs (see Chapter 2, Figure 2.2, for an illustration). For instance, the consonant /t/ is spoken with a longer VOT in English than in French and Spanish. This gives rise to the question of how, for instance, English–French bilinguals produce this consonant. Do they produce it with a VOT value characteristic of English when speaking English and with a VOT value characteristic of French when speaking French, or do their /t/ realizations differ from those of monolingual speakers of both languages, in so doing producing accented speech?

Flege and his colleagues addressed this question in a series of studies that all point towards the conclusion that the VOT value realized for the targeted language is influenced by the VOT value of the same consonant in the non-targeted language, and that this also holds when L1 is the test language. The results of one of these studies (Flege, 1987) are presented in Figure 7.6 (adapted from Flege, 2002). The participants in this study were English–French and French–English adult late bilinguals, the former American women who in adulthood had lived in Paris for 12 years on average, the latter French and Belgian women who had lived in Chicago for on average 12 years. They were asked to read aloud French and English phrases of the form *Tous les X* ("all X") and *Two little X* (with *X* the placeholder for a noun in the language of the rest of the phrase). Monolingual control participants were presented with these same phrases in their one language only.

As shown, the /t/ realizations of the bilinguals in both their languages clearly deviated from

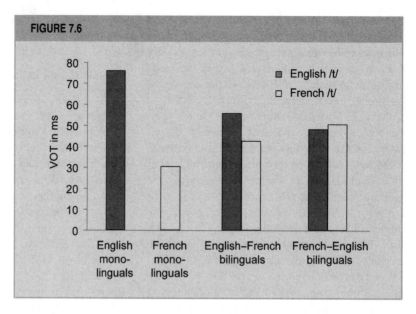

FIGURE 7.6

Mean VOT values for word-initial /t/ realizations in English and French by English–French and French–English bilinguals. The corresponding VOT values observed for English and French monolinguals are presented for comparison. Modified from Flege (2002). Copyright © Wissenschaftlicher Verlag Trier. Reproduced with permission.

those of monolingual speakers of these languages: The bilinguals' VOTs for the English /t/s were shorter than the English monolinguals' VOTs. In contrast, the bilinguals' VOTs for the French /t/s were longer than the corresponding VOTs in the /t/s produced by French monolinguals.

As noted above, cross-language influences in bilingualism are sometimes thought to result from competition between activated units in the different linguistic subsystems and at other times from differences between the memory representations of monolinguals and bilinguals/multilinguals. Whereas Mägiste adhered to the former account of cross-language transfer effects, Flege (2002) attributed his results to the existence of different /t/ representations in the phonetic system of monolinguals and bilinguals that have come about through the process of phonetic category assimilation described in Chapter 5 (p. 272). The core assumption of his speech learning model, which encompasses this assimilation hypothesis, is that L2 speech accents in, especially, late bilinguals do not result from the speech-learning equipment becoming corrupted with aging. Instead, they are thought to result from the fact that by the time L2 learning starts, strong phonetic categories have already been formed for L1 speech sounds. Depending on the degree of

similarity between the new L2 sounds to acquire and the corresponding L1 sounds, these extant L1 phonetic categories either "attract" the new L2 sounds or new categories are being created for them: The more similar the new L2 sound is to an L1 speech sound, the larger the chance that the former is attracted by the extant phonetic representation of the latter so that a merged category is formed that represents both. This process is called "phonetic category assimilation" (see Figure 5.12c for an illustration). Flege (2002) assumed that the /t/ sound accents in his French–English and English–French bilingual participants resulted from such merged representations. Particularly important in the present context is that the merged representations differ from the representations of the analogous sounds in the phonetic system of monolingual users of the languages in question, here French and English. As a consequence, the /t/ utterances of the French–English and English–French participants in *both* their L1 and L2 deviated from those of monolingual speakers of these languages.

Contrary to a process of assimilation, when the difference between the new L2 sound and the closest L1 sound is relatively large, the chances increase that a new representation for the L2 sound is formed in the phonetic system. According to Flege and his colleagues (e.g., Flege, 2002;

Flege et al., 2003), this process is also a cause of both L1 and L2 speech accents, because the representation of the closest L1 sound is pushed away somewhat from its original position in the phonetic system. This exaggerates the difference between the new L2 sound and its most similar sound in L1. This process is called "phonetic category dissimilation" (see Figure 5.12c for an illustration). Again exploiting the occurrence of VOT differences between languages, Flege and Eefting (1987) obtained evidence of such a dissimilation process in a study that compared Spanish–English bilinguals with monolinguals in both of these languages.

Accents in first language grammar

Some recent evidence of a grammatical accent in L1 due to a cross-language influence from L2 has already been presented in Chapter 4 (p. 210). It was described there how Spanish–English bilinguals immersed in an L2 English environment parsed one particular type of structurally ambiguous L1 Spanish sentences the way English monolinguals parse the English equivalents of these sentences, and different from the way Spanish monolinguals parse them (Dussias, 2006; Dussias & Sagarra, 2007). The critical sentences contained a complex noun phrase followed by a relative clause, for instance:

> *Alguien disparó contra el hijo de la actriz que estaba en el balcón* (*Someone shot the son of the actress who was on the balcony*)

Spanish favors a "high-attachment" analysis of this construction, assigning the head of the complex noun phrase (*el hijo*) the role of subject of the relative clause. English favors a "low-assignment" analysis, assigning the second noun in the complex noun phrase (*actress*) this role. Just like monolingual English speakers, the bilinguals immersed in their L2 English preferred a low-assignment analysis of sentences of this type, presented in L1 Spanish.

To examine cross-language grammatical influences of L2 on L1, Cook et al. (2003) exploited a research paradigm developed in the context of the competition model (e.g., MacWhinney et al., 1984). This is a model of sentence comprehension that attempts to explain how language users figure out the grammatical functions of the various constituents in a sentence. It assumes that language users exploit various types of cues in the sentence such as word order and subject-verb agreement in number and gender to do so. Languages differ from one another in which cues are the most reliable indicators of function and, accordingly, speakers of different languages differ between one another in what weight they give to each of the cues.

The most popular way to examine form–function mapping across languages involves the presentation of simple grammatical and ungrammatical sentences, typically containing two noun phrases and a verb, and asking the participants to identify the subject of the verb. By systematically manipulating different cues in the sentences and looking at the way conflicts ("competition"; hence the model's name) between the various cues are resolved, the researchers obtain information on the relative importance of the various cues in the test language. This methodology was first used in cross-linguistic studies with the main goal to identify differences between languages in the preferred function-assignment processes. Subsequently it was applied to find out whether bilinguals use the same cues in L2 form–function mapping as do native speakers of the language in question (see p. 212). Cook and his colleagues took the use of this methodology one step further, trying to find out whether bilinguals' form–function mapping in their *L1* differs from the mapping process in monolingual speakers of this language.

The participants in Cook et al. (2003) were adult Japanese–English, Spanish–English, and Greek–English bilinguals, all university students who studied L2 English in their respective countries, and matched Japanese, Spanish, and Greek monolingual controls. All participants were only tested in their L1. The experimental materials were manipulated on word order, animacy (that is, whether or not the nouns in a noun-verb-noun sequence refer to living beings), case, and number agreement. English translations

---

TABLE 7.3

Example materials used by Cook et al. (2003)

Word order manipulation:
N/V/N: The dog pats the tree
V/N/N: Watches the monkey the pen
N/N/V: The horse the rock kisses

Animacy manipulation:
N1 (animate)/V/N2 (inanimate): The bears kiss the tree
N1 (inanimate)/V/N2 (animate): The pencil smells the giraffe
N1 (animate)/V/N2 (animate): The dog pats the donkey

Case manipulation:
N1 (subject)/V/N2: The cow (subject) pats the monkey
N1/V/N2 (subject): The dog eats the donkey (subject)

Number agreement manipulation:
N1 (singular)/V/N2 (plural): The turtle smells the bears
N1 (plural)/V/N2 (singular): The dogs bites the monkey

Because English noun phrases do not have full surface case, the specification of surface case is indicated in brackets.

---

of some of the presented sentences are shown in Table 7.3.

The researchers predicted that the strength of the various cues would differ between the bilinguals and the monolinguals and, more precisely, that the differences would reflect an influence from L2 English in the bilinguals. For instance, because word order is an especially strong cue to function in English, the investigators expected the bilinguals to rely more on word order than the monolingual controls. In one respect the results were clear-cut: For all three languages differences were obtained between bilinguals and monolinguals in the way they processed the L1 sentences. This finding indeed suggests that knowledge of an L2 affects form–function mapping in L1. But unlike in the studies discussed above, the exact L2 knowledge structure that caused the L2 influence could not be identified. It was, for instance, not the case that the word order cue clearly received more weight in the bilinguals than in the L1 monolinguals. These findings thus suggest that the bilinguals, through their experience with L2 English, had become aware that languages other than their L1 exploit other features of the linguistic input to assign function than does their L1, but that they had not yet figured out the exact nature of the differences. The resulting uncertainty becomes manifest in

"accented" but variable function assignment in their L1.

Further evidence of an L2 influence on L1 concerns the violation of **selection restrictions**, and particularly those in the borderland between grammar and the lexicon: idiomatic verb usages in collocations such as *to make a decision* in English instead of *prendre un decision* in French or *een beslissing nemen* in Dutch (in both cases: "take a decision"). Both Laufer (2003a) and Altenberg (1991) examined the processing of L1 collocations containing verbs that either matched or mismatched their translation equivalents in L2. The bilingual participants in Laufer's study were Russian immigrants in Israel, with L1 Russian and L2 Hebrew. Their task was to judge whether Russian collocations like *Ja zakryl telvizor* ("I closed the television", as they say in Hebrew, whereas in Russia one switches off a television set) was correct or not and to correct it if it was not. Their performance was compared with that of Russian monolinguals in Moscow. Altenberg's study was a case study testing two German immigrants in the United States with German as L1 and English as, dominant, L2. They were shown German sentences that included collocations with acceptable (*Er brach sich das Bein*, "he broke his leg") or unacceptable verb usage (*Sein Fall wurde von einem Baum gebrochen*, "his fall was broken by a tree") and were asked to rate the acceptability of the sentences and, specifically, to judge whether the verb could be used this way in German. No German monolinguals were included for comparison. To detect possible influences of the L2, Laufer's L1 Russian sentences contained a large variety of different verbs. In contrast, the L1 German sentences in the Altenberg study either included the verb *nehmen* ("to take") or the verb *brechen* ("to break").

A potentially important difference between the two verbs tested by Altenberg (1991) is that the one (*nehmen*) is a non-cognate of its translation in English (*take*) whereas the other (*brechen*) shares a cognate relation with English *break*. The potential relevance of this difference relates to the fact that cross-language influence does not appear to occur randomly—with an equal probability for every linguistic unit in an utterance to be afflicted—but seems to be governed by regularities. In the search for the factors that promote transfer, similarity between a structure in the non-selected language and the language in use has been identified as a potentially critical one (e.g., Kellerman, 1983): Translation-equivalent structures in a bilingual's two languages that are similar are more likely to be affected by transfer than dissimilar structures. At a general level this could explain why there is more transfer between typologically close languages than between typologically distant languages. At the level of individual vocabulary items it would explain—and predict—differential susceptibility to cross-language influences of cognates and non-cognates. The relatively frequent occurrence of language switches in the neighborhood of a cognate, as examined in detail by Clyne (1967, 1972) and by many others after him (e.g., Broersma & De Bot, 2006), is one manifestation of this general phenomenon.

The results of both studies suggested that idiomatic verb usage in L1 collocations is influenced by the way the collocations' content is expressed in L2: Laufer's (2003a) Russian–Hebrew participants accepted about 40% of the incorrect Russian L1 collocations that were modeled on L2 as correct whereas the Russian monolinguals made few such errors. Similarly, Altenberg's (1991) two participants judged 53% of the unacceptable German L1 sentences as correct. Additional analyses by Laufer revealed that the amount of current use of L1 Russian, age of arrival in Israel, and length of residence in Israel all affected the degree of deterioration of L1 collocational knowledge: The deterioration was relatively large for the immigrants who still spoke Russian infrequently, had arrived in Israel at a young age, and had been living there for a relatively long time. Of these three variables, length of residence had the highest impact on performance. These same three variables have been shown to be important determinants of cross-language influence in other language domains, such as phonology (see pp. 269–272). Finally, the cognate manipulation in Altenberg's study also affected the results: Whereas on average 53% of the unacceptable German sentences

were considered correct, a huge difference emerged between the acceptability scores for the cognate *brechen* and the non-cognate *nehmen* (78% and 25% acceptance of incorrect sentences respectively). These data support the hypothesis that cross-language similarity determines the incidence of transfer.

Accents in first language semantics

A final linguistic domain in which an influence from L2 on L1 has been found is semantics. Languages differ from one another in how their vocabularies carve up conceptual space and the physical world into lexicalized concepts. As a consequence, it is generally the case that the referent of a particular word in one language and that of its closest translation equivalent in another language do not perfectly overlap. This was the reason why in Chapter 3 it was argued that to come to master the subtleties of a foreign vocabulary, direct, "de-contextualized" vocabulary acquisition techniques such as paired-associate learning and the keyword method must be augmented by contextual learning, through extensive reading in the target language or other forms of immersion in that language. Whereas the direct method in question swiftly provides an approximation of the new word's meaning in the form of the meaning of its closest translation equivalent in the learner's native language, through subsequent immersion learning the L1-specific parts must be chipped off from this model and its specific meaning components in the new language must be molded onto it. En route to (a closer approximation of) the targeted meaning, the learner will produce semantically accented speech in the form of word usages that in first language acquisition research have been called "overextensions" and "underextensions". An overextended word is one that is used too broadly (when, for instance, a child calls the sun a ball); an underextended word is one that is used too narrowly (when she would, for instance, only call a robin a bird, but not a heron). Differential word-to-meaning mapping across languages is more salient for some types of words than for others (e.g., it is more salient for words with abstract referents than for words with concrete referents) and is manifested most saliently in the existence of untranslatable words; that is, words referring to a concept that cannot be expressed in a single word in the other language but requires a circumlocution instead.

Semantic flaws similar to those of young children acquiring their mother tongue occur in the speech of L2 learners, such as the overextended use of Romance cognate words in learners of English discussed in Chapter 3 (p. 123). Another example concerns the semantic accents that L2 learners exhibit when they have to name pictures of common household objects such as jars, bottles, cups, and bowls. The demarcations between these objects or, more precisely, between the associated concepts, are not crystal clear with the effect that one and the same object might be called, say, a *cup* by some and a *bowl* by others. One and the same individual may even call this object a *cup* some of the time and a *bowl* at other times. Especially relevant in the present context is that languages differ in the way they have lexicalized these concepts. For instance, both Russian and English have separate words for glasses and cups (*stakany* and *chashki*, respectively, in Russian) but the exact coverage of these words differs between the two languages: Paper cups are called *stakanchiki* (small glasses) in Russian (the example is from Pavlenko, 2005). Malt and Sloman (2003) have shown that even very advanced L2 speakers of English demonstrate an influence from their L1 when naming pictures of common household objects in English, for instance calling a dish a *plate* because the object in question would typically be called the equivalent of *plate* in their L1.

A first indication that similar semantic accents may also occur in L1 through an influence of L2 is suggested by Isurin's (2000) study discussed earlier (pp. 353–355). In her participant S, a Russian child adopted by Americans when she was 9 years old, pairs of L1 Russian "convergent" words that are "divergent" in English were especially vulnerable to (partial) forgetting. For instance, in Russian there is just one word for both the concepts "ladder" and "staircase" (*lestnitza*), or for both "table" and "desk" (*stol*). In an

L1 Russian picture-naming task administered during her first year in the United States, S gradually started to fail to retrieve the Russian name for one of the two pictures depicting a converging pair in Russian. So for instance, she would say *lestnitza* to a picture of a staircase but fail to come up with this same Russian name when a picture of a ladder was shown (displaying the phenomenon of underextension introduced above). This failure appeared to coincide with the moment that S, after an earlier stage of naming both a picture of a staircase and of a ladder with one and the same English word (as if they constituted a converging pair in English), named only one of these pictures this way in English. Apparently, under the influence of L2 English, a semantic change had occurred such that the L1 word was assigned a meaning which was narrower (e.g., only "staircase") than its actual coverage (both "staircase" and "ladder").

Isurin's (2000) finding of a semantic accent in L1 as a consequence of differential word-to-meaning mapping in L1 and L2 was an unintentional one, a side-effect of the fortuitous inclusion of a couple of translation pairs with the above characteristic (convergent in L1, divergent in L2). An intentional demonstration of a similar effect was provided decades earlier, in two studies that examined color categorization in bilinguals. It has long been known that languages differ in the way they lexicalize the color continuum and vary widely in the number of color words they possess to describe this continuum. Examining the English and Zuni color systems, Lenneberg and Roberts (1956) were the first to observe an influence of a person's bilingualism on the way colors are labeled, Zuni–English bilinguals showing an English L2 accent in L1 Zuni color naming as compared with Zuni monolinguals. Ervin (1961b) and Caskey-Sirmons and Hickerson (1977) built on this observation in studies designed to probe the cause of these accents and examining other language pairs.

Ervin (1961b) examined color naming by Navajo–English bilinguals in both their languages and compared their performance with that of Navajo and English monolinguals. Both Navajo-dominant and English-dominant bilinguals were included, dominance being determined on the basis of their relative speed in naming pictures in each of their two languages. On the basis of a meticulous contrastive analysis of the color systems of Navajo and English, the author derived a set of predictions regarding the semantic shifts to occur in the color naming of the bilingual participants. For instance, the yellow range is easier to name in Navajo than in English. This is evidenced by the fact that *litso*, the Navajo "equivalent" of *yellow*, was the favored response of Navajo monolinguals to color stimuli across a much larger part of the color continuum than the range that excited English *yellow* in English monolinguals. It is also suggested by the fact that the commonality of Navajo monolinguals' *litso* responses at its peak (at the point that represented the focal color *litso*) was much larger than the commonality of English monolinguals' *yellow* responses at its peak: At this point 89% of the Navajo monolinguals responded with *litso* but only 34% of the English monolinguals responded with *yellow*.

Assuming an influence from the color's name in the non-response language, Ervin expected the response probabilities in the response language to differ in bilinguals as compared with monolinguals. For instance, she expected that, when presenting focal yellow and inviting a response in English, more bilinguals than English monolinguals would respond with *yellow*. Similarly, when presenting focal yellow and inviting a response in Navajo, bilinguals were predicted to produce fewer *litso* responses than monolingual Navajo controls. Collecting responses to hues across the complete color spectrum and in both languages, the majority of Ervin's predictions were borne out by the data, thus suggesting that bilingualism causes semantic shifts both from L1 to L2 and vice versa. The effects of the non-response language were smaller for bilinguals dominant in the response language than for those dominant in the non-response language, a finding that converges with similar effects of language dominance reported in Chapters 4 and 5.

Using a different methodology and focusing exclusively on an influence from L2 on L1, Caskey-Sirmons and Hickerson (1977) extended Ervin's (1961b) results to five other language pairs, all involving English as L2 and Korean, Japanese, Hindi, Cantonese, or Mandarin Chinese as L1. All bilingual participants were immigrants to the United States and had lived there for at least 2 years but generally much longer. Every bilingual participant was matched with a "monolingual" L1 speaker, a person who had immigrated to the United States from the same country as its bilingual counterpart but who had lived there relatively briefly (18 months at the most). In all, there were five monolingual and five bilingual participants per L1 test language. Instead of the production task used by Ervin—where the participants produced a color word in response to a color-patch stimulus—Caskey-Sirmons and Hickerson employed a two-step testing procedure designed to test color-word comprehension: They first elicited a list of basic color vocabulary in each participant's L1. In a second step each participant was presented with each of the L1 color words elicited in the first step and asked to map the focal area and range of each of them on a color chart that showed the whole color spectrum, ordered by hue on the horizontal dimension and brightness on the vertical dimension. To be able to assess an influence from L2 English on the bilinguals' L1, a group of native speakers of American English was also tested, using exactly the same procedure.

The response patterns clearly differed between the bilinguals and the monolinguals with which they were paired: The foci that the bilinguals mapped on the color chart showed more variation than those mapped by the monolinguals. Furthermore, the areas mapped by bilinguals were generally larger than the areas mapped by monolinguals. This general pattern is illustrated in Figure 7.7, which shows the data of the Korean monolinguals and the Korean–English bilinguals in diagrammatic representations of the color chart. The different numbers represent different colors. The positions of the numbers represent the associated colors' foci chosen by the participants. If a number occurs only once on a map (e.g., the number 5 on the monolingual map), this means that all participants mapped the same

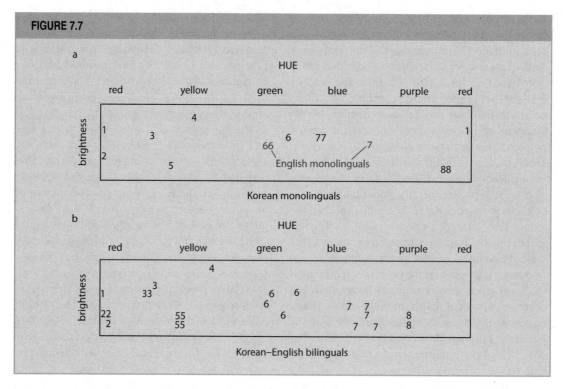

FIGURE 7.7

Diagrammatic representations of color charts onto which Korean monolinguals and Korean–English bilinguals mapped the focal area and range of each of a set of color words elicited before. The different numbers represent different colors. 1 = *punhong sek* ("pink"); 2 = *balgan sek* ("red"); 3 = *juhong sek* ("orange"); 4 = *noran sek* ("yellow"); 5 = *gal sek* ("brown"); 6 = *chorok sek* ("green"); 7 = *paran sek* ("blue"); 8 = *pora sek* ("purple"). For comparison, English monolinguals' mappings of green (6) and blue (7) are shown on the Korean monolinguals' chart. Adapted from Caskey-Sirmons and Hickerson (1977) with permission from University of Nebraska Press.

focal area for the associated color. If a number occurs more than once, this indicates that different focal areas were chosen for the associated color.

A quick glance at this figure immediately suggests the larger variability of the foci mapped by the bilinguals and the larger areas they mapped for the various color words. But most interestingly for our present purposes, as compared to the paired monolinguals, several changes were observed in the bilinguals' mappings that pointed at a shift towards the mappings common for English native speakers. In the bilinguals' sample such a shift was evident most clearly in the mapping of their L1 words for green (*chorok sek*) and blue (*paran sek*; numbers 6 and 7, respectively). For comparison, the mappings of the

native American-English participants' for *green* and *blue* are also placed on the Korean monolinguals' chart. It is evident that for a number of the Korean–English bilinguals the mapping of *chorok sek* ("green") has shifted towards the left of the chart, thus coming to resemble English L1 speakers' mapping for *green*. In contrast, the bilinguals' mapping of *paran sek* ("blue") has shifted to the right, thus coming to resemble English L1 speakers' mapping for *blue*. Because the group of Korean monolinguals were not true monolinguals but must also have acquired some knowledge of English during their, relatively short, stay in the United States, it is likely that the data reported for the bilinguals underestimated the actual influence of L2 on L1.

The above results led the authors to conclude

that, when acquiring a new language, the concepts associated with a pair of translations are gradually merged or generalized into one concept. As they put it: "the terminological categories of bilinguals become broader" (Caskey-Sirmons & Hickerson, 1977, p. 365). In other words, they explained the behavioral differences between monolinguals and bilinguals in terms of differences in the conceptual representations of color concepts in bilinguals and monolinguals. But this interpretation of the results is not the only possible one. I mentioned earlier that accented language, in all domains of language, can have two sources: One is that the memory representations of linguistic entities differ between monolinguals and bilinguals. The second assumes a processing difference between monolinguals and bilinguals and, specifically, that the accent arises from competition between memory structures occurring in bilinguals but not in monolinguals. Accordingly, in the studies on accents in L1 discussed in the previous sections both explanations have been advanced in explaining the data. This same indeterminacy applies to the semantic accents in color naming and color mapping. A Navajo–English bilingual may respond *tatLqid* ("green") to a color patch that most Navajo monolinguals would call *litso* ("yellow") but that many English monolinguals would call *green*, not because his concept of Navajo *litso* has changed in the course of becoming bilingual, but because the common English name for the depicted color (*green*) is co-activated with *litso*. *Green* then activates *tatLqid* through a connection that exists between them in memory and *tatLqid* emerges as response. This is in fact how Ervin (1961b) explained her results, discussed above. Similarly, in Caskey-Sirmons and Hickerson's study, the way the bilingual participants' delineated an L1 Korean color word on the color chart may have been influenced by co-activation of its closest translation in L2 English, which maps onto a somewhat different concept. But whatever the exact cause of the semantic accents observed in color naming and color mapping by bilinguals, they do, once again, show an influence of L2 on L1.

BILINGUALISM AND LINGUISTIC RELATIVITY

The relation between language and thought

In our discussion of how languages differ in the way they map words onto concepts and of the occurrence and origin of semantic accents in bilinguals' use of their first language, we have drifted imperceptibly into an area of research that has engaged scientists of all sorts, such as linguists, psychologists, philosophers, sociologists, and anthropologists, for a long time. The research area in question is the relation between language and thought. The middle decades of the previous century witnessed a surge of interest in this topic after Benjamin Lee Whorf (1897–1941), inspired by his master Edward Sapir (1884–1939), advanced his view that the language we speak influences our way of thinking. In its strongest form this view is known as **linguistic determinism**, which holds that the language we speak determines how we think about the world. In the years to follow this seminal work, a number of more nuanced versions of the theory have been contemplated, and after a waning interest during the 1970s and 1980s, the relation between language and thought has once again become the topic of a lively scientific debate (e.g., Boroditsky, 2001; Levinson, 1996, 2003; Lucy, 1992, 1997; see Gentner & Goldin-Meadow, 2003, for a complete volume).

The theory springs from the observation that there are innumerable ways to perceive the world around us and that languages differ from one another in the way they dissect this one world of ours into concepts and map these concepts onto linguistic structures. The theory then states that we perceive the world through the lens of our language, attending to and noticing those aspects of the world that are reflected in the distinctions encoded in our language and, conversely, ignoring, or even being blinded to, the phenomena that have not been laid down in our language:

We dissect nature along lines laid down by our native languages. The categories and types that we isolate from the world of phenomena we do not find there because they stare every observer in the face; on the contrary, the world is presented in a kaleidoscopic flux of impressions which has to be organized by our minds—and this means largely by the linguistic systems in our minds. We cut nature up, organize it into concepts, and ascribe significances as we do, largely because we are parties to an agreement to organize it in this way—an agreement that holds throughout our speech community and is codified in the patterns of our language.

(Whorf, cited by Crystal, 1987, p. 15).

It is easy to find evidence that different languages have carved up the surrounding world differently and, indeed, we have already witnessed such evidence earlier (p. 368). Recall, for instance, the convergence of English *ladder* and *staircase* into one word in Russian and the way different languages dissect the color spectrum into different lexicalized concepts. The plausibly best-known example is the large number of words that Inuit are reputed to have for snow; for instance, for snow that is falling down, for snow that has touched ground, for snow hard like ice, or for muddy snow (see Table 7.4 for another example of lexical diversity where English converges on the use of a single word). Similar differences

TABLE 7.4

Words for *hole* in Pintupi, an Australian aboriginal language

Yarla	a hole in an object
Pirti	a hole in the ground
Pirnki	a hole formed by a rock shelf
Kartalpa	a small hole in the ground
Yulpilpa	a shallow hole in which ants live
Mutara	a special hole in a spear
Nyarrkalpa	a burrow for small animals
Pulpa	a rabbit burrow
Makarnpa	a goanna burrow
Katarta	the hole left by a goanna when it has broken the surface after hibernation

Circumlocutions are required to convey the meaning of the above Pintupi Words in English (from Crystal, 1987, p. 15, with permission from Cambridge University Press).

between languages occur for linguistic structures other than those referring to nominal concepts, such as differences in what types of information are included in a language's verb forms, which reflect grammatical concepts such as tense, number, and gender. How widely languages may differ from one another in this respect is illustrated in the following quote:

To say that "the elephant ate the peanuts" in English, we must include tense—the fact that the event happened in the past. In Mandarin, indicating when the event occurred would be optional and couldn't be included in the verb. In Russian, the verb would need to include tense, whether the peanut-eater was male or female (though only in the past tense), and whether said peanut-eater ate all of the peanuts or just a portion of them. In Turkish, one would specify whether the event being reported was witnessed or hearsay.

(Boroditsky, Schmidt, & Phillips, 2003, p. 61).

Given the wealth of evidence to support it, that languages dissect the world differently is not a disputed claim. By implication, it is also not disputed that speakers of different languages must attend to different aspects of the world to learn and use their language correctly. What *is* disputed though is the theory's core assumption that these differences cause users of different languages to think about and perceive the world differently, to entertain different views of the world. This aspect of the theory comes in various versions. As already mentioned, according to the theory's strongest version, linguistic determinism, language truly *determines* thought in the sense that only the concepts that it expresses in its vocabulary and grammatical constructions can be grasped; concepts that are not reflected in a language's grammar or lexicon cannot be conceived by a speaker of this language. For instance, according to the strong version, a speaker of Hopi, an American-Indian language and one of the languages with which Whorf illustrated his theory, would lack a concept of time seen as a dimension because his language does not distinguish between various forms corresponding to the different tenses in English (Crystal, 1987). Similarly, a speaker of English, lacking a separate word for snow that is about to touch ground would lack the corresponding concept. The latter may be true initially, but it is also obvious from this example that this speaker of English, when explicitly confronted with this lexical gap, presumably has no problem whatsoever grasping the concept the moment the critical feature of this type of snow is pointed out. It is quite plausible that, similarly, a speaker of Hopi will come to master the concept of time as a dimension when it is explained, or, indirectly, during training on some task that highlights this way of thinking about time. Such findings would prove the strong version of the theory to be wrong.

In other words, even though the conceptual repertoire of speakers of a particular language is likely to depend on which distinctions are present and which ones are missing in this language, this does not necessarily imply that the concepts that are initially alien to them because they are not reflected in their language will forever be beyond their grasp. That such concepts can come to be understood successfully can be illustrated with an example from the domain of color terminology the reader has become familiar with in the previous section: Although the Dani, a tribe in New Guinea, have only two words for color in their language, they managed to learn the much more varied set of English color names without great trouble (Heider, 1972; Rosch, 1975). Apparently, there was little wrong with the Dani's ability to perceive colors and to organize the color spectrum similarly to the way native speakers of English do. It was just that they had never had a reason before to dissect the world of colors with English eyes and label it accordingly. Similarly, Boroditsky (2001) first substantiated the claim that native speakers of Mandarin Chinese on the one hand and English on the other hand talk about time differently; namely, as if it has a vertical or horizontal dimension, respectively. Next, she showed that it only takes a brief training in Mandarin-like time perception for English native speakers to also be able to think vertically about time. A more general argument

against the strong version, mentioned by Crystal (1987), is that translation between languages— which requires the transposition of conceptual content from one language to another—is largely possible (although it can be extremely demanding at times).

Given such counterevidence, linguistic determinism is unlikely to still be adhered to by anyone in this field of research. However, weaker, less deterministic, versions of the theory, known as **linguistic relativity**, have more recently been advanced that acknowledge that a language's peculiarities can influence thought and non-verbal behavior in subtle ways. These newer conceptions of the relation between language and thought are characterized by a more nuanced and refined approach to the issue. For instance, a distinction is made between the contents of thought and the processes of thinking, such as attending, remembering, or reasoning. Some researchers focus on the former, others on the latter, and yet others on both, examining which differences between languages relate to differences in conceptualization and which to differences in cognitive processes (Pavlenko, 2005). Gentner and Goldin-Meadow (2003) organized their volume, dedicated entirely to the relation between language and thought, in three main sections, thus making explicit that their domain of study can be defined and approached in different ways: (1) Language as lens: Does the language we acquire influence how we see the world? (2) Language as tool kit: Does the language we acquire augment our capacity for higher-order representation and reasoning? (3) Language as category maker: Does the language we acquire influence where we make our category distinctions?

Also, current work on the effect of language on thought specifies more carefully the type of data that would count as evidence that language influences thought. Many studies have exclusively used verbal tasks to assess whether language affects thought. This involves the danger that the collected evidence proves that language influences language rather than thought. To avoid the pending indeterminacy, evidence from non-verbal tasks such as classification, memory, sorting, and matching must also be taken into account

(Lucy, 1992, 1997). Furthermore, the newer work explicates the possibility that linguistic relativity may hold for some conceptual domains but not for others: Boroditsky (2001), Boroditsky, Ham, and Ramscar (2002), and Gentner and Boroditsky (2001) hypothesized that language may exert an especially strong influence on the formation of abstract nominal concepts (such as the concept of time), concepts representing abstract activities (e.g., to think), and relational concepts. The reason is that to acquire these concepts, the learner is primarily dependent on linguistic experience. In contrast, object concepts and concepts for concrete activities such as walking and eating can also be acquired from perceptual experience. Because perceptual experience but not language experience is largely shared by speakers of different languages, language-specific influences on thought are plausibly most obvious for the concepts that have to be acquired through language alone; that is, abstract and relational concepts. Finally, recent work often expresses the awareness that effects of language on thought are often confounded with effects of culture on thought, although there are ways to disentangle these effects (e.g., Bassetti, 2007; Ji et al., 2004).

In this debate regarding the relation between language and thought, bilingualism has until recently largely been ignored. The typical study involved a cross-linguistic comparison of some content of thought, or some process of thought, in monolingual speakers of two or more languages which differ in one selected aspect such as their grammatical tense, gender, or number system, or in the way they describe, for instance, time, spatial relations, or the color spectrum (see Boroditsky, 2003, and Pavlenko, 2005, for reviews). As noted by Pavlenko, in the study of linguistic relativity bilinguals are typically regarded "undesirable and messy" participants who should be excluded from experimental research to eliminate intervening variables (Pavlenko, 2005, p. 437). Pavlenko takes the opposite point of view that research on linguistic relativity should incorporate bilingualism as a test case because "it is quite possible that bilinguals are the only ones to experience directly the effects

of linguistic relativity" (p. 437), this being a direct consequence of their experience with two linguistic systems. Athanasopoulos (2006, p. 91) advocated the inclusion of bilinguals in studying the relation between language and thought on the ground that the majority of the world's population uses more than one language: "Consequently, an inquiry of the relationship between language and cognition in the human mind is surely incomplete without taking into account the mind's potential to accommodate more than one language. Researching the bilingual mind is central to our understanding of the human mind in general."

In bilingual studies on linguistic relativity, one of the interesting questions to pose is whether and to what extent bilinguals experience different conceptual worlds when communicating in their one or other language. Testimonies exist of **bicultural bilinguals** who experience a personal transformation into a different conceptual world when they switch to their other language (e.g., Wierzbicka, 1985; see Pavlenko, 2005, for a discussion). Such experiences clearly agree with the notion of linguistic relativity (as well as with the occurrence of "coordinate bilingualism" discussed on p. 129), especially when the experienced switch in personality occurring with a language switch does not require a simultaneous switch of sociocultural circumstances. At the same time such testimonies provide evidence against a strong, deterministic view of the theory which holds that the structure of the language acquired first determines one's conceptual world once and forever.

Other interesting questions are exactly which history of becoming bilingual leads to such a state of a "split personality" and whether in bicultural bilingualism there are intermediate states prior to this end state of experiencing two language-specific conceptual worlds. Is there, for instance, an initial stage of L2 acquisition in which the new language exploits the conceptual world associated with the L1 (cf. the form of bilingualism known as "subordinative" discussed on p. 129)? Can some pattern of gradual conceptual shift be detected en route to the state of dual conceptual worlds? Can certain acquisition contexts be identified that ultimately lead to a blended conceptual world shared by the two languages and different from the conceptual world of monolingual speakers of either language ("compound bilingualism"; see p. 129), one that represents some compromise between, or combination of, the "linguistically pure" conceptual worlds associated with the separate languages involved? Notice also that the emergence of such a mixed, language-independent conceptual world would support the notion of linguistic relativity because it would show that acquiring two languages results in a unique conceptual system that reflects both.

Some of the relevant evidence has already been presented in the previous section, where the way the color spectrum is split up lexically was shown to vary between languages and where bilinguals were shown to behave differently in color naming (Ervin, 1961b) and color identification (Caskey-Sirmons & Hickerson, 1977) in their L1 from monolingual control participants. That section also briefly referred to a study by Malt and Sloman (2003) which showed semantic accents when bilinguals were asked to name pictures of common household objects such as cups and bowls in their L2. A more recent study has shown similar semantic accents when bilinguals had to name pictures of such objects in L1 (Ameel, Storms, Malt, & Sloman, 2005). As mentioned, differences between the conceptual representations of monolinguals and bilinguals, perhaps in the form of a merger of analogous L1 and L2 concepts, may underlie this differential naming performance (see Ameel, Malt, Storms, & Van Assche, 2009, for a detailed investigation of how these representations might differ between monolinguals and bilinguals). If this account is correct (but see p. 371 for an alternative explanation) these color-naming and object-naming studies provide support for the linguistic relativity hypothesis.

In the next section I will detail a small set of studies that informed the debate on linguistic relativity by exploiting three grammatical features on which languages differ: gender, number, and tense. The focus will be on bilingual studies, but some cross-linguistic studies testing only mono-

linguals will also be included to set the stage for a similar study with bilinguals. It is hoped that the detailed description of the studies in question provides the reader with a clear idea of how to design studies that have the potential to inform the present discussion. For a more complete review of the conceptual domains that have been studied from the perspective of linguistic relativity theory and of the cross-language differences hypothesized to affect thinking in these domains, the reader is referred to Pavlenko (2005).

Evidence from cross-linguistic and bilingual studies

Grammatical and biological gender

One of the testing grounds for studying the possible influence of language on thought exploits the fact that **grammatical gender** systems differ significantly between languages, both in terms of the number of gender distinctions individual languages make and the degree to which, across languages, grammatical gender correlates with biological gender. "Gender" refers to a grammatical distinction which marks individual words in word classes such as nouns, pronouns, articles, adjectives, and verbs as "masculine", "feminine", and "neuter". These labels are somewhat misleading because they suggest a correlation with natural, biological gender; for instance, that a word with feminine gender refers to a female living being. There are languages in which biological and grammatical gender are indeed closely correlated, but in many languages no correlation at all exists between grammatical and biological gender, or grammatical gender is largely arbitrary. This arbitrariness is perhaps most clearly evident from the fact that the gender of the name of one and the same object may vary between languages so that the object may be feminine in one language, masculine in a second, and neuter in a third. For instance, the name for the sun is masculine in Spanish, neuter in Russian, and feminine in German (the example is from Boroditsky et al., 2003).

In addition to exhibiting a varied relation between grammatical and biological gender, languages vary widely in the extent to which they employ grammatical gender marking and in some languages hardly any gender marking occurs. For example, in English, grammatical gender only plays a role in selecting the third person pronouns *he, she,* and *it,* a selection that is largely, but not totally, based on natural gender. French distinguishes between masculine and feminine nouns, and a noun's gender determines the form of the associated definite or indefinite article (*le* and *un,* respectively, go with masculine nouns, and *la* and *une* go with feminine nouns; *le/un chapeau,* "the/a hat", versus *la/une maison,* "the/a house"), the associated adjective(s) (*le grand chapeau,* "the big hat", versus *la grande maison,* "the big house") and pronoun (*mon chapeau,* "my hat", versus *ma maison,* "my house"). In French a weak correlation exists between biological and grammatical gender. The latter also holds for German, which distinguishes between masculine, feminine, and neuter nouns. Dutch and Danish have a binary system that groups masculine and feminine nouns together in one category of nouns with a common gender, contrasting them with neuter nouns. Yet other languages, such as Russian and Latin, do without articles but reveal a noun's grammatical gender in the specific form the noun takes. Furthermore, in Russian the verb's form marks the sex of its actor. In Semitic languages biological gender plays a very significant role as, for instance, shown from the fact that in choosing the correct verb form in Hebrew the speaker must take his own gender or the gender of his interlocutor into account.

In a cross-linguistic study, Guiora (1983) studied the effect of a language's "gender loading" on the development of gender identity in its speakers. As defined by the author, the gender loading of a language is the extent to which it forces its speakers to take the sex of their addressees into account in order to choose the correct word forms. The author hypothesized that speakers of a language with a high gender loading develop a gender identity at a younger age than speakers of languages with a lower degree of gender loading. He examined this hypothesis in an experiment in which he compared the performance of three groups of children, aged 16 to 42 months, born and bred in three different monolingual language environments and lacking exposure to any other language. The languages concerned were Hebrew, English, and Finnish, and the testing took place in Israel, the USA, and Finland, respectively. The crucial difference between these three languages was the degree of gender loading they contained: In Finnish the sex of the participants in a conversation has no effect on word form whatsoever and in English and Hebrew it determines word form to a very modest and large degree, respectively. The dependent variable in this investigation was the children's performance on a non-verbal gender identity test, the Michigan Gender Identity Test. The data supported the investigator's hypothesis, demonstrating a clear effect of the ambient language's gender loading on the rate of attaining a gender identity: The growth curves in test performance differed for the three language groups, the children raised in a Hebrew environment showing a faster growth than those raised in an English environment, who, in turn, showed a faster growth than those raised in a Finnish environment. Accordingly, Guiora concluded that the specific linguistic structures to which a child is exposed can act as catalysts in the development of certain cognitive structures, in this specific case the cognitive structures that determine a person's gender identity.

In a more recent study, Boroditsky et al. (2003) posed the question of whether talking about inanimate and, therefore, sexless objects such as cupboards, bikes, and candles as if they were masculine or feminine might mislead people into thinking that inanimate objects have a gender. If such were to turn out to be the case, the reason might be that, unlike grammatical gender distinctions between the names of inanimate objects, other grammatical distinctions (e.g., singular versus plural inflections) *do* relate to actual differences in the environment (between one and more than of a particular type of entity). To learners of a language this might suggest that the grammatical gender of an inanimate object's name also reflects an inherent feature of the object and, specifically, its sex. Guided by this false assumption, when building a gendered noun's concept, the learner may search for properties of the noun's referent that match its gender, such as the sun's warmth for a German learner (*sun* being feminine in German), or its power for a Spanish learner (*sun* being masculine in Spanish).

To address this question, Boroditsky and her collaborators examined the mental representations of inanimate objects in Spanish–English and German–English bilinguals who were all highly proficient in L2 English. In Spanish and German, but not in English, nouns have a gender. The participants were presented with 24 object names in L2 English and were asked to name for each of them, in English, the first three adjectives that came to their mind. Importantly, the translation equivalents of the selected English object names had opposite genders in Spanish and German (half of the object names were masculine and half were feminine in each language). The question of interest was whether the grammatical gender of the object names in L1 German and L1 Spanish would be reflected in the L2 English adjectives provided by the participants: Would German speakers give relatively many masculine adjectives to the English object names with masculine German equivalents, and would Spanish speakers give relatively many feminine adjectives to these very same English object names? Similarly, would the reverse response pattern occur for the English object names with feminine German but masculine Spanish equivalents? English speakers, naive with respect to the purpose of the experiment, rated the adjectives generated by the participants as being feminine or masculine.

The results of this experiment provided affirmative answers to these questions, thus suggesting an influence of L1 grammatical gender on people's mental representations of inanimate objects. To illustrate the results, in response to *key*, with a masculine translation in German but a feminine translation in Spanish, the German speakers produced *hard, heavy, jagged, metal, serrated*, and *useful*, whereas Spanish speakers produced *golden, intricate, little, lovely, shiny*, and

tiny. Conversely, to *bridge*, feminine in German but masculine in Spanish, German speakers replied with *beautiful, elegant, fragile, peaceful, pretty*, and *slender*, whereas Spanish speakers produced *big, dangerous, long, strong, sturdy*, and *towering*. From this and corroborating evidence assembled in a series of further experiments—in which the investigators, among others, ruled out the possibility that the effects were due to the experimental groups' differential experience in culture rather than in language—the investigators (Boroditsky et al., 2003, p. 77) concluded that:

[. . .] even a fluke of grammar (the arbitrary designation of a noun as masculine or feminine) can have an effect on how people think about things in the world. Considering the many ways in which languages differ, our findings suggest that the private mental lives of people who speak different languages may differ much more than previously thought.

Boroditsky et al. (2003) looked at the effect of a gendered L1 (Spanish or German) on the representation of object concepts in a largely non-gendered L2 (English). A recent study by Bassetti (2007) examined the representation of object concepts in bilinguals whose two languages assign opposite gender to particular object nouns. The participants in this study were 9-year-old Italian monolingual and Italian–German bilingual children living in one and the same town in Italy, the latter fact minimizing the chances that differential cultural rather than linguistic experience might underlie any effect of bilingualism to emerge. The bilingual children had all acquired Italian from birth and were all balanced bilinguals. More than half of them were simultaneous bilinguals, having also acquired German from birth. The others had all started to learn German before the age of 4. The experimental materials consisted of drawings of familiar objects, all artifacts. The nouns for half of these objects were masculine in Italian and feminine in German, whereas for the remaining half the opposite held. For each object (e.g., a ball) a short sentence (e.g., *do you like a ball?*) was recorded twice, once spoken by a man and once spoken by a woman. On each trial an object drawing appeared on a computer screen while the associated sentence was first played in the one voice and next in the other voice, the order of the male and female voice determined randomly by the computer. The children were asked to imagine that the object on the screen could talk and to choose the most appropriate voice for each object by pressing either one of two keys on the computer's keyboard. All interactions with the child were exclusively in Italian. The results showed that the Italian monolingual children had a statistically significant preference for attributing voices consistently with Italian grammatical gender assignment (Italian preference: 71%; German preference: 19%; no preference: 10%). In numerical sense the Italian–German bilingual children also showed an "Italian" preference but a much weaker one (52%, 33%, and 14%, respectively), which was not statistically significant. The author concluded that the opposing grammatical gender of the test objects' names in Italian and German has resulted in conceptual representations of these objects that differ from those in the monolingual Italian children. Given the fact that this experiment controlled for differential cultural experience it is likely that indeed the linguistic difference between the two languages is the source of this difference in conceptual representation.

Grammatical number

In addition to differing in grammatical gender marking, languages differ in the way they mark **grammatical number**. Lucy (1992) has shown that the number-marking system of individual languages depends on two features of nouns; namely, whether or not their referents are animate (± animate) and whether or not they refer to discrete entities (±discrete). In English, nouns of both the +animate/+discrete class and the −animate/+discrete class always take a plural suffix when quantified and can be preceded directly by a numeral (they are so called "count nouns"; e.g., *two dogs*; *three bikes*), whereas −animate/−discrete nouns (so called "mass nouns" such as *sand*, *water*, and *flour*) cannot be

pluralized and require a "unitizer" (a unit of measurement) or "classifier" to be quantified (e.g., *two bags of flour* or *three glasses of water*, where *bags* and *glasses* are the unitizers). In other languages, such as Yucatec (a native Mexican language) and Japanese, plural marking of +animate/+discrete nouns is optional and −animate/+discrete nouns cannot take grammatical number, nor can they be directly preceded by a numeral but, just as −animate/−discrete nouns in English, are quantified with a classifier instead. In the words of Boroditsky (2003), these languages talk about objects as if they were substances or, in the words of Athanasopoulos and Kasai (2008), all inanimate nouns in such "classifier" languages are semantically unspecified with regard to individuation, just like mass nouns in English are. Yet other languages do not only mark the distinction between one (singular) and more than one (plural) in their grammatical number system (as English does obligatory with both +animate/+discrete and −animate/+discrete nouns but Japanese and Yucatec may do optionally only with +animate/+discrete nouns), but make a more fine-grained distinction between one, two, or more than two objects (Pavlenko, 2005).

Athanasopoulos (2006) investigated the consequence of this difference in grammatical number marking between languages for the performance of intermediate and advanced Japanese learners of L2 English on a picture-matching test introduced by Lucy (1992). For comparison, English and Japanese monolingual speakers were included as well. The test involved the presentation of a set of six drawn pictures on each trial. All pictures showed scenes that contained objects and animals corresponding to the above three different types of nouns, referred to as "animals" (+animate/+discrete), "implements" (−animate/+discrete), and "substances" (−animate/−discrete), respectively. One picture of each set concerned the target picture to which the other five, the "alternates", had to be compared. The target picture and each of the alternate pictures differed in the number or, in the case of a substance noun, the amount or number of portions of the depicted entity (e.g., zero bottles or one bottle; a small or a larger amount of food fed to the depicted pigs; one amount fed to the depicted pigs only, or one fed to the pigs and a second one to the chickens on the same picture). The task was to pick out the alternate picture that was "most like" the target picture.

Based on the results of Lucy's original study (a cross-language study with Yucatec and English monolinguals), Athanasopoulos predicted that English monolinguals would regard alternates that contained a difference in the number/amount of substances as more similar to the target picture than differences in the number of animals and implements. As a consequence, alternate pictures containing substance differences should be picked out relatively often. In contrast, Japanese monolinguals were predicted to regard both alternates that contained a difference in number/amount of substances and alternates containing a difference in the number of implements as more similar to the target picture than alternates containing a difference in the number of animals (thus treating implements as if they were substances). As a consequence, alternate pictures containing implement and substance differences should be picked out equally often. The data confirmed these predictions, replicating Lucy's main findings for a different pair of languages: The English monolinguals picked out the substance alternates about twice as often as the implement alternates. In contrast, the Japanese monolinguals selected the substance and implement alternates about equally often, treating these two types of alternates as if they did not differ from one another. Another way of putting this is that the English monolinguals demonstrated a special sensitivity to differences in both the numbers of animals and implements, whereas the Japanese monolinguals were only especially sensitive to a difference in the number of animals.

Of special interest were the data for the two groups of Japanese–English bilinguals. These showed that the advanced and intermediate Japanese learners of English showed the same response pattern as the English and Japanese monolinguals, respectively. Accordingly, with regard to the advanced bilinguals Athanasopoulos (2006, p. 94) concluded: "The evidence seems to suggest that L2 acquisition of grammatical number marking on [–animate/+discrete] noun phrases has influenced their cognitive disposition towards referents of that type of noun phrase." Regarding the intermediate bilinguals he concluded that "their cognitive disposition towards inanimate entities is still influenced by their knowledge of [–animate/–discrete] noun phrases" (p. 94). The cognitive mechanism involved in the cognitive change that is manifest in the advanced bilinguals is, so the author hypothesized, attention: ". . . language influences cognitive dispositions by directing speakers' attention to specific features of stimuli [. . .] the results indicate that highly proficient L2 speakers learn to redirect their attention to the distinctions made in their L2" (p. 95).

In the previous section we have seen that the grammatical gender of words that refer to inanimate objects influences language users' mental representations of these objects (Bassetti, 2007; Boroditsky et al., 2003). As we have just seen, it appears that a language's system of grammatical number also affects the mental representations of inanimate objects. This was already suggested earlier by cross-linguistic investigations conducted by Lucy and Gaskins (2001) and Imai and Gentner (1997). In Lucy and Gaskins' study monolingual speakers of either Yucatec or English were shown three objects on each trial, one being the target object (e.g., a plastic comb with a handle). The other two objects differed from the target either in shape (a plastic comb without a handle) or in material (a wooden comb with a handle). The participants' task was to select from the latter two objects the one they regarded most similar to the target. Yucatec speakers preferred the match in material, picking the plastic comb without the handle most often. In contrast, English speakers preferred the shape match, selecting the wooden comb with the handle more often. Apparently, in the object concepts of speakers of Yucatan the materials of which the objects in question are made are especially salient whereas in the object concepts of English speakers the objects' shapes appear to be represented more prominently. The authors attributed this difference to the different grammatical number systems of English and Yucatec described above. Specifically they proposed that the use of obligatory plural marking of inanimate objects in English directs English speakers' attention towards the shape of objects because an object's shape is a reliable perceptual indicator of individuation. In contrast, because of the absence of plural marking in the far majority of Yucatec nouns, the speakers' attention is not drawn to a perceptual analogue of individuation of the nouns' referents but to the referents' material properties instead. Imai and Gentner used the same triad-matching test examining Japanese and English monolinguals and using a more varied set of stimuli: they manipulated the type of object presented on a trial (simple: objects with simple shapes; complex: factory-made artifacts having complex shapes and specific functions) and also presented substance stimuli (e.g., a reverse C-shape in white Nivea cream as the target with a reverse C in transparent hair-gel as the same-shape alternate and a pile of Nivea cream as the same-material alternate). They found that both the Japanese and English monolinguals preferred the shape match when complex objects were presented. In contrast, for simple objects and substances the English monolinguals clearly preferred the shape-match responses over the material-match responses, whereas the Japanese monolinguals preferred the material-match responses.

Athanasopoulos and Kasai (2008) and Cook, Bassetti, Kasai, Sasaki, and Takahashi (2006) used a similar methodology, extending it to bilinguals. Athanasopoulos and Kasai tested English and Japanese monolinguals and intermediate and advanced Japanese learners of English. The monolingual participants were tested in their native country and half of the bilinguals were tested in the United Kingdom, the other half in Japan. The participants were presented with triads of novel artificial objects depicted on a screen, one object being the standard, the remaining two alternates of the standard. One of the alternates concerned the same object as the standard but of a different color; the other was a different object in the same color as the standard. The participants

were instructed to select from the two alternates the one that was "the same as" the standard. The authors predicted that as a consequence of obligatory plural marking of inanimate objects in English and the consequent focus on shape, the English monolinguals would more often than the Japanese monolinguals select the common-shape alternate (that is, the same object in a different color). This finding indeed materialized. But of particular interest, again, were the bilingual data. Similar to the results of Athanasopoulos (2006) discussed above, the advanced L2 English learners behaved like the English monolinguals and the intermediate L2 English learners behaved like the Japanese monolinguals. As concluded by the authors these findings suggest that the acquisition of an L2 with grammatical concepts that differ from the analogous L1 grammatical concepts causes changes in the learners' cognition.

The second bilingual study, by Cook and his colleagues (2006), confirmed these results and specified more precisely the type of concepts affected. Again Japanese learners of L2 English at two L2 proficiency levels were tested but no monolingual control groups were included. Instead, these researchers used exactly the same methodology as Imai and Gentner (1997; see above) had used with Japanese and English monolinguals and compared their own data with these earlier monolingual data. As mentioned, in that study both complex and simple objects were tested and substances were included as well. Just as the Japanese and English monolinguals in the monolingual study, both groups of L2 learners preferred the shape match for complex objects. However, for simple objects and substances, both learner groups preferred the material match, as the Japanese monolinguals did, but the group of learners with a higher level of proficiency in English manifested a larger shape-match preference than the group of lesser L2 proficiency, seemingly having shifted somewhat to the pattern observed for English monolinguals. The results of both bilingual studies thus converge on the conclusion that learning an L2 causes changes in conceptual representations.

Grammatical tense

As a final illustration of how the grammatical peculiarities of languages can shape the thought of their speakers, let us consider an unpublished study by Boroditsky et al. (2002). These researchers ingeniously made use of the fact that there are languages in which, unlike in English and many other languages, verbs do not contain tense markers. In other words, verb forms in these languages do not reveal whether the event or action that it describes has already taken place, is now taking place, or will take place in the future. One such language is Indonesian. Speakers of this language may use separate words to communicate time information, such as the Indonesian equivalents of *now* or *soon*, but doing so is optional and listeners must often infer time information from non-linguistic contextual information. The fact that the correct use of English verb forms forces its users to include the information when the event or action that it expresses took place, whereas speakers of Indonesian do not have to do so, plausibly implies that English and Indonesian speakers and listeners attend differently to time aspects of the things that are happening around them. This may result in differences in time cognition of speakers of English on the one hand and speakers of Indonesian on the other hand.

Boroditsky and her colleagues turned these hypotheses into a clever series of four experiments in which English and Indonesian monolinguals and Indonesian–English bilinguals took part. All experiments involved the presentation of photographs showing people who were either about to perform a particular action, were performing the action at this very moment, or had just completed it, the three conditions thus visualizing a future, present, or past event, respectively. Figure 7.8a illustrates each of these conditions (note that in the original study photographs instead of line drawings were presented). There were 90 different pictures in all, each of them showing 1 out of 10 different actions (e.g., kicking a ball, throwing a frisbee, eating a banana) performed by one out of three different actors. In two experiments, one testing monolinguals and

the second testing bilinguals, the participants were asked to judge (on a scale of 1 to 9) the similarity of two pictures presented to them on each trial. In half of the picture pairs one and the same actor performed the same action in different tenses (e.g., one and the same woman kicking a ball on one picture and about to kick a ball on the other picture; see Figure 7.8b, top). The other half of the picture pairs showed two different actors performing the same action in one and the same tense (e.g., one of the pictures showing a woman about to kick a ball; the second showing a man about to kick a ball; see Figure 7.8b, bottom).

Upon entering the laboratory, about half of the bilinguals were greeted and instructed in Indonesian. The remaining participants were greeted and instructed in English. The monolinguals were, obviously, greeted and instructed in their one language. For the rest the experiments were completely non-verbal. The authors predicted that English and Indonesian speakers should differ in the amount of attention devoted to the pictures' tense aspect, the English speakers attending more to it than the Indonesian speakers. The data, presented in Figure 7.9a, confirmed this prediction.

As shown, English monolinguals regarded the pictures involving different actors performing an action in the same tense as more similar than did the Indonesian monolinguals. The reverse pattern occurred for pictures with the same actor performing this action in different tenses. These findings suggest that the presence of tense markers on verbs in English but not in Indonesian does indeed result in differences in the way speakers of these languages think about tense and attend to tense aspects of the things happening around them. Specifically, time features about events and actions seem to be more salient for speakers of English than for speakers of Indonesian. Figure 7.9b presents the analogous bilingual data. The bilinguals greeted and instructed in English showed a pattern similar to that of the English monolinguals. For those tested in Indonesian, the difference between the two conditions disappeared. Because all bilingual participants were selected from one and the same

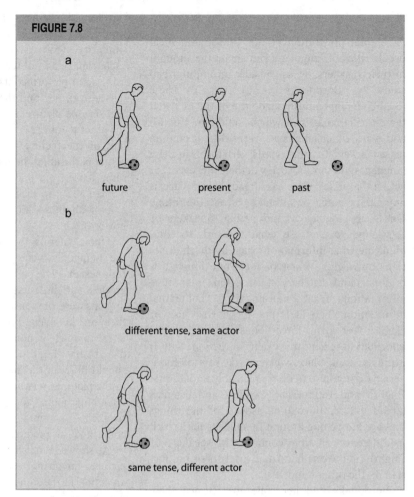

FIGURE 7.8

a

future   present   past

b

different tense, same actor

same tense, different actor

(a) Schematized illustrations of the photograph stimuli used by Boroditsky et al. (2002). All photographs showed people about to perform a particular action (future), performing the action this very moment (present), or having just completed it (past). (b) Schematized illustrations of the photograph pairs that the participants had to judge on degree of similarity on a scale of 1 to 9. In half of the presented photograph pairs one and the same actor performed the same action in different tenses (top). In the other half two different actors performed the same action in one and the same tense (bottom). Adapted from Boroditsky et al. (2002) with permission from the author.

population, it is unlikely that any other difference between them than being tested in different languages had caused the differential results for these two groups.

The first conclusion to draw from these data is that just changing the language of greetings and instructions—in an experiment that for the remainder is completely non-verbal—caused the participants to process the photographs differently and, by implication, to think differently during task performance. It is as if with a change of language they not only switched into another language mode (see pp. 288–291) but also into another mode of thinking. A second conclusion is that becoming bilingual alters the processes of thought. This conclusion follows from the fact that the response pattern of the bilinguals (all

with Indonesian as L1) in both language conditions differed from the results obtained with Indonesian monolinguals.

The goal of the remaining two experiments was to generalize these results to memory performance. The question posed was whether the differential experience of native speakers of English and Indonesian with grammatical tense leads to differences in their memory of the tense aspect of actions and events. One experiment tested English and Indonesian monolinguals, the second tested Indonesian–English bilinguals, and both consisted of a training phase followed by a test phase. On each trial in the training phase one picture out of the above set of 90 was presented. On each trial in the subsequent test phase three pictures were presented, one of them being one of

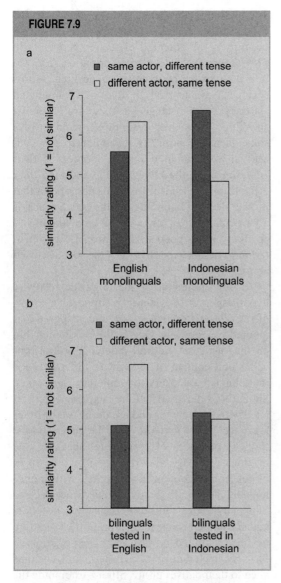

FIGURE 7.9

Average similarity ratings for different types of picture pairs by English and Indonesian monolinguals (a) and Indonesian–English bilinguals (b). From Boroditsky et al. (2002) with permission from the author.

the pictures presented during training, the other two differing from this target picture only in tense. The participants' task was to pick out the picture that had been presented during training. The authors predicted that recognition performance would be better for English mono-

linguals than for Indonesian monolinguals, for the reason that the former were hypothesized to attend more to the pictures' tense aspect during training. This prediction was borne out by the data. Regarding the data of the bilinguals, especially noteworthy was the finding that those instructed in English performed equally as well as the English monolinguals, whereas those instructed in Indonesian performed as poorly as the Indonesian monolinguals.

Because the bilingual groups' differential performance in all four experiments was triggered by just a slight brush of language (the language of greetings and instructions), the combined results of these studies constitute an especially striking demonstration of the power of language to affect people's thought while performing cognitive tasks. However, there is one specific conclusion that cannot be drawn on the basis of these data; namely, that bilingualism causes *permanent changes* in the content of conceptual representations. Recall that that was how Athanasopoulos and Kasai (2008), examining the effects of grammatical number marking on L2 learners' performance in the triad-matching task, explained their results. An explanation in terms of a permanent change in concepts cannot be accommodated with the fact that altering the language of instruction changes performance. Yet it is still possible that specific types of new linguistic experience *do* result in lasting changes in some specific conceptual domain. Exposure to a new language that marks grammatical number may constitute one sort of linguistic experience to bring about a lasting change in conceptual content. This is suggested by a recent grammatical number marking study by Athanasopoulos (2007), who, as did Boroditsky et al. (2002) in the domain of tense marking, manipulated the language in which the (Japanese–English) participants were instructed. An effect of bilingualism was again obtained, showing that the bilinguals' performance (again on the triad-matching task) had shifted to that of monolingual English speakers and away from that of monolingual Japanese speakers. Importantly though, in this study the language of instruction had no effect on the responses.

Conclusions

The studies discussed above suggest, first, that the specific linguistic structures encountered by native speakers of a language affect their thought processes and the content of their conceptual structures; second, that either language of a bilingual is like a magic wand that simply by being waved can reset the mental world of this bilingual into a different mode of thinking; third, that, possibly, bilingualism alters conceptual representations in some cognitive domains.

The above studies should have given you some sense of how to design both cross-linguistic and bilingual experiments that have the potential to inform the theory of linguistic relativity. The first step is to identify a particular linguistic contrast in two or more specific languages. The contrast in question may concern grammar, as in the above studies, but also some other aspect of language such as the way speakers of different languages talk about certain mental constructs, their choice of words and metaphors in doing so (see, e.g., Pavlenko, 2002, who discusses differences between Russian and English in how emotions are talked about; and see Boroditsky's, 2001, analysis of how speakers of English and Chinese use horizontal and vertical metaphors, respectively, to talk about time). Suitable contrasts to study may be relatively easy to find in pairs of languages that are typologically distant. It is unlikely to be a coincidence that the above studies have primarily used pairs and triads of distantly related languages (Finnish–English–Hebrew; Yucatan–English; Japanese–English; Indonesian–English). A second step is to identify some cognitive domain (e.g., the content of object concepts, the notions of past, present, and future) that may have been differentially affected by this linguistic contrast. A third and final step is to then design an experiment that has the power to reveal the hypothesized language-specific conceptualizations.

These three steps are shared by monolingual and bilingual experiments on linguistic relativity alike. The only difference between the two is whether monolingual speakers of the selected languages serve as participants or people who master both of them. Ideally, the bilingual experiments include monolinguals as well, because of the potential of such experiments to provide relatively detailed information (e.g., do bilinguals switch between two conceptual worlds that each is identical to that of monolingual speakers of the language they are currently speaking? Does their conceptual world involve some blend of both? Is it similar to the conceptual world of monolingual speakers of their L1, even when the bilinguals are speaking their L2?). It may be evident from this description that it takes detailed knowledge of the peculiarities of a particular pair of languages, a large amount of creativity, and a good sense of proper experimentation to design experiments of the sort discussed above.

In our discussion of the linguistic relativity hypothesis and the evidence to support it a couple of relevant related issues were underexposed and ignored, respectively. One is the possibility that not linguistic but cultural differences cause processes and content of thought to differ between monolingual speakers of different languages. Similarly, differential cultural experience correlated with the learning and use of the one or other language may underlie the language-specific thought processes of a bilingual speaking one or other language and the possible differences in conceptual content as compared with monolinguals. After all, many people who became bilingual in the course of their lives not only added a new language to their linguistic repertoire but also acquired novel cultural baggage along the way, including habits, beliefs, and customs alien to their native culture. Studies examining the effect of bilingualism on thought should try to control for this potential confound. This is not always easy but at the same time not totally impossible (e.g., Ji et al., 2004).

A second neglected issue is the question of why these contrasts between languages exist at all. While pondering over this question one readily comes up with the close relationship between language and culture as a major cause. Presumably, cultural diversity—correlated with environmental and geographical diversity—and the associated differences in the needs and habits of members of different cultural communities contribute importantly to linguistic diversity. That Inuit but not people living on the equator have a plethora of words for snow evidently has to do with the fact that (for the time being) snow is a much more salient substance in the Inuit environment than in the tropical rainforest. In conclusion then, the relation between language and culture is likely to work both ways: Cultural diversity gives rise to linguistic diversity, and language shapes the thought processes of its speakers in such a way that these speakers tie in conveniently with their culture.

THE COGNITIVE EFFECTS OF BILINGUALISM

The relation between early bilingualism and intelligence: A turning point in thought

The bilingual studies on linguistic relativity discussed above share a major goal—to learn more about bilingual cognition—with a second type of studies that approach this goal from a different theoretical angle and, accordingly, use a different methodology. As we have seen, the starting point of the studies conducted in the linguistic relativity research tradition is to identify a particular structural contrast in a pair of languages. The questions to then answer are whether and how this structural difference impacts on the thought of bilinguals who master these two languages, and in answering them the investigators look for language-specific differences in thought both within one and the same bilingual and between bilinguals and monolinguals.

The second type of studies looks at the effect of bilingualism per se on cognition, not at the way specific linguistic peculiarities of their two languages might mould bilinguals' thought processes. Designing studies of this type does not require the sophisticated linguistic knowledge that is required to transpose the linguistic relativity hypothesis into suitable experiments. Instead, what is (minimally) needed is a group of bilinguals, a carefully matched control group

of monolinguals, and a well-chosen task for them to perform. Task selection must be based on some informed hypothesis about how bilingualism might affect cognition; for instance, the hypothesis that the plausibly vaster conceptual world of bilinguals as compared to monolinguals is likely to lead to a relatively high skill in divergent thinking (see Kharkhurin, 2007, for evidence) or the hypothesis that always having to select the targeted one out of two possible lexical entries when expressing a particular lexical concept in speech plausibly results in superior processes of attention control (or "cognitive" control; I will use the terms interchangeably; see further on for evidence). The task to then choose or develop must be one that is known, or can be argued, to tap this aspect of cognition.

Because the effect of bilingualism per se is to be determined, not the effect of a specific structural contrast that exists between a specific pair of languages, generally any pair of languages involved in the bilingualism will do to address the question being posed and one and the same experiment may even include bilinguals who master different pairs of languages. Yet the size of the hypothesized effect may vary with the specific language pair(s) involved. For instance, one can imagine that divergent-thinking ability is boosted more if the bilingualism involves two distant languages than when two closely related languages are involved. Conversely, cognitive control might be enhanced especially in bilingualism involving two closely related languages, the similar cross-language structures entailing an increased risk of cross-linguistic interference, which must be coped with.

The chosen examples of how bilingualism might affect cognition—by enhancing divergent-thinking ability and cognitive control—suggest that bilingualism can be advantageous for cognition. Still, until well beyond the middle of the twentieth century the prevailing view was that bilingualism is detrimental for intelligence and cognitive functioning, especially when verbal tests are used to assess cognitive functioning. Because of a special interest in how bilingualism affects cognitive and linguistic *development*, the studies in question typically looked at the effect of bilingualism in children. A study by Peal and Lambert (1962) on the relation between child bilingualism and intelligence marks the turning point from regarding bilingualism a lamentable human condition to avoid whenever possible (which it generally cannot be) to a state that, under specific conditions, is beneficial for language competence and cognitive functioning in general.

The participants in the Peal and Lambert study were 10-year-old children from middle-class French schools in Canada's Montreal region (where at the time about 80% of the population was francophone) who had been selected on the basis of careful screening. The screening involved a number of tests to determine whether a child should be considered French monolingual or fully balanced French–English bilingual. Children who could not unambiguously be classified as monolingual or balanced bilingual were excluded as participants. (Incidentally, "monolingual" in this study did not mean the children in question had no knowledge whatsoever of English, and given the fact they were residents of a country where English is the national language it is likely that they had picked up quite of bit of English in the course of their lives.) The selected children were administered a number of tests that measured their verbal and non-verbal intelligence. Information on a number of background variables such as the children's and their parents' attitudes towards English and French, how well they did in school, their age, sex, and socioeconomic class was also collected.

Contrary to the authors' expectations, the bilingual children performed significantly better than the monolingual children on the vast majority of all tests and subtests, both those that measured verbal intelligence and the ones measuring non-verbal intelligence. The bilingual children outperformed the monolinguals in concept formation and in tasks that required mental flexibility, and bilinguals showed a more diversified set of mental abilities than the monolingual controls. These results also held when differences between the two groups in socioeconomic class, age, and sex were controlled. These results came as a big surprise to the investigators because a thorough review of the literature had led them to predict

that the monolinguals should perform better than the bilinguals on the tests that measured verbal intelligence, and that monolingual and bilingual children should not show any difference on the tests measuring nonverbal intelligence.

As observed by these and many later authors (e.g., Hakuta & Diaz, 1985; Reynolds, 1991), a plausible reason for the deviant results is that many of the earlier studies lacked experimental rigor, for instance by not matching the monolingual and bilingual groups on age, socioeconomic status, or amount of education. Other infelicities occurring in the earlier studies were that the tests were not always appropriately standardized or that the bilingual participants were not balanced and were tested in their weaker language. If bilingual test-takers experience difficulties with one of their languages and verbal intelligence is measured through this language, what else could be expected than lower scores on verbal intelligence? Similarly, it has been argued (Cummins, 1976, p. 23) that some minimal threshold of L2 proficiency should exist for bilingualism to become advantageous for cognitive functioning:

> ... there may be a threshold level of L2 competence which pupils must attain both in order to avoid cognitive disadvantages and allow the potentially beneficial aspects of becoming bilingual to influence their cognitive functioning. Those aspects of bilingualism which might accelerate cognitive growth seem unlikely to come into effect until the child has attained a certain minimum or threshold level of competence in his second language. Similarly, if a child [. . .] attains only a very low level of competence in his second language, his interaction with the environment through the medium of that language [. . .] is likely to be impoverished.

It may have been the case that the earlier studies have generally tested children whose linguistic competence in L2 happened to be below this threshold level. Finally, the participants' bilingualism had occasionally been determined in rather unorthodox ways: In some studies it had been determined on the basis of where the participants' parents were born and in one case it was even done by simply looking at the participants' names (Pintner, 1932; in Peal & Lambert, 1962). Even though some methodological weaknesses remained (see Hakuta & Diaz, 1985, for a discussion), in all these respects Peal and Lambert's investigation compared favorably with the earlier ones.

Looking for the reason why for the first time the evidence clearly pointed to a beneficial effect of bilingualism on intelligence, later publications (Lambert, 1977, 1981) highlighted one potentially crucial feature of Lambert and Peal's study: In the Montreal region both English and French are socially valued and respected languages, English being the national language and French the home language of the majority of the population. Therefore the acquisition of English by francophone children in this region does not involve the risk of the home language French getting corrupted as a consequence of a social pressure not to use it. In other words, the learning of English by French-Canadians does not involve the risk that their L1 French competence is lowered but truly enriches their linguistic repertoire with a new language; it adds a language onto one that does not suffer a cost (although, as we have seen on pp. 361–371, it may change through its contact with the new language). Lambert called this form of bilingualism **additive bilingualism**, and it is this form of bilingualism that he argued to be advantageous for cognitive functioning.

The counterpart of additive bilingualism is **subtractive bilingualism**, a form of bilingualism "experienced by ethnolinguistic minority groups who, because of national and educational policies and social pressures of various sorts, feel forced to put aside or subtract out their ethnic languages for a more necessary and prestigious national language" (Lambert, 1981, p. 12). In this form of bilingualism the L2 gradually replaces the L1. Because language serves to buttress thought, this form of bilingualism, weakening the native language, is detrimental for cognitive functioning for reasons that "it usually places youngsters in

a limbo where neither language is useful as a tool of thought and expression—a type of "semilingualism" (Lambert, 1981, p. 12). In conclusion, it appears that the bilingual French–English children in Peal and Lambert's (1962) study outperformed their monolingual French-speaking peers in intelligence because they had exploited the opportunity, provided by their environment, to become additive bilinguals. The reason why they, and not their monolingual peers, had exploited this opportunity presumably relates to the more favorable attitudes towards English and the English-Canadian community of these children and their parents (see Peal & Lambert, 1962, for a substantiation of this claim).

However, an alternative explanation of the results of Peal and Lambert (1962), of which the authors were well aware themselves, must be considered: that the relation between bilingualism and intelligence had worked the other way around. The more intelligent children may have been the ones to become bilingual, and because they were more intelligent they obviously performed better on the intelligence tests. Generally, a suitable way to determine the direction of causality between two variables is to design a longitudinal study in which one of two matched groups receives some treatment over an extended period of time and the other does not receive this treatment. To assess the effect of treatment, after some time performance of both groups on some task or set of tasks is compared. If the two groups perform differently on this task, the specific treatment is likely to have caused this difference.

A small set of longitudinal studies suggests that bilingualism can indeed improve cognitive functioning. One of these studies (Scott, 1973, in Lambert, 1981) concerned two groups of English-Canadian children. At the onset of the study the children in one group (the treatment group) had been given the opportunity to become functionally bilingual through immersion schooling in French over a couple of years, whereas the children in the other group (the control group) had not been given this opportunity but received their schooling exclusively in English, the conventional school language in Canada. The children in both groups were equated on IQ and social class background at the onset of the study. The second study concerned an experiment in which a random selection of schools in an area in New England, the home of many francophone Americans, were permitted to offer part of their elementary curriculum in French, the children's home language. A second group of schools, with children of similar intelligence and socio-economic backgrounds and, again, French as their home language, offered an all-English curriculum. When tested a number of years later, in both studies the group of children who had received (part of) their schooling in French, and had thus become functionally bilingual, out-performed the other group on tests that index some aspect of cognitive functioning, such as a math test or a test of divergent thinking. Interestingly, the children schooled in French also showed superior *English* language skills.

In a third longitudinal study (Kessler & Quinn, 1980, in Lambert, 1981), a group of Hispanic-American children were given the opportunity to learn subject matter in their home language Spanish and their performance on a number of tasks was compared to that of a socioeconomically more privileged group of middle-class, white, monolingual English-speaking children of the same age. Both groups received an extensive training program in science inquiry through discussions, films, and hypothesis testing. Despite being less privileged, the pupils in the Hispanic-American group outperformed those in the English-American group in problem-solving capacity, generating hypotheses of a much higher complexity and quality. Furthermore, while generating the hypotheses, the Spanish–English bilinguals used more complex linguistic structures than the English monolinguals. Thus, once again it appeared that bilingualism is the cause of enhanced cognitive functioning.

Finally, Hakuta and Diaz (1985) tackled the question of whether bilingualism improves cognitive functioning or whether superior cognition causes bilingualism in a slightly different way. They tested over 100 Spanish-dominant children aged between about 4 and 8 years and all enrolled in a bilingual education program of a number of public schools in Connecticut. The children were all tested twice (at Time 1 and Time 2), with an interval of 6 months in between the two test sessions. The tests included measures of their relative linguistic ability in Spanish and English and a measure of non-verbal cognitive ability. The measures of relative ability in the two languages provided an estimate of degree of bilingualism; that is, whether or not the children were balanced bilinguals and, if not, how large the proficiency difference between their two languages was. The investigators did not include a monolingual control group but were interested to find out whether degree of bilingualism at Time 1 predicted performance on the cognitive task at Time 2 or whether, instead, performance on the cognitive task at Time 1 predicted degree of bilingualism at Time 2. The data suggested that the relation between bilingualism and cognitive functioning works both ways, but "the model claiming degree of bilingualism to be the causal link was more consistent with our obtained data than the model claiming cognitive ability to be the causal variable" (Hakuta & Diaz, 1985, p. 340). In other words, the chances that a child becomes bilingual (in a bilingual environment) are greater if the child has strong cognitive skills than when it is endowed with lesser cognitive skills but, more so, bilingualism is the cause of enhanced cognitive ability.

An important conclusion to draw from all these studies is that allowing ethnic minority children to nurture their home language (instead of gradually having it replaced by the L2) and thus to "transform their subtractive experiences with bilingualism and biculturalism into additive ones" (Lambert, 1981, p. 13) improves their performance on a varied set of cognitive tasks. That minority children in circumstances of additive bilingualism even outperform monolingual children who are, in socioeconomic sense, more privileged, is an especially appealing result. Furthermore, all these studies suggest that the children's bilingualism was the *cause* of their relatively high levels of cognitive performance. Finally, there is some evidence to suggest that intelligence/high cognitive ability helps to become bilingual.

The beneficial effect of bilingualism on cognition: Further evidence and limitations

Since Peal and Lambert's (1962) seminal investigation, in many studies detailed knowledge has been gathered about the type of tasks on which bilinguals excel, and a number of factors have been identified that mediate and restrict the positive effect of bilingualism. But prior to elaborating on some of these it should be mentioned that bilingualism, even bilingualism of the additive form, brings about some minor drawbacks as well. This is especially the case when the fractional view of bilingualism is taken (see p. 340), which departs from the (flawed) assumption that a bilingual is two monolinguals in one person. For instance, several authors have shown that, as compared to the monolingual norm, bilingual children have relatively small vocabularies in their *separate* languages (see, e.g., Ben-Zeev, 1977a, 1977b; Bialystok, 1988; Eviatar & Ibrahim, 2000; Martin-Rhee & Bialystok, 2008; Rosenblum & Pinker, 1983; but see Pearson et al., 1993). The reason presumably is that having two words for one and the same concept and using both implies that bilinguals use each single word less often than monolinguals do. As a consequence it has been less well learned. This may also be the reason why word retrieval in adult bilinguals is slower and more effortful than in monolingual controls, as suggested by longer picture-naming latencies (e.g., Gollan et al., 2005; Ivanova & Costa, 2008; Mägiste, 1979), lesser verbal fluency (Gollan, Montoya, & Werner, 2002), and more "tip-of-the-tongue" states (Gollan & Silverberg, 2001) in bilinguals (but these effects may also result from greater lexical competition during word production in bilinguals than in monolinguals; see p. 362).

Ben-Zeev (1977a) hypothesized that the relative lack of experience with each separate language may also be reflected in relatively limited knowledge of grammatical rules, in each language separately, in bilingual children, but that this effect might be very short-lived because the "repetitiveness and redundancy in grammar compensate for inexperience" (Ben-Zeev, 1977a, p. 35). Similarly, she assumed that the vocabulary deficit will also diminish or disappear when, over the years, language experience increases, but because of the large size of a language's vocabulary one might expect the vocabulary deficit to last longer.

Other effects of bilingualism that from the fractional view of bilingualism may be considered detrimental have been presented in the earlier sections of this chapter. An example is the evidence of the ubiquitous accents (in phonology, grammar, and semantics) in the language use of bilinguals in both their L1 and L2, which result from interference due to co-activation of the non-targeted language and/or from the merging of L1 and L2 representations (p. 364). But from the holistic view of bilingualism (see p. 340), which acknowledges that the use of two languages produces a specific speaker-hearer in his or her own right (e.g., Cook, 1991; Grosjean, 1989), such results are non-normatively regarded as reflecting just differences between monolinguals and bilinguals; differences that obviously result from the bilingual experience. What is more, from the holistic point of view, what at first sight seems to be a drawback of bilingualism may be recognized as an advantage by a slight change in perspective. For instance, one may become aware of the fact that the two relatively small vocabularies bilingual children possess in each of their languages add up to the mastery of a range of concepts that outnumbers the concepts known by age-matched monolingual children. This is because a bilingual child's lexical-conceptual knowledge store includes both concepts shared between the languages as well as concepts specific to each separate language (cf. Umbel, Pearson, Fernández, & Oller, 1992). Furthermore, from a holistic point of view one might not only have an eye for the potentially harmful effects of having two words for one concept in terms of retrieval speed, but also for its potentially beneficial effects. It is to these, and other, advantageous effects of bilingualism that I will now turn.

Bilingualism and metalinguistic awareness

So what are the tasks that have revealed salutary effects of bilingualism and what aspects of superior cognitive functioning are tapped and indexed by these tasks? Many researchers in this field of study, and especially those who studied childhood bilingualism, have used tasks that are thought to index some form of **metalinguistic awareness**; that is, the ability "to reflect on and manipulate the structural features of language independent of meaning" (Bruck & Genesee, 1995, p. 307), "to look *at* language rather than *through* it to the intended meaning" (Cummins, 1978, p. 127), or to think about language rather than to think through language (Bialystok, 1992). Some metalinguistic tasks probe the test-taker's phonological awareness; that is, "the ability to reflect on and manipulate sublexical phonological units such as syllables, onsets, rimes and phonemes" (Bruck & Genesee, 1995, p. 308). To do so requires an understanding of the sound units that make up a word. Other metalinguistic tasks tap syntactic awareness; that is, the language user's ability to reflect on and manipulate syntactic structures. A further group of metalinguistic tasks probe word awareness; that is, the language user's understanding of the relation between words and their meanings and, especially, the arbitrary nature of this relation.

Some authors (e.g., Ben-Zeev, 1977a; Bruck & Genesee, 1995) have suggested that metalinguistic awareness is increased in bilingual children because their dual linguistic environment forces them to pay special attention to the structural aspects of language. Such a focus on structure would help them to separate the two systems and, thus, to minimize interlingual interference. As Bruck and Genesee (1995, p. 308) put it:

> The hypothesis that bilingualism or second language acquisition promotes metalinguistic awareness is based on the view that bilingualism provides a form of contrastive linguistics instruction which leads bilingual children to compare and analyse the structural aspects of language in more advanced ways than monolingual children.

Other aspects of cognitive performance may then benefit from this increased level of metalinguistic awareness in bilinguals, either indirectly through superior linguistic abilities, or directly, for instance because attention to structure is beneficial for cognitive functioning in general. According to Bialystok (e.g., 1988, 1992, 2001a, 2001b, 2004) metalinguistic tasks appeal to two cognitive processes that she calls the "analysis of representational structures" and "control of attentional processing" ("analysis" and "control", in short) and it is in the latter that she believes bilinguals excel (see below for details).

Word awareness in bilingual and monolingual children

The tasks that have been used to measure aspects of metalinguistic awareness are too numerous and varied to cover all of them here. Instead, by way of illustration I will confine myself to presenting those that were used in two influential early experimental studies (Ben-Zeev, 1977b; Ianco-Worrall, 1972), which were among the first to reveal beneficial effects of bilingualism. Specifically, both of them demonstrated that bilingualism boosts word awareness and, particularly, the awareness that a word's form and its meaning are not inseparable entities but have become associated merely through convention. This effect of bilingualism was first noticed by Leopold, who dedicated four volumes to the speech development of his daughter Hildegard who was raised according to the "one-person one-language principle" (Leopold, 1939, 1947, 1949a, 1949b). As summarized by Ianco-Worrall, from a very early age Hildegard "readily accepted new names for objects already denoted in one language and asked to be given the name in the second, or even a third, unfamiliar language" (Ianco-Worrall, 1972, p. 1391). This behavior suggests the awareness that the relation between a word's sound and meaning is arbitrary, that a particular thing (or living being or abstract concept) remains this very same thing if its name were to be changed into a completely different one.

A miscellaneous collection of advantageous effects has been attributed to this one insight. For instance, it is thought to be beneficial for abstract thinking (see Hakuta & Diaz, 1985, for a discussion), which is an ability that is likely to promote many facets of cognitive functioning. It is also thought to promote analytical thinking (e.g., Ben-Zeev, 1977b), to speed up semantic development (Ianco-Worrall, 1972), and others went so far as to regard the separation of word sound and word meaning as a liberating, emancipating attainment: "it frees the mind from the tyranny of words. It is extremely difficult for a monoglot to dissociate thought from words, but he who can express his ideas in two languages is emancipated" (Evans, 1953, in Peal & Lambert, 1962, pp. 19–20).

Ianco-Worrall (1972), seeking empirical support for Leopold's observations, hypothesized that the early separation of word sound from word meaning might have the effect that semantic development in bilingual children progresses at a faster rate than in monolingual children. She furthermore hypothesized that, if such were the case, bilingual children more often than monolingual children should perceive the relationship between words in terms of their semantic similarities rather than in terms of their acoustic attributes. The underlying assumption here appears to be that attention to form aspects of words is a developmentally earlier stage than attention to meaning aspects. In Chapter 3 (pp. 126–128) some evidence from multiple-choice recognition tasks was presented that supports this idea. It is furthermore supported by early word association studies, which have shown that younger children produce relatively many associations sharing a sound relation with the stimulus word, whereas in older children the number of associations sharing a semantic relation with the stimulus word increases (Entwisle, Forsyth, & Muus, 1964; Ervin, 1961a).

Ianco-Worrall tested these views in a semantic-phonetic preference test in which Afrikaans–English children (as Leopold's daughter, raised according to the one-person, one-language principle) and monolingual English and Afrikaans controls were presented with a set of standard words, each accompanied by two choice words. One of the latter two words was similar in sound to the standard (e.g., standard word: *cap*; choice word: *can*); the other was semantically related to the standard word (*hat*). The participants were asked to select the choice word most similar to the standard (e.g., "I have three words: *cap*, *can*, and *hat*. Which is more like *cap*, *can* or *hat*?"). All children were from two age groups: 4 to 6 years, and 7 to 9 years. The bilingual children were tested in both languages, their performance in Afrikaans and English being compared with that of the Afrikaans and English monolingual groups, respectively.

The investigator predicted that the older children would select the semantically related alternative more often than the younger children and that, within each age group, the bilingual children would select the semantic alternative more often than the monolingual controls. In agreement with these predictions, semantic preference indeed increased with age, but only in the monolinguals. The bilingual children did not show an age effect but the semantic preference was the dominant pattern in both age groups. From these data the author concluded that "bilinguals, brought up in a one-person, one-language home environment, reach a stage in semantic development, as measured by our test, some 2–3 years earlier than their unilingual peers" (Ianco-Worrall, 1972, p. 1398).

A second experiment provided a hint that this accelerated semantic development was related to (and possibly caused by) the bilingual children's relatively early awareness that the relation between word form and word reference is arbitrary. In this experiment all children were asked a set of questions, of three types: Questions that called for an explanation of word names (e.g., "Why is a dog called *dog*?"); questions that called for a judgment of whether or not word names could be interchanged (e.g., "Could you call a dog *cow* and a cow *dog*?"); and questions that called for an interchange of word names in play (e.g., "Let us play a game. Let us call a dog *cow*. Does this cow have horns? And does this cow give milk?"). The bilingual children outperformed their monolingual controls on the second type of questions, whereas performance of both groups on the remaining question types was similar. On the basis of the differential results regarding the second type of question the author concluded that bilingual children are aware of the arbitrary relation between a word and its meaning at a younger age than monolingual children.

In a similar study Ben-Zeev (1977b) provided converging evidence. Her participants were 5- to 8-year-old Hebrew–English bilingual children and matched Hebrew and English controls. One of the tests she administered was a so-called "symbol-substitution test", which consisted of seven items similar to the questions that Ianco-Worrall (1972) posed to her participants. All items were meant to determine the participants' ability to disconnect the conventional name of a referent and assign it another name; in other words, to find out to what extent they were aware that a name is not an intrinsic property of its referent. The items were of increasing difficulty (and increasingly bizarre). In the first two items, as in Ianco-Worrall's third type of questions, the name of an object/entity was substituted by the name of another object/entity. For instance, the experimenter showed a toy airplane to the child and said: "You know that in English this is named *airplane*. In this game it is named *turtle*. Can a turtle fly?" [Correct answer: yes]; "How does the turtle fly?" [Correct answer: with its wings]. The remaining items asked for a substitution that violated selection rules, a word from one grammatical class to be substituted by one of another grammatical class. For instance, the experimenter said: "For this game the way we say *I* is to say *macaroni*. So how do we say 'I am warm'?" [Correct answer: Macaroni am warm]. On both types of items the bilinguals performed better than the monolinguals, suggesting that it was easier for them to ignore the conventional meanings of words. Similar results have since been obtained by Bialystok (1988), testing French–English bilingual children.

Analysis vs. control

The above two studies exemplify a much larger number of studies that have shown an advanta-geous effect of bilingualism on some or other manifestation of linguistic awareness. But null effects of bilingualism have also been reported, even within the subset of studies that focused on word awareness, as the above studies did. Very occasionally a reversed effect has even been found, the monolinguals in fact performing better. Finally, in one study that exploited Ben-Zeev's (1977b) symbol substitution test (Rosenblum & Pinker, 1983), clear differences between monolinguals and bilinguals were obtained but these differences could not be qualified in terms of an advantage or disadvantage for either the bilinguals or the monolinguals. In two comprehensive reviews (Bialystok, 2001b, 2004), and building on her own experimental work (Bialystok, 1988, 1992), Bialystok managed to distill a regular pattern out of the ostensibly somewhat whimsical results and identified a couple of factors that seem to constrain the bilingual advantage.

A starting point in Bialystok's analysis is her observation—based on her review of the literature—that metalinguistic ability is not a "unitary achievement" (Bialystok, 2001b), because if it were the bilinguals might have been expected to excel on all tasks that putatively measure some aspect of metalinguistic awareness. They did not, however, not even on all tasks designed to index one subdomain of metalinguistic awareness: word awareness, syntactic awareness, or phonological awareness. Next, scrutinizing the processing requirements of all tasks dubbed "metalinguistic" she identified two types of processing involved in successful task performance: "analysis of representational structures" and "control of selective attention"—in short, "analysis" and "control". Bialystok regards any task that demands the involvement of one or both of these processes as a metalinguistic task. The more each of these types of processing must be deployed to perform the task properly, the more difficult the task.

Analysis of representational structures concerns children's ability to build increasingly detailed and explicit representational structures of linguistic information that initially is only stored in implicit representations. Implicit representations are thought to suffice for ordinary conversational uses of language but not for literate language use. For the literate use of language explicit representations are needed that can be consciously accessed and manipulated. Control of selective attention is the ability to direct attention to specific aspects of either an external stimulus or a mental representation during task performance. The control demands are especially high when the task environment contains a conflict or ambiguity between two (or more) possible mental representations of the task, and correct performance requires that one of them is attended to and the other ignored or suppressed. The higher the level of conflict between the competing representations, the more attention control must be exerted to maintain satisfactory levels of performance.

Scrutinizing the metalinguistic tasks on which monolinguals and bilinguals have been compared (tasks, thus, that require the involvement of at least one of these two processing components to some minimal degree), Bialystok (2001b, p. 178) discovered the following pattern:

> Simply put, tasks that are high in their demands for control of attention are solved better by bilinguals than monolinguals; tasks that are high in their demands for analysis of representations are not necessarily solved better by either group. The bilingual advantage, therefore, is in the ability to control attention when there is misleading information.

This analysis explains the bilingual children's superior performance on the symbol manipulation task presented above. In that task the misleading information to be inhibited is the conventional meaning of the substitute word (e.g., *turtle* in *can a turtle fly?*), where *turtle* is the substitute for *airplane*). For similar reasons, bilingual children are better than monolingual controls in accepting sentences such as "Apples grow on noses" as grammatically correct. To provide the correct response ("yes") the meaning of the sentence must be ignored and attention must be focused on the sentence's structure. Figure 7.10 organizes a larger set of metalinguistic tasks on the basis of the estimated analysis and control demands posed by each of them (from Bialystok, 2001b)

The conclusion that the bilingual advantage is the ability to control attention when there is misleading information in language tasks gives rise to the question of whether this advantage extends beyond the domain of language to other areas of cognitive functioning. The impact of an increased ability to control attention in non-linguistic tasks is potentially huge because attention control is required in all behavior that is not fully automated and thus, arguably, in the far majority of our everyday pursuits.

The above studies on the effects of bilingualism on metalinguistic task performance and the conclusions drawn from them have thus paved the way towards a new field of research that connects the study of bilingualism with the vast research field examining how humans exert attention control while performing cognitively demanding tasks and, especially, tasks that present some type of conflict. Ellen Bialystok was the first to see this possible connection and to start examining it. The general hypothesis underlying the ensuing experiments is that while controlling their languages bilinguals exploit more general processes and mechanisms of cognitive control (see also pp. 306–310) and that, as a consequence, they have become experts in cognitive control in general. If so, they should generally excel on tasks requiring cognitive control, even if the tasks in question are completely non-linguistic. A further hypothesis is that the beneficial effect of bilingualism on cognitive control in general extends beyond childhood into adulthood. In the next section I will present some of this work.

Bilinguals as experts in cognitive control

Evidence from the Simon task

To examine whether language control in bilinguals exploits more general processes and mechanisms of cognitive control, Ellen Bialystok and her colleagues compared the performance of bilinguals and monolingual controls of

FIGURE 7.10

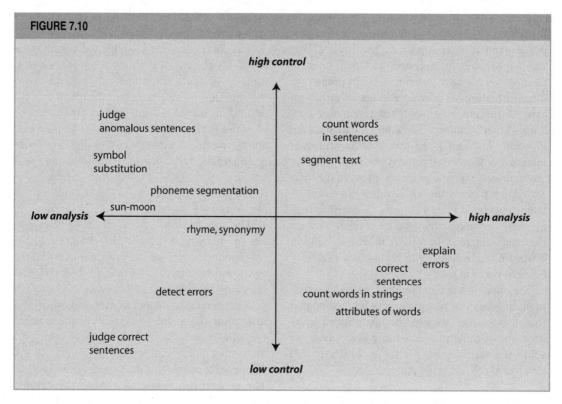

A number of metalinguistic tasks organized according to their estimated demands for analysis and control. From Bialystok (2001). Reproduced with permission from Cambridge University Press.

various ages on, among others, the "Simon task" (Bialystok, 2006; Bialystok, Craik, Klein, & Viswanathan, 2004; Bialystok et al., 2005a; Bialystok, Martin, & Viswanathan, 2005b; Martin-Rhee & Bialystok, 2008). This perceptual-motor task assesses the participants' skill in inhibiting or ignoring irrelevant spatial information, a skill that requires executive control. The participants are seated in front of a computer screen where stimuli (e.g., squares) in different colors are presented in different positions. In the standard set-up stimuli of two different colors are used, say blue and red, and the stimuli appear, in a randomized order, either on the right or the left side of the screen. The participants are instructed to press a key on the left-hand side of the key-board if the presented square's color is blue and to press a key on the right side when the square's color is red (or vice versa). In a congruent condition the stimulus's position on the screen matches

the position of the key to be pressed (e.g., red squares require pressing the right-hand key and a red square has just appeared on the right side of the screen); in an incongruent condition a stimulus's screen position and the position of the key to be pressed mismatch (e.g., the red square is presented on the left-hand side of the screen). Congruent and incongruent trials are presented in a mixed, unpredictable order. Typically, incongruent trials lead to longer response times (and more errors) than congruent trials. This effect is called the "Simon effect".

As mentioned, the starting point of Bialystok and her colleagues was the hypothesis that (active) bilingualism boosts cognitive control, and especially inhibitory control, outside the language domain, for reasons that bilingualism involves the incessant need to exert this type of control, inhibiting or ignoring one language to be able to speak the other. As we have already seen, earlier studies had provided evidence that balanced bilingual children are better than matched monolingual controls at metalinguistic language tasks that require the control of attention. Two of the questions the authors posed in the present set of new studies were whether this same advantage might also hold when a non-linguistic task has to be performed and if this would also be the case for balanced bilinguals of other age groups; that is, whether the bilingual advantage would sustain into adulthood. A further question built on the well-known fact that normal cognitive aging involves a decline of the mechanisms that enable cognitive control (e.g., Christ, White, Mandernach, & Keys, 2001). The authors wondered whether bilingualism might provide a "defense" against this decline of controlled processing with aging. Finally, they attempted to determine the neural correlates of a bilingual advantage in inhibiting irrelevant information.

Across these studies, a smaller Simon effect in bilinguals than in monolinguals was regarded as the main marker of more efficient inhibitory cognitive control in bilinguals. In addition, overall task performance was looked at as well because "the control processes required to perform the Simon task are involved in all trials, not just those explicitly containing conflict" (Martin-Rhee & Bialystok, 2008, p. 82). The reason is that the task incessantly requires a high level of vigilance on the part of the participants because they never know in advance what type of trial, congruent or incongruent, will be presented next. Therefore, in addition to a smaller Simon effect in bilinguals, bilinguals were expected to generally respond more rapidly than monolingual controls, on both congruent and incongruent trials.

To address these questions, across a number of studies Bialystok and her colleagues had monolingual children and young-adult, middle-aged, and older-adult monolinguals and matched groups of balanced bilinguals all perform the Simon task as described above. To be able to gather fine-grained knowledge on the relation between bilingualism and cognitive control, in addition to the congruent–incongruent manipulation the researchers included three further manipulations. First, they looked at the effect of increasing working memory demands in the Simon task, adding a condition with four rather than two colors and instructing the participants to press the left-hand key in reply to two of these colors and the right-hand key in reply to the remaining two colors. This manipulation increases working memory load because now the participants have to keep four instead of two associations between specific colors and keys in memory during task performance. Second, the researchers included a control condition in which the color stimulus to be responded to always appeared in the center of the screen (that is, without task-irrelevant spatial information). This manipulation was meant to rule out the possibility that a bilingual advantage to be obtained was merely due to overall faster responding of bilinguals rather than to increased efficiency of inhibitory control (as demonstrated by a smaller Simon effect and/or faster responding to congruent and incongruent trials). Third, the authors looked at the effect of task practice: If excessive practice in inhibitory control underlies the relatively small Simon effects in bilinguals (if these were to emerge at all), with increased practice on the Simon task the difference between the Simon effects obtained for monolinguals and bilinguals should become smaller.

The combined studies provided clear and consistent answers to the questions posed: First, excepting the population of young adults, specifically university undergraduates, among all participant populations the bilinguals generally showed reliably smaller Simon effects and/or performed better overall on the Simon task than monolinguals, indicating less disruption from misleading information, and thus superior inhibitory control. The authors regarded the absence of an effect of bilingualism in the university undergraduates as a ceiling effect: For these participants inhibitory control is at its peak so that bilingualism cannot boost it any further. Second, bilinguals were hampered less than monolinguals by an increase in working memory load, suggesting that the beneficial effect of bilingualism extends beyond improved inhibitory control to the improvement of other aspects of cognitive functioning. Third, as predicted, aging was associated with less-efficient executive control, as evidenced both by relatively large detrimental effects of increases in memory load and by increases in the Simon effect in the older-adult groups. Fourth, both these negative effects of aging were considerably smaller for bilinguals than for monolinguals, suggesting that bilingualism indeed attenuates the adverse effects of aging on executive control (and see Bialystok, Craik, & Freedman, 2007, for evidence that bilingualism delays the onset of symptoms of dementia). Fifth, in the majority of cases the possibility was excluded that the beneficial effects of bilingualism simply concerned a speed advantage by showing that the magnitude of the Simon effect (the primary signature of inhibitory control) always differed between monolinguals and monolinguals, except after extended practice. Sixth, practice reduced, and ultimately annihilated, the differences between bilinguals and monolinguals: After extended practice the adverse effect of increased load was equally large in both groups and the Simon effect was reduced to zero for both groups.

All in all, these findings constitute compelling evidence that the same executive processes are involved in managing the control over two languages as in performing the Simon task and, plausibly, other conflict tasks that require task-irrelevant information to be inhibited or ignored. Furthermore, the memory load data suggest that bilingualism also boosts memory capacity. (Bialystok, 2008, qualifies the latter conclusion by suggesting that this holds specifically for memory tasks that are primarily based on executive control. Memory tasks that are based primarily on verbal recall are performed more poorly by bilinguals than monolinguals, presumably as a consequence of bilinguals' lesser prior experience with, and therefore lesser vocabulary skills in, the language in which the recall test is administered; see p. 389.) Apparently, bilingualism yields benefits across a larger set of skills that all appeal to general executive processes. As summarized and concluded by Bialystok (2007, pp. 220–221):

> The research [. . .] reveals compelling evidence that bilinguals develop executive

control earlier and maintain their ability to control those functions longer than monolinguals. Given the fundamental centrality of these executive processes to our everyday cognitive life, this is an altogether promising outcome for bilinguals.

If these salutary effects of bilingualism are indeed caused by the incessant use of more general, non-bilingualism-specific, control processes, expertise in other domains that exploit these same control processes should similarly affect performance on the Simon task. A final result of the above studies confirms this hypothesis: Bialystok et al. (2005b) split up a participant group of young adults, college undergraduates, into a subgroup of youngsters who spent much time playing video games on the computer and a subgroup who played computer games infrequently. Recall that the group of young adults was the only group that, overall, did not show an effect of bilingualism on performance in the Simon task. Again a clear-cut result emerged, and one that will be reassuring for all those parents who have worried about the possibly harmful effects of excessive computer game play on their (especially male) offspring: Performance on the Simon task was considerably better in the group who played video games frequently, suggesting that gaming improves executive control (see also Bialystok, 2006). Similary, Green and Bavelier (2003) have shown that playing action video games modifies visual selective attention. Whatever mental havoc excessive gaming may cause, apparently there are beneficial effects on cognition as well. What this result also demonstrates is that there are other ways to become an expert in inhibitory control than having the good fortune to grow up in a bilingual home.

Evidence from other tasks

Child studies. Although the conclusion seems warranted that bilingualism boosts cognitive control, the exact nature of the benefit and the processes and mechanisms that underlie this advantage are not yet fully understood. To augment and refine our knowledge about these processes and mechanisms, researchers have begun to compare the performance of bilinguals and monolinguals on other tasks that require some form of cognitive control different from the requirements posed by the Simon task. This way the limits of the bilingual advantage can be pinpointed and the exact sources of the advantage can be charted step by step. To this end Martin-Rhee and Bialystok (2008) not only administered the Simon task but also a Stroop-like task, the "day–night" task, in which their participants, monolingual and bilingual children of about 4.5 years old, were instructed to say "night" to a picture of a bright sun and "day" to a picture of a dark moonlit sky.

The choice of the day–night task was based on a categorization of inhibitory control tasks into two types, each associated with a specific type of stimulus display: tasks that require "interference suppression" and those that require "response inhibition". The former type of tasks are associated with so-called "bivalent displays", the latter with "univalent" displays. In bivalent displays there are two perceptual features that may converge on one and the same response (on congruent trials) or that each summons a different response tendency (on incongruent trials). In univalent displays there are two response options to one and the same stimulus feature, a habitual one and an arbitrary one. The Simon task is an instance of an interference-suppression task because the color and the position of the stimulus concern two potentially competing features and the display is thus bivalent. Correct task performance requires that the task-irrelevant feature (position) is suppressed. The "day–night" task (as the classical Stroop task) is an instance of a response-inhibition task: The habitual response to provide the common name of the picture must be inhibited in order to come up with the requested response, the one based on an arbitrary agreement.

The bilingual advantage turned out to be limited to the Simon task and not to extend to the day–night task. These data thus suggest that bilingual children outperform their monolingual peers on tasks that require attention to be selectively directed to specific cues in conflict situations, inhibiting attention to the distracting cue, but not on tasks that require the inhibition of a habitual response. In other words, inhibitory processes are not generally enhanced in bilingual children. The authors (Martin Rhee & Bialystok, 2008, p. 85) attributed this selective advantage to the nature of the specific bilingual experience, which resembles the demands of bivalent tasks:

> For bilinguals, their two linguistic systems function as bivalent representations, offering different, potentially competing response options to the same intention or goal. To manage this conflict, bilinguals must attend to the relevant language system and ignore the unwanted system to assure fluency in speech production.

The data suggest that practicing this form of attention control through bilingualism then transfers to increased levels of attention control in similar non-language tasks.

This analysis receives support from a study that assessed the generality of the bilingual advantage by administering a much larger battery of tasks, nine in all, that were all hypothesized to index some aspect of executive functioning and that all involve some form of inhibition (Carlson & Meltzoff, 2008). The participants were three groups of kindergarten children: (1) a group of Spanish–English bilingual children who had been exposed to both languages from birth. (2) A group of L1 English children who attended immersion elementary schools where they were instructed in English for half the day and in either Spanish or Japanese for the rest of the day. At the time of testing this immersion experience had lasted about 6 months. (3) A control group of L1 English children attending traditional English schools. Despite the fact that the children in the bilingual group had relatively low scores on a test of verbal ability and had parents with relatively low education levels, their scores on all tests equaled those of the other groups. But when verbal ability and parental education level were statistically controlled for, the composite executive-functioning score based on all nine subtests together showed superior performance for the bilingual group as compared to the other groups. The performance of the immersion and control groups did not differ from one another.

Each of the individual tests also suggested an advantage for the bilingual group, but the effect was only statistically significant on a subset of them. It appeared that the shared feature of the tests in this subset was that they all required inhibition of attention to misleading contextual information. This hypothesis was confirmed by the results of a factor analysis on the data of all nine tests. This analysis revealed two distinct factors that the researchers interpreted as measuring the children's ability to manage conflicting attentional demands and the ability to control impulses, respectively. The bilingual advantage exclusively occurred on the tasks that loaded on the first of these two factors. In conclusion then, it appears that the bilingual advantage does not apply to all circumstances that require inhibitory control but to circumstances in which distracting information must be inhibited or ignored. A further conclusion to draw from Carlson and Meltzoff's (2008) study is that the bilingual advantage, not surprisingly, depends on the degree of bilingualism. This follows from the fact that the immersion group, after 6 months of L2 experience, did not yet show any advantage in executive functioning as compared with the control group.

Still, a recent study in which infants were tested suggested that for other aspects of executive function a bilingual advantage may not take more than about half a year of bilingual experience to occur (Kovács & Mehler, 2009). In this study a group of 7-month-old bilingual infants raised with two languages from birth and a group of matched monolingual 7-month-olds were trained to anticipate a reward stimulus (a puppet) on one side of a screen. This training phase was followed by a number of trials in which the reward stimulus appeared on the other side of the screen. The bilingual infants, but not their monolingual age-mates, managed to redirect their anticipatory looks to this other position on the screen after the puppet's position switch, a finding the authors attributed to superior cognitive control in the bilingual infants. Importantly, not only does this finding show that advantageous effects of bilingualism on cognitive control may take a relatively short period of bilingual experience to become manifest, but it also shows that for a bilingual advantage (at least the one tapped in this task) to develop no experience in bilingual *output* is required. After all, infants this age do not produce speech yet (except in the form of babbling; see Table 2.1, p. 21). It thus seems that a relatively short period of just perceiving and processing speech *input* in two languages already has a positive effect on cognitive control.

Adult studies. As mentioned earlier, the common bilingual advantage in the Simon task had not turned up in a comparison of monolingual and bilingual young adult college undergraduates. The reason may be that young adults in general are at a peak of their executive control abilities and that the null effect of bilingualism reflects asymptotic performance in both groups. That bilingualism can nevertheless boost executive control even in this age group was recently demonstrated by Costa, Hernández, and Sebastián-Gallés (2008). The participants in this study were all young adults and consisted of a group of early highly proficient Catalan–Spanish bilinguals and a control group of Spanish monolinguals matched with the bilinguals on age and educational level. The researchers had all of them perform the "attentional network task" (ANT) developed by Fan, McCandliss, Sommer, Raz, and Posner (2002). This task has been designed to reflect three types of attentional processes that are assumed to each be taken care of by a different set of brain structures: executive control (monitoring performance and resolving conflict), alerting (to become and stay alert), and orienting (selecting a subset of information from sensory input). In the ANT task participants must indicate whether an arrow (→ or ←) that is embedded between four flanker arrows, two on each side, points towards the right or the left. In a congruent condition the flanker arrows point in the same direction as the target arrow (→→→→→ or ←←←←←); in an incongruent condition the pointing direction differs between the target and the flankers (→→←→→; or ←←→←←). Just as the incongruent condition in the Simon task, the incongruent condition usually produces slower responses than the congruent condition. This congruency effect is attributed to the fact that a conflict must be resolved in the incongruent condition; namely, between the opposite pointing directions of target and flankers. The attention process assumed to be involved in resolving the conflict is executive control. The involvement of the second process, alerting, is manipulated by presenting or not presenting an alerting cue (an asterisk) prior to target presentation. The third process, orienting, is manipulated by having or not having the cue indicate the position where the target subsequently appears. Costa and his colleagues wondered which one(s) of these manipulations (congruency, the presence or absence of a cue, cue position) affects the performance of bilinguals and monolinguals differently, thus suggesting the differential efficiency of one or more of the three different attention mechanisms involved.

In agreement with the analogous findings of Bialystok and her collaborators with the Simon task, the bilinguals suffered less interference from incongruent flankers than the monolinguals did, again suggesting that they are better at resolving conflict in a situation where there is misleading information. It is particularly noteworthy that this finding materialized even though all participants were young adults, and thus at the peak of a human's executive skills. Also, as in the Simon task studies, the bilinguals were faster overall than the monolinguals. A further finding of interest was that bilinguals benefited more from the presence of an alerting cue than monolinguals, indicating that the alerting mechanism works more efficiently in bilinguals. The third manipulation (cue position) did not differentiate between bilinguals and monolinguals, suggesting that the third attentional process, orienting, does not benefit from bilingual experience. To summarize, it appears from this study that the executive control and alerting components of the brain's attentional network work more efficiently in bilinguals than in monolinguals.

A second recent study, by Colzato, Bajo, Van den Wildenberg, and Paolieri (2008), probed

into the nature of the bilingual advantage by contrasting two ways in which the human control system may safeguard itself against outputting unintended responses: through "active" or "reactive" inhibition. In the authors' terminology, active inhibition is executed if some central inhibitory system directly *inhibits* (deactivates) memory nodes associated with non-target responses (e.g., the node for Spanish *mesa*, "table", when a Spanish–English bilingual intends to speak English, not Spanish), thus making these responses less available. Conversely, reactive inhibition is operative if the current goal, for instance, the intention to speak English, *boosts* the activation in the memory nodes representing the targeted responses (here, the nodes representing English words). Through lateral inhibition along inhibitory connections between targeted and non-targeted memory nodes (e.g., between the nodes for *table* and *mesa*) the activation level in the non-target nodes is then lowered, making the associated responses less available. According to this view, inhibitory effects do not result from actual inhibition exerted by an inhibitory control system but from a control mechanism that works through facilitation. The process of lateral inhibition between word nodes representing translation equivalents presupposed by this view is more often assumed in models of bilingual word processing (see p. 177). These two views on bilingual language control are illustrated in Figure 7.11. (Notice that the present authors' definition of active and reactive inhibition deviates from our use of the terms "proactive" and "reactive" control in Chapter 6. The term "proactive" control was used there to refer to a process whereby the intention to speak one language and not the other boosts the activation of the memory nodes in the targeted language, thereby rendering them more available. In other words, the process involved is the first step in what the present authors call "reactive inhibition". In contrast, "reactive control" as we used the term concerned a process operating on the imminent output of the language system, preventing elements of the non-selected language from emerging in speech.)

Colzato and collaborators examined the

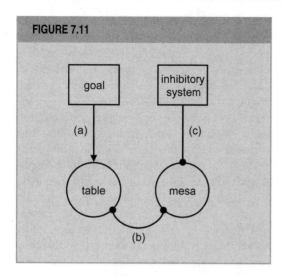

FIGURE 7.11

Two possible ways in which the human control system may safeguard itself against outputting unintended responses: (1) The current goal boosts the activation of the targeted memory nodes (a). The activated targeted nodes then inhibit non-targeted nodes through reactive inhibitory connections (b). (2) A central inhibitory system directly inhibits non-targeted memory nodes (c). From Colzato et al. (2008). Copyright © 2008 American Psychological Society.

nature of the bilingual advantage by comparing the performance of adult balanced Dutch–English bilinguals and Spanish monolinguals on three non-verbal cognitive control tasks that, according to the authors, differ from one another in the type of inhibition they appeal to, active or reactive. I will refrain from explaining these tasks and their rationale because doing so would take an inordinate amount of space. Instead I will confine myself to mentioning the authors' conclusion that the pattern of results was consistent with a reactive-inhibition account of bilingual control. More precisely, the authors concluded that bilinguals are better than monolinguals in maintaining action goals, which boost activation in the goal-relevant memory representations.

To conclude this review of studies that attempted to delineate the set of circumstances under which bilinguals outperform monolinguals on non-verbal control tasks, one such study must not be overlooked. It included bilinguals of a type ignored so far, and provided important new information on the limits and source of the bilingual advantage. The bilinguals in question did not master two spoken languages, as those in the studies discussed above, but one spoken language and one sign language. Like "unimodal" bilinguals (who master two spoken languages), such "bimodal" bilinguals have acquired two full linguistic systems (see pp. 53–54 for a substantiation of the claim that sign languages are fully fledged languages). But unlike unimodal bilinguals, bimodal bilinguals can produce words from both languages simultaneously, one through vocal speech, the second through signing. In other words, the physical restriction that words can only be uttered vocally one at the time *forces* lexical selection in unimodal bilinguals, whereas the physical possibility of speaking and signing at the same time does not do so. An investigation by Emmorey, Borinstein, Thompson, and Gollan (2008a) showed that the simultaneous production of words across two modalities in bimodal bilinguals is not only a theoretical possibility but in fact happens in actual practice.

Emmorey, Luk, Pyers, and Bialystok (2008b) wondered whether the bilingual advantage in cognitive control might result from the fact that unilingual bilinguals are always forced to select one language in speech and that knowing two languages per se does not contribute to the advantage. If so, unlike unimodal bilinguals, bimodal bilinguals should not exhibit better performance than monolinguals on non-verbal control tasks. The researchers examined this hypothesis by comparing the performance of monolinguals, unimodal bilinguals, and bimodal bilinguals on two "flanker tasks" and one control task. One of the flanker tasks was similar to the one included in Costa et al.'s study (2008; see above), except that the stimuli were built not from arrows but from chevron heads: The stimuli in the congruent condition consisted of a series of chevrons all pointing in the same direction, one of them, printed in red, being the target, the other the flankers (e.g., <<<<<). In the incongruent condition the flankers pointed in the opposite direction from the target (<< ><<). On each trial the participants had to indicate, by pressing one of two buttons, whether the target chevron pointed towards the right or the left. In the second flanker task the target, again a red chevron, was flanked on either side by two red flankers. In a "go" condition the flankers were diamonds (◊◊>◊◊). In a "no-go" condition they were red Xs (XX>XX). In the "go" condition the participants had to indicate in what direction the chevron pointed by pressing the appropriate button. In the "no-go" condition they had to withhold their response. Finally, on each trial in the control task a single chevron was presented and the participants had to indicate whether it pointed to the right or the left.

The results provided clear support for the hypothesis that the superior cognitive control in unimodal bilinguals does not result from their knowing two languages but from the requirement to unrelentingly and inevitably select one language: Unimodal but not bimodal bilinguals responded faster than monolinguals on both congruent and incongruent trials in the first of the above flanker tasks and on the "go" trials in the second. On the control task, in which there was no conflict to resolve or response to withhold, all three groups responded equally fast. The authors concluded that the bilingual advantage in cognitive control results from the unimodal bilingual's experience in controlling two languages in the same modality. As mentioned above, the authors attributed the effect specifically to the requirement of *output* control in unimodal bilinguals. Notice, however, that the results of the study performed by Kovács and Mehler (2009; see the above section on child studies) with preverbal infants as participants suggest that input control might contribute to the unimodal bilinguals' advantage as well.

All in all, it can be concluded that the combined child and adult studies discussed above clearly suggest that (unimodal) bilingualism brings superior cognitive control that is already manifest in very early childhood and lasts in adulthood. These studies have also begun to reveal which subcomponents of the multifaceted skill of cognitive control are the ones to benefit from the bilingual experience. While this evidence was being gathered, other researchers started to map the brain areas involved in this cognitive advantage. The results from the pertinent studies will be presented in Chapter 8.

SUMMARY

- The multiple languages of a bilingual or multilingual all interact with one another both during acquisition and use. The inevitable consequence of this fact is that the linguistic utterances of bilinguals and multilinguals differ from those of monolingual speakers of the languages involved. In other words, multilingualism does not equal multiple monolingualism.
- The cross-linguistic influence of a multilingual speaker's currently non-selected languages on the currently selected one is determined by a number of factors: the typological distance between the non-selected languages and the selected language; the foreign language status, strength, and proportion of recent use of the non-selected languages; the order of acquisition of the selected and non-selected languages; the multilingual's current language mode; the speaker's proficiency in the selected language.
- Degree of loss of L2 vocabulary acquired at some point in the past but not used recently depends on the level of L2 proficiency originally attained, the duration of elapsed time since acquisition, the spacing of the training sessions during acquisition, and specific features of the learning materials. Part of the vocabulary originally acquired beyond some minimal threshold level seems to be immune to loss and can still be retrieved from memory after decades of non-use.
- The savings paradigm is a highly sensitive technique to detect residues of seemingly lost knowledge acquired in the remote past. It involves the brief relearning of materials (e.g., a set of L2 words) likely to be known in the past but seemingly lost and the (equally brief) learning of

matched materials unlikely to be known before (e.g., another set of L2 words). The test scores on a subsequent cued recall test for the former materials are typically substantially higher than those for the latter materials even when the test is administered after decades of disuse of the former materials. This finding suggests that prior knowledge is not lost but unavailable, and that it takes little to reactivate it.

- The L1 can be completely lost and replaced by an L2 when at a young age the L1 learner is abruptly cut off from further L1 input, as sometimes happens in adoption. Such "catastrophic forgetting", presumably caused by a process of retroactive interference from the L2, has successfully been imitated in computational modeling.

- A comparison of studies on L1 and L2 loss suggests that an unused L1 is more susceptible to forgetting than an unused L2. However, to legitimately draw this conclusion studies need to be designed that rule out an explanation of the differential loss of L1 and L2 in terms of a number of potentially confounding variables: the amount of continued exposure to the corroded language in between initial learning and later testing; the types of linguistic knowledge that are examined during testing; the originally acquired level of fluency in the corroded language; the test methods used to assess the degree of loss. Only if differential loss is observed for L1 and L2 if these variables have been controlled for can it be concluded that L1 is more easily lost than L2.

- As compared with the speech of monolingual language users, bilingual speech in both L1 and L2 is characterized by an accent in all domains of language: phonology, grammar, and semantics. There are two possible sources of these accents: memory structures that differ between monolinguals and bilinguals or response competition caused by activated structures in the non-response language in bilinguals.

- Languages differ from one another on many structural dimensions including whether and how they mark grammatical gender, number, and tense. Cross-linguistic studies have shown that the specific linguistic structures encountered by native speakers of a language affect their thought processes and the content of their conceptual structures. Bilingual studies have shown that a switch of language may change bilinguals' processes of thought, and that the content of thought in at least some conceptual domains may differ between bilinguals and monolinguals.

- A form of bilingualism called "additive" is advantageous for cognitive functioning. This form of bilingualism emerges when an L2 is added onto the native language instead of gradually replacing it. A form of bilingualism called "subtractive" is detrimental for cognitive functioning. In this form of bilingualism, due to social pressure and educational policy the use of the native language is discouraged and, consequently, it is gradually replaced by L2.

- So-called "metalinguistic" tasks appeal to the language user's ability to step back from the meaning-conveying function of language and to reflect on the structural aspects of linguistic expressions. Metalinguistic ability has been analyzed in two component abilities: analysis of representational structures and control of selective attention. It is hypothesized that bilinguals outperform monolinguals on metalinguistic tasks that appeal to the second of these abilities.

- The Simon task is a non-verbal perceptual-motor task that assesses the ability to inhibit or ignore irrelevant spatial information, a skill that requires cognitive control. Bilinguals of all age groups, excepting young adults, outperform matched monolinguals on this task, suggesting superior cognitive control in bilinguals. Furthermore, the adverse effects of aging on cognitive control are smaller in bilinguals than in monolinguals, suggesting that bilingualism attenuates the detrimental effect of aging on cognitive control. These results suggest that bilingualism boosts cognitive control. The absence of a bilingual advantage in young adults is probably due to the fact that at this age cognitive control is at its peak and cannot be boosted further by bilingualism.

- The finding that bilingualism brings along superior performance on non-verbal tasks requiring cognitive control suggests that language control in bilinguals exploits more general processes and mechanisms of cognitive control.
- Two forms of cognitive control can be distinguished: (1) The ability to direct attention selectively to specific information in conflict situations while inhibiting or ignoring misleading contextual information. (2) The ability to suppress habitual responses, in other words, to control impulses. Studies that compared monolingual and bilingual children and adults on tests tapping the first of these two types of ability suggest that it is boosted by bilingualism. Studies that compared monolingual and bilingual children on tasks tapping the second ability suggest that it is not affected by bilingualism. In addition, it has been shown that bilingual adults react to alerting signals in the environment more efficiently than monolingual adults.
- There are two ways in which the human control system may safeguard itself against outputting unintended responses: (1) It may directly deactivate memory nodes associated with non-target responses, thus making these responses less available. (2) It may boost the activation in the memory nodes that mediate the targeted responses. Through lateral inhibition along inhibitory connections between targeted and non-targeted memory nodes the activation level in the non-target nodes is then lowered, making the associated responses less available.
- Unlike bilinguals mastering two spoken languages ("unimodal" bilinguals), bilinguals who master one spoken and one sign language ("bimodal" bilinguals) are not better than monolinguals at non-verbal tasks requiring cognitive control. This suggests that the bilingual advantage manifested by unimodal bilinguals does not result from knowing two languages per se, but from the fact that these bilinguals are forced to always select one language in speech. This control requirement is less stringent in bimodal bilingualism because the distinct motor systems involved in signing and speaking allow simultaneous production in both modalities.

Bilingualism and the Brain

INTRODUCTION AND PREVIEW

In the previous chapters, the way bilinguals and multilinguals process language has been dealt with in detail and much has also been said about the type of knowledge structures that underlie bilingual language processing. But one important and topical research area has clearly been underexposed so far—the study of the brain structures that subserve bilingual and multilingual functioning. This neglect is remedied in this final chapter. The emergence of functional neuroimaging techniques in the last decade of the twentieth century boosted research in this field and the results of the pertinent studies have refined and extended the conclusions drawn from earlier neuropsychological and behavioral studies probing into the brain basis of bilingualism.

It is an established fact that the human brain's two hemispheres are not equally involved in language processing, but that in the vast majority of the human population the left cerebral hemisphere predominantly subserves linguistic behavior; in other words, language is "lateralized" in the left hemisphere in most people. This conclusion has primarily been based on studies that examined language processing in monolingual language users. (More precisely, these studies investigated native language processing in language users who were considered monolingual, while it was usually ignored that the language users in question might also have mastered one or more other languages to at least some degree.) Monolingual studies have also revealed the specific areas in the left hemisphere that play a role in language processing. In addition, they have shown that certain types of language processing—among others, the processing of indirect forms of language such as metaphors or irony—recruit areas in the right hemisphere.

Two questions have dominated—and continue to dominate—the study of the bilingual brain. The first is what parts of the brain are recruited when bilinguals process language and, specifically, whether these might differ from the regions involved in monolingual language processing. A substantial portion of the older studies addressing this question have focused on language lateralization in bilinguals, trying to find out whether language is left-lateralized to the same degree as it is in monolinguals or whether perhaps language is processed more bilaterally in bilinguals. The second main question posed in the study of the bilingual brain is what brain regions are involved in bilingual language control; that is, the bilingual's ability to maintain the use of one of his or her languages in circumstances where unilingual output is required and to switch between the languages if such is demanded by the circumstances.

In two separate sections, this chapter provides the results of studies that have addressed these questions: what are the language areas in the bilingual brain and what brain areas are specifically involved in bilingual control? To set the stage for presenting the bilingual work, the so-called "classical language areas" will first be introduced: the brain regions in the left hemisphere that about 150 years ago were first found to be involved in language processing. In this same section the various views on the functions these areas have in language processing will be presented and some attention given to the contribution of the right hemisphere to language processing.

As mentioned above, functional neuroimaging studies have contributed importantly to our current knowledge about the neural substrate of bilingualism. I will present the essence of the techniques used in these studies (and of a number of structural imaging techniques) in the methods part of the Methods and Nomenclature section. The common behavioral methods to examine language lateralization will also be presented in this part. The second (nomenclature) part of this section describes the conventions used in labeling brain areas. Without some basic knowledge of these conventions, grasping the core message in neuroimaging publications can be extremely challenging for the reader. In neuroimaging studies, in principle, the same tasks are used as all those employed in the behavioral studies on bilingualism that were reviewed in the preceding chapters, which renders a separate task section superfluous.

METHODS AND NOMENCLATURE

Methods

Knowledge about the way the brain represents and processes language is gathered in two main lines of study. The first concerns clinical neuropsychological studies on patients with language disorders resulting from brain damage caused by, for instance, a stroke, a brain tumor, trauma, or some degenerative brain disease. Deficits in language comprehension and/or production due to neurological damage are collectively known as aphasia. Since the pioneering work of Paul Broca (1824–1880) and Carl Wernicke (1848–1905) it is known that lesions in specific parts of the brain lead to specific language disorders, suggesting that specific parts of the brain subserve different aspects of linguistic functioning. Although one and a half centuries of aphasia research still has not settled the debate on the exact function of each of the various brain structures involved in language representation and processing, the brain areas identified by Broca and Wernicke as components of the language system feature in all contemporary views on the brain's language network (see further on).

In the era of Broca and Wernicke, the damaged brain area causing the language disorder could only be identified post mortem, during autopsy. Nowadays the afflicted area can be detected in vivo by means of a number of non-invasive brain-scanning techniques, collectively known as "structural imaging" techniques, with which the brain's anatomical structures can be revealed, intact and damaged. ("Non-invasive" means that the technique does not require that some substance, for instance some fluid or measuring device, is inserted in the body.) If a damaged structure is detected, the specific characteristics of the functional disorder then point to the functional role of this structure. One of these techniques is computed tomography (CT), an advanced application of the X-ray technique which reconstructs three-dimensional images of brain structures from the two-dimensional images produced by the conventional X-ray technique. CT exploits the fact that the amount of radiation absorbed by neural tissue varies with tissue density, with high-density tissue absorbing more radiation than low-density tissue. A second technique to reveal brain structures is magnetic resonance imaging (MRI), which exploits the magnetic properties of the elements in organic tissue by temporarily changing the orientation of certain atoms (e.g., hydrogen) by means of a strong magnetic field and then detecting the magnetic field that is generated when the atoms return to their original position. The specific characteristics of these magnetic fields vary with the density of the hydrogen atoms in the various brain tissues, thus enabling the detection of brain structures. The spatial resolution of MRI scans is far better than that of CT scans: MRI scans provide images of brain structures that are less than 1 mm apart, whereas brain structures must be about 5 mm apart for them to be discriminated on CT scans. MRI scans reveal the distinction between **gray matter** (regions of the nervous system that primarily contain the cell bodies) and **white matter** (areas of the nervous system that primarily contain axons; these axons are coated with **myelin**, a whitish substance). A third structural imaging technique, **diffusion tensor imaging**, uses an MRI scanner to provide images of white matter pathways in the brain. It measures the density and motion of water in the axons. (For more details about these techniques see Gazzaniga, Ivry, & Mangun, 2009, and Kolb & Whishaw, 2001, which provided the basis for the above summary of these neuroimaging techniques.)

Conclusions on the role of particular brain structures in linguistic functioning that are based on brain damage must be met with caution. The reason is that the disorder caused by the damaged structure does not unambiguously point at the structure's normal function. In terms of an analogy used by Gazzaniga et al. (2009, p. 148):

[. . .] allowing the spark plugs to decay or cutting the line distributing the gas to the pistons will cause an automobile to stop running, but this does not mean that spark plugs and distributors do the same thing; rather, their removal has similar functional consequences.

To illustrate the ambiguity with a specific language disorder, consider one of the characteristic symptoms of damage to Broca's area, a brain area located in the inferior part of the left frontal lobe (see p. 420). Damage to this area typically results in telegraphic speech: simple short sentences that lack inflections and words with syntactic functions such as articles, prepositions, pronouns, and auxiliaries. It is therefore tempting to conclude that Broca's area is the site of grammar. However, alternative accounts are possible, for instance that these symptoms are a manifestation of a working memory deficit while grammatical knowledge is intact (see pp. 421–422). To discover the functionality of the various parts of the brain involved in language representation and processing, studying the effects of brain lesions on language use must therefore be complemented with examinations of how the healthy brain processes language. This concerns the second main line of study referred to above: The measurement of brain activity while neurologically intact people perform language tasks. The measurement techniques in question, collectively known as "functional imaging" techniques, either detect the brain's electrical activity (or correlates thereof) or its metabolic activity while participants perform the task at hand (a language task or a task that taps into another cognitive domain). In addition to being used with neurologically intact people, these techniques can also be exploited in clinical populations to see how electrical or metabolic activity deviates from the patterns observed in healthy individuals.

Electrical and magnetic signals

One of the techniques that exploit the brain's electrical activity while it is busy performing some task concerns the registration of "event-related potentials" (ERPs). It makes use of the fact that the electrical activity of the brain is modulated by sensory, motor, and cognitive events. In the participants of these studies, an electroencephalogram (EEG) is registered that records the electrical activity of thousands or millions of neurons in the **cortex** by means of a number of recording electrodes placed over the scalp. A reference electrode is placed at some distance from these electrodes and the potential

FIGURE 8.1

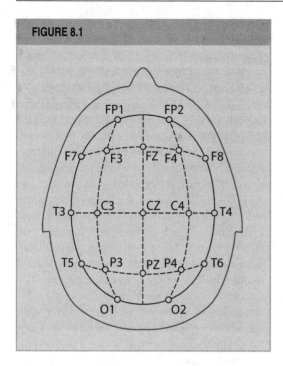

Electrode positions and names according to the 10-20 electrode system. F = frontal; T = temporal; P = parietal; O = occipital; C = central; FP = frontal pole; Z = 0/zero.

differences between the recording electrodes and the reference electrode are recorded. While the EEG is registered, once in a while a stimulus of a specific type is presented (the so-called "event"). This produces a small voltage change in the EEG signal, the ERP. The voltage change caused by a single trial is too small to be detected, but when a number of stimuli of the same type are presented, and the voltage changes caused by all of them are averaged, the voltage changes caused by the critical stimuli can be separated from the background noise and can be related to a specific cognitive process (such as syntactic or semantic analysis).

The electrode positions and names used in EEG/ERP registration are standardized. Figure 8.1 illustrates the original 10-20 international system (Jasper, 1958), which includes 19 electrodes.

All electrode names consist of one or more letters in combination with a number. Electrodes placed on the left part of the scalp, above the

left hemisphere, have odd numbers; those placed on the right part of the scalp have even numbers. Electrodes placed on the midline of the head are labeled with a Z (for 0/zero, to avoid confusion with the letter O). The letters F, P, T, and O refer to the four main parts of the cerebral hemispheres, called lobes, above which the electrodes are positioned: the **frontal, parietal, temporal, and occipital** lobe. The upper part of Figure 8.2a provides a "lateral" view of the four lobes of the *left* hemisphere, looking at them from the side of the brain, as illustrated in Figure 8.2b. The lower part of Figure 8.2a provides a "medial" view of the four lobes of the *right* hemisphere, looking at them from the middle of the brain, as illustrated in Figure 8.2b. The electrodes with the letters Fp are located above the "frontal pole", the most anterior area of the frontal lobe. The electrodes labeled with a C lie above the "central **sulcus**" or "central **fissure**", the cleft that divides the frontal and parietal lobes. (In addition to lateral and medial views of the brain, journal articles often present illustrations of the brain looking at it from above or below; these views are called "dorsal" and "ventral", respectively.) The "lateral sulcus", the cleft that divides the frontal and temporal lobes, is also called the "Sylvian fissure". As we shall see, areas on both sides of this sulcus (so called "perisylvian areas") are usually recruited during language processing.

The 19 electrodes in the original 10-20 standard system suffice to detect variations in the EEG pattern that are associated with different states of consciousness (such as an alert state, drowsiness, and deep sleep) and to detect deviations from these various normal states caused by congenital abnormalities or afflictions such as epilepsy. However, ERP research often requires a higher density of electrodes. Extensions of the 19 electrodes system, up to 256 electrodes, have therefore been developed in which additional electrodes are placed in between and beyond those in the original system and the electrodes in the original system are accordingly renumbered.

The ERP signal incited by a particular stimulus (the "event") and extracted from the

FIGURE 8.2

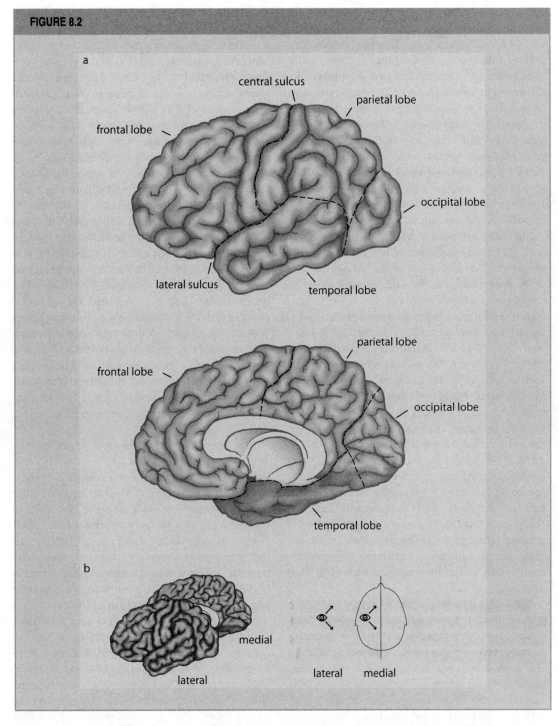

(a) The frontal, parietal, occipital, and temporal lobes of the cerebral cortex as seen from a lateral view of the left hemisphere (top) and from a medial view of the right hemisphere (bottom). (b) The terms "lateral" and "medial" explained.

EEG consists of a wave pattern of positive and negative peaks called "components" (see pp. 43 and 249 for illustrations). Different components reflect different cognitive processes and each component is characterized by a number of features. The first characteristic of a component is its polarity; that is, whether it concerns a positive or negative voltage change relative to the baseline. Positive and negative voltage changes are generally (not always), and counterintuitively, plotted downward and upward, respectively. The second of a component's characteristics is its latency, the time duration, expressed in milliseconds, between stimulus presentation and the moment the component reaches its peak voltage level. The third characteristic is the component's amplitude; that is, the size of the voltage change at its maximum. Finally, the topography of a component, often visualized in a so-called topographical map, refers to where on the skull's surface (at what electrode positions) the associated electrical activity is detected. If two different stimulus types (e.g., nouns versus function words such as articles or prepositions) show different topographical maps, this suggests that the two stimulus types are processed by different neural systems. However, the exact structures involved are not revealed by the associated topographical maps. The reason is that electric signals are distorted during the trajectory from their neural source to the scalp through the brain tissue in between the two. ERP components can be "exogenous" or "endogenous". Exogenous components reflect physical features of the stimulus such as its intensity, whereas endogenous components index the cognitive effects of the stimulus.

ERP components are often named after their polarity and latency so, for instance, the P600 is a component with a positive polarity that typically peaks at 600 ms after the onset of the stimulus. It is evoked by a number of syntactic anomalies such as a violation of grammatical number agreement between a sentence's subject and verb (e.g., Hagoort, Brown, & Groothusen, 1993; Osterhout & Holcomb, 1992) and by syntactic ambiguities (e.g., Kotz, Holcomb, & Osterhout, 2008). In contrast, the N400 is a component with a negative polarity that typically peaks at 400 ms after stimulus onset. It is evoked by every content word in a sentence, is generally thought to index semantic processing, and is modulated by various factors such as how well the word fits the context semantically and its frequency of occurrence (Kutas & Hillyard, 1980). The latency of a particular component can vary as a function of factors such as the age of the participants and their level of expertise in the domain tapped by the experimental task. In other words, the latency part of a particular component's name (e.g., 400) is not a perfectly reliable marker of the time it takes the cognitive process underlying this component to develop. An alternative to naming components after their polarity and latency is to use names that refer to the cognitive functions the components are assumed to index. For instance, the P600 is also called the syntactic positive shift (SPS) because it is assumed to reflect syntactic processing. A drawback of this naming convention is that the initial hypothesis regarding the component's function may eventually turn out to be incorrect, or that the component is not only aroused by the cognitive operation suggested by its name but by other cognitive processes as well.

The specific combination of values on the above-mentioned four features that typify individual ERP components provides information on the nature, strength, and development of the cognitive operations that underlie the various components. For instance, if two of an ERP signal's components differ in polarity and topography, this suggests that the two components are generated by qualitatively different cognitive processes (e.g., syntactic vs. semantic analysis) that are subserved by different neural networks. A component's latency and amplitude indicate how the underlying cognitive process develops over time and to what extent it is implicated, respectively (Hagoort & Ramsey, 2004; Hahne & Friederici, 2001). As compared with behavioral measures (such as registering the time it takes participants to produce a particular vocal or manual response to a stimulus), an advantage of the ERP methodology is that components show up in the signal without participants having to respond overtly to the stimulus. The participants' task may, for instance, simply be to listen to sentences. Not requesting an overt response guarantees that the ERP signal is not contaminated by any contribution of such a response to the signal and provides a relatively pure marker of the underlying cognitive process of interest. A further advantage of the ERP methodology is its high temporal resolution, which means that the cognitive process of interest leaves its mark on the signal within milliseconds after its onset. In this respect the ERP technique compares favorably with techniques that measure the brain's metabolic activity during cognitive processing (see below). A specific disadvantage of the ERP technique has already been mentioned, namely that the signal that it produces has a low spatial resolution. This means that the electrical activity detected at the scalp does not provide reliable information about the exact location of the signal's neural source, the brain structure that causes it. As we will see below, in this respect the common techniques to detect the brain's metabolic activity are superior to ERP measurement, but also **magneto-encephalography (MEG)** fares better than ERP measurement in source localization.

MEG is related to EEG/ERP but it measures the magnetic correlate of the electrical activity in the neurons upon the presentation of a critical stimulus (again called the "event"). It was mentioned above that in ERP research a voltage change caused by a single trial is too small to be detected but that averaging over a number of trials of the same type reveals a voltage change that can be related to a cognitive process. Similarly, in MEG studies the magnetic field aroused by an individual stimulus is too small to be observed, but averaging over a series of similar trials produces a measurable event-related magnetic field. The magnetic activity is registered by means of tens to hundreds of sensors in a helmet-like MEG scanner that surrounds the participant's head. The temporal resolution of the MEG signal is as good as that of the ERP signal and, in comparison to ERP measurement, MEG has the advantage that it is relatively easy to localize the signal's neural source. This advantage is due to the fact that, unlike electric signals, magnetic signals are not distorted on their way from a deeper neural source through more superficially located brain tissue to the scalp (Gazzaniga et al., 2009). However, a disadvantage is that MEG can only detect the neural activity flowing parallel to the skull's surface whereas EEG can also detect neural activity flowing at a right-angle to the skull (e.g., Hagoort & Ramsey, 2004). Because in the sulci of the brain in particular the activity flows parallel to the surface of the skull, it is especially the activation flow in the sulci that is detected by means of MEG.

Hemodynamic signals

Whereas EEG and MEG measure neural activity directly, the remaining functional imaging techniques to introduce here, **positron emission tomography (PET)** and **functional magnetic resonance imaging (fMRI)**, do so indirectly by inferring neural activity in a specific brain region from the increased blood supply to that region when it is involved in some cognitive task. The increased blood supply provides active neurons with the additional energy, in the form of oxygen and glucose, that they need to do their specialized work. The medical term for the dynamic regulation of the blood flow in the brain is "hemodynamics" and the change in blood flow related to neural activity is called the "hemodynamic response"; hence the name of the signals produced by these techniques: "hemodynamic signals".

To produce a PET image of the parts of the brain that are active while a specific task is being performed, a small amount of water labeled with a radioactive element (an "isotope") is injected into the bloodstream while the participant is engaged in the task. In cognitive activation studies most often a radioactive form of oxygen, oxygen-15, is used, which subsequently accumulates in different brain areas in direct proportion to the amount of blood supply to those areas. The nuclei of oxygen-15 isotopes are unstable and emit a positron from their nucleus during decay. This positron collides with an electron in the blood. During this collision the mass of positron and electron is converted into two photons that move in opposite directions and are simultaneously detected by two of the photon detectors that encircle the participant's head and that together constitute the PET camera. The simultaneous detections are counted and the total count during 1 minute following the injection is converted into an image of the blood flow in the brain: The larger the simultaneous photons count, the more collisions between positron and electron in the blood must have taken place and, hence, the more blood there must have been in the region where the collisions took place. This, in turn, provides an indirect measure of neural activity in that region. The measure in which the results of PET studies are usually expressed is the so-called "regional cerebral blood flow" (rCBF); that is, the distribution of the blood supply in the brain. Because it takes relatively long—around 60 seconds—to get a clear image of the increase in rCBF as a consequence of increased neural activity, as compared with the ERP method described above, the temporal resolution of PET is rather poor. Its spatial resolution is relatively good however, revealing active brain regions of a volume of 5–10 mm^3.

PET studies typically compare changes in metabolic activity in specific brain areas in at least two conditions: an experimental condition and some control or baseline condition. The control condition can be a resting state in which the participants do not have to perform any task, or it may involve a task that differs from the experimental task in one or more critical respects. For example, in a bilingual study the comparison might be between picture naming in L1 (the control condition) and L2 (the experimental condition) or between word naming in L1 (control) and translating L1 words into L2 (experimental). Ideally, the control and experimental conditions only differ from one another in the specific cognitive component that is being examined. The blood supply to a specific region measured in the control condition—as inferred from the photon count based on positron–electron collisions taking place in that region—is then subtracted

from the blood supply to the same region in the experimental condition. A statistically significant difference in blood supply to one or more regions in the two conditions indicates that these brain regions are recruited by the cognitive component under study.

Just as PET, fMRI makes use of the fact that active parts of the brain are supplied with more blood than inactive parts, but whereas PET requires the injection of radioactive elements into the bloodstream, fMRI is non-invasive. It exploits the physical properties of elements that occur naturally in blood, specifically the magnetic properties of iron-holding hemoglobin in the blood cells, and makes use of the MRI scanners that are also used for structural MRI (see above). Hemoglobin transports oxygen through the blood. The oxygen is absorbed by active brain areas and as a consequence the hemoglobin becomes deoxygenated. Deoxygenated hemoglobin has so-called "paramagnetic" properties and can be detected by the fMRI equipment. More precisely, the equipment measures the ratio between oxygenated and deoxygenated hemoglobin. This ratio is called the BOLD signal (for "blood oxygenation level dependent"). Even though active areas consume extra oxygen, this ratio is higher, not lower, in brain areas with increased neuronal activity. In other words, the proportion of oxygenated hemoglobin is relatively large in active brain tissue even though active tissue absorbs a relatively large amount of oxygen. This phenomenon—paradoxical at first sight—is explained by assuming that the absorption of oxygen by active cells results in an immediate increase of blood flow to that part of the brain, so much so that not all of the additionally supplied oxygen can be absorbed, and a local surplus of oxygen is created. Like PET studies, fMRI studies typically compare brain activity in an experimental condition and some well-chosen control condition that is assumed to involve the same cognitive processing components as the experimental task except for the one critical cognitive component being examined. The subtraction procedure subsequently reveals the brain area(s) recruited by this component.

A clear advantage of fMRI as compared with PET is that the fMRI method's non-invasive character permits more trials per participant than PET, where the fact that radioactive material has to be injected causes a constraint on the number of data points that can be collected from an individual participant. This allows for more advanced experimental designs with fMRI (see e.g., Gazzaniga et al., 2009, and Hagoort & Ramsey, 2004, for details). Furthermore, the spatial resolution of fMRI scans is better than that of PET scans, revealing structures of 3 mm³ in volume. In comparison to EEG/ERP and MEG, the temporal resolution of fMRI is poor, but better than of PET, taking a couple of seconds. Finally, for an image to be created by means of PET, a participant must perform a particular task for at least 40 seconds, and most fMRI studies employ a design in which the task is performed during 20 to 30 seconds and the fMRI signal is summed over this time duration. However, with fMRI it is also possible to measure the BOLD signal time-locked to a single stimulus, a method that is known as "event-related fMRI". Just as in ERP studies, averaging over a number of repetitions of the stimulus produces a measurable signal.

Further methods

In the introduction to this chapter I mentioned that, in the vast majority of monolingual language users, the left hemisphere plays a predominant role in language processing; that is, language is lateralized to the left hemisphere. In addition I introduced the idea that hemispheric lateralization in bilinguals, for one or both languages, is less pronounced than in monolinguals—in other words, that language is more bilaterally localized in bilinguals. Since its emergence around 1990, functional neuroimaging has become an increasingly popular method to test this idea. Different language lateralization in monolinguals and bilinguals would show from different distributions of neural activity in the two hemispheres when participants from these two populations perform one and the same language task. The possibility of differential

language lateralization in monolinguals and bilinguals has also been investigated, and continues to be, by means of older methods. The oldest one is the post mortem study of the site of brain lesions in bilingual aphasic patients. If language lateralization differs between monolinguals and bilinguals, the lesion site should differ between monolingual and bilingual aphasic patients. For instance, if the specific form the monolingual–bilingual lateralization difference takes is that both languages of a bilingual are more often subserved by the right hemisphere in bilinguals than in monolinguals (see pp. 429–432 for a number of different views on how language lateralization might differ between monolinguals and bilinguals), the incidence of so-called "crossed aphasia"—aphasia following a lesion in the right instead of the left hemisphere—should be larger in bilinguals than in monolinguals.

In addition to the lesion paradigm and the recent neuroimaging techniques, three non-invasive behavioral techniques to examine cerebral lateralization of language (and other cognitive functions) exist that emerged around 1970: the "dichotic listening paradigm", the "tachistoscopic viewing paradigm", and the "verbal–manual interference paradigm". In the dichotic listening paradigm two different auditory inputs, each for instance consisting of a series of words, are presented simultaneously, one to the left ear, the other to the right ear. The stimuli presented to the right ear are predominantly processed by the left hemisphere and those presented to the left ear are predominantly processed by the right hemisphere. Immediately after stimulus presentation the participants have to recall as many as possible of the items presented to both ears. Left hemisphere specialization or dominance for language processing would show from better recall performance for the stimuli presented to the right ear than for those presented to the left ear.

In the tachistoscopic viewing paradigm visual stimuli such as written words are very briefly and randomly presented in the left or right visual field while participants fixate their eyes on a fixation point in the center of the field. This manner of stimulus presentation can nowadays be pro-grammed on a computer, but because these were not widely available when this paradigm was first developed a piece of equipment called a "tachistoscope" was used for this purpose, hence the paradigm's name (the word *tachistoscope* derives from the Greek words for *rapid* and *vision*). The visual information presented in the right visual field is sent directly to the left hemisphere, whereas the information presented in the left visual field is sent to the right hemi-sphere. The degree of involvement of each hemi-sphere in language processing is inferred from the recognition score (and recognition speed) for the words presented to the one or the other visual half-field. Left hemisphere dominance for language would show from higher recognition scores for items presented in the right visual field than for items presented in the left visual field.

Finally, the verbal–manual interference paradigm exploits the fact that in most people the left hemisphere not only dominates language use but also controls the dominant right hand. In experiments that implement this paradigm, participants are first asked to tap a key as rapidly as possible with one of their index fingers for some length of time and then to do this with the other index finger. The tapping rate for each index finger is measured. Following this control condi-tion the participants perform the finger-tapping task once again but this time they concurrently have to perform some verbal task. If language primarily resides in the left hemisphere, finger tapping with the right index finger, controlled by the left hemisphere, should exhibit strong inter-ference from the concurrent verbal task and the tapping rate should be lower than in the control condition. Although interference from the con-current verbal task will also emerge when tapping is done with the left index finger (performance under dual-task conditions is generally poorer than when the participants can concentrate on a single task), the interference effect (the difference between the tapping rates in the control and experimental conditions) should be largest in the right-finger tapping condition. The size of the interference effect in the right-index-finger- and

left-index-finger tapping conditions thus provides a measure of the degree of cerebral asymmetry of language.

All three paradigms can be used to test the hypothesis that language lateralization differs between monolinguals and bilinguals by simply comparing the performance of monolinguals and bilinguals in an experiment that implements one of these paradigms. In addition, all three paradigms provide information on the precise nature of the lateralization difference. For instance, if language is less lateralized in bilinguals than in monolinguals (that is, the two hemispheres are more evenly involved in lan-guage processing in bilinguals), the size difference between the interference effects in the right and left tapping conditions should be smaller in bilinguals than in monolinguals. In contrast, if the cerebral lateralization of language is as asymmetric in bilinguals as in monolinguals but it is the right rather than the left hemisphere that dominates language processing in bilinguals, the interference caused by a concurrent verbal task on the rate of finger tapping should be largest when the tapping must be done with the left index finger. Yet further possibilities (e.g., left lateralization for the L1 and right lateralization for the L2) can also be inferred from the pattern of interference effects to emerge. A limitation of all three techniques is that, unlike the neuro-imaging techniques, they do not provide any information on the exact locus of processing within a hemisphere.

Just as the various functional neuroimaging techniques, the above three behavioral paradigms to localize language (and other cognitive func-tions) in the brain can be used, and in fact are predominantly used, with healthy participants. A couple of further techniques are invasive and are sometimes applied to neurologically damaged patients prior to neurosurgery. One of them is direct electrical stimulation of the brain. It was developed in the 1940s by the Canadian neuro-surgeon Wilder Penfield and has been used since during neurosurgical operations to precisely demarcate the cortical areas that subserve specific cognitive functions. This way decisions can be made concerning the best way to perform the surgery, thus reducing the risk of negative side effects. The technique involves the application of a weak electrical current to the brain of the conscious patient by means of a bipolar electrode. This causes a transient inhibition of the function subserved by the stimulated brain region. While the current is applied, the patient must perform some cognitive task, for instance provide the names of depicted objects. If task performance fails during electrical stimulation but is unhampered otherwise it can be concluded that the stimulated brain area is normally involved in the cognitive function tapped by the task. By applying currents systematically to neighboring areas, the borders of the area subserving the function can be charted. Ojemann and his colleagues (e.g., Calvin & Ojemann, 1994; Ojemann & Whitaker, 1978) have employed electrical stimulation to locate the brain tissue involved in language processing in both monolinguals and bilinguals (see Fabbro, 1999, for a more detailed description of the technique).

A second technique used with patients is the Wada test, named after Juhn Wada, who first used it around 1960 to determine which hemisphere was dominant for language in patients who were about to undergo neurosurgery. The barbiturate amobarbital is injected to one hemisphere via an artery (the carotid artery) that leads into this hemisphere. This causes a temporary anesthesia of this hemisphere which lasts several minutes, and a language test is administered within this period to determine the role of this hemisphere in language processing. Some time later the procedure is repeated, now injecting the artery that leads into the other hemisphere. Comparing the performance of the patient on the language test in the two conditions reveals which of the two hemispheres is dominant for language.

Functional specialization of the two hemispheres can also be examined on "split-brain" patients. These patients have undergone surgery in which a large part of the corpus callosum, a white matter tract that connects the two hemispheres with one another and that consists of hundreds of millions of axons, is cut through to relieve the symptoms of epilepsy. As a result of disconnecting the two hemispheres in this way, the communication between the two hemispheres is impaired. Differential involvement of the two hemispheres in language processing can then be examined by presenting language materials, for instance words or sentences, in either the left visual field or the right visual field and asking the patient to perform certain language tasks (e.g., provide the meanings of the words). The technique can obviously be applied with both monolinguals and bilinguals who have undergone this type of surgery, but given the low incidence of split-brain patients the chances are small that sufficiently large numbers of matched monolingual and bilingual patients will be found to inform the differential lateralization debate.

Finally, transcranial magnetic stimulation (TMS) is a non-invasive technique that creates transient virtual brain lesions by briefly disrupting neural processing. It involves the generation of a strong electrical current in a device held by the researcher against the participant's head. This current generates a magnetic field, which passes through the skin and skull and causes the neurons in the underlying brain region to fire. By stimulating the neurons in this way, their normal activity is disrupted briefly, as indicated from performance failures on tasks that tap into the cognitive function subserved by the stimulated region. The method was originally developed for clinical purposes but can be used with neurologically intact people as well. A recent report on two bilinguals who received a TMS treatment for major depression (Holzheimer, Fawaz, Wilson, & Avery, 2005) provided a first indication that the technique might be useful for examining language processing in bilinguals.

Nomenclature

In publications on cognitive neuroscience the various regions of the cerebral cortex are labeled according to three conventions. The first concerns a labeling of the main divisions of the cerebral hemispheres formed by the brain's main gyri and sulci. Figure 8.2a above illustrated this convention, except that the complete nomenclature makes more fine-grained divisions than in terms

FIGURE 8.3

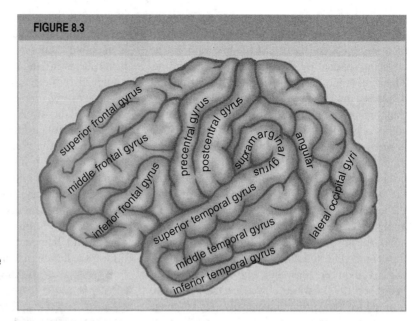

The main gyri and sulci of the cerebral cortex as seen from a lateral view of the left hemisphere.

of just the four main lobes and the main sulci shown there. These subdivisions are shown in Figure 8.3, which provides a lateral view of the left hemisphere.

To extend the degree of precision in indicating specific brain areas, conventional names are used for the top, bottom, front, and back of the brain as a whole and of its anatomical subregions. The top part is referred to as either "superior" or "dorsal"; the bottom part is called "inferior" or "ventral"; the front is labeled "anterior" or "rostral"; the back is named "posterior" or "caudal". This convention is illustrated in Figure 8.4a for the cerebral cortex as a whole and in Figure 8.4b for the left temporal lobe. Notice that, as a consequence of this convention, the orientation of different subregions indicated by the same name, say, superior, may differ (cf. the orientation of the area called superior in Figures 8.4a and 8.4b). According to this naming convention, a specific brain area might thus be referred to as the "left posterior (or "caudal") middle frontal gyrus" and another might be called the "anterior (or "rostral") left middle temporal gyrus". Alternatively, acronyms of the full names are used, such as LIFG for "left inferior frontal gyrus" or STG for "superior temporal gyrus". It is important to realize that in these designations

"left" and "right" refer to the left and right hemispheres, not to the left or right part of a specific region in either the left or right hemisphere.

The second way of labeling specific brain areas is according to the so-called "cytoarchitectonics" of the brain; that is, in terms of the micro-anatomy of the different cell types and their organization and distribution in the brain. The person best known for this approach is Korbinian Brodmann, who about a century ago (in 1909) subdivided the cerebral cortex into 52 areas based on minute microscopic examination of the cell structures in the cortex. Up to this day the numbering system introduced by Brodmann is used widely in neuroscience and the pertinent publications refer to the areas that he distinguished by means of numbered "Brodmann areas" (BAs). Figure 8.5a shows Brodmann areas on a lateral view of the left hemisphere. Other Brodmann areas are located inside the brain; these are shown in Figure 8.5b on a medial view of the right hemisphere. According to this naming convention, Broca's area (in the left inferior frontal gyrus) would be indicated by BAs 44 and 45, and a second area well known for its involvement in language processing, Wernicke's area (in the left superior temporal gyrus) would be referred to as BA 22. Most

FIGURE 8.4

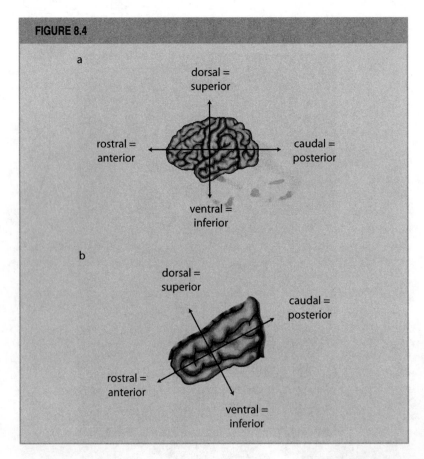

Conventional names for the top, bottom, front, and back of the cerebral cortex as a whole and of its subregions, as illustrated on a lateral view of (a) the left hemisphere and (b) the left temporal lobe.

Brodmann areas occur symmetrically in both hemispheres.

Finally, the third convention is to refer to brain areas according to their function. For instance, the "motor cortex" (BA 4, on the anterior side of the central sulcus) is recruited during the execution of movements, the "somatosensory cortex" (BAs 1, 2, and 3, posterior to the central sulcus) represents sensory information such as smells and touch, and the "primary visual cortex" (BA 17, in the medial posterior part of the occipital lobe) processes visual information. When the convention was described above to name ERP components after their function it was mentioned that it involves the risk that the initial hypothesis regarding the component's function may later turn out to be wrong. Labeling brain areas according to the function they are thought to serve involves the same risk. For instance, because damage to Broca's area is often corre-lated with speech devoid of syntax, one might consider calling it the "syntax cortex", but as already alluded to above, the syntactic problems exhibited by most people with Broca's aphasia may have a different cause than corrupted syntactic knowledge, such as a shortage of computational resources (e.g., Kolk & Heeschen, 1990) or a general problem of unifying smaller linguistic entities into larger wholes (Hagoort, 2005). A further comment on labeling brain areas by their function is that many brain functions are subserved by networks consisting of different non-neighboring brain regions. The consequence would be that the chosen name should be assigned to each of these regions.

A couple of further technical terms help to grasp the essence of neuroimaging publications. These publications often illustrate where neural activity is located on brain slices that cut up the brain according to three different orientations:

FIGURE 8.5

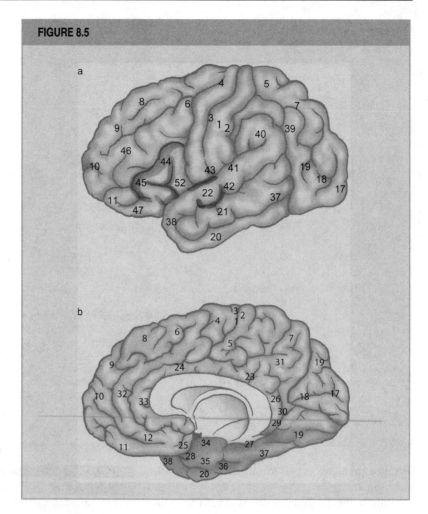

Brodmann areas as seen from (a) a lateral view of the left hemisphere and (b) a medial view of the right hemisphere.

"coronal", "sagittal", and "axial". These are illustrated in Figure 8.6. Axial orientations are also known as "transversal" or "horizontal". Two further terms that one encounters in these publications are "voxels" and "regions of interest" (ROIs). Voxels are cube-shaped elements in which brain signals are recorded. ROIs are the brain regions the researcher focuses on in the data analyses, and usually cover many voxels. They are chosen on the basis of established knowledge and informed hypotheses about the brain regions that might be involved when the participants perform the specific experimental task being used. For instance, in studies on language processing the selected ROIs will typically include Broca's area and Wernicke's area.

LANGUAGE AREAS IN THE BRAIN AND THEIR FUNCTION

The classical language areas: Broca's area, Wernicke's area, and their connection

As already mentioned, from post mortem investigations of the brains of aphasic patients it has long been known that there are at least two areas in the left hemisphere that are recruited during language use. Broca (1861) described a patient who was completely unable to speak while his comprehension was relatively good. Post mortem examination of this patient's brain showed that

FIGURE 8.6

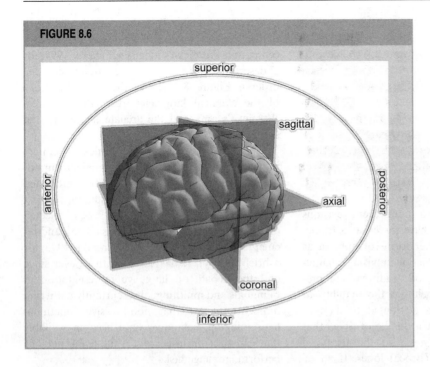

Conventional names for the three types of cut-through sections of the brain used in neuroimaging studies.

he had a lesion in the middle posterior part of the inferior frontal gyrus in the left hemisphere (BAs 44 and 45). About a decade later Wernicke (1874) reported on a patient who exhibited the opposite behavioral pattern, demonstrating poor understanding of spoken language while at the same time producing fluent but unintelligible speech. An autopsy on this patient's brain showed a lesion in the left superior temporal gyrus (BA 22). The brain's language areas identified in these pioneering studies are now called Broca's area and Wernicke's area and, together with the "arcuate fasciculus" (see below), they are often called the classical language areas. About another decade later, Lichtheim (1885) developed a functional model of language that encompassed three language centers in the brain, two of them being Broca's area and Wernicke's area. According to this model, Broca's area stores the motor representations of words and Wernicke's area represents the auditory forms of words (that is, their phonological representations). The third language center, the "concept center", was thought to store conceptual representations. In the model the auditory and motor areas were connected directly as well as indirectly via the concept center.

Lichtheim's model has been extremely influential in aphasia research for over a century, serving as a productive framework for advancing hypotheses on various forms of aphasia. Damage to Broca's area was thought to lead to a pattern of symptoms that are now collectively known as "Broca's aphasia". Consistent with Lichtheim's hypothesis that Broca's area stores the motor representations of words, the speech of patients with lesions in this area is very effortful, non-fluent, and poorly articulated. A further characteristic of the speech of these patients is that the sentences they utter are telegraphic and "agrammatic"; that is, they are simple and short and devoid of grammatical markers and function words. Because Lichtheim's model deals with the storage of various types of *word* knowledge, not syntax, it cannot readily account for this particular symptom of Broca's aphasia. A final salient characteristic of the linguistic behavior of Broca's aphasic patients is that their comprehension is relatively good, just as it was in Broca's original patient, although they typically run into comprehension problems when the sentences to process are grammatically complex. The general hypothesis that emerged from this behavioral pattern was that Broca's area supports speech production. In contrast, "Wernicke's aphasia", caused by damage to Wernicke's area, is characterized by the opposite behavioral pattern: As already noticed by Wernicke, damage to this area results in fluent but nonsensical speech accompanied by severe comprehension problems. This led to the hypothesis that Wernicke's area is the site of speech comprehension.

Lichtheim's model and more recent revisions of it (Geschwind, 1970) have served as a framework to account for other forms of aphasia as well. For instance, "conduction aphasia", characterized by relatively good auditory comprehension and fluent speech but the inability to repeat speech, has been attributed to damage to the arcuate fasciculus, a bundle of fibers that connects the language areas in the temporal (Wernicke) and frontal (Broca) lobes. If all of these areas are damaged, "global aphasia" emerges, characterized by overall poor linguistic performance. Other forms of aphasia that have been explained in terms of the model are "transcortical motor aphasia" and "transcortical sensory aphasia". The former has been attributed to damage to the brain structures between the concept center and Broca's area; the latter to damage to brain structures between the concept center and Wernicke's area (see Fabbro, 1999, for a description of the associated functional disorders). Figure 8.7 shows the brain locations of the classical language areas: Broca's area, Wernicke's area and the arcuate fasciculus that connects them.

In between Broca's and Wernicke's seminal publications, the idea that a bilingual's or multilingual's multiple languages might be represented in different brain areas was suggested for the first time (Scoresby-Jackson, 1867), was rejected about three decades later by Pitres (1895), and re-emerged again in the 1970s (see Paradis, 1995, for a brief history). It has stayed with us ever since and the debate on language representation in bilinguals and multilinguals is currently gathering momentum now that non-invasive functional neuroimaging techniques have become available that can spot brain activity while living persons perform language tasks.

Functional equivocality of the classical language areas

The view that Broca's and Wernicke's areas subserve speech production and comprehension, respectively, is no longer widely accepted because

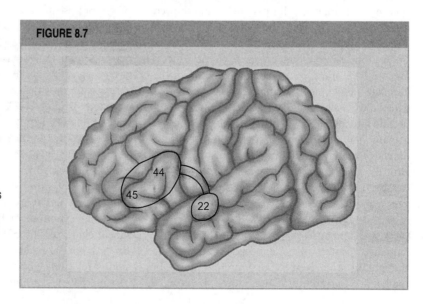

FIGURE 8.7

The classical language areas in the brain: Broca's area (BAs 44 and 45), Wernicke's (BA 22), and the arcuate fasciculus, the connection between Broca's and Wernicke's areas.

a substantial amount of evidence against this division of labor between these two brain areas has accumulated during the past decades. This counterevidence comes from both lesion studies and, since around 1990, increasingly from neuro-imaging studies in which language processing in neurologically healthy people is examined. In a review of the latter type of studies, both PET and fMRI, Stowe, Haverkort, and Zwarts (2005) concluded that it is beyond any doubt that the left inferior frontal gyrus (encompassing Broca's area) and the superior temporal gyrus (encompassing Wernicke's area) are indeed essential for language use but that the hypothesis that the former subserves language production and the latter language comprehension is not supported by the evidence. The production/comprehension model predicts that tasks that only involve comprehension and tasks that only involve production selectively activate Wernicke's area and Broca's area, respectively. Yet many of the studies that employed either comprehension or production tasks showed activation in both areas. This result emerged both from studies that examined the processing of single words and from those investigating sentence processing. The authors therefore concluded that Broca's and Wernicke's areas contribute in some way to both comprehension and production (Stowe et al., 2005).

A second view on the different functional roles of Broca's area and Wernicke's area, which became popular around 1970, is that the former is the site of syntactic knowledge, supporting syntactic processing in both production and comprehension, whereas the latter stores word meanings and subserves lexical semantic processing. Consistent with this view is the finding that the speech of people with Broca's aphasia is characterized by a lack of grammar. It also agrees with the observation that many of these patients cannot fully grasp the meanings of sentences if full understanding cannot be solely based on the meanings of the constituent words combined with general world knowledge but requires grammatical analysis as well (e.g., Caramazza & Zurif, 1976). However, the neuroimaging data reviewed by Stowe et al. (2005) also cast doubt on

the validity of this hypothesis. On the one hand, studies manipulating the semantics of the presented stimulus materials have shown that these manipulations not only influence the activation in Wernicke's area but also in Broca's area and, on the other hand, stimulus materials that obviously require syntactic analysis do not always activate Broca's area. A further review of neuroimaging studies that searched for the neural substrate of syntax in the normal population (Kaan & Swaab, 2002) similarly led to the conclusion that Broca's area is not always involved in syntactic processing and, conversely, that many parts of the temporal lobe, including Wernicke's area, also support syntactic processing.

A number of lesion studies also provide evidence against the idea that Broca's area is the site of syntax. It has for instance been shown that patients performing poorly on tests of mopho-syntax shared damage to Wernicke's area but not to Broca's area, while some patients with a lesion in Broca's area did not show severe problems with morpho-syntax (Dronkers, Wilkins, Van Valin, Redfern, & Jaeger, 1994). Furthermore, patients with lesions in Broca's area who exhibit agrammatic symptoms do not *consistently* do so under all circumstances but especially under computationally taxing circumstances (Haarman & Kolk, 1994). The dependency of agrammatic symptoms on computational load suggests that Broca's area is not the site where grammatical knowledge is stored, because if it were, the linguistic expressions of the afflicted persons should *invariably* be agrammatic, irrespective of the current computational demands. All in all it appears that the view that Broca's and Wernicke's areas subserve syntactic and semantic processing, respectively, does not fare any better in accounting for the evidence than the view that they support speech production and comprehension, respectively.

Stowe et al. (2005) discussed a third view on the function of Broca's area, one that is consistent with the variability of agrammatical performance in patients with lesions in this area. It holds that Broca's area supports some type of computation on knowledge units retrieved from knowledge stores elsewhere in the brain and that it maintains these knowledge units for the duration of the computation. In other words, according to this view, Broca's area is a working memory system that temporarily stores and processes information, be it syntactic or of any other type, linguistic or non-linguistic. A specific version of this view is advanced by Hagoort (2005), who approached the question of which brain areas are committed to language from a different perspective than is mostly adopted. He started out by noting that researchers generally address this question from an experimental-task perspective, trying to find out what brain areas are involved during the execution of specific language tasks (e.g., verb generation, picture naming, word reading). To be able to make better sense of the steadily increasing body of data gathered in neuroimaging studies, he then proposed a "design perspective" instead; that is, an approach that starts out by charting the various cognitive components that enable language use, both comprehension and production. After these components have been identified, hypotheses are put forward about the brain regions that subserve them.

Adopting this approach, Hagoort (2005) hypothesized the existence of three such components, which he called "memory", "unification", and "control", and that together he referred to as the MUC framework. In his terminology, "memory" refers to long-term memory information, specifically information in the mental lexicon. Importantly, Hagoort adheres to the view that the mental lexicon not only contains information on the phonological, phonetic, syntactic, and conceptual properties of words, but also so-called "structural frames" that enable grammatical analysis of sentences. This is in line with a class of linguistic theories, called "lexicalist", that no longer assume a distinction between lexical items on the one hand and syntactic rules on the other hand (e.g., Jackendoff, 2002; Vosse & Kempen, 2000). Instead, all grammatical information, including the knowledge that enables syntactic parsing, is assumed to be stored in the mental lexicon. In addition to storing information, the memory component is thought to be involved in retrieving it. Hagoort

uses the term "unification" to refer to the process of integrating the information retrieved from the lexicon, be it syntactic, semantic, or phonological information, into a representation of multiword expressions. Finally, the control component sees to it that the language system operates in agreement with the current communicative circumstances and the goals of the interlocutors. For instance, it enables a bilingual (or bi-dialectal) speaker in unilingual settings to produce output in the selected language (or dialect) or to switch languages in translation settings and a monolingual speaker to select the contextually appropriate register (e.g., formal or casual; child directed speech, "motherese", or adult directed speech). In short, according to Hagoort's design perspective, linguistic behavior involves a specific type of computation on specific types of linguistic knowledge structures with a specific goal in mind.

Assuming that the language system indeed consists of these three functional components, what are the brain areas that subserve them? On the basis of a review of the neuroimaging literature, Hagoort (2005) pointed to the left inferior frontal gyrus (including Broca's area, BAs 44 and 45, but also covering BA 47) as the unification site and localized the memory function in a large region in the left temporal lobe (including Wernicke's area, BA 22, in the superior temporal gyrus but also covering more anterior and inferior regions: BA 38, also called the "temporal pole", and BA 21 in the middle temporal gyrus). Interestingly, different subregions within the left inferior frontal gyrus appear to be specialized for unification of different types of information: phonological, syntactic, and semantic (see e.g., Stowe et al., 2005, and Paulesu et al., 1997). Finally, Hagoort localized the control function in a network in the frontal lobe containing the anterior cingulate cortex (ACC; BA 24 and BA 32) and the dorsolateral prefrontal cortex (DLPFC, BA 46 and BA 9). Later on (pp. 435–437). I will provide more details on these two regions, which are generally assumed to be involved in executive control and to be domain independent (that is, not specific for language). They also appear to play a crucial role

FIGURE 8.8

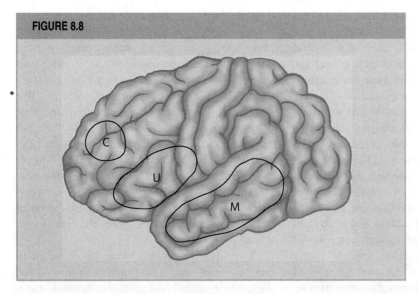

The brain regions assumed to subserve the memory (M), unification (U), and control (C) components in Hagoort's (2005) MUC model of language use.

in bilingual language control; that is, the ability of a bilingual to produce unilingual output whenever such is required, mixed language output under circumstances where language mixing is common and natural and does not hamper communication, and to translate between the two languages whenever the bilingual speaker wishes to do so.

With the exception of the ACC, the brain's language-processing regions that are assumed in the MUC model are indicated in Figure 8.8, which shows a lateral view of the left hemisphere (the ACC lies within the brain and can be seen in Figure 8.9, p. 437). These regions coincide with language regions revealed in three further recent reviews of the neuroimaging literature on language processing (Démonet, Thierry, & Cardebat, 2005; Indefrey & Levelt, 2004, which specifically focuses on the neural substrate of speech production; Stowe et al., 2005), so there can be no doubt that they are all crucial for language processing. Depending on the exact characteristics of the task and stimulus materials used in a specific study (e.g., auditory or visual, recognition/ comprehension or production; spoken or written output; alphabetic or logographic reading materials) additional areas will be activated. For instance, the primary auditory cortex (BA 41 in the posterior part of the superior temporal gyrus) will be activated with auditory input; the primary

visual cortex (BA 17 in the posterior part of the occipital lobe) will be involved when visual language material is input; the motor cortex (BA 4) will be activated in all tasks that require speech output; and regions in the right hemisphere will be more heavily involved while reading logographic print than while reading alphabetic print.

So far I have presented three views on the function of Broca's area (it is committed to speech production; it is the site of syntactic knowledge; it is some sort of working memory system) and two views on the role of Wernicke's area (it subserves comprehension or lexical-semantic processing). These views by no means exhaust the set of hypotheses about the function of these language areas that have been proposed. A further hypothesis concerning the role of a large region in the left temporal lobe, roughly covering the brain area that Hagoort (2005) assigned the memory function and including Wernicke's area, was advanced by Damasio, Grabowski, Tranel, Hichwa, and Damasio (1996). These researchers hypothesized that the left temporal lobe is committed to word retrieval and, furthermore, that different parts of it are specialized for retrieving different types of words. To test these ideas they presented a group of patients with lesions throughout the brain with a set of photographs showing faces of well-known people, animals, or tools, and asked them to name the entities on the photographs. The performance of the patients was compared with that of a control group of neurologically healthy people and the patients showing abnormal naming performance relative to this control group (30 out of 127) were singled out for further examination. It was obvious that the naming deficit was not caused by damaged conceptual knowledge because the patients' responses clearly showed that they knew the depicted entities perfectly well. For instance, presented with the picture of a skunk a patient might say: "Oh, that animal makes a terrible smell if you get too close to it; it is black and white, and gets squashed on the road by cars sometimes." Brain scans were subsequently made to locate the damaged brain areas. Of the 30 selected patients (those who had shown abnormal naming behavior), 29 had damage to the left temporal lobe, thus indicating that word retrieval is indeed subserved by this brain area. But more spectacularly, and confirming the second hypothesis, the scans revealed that the exact site of the lesion was correlated with a specific word retrieval deficit: Patients with a lesion in the most anterior part of the left temporal lobe, the temporal pole, exhibited impaired naming of persons; those with a lesion in the middle of the left inferior temporal gyrus showed impaired naming of animals; finally, those with a lesion in the posterior part of the left inferior, middle, and superior temporal gyri exhibited impaired naming of tools. A subsequent PET study with brain-intact participants corroborated the results of the lesion study: The brain region activated while the participants named persons was the one that was damaged in the patients who exhibited abnormal performance in naming persons, and the same correspondence between the patient data and those of the brain-intact participants held for naming animals and tools.

As mentioned, the three left temporal lobe areas that Damasio et al. (1996) showed to be involved in word retrieval together largely coincide with the area that subserves the memory component in Hagoort's (2005) MUC model. Yet it is obvious that in the MUC model it serves a different function. Recall that Hagoort

hypothesized that this area stores and retrieves various aspects of lexical information, including the phonological forms (names) and syntactic and conceptual specifications of all the words known by the language user. In contrast, Damasio and her collaborators assumed that* the three subregions they delineated are what they called "intermediary" regions that do not themselves contain the names of persons, animals, and tools, but knowledge on how to *reconstruct* these names, and that the regions in question mediate between activated concepts elsewhere in the brain and the representation of the corresponding names, again elsewhere in the brain.

To provide yet a further example of the multiplicity of ideas about the function of Broca's and Wernicke's areas and the surrounding brain tissue, I will call to mind a three-step model of sentence comprehension presented elsewhere in this book (p. 215): early local, automatic, syntactic structure building, followed by lexical-semantic integration, followed by syntactic revision and integration (Hahne & Friederici, 1999). These three processing steps are reflected in three different ERP components: the ELAN (for early left anterior negativity), N400, and P600, which show up in the ERP signal about 150–200 ms, 300–500 ms, and around 600 ms, respectively, after the onset of the critical stimulus and are characterized by a different topography. ERP research on aphasic patients has shown that these components are modulated in aphasic patients (e.g., Friederici, von Cramon, & Kotz, 1999; see Kotz & Friederici, 2003, for a review). Together with fMRI studies of patients with lesions in frontal and anterior temporal regions in the left hemisphere and in the basal ganglia (e.g., Friederici, Hahne, & von Cramon, 1998), these results have led to the suggestion that early syntactic structure building is subserved by a part of Broca's area in the left inferior frontal gyrus (BA 44) as well as by the anterior part of the left superior temporal gyrus (Friederici & Kotz, 2003), and that later syntactic integration and revision is supported by the basal ganglia and a more posterior part of the left superior temporal gyrus (Wernicke). (The basal ganglia are a collection of subcortical brain structures that play an important role in the control of movement and that also appear to be involved in language control in bilinguals; see further on.) In other words, this model holds that different types of syntactic processing are supported by different parts of the left temporal lobe and that a part of Broca's area is involved in one of these types of syntactic processing. As such, it differs from all of the views on the function of the inferior frontal and superior temporal areas discussed above.

A final illustration of the great diversity of views on the function of the classical language areas in the left hemisphere concerns the declarative/procedural memory model developed by Ullman and his colleagues (Ullman, 2001; Ullman et al., 1997). It builds on a common distinction in theories on memory; namely, between a system that is involved in the learning, representation, and use of facts and events on the one hand ("declarative" memory) and a system involved in the learning and control of motor and cognitive skills and habits on the other hand ("procedural" memory). The learning and recall of information in declarative memory is accessible to consciousness, whereas information in procedural memory is non-conscious. For this reason, declarative and procedural memory are also referred to as "explicit" and "implicit" memory, respectively. According to Ullman, lexical knowledge—that is, knowledge of the sounds and meanings of words—is part of explicit declarative memory and primarily rooted in temporal lobe structures, including Wernicke's area. In contrast, grammar, a rule-based aspect of language, is thought to be a component of procedural memory and to be subserved by left frontal structures and the basal ganglia, including Broca's area. Particularly relevant in view of our interest in bilingualism is Ullman's suggestion—which he underpins with lesion data—that a dysfunction of procedural memory can be compensated by an increased dependence on declarative memory in the sense that linguistic structures that are normally computed by the procedural system (e.g., regular past tenses of verbs) are memorized by declarative memory. Alternatively, these structures are constructed by explicit rules

contained by declarative memory. Ullman posits that in languages that are learned later in life the two memory systems play a different role than in L1 because "later exposure to language may impair the ability of the procedural memory system to learn or compute aspects of grammar. Instead, linguistic forms that are computed grammatically in procedural memory in L1 may depend largely on declarative/lexical memory in L2" (Ullman, 2001, p. 117). The later the age of first exposure to the L2, the larger the role of declarative memory in grammatical processing is assumed to be.

When earlier on in this chapter I introduced the various methods that are used to identify the language areas in the brain, I mentioned the need for complementing studies of damaged brains with those examining the brains of neurologically intact people because of the equivocality of the clinical evidence. The above discussion, based to a large extent on neuroimaging studies that investigated language processing in healthy people, demonstrates that this source of evidence suffers from the same indeterminacy. Both lines of study clearly designate the same brain regions as those that are unmistakably involved in language processing. However, neither one discloses the exact role of each of them and, interestingly, some of the proposed accounts (Hagoort, 2005; Ullman, 2001) assume a type of operation for a specific area which suggests that it is committed to other, non-linguistic, domains of cognition as well rather than being specialized for language processing. For instance, the left inferior frontal gyrus was considered to be a domain-general working memory system or a procedural memory system, and it is well known that the control system assumed in Hagoort's MUC model is involved in executive control in general (pp. 435–437). Further on we will see that it also plays a major role in language control in bilinguals.

The involvement of the right hemisphere in language processing

So far the focus has been on brain areas in the left hemisphere, in agreement with the general view that of the two hemispheres the left one is specialized for language processing. This view, known as language lateralization, has its origins in Broca's finding (1861) that a circumscribed lesion in the left frontal cortex, with the rest of the cerebral cortex undamaged, resulted in a severe speech production disorder. After verifying that the observed functional disorder did not concern an isolated idiosyncratic case, Broca concluded that the language function is subserved exclusively by the left hemisphere. As related by Fabbro (1999), Broca's finding and its theoretical implications caused quite some excitement at the time, because since Aristotle all classic theories had assumed hemispheric symmetry of brain function. It follows from Broca's finding that this view of cerebral symmetry cannot be correct because a circumscribed lesion in one hemisphere could then never result in the complete loss of a specific function. After all, the homologous area in the intact hemisphere should continue to support this function.

Since those early days, the idea that the left hemisphere is specialized in language processing in the majority of people (about 90–95% of right-handed people and about 70% of left-handed people) has received support from a wealth of studies, including neuroimaging studies and studies that employed the various behavioral paradigms designed to study cerebral asymmetry (the dichotic listening, tachistoscopic viewing, and verbal–manual interference paradigms presented earlier). Nevertheless, there is plenty of evidence to suggest that the right hemisphere is involved in language processing as well. Some of these sources of evidence can easily be reconciled with the notion of left hemisphere specialization for language. For instance, as compared with a control condition in which participants do not have to perform any task, during the reading of sentences a large area of the occipital lobe of both the left *and* the right hemisphere is activated (e.g., Stowe et al., 2005). Rather than concluding that this finding shows the right occipital lobe is involved in *language* processing, the more obvious conclusion is that this activation reflects the task's visual component: Reading involves vision and it is a well-established fact that the occipital lobe, both left and right, subserves vision. This account is supported by the fact that the activation in the occipital lobe disappears when the sentence-reading condition is compared with a visual control condition (and the occipital lobe activation is thus removed in the subtraction procedure).

Providing a further example, Tan et al. (2001) have shown that several areas in the right hemisphere are strongly activated during the processing of logographic Chinese characters. The authors ascribed this effect to the fact that the right hemisphere is specialized in processing visual-spatial information and it is very detailed visual-spatial processing that is required to be able to tell Chinese logographic characters apart. Importantly, the Chinese characters also activated the common language areas in the left hemisphere, again pointing at the specialist language function of these areas. Similarly, Buchweitz, Mason, Hasegawa, and Just (2009) compared the brain activation of Japanese L1 speakers reading Japanese syllabic hiragana vs. Japanese logographic kanji, and showed that reading kanji was associated with a relatively high level of activation in occipito-temporal areas of the right hemisphere. (Conversely, reading hiragana showed more activation in areas in both the left and right hemisphere that are associated with phonological processing.)

But less obvious demonstrations of right hemisphere activation during language processing have also been shown, in both the temporal lobe and the frontal lobe. In reviewing the pertinent studies, Stowe and her colleagues (2005) concluded that the right hemisphere is involved in the processing of lexically ambiguous words and indirect forms of language use such as metaphors, suggesting that the right hemisphere provides an alternative interpretation when the initially constructed meaning turns out to be incompatible with contextual information. Furthermore, it appears that neural tissue in the right hemisphere is recruited when for some reason or other the processing demands increase; for instance, because the linguistic material to process is complex or the input speech is presented in a compressed fashion and therefore hard to decipher. In fact, right hemisphere activation during the processing of lexical ambiguities or indirect language just mentioned may also reflect computational load. Further support for a computational load account of right hemisphere involvement, also mentioned by these authors, concerns the fact that a number of special populations (elderly people, those who stutter, people with autism or schizophrenia, and—especially important in view of our interest in bilingualism—second language learners), often show more right hemisphere activation than the standard population. These special groups of people can all be argued to have fewer cognitive resources to spare than required for the language task at hand and additional right hemisphere processing may compensate for this insufficiency.

This view on right hemisphere involvement during language processing strongly resembles the one that Michel Paradis (1997, 2004) has fervently advocated to account for evidence of differential right hemisphere involvement in bilinguals as compared with monolinguals (see also, e.g., Fabbro, 1999, 2001). He, however, added the relevant new perspective that right hemisphere involvement under specific circumstances in no way jeopardizes the idea that language is processed exclusively by the left hemisphere because, according to him, the compensatory processes involved are entirely nonlinguistic. In his words: "Increased right hemisphere involvement [. . .] does not reflect the representation or processing of the language system [. . .], but, on the contrary, whatever nonlinguistic competence is substituted for it" (Paradis, 1997, p. 338). The non-linguistic competence he is referring to is the ability to exploit pragmatic and metalinguistic knowledge in communication. In other words, whether or not one regards right hemisphere activation during language processing as evidence against the view that language is exclusively subserved by the left hemisphere depends on one's definition of language. If pragmatic and metalinguistic knowledge is excluded from the definition, right hemisphere activation during language use is fully consistent with the view that only the left hemisphere is involved in language processing.

LANGUAGE AREAS IN THE BILINGUAL BRAIN

Introduction

Soon after Broca's seminal discoveries the question was raised of whether a bilingual's two languages (and a multilingual's multiple languages) are subserved by the same brain areas as those committed to language in monolingual speakers. If all of a person's languages recruit neurons in a particular brain region, damage to this region should have an equal impact on all of them. If, instead, the different languages are subserved by different brain areas, a lesion should provoke a disorder of the language that is normally subserved by the afflicted area while the other language(s) should remain unaffected. As it happened, soon after Broca's influential publication, Scoresby-Jackson (1867) reported the case of a bilingual patient who exhibited selective loss of one language following brain injury. This led him to speculate that the two languages of a bilingual are stored in different cortical areas. Specifically he speculated that a bilingual's native language is stored in Broca's area whereas later languages are stored in a brain area anterior to Broca's area (Fabbro, 2001). A couple of decades later Pitres (1895) rejected this account on logical grounds. In his reasoning he departed from the assumption that there are four brain areas that subserve language, namely two sensory centres, for auditory and visual images, and two motor centers, for graphic and phonetic motor images (Pitres, 1895, as cited by Ijalba, Obler, & Chengappa, 2004; see also Paradis, 1995, 1997). He then argued that selective loss of one language would imply that the aphasia-causing event had accidentally damaged all four of these regions while at the same time leaving the corresponding areas supporting the other language intact. That brain trauma could ever result in such a specific distribution of lesions across the brain's language areas is highly unlikely. So what else might have caused the selective loss of one language as observed by Scoresby-Jackson, and since then by many others?

As an alternative to an explanation in terms of the selective destruction of the neural substrate of the apparently lost language, Pitres (1895) suggested that this language was in fact not lost but unavailable due to a functional impairment. Specifically, he hypothesized that it was inhibited because of what he called "inertia" of the language centers. This hypothesis provides a natural explanation of the fact that many aphasic patients who exhibit selective loss immediately after the insult subsequently show a recovery of the affected language within a time span too short for it to have been relearned within the interval between its apparent loss and return (this recovery pattern in bilingual aphasia is known as "sequential recovery" or "successive recovery"). This fast recovery clearly suggests that the language was not lost but only temporarily unavailable. Similarly, selective permanent loss (known as "selective recovery") can be explained in terms of permanent inhibition of one of the languages rather than in terms of its selective loss. This explanation of recovery patterns in terms of a functional deficit is common in contemporary views on bilingual aphasia (e.g., Green, 1986; Paradis, 2001; see also p. 295). The relevant point to stress here is that the occurrence of selective loss of one language does not enforce the conclusion—drawn by Scoresby-Jackson (1867)—that the multiple languages of bilinguals and multilinguals are subserved by neural tissue in spatially different brain regions. Instead, it is compatible with the view that a bilingual's two languages recruit different circuits of neurons within the same brain regions. In the words of another scholar from the olden times: "[. . .] within the same area, the same elements are active, though in different combinations and interacting with a differential linguistic constellation" (Minkowski, 1927, p. 229, as cited by Fabbro, 2001, p. 212). On this account, the (temporary) loss of one language may reflect the (temporary) inhibition of the neural circuit that subserves this language within (one of) the common language area(s) in the left hemisphere and suggests that the brain mechanism that regulates the activation and inhibition of this neural circuit is damaged (see pp. 437–440 for details).

After Pitres (1895), the view that all of a multilingual's languages are subserved by the same brain regions dominated the field for many decades (see Paradis, 1995, 1997, for reviews) and many researchers shifted their interest towards the question of what factors might determine the exact recovery pattern exhibited in bilingual aphasia: the order in which, or the age at which, the languages were acquired; the frequency of use of each of the languages prior to the insult; the level of proficiency originally gained in each language (see Ijalba et al., 2004, for a discussion). Around 1970, however, after the introduction of a set of non-invasive techniques to study cerebral lateralization of cognitive functions in both neurologically intact individuals and people with brain damage (the dichotic listening, tachistoscopic viewing, and verbal–manual interference paradigms introduced before; pp. 413–414), an upsurge of studies on language localization in the bilingual brain can be witnessed. This time the specific question being posed was whether language might be lateralized differently in bilinguals and monolinguals (instead of recruiting different neural tissue within the same, left, hemisphere) and, if so, whether this holds for both of a bilingual's languages or for just one of them. The suggestion that there might be a higher incidence of crossed aphasia (aphasia caused by a lesion in the *right* hemisphere) in bilinguals than in monolinguals (Gloning & Gloning, 1965; but see Karanth & Rangamani, 1988, for counterevidence) presumably contributed to this renewed interest in language localization in bilinguals. After all, cases of crossed aphasia indicate that language is subserved by neural structures in the right hemisphere of the afflicted patients, and a higher incidence of the phenomenon in bilinguals would thus suggest that the right hemisphere more often subserves language in bilinguals than in monolinguals (see Solin, 1989, for a review). In the next section I will discuss the results of studies that examined language lateralization in bilinguals by using the common behavioral lateralization paradigms. Functional neuroimaging studies that looked at language localization in bilinguals will be discussed afterwards.

Language lateralization in bilinguals: Evidence from behavioral lateralization paradigms

In two commentaries on a large number of studies in which language lateralization in bilinguals was examined by means of the dichotic listening, tachistoscopic viewing, and verbal–manual interference paradigms, Paradis (1990, 2003) concluded that this body of studies has not advanced our knowledge of language lateralization in bilinguals "one bit" but just produced "a clutter of inherently uninterpretable contradictory results" (Paradis, 2003, p. 441) and that successive studies aimed at clarification of the issue only created more confusion. He based this harsh judgment on his observation that the experimental methods used in these studies lack validity. To be valid, he argued, four conditions must be fulfilled: (1) It must be demonstrated that the instrument (e.g., the dichotic listening procedure) does indeed measure degree of cerebral laterality (e.g., that in monolinguals language is more lateralized than in bilinguals). (2) It must be clearly defined what aspect of language is alleged to be differently lateralized in bilinguals and monolinguals, for instance, grammar or vocabulary. (3) It must be demonstrated that the stimuli that are used do indeed tap into that particular aspect of language. (4) It must be explicitly argued why it is that for this specific aspect of language lateralization should differ between monolinguals and bilinguals (Paradis, 2003).

According to Paradis, the prototypical study on bilingual language lateralization does not meet these requirements. As a consequence, a gamut of divergent data patterns emerged from the individual studies that have led to equally many different, and often contradictory, claims about language lateralization in bilinguals as compared with monolinguals. To mention just a few of the 14 listed by Paradis (2003): Greater *right* hemisphere involvement is assumed (1) for both languages of (all) bilinguals; (2) only for the second language of bilinguals; (3) only in late bilinguals; (4) only in early bilinguals; (5) only in second languages acquired informally. But also greater *left* hemisphere involvement has been claimed for the second language (5), as well as similar language localization in bilinguals and monolinguals (6). To reconcile a specific pattern of results with the (most popular) hypothesis that the right hemisphere is more involved in language processing in bilinguals than in monolinguals, the hypothesis has been narrowed down *ad absurdum* to extremely restricted subgroups of people "such as proficient female late acquirers in informal settings, provided they keep their eyes closed [. . .] or block one nostril" (Paradis, 1990, p. 578). If this is indeed the state of affairs in bilingual language lateralization research, it is easy to see why Paradis has likened the whole enterprise of trying to identify language lateralization differences between monolinguals and bilinguals to a futile search for the mythical Loch Ness Monster (Paradis, 1992, 2003) and urged the bilingual research community "to move on to more productive research" (Paradis, 1990, p. 576).

In an attempt to create order in this apparently chaotic body of experimental data, Vaid and her colleagues conducted meta-analyses on selected bilingual lateralization studies (Hull & Vaid, 2006; Vaid & Hall, 1991). They noted that the considerable variability of the experimental results is not all that surprising given the large variety in participant characteristics (e.g., in L2 onset age and fluency level) and in paradigm and task characteristics across studies. Meta-analyses provide a way to detect "underlying patterns across large quantities of disparate data points by standardizing statistical outcomes and minimizing the influences of researcher bias, paradigm bias, procedural bias, and reliance on particular methodologies" (Hull & Vaid, 2006, p. 439). In addition, they provide a means to evaluate the magnitude of the effects of different variables and to compare these effects.

As theoretical starting point, Vaid and her colleagues reviewed the literature and identified the five most common hypotheses on brain lateralization in bilinguals (Hull & Vaid, 2005; Vaid & Hall, 1991). Their meta-analyses should subsequently reveal which one of these hypotheses received support from the data. According to the *L2 hypothesis*, the right hemisphere is more involved when bilinguals process their L2 than when they process their L1. When they process their L1 the left hemisphere is involved to an equal extent as in language processing by monolinguals. The *balanced bilingual hypothesis* states that during language processing proficient bilinguals exploit their right hemisphere more than monolinguals and that this holds for both languages. The *stage of L2 acquisition hypothesis* (Obler, 1981) posits that during the initial stages of L2 acquisition the right hemisphere is relatively much involved in processing this language and that left hemisphere involvement gradually increases with increasing L2 fluency. The *manner of L2 acquisition hypothesis* posits that if the L2 was acquired primarily in an informal manner— that is, in naturalistic communicative contexts involving interaction with other interlocutors— there is more right hemisphere involvement than when it was acquired in formal settings. Finally, the *age of L2 acquisition hypothesis* (Vaid & Genesee, 1980) states that the closer in time the acquisition of an L2 is to L1 acquisition, the more similar the lateralization pattern for the two languages should be. In other words, early bilinguals should show a similar lateralization pattern for their two languages, whereas late bilinguals should show a disparate pattern for their two languages.

The results of the earliest meta-analysis (Vaid & Hall, 1991), which included a total of 59 studies testing brain-intact participants, suggested that, overall, language lateralization is similar in bilinguals and monolinguals and that the left hemisphere dominates language processing in both populations. However, a comparison *within* bilinguals that took age of L2 acquisition and level of L2 proficiency into account showed that level of L2 proficiency did not modulate the pattern of lateralization, but that age of L2 acquisition did, the early bilinguals exhibiting less left hemisphere lateralization (that is, more bilateral hemispheric involvement) than the late bilinguals. But, as noted by Hull and Vaid (2006), this early meta-analytic study suffered from a couple of shortcomings: Three-quarters of the included studies had not directly compared language laterality in bilinguals and monolinguals but had tested bilinguals only. Furthermore, of

the studies that had included a monolingual comparison group, the language of this control group was the bilingual participants' L1 in some cases but their L2 in other cases. In still other cases the data of the bilinguals' two languages were collapsed and then compared with those of the monolingual control group.

In the 2006 study these problems were addressed by exclusively including studies that encompassed a bilingual–monolingual comparison and in which the language of test taking was always the monolinguals' one and only language and the bilinguals' L1. Furthermore, as in the 1991 study, only studies that tested brain-intact participants were included. A total of 23 studies met all the selection criteria and were included in the meta-analysis. In view of the different hypotheses on bilingual language lateralization presented above, one consequence of the selection procedure should be emphasized at this point: Even though the majority of the hypotheses focus on the locus of bilinguals' L2, the design of the study can only reveal lateralization patterns for their L1. The variables examined in the meta-analysis were language experience (monolingual vs. bilingual), experimental paradigm, and, among the bilinguals, L2 proficiency (proficient vs. non-proficient) and age of L2 acquisition (early, before age 6, vs. late, after age 6). The experimental paradigms that were compared concerned the three common lateralization paradigms introduced before: dichotic listening, tachistoscopic viewing (called the "visual hemifield" paradigm in this specific study), and verbal–manual interference (called the "dual-task" paradigm here). Due to the relatively small number of selected studies, no potentially important finer-grained distinctions between the studies were examined, such as the type of stimuli (e.g., words or sentences) and the exact task used (e.g., word recall or word identification).

A first noteworthy finding emerging from the 2006 meta-analysis was that the three lateralization paradigms produced different sets of results, thus indicating that Paradis' (1990, 2003) concern about the validity of the paradigms used to examine lateralization of language was justified. Specifically, the dichotic listening paradigm showed left hemisphere dominance in both monolinguals and bilinguals, whereas the visual hemifield and dual-task paradigms resulted in data patterns suggesting bilateral involvement and less left hemisphere lateralization in both groups. A further finding was that, in agreement with the common view on language lateralization, monolinguals as a group (and collapsed across paradigms) were moderately left hemisphere dominant for language. Additional subgroup analyses among the bilinguals revealed that early bilinguals, who were all fluent bilinguals, showed bilateral hemispheric involvement (in their L1; see above), whereas late bilinguals were left hemisphere dominant (in their L1) and did not differ from monolinguals. Both of these findings converged with the results obtained in the earlier meta-analysis (Vaid & Hall, 1991). Finally, when age of L2 acquisition was controlled, no effect of L2 proficiency (on L1 laterality) materialized. In other words, L2 acquisition age on its own sufficed to explain lateralization differences among the bilinguals' L1.

The most interesting of these results is the finding that the early bilinguals' L1 seems to be more bilaterally localized than the one and only language of monolinguals. As noted by the authors, this finding "presents a compelling argument that there is something special about early exposure to multiple languages that affects neurofunctional organisation" (Hull & Vaid, 2006, p. 459). That the L1 of late bilinguals is localized the same way as the language of monolinguals—namely, predominantly in the left hemisphere—is less of a surprise, because at least during the first 6 years of life the language acquisition history of the late bilinguals in the above study was identical to that of monolinguals. The moment the late bilinguals were first exposed to dual-language input, the development of the L1 and the brain were both well on the way.

As mentioned, the above study was designed to reveal the lateralization pattern for the bilingual participants' L1, not their L2. As a corollary, somewhat ironically in view of the authors' goals to contrast the above hypotheses about language lateralization in bilinguals, the majority of the predictions derived from these hypotheses in fact

could not be tested. One of them is the idea that the right hemisphere is more involved in L2 processing than in L1 processing (the "L2 hypothesis"). A second is that this holds especially for the initial stages of L2 acquisition (the "stage of L2 acquisition hypothesis"). A third is that the two languages of early bilinguals show the same lateralization pattern while those of late bilinguals show a more disparate lateralization pattern (the "age of L2 acquisition hypothesis"). Further meta-analyses that examine the lateralization patterns in both L1 and L2 of various bilingual populations (early and late learners; fluent and non-fluent bilinguals) will have to be performed to complement the above findings.

To conclude this discussion of the behavioral bilingual language lateralization studies, three comments are in order. The first two echo Paradis's skepticism with regard to the three main paradigms used in this field and the way they are implemented in individual studies: The fact that the three paradigms produce different data patterns indicates that they do not all measure the same thing. Therefore, to be able to make any legitimate claims about language lateralization on the basis of data gathered by means of these paradigms we would first need to know which one of them measures what it purports to measure. The second comment concerns the nature of the stimulus materials used in these studies. Most of them have used word stimuli and, indeed, this also held for the majority of studies included in the above meta-analyses. As argued by Paradis (2003), of the various components of the language system, phonology, morphology, grammar, and vocabulary, the latter qualifies least as a component specific to (human) language. He substantiated this claim with a number of arguments; for instance, that vocabulary is subserved by a memory system different from the one that subserves the other language components (namely by declarative and procedural memory, respectively; see e.g., Ullman, 2001, discussed above). Furthermore, anthropoids such as gorillas and chimpanzees are quite successful at learning vocabulary but fail to learn any grammar. It has been claimed that the same holds for children growing up deprived of linguistic input (pp. 48–53). For these and other reasons Paradis concluded that by presenting isolated words as stimuli, these studies have used the least suitable type of stimulus to examine the location of language in the brain. A final comment to make here is that, even if the above three lateralization paradigms are at all suitable to reveal differential hemispheric involvement in language processing in monolinguals and bilinguals, they are surely unsuitable to disclose within-hemispheric differences between these two populations. In this respect, functional neuroimaging techniques are more promising. It is to these that I will now turn.

Localizing language in the bilingual brain: Functional neuroimaging studies

In line with the conclusions drawn from the above meta-analyses of studies using the behavioral lateralization paradigms (Hull & Vaid, 2005; Vaid & Hall, 1991), from the first moment neuroimaging studies on the neural substrate of bilingualism started to appear in the literature the possibility was pondered that the age at which a bilingual speaker is first exposed to an L2 might affect bilingual cerebral language organization. For this reason, Kim et al. (1997) tested both a group of adult early bilinguals, exposed to two languages during infancy, and a group of adult late bilinguals, first exposed to an L2 in early adulthood. They used fMRI as the neuroimaging technique and focused their data analyses on Broca's area in the left inferior frontal gyrus and Wernicke's area in the left superior temporal gyrus (see Figure 8.7). The task performed by the participants while being scanned was silent sentence generation; specifically, they were asked to describe events that occurred the previous day. A rather spectacular interaction between age of acquisition on the one hand and pattern of brain activation on the other occurred: In early bilinguals the two languages gave rise to activation in exactly the same subregion within Broca's area, whereas in late bilinguals L1 and L2 activated neighboring locations within Broca's area (in fact supporting, in a slightly different form, Scoresby-Jackson's, 1867, speculations regarding differential cortical localization for L1

and L2; see p. 427). In contrast, the two languages of both early and late bilinguals activated the same region within Wernicke's area. The spatial separation between the two languages in Broca's area in late but not early bilinguals led the authors to conclude that age of language acquisition affects the functional organization of language in the brain. A similar conclusion was drawn in a recent trilingual study in which the analyses were also concentrated on Broca's and Wernicke's area (Bloch et al., 2009). Interestingly, in this study it was also found that in early bilinguals a third language, acquired late, activated exactly the same brain regions as the two early languages did.

But soon after Kim et al.'s (1997) seminal study, other publications reported the conclusion that both languages recruit the same brain regions, not only in early bilinguals but also in late ones. For instance, Chee, Tan, and Thiel (1999) examined brain activation in early and late adult Mandarin–English bilinguals while they performed various silent word generation tasks in response to visual cues (e.g., stimulus cue: *cou*; response: *couple*). Whereas Kim and colleagues had only chosen Broca's and Wernicke's areas as regions of interest, Chee and collaborators focused their analyses on other brain areas as well, in both the left and right hemisphere, that previous studies had shown to be involved in linguistic behavior. They found that word generation in Mandarin and English, in early and late bilinguals alike, aroused exactly the same pattern of brain activation, involving dorsolateral prefrontal areas (that are typically associated with bilingual language control and executive control in general; see pp. 435–446), inferior frontal areas (including Broca's area), the supplementary motor area (an area anterior to the central sulcus that is involved in motor actions and thus also in speech), and occipital and parietal regions in both hemispheres. This common activation pattern for the two languages is particularly noteworthy in view of the fact that Chinese and English use different writing systems and other studies have shown that the processing of Chinese characters recruits different cortical regions than the processing of alphabetic symbols (e.g., Tan et al., 2001, 2003; see also Buchweitz et al., 2009 for a similar result in a comparison of Japanese syllabic hiragana and Japanese logographic kanji).

In agreement with the latter results, Illes et al. (1999) found similar patterns of activation, in left and right frontal regions, when adult fluent late English–Spanish bilinguals performed a semantic categorization task to series of visually presented words (does the word refer to a concrete or an abstract entity?). For both English and Spanish words, the activation in these areas was larger than the activation observed when, in a separate control condition, non-semantic decisions had to be made to these same words (is the word printed in upper case or lower case?). A pattern of converging activation in largely the same brain regions for different languages has also been demonstrated for multilingualism, in a study wherein Dutch–English–French trilinguals, all relatively fluent late learners of English and French, performed a word fluency task, a picture-naming task, and a reading comprehension task (Vingerhoets et al., 2003)

What may have caused the different pattern of results between these studies and, specifically, why did age of acquisition not have the same effect in all studies? One cause of the deviant results might be the use of different tasks. Plausibly, different activation patterns between a bilingual's two languages only hold for specific language tasks, tapping specific aspects of language. But the above studies may also accidentally have differed with respect to one further variable, one that has repeatedly been shown to determine the pattern of brain activation when bilinguals process their native or their second language: the level of attained L2 proficiency in late bilinguals. Perani et al. (1998) hypothesized that the differential activation of a number of brain regions during L1 and L2 processing they had observed in an earlier study might have been due to the fact the participants in that study had not only been late bilinguals, but were at the same time not proficient in their L2. To find out whether perhaps the lesser proficiency in L2 than in L1 had been the cause of the different activation patterns for the two languages, the researchers now manipulated the age of acquisition variable while keeping the L2 proficiency level constant, at a high level, across the two age of acquisition conditions: before age 4 (early) and after the age of 10 (late). The task to be performed by the participants was listening to stories, the same task as used in the earlier study. This time, not only the early bilinguals but also the late ones showed similar activation patterns for the two languages and the authors concluded that "attained proficiency is more important than age of acquisition as a determinant of the cortical representation of L2" (Perani et al., 1998, p. 1841).

In subsequent reviews of studies that employed both comprehension and production tasks, at both the word and sentence level, and probing different linguistic domains (semantics and grammar), it was concluded that, generally, attained L2 proficiency is a stronger determinant of the cerebral organization of language than age of acquisition (Abutalebi, 2008; Abutalebi, Cappa, & Perani, 2001, 2005). The authors furthermore concluded that grammatical processing may be excepted from this general conclusion, because in at least one study, by Wartenburger et al. (2003), a high level of L2 proficiency did not preclude the occurrence of an age of acquisition effect while participants performed a grammatical task. In this study three groups of Italian–German bilinguals were presented with sentences that were grammatically and semantically correct or contained a grammatical or semantic violation and were asked to perform correctness judgments while fMRI scans were made. Three groups participated: a group of simultaneous early bilinguals with a high level of proficiency in both languages; a group of late bilinguals who were all equally proficient in L2 (and L1) as the early bilinguals; a group of late bilinguals with a lesser level of L2 proficiency. Whereas the pattern of brain activation for the semantic judgments largely depended on the participants' L2 proficiency level, age of acquisition mainly affected the activation pattern observed during the grammatical judgment task: The activation pattern observed for the late but proficient bilinguals performing the semantic task closely resembled that of the early bilinguals, in both languages, whereas the late but less-proficient bilinguals showed a pattern of activation over a more extended set of brain areas, in both hemispheres, when they processed their second language. In contrast, whereas the grammatical task engaged exactly the same pattern of brain activation for the two languages in the early bilinguals, in both groups of late bilinguals more extended brain areas in, especially, the left hemisphere were activated during grammatical processing in L2 as compared with L1, and this pattern was largely the same for these two participant groups.

So far it seems that age of acquisition selectively influences bilingual cerebral organization of grammar, whereas attained level of L2 proficiency selectively influences bilingual cerebral organization of semantics. Further studies, however, suggest that this conclusion does not do justice to all of the experimental evidence. To mention just one of the studies that have shown results inconsistent with this conclusion, Xue, Dong, Jin, Zhang, and Wang (2004) compared the brain activity for L1 and L2 processing in late second language learners performing a semantic judgment task. The participants were 10–12 years old, native speakers of Chinese who began learning L2 English when they were 8 years old and, importantly, had all only reached a low level of proficiency in English. Despite the fact that a semantic task was used (which the above results have shown to be sensitive to L2 proficiency), the same pattern of activation occurred for strong L1 and weak L2, suggesting that "there are shared neural substrates for semantic processing of L1 and L2 even when one is at a very low L2 proficiency level" (Xue et al., 2004, p. 791). Apparently, in addition to age of acquisition and attained level of proficiency, there are other factors that affect the pattern of brain activation; for instance, the amount of exposure to the L2 (see e.g., Perani & Abutalebi, 2005, and Vingerhoets et al., 2003).

As we have seen above (p. 429), if a specific scientific debate cannot be settled on the basis of individual studies, meta-analyses can provide a way out of the indeterminacy by creating order in the variability of potentially important factors and taking these into account in analyzing the data. For this reason, Indefrey (2006) conducted a meta-analysis of 30 hemodynamic experiments (PET and fMRI) that had all compared activation patterns for L1 and L2 while making use of one of three types of tasks: tasks that require the production of words, semantic decisions to written words, or the grammatical and semantic analysis of written or spoken input sentences. In addition to this variation in tasks, three participant variables were taken into account in the meta-analysis: L2 age of acquisition, L2 proficiency, and amount of L2 exposure. Indefrey's main goal was to identify reliable neural differences between the activation patterns during L1 and L2 processing. The differences that emerged were coded according to a reference system the author had used earlier in a study that attempted to determine the brain regions involved in speech production (Indefrey & Levelt, 2004) and that contains 114 brain regions together covering the whole brain.

Despite the large number of brain regions focused on, across all experiments only 15 differences between activated regions for L1 and L2 emerged from the analysis and these all concerned differences in the *strength* of activation, not the location of activation. Of these differences, 13 concerned reliably stronger activation in a particular area during L2 processing, but this differential activation only occurred for specific tasks and specific bilingual subgroups. (In the remaining two cases stronger activation in L1 was observed.) All three participant variables appeared to play a role in the activation differences between L1 and L2 observed in the word production tasks. In contrast, differential activation in L1 and L2 appeared only to be related to L2 proficiency in the tasks requiring semantic decisions to words and only to L2 age of acquisition in the tasks that tapped syntactic processing in sentence comprehension. The latter two findings agree with the task-specific effects of L2 age of acquisition and L2 proficiency in Wartenburger et al.'s (2003) study discussed above. But perhaps the most noteworthy finding was that no L2-specific regions of activation were discovered, but only *strength* of activation differences within regions activated for both L1 and L2. A further finding of interest was that these strength of activation differences between L1 and L2 primarily showed up in the posterior part of the left inferior frontal gyrus (IFG; Broca's area). Temporal lobe areas (including Wernicke's area) were on the whole not more activated in L2 than L1. The functional roles that Indefrey assigns to the left posterior IFG and to temporal lobe regions are non-lexical compositional and lexical processes, respectively (cf. the "unification" and "memory" functions attributed to these areas in Hagoort's, 2005, MUC model; see p. 422). If this functional interpretation of these areas is correct, the activation strength differences between L1 and L2 processing in the left posterior IFG suggest more effortful, less efficient, compositional processes (e.g., grammatical analysis) in L2 than in L1.

If the functional neuroimaging studies discussed above have made one thing clear it is that, to be able to make sense of the data, many variables need to be taken into account because they all might influence the (strength and/or locus of the) pattern of differential brain activation for L1 and L2: the specific task the participants have to perform while being scanned (comprehension or production; auditory or visual; at the word level or sentence level; one that taps semantic processing, grammatical processing, or both), and participant characteristics such as L2 acquisition age, L2 proficiency, and amount of L2 exposure. Other factors that presumably play a role in differential activation for L1 and L2 is whether or not they employ the same writing system (e.g., Buchweitz et al., 2009) and, correlated with this, whether a bilingual's two languages are typologically close or distant.

One specific aspect of the neuroimaging data that needs to be better understood to be able to make sense of them is what it is exactly that causes a region to be activated at different levels under different circumstances. That this question is not trivial shows from the following quote from Indefrey (2006, p. 297):

Once an area becomes involved in a linguistic task, its activation level might be initially positively correlated with performance but might show a negative correlation after years of practice. The positive correlation might simply reflect [. . .] the degree of effort put into the task. By contrast, a negative correlation might be explained by assuming that the neural structures support the linguistic process involved in the task more effectively [. . .].

In other words, if only little activation in a specific brain area is observed during task performance this does not necessarily indicate the area is not central for task performance. To the contrary, it may be that the area is extremely central for the task at hand but has been involved often enough to do its job extremely efficiently. A similar relation between amount of practice on a task and activation in a specific brain area has been assumed for the *extent* (rather than the strength) of activation: "[. . .] it is generally accepted that the cortical area that subserves a skill gets less extensive as the skill gets more automatized" (Paradis, 1995, p. 212).

Two final remarks are in order here. One is that in neuroimaging studies that search for differences in the locus and strength of brain activation during L1 and L2 processing, surprisingly few words are spent on discussing the implication of the results for the differential lateralization debate. Whatever the reason for this textual lacuna, generally the data seem to provide little support for the view that a bilingual's two languages are differentially lateralized. Instead, the same areas in the left hemisphere seem to subserve both. The second remark is a related one, namely that in these neuroimaging studies monolingual control groups are generally missing, so that it is impossible to determine whether language is differently lateralized in monolinguals and bilinguals.

LANGUAGE CONTROL IN BILINGUALS

Chapter 6 dealt with the question of how bilinguals manage to either produce unilingual speech or to switch between their two languages depending on the prevailing circumstances.

Several views on language maintenance and switching—together known as "language control"—were presented there, among them the idea that language control is secured by reactive suppression of the language that is currently not targeted. The view in question, known as the inhibitory control model (pp. 307–310), encompassed the idea that language control is effected by a general executive control system rather than by a specialized system dedicated exclusively to language control in bilinguals. Two sources of evidence that point towards this conclusion were presented: (1) the fact that bilinguals outperform monolinguals on non-linguistic tasks that require a high level of executive control, such as the Simon task (see pp. 393–396). (2) The similarity of the behavioral response patterns obtained when bilinguals switch between their stronger and weaker language and when monolinguals (or bilinguals) switch between an easy and a more difficult task, both performed in the same language. An example of such a pair of tasks is when participants have to switch between reading the words and naming the colors of Stroop stimuli (words printed in various colors; word reading is easy, color naming is more difficult).

If it could be shown that language maintenance and switching in bilinguals recruit the same brain areas as do tasks that are known to require general executive control, this would undoubtedly constitute the most compelling evidence that one and the same control system is implicated. It is well known that two regions in the frontal lobes play a central role in executive control: the dorsolateral prefrontal cortex (DLPFC) and the anterior cingulate cortex (ACC), which were both already introduced before in the context of Hagoort's (2005) MUC model of language processing (pp. 422–423). Figure 8.9 shows their location in the brain. The ACC is the anterior part of the so-called cingulate cortex that encircles the corpus callosum.

A series of fMRI studies that examined the way executive control is exerted in conflict tasks such as the classical Stroop task (Carter et al., 2000; Egner & Hirsch, 2005; Kerns et al., 2004; MacDonald et al., 2000) has revealed a division of labor between these two brain areas: The DLPFC appears to be involved in implementing and maintaining control whereas the ACC monitors performance and, when it encounters a response conflict, signals to the DLPFC to increase its level of control so that errors can be prevented. In the classical Stroop task this happens upon the presentation of an incongruent trial, where the word and the color in which it is printed mismatch and thus lead to different response tendencies. In view of our interest in bilingualism, a couple of findings in this set of studies are of special relevance. MacDonald et al. (2000) observed that when the participants were instructed to name the color of the stimulus to be presented on the upcoming trial, activity was observed in the left DLPFC whereas no such activity was observed when they were told they should read the word to appear next. This finding thus suggests that only the more difficult task, color naming, requires top-down control and that it is the DLPFC that implements this type of control. It is tempting to predict that, similarly, the DLPFC in the brain of an unbalanced bilingual who is forced by the current circumstances to use his or her weaker language is activated, while it is not (or less) activated under circumstances wherein the stronger language must be used. After all, a bilingual's use of the weaker or stronger language can be likened to executing a relatively difficult and a relatively easy task, respectively. A second relevant finding of MacDonald and his colleagues was that the ACC did not show any instruction-related modulation of activation but, instead, responded to the congruency manipulation of the Stroop stimuli: It showed a higher level of activation upon the presentation of an incongruent stimulus (e.g., the word *red* printed in blue) than upon the presentation of a congruent stimulus (e.g., the word *red* printed in red). This was one of the findings that led the authors to suggest that the ACC's role is to monitor performance and to signal response conflict. Because a bilingual's two names for one and the same concept can be likened to the two conflicting responses on an incongruent Stroop trial, it does not seem far-fetched to hypothesize that the ACC has a role to play in bilingual language control as well.

FIGURE 8.9

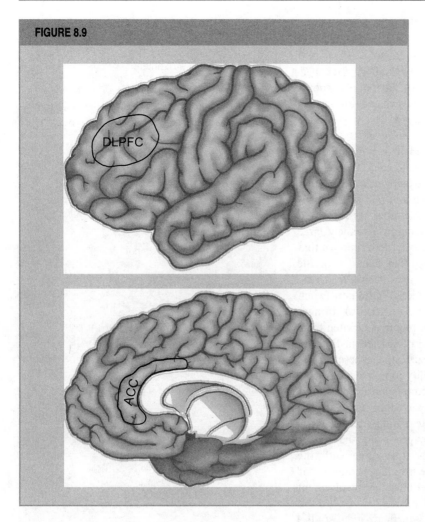

Two frontal brain regions that play a central role in executive control: the dorsolateral prefrontal cortex (DLPFC) and the anterior cingulate cortex (ACC) as seen on a lateral view of the left hemisphere and a medial view of the right hemisphere, respectively.

If bilingual language control is effected by the brain's control system that secures executive control in general, the frontal lobes, and specifically the DLPFC and ACC, should also be involved in language maintenance and switching in bilinguals. Evidence that such is indeed the case has been gathered in both neuropsychological studies testing patients and in neuroimaging studies with neurologically intact participants. In the two final sections of this chapter I will discuss the relevant evidence from neuropsychological studies and neuroimaging studies, respectively. The combined evidence suggests that, in addition to the DLPFC and ACC, a third, subcortical, brain structure, the caudate nucleus, is involved

in bilingual language control (and perhaps other subcortical areas as well; see below for details). Interestingly, the caudate nucleus is also considered to be part of the brain's general executive control system.

Neuropsychological evidence

Meuter, Humphreys, and Rumiati (2002) compared the language maintenance and switching performance of an Urdu–English bilingual patient (FK) with bilateral damage to the middle and superior frontal gyri with that of a control group of neurologically intact bilinguals. Notice that the area covered by the middle and superior frontal gyri includes the DLPFC area (cf. Figure 8.3 and the top part of Figure 8.9). In agreement with the view that the frontal lobe is involved in executive control, FK exhibited poor performance on a number of tasks that are known to require executive control (such as color naming in the classical Stroop task). The participants were presented with sequences of the Arabic numerals 1 to 9 presented in a random order. Depending on the background color, the numeral had to be named in the participants' one or other language. Language switch and non-switch trials occurred in an unpredictable order. As compared with the controls, FK made an extremely large number of errors and the exact error pattern that emerged strongly suggested that he had a specific problem in maintaining, and switching to, Urdu, his weaker language: In series of Urdu non-switch trials he often inadvertently switched to stronger English and on trials that required a switch from English to Urdu he often persevered in English. The authors hypothesized that these errors resulted from FK's inability to marshal and sustain the resources required to suppress dominant English over a longer period of time and to establish (on an English-to-Urdu switch trial) the new task set required for producing the weaker language. These findings thus agree with the above suggestion that the installment and use of the weaker language require the involvement of the DLPFC, damaged in FK.

The joint results of two further patient studies also indicate that bilingual language control is regulated by frontal brain structures. One of these studies (Fabbro et al., 2000) again points at a role for the DLPFC, but at the same time it indicates that the ACC is also involved. The second study (Abutalebi, Miozzo, & Cappa, 2000) suggests that a third frontal brain structure is implicated as well: the left caudate nucleus. The caudate nuclei (one in each hemisphere) are part of the basal ganglia, a collection of neuronal groups that lie within the forebrain just below the white matter of the cortex and play an important role in the control of movement (the other two basal ganglia structures are the globus pallidus and the putamen). The upper part of Figure 8.10 shows their location in the brain on an axial brain slice (the

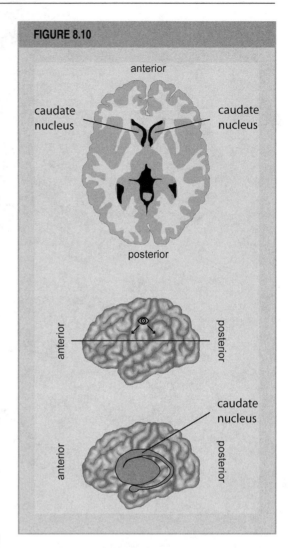

FIGURE 8.10

The location of the caudate nuclei in the brain. The caudate nuclei are part of a group of subcortical structures called the basal ganglia. The lower part of the figure shows the basal ganglia projected onto the brain.

middle part of the figure showing the approximate position of this axial slice). The lower part of Figure 8.10 shows the basal ganglia projected onto the brain and indicates which part of it concerns the (left) caudate nucleus.

The patient examined by Fabbro and his colleagues was a Friulan–Italian bilingual man with a lesion in the left ACC and in the white matter of prefrontal and frontal areas of the left hemisphere. A detailed neurolinguistic assessment including comprehension and production tests in both languages showed that he did not exhibit any aphasic symptoms in either language, suggesting that the language system proper was not damaged. In addition, tests that required him to translate words and sentences between the two languages showed that he was perfectly capable of doing so, suggesting that, if bilinguals have developed a separate translation system (cf. p. 321), this system was also still intact. The patient, however, failed to maintain the use of the language specified by the experimenter. When on the first testing day the examiner addressed him in Italian (the patient's L2) and asked him to speak Italian exclusively, only slightly more than 50% of the patient's utterances were in Italian and the remaining utterances were in L1 Friulan (an utterance being defined as a complete sentence). Similarly, when on the next day he was asked to speak in L1 Friulan exclusively, about half of his utterances were in L2 Italian. This pattern of repeated language switching occurred despite the fact the patient was continuously reminded of the requirement to stay in one language. He displayed this same pathological language alternation outside the laboratory, even when his interlocutors were monolingual. It thus seems that, just like the patient tested by Meuter et al. (2002), this patient failed to sustain the resources to suppress the non-target language or, alternatively, to maintain the target language, except that this time the problem was manifest for *both* languages. Interestingly, language mixing (defined by the authors as intermingling the two languages *within* a single utterance) hardly occurred. The fact that their patient did not exhibit aphasic symptoms in any of the two languages and was capable of translating between the two led the authors to suggest that the system responsible for maintaining a language is neurofunctionally separate and independent of the linguistic system and the translation system, and is part of a more general control system underlying the selection of different behaviors (Fabbro et al., 2000). Furthermore, the nearly complete absence of language mixing within utterances, combined with the observation of pathological within-utterance language mixing

in other patients (see below), indicates that pathological between- and within-utterance switching is caused by damage to (partially) different brain structures.

Abutalebi et al. (2000) obtained evidence to suggest that pathological within-utterance language mixing is caused by damage to the left caudate nucleus (also simply called the "caudate"). Their participant, AH, was a trilingual woman with Armenian as L1, English as L2, and Italian as L3. After suffering a stroke that damaged the white matter adjacent to the left caudate she could no longer hold a conversation in one language but involuntarily switched between languages, mixing elements of more than one language within a single utterance (producing sentences such as: *Oggi I cannot say il mio nome to you*, "Today I cannot say my name to you" or *I bambini steal the biscuits*, "The children steal the biscuits"). Characteristic features of these mixed utterances were that they were semantically appropriate, that a switch never occurred within a noun phrase, and that there was always morphological agreement between adjacent structures of different languages (e.g., Italian: *I bambini*, English: *steal*, both plural), suggesting that the speech production stage in which semantic and syntactic information is retrieved was not disrupted by the lesion. Picture-naming tasks administered in all three languages confirmed AH's inability to sustain unilingual output, showing switching to one or both other language in all three language conditions. As noted by the authors, these joint findings suggest that the lesion disrupted a late stage in word retrieval—namely, lexical selection between cross-language lexical alternatives—and, thus, that the left caudate nucleus is part of the network that is responsible for language selection in bilinguals.

To summarize, the joint results of the above neuropsychological studies provide a first set of indications that three brain regions are involved in bilingual language control: the left DLPFC, ACC, and caudate nucleus. The fact that these structures are known to be recruited during executive control tasks in studies that do not examine bilingualism suggests that bilingual language control is effected, at least partly, by a general executive control system. A set of neuro-imaging studies, to be presented next, provides converging evidence that such is case. In these studies both behavioral and brain responses were gathered, but in the ensuing discussion the behavioral data will be ignored. In addition, the discussion will focus on the brain regions that are generally assumed to play a role in executive control, ignoring activation in common language areas such as Broca's area and Wernicke's area (which were primarily dealt with on pp. 432–435).

Evidence from neuroimaging studies

Production tasks: Picture naming and digit naming

Much of the pertinent neuroimaging evidence has been gathered in studies that tested word production by means of a picture-naming task in which the bilingual participants named the picture stimuli in their L1, their L2, or switched between their L1 and L2. Hernandez et al. (2000, 2001) and Hernandez (2009) used fMRI to observe neural activity during unilingual and language-mixed picture naming by early and relatively balanced Spanish–English bilinguals. Spanish was their L1 and they all had been first exposed to English upon entering school at age 5. At the time of testing, when they were in their early twenties, their L2 English was slightly stronger than their L1 Spanish. In the unilingual blocks of trials the participants named a set of pictures in one and the same language, either English or Spanish. In the language-mixed blocks, picture naming switched between English and Spanish in a predictable pattern (S, E, S, E, S, etc.). In addition to the experimental part in which the participants either produced unilingual responses in a block of trials (no-switching) or switched between their two languages within a block (switching), the 2001 study included a pair of no-switching/switching conditions in which the participants *always* produced responses in one and the same language, also in the switching condition. In this part of the experiment the participants were shown pictures of a person or

animal performing some action (e.g., a crawling baby, a barking dog, an eating boy) and they were asked to either name the action (crawl, bark, eat) or the agent of the action (baby, dog, boy). A block of trials consisted of action-naming trials only, agent-naming trials only, or the invited responses alternated predictably between action naming and agent naming. In all three studies the type of response to produce on a specific trial was indicated by a verbal cue: the word "say" or "diga" when the picture had to be named in English or Spanish, respectively and, in the 2001 study, the word "to" or "the" when the action or agent had to be named.

In addition to activation in brain areas commonly involved in language processing, the 2000 study showed activation in the DLPFC of the left hemisphere during picture naming in all participants, and in the majority of the participants the homologous area in the right hemisphere was also activated. This activation was significantly higher than the activation observed in the analogous control condition (in which the participants just stared at a set of four Xs followed by a non-object). Activation in the DLPFC was observed in both the unilingual condition and in the language-switching condition, but the intensity of activation was higher in the switching condition and, in addition, the activated area was larger in the switching condition. A similar pattern of results was obtained in the 2001 study (wherein the control condition was one in which the participants were instructed to take a rest) and in the 2009 study (which did not include a control condition but only involved a direct comparison between the unilingual and switching conditions). The increased activity in the DLPFC in the language-switching conditions led the authors to conclude that switching between languages in picture naming involves an increase in general executive processing as compared with the amount of executive processing required for unilingual picture naming. Interestingly, the within-language task pair of the 2001 study also revealed activation in the DLPFC, in both the switching and no-switching conditions, but here the switching condition did not show an increase in activation. The authors hypothesized this might be because the within-language switching task in question is relatively easy and, therefore, requires less involvement of the executive control mechanism than switching between languages does.

When I introduced the current view on the role of the DLPFC in executive control (namely, that it implements and maintains top-down control under demanding circumstances; e.g., MacDonald et al., 2000; see p. 436 above), I suggested that in unbalanced bilinguals the DLPFC might be more involved when they must use their weaker language than when they must use their stronger language. A further study (Hernandez & Meschyan, 2006), which tested a different bilingual population than the one examined in the above three studies, provides support for this idea. Recall that the participants in the above three studies were all relatively balanced early bilinguals with Spanish as L1 and English as L2. In contrast, the participants in Hernandez and Meschyan's study were all late Spanish–English bilinguals who had started to learn English after their arrival in the United States at age 18. At the time of testing (in their early twenties), their L1 Spanish was still clearly the dominant language. They were asked to name blocks of pictures in either L1 Spanish or L2 English while fMRI scans were being made. The scans showed increased activity in, among others, the DLPFC during picture naming in (weaker) L2 English as compared with picture naming in (stronger) L1 Spanish. Consistent with the results obtained in the monolingual Stroop tasks discussed earlier (p. 436) these results thus suggest that a more difficult task requires more top-down executive control and that it is the DLPFC that subserves this type of control. Interestingly, the ACC—the second brain region the monolingual Stroop studies had identified as a component of the executive control network—was also more highly activated in L2 English picture naming. The combined findings thus point to a role of a general executive control mechanism in bilingual language control and a larger role of this mechanism when the weaker language must be used.

In a German–French picture-naming study, Abutalebi et al. (2008) extended the above results by showing that the left caudate is also involved in bilingual language control, a conclusion that part of this group of researchers had already drawn earlier on the basis of the language-mixing behavior of a trilingual patient with damage to the left caudate (Abutalebi et al., 2000; see p. 439). As Hernandez et al. (2001), these researchers compared language switching with switching between two tasks that were both performed in the same language. All participants were adult late bilinguals with German as L1 and highly fluent in L2 French. The two tasks in the within-language switching condition were either to produce the L1 German name of the depicted object or to produce, also in L1, a verb related to the depicted object. In addition to this monolingual task-switching condition, a bilingual language-switching condition was included in which the presented object had to be named in either L1 German or L2 French. Finally, a monolingual simple naming condition was included, in which on all trials the presented object had to be named in L1. This design allowed the comparison of the neural structures involved in switching between two same-language tasks on the one hand and switching between two languages on the other hand. It also enabled the researchers to compare the brain activity in the two language conditions of the language-switching condition, and to compare the activation in either one of the two switching conditions on the one hand and in the simple naming condition on the other hand. In all cases the naming responses had to be produced out loud and the type of response requested on a trial was cued by a visual word cue: "name" or "verb" in the task-switching condition; "Deutch" or "Français" in the language-switching condition; and "name" in the simple naming condition.

One finding of interest was that, as compared with the simple naming condition, the language-switching condition showed activation in a more extensive network of brain areas than did the task-switching condition. Focusing on the brain regions typically associated with executive control (and ignoring the activation in the common language areas; e.g., BA 22, Wernicke, and BA 44 and 45, Broca), task switching but not simple naming showed activation in the left DLPFC

(BA 9 and BA 46) and the right ACC. The comparison of L1 naming in the language-switching condition with simple naming (also in L1) showed activation in these same areas but, in addition, the left ACC and the left and right caudate were also activated. These results were confirmed in a direct comparison of the task-switching and language-switching conditions. The authors concluded that the exact executive control processes differ between the language-switching and task-switching conditions, and that the differences are due to the specific requirement in the language-switching condition to regulate the activation in the two language subsystems. The brain activation patterns suggest that the ACC and the caudate nucleus subserve this activation regulation. Finally, a direct comparison between naming in L1 vs. L2 in the language-switching condition revealed that the left and right ACC, a part of the left DLPFC (BA 46), and the left and right caudate nucleus were more highly activated in L2 naming than in L1 naming. The authors hypothesized that these differences between naming in L1 and L2 are due to the differential processing demands of these two conditions, word production in the weaker L2 requiring relatively many controlled processing resources whereas word production in the stronger L1 is relatively automatic. This hypothesis is in agreement with the above conclusion, based on the results of Hernandez and Meschyan (2006), that a general executive control mechanism is relatively strongly involved during speech production in the weaker language, although there this only showed from increased activation in the DLPFC and ACC, not the caudate.

By using *event-related* fMRI, a further study has provided the insight that bilingual language control can be dissected into two different components that recruit different networks of brain areas. As described earlier (p. 412), in many fMRI studies the participant performs a particular task for a certain duration of time, say 20 to 30 seconds, and the fMRI signal (the hemodynamic response) is summed over this time duration. The picture-naming studies discussed above all used this procedure. With this procedure it is not possible to distinguish, within a series of language-mixed trials, between neural responses to switch trials on the one hand and non-switch trials on the other hand. In contrast, in event-related fMRI it is possible to measure the hemodynamic signal incited by a single stimulus, and thus to compare the neural responses to switch and non-switch trials.

In a Chinese–English study, Wang, Kuhl, Chen, and Dong (2009) used event-related fMRI to obtain support for their hypothesis that two neural components of bilingual language control must be distinguished. As compared with language-pure blocks, stimulus blocks of language-mixed trials require "sustained" (or "state-related") control because of the incessant need to stay alert; after all, every next trial may require a system reset. Furthermore, within a block of language-mixed trials, each time a stimulus is presented that requires a language switch, a fleeting moment of "transient" (or "item-related") control is required to effect the switch. Wang and colleagues probed the neural substrate of sustained control by comparing the fMRI signals for blocks of language-mixed trials with those observed for blocks of same-language trials. To reveal the neural structures involved in transient control, they compared the fMRI signals to switch and non-switch trials within language-mixed blocks. The stimuli were the digits 1 to 9, to be named in Chinese or English. These two types of comparisons revealed the involvement of different neural networks, thus supporting the hypothesis that bilingual language control indeed encompasses these two components. Specifically, sustained control induced bilateral activation in frontal areas including the DLPFC, whereas transient control induced a left-lateralized pattern of activation over both frontal and parietal areas. One subregion of the left DLPFC, BA 46, showed increased activation in both sustained and transient control. Contrary to some of the studies discussed above, no activation was observed in the ACC and the caudate. The authors hypothesized the reason might be that digit naming involves more automatic retrieval than picture naming, the task used in the above studies. In other words, they suggested that different bilingual production tasks require different levels of bilingual language control, and that the ACC and caudate only become implicated when more control is required to perform the task.

Production tasks: Word generation and translation

Two studies that included a bilingual task *pur sang*—namely, word translation—strengthen the emerging general picture that the prefrontal cortex, ACC, and caudate all have a role to play in bilingual language control, even though neither one of them on its own has shown an influence of all three structures at the same time. In addition, a third study that examined sentence translation indicated a role for a basal ganglia structure different from the caudate: the globus pallidus. In Klein et al. (1995), English–French bilinguals performed three different word generation tasks: Words were presented aurally to both ears and the participants had to generate out loud, in three different conditions, a word similar in meaning to the presented word, in the same language (the synonym task), a word with a similar sound, again in the same language (the rhyme task), or a translation in the other language (the translation task). French and English stimulus repetition tasks, in which the participants simply repeated the presented stimuli, served as control conditions. The three conditions showed a strikingly similar pattern of results: When the activation patterns obtained in the control conditions were subtracted from those in the experimental conditions, in all three of the latter significant activation was observed in the (left) prefrontal cortex and ACC (in addition to weaker activation in a number of other regions that are commonly associated with language processing). The fact that the two within-language generation tasks and the translation task showed similar activation patterns suggests that the same general control system is involved in all three of them.

In a related study, Price et al. (1999) tested German–English bilinguals in a word translation task similar to the one used by Klein and her colleagues, presenting the words to be translated visually rather than aurally and using a word-reading task as the control task. Whereas Klein and collaborators had observed increased activation in the left DLPFC and the ACC in translation as compared with the control task, these authors observed (again compared to the control task) increased activation in the ACC and two subcortical structures, among them the left and right caudate (the other one being the putamen), but not in the DLPFC. Because prefrontal activation has been shown to decrease with over-learning or practice, the authors suggested that differential involvement of the DLPFC in the two studies might result from a difference in L2 proficiency of the participants in the two studies. Specifically, they suggested that the L2 proficiency level of the participants in Klein and colleagues' study may have been lower than in their own study. Although independent evidence that the participants in these two studies were indeed not comparable in proficiency is lacking, this analysis is in agreement with the findings, discussed above, that the DLPFC is implicated more in a difficult task (e.g., color naming in a Stroop task, MacDonald et al., 2000; bilingual picture naming in the weaker language, Hernandez & Meschyan, 2006) than in an easier task (word naming and picture naming in the stronger language, respectively).

The above analysis is also in agreement with the results of Lehtonen et al. (2005), an fMRI study that searched for the neural substrate of sentence translation, which is a more complex task than word translation is. In this study, Finnish–Norwegian bilinguals silently translated sentences from Finnish to Norwegian and a condition in which sentences simply had to be read in silence served as the control condition. When the activation in the control task was subtracted from the activation observed in the translation task, residual left prefrontal activation showed in the translation task (although it was localized somewhat more ventrally than in the study by Klein and colleagues). In addition, activation in a basal ganglia structure, the left globus pallidus, was observed in the translation task. In conclusion, these three translation studies together suggest that the specific control operations involved in translation recruit part of the prefrontal cortex, the ACC, and basal ganglia structures in, predominantly, the left hemisphere.

As discussed in Chapter 6, of all forms of language usage exhibited by bilinguals, the one that doubtlessly challenges the executive control system most is simultaneous interpreting of full texts. It may therefore be expected that a comparison of brain activity in simultaneous translation of full text and in translating isolated words or sentences would reveal a more extended pattern of activation in simultaneous interpreting, especially in the brain's executive control areas. However, the few studies that have investigated brain activity in simultaneous interpreting (Tommola, Laine, Sunnari, & Rinne, 2000/2001; Rinne et al., 2000) have not examined this specific question but compared brain activity in simultaneous interpreting (in both translation directions) and within-language shadowing of aurally presented text (in both languages; in shadowing the speech input must simply be repeated). In addition, they compared the activation patterns for interpreting from the stronger to the weaker language and vice versa, showing that interpreting into the weaker language activates more brain regions than interpreting from the weaker to the stronger language. Because interpreting from the stronger to the weaker language is generally considered to be more demanding than interpreting in the reverse direction, this result is consistent with the common finding that extent of brain activation is correlated with task difficulty: the more difficult the task, the more extended the pattern of activation. Of specific relevance in the present context is that, as compared with shadowing, simultaneous interpreting specifically recruited neurons in the left DLPFC, one of the areas that Klein and colleagues (1995) had found to be involved in word translation.

Summing up, the neuroimaging and neuropsychological studies presented in this section so far provide converging evidence that the DLPFC, ACC and caudate, and especially those in the left hemisphere, are involved in bilingual language control. In addition, a couple of studies indicated that other basal ganglia structures than the ACC—namely, the putamen and globus pallidus—are also occasionally involved. The joint evidence also indicates that the more difficult the task is to perform (because the task itself is a relatively complex one or the participant has a relatively low level of proficiency in the test language), the larger the chance that all of these structures are implicated and/or that a specific structure is activated relatively highly.

Comprehension tasks

In the neuroimaging studies just discussed, the bilingual participants always had to perform a production task, most often picture naming. Two further studies examined the neural substrate involved in language switching by using comprehension tasks. Together they indicate that the involvement of (part of) the DLPFC, the caudate and the ACC of, especially, the left hemisphere in bilingual language control is not confined to production tasks but can be witnessed in comprehension tasks as well. In an fMRI study, Crinion et al. (2006) examined the brain responses of one group of Japanese–English bilinguals and a second group of German–English bilinguals while they made semantic decisions to (printed) target words that were preceded by either a related prime or an unrelated (printed) prime (e.g., related: *bathtub–shower*; unrelated: *spoon–shower*). Prime and target were in the same language (e.g., English: *trout–salmon*; German: *Forelle–Lachs*) or in different languages (e.g., *trout–Lachs* or *Forelle–salmon*). To see whether any effects to be obtained would generalize across studies using different techniques, a PET study with a second group of German–English bilinguals was also performed. The finding that is of special interest in the present context was that in all participant groups the left caudate responded to the relatedness manipulation, but only when prime and target were in the same language. In this condition the left caudate was activated less when related pairs were presented than when unrelated pairs were shown. When prime and target belonged to different languages, the level of activation in the left caudate was the same in the related and unrelated conditions, in both cases equaling the level of activation in the unrelated same-language condition. The authors concluded that the left caudate "plays a universal role in monitoring and controlling the language in use" (Crinion et al., 2006, p. 1537).

Abutalebi et al. (2007) examined the neural correlates of language switching during comprehension by means of *event-related* fMRI (cf. Wang et al.'s, 2009, digit-naming study). They had early Italian–French bilinguals passively listen to narratives that contained a number of sudden and unpredictable switches to the other language. These language switches were the "events" that incited the hemodynamic response measured by means of the event-related fMRI technique. The participants were native speakers of Italian who had lived in a predominantly L2 French environment since their childhood and were exposed more to L2 French than to L1 Italian. Plausibly therefore, L1 Italian was the weaker language of the two (although behavioral tests suggested they were balanced bilinguals). Switching into the less-exposed L1 led to activation in many brain regions, predominantly in the left hemisphere. Among the activated areas were the left ACC, a part of the left DLPFC (BA 9), and the left caudate. Switching into the more-exposed L2 showed a less-extended pattern of activation and a direct comparison between the two directions of switching showed that switching into L1 selectively engaged the caudate and ACC. The authors drew two main conclusions from these data: (1) that the brain's executive control network not only subserves language control in bilingual speech production but also in bilingual auditory comprehension, and (2) that the selective activation in the caudate and ACC upon a switch to the less-exposed (and presumably weaker) language might reflect the enhanced level of control required for processing this language. Note that this latter conclusion echoes the one drawn by Wang et al. (2009; see above), who hypothesized that the reason they did not observe any activation in the ACC and the caudate in their digit-naming task might be that this task involves more automatic (less controlled) retrieval processes than picture naming, the task used in similar production studies.

A final comprehension study to present here also illustrates the general picture emerging from the above studies: that the separate components of the brain's executive control network are not always all involved simultaneously in tasks that require bilingual language control. In a Dutch–English study, Van Heuven, Schriefers, Dijkstra, and Hagoort (2008) tried to detect the locus of the language conflict that bilinguals experience when they receive cross-language ambiguous input: the conflict might occur during stimulus processing, during response generation, or during both. In addition they aimed to identify the brain structures involved in resolving language conflict, and wondered whether these might be the same structures as those involved in general executive control. As experimental tasks they used two versions of the visual lexical decision task (see p. 157 for details) and the critical, ambiguous, stimuli were Dutch–English interlexical homographs (words that mean something different in Dutch and English; e.g., *kind*, meaning "child" in Dutch; see p. 156 for details). As compared with non-homographic control words, the interlexical homographs were hypothesized to lead to both stimulus-based and response-based language conflict in one of the task versions, whereas in the other task version they were hypothesized to give rise to stimulus-based conflict only (see the original study for details). The task version that was argued to involve response-based conflict in addition to stimulus-based conflict, but not the one argued to only involve a conflict at the stimulus level, showed a higher level of activation for homographs than controls in the ACC and the left caudate. In contrast, in both task versions homographs showed more activation in a part of DLPFC (BA 46). These joint findings thus suggest that the ACC and left caudate were recruited to resolve the conflict between two possible responses whereas the DLPFC was involved in resolving the conflict caused by input ambiguity.

All in all, the results of this small set of comprehension studies warrant the conclusion that the DLPFC, ACC, and caudate, especially in the left hemisphere, regulate bilingual language control not only in production tasks but also in comprehension tasks, and that the chance each individual one of these neural structures becomes implicated in task performance increases with increases in task difficulty. But the most important, overarching, conclusion that can be drawn from the bilingual production and comprehension studies together is that bilingual language control seems to be subserved by a network of brain structures that subserves executive control in general.

And with these words this long journey through the multifaceted study of language and cognition in bilinguals and multilinguals comes to an end.

Glossary

In compiling this glossary I have made use of the following sources: Carroll (2004), Crystal (1987), Gazzaniga, Ivry, and Mangun (2009), Harley (2008), Hartmann and Stork (1972), Kolb and Whishaw (2001), Richards, Platt, and Platt (1992), Taylor and Taylor (1990), and Whitney (1998).

Abstract words: See **Word concreteness**.

Additive bilingualism: The bilingualism that emerges under circumstances in which the first language is maintained and supported while a second language is being learned, and there is no pressure to replace the first language with the new language. Under these circumstances the new language truly enriches the linguistic repertoire of the language user, which in turn is advantageous for cognitive functioning. This form of bilingualism arises, for instance, when a foreign language is learned in school or when in a bilingual country native speakers of the national, majority language are taught the language of the minority. In contrast, when a new language is acquired that is more prestigious than the native language, and there is social pressure to no longer use the native language or to use it less, the new language may gradually replace the native language. This form of bilingualism is called **subtractive bilingualism** and has been found to be detrimental for cognitive functioning, presumably because neither language is ultimately sufficiently well developed to support thought.

Affix: A bound **morpheme** that cannot stand on its own but is added to the root or stem of a word thus changing its meaning or function (e.g., *un-*, *re-*, *-ness*, *-ing*). If it occurs before the root it is called a prefix. If it is attached to the root's end it is called a suffix.

Affricates: Consonants produced by an initial complete closure of the vocal tract followed by a gradual release of the air (e.g., the /ts/ in German *zu*).

Age of acquisition (AoA) effects: In second language use, the age at which the language was acquired determines the level of proficiency ultimately achieved. Typically, the earlier in life the language is learned, the higher the ultimate proficiency.

Allophones: Phonetic variants of one and the same **phoneme**. One source of this variance is the linguistic context of the phoneme. For example, exemplars of the /l/ phoneme occurring before vowels sound different from those occurring before consonants, and the /p/ phoneme occurring as the only consonant at the beginning of words (e.g., /pope/) is different from the /p/ occurring in word-initial consonant clusters (/spider/).

Alphabet: A writing system in which the graphic signs (its letters) represent the language's **phonemes**.

Alveolar-palatal: Said of consonants that are articulated by letting the tongue make contact with the bony ridge behind the upper teeth.

Antonym: A word that has the opposite meaning from another word (e.g., *large* is an antonym of *small* and *cheap* is an antonym of *expensive*).

Aphasia: A language disorder caused by brain damage, affecting a person's ability to produce or understand language, or both.

Articulatory suppression: An experimental technique that examines the role of phonological short-term memory in learning by having the participants utter a particular sound repeatedly while learning verbal material. This activity disrupts the rehearsal of the materials to be learned and adversely affects retention.

Base language: Except in translation situations, bilinguals usually select one language for communication, even when their interlocutors master the same two languages. The selected language is called the "base language". It is also referred to as the "language-in-use". The non-selected language is sometimes called the **guest language** because base language speech may be intermingled with words or larger linguistic constructions from the non-selected language. The more highly activated the guest language's memory system, the larger the incidence of such "guests" (or "**code switches**"). See also **Language-mode theory**.

Bicultural bilinguals: Speakers of two languages who know, and identify with, the social habits, beliefs, customs, etc. of native speakers of both languages. It is possible to be bilingual without being bicultural.

Bilabial: Said of a consonant that is articulated by closing the lips.

Bilingual aphasia: A language disorder in bilinguals resulting from brain damage and affecting their ability to produce speech and/or to comprehend written and/or spoken language in one or both languages or their ability to produce unilingual speech. Various types of bilingual aphasic syndromes and recovery patterns occur. One type is characterized by pathological **blending** or language mixing. Three further types are characterized by **selective recovery**, **sequential recovery**, and **differential recovery**. Selective recovery means that one language recovers fully but the second shows lasting aphasic symptoms. In sequential recovery both languages recover but one of them only begins to reappear after the other has already been restored. In differential recovery both languages recover in parallel but at a different speed. All four types can be explained in terms of a failing control mechanism: Blending may result from the mechanism's failure to inhibit the currently inappropriate linguistic subsystem as long as required. Selective and sequential recovery may result from the mechanism's permanent and temporary inhibition, respectively, of one of the two linguistic subsystems. Differential recovery may result from the control mechanism exerting a disproportionate amount of inhibition on one of the two linguistic subsystems.

Bilingual first language acquisition (BFLA); also **Simultaneous bilingualism**: Being exposed to bilingual input, and thus acquiring two languages, from birth. The development of bilingualism in these children, who can be said to have two native languages, differs from the developing bilingualism in early **sequential bilingualism**, in which the child is first exclusively exposed to one language and, at some later point in time, starts receiving bilingual input. Late learners of a second language are all sequential bilinguals. It has been suggested that, as compared with early and late sequential bilingualism, in BFLA the two languages develop relatively independently of one another.

Bilingual mode: See **Language-mode theory**.

Bilingual Stroop task: The bilingual version of the common **Stroop task**. A typical experiment includes an interlingual incongruent condition and an intralingual incongruent condition in addition to a neutral condition. In a neutral condition a non-conflict stimulus is presented, for instance a color patch. In the intralingual incongruent condition the printed word and the invited response are in the same language (e.g., stimulus word: *blue*; response: *green*). In the interlingual incongruent condition the language of stimulus and response differ (e.g., a Spanish–English bilingual is shown the word *blue* and must say *verde*). Responses are typically slower in the intralingual incongruent condition than in the neutral condition. This is the **Stroop effect**. The **interlingual Stroop effect** is the difference in response time between the interlingual incongruent condition and the neutral condition.

Blending: The production of language-mixed speech by bilinguals. Pathological blending is a symptom of one form of **bilingual aphasia**.

Borrowing: A word or phrase taken from one language and used in another language. When the borrowing is a single word it is called a **loan word**. Borrowings may be pronounced the way they are pronounced in the original language, but they can also be adapted to the phonology of the host language.

Categorical perception: The phenomenon that listeners can hear the difference between two speech sounds that represent two different **phonemes** but often fail to discriminate between two speech sounds that are variants of one and the same phoneme. This holds even if the acoustic differences between the two phonemes on the one hand and the two variants of the same phoneme on the other hand are equally large.

Child directed speech (CDS): Speech directed at very young children. It is characterized by exaggerated intonation and clear articulation, is spoken slowly, and the sentences are typically very short. CDS is sometimes called **motherese**.

Classifier: A word used with a noun that indicates the semantic class to which the noun belongs. For instance, *sek* in Korean signifies that the preceding noun refers to a color (e.g., *paran sek*, "blue"; *juhong sek*, "orange"). Also, an **affix** attached to a free **morpheme** that indicates the syntactic class to which the word composed of affix and free morpheme belongs. For instance, the affix *-mente* attached to a free morpheme in Italian or Spanish indicates that the word in question is an adverb.

Code switch: Changing from the use of one language to another. See also **Language-switching paradigm**.

Cognates: Words that share all or a large part of their phonological and/or orthographic form with their translation in another language. For instance, the French and English *rose* and *rose* are cognates.

Cohort: A set of representations in the mental lexicon that become activated upon the presentation of a spoken word to the listener. The set of activated elements are the phonological representations of the input word and of words that sound similar to the input word. The word "cohort" is derived from the cohort model of spoken word recognition that assumes this multiple-activation process to take place.

Competence: In linguistics, competence refers to the (largely unconscious) knowledge people have of their language(s) or, in a more narrow sense, of the grammar of their language(s). The term contrasts with **performance**, which refers to the actual use of this knowledge in language production and comprehension. Performance failures may occur even if the underlying knowledge (competence) is in place (due to, for instance, limited working memory capacity).

Compound bilingualism: According to one view on how word knowledge is stored in bilingual memory, the two languages of the bilingual share a single conceptual system (that is, the system storing the meanings of words). L1 and L2 words access this one conceptual system directly and independently of one another. This set-up is referred to as "compound bilingualism". According to a view known as **subordinative bilingualism** there is also just one conceptual system but it is accessed directly by L1 words only. L2 words access the conceptual system indirectly, via the L1 word form representations. According to a view known as **coordinate bilingualism** the bilingual has two conceptual systems, one for each language. It has been suggested that different acquisition contexts lead to these different forms of bilingual memory representation; for instance, coordinate bilingualism might arise under circumstances where the two languages are acquired in two distinct cultural settings.

Computed tomography (CT): A neuroimaging technique that uses computer algorithms to reconstruct two-dimensional images produced by means of the conventional X-ray technique into three-dimensional images of brain structures.

Conceptualizing: The first steps in the speech-production process comprising the conception of the intention to express a particular thought into words, the selection of the required non-verbal information from the relevant memory stores, and the ordering of this information for expression. The output of these processing operations is called the **preverbal message**.

Conceptually mediated translation: A form of translation that exploits the same knowledge structures and language-processing operations as used in monolingual language comprehension and production, and that does not require the use of specialized translation strategies nor specific knowledge regarding translation-equivalent linguistic structures. According to this view, any person who masters two languages both productively and receptively can translate between them (cf. **Transcoding**).

Concrete words: See **Word concreteness**.

Consecutive interpreting: A form of speech-to-speech translation in which the interpreter alternates between listening to the **source language** and providing an oral rendition of it in the **target language** (cf. **Simultaneous interpreting**).

Context availability: Given a particular word, a measure of how easy it is to think of a context in which the word might occur.

Continued word association: See **Word association (discrete)**.

Coordinate bilingualism: See **Compound bilingualism**.

Cortex: The newest layer of neurons overlying the forebrain and composed of about six layers of neurons.

Critical period hypothesis: The premise that there is a limited period of heightened linguistic sensitivity early in life during which the language learner must be exposed to language in order to reach full linguistic competence. The hypothesis predicts a low level of linguistic performance in all language users who began learning the language after the closure of this time window early in life.

Cross-language neighborhood: See **Neighborhood**.

Cross-linguistic influence: also "cross-linguistic transfer": The influence of the non-selected language on the selected language in language use by bilinguals (and multilinguals), or the influence of an earlier acquired language (e.g., the L1) on the acquisition of a new language (e.g., L2). Cross-linguistic influence can have positive as well as negative effects on language use and acquisition, speeding up or slowing down language use and facilitating the acquisition of a particular structure in the new language or misleading the learner. An example of positive and negative transfer in L2 vocabulary acquisition is when the learner assumes that similar forms mean the same thing across languages. This facilitates the learning of **cognates** but interferes with the learning of **false cognates** or **false friends**.

Cross-modal priming: See **Word priming technique**.

Cued recall: A recall test of previously learned foreign vocabulary in which on each trial a retrieval cue is presented. In **receptive cued recall** the newly learned foreign word serves as retrieval cue and the corresponding native word must be retrieved from memory. In **productive cued recall** the native word is the retrieval cue and the newly learned foreign word must be retrieved.

Cued translation: See **Translation production**.

Delayed recall: See **Immediate recall**.

Differential recovery: See **Bilingual aphasia**.

Diffusion tensor imaging: A neuroimaging technique that uses an MRI scanner to provide images of **white matter** pathways in the brain. It measures the density and motion of water in the axons of neurons.

Distributed memory representation: See **Localist memory representation**.

Dual-coding theory: A theory of memory storage and representation that assumes the existence of both a verbal and an image system in memory. The theory can explain why the **keyword method** is an effective method for acquiring foreign vocabulary: During keyword learning both a verbal and an image code of the new item are stored in memory and both of them support recall. The theory can also account for the effect of **word concreteness** in foreign vocabulary learning because **concrete words** but not **abstract words** foster the storage of both a verbal and an image code in memory.

Ear–voice span: In simultaneous interpreting, the lag between the moment a **source language** fragment is spoken by the speaker and the moment the equivalent of this fragment emerges in the interpreter's aural rendition of the source language in the **target language**.

EEG (electroencephalography): A technique for measuring the electrical activity of the brain by means of electrodes that are placed on the scalp.

ELAN: See **LAN**.

ERP (event-related potential): A small voltage change in the brain's electrical activity that is induced by a particular stimulus (the "event"). The ERP is measured at the scalp by means of electroencephalography (**EEG**) and it is measured time-locked to the stimulus. Different ERPs (or ERP "components") are characterized by their *polarity* (they can be positive or negative, indicated by P or N, respectively), *latency* (the time interval, expressed in milliseconds, between the onset of the stimulus and the moment a voltage peak shows in the signal), *amplitude* (the size of the voltage change relative to some baseline), and *topography* (the places on the scalp where the electrical activity is detected). Components are often named according to their polarity and latency (e.g., N400; P600).

Extensional meaning: See **Referential meaning**.

Eye–mind hypothesis: The hypothesis that at every moment in time while reading the mind processes the word or segment on which the eyes are fixating.

Eye-movement recording (as applied in reading research): An experimental technique that registers the participants' forward and backward eye movements and eye fixations while they read a text, documenting where exactly they are looking at and for how long.

Eye-movement tracking paradigm (as applied in the study of spoken language comprehension): Participants are presented with spoken instructions to manipulate objects on a visual display. They wear a headband with equipment that tracks their eye movements while they carry out the instructions (e.g., *Pick up the candy and put it above the fork*). The time to initiate an eye movement to a target object on the display and the proportion of trials in which eye movements are made to other objects on the display reveal information on how spoken words are recognized.

False cognate: See **False friend**.

False friend; also **Pseudocognate** or **False cognate**: A word from which the written (or spoken) form closely resembles the form of a word in another language but that shares no meaning with it; the resemblance is accidental (e.g., English *juice* and Spanish *juicio*, "judge").

Familiarization paradigm: See **Habituation paradigm**.

Fissure: See **Sulcus**.

fMRI: See **Functional magnetic resonance imaging**.

Foreign language effect: The phenomenon that the learner's L2 (or another language acquired after native L1, but *not* native L1) is the source of cross-language interference on the currently acquired foreign language, say L4.

Formant: A term used in acoustic phonetics to indicate a concentration of acoustic energy in a particular frequency range in a speech sound. A speech sound's formants can be visualized in **spectrograms** of the speech signal. Vowels are characterized by the frequency ranges of the first two formants.

Formulator: A component of the speech production architecture that translates the **preverbal message**—that is, the output of **conceptualizing**—into a linguistic structure.

Fricatives: Consonants produced by constricting but not fully closing the vocal tract. The air that is forced through the constriction produces a hissing noise. Examples are /s/, /z/, /f/, and /v/.

Frontal lobe: The part of the **cortex** that is located in front of the central **sulcus** and above the lateral sulcus (see Figure 8.2). It contains the motor cortex and the prefrontal cortex.

Functional magnetic resonance imaging (fMRI): A neuroimaging method that exploits **magnetic resonance imaging** (MRI) for measuring blood flow changes in the brain that are correlated with local changes in neural activity. When neurons are active, their consumption of oxygen increases and the local response to this increase in oxygen use is an increased blood flow to the region of active neurons, called the "hemodynamic response", which lasts a couple of seconds. It is this response that is detected by means of the fMRI technique.

Gating: A **perceptual identification** procedure in which listeners are presented with gradually increasing fragments of spoken words and are asked to guess the words from the fragments. The primary variable of interest is the "gate duration" (that is, the length of the spoken fragment) at which the target word is first guessed correctly.

Generalized lexical decision; also **Language-neutral lexical decision**: A bilingual version of the **lexical decision** task in which a "yes" response must be given if the presented letter string is a word in *either one* of the participant's two languages. If this is not the case, a "no" response must be given. In **language-specific lexical decision** a "yes" response must only be given to letter strings that are words in the language specified by the experimenter. The correct response to letter strings that are words in the other language is a "no" response.

Go/no-go task: A class of tasks in which the participants have to translate the outcome of the cognitive process of interest in an overt response on some trials ("go") but withhold a response on other trials ("no-go"). For instance, in the **language go/no-go task** the (bilingual) participants must produce an overt response whenever a stimulus is a word in one language and refrain from responding when it is a word in the other language.

Grammatical encoding: A component of the speech production process that retrieves grammatical information from **lemmas** in the mental lexicon from which it can then build syntactic constructions (cf. **Phonological encoding**).

Grammatical gender: A grammatical concept that marks words such as nouns, adjectives, articles, and pronouns according to a distinction between masculine, feminine, and neuter. In some languages a strong correlation exists between grammatical gender and natural, biological, gender, but in most languages no, or only a weak, correlation exists between grammatical and natural gender. Languages vary in the number of gender distinctions they make. For instance, German has three (masculine, feminine, and neuter), whereas French has two (masculine and feminine). A word's gender may show in the form of the article and adjective (e.g., French: *un/ le grand jardin* vs. *une/la grande voiture*, "a/the big garden" vs. "a/the big car") whereas in other languages it also shows in the form of the noun (Italian: *un/il giardino grande*; *una/la macchina granda*).

Grammatical number: A grammatical concept that expresses the contrasts singular, dual, and plural. In many languages verb forms show agreement with the number (and person) of the subject (*her dress [singular] looks [singular] nice*; *her dresses [plural] look [plural] nice*).

Grapheme: The smallest contrastive unit in the writing system of a language. It is the written equivalent of a **phoneme**.

Gray matter: Those areas of the nervous system that predominantly contain the cell bodies, which look grayish.

Guest language: See **Language-mode theory**.

Habituation paradigm; also **Familiarization paradigm**: A popular experimental method used to examine the perceptual discrimination abilities of babies, which makes use of the fact that babies pay more attention to novel stimuli than to familiar stimuli. It involves a habituation or familiarization phase followed by a test phase. In the habituation phase the infant participants are repeatedly presented with one and the same stimulus, say a speech sound. When this sound is first presented, it will arouse the infant's attention. Attention will subsequently gradually lessen. When it is back at some baseline level the test phase follows in which a new speech sound is presented. If this arouses the child's attention again the conclusion can be drawn that the child detected the difference between the stimuli presented during habituation and at test. See the **head-turn procedure**, the **heart-rate paradigm**, and the **preferential looking technique** for specific versions of this general method.

Head-turn procedure: An experimental technique used in the study of infant speech perception which makes use of the fact that infants look at the place where an interesting new sound comes from and stop looking when the novelty of the sound wears off. Looking time thus indexes listening time and both index attention time. Whereas in the **preferential looking technique** the stimuli are emitted from one loudspeaker, the head-turn procedure makes use of two loud-speakers that are located left-front and right-front of the infant. In a familiarization phase the infants are trained to turn their heads towards a light that flashes near the one or the other loud-speaker while a stimulus set is emitted from *both* speakers. The speech stimuli presented during the subsequent test phase are either the ones pre-sented during familiarization or novel ones. The test stimuli are again accompanied by a flashing light but this time they are only played from one loudspeaker at a time (the one where the light flashes). The question of interest is whether the time the infant looks in the direction of the sound-emitting speaker differs when the sound is the familiar one than when it is a novel one. If it does, it can be concluded that the infant notices the difference between the two.

Heart-rate paradigm: An experimental technique used in the study of infant speech perception, which exploits the fact that an increase in atten-tion is accompanied by an increase in heartbeat. Changes in a cardiogram that occur the moment a familiar speech sound, for instance, is replaced by a novel speech sound thus suggest increased attention. In turn, the increased attention indi-cates the infant has noticed the difference between the two speech sounds.

Hebbian learning: A learning principle stating that co-activated memory units (or "nodes") become linked with one another, as succinctly expressed in the maxim "what fires together wires together". The more often memory nodes fire together, the stronger the bond between them becomes. The simultaneous firing of memory nodes is called **resonance**. Hebbian learning can explain the formation of language subsets in bilingual memory.

High-amplitude sucking paradigm (HAS): An experimental technique used to examine fluctu-ations of attention in babies. It exploits the fact that the rate at which infants suck on a pacifier varies with the amount of attention they pay to a particular stimulus: The higher the level of attention, the higher the sucking rate.

Homograph effect: In studies of bilingual word recognition, the finding that the response time to **interlexical homographs** differs from the response time to non-homographic control words. The direction of the effect (positive or negative) varies with the constellation of the stimulus set and the exact task demands.

Homonym: One of two words with an identical form but different meanings (e.g., *bank*, "financial institution" or "landscape feature").

Homonymy; also **Lexical ambiguity**: The phenom-enon that one and the same word form has multiple meanings (e.g., *bank*, "financial institu-tion" or "landscape feature").

Homophone effect: In studies of bilingual word recognition, the finding that the response time to **interlexical homophones** differs from the response time to non-homophonic control words.

Hyponym: A word referring to an exemplar of a class of objects, persons, or animals. For instance, *chair* is a hyponym of *furniture* and *lion* is a hyponym of *mammal*.

Immediate recall: Testing the retention of learned material, for instance, foreign language vocabu-lary, immediately after acquisition. In **delayed recall** retention is tested at some later point in time.

Incidental vocabulary learning: The vocabulary learning that occurs when the participants per-form particular language-processing tasks that are not directly aimed at committing lexical information to memory. The participants are not informed that their retention of vocabulary will be tested afterwards and they are therefore unlikely to focus on the meaning and form of individual words (cf. **Intentional vocabulary learning**).

Intensional meaning: See **Referential meaning**.

Intentional vocabulary learning: The vocabulary learning that occurs when learners perform activities that are deliberately aimed at commit-ting lexical information to memory. The term is also used for vocabulary learning in studies in which the participants are informed that their retention will subsequently be tested (cf. **Incidental vocabulary learning**).

Interlexical homograph: also called "interlingual homograph" or "interlanguage homograph"): A word that has an orthographic form identical to that of a word in another language while not sharing meaning with it (e.g., French *coin*, "corner", and English *coin*). An "interlexical homographic neighbor" is a word whose written form is not identical but closely similar to a word in another language.

Interlexical homophone: A word that sounds the same as a word in another language while not sharing meaning with it (e.g., French *mot*, "word", and English *mow*). An "interlexical homophonic neighbor" is a word that sounds similar to, but not exactly the same as, a word in another language.

Interlingual Stroop effect: See **Bilingual Stroop task**.

Keyword method: A method of foreign language vocabulary learning in which for the foreign word to be learned (e.g., French *arbre*, "tree") a similar-sounding native language word is thought up (*arbor*). This word is the so-called keyword. Next, a mental image is created in which the meanings of the keyword and the new vocabulary item interact (e.g., the image of an arbor shaded by a tree). During recall this image is retrieved from memory and the targeted foreign word can be "read off" from it. In the **verbiage** version of the method the learner constructs native language sentences containing a keyword and the native translation of the targeted foreign words (e.g., to learn Italian *forbice*, "scissors", the sentence *Scissors are forbidden for children*, in which *forbidden* is the keyword for *forbice*).

LAN (left anterior negativity): An **ERP** component with a negative polarity measured at electrodes positioned above the anterior region of the left hemisphere and that occurs between 300 ms and 500 ms after the onset of the critical word in a sentence. Sometimes it occurs earlier, between 100 ms and 250 ms after word onset. It is then called **ELAN** (early left anterior negativity). It is thought to index an early stage of automatic sentence-structure building (cf. **P600**).

Language cue: A piece of information in the **preverbal message** that specifies the language a bilingual intends to use in a specific situation.

Language decision task: An experimental task in which bilingual participants are presented with words in their two languages and have to decide for each word to which language it belongs.

Language go/no-go task: See **Go/no-go task**.

Language-mode theory: A theory on the relative activation levels of a bilingual's two mental linguistic subsystems, one for each language. Except during translation, one language is always selected as the main language for communicative interaction. This language is called the **base language** (or Language A) and the associated linguistic subsystem is maximally activated. The activation of the other subsystem, the one storing the so-called **guest language** (or Language B), varies with the contextual circumstances, including the linguistic abilities of the interlocutors. If the interlocutors are fully monolingual so that unilingual output must be produced to avoid a communicative breakdown, the guest language's subsystem is deactivated as best as possible and the bilingual speaker is said to be in a **monolingual mode**. The behavioral effect of this activation state is that few code switches into the guest language occur. If the bilingual speaker is communicating with interlocutors who master the same two languages, the guest language subsystem may be activated above this minimum level. The behavioral effect of this activation state is that more code switching occurs. The bilingual speaker is said to be in a **bilingual mode** if the guest language is also relatively highly activated (but still less so than the base language). This may occur under circumstances in which frequent code switching does not hamper the conversation flow. The theory comprises the assumption that, depending on the contextual circumstances, a bilingual can choose any position on a continuum (the "language-mode continuum") between the monolingual and bilingual language modes.

Language-neutral lexical decision: See **Generalized lexical decision**.

Language-nonselective lexical access: In comprehension studies, the view that when a bilingual reads or hears a word in one of his or her languages, representations of words of *both* languages are activated in the mental lexicon and compete for selection. In production studies the term refers to the view that a lexical concept activates the **lemmas** of words in both of a bilingual's languages. In contrast, according to the **language-selective lexical access** view, a word input only activates representations of words belonging to the same language as the input word (in comprehension), or a lexical concept only activates lemmas in the currently targeted language (in production).

Language-selective lexical access: See **Language-nonselective lexical access**.

Language-specific lexical decision: See **Generalized lexical decision**.

Language-switching effect: See **Language-switching paradigm**.

Language-switching paradigm: An experimental technique in which at predictable or unpredictable moments a language input presented to a bilingual participant changes from the one language to the other (in comprehension) or a bilingual participant is forced to change the output language from one moment to the next (in production). The recognition or production of the word involving a language switch typically takes longer than the recognition or production of a matched word in the same language as the previous word. This response-time difference between no-switch and switch words is the **language-switching effect** or "switch cost". Spontaneous language switching in natural conversations, usually called "code switching" or "language mixing", does not necessarily involve a switch cost.

Language tag: A piece of information in a word's representation in the mental lexicon of a bilingual (or multilingual) that specifies the language to which the word belongs.

Lemma: According to some models of lexical representation, that part of a lexical entry that comprises the word's meaning and syntactical specifications. In other models the term only comprises the syntactic information associated with a word, for instance that it concerns a count noun with female **grammatical gender**.

Lemma selection: That part of the word-production process during which one **lemma** out of a larger set of lemmas that are activated by some conceptualized content (called the "semantic cohort") is selected for further processing, specifically for **phonological encoding**.

Lexeme: According to some models of lexical representation, that part of the lexical entry that contains the word's morphological and phonological properties. The term is also used in a more narrow sense, only covering the word's phonological form.

Lexical access: In comprehension studies, used in a narrow sense the term refers to the stage during word recognition in which, following a match between an input word and a representation in the mental lexicon, all the information stored with this representation, including its syntactical and morphological specifications and its meaning, becomes available for further processing. In a broader sense it is also used to cover the earlier stage in which an input word is matched onto its lexical representation. In production studies "lexical access" is used to refer to all the processing that occurs between the conceptualization of a specific lexical concept and the moment the corresponding lexical element (or **lemma**) is selected for actual production.

Lexical ambiguity: See **Homonymy**.

Lexical decision: A popular experimental task to study word recognition: A number of words and **pseudowords** (e.g., *hand, plete, floor, music, flike,* etc.) are presented to the participants one by one, and they have to decide for each of these stimuli whether or not it constitutes a word, notifying their decision by pressing a "yes" or a "no" button.

Linguistic determinism: The view that a speaker's language, through the specific grammatical structures and semantic classifications that it exploits, determines his or her view of the world. As a consequence, speakers of different languages will think differently. Because it was put forward by the American anthropological linguists Sapir and Whorf, it is also known as the Sapir-Whorf hypothesis. A weaker version of the theory, called linguistic relativity, holds that a language's specific structures influence (rather than determine) the way its speakers view the world and think.

Linguistic relativity: See **Linguistic determinism**.

Loan word: See **Borrowing**.

Localist memory representation: A memory representation for which a one-to-one relation holds between the representing structure and the information that it represents. For instance, a word's meaning is represented in a single memory unit ("node"). Instead, in a **distributed memory representation** the represented information is spread out over multiple memory nodes so that, for instance, a particular word's meaning is represented across, say, 50 memory nodes.

Magnetic resonance imaging (MRI): A neuroimaging technique that enables the production of a structural map of the brain by exploiting the magnetic properties of organic tissue: A strong magnetic field alters the orientation of certain atoms. When the magnetic field is removed the atoms will return to a randomly distributed orientation, generating a small magnetic field in the process. This magnetic field is picked up by detectors.

Magneto-encephalography (MEG): The recording, by magnetic detectors placed around the scalp, of the magnetic correlate of the electronic activity in active neurons. Like the **ERP** signal, the MEG signal can be measured in response to a specific stimulus, thus producing a so-called "event-related field".

Malapropism: A type of speech error where a word with a similar sound is substituted for the intended word (e.g., *evaporate* for *evacuate*). In addition to many shared phonemes, malapropisms often have the same stress pattern and number of syllables as the intended word, and they typically belong to the same grammatical class. In foreign language learning, substitutions of this type are sometimes called **synforms**.

Masked priming: See **Semantic priming technique**.

Matthew effect: The phenomenon that an abundance of something brings about more abundance, as expressed in the maxim "the rich get richer". It also applies to foreign language knowledge: The more of it one has, the easier it is to acquire new foreign language knowledge. The term derives from a saying of the apostle Matthew: "to one that has shall be given".

Mean length of utterance (MLU): The mean number of **morphemes**, both bound and free, averaged over a sample of utterances produced by a child at a certain age. It is used as a measure of the stage of language development the child has reached.

Metalinguistic awareness: The ability to reflect on and manipulate linguistic structures independent of their meaning.

Modularity of mind theory: Central in this theory is the concept of mental modules, information-processing devices that perform basic cognitive functions on incoming information, such as recognizing faces or words, and that are characterized by a number of features: Modules tend to operate in a "domain-specific" way (which means that they only respond to input of a particular type, say faces or words), they operate fast and mandatorily, and they are "informationally encapsulated". The latter concept means that modules are impenetrable by information delivered by "higher" cognitive processes such as thinking, problem solving, or making inferences, and cannot exploit the background knowledge these higher cognitive processes make use of.

Monolingual mode: See **Language-mode theory**.

Mora: A minimal rhythmical unit in speech about the length of a short syllable.

Morpheme: The smallest linguistic unit that bears meaning. "Free" morphemes can occur on their own (e.g., *great* or *shark*). "Bound" morphemes cannot stand on their own but are attached to free morphemes, modifying their meaning (e.g., *-ness*, and *-s* in *greatness* and *sharks*).

Morphology: The study of word structure, of how words are built up from morphemes.

Motherese: See **Child directed speech**.

Moving-window technique: A procedure to study reading processes. A text appears on the screen in successive segments ("windows") while earlier and later segments are replaced by groups of dashes, each group representing a word and each single dash representing a letter. For instance, the current presentation of the segment *landed* in the sentence *A heron has just landed in my garden* would look as follows: - ----- --- ---- *landed* -- -- ------. In another version of the task the segments revealed in the previous windows remain on the screen: *A heron has just landed* -- -- ------.

Myelin: A substance that surrounds the axons of neurons and that speeds up the conduction of action potentials.

Natural translation: The translating done in everyday circumstances by bilinguals of all ages without any professional training in translating.

N400: An **ERP** with a negative polarity that is elicited by any content word and that is maximal at about 400 ms after the onset of the word. It is larger in amplitude the more difficult it is to integrate the word's meaning with the meaning of the surrounding linguistic context. In word-priming experiments (see **Semantic priming technique**) it is larger for words preceded by an unrelated prime word than for words preceded by a related word prime. In a sentence context it is larger for words that violate lexical-semantic constraints (as in *The girl comforted the clock*) than for words that fit the context semantically (*The girl comforted the baby*). The **N400 effect** is the difference in amplitude of the N400 for related and unrelated content words, or for contextually appropriate and inappropriate content words.

N400 effect: See **N400**.

Neighbor: See **Neighborhood**.

Neighborhood: A word's lexical neighborhood is the set of words in a language user's mental lexicon that all share most of their (orthographic and/or phonological) form with it. For instance, the orthographic neighborhood of written *land* contains the words *band*, *sand*, *lane*, *hand*, *lank*, and *and*, all called **neighbors** of *land*. In bilinguals the **cross-language neighborhood** of a given word consists of all the words in the other one of the two known languages that share most of their form with it. For instance, in a Dutch–English bilingual the cross-language neighborhood of English *land* comprises Dutch *mand*, *zand*, *pand*, *lans*, *land*, and *band*.

Occipital lobe: The part of the **cortex** located at the back of the brain (see Figure 8.2). It is primarily involved in the processing of visual information.

Off-line task: See **On-line task**.

On-line task: An experimental task that taps the mental process of interest the very moment it takes place. In contrast, an **off-line task** only measures the mental process of interest afterwards.

P600; also **Syntactic positive shift**: An ERP component with a positive polarity and a latency of about 600 ms that occurs when words violate syntactic rules in sentences. It is thought to reflect an attention-demanding syntactic integration process (cf. **ELAN** and **LAN**).

Paired-associate learning: A general learning method in which pairs of stimuli are presented during training. Two versions of the methodology are used in foreign language vocabulary acquisition. In **picture–word association** one of the two elements in each stimulus pair is the foreign word to acquire, the other a picture depicting its meaning. In **word–word association** the stimulus pairs consist of a foreign word and its translation in the native language.

Paradigmatic relation: The "vertical" relationship between linguistic elements that can substitute for one another in a linguistic structure, for instance, *boastful*, *handsome*, *generous* in my *boastful/handsome/generous colleague*. Words that are paradigmatically related generally belong to the same grammatical class (cf. **Syntagmatic relation**).

Parietal lobe: The part of the **cortex** that is located behind the central **sulcus**, in front of the **occipital lobe** and above the posterior part of the **temporal lobe** (see Figure 8.2).

Parsing: Uncovering the grammatical structure of a sentence. In the process the sentence's constituent parts such as subject, verb, and object are revealed.

Perceptual identification task: A common task to study word recognition. The word stimuli are presented "degraded" or "masked"; that is, they cannot be perceived readily and automatically. Several procedures are used to degrade the stimuli, for instance they are presented very briefly while they are preceded and followed by a pattern mask (called a "forward" and "backward" mask, respectively).

Performance: See **Competence**.

PET: See **Positron emission tomography**.

Phoneme: The smallest contrastive unit in the sound system of a language. In English, /b/ and /p/ are two phonemes because, for instance, *bun* and *pun* or *bear* and *pear* mean different things. Changing a phoneme changes the meaning of a word. It is convention to mark phonemes by putting them between two slashes, as in /d/.

Phonetic category assimilation: An L2 speech learning process assumed by J. E. Flege (e.g., Flege, 2002) in his speech learning model. The model assumes that during the development of the L2 sound system the phonetic categories of the L2 are stored in the memory system that already holds the L1 phonetic categories, and that the degree of similarity between a new L2 category and the stored L1 categories determines whether or not a separate category for the L2 sound is formed. If the new sound is similar to a stored L1 sound, the phonetic category that stores this L1 sound attracts the new L2 sound. During this process the attracting L1 category shifts somewhat in phonemic space towards a position that reflects the acoustic characteristics of the L2 sound. This process is called "phonetic category assimilation". If the new L2 sound is very dissimilar from all stored L1 sounds, a separate phonetic category for the L2 sound is formed. In order to obtain maximal distinctiveness between the new L2 sound and the closest L1 sound, the two adopt exaggerated values on the phonetic characteristics that distinguish them. This process is called **phonetic category dissimilation**.

Phonetic category dissimilation: See **Phonetic category assimilation**.

Phonetics: The scientific study of how speech sounds are produced, perceived, and what their physical properties are.

Phonological encoding: A processing component of speech production during which a phonetic plan is built for each **lemma** and the utterance as a whole. During this process, the lexical entries' **lexemes** are accessed and the elements in the grammatical encoder's output are morphologically and phonologically adapted to their linguistic environment (cf. **Grammatical encoding**).

Phonotactical typicality (a characteristic of foreign language words): The degree to which the phonotactical structure of a foreign language word resembles the sound structure of L1 words. Foreign words with a phonotactical structure akin to L1 words are easier to learn than those with an atypical phonotactical structure. See **Phonotactics** for further clarification.

Phonotactics: (A description of) the specific sequences of phonemes that can occur in a language and their positional constraints. For instance, in English the phoneme sequence /spr/ occurs but only at the beginning, not at the end, of words.

Picture-naming task: A popular task to study word production. In the simplest version of the task the participants are presented with pictures that depict lexicalized concepts and are instructed to name each of them as rapidly as possible. In the **picture–word interference task** the picture is accompanied by a word and the relation between picture and word is systematically varied (e.g., a picture of a cat is accompanied by the word *dog*). This word can have an interfering or a facilitative effect on picture naming, depending on the type of relation between picture and word.

Picture–word association: See **Paired-association learning**.

Picture–word interference task: See **Picture-naming task**.

Place of articulation: The location in the vocal tract where the airflow is constricted during the production of a consonant (e.g., at the lips or the alveolar ridge, the ridge just behind the upper teeth).

Plosive: A consonant produced by the sudden release of air following a complete closure of the vocal tract (e.g., the /p/, /t/, and /k/, as in *pet*, *top*, and *kid* are plosives).

Positron emission tomography (PET): A neuroimaging method that detects changes in neural activity by measuring correlated blood flow changes in the brain. A radioactive element is injected into the bloodstream and subsequently the photons that are produced during the decay of the radioactive element are counted. The larger the number of photons detected in a specific brain area, the more blood there is in that region, and thus the more active that area.

Preferential listening technique: See **Preferential looking technique**.

Preferential looking technique: An experimental technique used in the study of infant speech perception that makes use of the fact that infants look at the place where an interesting new sound comes from and stop looking when the novelty of the sound wears off. The speech stimulus is accompanied by some visual stimulus, typically presented on a screen, to attract the infant's attention and the source emitting the speech stimulus is located near the screen. Looking time is assumed to index listening time and both are assumed to index attention time. The technique is also called the **preferential listening technique** (cf. **Head-turn procedure**).

Preverbal message: See **Conceptualizing**.

Productive cued recall: See **Cued recall**.

Progressive demasking: A perceptual identification procedure (see **perceptual identification task**) in which the visual presentation of a target word and a mask alternate. During this alternation process the presentation duration of the target gradually increases and that of the mask gradually decreases. The procedure stops the moment the participant can identify the target.

Pseudocognate: See **False friend**.

Pseudowords: Meaningless letter strings that are used as stimuli in a **lexical decision** experiment and obey the orthography and phonology of the test language. They differ from real words only in that they lack meaning.

Rapid serial visual presentation (RSVP): A technique used in reading research. Segments of text are presented one by one on a screen at a fixed rate and at the same location. Unlike in **self-paced reading**, the experimenter determines the presentation speed of the reading materials.

Receptive cued recall: See **Cued recall**.

Referent: The object, entity, or person in the world to which a particular word refers.

Referential meaning: Knowledge regarding the entities or events in the external world to which a word refers (also called **extensional meaning**). It contrasts with **intensional meaning**—the relation of a word to other words in the lexicon, such as its **antonyms**, **synonyms**, and **hyponyms**.

Resonance: The simultaneous activation of specific memory nodes when a certain stimulus is presented. Resonance causes the resonating memory nodes to become connected. See also **Hebbian learning**.

Retroactive interference: The interference of later learning on previous learning. Learning new things somehow overwrites or obscures earlier knowledge.

Rote-rehearsal learning: A foreign language vocabulary learning technique that uses the **word–word association** presentation procedure and in which the participants are instructed to silently rehearse the words within the word pairs.

Saccade: A ballistic movement of the eyes between two eye fixations, for instance while reading.

Segmental: Regarding the "segments" of speech; that is, a language's vowels and consonants (cf. **Suprasegmental**).

Selection restrictions: Constraints on the way linguistic units (e.g., phonemes, words) can combine with other units in particular environments.

Selective recovery: See **Bilingual aphasia**.

Self-paced reading: A technique used in reading research. The participant summons each segment of text onto the monitor in front of him/her by pressing a key. The interval between two successive key presses is measured and is regarded the reading time for the segment. In one version of the task every new segment replaces the preceding fragment so that at any moment in time just one segment is on the screen. Successive fragments may occur in the same position on the screen or move across the screen. See also **Moving-window technique**.

Semantic memory: That part of long-term memory that stores knowledge independent of the experience that led to this knowledge. The term also refers to knowledge of this type. Knowledge of words, their **referential** and **intensional meaning**, is part of semantic memory. The term contrasts with episodic memory, which is that part of long-term memory that contains knowledge of personal experiences, "episodes". Not only our experiences in daily life outside the laboratory are called episodes, but also, for instance, our participation in a laboratory experiment, for example, as a participant in a **paired-associate learning** experiment. Unlike semantic memory representations, episodic memory representations contain information about the time and place the events took place and the circumstances under which they took place.

Semantic priming effect: See **Semantic priming technique**.

Semantic priming technique: An experimental procedure to examine the connections between entries in the mental lexicon. A target word is preceded by a semantically related prime word, an unrelated prime word, or a "neutral" prime, and the effect of the prime on target processing is measured. The **semantic priming effect** is the finding that a target preceded by a semantically related prime is responded to faster than a target preceded by an unrelated or neutral prime. In **masked priming** the prime word is visually degraded (e.g., by presenting it very briefly or interspersed between two noise signals) in order to prevent conscious perception of the prime.

Sequential bilingualism: See **Bilingual first language acquisition**.

Sequential recovery: See **Bilingual aphasia**.

Simultaneous bilingualism: See **Bilingual first language acquisition**.

Simultaneous interpreting: A form of speech-to-speech translation in which the interpreter simultaneously listens to the **source language** segment that is currently being spoken by the speaker and provides an oral rendition of an earlier input segment in the **target language** (cf. **Consecutive interpreting**).

Source language: The input language in translation. The output language is called the **target language**.

Spectrogram: A visual rendition of a speech fragment on a piece of paper produced by a technical instrument called a **spectrograph**. A spectrogram shows an analysis of speech sounds in the constituent sound waves, their intensity, and how they develop over time. The horizontal and vertical axes of a spectrogram represent time and frequency of the constituent sound waves, respectively. The intensity of the speech at any moment in time is indicated by the degree of blackness of the marks on the paper: the higher the intensity, the blacker the markings.

Spectrograph: A device used to study the physical properties of speech sounds. It creates a **spectrogram**.

Stroop effect: See **Stroop task**.

Stroop task: A popular task to study the ability to ignore part of a stimulus. The participants are presented with color words printed in different colors and must name the words' ink-colors and ignore their names. When the color of the word and its name are incongruent (e.g., the word *red* printed in green ink) the color name response is slower than when they are congruent. This difference in response time is the **Stroop effect**. In another version of the task the words have to be read and the colors ignored. To study language processing and representation in bilinguals, the **bilingual Stroop task** has been used.

Sublexical: Said of the linguistic units that words are composed of. Phonemes and common phoneme sequences (see **Phonotactics**) are thus sublexical linguistic units.

Subordinative bilingualism: See **Compound bilingualism**.

Subtractive bilingualism: See **Additive bilingualism**.

Sulcus; also **Fissure**: A cleft in the **cortex** formed by the folding of the cortex.

Suprasegmental: An aspect of the speech signal that is superimposed over more than one speech segment; that is, over more than one vowel or consonant, e.g., stress and pitch (cf. **Segmental**).

Syllable: A rhythmical unit of speech. Syllables can be divided into an onset and a "rime" and, in turn, the rime can often be further divided into a "nucleus" and a "coda". For instance, the word *perpendicular* consists of the syllables *per*, *pen*, *di*, *cu*, and *lar*. The onset, nucleus, and coda of *per* are *p*, *e*, and *r*, respectively, and *er* is its rime.

Synform (for "similar lexical form"): A foreign language word that is similar in form, but not in meaning, to another word in this language and that a foreign language learner may therefore accidentally substitute for the targeted similar word. For instance, a learner of Hebrew might use the word *halvaja*, "funeral" when *halva'a*, "loan" was intended; cf. **Malapropism**).

Synonym: A word with the same, or nearly the same, meaning as another word.

Syntactic positive shift: See **P600**.

Syntagmatic relation: The "horizontal" relationship between linguistic elements in linguistic constructions; for instance, between *beautiful* and *weather* in *beautiful weather*, or between *get* and *behind* in *get behind*. The term derives from "syntagma", a general term for any string of linguistic units that together form a more complex linguistic unit. The units constituting a syntagmatic relation typically belong to different grammatical classes (cf. **Paradigmatic relation**).

Syntax-first models: Models of **parsing** that assume the parser initially automatically applies a universal parsing strategy that assigns the simplest possible structure to the sentence on the basis of syntactical information only, ignoring syntax-external sources of information such as contextual-semantic and lexical information. Only later, if and when this strategy encounters a deadlock, may other sources of information be implicated in a reanalysis of the sentence. This type of model is consistent with **modularity of mind theory**. They differ from "interactive parsing" models, which assume that in assigning a structural analysis to a sentence the parser exploits syntax-external sources of information immediately.

Target language: The output language in translation. The term is also used in a more general sense to refer to the language a bilingual intends to use under specific (naturalistic or experimental) circumstances.

Temporal lobe: The part of the **cortex** bounded by the lateral **sulcus**, the inferior part of the **parietal lobe** and the anterior part of the **occipital lobe** (see Figure 8.2).

Thematic role: The semantic role of a noun phrase in a sentence, for instance whether it is the actor ("agent") or the recipient ("patient") of the action expressed by the verb. Alternative names are "theta role" and "case role".

Tip-of-the-tongue phenomenon: A failure to retrieve a particular word (typically of low frequency) from memory while at the same time the speaker knows that he or she knows the word. In this "feeling-of-knowing" state a number of the word's features can usually be retrieved, such as its first letter or how many syllables it has.

Transcoding: A translation procedure in which structures in the **source language** are directly replaced by the corresponding **target language** structures, exploiting the fact that earlier translation experience has led to direct connections between translation-equivalent memory structures. If an input activates a source language structure, the corresponding target language structure is automatically activated due to spreading activation across the link between them (cf. **Conceptually mediated translation**).

Translation priming effect: The finding that bilinguals process a word faster when it is preceded by its translation in the other language than when it is preceded by an unrelated word in the other language.

Translation production: An experimental task in which on each trial a stimulus word is presented, which the bilingual participant has to translate into the other language. In **cued translation** the stimulus word presented for translation is accompanied by a cue that reveals part of the identity of its translation; for instance, its first letter may be given as cue.

Translation recognition: An experimental task in which pairs of words are presented to the bilingual participants, each pair consisting of an L1 word and an L2 word. A pair may consist of actual translations or of words that are not translations of one another. The participants must indicate for each pair whether or not it consists of translations.

Typological distance: "Typological linguistics" is the study of the structural similarities and differences among languages according to their phonology, grammar, and vocabulary. The typological distance between a pair of languages is the extent to which they share structures in these linguistic domains.

Uninstructed learning; also "unstructured learning" or "own-strategy learning": A form of **word–**word association foreign vocabulary learning in which the participants receive no specific instruction on how to process the stimulus pairs but are free to choose their own learning strategy.

Universal grammar (UG): A grammar that specifies the form that the grammar of individual languages can take. The term is also used to refer to a universal and innate human language faculty that is postulated by some linguistic theories. The assumed language faculty is thought to consist of innate knowledge regarding the forms that the grammars of natural languages may take.

Verbiage: See **Keyword method**.

Vocabulary breadth: The number of words that a language user knows to at least some extent. **Vocabulary depth** concerns the degree to which individual words are known; what different types of knowledge regarding the word are known (e.g., semantic, syntactic, pragmatic).

Vocabulary depth: See **Vocabulary breadth**.

Voice onset time (VOT): The time between the release of the air and the moment the vocal cords start to vibrate when a speaker produces a consonant.

White matter: Regions of the nervous system that primarily contain axons. Axons are coated with **myelin** that has a whitish appearance.

Word association (discrete): An experimental procedure to reveal connections between word representations in memory. A series of prompt words are presented to the participants one by one and they are asked to say the first word that comes to mind after hearing or seeing the prompt word. In **continued word association** the participants generate as many words as possible for each of the prompt words within a certain unit time.

Word concreteness: A semantic word variable that distinguishes between **concrete** and **abstract words**. Concrete words refer to physical entities that can be perceived by (at least one of) the senses (e.g., *paperclip*, *basket*). Abstract words refer to non-physical entities and cannot be perceived by any of the senses (e.g., *hate*, *indulgence*).

Word frequency: A measure of how frequently a word occurs in speech or text. A word's frequency of occurrence is usually determined on the basis of a word count of speech or text corpora.

Word imageability: A semantic word variable that reflects how easy it is to form a mental image of the referent of the word. The variable is highly correlated with **word concreteness**: Concrete words are generally easy to imagine. For abstract words this is hard.

Word naming: A popular experimental task to study word recognition. A number of printed words are presented one by one and the participants are asked to read each of them aloud. Response latencies and reading accuracy are registered.

Word priming technique; see also **Semantic priming technique**: An experimental technique in which a word target is preceded by a prime (usually a word or a sentence fragment) and the effect of the prime on processing the target is measured. In **cross-modal priming**, prime and target are presented in different modalities, for instance, the prime aurally, the target visually.

Word–word association: See **Paired-associate learning**.

References

Abrahamsson, N., & Hyltenstam, K. (2009). Age of onset and nativelikeness in a second language: Listener perception versus linguistic scrutiny. *Language Learning, 59,* 249–306.

Abu-Rabia, S., & Kehat, S. (2004). The critical period for second language pronunciation: Is there such a thing? Ten case studies of late starters who attained a native-like Hebrew accent. *Educational Psychology, 24,* 77–98.

Abutalebi, J. (2008). Neural aspects of second language representation and language control. *Acta Psychologica, 128,* 466–478.

Abutalebi, J., Annoni, J.-M., Zimine, I., Pegna, A. J., Seghier, M. L., Lee-Jahnke, H., et al. (2008). Language control and lexical competition in bilinguals: An event-related fMRI study. *Cerebral Cortex, 18,* 1496–1505.

Abutalebi, J., Brambati, S. M., Annoni, J. M., Moro, A., Cappa, S. M., & Perani, D. (2007). The neural cost of the auditory perception of language switches: An event-related functional magnetic resonance imaging study in bilinguals. *The Journal of Neuroscience, 27,* 13762–13769.

Abutalebi, J., Cappa, S. F., & Perani, D. (2001). The bilingual brain as revealed by functional neuroimaging. *Bilingualism: Language and Cognition, 4,* 179–190.

Abutalebi, J., Cappa, S. F., & Perani, D. (2005). What can functional neuroimaging tell us about the bilingual brain? In J. F. Kroll & A. M. B. de Groot (Eds.), *Handbook of bilingualism: Psycholinguistic approaches* (pp. 497–515). New York: Oxford University Press.

Abutalebi, J., Miozzo, A., & Cappa, S. F. (2000). Do subcortical structures control "language selection" in polyglots? Evidence from pathological language mixing. *Neurocase, 6,* 51–56.

Adamowicz, A. (1989). The role of anticipation in discourse: Text processing in simultaneous interpreting. *Polish Psychological Bulletin, 20,* 153–160.

Ahukanna, J. G. W., Lund, N. J., & Gentile, J. R. (1981). Inter- and intra-lingual interference effects in learning a third language. *Modern Language Journal, 65,* 281–287.

Aitchison, J. (1987). *Words in the mind: An introduction to the mental lexicon.* Oxford, UK: Basil Blackwell.

Allport, A., MacKay, D. G., Prinz, W., & Scheerer, E. (1987). *Language perception and production: Relationships between listening, speaking, reading, and writing.* London: Academic Press.

Allport, A., Styles, E. A., & Hsieh, S. (1994). Shifting intentional set: Exploring the dynamic control of tasks. In C. Umiltà & M. Moscovitch (Eds.), *Attention and performance XV: Conscious and nonconscious information processing* (pp. 421–452). Hillsdale, NJ: Erlbaum.

Altarriba, J., & Basnight-Brown, D. M. (2007). Methodological considerations in performing semantic- and translation-priming experiments across languages. *Behavior Research Methods, 39,* 1–18.

Altarriba, J., & Mathis, K. M. (1997). Conceptual and lexical development in second language acquisition. *Journal of Memory and Language, 36,* 550–568.

Altenberg, E. P. (1991). Assessing first language vulnerability to attrition. In H. W. Seliger & R. M. Vago (Eds.), *First language attrition* (pp. 189–206). Cambridge, UK: Cambridge University Press.

Ameel, E., Malt, B. C., Storms, G., & Van Assche, F. (2009). Semantic convergence in the bilingual lexicon. *Journal of Memory and Language, 60,* 270–290.

Ameel, E., Storms, G., Malt, B. C., & Sloman, S. A. (2005). How bilinguals solve the naming problem. *Journal of Memory and Language, 53,* 60–80.

Ammerlaan, T. (1997). "Corrosion" or "loss" of immigrant Dutch in Australia: An experiment on first language attrition. In J. Klatter-Folmer & S. Kroon (Eds.), *Dutch overseas* (pp. 69–79). Tilburg, The Netherlands: Tilburg University Press.

Anderson, L. (1994). Simultaneous interpretation: Contextual and translation aspects. In S. Lambert & B. Moser-Mercer (Eds.), *Bridging the gap: Empirical research in simultaneous interpretation* (pp. 101–120). Amsterdam/Philadelphia: Benjamins.

Andrews, S. (1989). Frequency and neighborhood effects on lexical access: Activation or search? *Journal of Experimental Psychology: Learning, Memory, and Cognition, 15,* 802–814.

Ardal, S., Donald, M. W., Meuter, R., Muldrew, S., & Luce, M. (1990). Brain responses to semantic incongruity in bilinguals. *Brain and Language, 39,* 187–205.

Athanasopoulos, P. (2006). Effects of the grammatical representation of number on cognition in bilinguals. *Bilingualism: Language and Cognition, 9,* 89–96.

Athanasopoulos, P. (2007). Interaction between grammatical categories and cognition in bilinguals: The role of proficiency, cultural immersion, and language instruction. *Language and Cognitive Processes, 22,* 689–699.

Athanasopoulos, P., & Kasai, C. (2008). Language and thought in bilinguals: The case of grammatical number and nonverbal classification preferences. *Applied Psycholinguistics, 29,* 105–123.

Atkinson, R. C. (1972). Optimizing the learning of a second-language vocabulary. *Journal of Experimental Psychology, 96,* 124–129.

Atkinson, R. C. (1975). Mnemotechnics in second-language learning. *American Psychologist, 30,* 821–828.

Atkinson, R. C., & Raugh, M. R. (1975). The application of the mnemonic keyword method to the acquisition of a Russian vocabulary. *Journal of Experimental Psychology: Human Learning and Memory, 104,* 126–133.

Au, T. K., Knightly, L. M., Jun, S.-A., & Oh, J. S. (2002). Overhearing a language during childhood. *Psychological Science, 13,* 238–243.

Baars, B. J., Motley, M. T., & MacKay, D. G. (1975). Output editing for lexical status in artificially elicited slips of the tongue. *Journal of Verbal Learning and Verbal Behavior, 14,* 382–391.

Bach, M. J., & Underwood, B. J. (1970). Developmental changes in memory attributes. *Journal of Educational Psychology, 61,* 292–296.

Baddeley, A. (2000). The episodic buffer: A new component of working memory? *Trends in Cognitive Sciences, 4,* 417–423.

Baddeley, A., Gathercole, S., & Papagno, C. (1998). The phonological loop as a language learning device. *Psychological Review, 105,* 158–173.

Baddeley, A. D. (1986). *Working memory.* Oxford, UK: Oxford University Press.

Baddeley, A. D., & Hitch, G. J. (1974). Working memory. In G. H. Bower (Ed.), *The psychology of learning and motivation* (Vol. 8, pp. 47–89). New York: Academic Press.

Baddeley, A. D., Papagno, C., & Vallar, G. (1988). When long-term learning depends on short-term storage. *Journal of Memory and Language, 27,* 586–595.

Bahrick, H. P. (1984). Semantic memory content in permastore: Fifty years of memory for Spanish learned in school. *Journal of Experimental Psychology: General, 113,* 1–29.

Bahrick, H. P., & Phelps, E. (1987). Retention of Spanish vocabulary over 8 years. *Journal of Experimental Psychology: Learning, Memory, and Cognition, 13,* 344–349.

Bajo, M. T., Padilla, F., & Padilla, P. (1999). *Comprehension processes in simultaneous interpreting.* Proceedings of the 2nd International Congress of the European Society for Translation Studies, Granada, September, 1999.

Bajo, M. T., Puerta-Melguizo, M. C., & Macizo, P. (2003). The locus of semantic interference in picture naming. *Psicológica, 24,* 31–55.

Balota, D. A., & Chumbley, J. I. (1984). Are lexical decisions a good measure of lexical access? The role of word frequency in the neglected decision stage. *Journal of Experimental Psychology: Human Perception and Performance, 10,* 340–357.

Balota, D. A., & Chumbley, J. I. (1985). The locus of word-frequency effects in the pronunciation task: Lexical access and/or production? *Journal of Memory and Language, 24,* 89–106.

Banta, F. G. (1981). Teaching German vocabulary: The use of English cognates and common loan words. *The Modern Language Journal, 65,* 129–136.

Basnight-Brown, D. M., & Altarriba, J. (2007). Differences in semantic and translation priming across languages: The role of language direction and language dominance. *Memory & Cognition, 35,* 953–965.

Bassetti, B. (2007). Bilingualism and thought: Grammatical gender and concepts of objects in Italian-German bilingual children. *International Journal of Bilingualism, 11,* 251–273.

Bates, E., McNew, S., MacWhinney, B., Devescovi, A., & Smith, S. (1982). Functional constraints on sentence processing: A cross-linguistic study. *Cognition, 11*, 245–299.

Beaton, A., Gruneberg, M., & Ellis, N. (1995). Retention of foreign vocabulary learned using the keyword method: A ten-year follow-up. *Second Language Research, 11*, 112–120.

Beaton, A. A. (2005). Memory for foreign vocabulary after two decades: A single case study revisited. *Cognitive Technology, 10*, 29–32.

Beaton, A. A., Gruneberg, M. M., Hyde, C., Shufflebottom, A., & Sykes, R. N. (2005). Facilitation of receptive and productive foreign vocabulary learning using the keyword method: The role of image quality. *Memory, 13*, 458–471.

Beauvillain, C., & Grainger, J. (1987). Accessing interlexical homographs: Some limitations of a language-selective access. *Journal of Memory and Language, 26*, 658–672.

Benedict, H. (1979). Early lexical development: Comprehension and production. *Journal of Child Language, 6*, 183–200.

Ben-Zeev, S. (1977a). Mechanisms by which childhood bilingualism affects understanding of language and cognitive structures. In P. A. Hornby (Ed.), *Bilingualism: Psychological, social, and educational implications* (pp. 29–55). New York: Academic Press.

Ben-Zeev, S. (1977b). The influence of bilingualism on cognitive strategy and cognitive development. *Child Development, 48*, 1009–1018.

Best, C. T. (1994). The emergence of native-language phonological influences in infants: A perceptual assimilation model. In J. C. Goodman & H. C. Nusbaum (Eds.), *The development of speech perception: The transition from speech sounds to spoken words* (pp. 167–224). Cambridge, MA: MIT Press.

Best, C. T., & McRoberts, G. W. (2003). Infant perception of non-native consonant contrasts that adults assimilate in different ways. *Language and Speech, 46*, 183–216.

Best, C. T., McRoberts, G. W., & Sithole, N. M. (1988). Examination of perceptual reorganization for nonnative speech contrasts: Zulu click discrimination by English-speaking adults and infants. *Journal of Experimental Psychology: Human Perception and Performance, 14*, 345–360.

Bialystok, E. (1988). Levels of bilingualism and levels of linguistic awareness. *Developmental Psychology, 24*, 560–567.

Bialystok, E. (1992). Selective attention in cognitive processing: The bilingual edge. In R. J. Harris (Ed.), *Cognitive processing in bilinguals* (pp. 501–513). Amsterdam: Elsevier Science Publishers.

Bialystok, E. (2001a). *Bilingualism in development: Language, literacy, & cognition.* New York: Cambridge University Press.

Bialystok, E. (2001b). Metalinguistic aspects of bilingual processing. *Annual Review of Applied Linguistics, 21*, 169–181.

Bialystok, E. (2004). The impact of bilingualism on language and literacy development. In T. K. Bhatia & W. C. Ritchie (Eds.), *The handbook of bilingualism* (pp. 577–601). Malden, MA: Blackwell Publishing.

Bialystok, E. (2006). Effect of bilingualism and computer video game experience on the Simon task. *Canadian Journal of Experimental Psychology, 60*, 68–79.

Bialystok, E. (2007). Cognitive effects of bilingualism: How linguistic experience leads to cognitive change. *The International Journal of Bilingual Education and Bilingualism, 10*, 210–223.

Bialystok, E. (2008). Bilingualism: The good, the bad, and the indifferent. *Bilingualism, Language and Cognition, 12*, 3–11.

Bialystok, E., Craik, F. I. M., & Freedman, M. (2007). Bilingualism as a protection against the onset of symptoms of dementia. *Neuropsychologia, 45*, 459–464.

Bialystok, E., Craik, F. I. M., Grady, C., Chau, W., Ishii, R., Gunji, A., & Pantev, C. (2005a). Effect of bilingualism on cognitive control in the Simon task: Evidence from MEG. *NeuroImage, 24*, 40–49.

Bialystok, E., Craik, F. I. M., Klein, R., & Viswanathan, M. (2004). Bilingualism, aging, and cognitive control: Evidence from the Simon task. *Psychology and Aging, 19*, 290–303.

Bialystok, E., Martin, M. M., & Viswanathan, M. (2005b). Bilingualism across the lifespan: The rise and fall of inhibitory control. *International Journal of Bilingualism, 9*, 103–119.

Bierwisch, M., & Schreuder, R. (1992). From concepts to lexical items. *Cognition, 42*, 23–60.

Bijeljac-Babic, R., Biardeau, A., & Grainger, J. (1997). Masked orthographic priming in bilingual word recognition. *Memory & Cognition, 25*, 447–457.

Bijeljac-Babic, R., Nassurally, K., Havy, M., & Nazzi, T. (2009). Infants can rapidly learn words in a foreign language. *Infant Behavior & Development, 32*, 476–480.

Birdsong, D. (1999). Introduction: Whys and why nots of the critical period hypothesis for second language acquisition. In D. Birdsong (Ed.), *Second language acquisition and the critical period hypothesis* (pp. 1–22). Mahwah, NJ: Erlbaum.

Birdsong, D. (2005). Interpreting age effects in second language acquisition. In J. F. Kroll &

A. M. B. de Groot (Eds.), *Handbook of bilingualism: Psycholinguistic approaches* (pp. 109–127). New York: Oxford University Press.

Birdsong, D. (2006). Age and second language acquisition and processing: A selective overview. *Language Learning, 56*, 9–48.

Birdsong, D., & Flege, J. E. (2001). Regular–irregular dissociations in L2 acquisition of English morphology. In *BUCLD 25: Proceedings of the 25th Annual Boston University Conference on Language Development* (pp. 123–132). Boston, MA: Cascadilla Press.

Birdsong, D., & Molis, M. (2001). On the evidence for maturational constraints in second-language acquisition. *Journal of Memory and Language, 44*, 235–249.

Blank, M. A. (1980). Measuring lexical access during sentence processing. *Perception & Psychophysics, 28*, 1–8.

Bley-Vroman, R. (1988). The fundamental character of foreign language learning. In W. Rutherford & M. Sharwood Smith (Eds.), *Grammar and second language teaching: A book of readings* (pp. 19–30). Rowley, MA: Newbury House.

Bloch, C., Kaiser, A., Kuenzli, E., Zappatore, D., Haller, S., et al. (2009). The age of second language activation determines the variability in activation elicited by narration in three languages in Broca's and Wernicke's area. *Neuropsychologia, 47*, 625–633.

Bloem, I., & La Heij, W. (2003). Semantic facilitation and semantic interference in word translation: Implications for models of lexical access in language production. *Journal of Memory and Language, 48*, 468–488.

Bloem, I., Van den Boogaard, S., & La Heij, W. (2004). Semantic facilitation and semantic interference in language production: Further evidence for the conceptual selection model of lexical access. *Journal of Memory and Language, 51*, 307–323.

Blumenfeld, H. K., & Marian, V. (2007). Constraints on parallel activation in bilingual spoken language processing: Examining proficiency and lexical status using eye-tracking. *Language and Cognitive Processes, 22*, 633–660.

Bock, J. K. (1995). Sentence production: From mind to mouth. In J. L. Miller & P. D. Eimas (Eds.), *Handbook of perception and cognition: Speech, language, and communication* (Vol. 11, pp. 181–216). San Diego, CA: Academic Press.

Bock, J. K., & Miller, C. A. (1991). Broken agreement. *Cognitive Psychology, 23*, 45–93.

Bock, K. (1996). Language production: Methods and methodologies. *Psychonomic Bulletin & Review, 3*, 395–421.

Bock, K., & Levelt, W. (1994). Language production: Grammatical encoding. In M. A. Gernsbacher (Ed.), *Handbook of psycholinguistics* (pp. 945–984). New York: Academic Press.

Bogaards, P. (2001). Lexical units and the learning of foreign language vocabulary. *Studies in Second Language Acquisition, 23*, 321–343.

Bongaerts, T. (1999). Ultimate attainment in L2 pronunciation: The case of very advanced late L2 learners. In D. Birdsong (Ed.), *Second language acquisition and the critical period hypothesis* (pp. 133–159). Mahwah, NJ: Erlbaum.

Bongaerts, T., Van Summeren, C., Planken, B., & Schils, E. (1997). Age and ultimate attainment in the pronunciation of a foreign language. *Studies in Second Language Acquisition, 19*, 447–465.

Boroditsky, L. (2001). Does language shape thought? Mandarin and English speakers' conceptions of time. *Cognitive Psychology, 43*, 1–22.

Boroditsky, L. (2003). Linguistic relativity. In L. Nadel (Ed.), *Encyclopedia of cognitive science* (pp. 917–921). London: Macmillan.

Boroditsky, L., Ham, W., & Ramscar, M. (2002). *What is universal in event perception? Comparing English and Indonesian speakers.* Proceedings of the 24th Annual Meeting of the Cognitive Science Society, Fairfax, VA.

Boroditsky, L., Schmidt, L. A., & Phillips, W. (2003). Sex, syntax, and semantics. In D. Gentner & S. Goldin-Meadow (Eds.), *Language in mind: Advances in the study of language and thought* (pp. 61–79). Cambridge, MA: MIT Press.

Bosch, L., & Sebastián-Gallés, N. (1997). Native-language recognition abilities in 4-month-old infants from monolingual and bilingual environments. *Cognition, 65*, 33–69.

Bosch, L., & Sebastián-Gallés, N. (2001). Evidence of early language discrimination abilities in infants from bilingual environments. *Infancy, 2*, 29–49.

Bosch, L., & Sebastián-Gallés, N. (2003a). Language experience and the perception of a voicing contrast in fricatives: Infant and adult data. In M. J. Solé, D. Recasens, & J. Romero (Eds.), *Proceedings of the 15th International Congress of Phonetic Sciences* (pp. 1987–1990). Barcelona: Causal Productions.

Bosch, L., & Sebastián-Gallés, N. (2003b). Simultaneous bilingualism and the perception of a language-specific vowel contrast in the first year of life. *Language and Speech, 46*, 217–243.

Bosch, L., & Sebastián-Gallés, N. (2005). Developmental changes in the discrimination of vowel contrasts in bilingual infants. In J. Cohen, K. McAlister, K. Roltad, & J. MacSwan (Eds.), *Proceedings of the 4th International Symposium on*

Bilingualism (pp. 354–363). Somerville, MA: Cascadilla Press.

Bosman, A. M. T., & Van Orden, G. C. (1997). Why spelling is more difficult than reading. In C. A. Perfetti, L. Rieben, & M. Fayol (Eds.), *Learning to spell: Research, theory, and practice across languages* (pp. 173–194). Hillsdale, NJ: Erlbaum.

Botha, R. (2007). On homesign systems as a potential window on language evolution. *Language & Communication, 27*, 41–53.

Boudreault, P., & Mayberry, R. I. (2006). Grammatical processing in American Sign Language: Age of first-language acquisition effects in relation to syntactic structure. *Language and Cognitive Processes, 21*, 608–635.

Brauer, M. (1998). Stroop interference in bilinguals: The role of similarity between the two languages. In A. F. Healy & L. E. Bourne (Eds.), *Foreign language learning: Psycholinguistic studies on training and retention* (pp. 317–337). Mahwah, NJ: Erlbaum.

Broca, P. (1861). Perte de la parole. Ramollissement chronique en destruction partielle de lobe antérieur gauche de cerveau. *Bulletin de la Société d'Anthropologie, 2*, 235–238.

Broersma, M. (2002). Comprehension of non-native speech: Inaccurate phoneme processing and activation of lexical competitors. *Proceedings of the 7th International Conference on Spoken Language Processing* (pp. 261–264). Center for Spoken Language Research, University of Colorado, Boulder [CD-ROM].

Broersma, M. (2005). *Phonetic and lexical processing in a second language*. Unpublished Ph.D. Thesis, Radboud University Nijmegen, The Netherlands.

Broersma, M. (2006). *Accident-execute: Increased activation in nonnative listening*. Paper presented at Interspeech 2006-ICSLP, Ninth International Conference on Spoken Language Processing, Pittsburgh, PA.

Broersma, M., & De Bot, K. (2006). Triggered codeswitching: A corpus-based evaluation of the original triggering hypothesis and a new alternative. *Bilingualism: Language and Cognition, 9*, 1–13.

Brown, C. M., & Hagoort, P. (1993). The processing nature of the N400: Evidence from masked priming. *Journal of Cognitive Neuroscience, 5*, 34–44.

Brown, R., & McNeil, D. (1966). The "tip of the tongue" phenomenon. *Journal of Verbal Learning and Verbal Behavior, 5*, 325–337.

Bruck, M., & Genesee, F. (1995). Phonological awareness in young second language learners. *Journal of Child Language, 22*, 307–324.

Brysbaert, M., Van Dyck, G., & Van de Poel, M. (1999). Visual word recognition in bilinguals: Evidence from masked phonological priming. *Journal of Experimental Psychology: Human Perception and Performance, 25*, 137–148.

Buchweitz, A., Mason, R. A., Hasagawa, M., & Just, M. A. (2009). Japanese and English sentence reading comprehension and writing systems: An fMRI study of first and second language effects on brain activation. *Bilingualism: Language and Cognition, 12*, 141–151.

Burnham, D. K. (1986). Developmental loss of speech perception: Exposure to and experience with a first language. *Applied Psycholinguistics, 7*, 207–239.

Butler, Y. G., & Hakuta, K. (2004). Bilingualism and second language acquisition. In T. K. Bhatia & W. C. Ritchie (Eds.), *The handbook of bilingualism* (pp. 114–144). Malden, MA: Blackwell Publishing.

Butterworth, B. (1989). Lexical access in speech production. In W. Marslen-Wilson (Ed.), *Lexical representation and process* (pp. 108–135). Cambridge, MA: MIT Press.

Calvin, W. H., & Ojemann, G. A. (1994). *Conversations with Neil's brain. The neural nature of thought and language*. New York: Addison Wesley.

Campos, A., Amor, A., & González, M. A. (2002). Presentation of keywords by means of interactive drawings. *The Spanish Journal of Psychology, 5*, 102–109.

Campos, A., Amor, A., & González, M. A. (2004). The importance of the keyword-generation method in keyword mnemonics. *Experimental Psychology, 51*, 1–7.

Campos, A., González, M. A., & Amor, A. (2004). Different strategies for keyword generation. *Journal of Mental Imagery, 28*, 51–58.

Caramazza, A. (1997). How many levels of processing are there in lexical access? *Cognitive Neuropsychology, 14*, 177–208.

Caramazza, A., & Brones, I. (1979). Lexical access in bilinguals. *Bulletin of the Psychonomic Society, 13*, 212–214.

Caramazza, A., & Zurif, E. B. (1976). Dissociation of algorithmic and heuristic processes in language comprehension: Evidence from aphasia. *Brain and Language, 3*, 572–582.

Carlson, S. M., & Meltzoff, A. N. (2008). Bilingual experience and executive functioning in young children. *Developmental Science, 11*, 282–298.

Carroll, D. W. (2004). *Psychology of language* (4th Ed.). Belmont, CA: Wadsworth.

Carroll, J. B. (1978). Linguistic abilities in translators and interpreters. In D. Gerver & H. W. Sinaiko (Eds.), *Language interpretation and communication* (pp. 119–129). New York: Plenum Press.

Carroll, S. E. (1992). On cognates. *Second Language Research, 8*, 93–119.

Carter, C. S., Macdonald, A. M., Botvinick, M., Ross, L. L., Stenger, V. A., Noll, D., & Cohen, J. D. (2000). Parsing executive processes: Strategic vs. evaluative functions of the anterior cingulate cortex. *Proceedings of the National Academy of Sciences, 97*, 1944–1948.

Caskey-Sirmons, L. A., & Hickerson, N. P. (1977). Semantic shift and bilingualism: Variation in the color terms of five languages. *Anthropological Linguistics, 19*, 358–367.

Cenoz, J. (2001). The effect of linguistic distance, L2 status and age on cross-linguistic influence in third language acquisition. In J. Cenoz, B. Hufeisen, & U. Jessner (Eds.), *Cross-linguistic influence in third language acquisition: Psycholinguistic Perspectives* (pp. 8–20). Clevedon, UK: Multilingual Matters.

Cenoz, J. (2003). The role of typology in the organization of the multilingual lexicon. In J. Cenoz, B. Hufeisen, & U. Jessner (Eds.), *The multilingual lexicon* (pp. 103–116). The Netherlands: Kluwer Academic Publishers.

Chambers, K. E., Onishi, K. H., & Fisher, C. (2003). Infants learn phonotactic regularities from brief auditory experience. *Cognition, 87*, B69–B77.

Chee, M. W. L., Tan, E. W. L., & Thiel, T. (1999). Mandarin and English single word processing studied with functional magnetic resonance imaging. *The Journal of Neuroscience, 19*, 3050–3056.

Chen, H.-C. (1990). Lexical processing in a non-native language: Effects of language proficiency and learning strategy. *Memory & Cognition, 18*, 279–288.

Chen, H.-C., & Ho, C. (1986). Development of Stroop interference in Chinese–English bilinguals. *Journal of Experimental Psychology: Learning, Memory, and Cognition, 12*, 397–401.

Chen, H.-C., & Leung, Y.-S. (1989). Patterns of lexical processing in a nonnative language. *Journal of Experimental Psychology: Learning, Memory, and Cognition, 15*, 316–325.

Chen, H.-C., & Ng, M.-L. (1989). Semantic facilitation and translation priming effects in Chinese–English bilinguals. *Memory & Cognition, 17*, 454–462.

Chernov, G. (1994). Message redundancy and message anticipation in simultaneous interpretation. In S. Lambert & B. Moser-Mercer (Eds.), *Bridging the gap: Empirical research in simultaneous interpretation* (pp. 139–153). Amsterdam/Philadelphia: John Benjamins.

Cheung, H. (1996). Nonword span as a unique pre-

dictor of second-language vocabulary learning. *Developmental Psychology, 32*, 867–873.

Christ, S. E., White, D. A., Mandernach, T., & Keys, B. A. (2001). Inhibitory control across the life span. *Developmental Neuropsychology, 20*, 653–669.

Christoffels, I. K., & De Groot, A. M. B. (2004). Components of simultaneous interpreting: Comparing interpreting with shadowing and paraphrasing. *Bilingualism: Language and Cognition, 7*, 227–240.

Christoffels, I. K., & De Groot, A. M. B. (2005). Simultaneous interpreting: A cognitive perspective. In J. F. Kroll & A. M. B. de Groot (Eds.), *Handbook of bilingualism: Psycholinguistic approaches* (pp. 454–479). New York: Oxford University Press.

Christoffels, I. K., De Groot, A. M. B., & Kroll, J. F. (2006). Memory and language skills in simultaneous interpreters: The role of expertise and language proficiency. *Journal of Memory and Language, 54*, 324–345.

Christoffels, I. K., De Groot, A. M. B., & Waldorp, L. J. (2003). Basic skills in a complex task: A graphical model relating memory and lexical retrieval to simultaneous interpreting. *Bilingualism: Language and Cognition, 6*, 201–211.

Christophe, A., & Morton, J. (1998). Is Dutch native English? Linguistic analysis by 2-month-olds. *Developmental Science, 1*, 215–219.

Chwilla, D. J., Brown, C. M., & Hagoort, P. (1995). The N400 as a function of the level of processing. *Psychophysiology, 32*, 274–285.

Clahsen, H., & Felser, C. (2006a). Grammatical processing in language learners. *Applied Psycholinguistics, 27*, 3–42.

Clahsen, H., & Felser, C. (2006b). How native-like is non-native language processing? *Trends in Cognitive Sciences, 10*, 564–569.

Clark, E. V. (1987). The principle of contrast: A constraint on language acquisition. In B. MacWhinney (Ed.), *Mechanisms of language acquisition* (pp. 1–34). Hillsdale, NJ: Erlbaum.

Clark, E. V. (1988). On the logic of contrast. *Journal of Child Language, 15*, 317–335.

Clyne, M. (1967). *Transference and triggering: Observations on the language assimilation of postwar German-speaking migrants in Australia*. Den Haag: Martinus Nijhoff.

Clyne, M. (1972). *Perspectives on language contact: Based on a study of German in Australia*. Melbourne: Hawthorn.

Clyne, M. (1997). Some of the things trilinguals do. *The International Journal of Bilingualism, 1*, 95–116.

Cochran, B. P., McDonald, J. L., & Parault, S. J. (1999). Too smart for their own good: The disadvantage of a superior processing capacity for adult language learners. *Journal of Memory and Language, 41*, 30–58.

Cohen, A. D. (1987). The use of verbal and imagery mnemonics in second-language vocabulary learning. *Studies in Second Language Acquisition, 9*, 43–62.

Colomé, A. (2001). Lexical activation in bilinguals' speech production: Language-specific or language-independent? *Journal of Memory and Language, 45*, 721–736.

Coltheart, M. (1999). Modularity and cognition. *Trends in Cognitive Sciences, 3*, 115–120.

Colzato, L. S., Bajo, M. T., Van den Wildenberg, W., & Paolieri, D. (2008). How does bilingualism improve executive control? A comparison of active and reactive inhibition mechanisms. *Journal of Experimental Psychology: Learning, Memory, and Cognition, 34*, 302–312.

Conboy, B. T., & Mills, D. L. (2006). Two languages, one developing brain: Event-related potentials to words in bilingual toddlers. *Developmental Science, 9*, F1–F12.

Conklin, K., & Mauner, G. (2003). Investigating bilingual lexical access: Processing French-English homographs in sentential contexts. *Proceedings of the 4th International Symposium on Bilingualism.* Arizona, April.

Cook, V. (1991). The poverty-of-the-stimulus argument and multicompetence. *Second Language Research, 7*, 103–117.

Cook, V. (Ed.) (2003a). *Effects of the second language on the first.* Clevedon, UK: Multilingual Matters.

Cook, V. (2003b). Introduction: The changing L1 in the L2 user's mind. In V. Cook (Ed.), *Effects of the second language on the first* (pp. 1–18). Clevedon, UK: Multilingual Matters.

Cook, V., Bassetti, B., Kasai, C., Sasaki, M., & Takahashi, J. A. (2006). Do bilinguals have different concepts? The case of shape and material in Japanese L2 users of English. *International Journal of Bilingualism, 10*, 137–152.

Cook, V., Iarossi, E., Stellakis, N., & Tokumaru, Y. (2003). Effects of the L2 on the syntactic processing of the L1. In V. Cook (Ed.), *Effects of the second language on the first* (pp. 193–213). Clevedon, UK: Multilingual Matters.

Costa, A. (2005). Lexical access in bilingual production. In J. F. Kroll & A. M. B. de Groot (Eds.), *Handbook of bilingualism: Psycholinguistic approaches* (pp. 308–325). New York: Oxford University Press.

Costa, A., & Caramazza, A. (1999). Is lexical selection in bilingual speech production language-specific? Further evidence from Spanish–English and English–Spanish bilinguals. *Bilingualism: Language and Cognition, 2*, 231–244.

Costa, A., Caramazza, A., & Sebastián-Gallés, N. (2000). The cognate facilitation effect: Implications for models of lexical access. *Journal of Experimental Psychology: Learning, Memory, and Cognition, 26*, 1283–1296.

Costa, A., Colomé, A., Gómez, O., & Sebastián-Gallés, N. (2003). Another look at cross-language competition in bilingual speech production: Lexical and phonological factors. *Bilingualism: Language and Cognition, 6*, 167–179.

Costa, A., Hernández, M., & Sebastián-Gallés, N. (2008). Bilingualism aids conflict resolution: Evidence from the ANT task. *Cognition, 106*, 59–86.

Costa, A., Kovacic, D., Franck, J., & Caramazza, A. (2003). On the autonomy of the grammatical gender systems of the two languages of a bilingual. *Bilingualism: Language and Cognition, 6*, 181–200.

Costa, A., Miozzo, M., & Caramazza, A. (1999). Lexical selection in bilinguals: Do words in the bilingual's two lexicons compete for selection? *Journal of Memory and Language, 41*, 365–397.

Costa, A., Roelstraete, B., & Hartsuiker, R. J. (2006). The lexical bias effect in bilingual speech production: Evidence for feedback between lexical and sublexical levels across languages. *Psychonomic Bulletin & Review, 13*, 972–977.

Costa, A., & Santesteban, M. (2004a). Bilingual word perception and production: Two sides of the same coin? *Trends in Cognitive Sciences, 8*, 253.

Costa, A., & Santesteban, M. (2004b). Lexical access in bilingual speech production: Evidence from language switching in highly proficient bilinguals and L2 learners. *Journal of Memory and Language, 50*, 491–511.

Costa, A., Santesteban, M., & Caño, A. (2005). On the facilitatory effects of cognate words in bilingual speech production. *Brain and Language, 94*, 94–103.

Costa, A., Santesteban, M., & Ivanova, I. (2006). How do highly proficient bilinguals control their lexicalization process? Inhibitory and language-specific selection mechanisms are both functional. *Journal of Experimental Psychology: Learning, Memory, and Cognition, 32*, 1057–1074.

Crinion, J., Turner, R., Grogan, A., Hanakawa, T., Noppeney, U., Devlin, J. T., Aso, T., Urayama, S., Fukuyama, H., Stockton, K., Usui, K., Green, D. W., & Price, C. J. (2006). Language control in the bilingual brain. *Science, 312*, 1537–1540.

Cristoffanini, P., Kirsner, K., & Milech, D. (1986). Bilingual lexical representation: The status of Spanish–English cognates. *The Quarterly Journal of Experimental Psychology, 38A*, 367–393.

Crutch, S. J., & Warrington, E. K. (2005). Abstract and concrete concepts have structurally different representational frameworks. *Brain, 128,* 615–627.

Crystal, D. (1987). *The Cambridge encyclopaedia of language.* Cambridge, UK: Cambridge University Press.

Cuetos, F., & Mitchell, D. C. (1988). Cross-linguistic differences in parsing: Restrictions on the use of the Late Closure strategy in Spanish. *Cognition, 30,* 73–105.

Cummins, J. (1976). The influence of bilingualism on cognitive growth: A synthesis of research findings and explanatory hypotheses. *Working Papers on Bilingualism, 9,* 1–43.

Cummins, J. (1978). Metalinguistic development of children in bilingual education programs: Data from Irish and Canadian Ukranian–English programs. In M. Paradis (Ed.), *The Fourth Lacus Forum* (pp. 29–40). Columbia, SC: Hornbeam Press.

Curtiss, S. (1977). *Genie: A psycholinguistic study of a modern-day "wild child".* New York: Academic Press.

Curtiss, S. (1988). The special talent of grammar acquisition. In L. K. Obler & D. Fein (Eds.), *The exceptional brain: Neuropsychology of talent and special abilities* (pp. 364–386). New York: Guilford Press.

Curtiss, S., Fromkin, V., & Krashen, S. (1978). Language development in the mature (minor) right hemisphere. *ITL: Review of Applied Linguistics, 39–40,* 23–37.

Curtiss, S., Fromkin, V., Krashen, S., Rigler, D., & Rigler, M. (1974). The linguistic development of Genie. *Language, 50,* 528–554.

Cutler, A. (2005). The lexical statistics of word recognition problems caused by L2 phonetic confusion. In *Proceedings of the 9th European Conference on Speech Communication and Technology,* Lisbon, September 2005.

Cutler, A., & Butterfield, S. (1992). Rhythmic cues to speech segmentation: Evidence from juncture misperception. *Journal of Memory and Language, 31,* 218–236.

Cutler, A., Mehler, J., Norris, D., & Segui, J. (1986). The syllable's differing role in the segmentation of French and English. *Journal of Memory and Language, 25,* 385–400.

Cutler, A., Mehler, J., Norris, D., & Segui, J. (1989). Limits on bilingualism. *Nature, 340,* 229–230.

Cutler, A., Mehler, J., Norris, D., & Segui, J. (1992). The monolingual nature of speech segmentation by bilinguals. *Cognitive Psychology, 24,* 381–410.

Cutler, A., & Norris, D. (1988). The role of strong syllables in segmentation for lexical access.

Journal of Experimental Psychology: Human Perception and Performance, 14, 113–121.

Cziko, G. A. (1980). Language competence and reading strategies: A comparison of first- and second-language oral reading errors. *Language Learning, 30,* 101–114.

Dahan, D., & Tanenhaus, M. K. (2004). Continuous mapping from sound to meaning in spoken-language comprehension: Immediate effects of verb-based thematic constraints. *Journal of Experimental Psychology: Learning, Memory, and Cognition, 30,* 498–513.

Damasio, H., Grabowski, T. J., Tranel, D., Hichwa, R. D., & Damasio, A. R. (1996). A neural basis for lexical retrieval. *Nature, 380,* 499–505.

Daneman, M., & Carpenter, P. A. (1980). Individual differences in working memory and reading. *Journal of Verbal Learning and Verbal Behavior, 19,* 450–466.

Daneman, M., & Green, I. (1986). Individual differences in comprehending and producing words in context. *Journal of Memory and Language, 25,* 1–18.

Daoussis, L., & McKelvie, S. J. (1986). Musical preferences and effects of music on a reading comprehension test for extraverts and introverts. *Perceptual and Motor Skills, 62,* 283–289.

Darò, V., & Fabbro, F. (1994). Verbal memory during simultaneous interpretation: Effects of phonological interference. *Applied Linguistics, 15,* 365–381.

Davis, M. H., Di Betta, A. M., MacDonald, M. J. E., & Gaskell, M. G. (2008). Learning and consolidation of novel spoken words. *Journal of Cognitive Neuroscience, 21,* 803–820.

De Angelis, G. (2005). Interlanguage transfer of function words. *Language Learning, 55,* 379–414.

De Bot, K. (1992). A bilingual production model: Levelt's "speaking" model adapted. *Applied Linguistics, 13,* 1–24.

De Bot, K. (1998). The psycholinguistics of language loss. In G. Extra & L. Verhoeven (Eds.), *Bilingualism and migration* (pp. 345–361). Berlin: De Gruyter.

De Bot, K. (2000). Simultaneous interpreting as language production. In B. Englund Dimitrova & K. Hyltenstam (Eds.), *Language processing and simultaneous interpreting* (pp. 65–88). Amsterdam: Benjamins.

De Bot, K., Lowie, W., & Verspoor, M. (2007). A Dynamic Systems Theory approach to second language acquisition. *Bilingualism: Language and Cognition, 10,* 7–21.

De Bot, K., Martens, V., & Stoessel, S. (2004). Finding residual lexical knowledge: The "savings" approach to testing vocabulary. *International Journal of Bilingualism, 8,* 373–382.

De Bot, K., & Schreuder, R. (1993). Word production and the bilingual lexicon. In R. Schreuder & B. Weltens (Eds.), *The bilingual lexicon* (pp. 191–214). Amsterdam/Philadelphia: John Benjamins.

De Bot, K., & Stoessel, S. (2000). In search of yesterday's words: Reactivating a long-forgotten language. *Applied Linguistics, 21,* 333–353.

De Bot, K., & Weltens, B. (1995). Foreign language attrition. *Annual Review of Applied Linguistics, 15,* 151–164.

De Groot, A. M. B. (1984). Primed lexical decision: Combined effects of the proportion of related prime-target pairs and the stimulus onset asynchrony of prime and target. *The Quarterly Journal of Experimental Psychology, 36A,* 253–280.

De Groot, A. M. B. (1989). Representational aspects of word imageability and word frequency as assessed through word association. *Journal of Experimental Psychology: Learning, Memory, and Cognition, 15,* 824–845.

De Groot, A. M. B. (1992a). Bilingual lexical representation: A closer look at conceptual representations. In R. Frost & L. Katz (Eds.), *Orthography, phonology, morphology, and meaning* (pp. 389–412). Amsterdam: Elsevier Science Publishers.

De Groot, A. M. B. (1992b). Determinants of word translation. *Journal of Experimental Psychology: Learning, Memory, and Cognition, 18,* 1001–1018.

De Groot, A. M. B. (1993). Word-type effects in bilingual processing tasks: Support for a mixed-representational system. In R. Schreuder & B. Weltens (Eds.), *The bilingual lexicon* (pp. 27–51). Amsterdam/Philadelphia: John Benjamins.

De Groot, A. M. B. (1995). Determinants of bilingual lexicosemantic organisation. *Computer Assisted Language Learning, 8,* 151–180.

De Groot, A. M. B. (1997). The cognitive study of translation and interpretation. In J. H. Danks, G. M. Shreve, S. B. Fountain, & M. K. McBeath (Eds.), *Cognitive processes in translation and interpreting* (pp. 25–56). Thousand Oaks, CA: Sage Publications.

De Groot, A. M. B. (2002). Lexical representation and lexical processing in the L2 user. In V. Cook (Ed.), *Portraits of the L2 user* (pp. 32–63). Clevedon, UK: Multilingual Matters.

De Groot, A. M. B. (2006). Effects of stimulus characteristics and background music on foreign language vocabulary learning and forgetting. *Language Learning, 56,* 463–506.

De Groot, A. M. B., Borgwaldt, S., Bos, M., & Van den Eijnden, E. (2002). Lexical decision and word naming in bilinguals: Language effects and task effects. *Journal of Memory and Language, 47,* 91–124.

De Groot, A. M. B., & Comijs, H. (1995). Translation recognition and translation production: Comparing a new and an old tool in the study of bilingualism. *Language Learning, 45,* 467–509.

De Groot, A. M. B., Dannenburg, L., & Van Hell, J. G. (1994). Forward and backward word translation by bilinguals. *Journal of Memory and Language, 33,* 600–629.

De Groot, A. M. B., Delmaar, P., & Lupker, S. J. (2000). The processing of interlexical homographs in translation recognition and lexical decision: Support for non-selective access to bilingual memory. *The Quarterly Journal of Experimental Psychology, 53A,* 397–428.

De Groot, A. M. B., & Hoeks, J. C. J. (1995). The development of bilingual memory: Evidence from word translation by trilinguals. *Language Learning, 45,* 683–724.

De Groot, A. M. B., & Keijzer, R. (2000). What is hard to learn is easy to forget: The roles of word concreteness, cognate status, and word frequency in foreign-language vocabulary learning and forgetting. *Language Learning, 50,* 1–56.

De Groot, A. M. B., & Nas, G. L. J. (1991). Lexical representation of cognates and noncognates in compound bilinguals. *Journal of Memory and Language, 30,* 90–123.

De Groot, A. M. B., & Poot, R. (1997). Word translation at three levels of proficiency in a second language: The ubiquitous involvement of conceptual memory. *Language Learning, 47,* 215–264.

De Groot, A. M. B., & Van den Brink, R. C. L. (2008). Apprentissage du vocabulaire d'une langue étrangère: le stade de la dénomination. In M. Kail, M. Fayol, & M. Hickmann (Eds.), *Apprentissage des langues* (pp. 303–315). Paris: CNRS Éditions.

De Groot, A. M. B., & Van Hell, J. G. (2005). The learning of foreign language vocabulary. In J. F. Kroll & A. M. B. de Groot (Eds.), *Handbook of bilingualism: Psycholinguistic approaches* (pp. 9–29). New York: Oxford University Press.

Dehaene, S., Dupoux, E., Mehler, J., Cohen, L., Paulesu, E., Perani, D., et al. (1997). Anatomical variability in the cortical representation of first and second language. *NeuroReport, 8,* 3809–3815.

De Houwer, A. (2005). Early bilingual acquisition: Focus on morphosyntax and the Separate Development Hypothesis. In J. F. Kroll & A. M. B. de Groot (Eds.), *Handbook of bilingualism: Psycholinguistic approaches* (pp. 30–48). New York: Oxford University Press.

De Houwer, A., Bornstein, M. H., & De Coster, S.

(2006). Early understanding of two words for the same thing: A CDI study of lexical comprehension in infant bilinguals. *International Journal of Bilingualism, 10,* 331–347.

DeKeyser, R., & Larson-Hall, J. (2005). What does the critical period really mean? In J. F. Kroll & A. M. B. de Groot (Eds.), *Handbook of bilingualism: Psycholinguistic approaches* (pp. 88–108). New York: Oxford University Press.

DeKeyser, R. M. (2000). The robustness of critical period effects in second language acquisition. *Studies in Second Language Acquisition, 22,* 499–533.

Dell, G. S. (1986). A spreading activation theory of retrieval in sentence production. *Psychological Review, 93,* 283–321.

Dell, G. S., & Reich, P. A. (1981). Stages in sentence production: An analysis of speech error data. *Journal of Verbal Learning and Verbal Behavior, 20,* 611–629.

Démonet, J.-F., Thierry, G., & Cardebat, D. (2005). Renewal of the neurophysiology of language: Functional neuroimaging. *Physiological Reviews, 85,* 49–95.

Derwing, T. M., & Munro, M. J. (1997). Accent, intelligibility, and comprehensibility: Evidence from four L1s. *Studies in Second Language Acquisition, 19,* 1–16.

Desrochers, A., Wieland, L. D., & Coté, M. (1991). Instructional effects in the use of the mnemonic keyword method for learning German nouns and their grammatical gender. *Applied Cognitive Psychology, 5,* 19–36.

Dewaele, J.-M. (1998). Lexical inventions: French interlanguage as L2 versus L3. *Applied Linguistics, 19,* 471–490.

Dewaele, J.-M. (2001). Activation or inhibition? The interaction of L1, L2 and L3 on the language mode continuum. In J. Cenoz, B. Hufeisen, & U. Jessner (Eds.), *Cross-linguistic influence in third language acquisition: Psycholinguistic perspectives* (pp. 69–89). Clevedon, UK: Multilingual Matters.

Dijkstra, T. (2005). Bilingual visual word recognition and lexical access. In J. F. Kroll & A. M. B. de Groot (Eds.), *Handbook of bilingualism: Psycholinguistic approaches* (pp. 179–201). New York: Oxford University Press.

Dijkstra, T., De Bruijn, E., Schriefers, H., & Ten Brinke, S. (2000a). More on interlingual homograph recognition: Language intermixing versus explicitness of instruction. *Bilingualism: Language and Cognition, 3,* 69–78.

Dijkstra, T., Grainger, J., & Van Heuven, W. J. B. (1999). Recognition of cognates and interlingual homographs: The neglected role of phonology. *Journal of Memory and Language, 41,* 496–518.

Dijkstra, T., Timmermans, M., & Schriefers, H. (2000b). On being blinded by your other language: Effects of task demands on interlingual homograph recognition. *Journal of Memory and Language, 42,* 445–464.

Dijkstra, T., & Van Heuven, W. J. B. (1998). The BIA model and bilingual word recognition. In J. Grainger & A. M. Jacobs (Eds.), *Localist connectionist approaches to human cognition* (pp. 189–225). Mahwah, NJ: Erlbaum.

Dijkstra, T., & Van Heuven, W. J. B. (2002). The architecture of the bilingual word recognition system: From identification to decision. *Bilingualism: Language and Cognition, 5,* 175–197.

Dijkstra, T., Van Jaarsveld, H., & Ten Brinke, S. (1998). Interlingual homograph recognition: Effects of task demands and language intermixing. *Bilingualism: Language and Cognition, 1,* 51–66.

Dillinger, M. (1994). Comprehension during interpreting: What do interpreters know that bilinguals don't? In S. Lambert & B. Moser-Mercer (Eds.), *Bridging the gap: Empirical research in simultaneous interpretation* (pp. 155–189). Amsterdam/Philadelphia: John Benjamins.

Doctor, E. A., & Klein, D. (1992). Phonological processing in bilingual word recognition. In R. J. Harris (Ed.), *Cognitive processing in bilinguals* (pp. 237–252). Amsterdam: Elsevier Science Publishers.

Dornic, S. (1978). The bilingual's performance: Language dominance, stress and individual differences. In D. Gerver & H. Sinaiko (Eds.), *Language interpretation and communication* (pp. 259–271). New York: Plenum.

Dronkers, N. F., Wilkins, D. P., Van Valin, R. D., Redfern, B. B., & Jaeger, J. J. (1994). A reconsideration of the brain areas involved in the disruption of morphosyntactic comprehension. *Brain & Language, 47,* 461–462.

Dufour, R., & Kroll, J. F. (1995). Matching words to concepts in two languages: A test of the concept mediation model of bilingual representation. *Memory & Cognition, 23,* 166–180.

Durgunoğlu, A. Y., & Roediger, H. L. (1987). Test differences in accessing bilingual memory. *Journal of Memory and Language, 26,* 377–391.

Dussias, P. E. (2003). Syntactic ambiguity resolution in L2 learners: Some effects of bilinguality on L1 and L2 processing strategies. *Studies in Second Language Acquisition, 25,* 529–557.

Dussias, P. E. (2006). *Understanding sentences in two languages.* Rovereto Workshop on Bilingualism, Sep 28– Oct 1, Rovereto, Italy.

Dussias, P. E., & Cramer, T. R. (2006). The role of L1 verb bias in L2 sentence parsing. In

D. Bamman, T. Magnitskaia, & C. Zaller (Eds.), *BUCLD 30 Proceedings* (pp. 166–177). Somerville, MA: Cascadilla Press.

Dussias, P. E., & Cramer Scaltz, T. R. (2008). Spanish–English L2 speakers' use of subcategorization bias information in the resolution of temporary ambiguity during second language reading. *Acta Psychologica, 128*, 501–513.

Dussias, P. E., & Sagarra, N. (2007). The effect of exposure on syntactic parsing in Spanish–English bilinguals. *Bilingualism: Language and Cognition, 10*, 101–116.

Duyck, W., & Brysbaert, M. (2004). Forward and backward number translation requires conceptual mediation in both balanced and unbalanced bilinguals. *Journal of Experimental Psychology: Human Perception and Performance, 30*, 889–906.

Duyck, W., & Brysbaert, M. (2008). Semantic access in number word translation: The role of crosslingual lexical similarity. *Experimental Psychology, 55*, 102–112.

Duyck, W., Diependaele, K., Drieghe, D., & Brysbaert, M. (2004). The size of the cross-lingual masked phonological priming effect does not depend on second language proficiency. *Experimental Psychology, 51*, 1–9.

Duyck, W., Van Assche, E., Drieghe, D., & Hartsuiker, R. J. (2007). Visual word recognition by bilinguals in a sentence context: Evidence for non-selective lexical access. *Journal of Experimental Psychology: Learning, Memory, and Cognition, 33*, 663–679.

Dyer, F. N. (1971). Color-naming interference in monolinguals and bilinguals. *Journal of Verbal Learning and Verbal Behavior, 10*, 297–302.

Ebbinghaus, H. (1885). *Über das Gedächtnis. Untersuchungen zur experimentellen Psychologie* (On memory: Investigations in experimental psychology). Leipzig: Duncker & Humblot.

Egner, T., & Hirsch, J. (2005). Cognitive control mechanisms resolve conflict through cortical amplification of task-relevant information. *Nature Neuroscience, 8*, 1784–1790.

Ehri, L. C., & Ryan, E. B. (1980). Performance of bilinguals in a picture–word interference task. *Journal of Psycholinguistic Research, 9*, 285–302.

Eimas, P. D. (1974). Auditory and linguistic processing of cues for place of articulation by infants. *Perception and Psychophysics, 16*, 513–521.

Eimas, P. D. (1975). Auditory and phonetic coding of the cues for speech: Discrimination of the [r–l] distinction by young infants. *Perception and Psychophysics, 18*, 341–347.

Eimas, P. D., & Miller, J. L. (1991). A constraint on the discrimination of speech by young infants. *Language and Speech, 34*, 251–263.

Eimas, P. D., Siqueland, E. R., Jusczyk, P., & Vigorito, J. (1971). Speech perception in infants. *Science, 171*, 303–306.

Elhelou, M. W. A. (1994). Arab children's use of the keyword method to learn English vocabulary words. *Educational Research, 36*, 295–302.

Ellis, A. W., & Lambon Ralph, M. A. (2000). Age of acquisition effects in adult lexical processing reflect loss of plasticity in maturing systems: Insights from connectionist networks. *Journal of Experimental Psychology: Learning, Memory, and Cognition, 26*, 1103–1123.

Ellis, N., & Beaton, A. (1993a). Factors affecting the learning of foreign language vocabulary: Imagery keyword mediators and phonological short-term memory. *The Quarterly Journal of Experimental Psychology, 46A*, 533–558.

Ellis, N. C. (1995). The psychology of foreign language vocabulary acquisition: Implications for CALL. *Computer Assisted Language Learning, 8*, 103–128.

Ellis, N. C., & Beaton, A. (1993b). Psycholinguistic determinants of foreign language vocabulary learning. *Language Learning, 43*, 559–617.

Ellis, N. C., & Sinclair, S. G. (1996). Working memory in the acquisition of vocabulary and syntax: Putting language in good order. *The Quarterly Journal of Experimental Psychology, 49A*, 234–250.

Elman, J. L. (1990). Finding structure in time. *Cognitive Science, 14*, 179–211.

Elman, J. L. (1993). Learning and development in neural networks: The importance of starting small. *Cognition, 48*, 71–99.

Elston-Güttler, K. E., Gunter, T. C., & Kotz, S. A. (2005). Zooming into L2: Global language context and adjustment affect processing of interlingual homographs in sentences. *Cognitive Brain Research, 25*, 57–70.

Emmorey, K., Bellugi, U., Friederici, A., & Horn, P. (1995). Effects of age of acquisition on grammatical sensitivity: Evidence from on-line and off-line tasks. *Applied Psycholinguistics, 16*, 1–23.

Emmorey, K., Borinstein, H. B., Thompson, R., & Gollan, T. H. (2008a). Bimodal bilingualism. *Bilingualism: Language and Cognition, 11*, 43–61.

Emmorey, K., Luk, G., Pyers, J. E., & Bialystok, E. (2008b). The source of enhanced cognitive control in bilinguals: Evidence from bimodal bilinguals. *Psychological Science, 19*, 1201–1206.

Entwisle, D., Forsyth, D., & Muus, R. (1964). The syntactic-paradigmatic shift in children's word associations. *Journal of Verbal Learning and Verbal Behavior, 3*, 19–29.

Erickson, D. M, Mattingly, I. G., & Turvey, M. T.

(1977). Phonetic activity in reading: An experiment with Kanji. *Language and Speech, 20,* 384–403.

Ervin, S. (1961a). Changes with age in the verbal determinants of word-association. *American Journal of Psychology, 74,* 361–372.

Ervin, S. M. (1961b). Semantic shift in bilingualism. *American Journal of Psychology, 24,* 233–241.

Ervin, S. M., & Osgood, C. E. (1954). Second language learning and bilingualism. *Journal of Abnormal and Social Psychology, Supplement, 49,* 139–146.

Escudero, P. (2007). Multilingual sound perception and word recognition. *Stem, Spraak en Taalpathologie, 15,* 93–103.

Eviatar, Z., & Ibrahim, R. (2000). Bilingual is as bilingual does: Metalinguistic abilities of Arabic-speaking children. *Applied Psycholinguistics, 21,* 451–471.

Eysenck, H. (1967). *The biological basis of personality.* Springfield, IL: Thomas.

Fabbro, F. (1999). *The neurolinguistics of bilingualism: An introduction.* Hove, UK: Psychology Press.

Fabbro, F. (2001). The bilingual brain: Cerebral representation of languages. *Brain and Language, 79,* 211–222.

Fabbro, F., & Darò, V. (1995). Delayed auditory feedback in polyglot simultaneous interpreters. *Brain and Language, 48,* 309–319.

Fabbro, F., Gran, B., & Gran, L. (1991). Hemispheric specialization for semantic and syntactic components of language in simultaneous interpreters. *Brain and Language, 41,* 1–42.

Fabbro, F., Skrap, M., & Aglioti, S. (2000). Pathological switching between languages after frontal lesions in a bilingual patient. *Journal of Neurological and Neurosurgical Psychiatry, 68,* 650–652.

Fan, J., McCandliss, B. D., Sommer, T., Raz, A., & Posner, M. I. (2002). Testing the efficiency and independence of attentional networks. *Journal of Cognitive Neuroscience, 14,* 340–347.

Fang, S.-P., Tzeng, O. J. L., & Alva, L. (1981). Intralanguage vs. interlanguage Stroop effects in two types of writing systems. *Memory & Cognition, 9,* 609–617.

Favreau, M., & Segalowitz, N. S. (1983). Automatic and controlled processes in the first- and second-language reading of fluent bilinguals. *Memory & Cognition, 11,* 565–574.

Fay, D., & Cutler, A. (1977). Malapropisms and the structure of the mental lexicon. *Linguistic Inquiry, 8,* 505–520.

Felix, U. (1993). The contribution of background music to the enhancement of learning in suggestopedia: A critical review of the literature. *Journal of the Society for Accelerative Learning and Teaching, 18,* 277–302.

Felser, C., Roberts, L., Gross, R., & Marinis, T. (2003). The processing of ambiguous sentences by first and second language learners of English. *Applied Psycholinguistics, 24,* 453–489.

Fennell, C. T., Byers-Heinlein, K., & Werker, J. F. (2007). Using speech sounds to guide word learning: The case of bilingual infants. *Child Development, 78,* 1510–1525.

Fenson, L., Dale, P. S., Reznick, J. S., Thal, D., Bates, E., Hartung, J. P., Pethick, S., & Reilly, J. S. (1993). *The MacArthur Communicative Development Inventories: User's guide and technical manual.* San Diego, CA: Singular Publishing Group.

Fenson, L., Pethick, S., Cox, R. C., Cox, J. L., Dale, P. S., & Reznick, J. S. (2000). Short-form versions of the MacArthur Communicative Development Inventories. *Applied Psycholinguistics, 21,* 95–116.

Ferré, P., Sánchez-Casas, R., & Guasch, M. (2006). Can a horse be a donkey? Semantic and form interference effects in translation recognition in early and late proficient and nonproficient Spanish–Catalan bilinguals. *Language Learning, 56,* 571–608.

Ferreira, F., & Clifton, C. Jr. (1986). The independence of syntactic processing. *Journal of Memory and Language, 25,* 348–368.

Finkbeiner, M., Almeida, J., Janssen, N., & Caramazza, A. (2006). Lexical selection in bilingual speech production does not involve language suppression. *Journal of Experimental Psychology: Learning, Memory, and Cognition, 32,* 1075–1089.

Finkbeiner, M., Forster, K. I, Nicol, J., & Nakamura, K. (2004). The role of polysemy in masked semantic and translation priming. *Journal of Memory and Language, 51,* 1–22.

Finkbeiner, M., Gollan, T. H., & Caramazza, A. (2006). Lexical access in bilingual speakers: What's the (hard) problem? *Bilingualism: Language and Cognition, 9,* 153–166.

Flege, J. (1987). The production of "new" and "similar" phones in a foreign language: Evidence for the effect of equivalence classification. *Journal of Phonetics, 15,* 47–65.

Flege, J., Munro, M., & MacKay, J. (1995b). The effect of age of second language learning on the production of English consonants. *Speech Communication, 16,* 1–26.

Flege, J. E. (1999). Age of learning and second language speech. In D. Birdsong (Ed.), *Second language acquisition and the critical period hypothesis* (pp. 101–131). Mahwah, NJ: Erlbaum.

Flege, J. E. (2002). Interactions between the native

and second-language phonetic systems. In P. Burmeister, T. Piske, & A. Rohde (Eds.), *An integrated view of language development: Papers in honor of Henning Wode* (pp. 217–244). Trier: Wissenschaftlicher Verlag.

Flege, J. E. (2005). *Origins and development of the Speech Learning Model.* 1st ASA Workshop on L2 Speech Learning. Vancouver, BC, April 14–15.

Flege, J. E, & Eefting, W. (1987). The production and perception of English stops by Spanish speakers of English. *Journal of Phonetics, 15,* 67–83.

Flege, J. E., Frieda, E. M., & Nozawa, T. (1997). Amount of native-language (L1) use affects the pronunciation of an L2. *Journal of Phonetics, 25,* 169–186.

Flege, J. E., Munro, M. J, & MacKay, I. R. A. (1995a). Factors affecting degree of perceived foreign accent in a second language. *Journal of the Acoustical Society of America, 97,* 3125–3134.

Flege, J. E., Schirru, C., & MacKay, I. R. A. (2003). Interaction between the native and second language phonetic subsystems. *Speech Communication, 40,* 467–491.

Flege, J. E., Yeni-Komshian, G. H., & Liu, S. (1999). Age constraints on second-language acquisition. *Journal of Memory and Language, 41,* 78–104.

Fodor, J. A. (1983). *The modularity of mind.* Cambridge, MA: MIT Press.

Fodor, J. A. (1985). Précis of "The Modularity of Mind". *Behavioral and Brain Sciences, 8,* 1–42.

Fouts, R. S., Fouts, D. H., & Van Cantfort, T. E. (1989). The infant Loulis learns signs from cross-fostered chimpanzees. In R. A. Gardner, B. T. Gardner, & T. E. Van Cantfort (Eds.), *Teaching sign language to chimpanzees* (pp. 280–292). Albany, NY: State University of New York Press.

Francis, W. S. (1999). Cognitive integration of language and memory in bilinguals: Semantic representation. *Psychological Bulletin, 125,* 193–222.

Francis, W. S. (2005). Bilingual semantic and conceptual representation. In J. F. Kroll & A. M. B. de Groot (Eds.), *Handbook of bilingualism: Psycholinguistics approaches* (pp. 251–267). New York: Oxford University Press.

Francis, W. S., & Gallard, S. L. K. (2005). Concept mediation in trilingual translation: Evidence from response time and repetition priming patterns. *Psychonomic Bulletin & Review, 12,* 1082–1088.

Frantzen, D. (2003). Factors affecting how second language Spanish students derive meaning from context. *The Modern Language Journal, 87,* 168–199.

Frazier, L. (1987). Sentence processing: A tutorial review. In M. Coltheart (Ed.), *Attention and performance XII: The psychology of reading* (pp. 559–586). Mahwah, NJ: Erlbaum.

Frazier, L., & Rayner, R. (1982). Making and correcting errors during sentence comprehension: Eye movements in the analysis of structurally ambiguous sentences. *Cognitive Psychology, 14,* 178–210.

French, L. M., & O'Brien, I. (2008). Phonological memory and children's second language grammar learning. *Applied Psycholinguistics, 29,* 463–487.

French, R. M. (1998). A simple recurrent network model of bilingual memory. *Proceedings of the 20th Annual Cognitive Science Society Conference* (pp. 368–373). Hillsdale, NJ: Erlbaum.

French, R. M., & Jacquet, M. (2004). Understanding bilingual memory: Models and data. *Trends in Cognitive Sciences, 8,* 87–93.

French, R. M., & Ohnesorge, C. (1995). Using non-cognate interlexical homographs to study bilingual memory organization. *Proceedings of the 17th Annual Cognitive Science Conference* (pp. 31–36). Hillsdale, NJ: Erlbaum.

Frenck, C., & Pynte, J. (1987). Semantic representation and surface forms: A look at across-language priming in bilinguals. *Journal of Psycholinguistic Research, 16,* 383–396.

Frenck-Mestre, C. (2002). An on-line look at sentence processing in the second language. In R. H. Heredia & J. Altarriba (Eds.), *Bilingual sentence processing* (pp. 217–236). Amsterdam: Elsevier Science Publishers.

Frenck-Mestre, C. (2005a). Ambiguities and anomalies: What can eye movements and event-related potentials reveal about second language sentence processing? In J. F. Kroll & A. M. B. de Groot (Eds.), *Handbook of bilingualism: Psycholinguistic approaches* (pp. 268–281). New York: Oxford University Press.

Frenck-Mestre, C. (2005b). Eye-movement recording as a tool for studying syntactic processing in a second language: A review of methodologies and experimental findings. *Second Language Research, 21,* 175–198.

Frenck-Mestre, C., & Prince, P. (1997). Second language autonomy. *Journal of Memory and Language, 37,* 481–501.

Frenck-Mestre, C. & Pynte, J. (1997). Syntactic ambiguity resolution while reading in second and native languages. *The Quarterly Journal of Experimental Psychology, 50A,* 119–148.

Friederici, A. D., Hahne, A., & von Cramon, D. Y. (1998). First-pass versus second-pass parsing processes in a Wernicke's and a Broca's aphasic: Electro-physiological evidence for a double dissociation. *Brain and Language, 62,* 311–341.

Friederici, A. D., & Kotz, S. A. (2003). The brain

basis of syntactic processes: Functional imaging and lesion studies. *NeuroImage, 20*, S8–S17.

Friederici, A. D., von Cramon, D. Y., & Kotz, S. A. (1999). Language related brain potentials in patients with cortical and subcortical left hemisphere lesions. *Brain, 122*, 1033–1047.

Friederici, A. D., Steinhauer, K., & Pfeifer, E. (2002). Brain signatures of artificial language processing: Evidence challenging the critical period hypothesis. *Proceedings of the National Academy of Sciences, 99*, 529–534.

Friedrich, M., & Friederici, A. D. (2004). N400-like semantic incongruity effect in 19-months-olds: Processing known words in picture contexts. *Journal of Cognitive Neuroscience, 16*, 1465–1477.

Fromkin, V. A., Krashen, S., Curtiss, S., Rigler, D., & Rigler, M. (1974). The development of language in Genie: A case of language acquisition beyond the "critical period". *Brain and Language, 1*, 81–107.

Frost, R. (1998). Toward a strong phonological theory of visual word recognition: True issues and false trails. *Psychological Bulletin, 123*, 71–99.

Frost, R., & Katz, L. (Eds.). (1992). *Orthography, phonology, morphology, and meaning*. Amsterdam: North Holland.

Furnham, A., & Allass, K. (1999). The influence of musical distraction of varying complexity on the cognitive performance of extraverts and introverts. *European Journal of Personality, 13*, 27–38.

Furnham, A., & Bradley, A. (1997). Music while you work: The differential distraction of background music on the cognitive test performance of introverts and extraverts. *Applied Cognitive Psychology, 11*, 445–455.

Gais, S., Lucas, B., & Born, J. (2006). Sleep after learning aids memory recall. *Learning & Memory, 13*, 259–262.

García-Albea, J. E., Sánchez-Casas, R., & Igoa, J. M. (1998). The contribution of word form and word meaning to language processing in Spanish: Some evidence from monolingual and bilingual studies. In D. Hillert (Ed.), *Sentence processing: A cross-linguistic perspective* (pp. 183–209). New York: Academic Press.

Gardner, B. T., & Gardner, R. A. (1975). Evidence for sentence constituents in the early utterances of child and chimpanzee. *Journal of Experimental Psychology: General, 104*, 244–267.

Gardner, R. A., & Gardner, B. T. (1969). Teaching sign language to a chimpanzee. *Science, 165*, 664–672.

Gass, S., & Varonis, E. M. (1984). The effect of familiarity on the comprehensibility of nonnative speech. *Language Learning, 34*, 65–87.

Gathercole, S. E., & Baddeley, A. D. (1989). Evaluation of the role of phonological STM in the development of vocabulary in children: A longitudinal study. *Journal of Memory and Language, 28*, 200–213.

Gathercole, S. E., & Baddeley, A. D. (1990). The role of phonological memory in vocabulary acquisition: A study of young children learning new names. *British Journal of Psychology, 81*, 439–454.

Gathercole, S. E., & Baddeley, A. D. (1993). *Working memory and language*. Hillsdale, NJ: Erlbaum.

Gathercole, S. E., & Thorn, A. S. C. (1998). Phonological short-term memory and foreign-language learning. In A. F. Healy & L. E. Bourne (Eds.), *Foreign-language learning: Psycholinguistics studies on training and retention* (pp. 141–185). Mahwah, NJ: Erlbaum.

Gazzaniga, M. S., Ivry, R. B., & Mangun, G. R. (2009). *Cognitive Neuroscience: The biology of the mind* (3rd ed.). New York/London: Norton & Company.

Gekoski, W. L. (1980). Language acquisition context and language organization in bilinguals. *Journal of Psycholinguistic Research, 9*, 429–449.

Genesee, F., Nicoladis, E., & Paradis, J. (1995). Language differentiation in early bilingual development. *Journal of Child Language, 22*, 611–631.

Gentner, D., & Boroditsky, L. (2001). Individuation, relativity and early word learning. In M. Bowerman & S. C. Levinson (Eds.), *Language acquisition and conceptual development* (pp. 215–256). Cambridge, UK: Cambridge University Press.

Gentner, D., & Goldin-Meadow, S. (2003). (Eds.). *Language in mind: Advances in the study of language and cognition*. Cambridge, MA: MIT Press.

Gerard, L. D., & Scarborough, D. L. (1989). Language-specific lexical access of homographs by bilinguals. *Journal of Experimental Psychology: Learning, Memory, and Cognition, 15*, 305–315.

Gerhand, S. J., Deregowski, J. B., & McAllister, H. (1995). Stroop phenomenon as a measure of cognitive functioning of bilingual (Gaelic/English) subjects. *British Journal of Psychology, 86*, 89–92.

Gerken, L. A. (1994). Child phonology: Past research, present questions, future directions. In M. A. Gernsbacher (Ed.), *Handbook of psycholinguistics* (pp. 781–820). San Diego, CA: Academic Press.

Gerver, D. (1974). Simultaneous listening and speaking and retention of prose. *The Quarterly Journal of Experimental Psychology, 26*, 337–342.

Gerver, D. (1976). Empirical studies of simultaneous

interpretation: A review and a model. In R. W. Brislin (Ed.), *Translation: Application and research* (pp. 165–207). New York: Gardner Press.

Gerver, D., Longley, P., Long, J., & Lambert, S. (1984). Selecting trainee conference interpreters: A preliminary study. *Journal of Occupational Psychology, 57*, 17–31.

Geschwind, N. (1970). The organization of language in the brain. *Science, 170*, 940–944.

Gibson, M., & Hufeisen, B. (2003). Investigating the role of prior foreign language knowledge: Translating from an unknown into a known foreign language. In J. Cenoz, B. Hufeisen, & U. Jessner (Eds.), *The multilingual lexicon* (pp 87–102). Netherlands: Springer.

Gile, D. (1995). *Basic concepts and models for interpreter and translator training*. Amsterdam/Philadelphia: John Benjamins.

Gile, D. (1997). Conference interpreting as a cognitive management problem. In J. H. Danks, G. M. Shreve, S. B. Fountain., & M. K. McBeath (Eds.), *Cognitive processes in translation and interpreting* (pp. 196–214). Thousand Oaks, CA: Sage Publications.

Glaser, M. O., & Glaser, W. R. (1982). Time course analysis of the Stroop phenomenon. *Journal of Experimental Psychology: Human Perception and Performance, 8*, 875–894.

Gloning, I., & Gloning, K. (1965). Aphasien by polyglotten. *Wiener Zeitschrift für Nervenheilkunde, 22*, 362–397.

Glushko, R. J. (1979). The organization and activation of orthographic knowledge in reading aloud. *Journal of Experimental Psychology: Human Perception and Performance, 5*, 674–691.

Goldin-Meadow, S. (2003). *The resilience of language. What gesture creation in deaf children can tell us about how all children learn language*. New York: Psychology Press.

Goldin-Meadow, S. (2005). Watching language grow. *Proceedings of the National Academy of Sciences, 102*, 2271–2272.

Goldin-Meadow, S., Butcher, C., Mylander, C., & Dodge, M. (1994). Nouns and verbs in a self-styled gesture system: What's in a name? *Cognitive Psychology, 27*, 259–319.

Goldman-Eisler, F. (1972). Segmentation of input in simultaneous translation. *Journal of Psycholinguistic Research, 1*, 127–140.

Goldowsky, B. N., & Newport, E. L. (1993). Modeling the effects of processing limitations on the acquisition of morphology: The less is more hypothesis. In E. Clark (Ed.), *The proceedings of the 24th annual Child Language Research Forum* (pp. 124–138). Stanford, CA: CSLI Publications.

Gollan, T. H., & Acenas, L.-A. (2004). What is a TOT? Cognate and translation effects on tip-of-the-tongue states in Spanish–English and Tagalog–English bilinguals. *Journal of Experimental Psychology: Learning, Memory, and Cognition, 30*, 246–269.

Gollan, T. H., & Ferreira, V. S. (2009). Should I stay or should I switch? A cost–benefit analysis of voluntary language switching in young and aging bilinguals. *Journal of Experimental Psychology: Learning, Memory, and Cognition, 35*, 640–665.

Gollan, T. H., Forster, K. I., & Frost, R. (1997). Translation priming with different scripts: Masked priming with cognates and noncognates in Hebrew–English bilinguals. *Journal of Experimental Psychology: Learning, Memory, and Cognition, 23*, 1122–1139.

Gollan, T. H., Montoya, R. J., Fennema-Notestine, C., & Morris, S. K. (2005). Bilingualism affects picture naming but not picture classification. *Memory and Cognition, 33*, 1220–1234.

Gollan, T. H., Montoya, R. J., & Werner, G. A. (2002). Semantic and letter fluency in Spanish–English bilinguals. *Neuropsychology, 16*, 562–576.

Gollan, T. H., & Silverberg, N. B. (2001). Tip-of-the-tongue states in Hebrew–English bilinguals. *Bilingualism: Language and Cognition, 4*, 63–84.

Gomez, R. L., & Gerken, L. (1999). Artificial grammar learning by 1-year-olds leads to specific and abstract knowledge. *Cognition, 70*, 109–135.

Gopher, D. (1992). The skill of attention control: Acquisition and execution of attention strategies. In D. E. Meyer & S. Kornblum (Eds.), *Synergies in experimental psychology, artificial intelligence, and cognitive neuroscience (Attention and Performance, 9*, pp. 299–322). Cambridge, MA: MIT Press.

Gopher, D., Weil, M., & Siegel, D. (1989). Practice under changing priorities: An approach to training of complex skills. *Acta Psychologica, 71*, 147–179.

Goulden, R., Nation, P., & Read, J. (1990). How large can a receptive vocabulary be? *Applied Linguistics, 11*, 341–363.

Grainger, J. (1990). Word frequency and neighborhood frequency effects in lexical decision and naming. *Journal of Memory and Language, 29*, 228–244.

Grainger, J. (1993). Visual word recognition in bilinguals. In R. Schreuder & B. Weltens (Eds.), *The bilingual lexicon* (pp. 11–25). Amsterdam/Philadelphia: John Benjamins.

Grainger, J., & Beauvillain C. (1987). Language blocking and lexical access in bilinguals. *The Quarterly Journal of Experimental Psychology, 39A*, 295–319.

Grainger, J., & Dijkstra, T. (1992). On the representation and use of language information in bilinguals. In R. J. Harris (Ed.), *Cognitive processing in bilinguals* (pp. 207–220). Amsterdam: Elsevier Science Publishers.

Grainger, J., & Jacobs, A. M. (1996). Orthographic processing in visual word recognition: A multiple read-out model. *Psychological Review, 103*, 518–565.

Grainger, J., O'Regan, J. K., Jacobs, A. M., & Segui, J. (1989). On the role of competing word units in visual word recognition: The neighborhood frequency effect. *Perception & Psychophysics, 45*, 189–195.

Grainger, J., & Segui, J. (1990). Neighborhood frequency effects in visual word recognition: A comparison of lexical decision and masked identification latencies. *Perception & Psychophysics, 47*, 191–198.

Granger, S. (1993). Cognates: An aid or a barrier to successful L2 vocabulary development? *ITL Review of Applied Linguistics, 99–100*, 43–56.

Green, C. S., & Bavelier, D. (2003). Action video game modifies visual selective attention. *Nature, 423*, 534–537.

Green, D. W. (1986). Control, activation, and resource: A framework and a model for the control of speech in bilinguals. *Brain and Language, 27*, 210–223.

Green, D. W. (1993). Towards a model of L2 comprehension and production. In R. Schreuder & B. Weltens (Eds.), *The bilingual lexicon* (pp. 249–277). Amsterdam/Philadelphia: John Benjamins.

Green, D. W. (1998). Mental control of the bilingual lexico-semantic system. *Bilingualism: Language and Cognition, 1*, 67–81.

Green, D. W. (2002). Representation and control: Exploring recovery patterns in bilingual aphasics. In F. Fabbro (Ed.), *Advances in the neurolinguistics of bilingualism: Essays in honour of Michel Paradis* (pp. 239–259). Udine, Italy: Udine University Press.

Green, D. W. (2005). The neurocognition of recovery patterns in bilingual aphasics. In J. F. Kroll & A. M. B. de Groot (Eds.), *Handbook of bilingualism: Psycholinguistic approaches* (pp. 516–530). New York: Oxford University Press.

Green, D.W., & Price, C. (2001). Functional imaging in the study of recovery patterns in bilingual aphasics. *Bilingualism: Language and Cognition, 4*, 191–201.

Greidanus, T., & Nienhuis, L. (2001). Testing the quality of word knowledge in a second language by means of word associations: Types of distractors and types of associations. *The Modern Language Journal, 85*, 567–577.

Griffin, G., & Harley, T. A. (1996). List learning of second language vocabulary. *Applied Psycholinguistics, 17*, 443–460.

Grimshaw, G. M., Adelstein, A., Bryden, M. P., & MacKinnon, G. E. (1998). First-language acquisition in adolescence: Evidence for a critical period for verbal language development. *Brain and Language, 63*, 237–255.

Grosjean, F. (1985). Polyglot aphasics and language mixing: A comment on Perecman (1984). *Brain and Language, 26*, 349–355.

Grosjean, F. (1988). Exploring the recognition of guest words in bilingual speech. *Language and Cognitive Processes, 3*, 233–274.

Grosjean, F. (1989). Neurolinguists beware! The bilingual is not two monolinguals in one person. *Brain and Language, 36*, 3–15.

Grosjean, F. (1994). Individual bilingualism. In *The encyclopedia of language and linguistics* (pp. 1656–1660). Oxford, UK: Pergamon Press.

Grosjean, F. (1995). A psycholinguistic approach to code-switching: The recognition of guest words by bilinguals. In L. Milroy & P. Muysken (Eds.), *One speaker, two languages* (pp. 259–275). Cambridge, UK: Cambridge University Press.

Grosjean, F. (1997a). Processing mixed language: Issues, findings, and models. In A. M. B. de Groot & J. F. Kroll (Eds.), *Tutorials in bilingualism: Psycholinguistic perspectives* (pp. 225–254). Mahwah, NJ: Erlbaum.

Grosjean, F. (1997b). The bilingual individual. *Interpreting, 2*, 163–187.

Grosjean, F. (1998). Studying bilinguals: Methodological and conceptual issues. *Bilingualism: Language and Cognition, 1*, 131–149.

Grosjean, F. (2001). The bilingual's language modes. In J. Nicol (Ed.), *One mind, two languages: Bilingual language processing* (pp. 1–22). Oxford, UK: Blackwell.

Gruneberg, M. (1987/2004). *Linkword Italian.* London: Corgi.

Gruneberg, M., & Morris, P. (Eds.) (1992). *Aspects of memory, Vol. 1: The practical aspects.* London/New York: Routledge.

Gruneberg, M., & Sykes, R. (1996). The use of mnemonic strategies in the learning of non roman foreign language alphabets. *Language Learning Journal, 13*, 82–83.

Gruneberg, M. M. (1998). A commentary of the keyword method of learning foreign languages. *Applied Cognitive Psychology, 12*, 529–532.

Gruneberg, M. M., & Pascoe, K. (1996). The effectiveness of the keyword method for receptive and productive foreign vocabulary learning in the elderly. *Contemporary Educational Psychology, 21*, 102–109.

Gruneberg, M. M., Sykes, R. N., & Gillett, E.

(1994). The facilitating effects of mnemonic strategies on two learning tasks in learning disabled adults. *Neuropsychological Rehabilitation*, *4*, 241–254.

Guiora, A. Z. (1983). Language and concept formation: A cross-lingual analysis. *Behavior Science Research*, *18*, 228–256.

Haarman, H. J., & Kolk, H. H. J. (1994). On-line sensitivity to subject–verb agreement violations in Broca's aphasics: The role of syntactic complexity and time. *Brain and Language*, *46*, 493–516.

Haberlandt, K. (1994). Methods in reading research. In M. A. Gernsbacher (Ed.), *Handbook of psycholinguistics* (pp. 1–31). San Diego, CA: Academic Press.

Hagoort, P. (2005). On Broca, brain, and binding: A new framework. *Trends in Cognitive Sciences*, *9*, 416–423.

Hagoort, P., Brown, C. M., & Groothusen, J. (1993). The Syntactic Positive Shift (SPS) as an ERP measure of syntactic processing. *Language and Cognitive Processes*, *8*, 439–483.

Hagoort, P., & Ramsey, N. (2004). De gereedschapskist van de cognitieve neurowetenschap [The toolkit of the cognitive neurosciences]. In F. Wijnen & F. Verstraten (Eds.), *Het brein te kijk: Verkenning van de cognitieve neurowetenschappen* [*The brain exposed: Exploration of the cognitive neurosciences*] (pp. 39–67). Amsterdam: Harcourt Assessment BV.

Hahne, A., & Friederici, A. D. (1999). Electrophysiological evidence for two steps in syntactic analysis: Early automatic and late controlled processes. *Journal of Cognitive Neuroscience*, *11*, 193–204.

Hahne, A., & Friederici, A. D. (2001). Processing a second language: Late learners' comprehension mechanisms as revealed by event-related brain potentials. *Bilingualism: Language and Cognition*, *4*, 123–141.

Haigh, C. A., & Jared, D. (2007). The activation of phonological representations by bilinguals while reading silently: Evidence from interlingual homophones. *Journal of Experimental Psychology: Learning, Memory, and Cognition*, *33*, 623–644.

Hakuta, K., & Diaz, R. M. (1985). The relationship between degree of bilingualism and cognitive ability: A critical discussion and some new longitudinal data. In K. E. Nelson (Ed.), *Children's language, Vol. 5* (pp. 319–344). Hillsdale, NJ: Erlbaum.

Hakuta, K., Bialystok, E., & Wiley, E. (2003). Critical evidence: A test of the Critical-Period Hypothesis for second-language acquisition. *Psychological Science*, *14*, 31–38.

Hall, C. J. (2002). The automatic cognate form assumption: Evidence for the parasitic model of vocabulary development. *International Review of Applied Linguistics in Language Teaching*, *40*, 69–87.

Hamers, J. F., & Blanc, M. H. A. (1989). Bilinguality and bilingualism. Cambridge, UK: Cambridge University Press.

Hammarberg, B. (2001). Roles of L1 and L2 in L3 production and acquisition. In J. Cenoz, B. Hufeisen, & U. Jessner (Eds.), *Cross-linguistic influence in third language acquisition: Psycholinguistic perspectives* (pp. 21–41). Clevedon, UK: Multilingual Matters.

Hansen, L. (2001). Language attrition: The fate of the start. *Annual Review of Applied Linguistics*, *21*, 60–73.

Hansen, L., Umeda, Y., & McKinney, M. (2002). Savings in the relearning of second language vocabulary: The effects of time and proficiency. *Language Learning*, *52*, 653–678.

Harley, T. A. (2008). *The psychology of language: From data to theory* (3rd ed.). Hove, UK: Psychology Press.

Harrington, M. (1992). Working memory capacity as a constraint on L2 development. In R. J. Harris (Ed.), *Cognitive processing in bilinguals* (pp. 123–135). Amsterdam: Elsevier Science Publishers.

Harris, B. (1980). How a three-year-old translates. In *Patterns of bilingualism* (pp. 370–393). [RELC Anthology series 8.] Singapore: National University of Singapore Press.

Harris, B., & Sherwood, B. (1978). Translating as an innate skill. In D. Gerver & H. W. Sinaiko (Eds.), *Language interpretation and communication* (pp. 155–170). New York: Plenum Press.

Hartmann, R. R. K., & Stork, F. C. (1972). *Dictionary of language and linguistics*. London: Applied Science Publishers Ltd.

Hatch, E. (1974). Research on reading a second language. *Journal of Reading Behavior*, *6*, 53–61.

Hatzidaki, A. (2007). *Interaction between languages in verb- and pronoun agreement in bilingual sentence production*. Unpublished Ph.D. thesis, The University of Edinburgh, UK.

Hazenberg, S., & Hulstijn, J. H. (1996). Defining a minimal receptive second-language vocabulary for non-native university students: An empirical investigation. *Applied Linguistics*, *17*, 145–163.

Heider, E. R. (1972). Universals in color naming and memory. *Journal of Experimental Psychology*, *93*, 10–20.

Henning, G. H. (1973). Remembering foreign language vocabulary: Acoustic and semantic parameters. *Language Learning*, *23*, 185–196.

Henriksen, B. (1999). Three dimensions of vocabulary development. *Studies in Second Language Acquisition, 21*, 303–317.

Hermans, D., Bongaerts, T., De Bot, K., & Schreuder, R. (1998). Producing words in a foreign language: Can speakers prevent interference from their first language? *Bilingualism: Language and Cognition, 1*, 213–229.

Hernandez, A., Li, P., & MacWhinney, B. (2005). The emergence of competing modules in bilingualism. *Trends in Cognitive Sciences, 9*, 220–225.

Hernandez, A. E. (2009). Language switching in the bilingual brain: What's next? *Brain & Language, 109*, 133–140.

Hernandez, A. E., Dapretto, M., Mazziotta, J., & Bookheimer, S. (2001). Language switching and language representation in Spanish–English bilinguals: An fMRI study. *NeuroImage, 14*, 510–520.

Hernandez, A. E., Martinez, A., & Kohnert, K. (2000). In search of the language switch: An fMRI study of picture naming in Spanish–English bilinguals. *Brain and Language, 73*, 421–431.

Hernandez, A. E., & Meschyan, G. (2006). Executive function is necessary to enhance lexical processing in a less proficient L2: Evidence from fMRI during picture naming. *Bilingualism: Language and Cognition, 9*, 177–188.

Hirsh, K. W., Morrison, C. M., Gaset, S., & Carnicer, E. (2003). Age of acquisition and speech production in L2. *Bilingualism: Language and Cognition, 6*, 117–128.

Hirst, W., Spelke, E. S., Reaves, C. C., Caharack, G., & Neisser, U. (1980). Dividing attention without alternation or automaticity. *Journal of Experimental Psychology: General, 109*, 98–117.

Hogaboam, T. W., & Perfetti, C. A. (1975). Lexical ambiguity and sentence comprehension. *Journal of Verbal Learning and Verbal Behavior, 14*, 265–274.

Hogben, D., & Lawson, M. J. (1997). Reexamining the relationship between verbal knowledge background and keyword training for vocabulary acquisition. *Contemporary Educational Psychology, 22*, 378–389.

Holtzheimer, P., Fawaz, W., Wilson, C., & Avery, D. (2005). Repetitive transcranial magnetic stimulation may induce language switching in bilingual patients. *Brain and Language, 94*, 274–277.

Horowitz, L. M., & Gordon, A. M. (1972). Associative symmetry and second-language learning. *Journal of Educational Psychology, 63*, 287–294.

Hoshino, N., & Kroll, J. F. (2007). Cognate effects in picture naming: Does cross-language activation survive a change of script? *Cognition, 106*, 501–511.

Hu, C.-F. (2003). Phonological memory, phonological awareness, and foreign language word learning. *Language Learning, 53*, 429–462.

Huckin, T., & Coady, J. (1999). Incidental vocabulary acquisition in a second language. *Studies in Second Language Acquisition, 21*, 181–193.

Hull, R., & Vaid, J. (2005). Clearing the cobwebs from the study of the bilingual brain: Converging evidence from laterality and electrophysiological research. In. J. F. Kroll & A. M. B. de Groot (Eds.), *Handbook of bilingualism: Psycholinguistic approaches* (pp. 480–496). New York: Oxford University Press.

Hull, R., & Vaid, J. (2006). Laterality and language experience. *Laterality, 11*, 436–464.

Hulstijn, J. (1997). Mnemonic methods in foreign vocabulary learning: Theoretical considerations and pedagogical implications. In J. Coady & T. Huckin (Eds.), *Second language vocabulary acquisition* (pp. 203–224). New York: Cambridge University Press.

Hulstijn, J. H., Hollander, M., & Greidanus, T. (1996). Incidental vocabulary learning by advanced foreign language students: The influence of marginal glosses, dictionary use, and reoccurrence of unknown words. *The Modern Language Journal, 80*, 327–339.

Humphreys, G. W., Riddock, M. J., & Quinlan, P. T. (1988). Cascade processes in picture identification. *Cognitive Neuropsychology, 5*, 67–104.

Hyltenstam, K., Bylund, E., Abrahamsson, N., & Park, H.-S. (2009). Dominant-language replacement: The case of international adoptees. *Bilingualism: Language and Cognition, 12*, 121–140.

Ianco-Worrall, A. D. (1972). Bilingualism and cognitive development. *Child Development, 43*, 1390–1400.

Ijalba, E., Obler, L. K., & Chengappa, S. (2004). Bilingual aphasia. In T. K. Bhatia & W. C. Ritchie (Eds.), *The handbook of bilingualism* (pp. 71–89). Malden, MA: Blackwell Publishing.

Illes, J., Francis, W. S., Desmond, J. E., Gabrieli, J. D. E., Glover, G. H., et al. (1999). Convergent cortical representation of semantic processing in bilinguals. *Brain and Language, 70*, 347–363.

Imai, M., & Gentner, D. (1997). A cross-linguistic study of early word meaning: Universal ontology and linguistic influence. *Cognition, 62*, 169–200.

Indefrey, P. (2006). A meta-analysis of hemodynamic studies on first and second language processing: Which suggested differences can we trust and what do they mean? *Language learning, 56*, 279–304.

Indefrey, P., & Levelt, W. J. M. (2004). The spatial and temporal signatures of word production components. *Cognition, 92*, 101–144.

Isham, W. P. (1994). Memory for sentence form after simultaneous interpretation: Evidence both for and against deverbalization. In S. Lambert & B. Moser-Mercer (Eds.), *Bridging the gap: Empirical research in simultaneous interpretation* (pp. 191–211). Amsterdam/Philadelphia: John Benjamins.

Isham, W. P. (2000). Phonological interference in interpreters of spoken-languages: An issue of storage or process? In B. Englund Dimitrova & K. Hyltenstam (Eds.), *Language processing and simultaneous interpreting* (pp. 133–149). Amsterdam: John Benjamins.

Isham, W. P., & Lane, H. (1993). Simultaneous interpretation and the recall of source-language sentences. *Language and Cognitive Processes, 8*, 241–264.

Isurin, L. (2000). Deserted island or a child's first language forgetting. *Bilingualism: Language and Cognition, 3*, 151–166.

Isurin, L., & McDonald, J. L. (2001). Retroactive interference from translation equivalents: Implications for first language forgetting. *Memory & Cognition, 29*, 312–319.

Ivanova, I., & Costa, A. (2008). Does bilingualism hamper lexical access in speech production? *Acta Psychologica, 127*, 277–288.

Jackendoff, R. (2002). *Foundations of language: Brain, meaning, grammar, evolution.* Oxford, UK: Oxford University Press.

Jackson, G. M., Swainson, R., Cunnington, R., & Jackson, S. R. (2001). ERP correlates of executive control during repeated language switching. *Bilingualism: Language and Cognition, 4*, 169–178.

Jackson, G. M., Swainson, R., Mullin, A., Cunnington, R., & Jackson, S. R. (2004). ERP correlates of a receptive language-switching task. *The Quarterly Journal of Experimental Psychology, 57A*, 223–240.

Jacobs, A. M., & Grainger, J. (1994). Models of visual word recognition—Sampling the state of the art. *Journal of Experimental Psychology: Human Perception and Performance, 20*, 1311–1334.

Jared, D., & Kroll, J. F. (2001). Do bilinguals activate phonological representations in one or both of their languages when naming words? *Journal of Memory and Language, 44*, 2–31.

Jared, D., Levy, B. A., & Rayner, K. (1999). The role of phonology in the activation of word meanings during reading: Evidence from proofreading and eye movements. *Journal of Experimental Psychology: General, 128*, 219–264.

Jared, D., McRae, K., & Seidenberg, M. S. (1990). The basis of consistency effects in word naming. *Journal of Memory and Language, 29*, 687–715.

Jared, D., & Szucs, C. (2002). Phonological activation in bilinguals: Evidence from interlingual homograph naming. *Bilingualism: Language and Cognition, 5*, 225–239.

Jasper, H. H. (1958). Report to the committee on methods of clinical examination in electroencephalography. Appendix: The ten-twenty system of the International Federation. *Electroencephalography and Clinical Neurophysiology, 10*, 371–375.

Jescheniak, J. D., & Levelt, W. J. M. (1994). Word frequency effects in speech production: Retrieval of syntactic information and of phonological form. *Journal of Experimental Psychology: Learning, Memory, and Cognition, 20*, 824–843.

Jescheniak, J. D., & Schriefers, H. (1998). Discrete serial versus cascaded processing in lexical access in speech production: Further evidence from the coactivation of near-synonyms. *Journal of Experimental Psychology: Learning, Memory, and Cognition, 24*, 1256–1274.

Jessner, U. (1999). Metalinguistic awareness in multilinguals: Cognitive aspects of third language learning. *Language Awareness, 8*, 201–209.

Jessner, U. (2003). A dynamic approach to language attrition in multilingual systems. In V. Cook (Ed.), *Effects of the second language on the first* (pp. 234–246). Clevedon, UK: Multilingual Matters.

Ji, L.-J., Zhang, Z., & Nisbett, R. E. (2004). Is it culture or is it language? Examination of language effects in cross-cultural research on categorization. *Journal of Personality and Social Psychology, 87*, 57–65.

Jiang, N. (1999). Testing processing explanations for the asymmetry in masked cross-language priming. *Bilingualism: Language and Cognition, 2*, 59–75.

Jiang, N. (2000). Lexical representation and development in a second language. *Applied Linguistics, 21*, 47–77.

Jiang, N. (2004). Morphological insensitivity in second language processing. *Applied Psycholinguistics, 25*, 603–634.

Jiang, N., & Forster, K. I. (2001). Cross-language priming asymmetries in lexical decision and episodic recognition. *Journal of Memory and Language, 44*, 32–51.

Johnson, J. S., & Newport, E. L. (1989). Critical period effects in second language learning: The influence of maturational state on the acquisition of English as a second language. *Cognitive Psychology, 21*, 60–99.

Jones, L. (2004). Testing L2 vocabulary recognition and recall using pictorial and written test items. *Language Learning & Technology, 8*, 122–143.

Jones, P. E. (1995). Contradictions and unanswered questions in the Genie case: A fresh look at the linguistic evidence. *Language & Communication, 15*, 261–280.

Junker, D. A., & Stockman, I. J. (2002). Expressive vocabulary of German–English bilingual toddlers. *American Journal of Speech-Language Pathology, 11*, 381–394.

Jusczyk, P. W., & Aslin, R. N. (1995). Infants' detection of the sound patterns of words in fluent speech. *Cognitive Psychology, 29*, 1–23.

Jusczyk, P. W., Friederici, A. D., Wessels, J. M. I, Svenkerud, V. Y., & Jusczyk, A. M. (1993). Infants' sensitivity to the sound patterns of native language words. *Journal of Memory and Language, 32*, 402–420.

Jusczyk, P. W., Pisoni, D. B., Walley, A., & Murray, J. (1980). Discrimination of relative onset time of two-component tones by infants. *Journal of Acoustical Society of America, 67*, 262–270.

Just, M. A., & Carpenter, P. A. (1992). A capacity theory of comprehension: Individual differences in working memory. *Psychological Review, 99*, 122–149.

Kaan, E., & Swaab, T. Y. (2002). The brain circuitry of syntactic comprehension. *Trends in Cognitive Sciences, 6*, 350–356.

Karanth, P., & Rangamani, G. N. (1988). Crossed aphasia in multilinguals. *Brain and Language, 34*, 169–180.

Kellerman, E. (1977). Towards a characterization of the strategy of transfer in second language learning. *Interlanguage Studies Bulletin, 2*, 58–145.

Kellerman, E. (1983). Now you see it, now you don't. In S. M. Gass & L. Selinker (Eds.), *Language transfer in language learning* (pp. 112–134). Rowley, MA: Newbury House.

Kemler-Nelson, D. G., Jusczyk, P. W., Mandel, D. R., Myers, J., Turk, A., & Gerken, L. A. (1995). The Head-Turn Preference Procedure for testing auditory perception. *Infant Behavior and Development, 18*, 111–116.

Kempen, G., & Huijbers, P. (1983). The lexicalization process in sentence production and naming: Indirect election of words. *Cognition, 14*, 185–209.

Kempen, G., Olsthoorn, N., & Sprenger, S. (2009). *Entanglement of grammatical encoding and decoding in language production and comprehension.* Unpublished manuscript.

Kerkhofs, R., Dijkstra, T., Chwilla, D. J., & De Bruijn, E. R. A. (2006). Testing a model for bilingual semantic priming with interlingual homographs: RT and N400 effects. *Brain Research, 1068*, 170–183.

Kerns, J. G., Cohen, J. D., MacDonald III, A. W., Cho, R. Y., Stenger, V. A., & Carter, C. S. (2004). Anterior cingulate conflict monitoring and adjustments in control. *Science, 303*, 1023–1026.

Kharkhurin, A. V. (2007). The role of cross-linguistic and cross-cultural experiences in bilingual's divergent thinking. In I. Kecskes & L. Albertazzi (Eds.), *Cognitive aspects of bilingualism* (pp. 175–210). Dordrecht, Netherlands: Springer.

Kieras, D. (1978). Beyond pictures and words: Alternative information-processing models for imagery effects in verbal memory. *Psychological Bulletin, 85*, 532–554.

Kim, K. H. S., Relkin, N. R., Lee, K.-M., & Hirsch, J. (1997). Distinct cortical areas associated with native and second languages. *Nature, 388*, 171–174.

Kirsner, K., Lalor, E., & Hird, K. (1993). The bilingual lexicon: Exercise, meaning, and morphology. In R. Schreuder & B. Weltens (Eds.), *The bilingual lexicon* (pp. 215–248). Amsterdam/Philadelphia: John Benjamins.

Kirsner, K., Smith, M. C., Lockhart, R. S., King, M. L., & Jain, M. (1984). The bilingual lexicon: Language-specific units in an integrated network. *Journal of Verbal Learning and Verbal Behavior, 23*, 519–539.

Kiyak, H. A. (1982). Interlingual interference in naming color words. *Journal of Cross-Cultural Psychology, 13*, 125–135.

Klein, D., Milner, B., Zatorre, R. J., Meyer, E., & Evans, A. C. (1995). The neural substrates underlying word generation: A bilingual functional-imaging study. *Proceedings of the National Academy of Sciences, 92*, 2899–2903.

Klima, E. J., & Bellugi, U. (1979). *The signs of language.* Cambridge, MA: Harvard University Press.

Kohonen, T. (1982). Self-organized formation of topologically correct feature maps. *Biological Cybernetics, 43*, 59–69.

Kolb, B., & Whishaw, I. Q. (2001). *An introduction to brain and behavior.* New York: Worth Publishers.

Kolers, P. A. (1963). Interlingual word association. *Journal of Verbal Learning and Verbal Behavior, 2*, 291–300.

Kolers, P. A. (1966). Reading and talking bilingually. *American Journal of Psychology, 79*, 357–376.

Kolk, H. H. J., & Heeschen, C. (1990). Adaptation symptoms and impairment symptoms in Broca's aphasia. *Aphasiology, 4*, 221–131.

Kotz, S. A. (2009). A critical review of ERP and fMRI evidence on L2 syntactic processing. *Brain & Language, 109*, 68–74.

Kotz, S. A., & Friederici, A. D. (2003). Electrophysiology of normal and pathological language processing. *Journal of Neurolinguistics, 16*, 43–58.

Kotz, S. A., Holcomb, P. J., & Osterhout, L. (2008). ERPs reveal comparable syntactic sentence processing in native and non-native readers of English. *Acta Psychologica, 128,* 514–527.

Kovács, A. M., & Mehler, J. (2009). Cognitive gains in 7-month-old bilingual infants. *Proceedings of the National Academy of Sciences, 106,* 6556–6560.

Krashen, S. (1989). We acquire vocabulary and spelling by reading: Additional evidence for the input hypothesis. *Modern Language Journal, 73,* 450–464.

Krashen, S. (1993). *The power of reading.* Englewood, NJ: Libraries Unlimited.

Kroll, J. F. (1993). Accessing conceptual representations for words in a second language. In R. Schreuder & B. Weltens (Eds.), *The bilingual lexicon* (pp. 53–81). Amsterdam/Philadelphia: John Benjamins.

Kroll, J. F., & Curley, J. (1988). Lexical memory in novice bilinguals: The role of concepts in retrieving second language words. In M. M. Gruneberg, P. E. Morris, & R. N. Sykes (Eds.), *Practical aspects of memory: Current research and issues, Vol. 2: Clinical and educational implications* (pp. 389–395). Chichester, UK: John Wiley & Sons.

Kroll, J. F., & De Groot, A. M. B. (1997). Lexical and conceptual memory in the bilingual: Mapping form to meaning in two languages. In A. M. B. de Groot & J. F. Kroll (Eds.), *Tutorials in bilingualism: Psycholinguistic perspectives* (pp. 169–199). Mahwah, NJ: Erlbaum.

Kroll, J. F., Dijkstra, A., Janssen, N., & Schriefers, H. (2000). *Selecting the language in which to speak: Experiments on lexical access in bilingual production.* Paper presented at the 41st Annual meeting of the Psychonomic Society, New Orleans, LA.

Kroll, J. F., & Dussias, P. E. (2004). The comprehension of words and sentences in two languages. In T. K. Bhatia & W. C. Ritchie (Eds.), *The handbook of bilingualism* (pp. 169–200). Malden, MA: Blackwell Publishing.

Kroll, J. F., Michael, E., & Sankaranarayanan, A. (1998). A model of bilingual representation and its implications for second language acquisition. In A. F. Healy & L. E. Bourne (Eds.), *Foreign language learning: Psycholinguistic studies on training and retention* (pp. 365–395). Mahwah, NJ: Erlbaum.

Kroll, J. F., Michael, E., Tokowicz, N., & Dufour, R. (2002). The development of lexical fluency in a second language. *Second Language Research, 18,* 137–171.

Kroll, J. F., & Sholl, A. (1992). Lexical and conceptual memory in fluent and nonfluent bilinguals. In R. J. Harris (Ed.), *Cognitive processing in bilinguals* (pp. 191–203). Amsterdam: Elsevier Science Publishers.

Kroll, J. F., & Stewart, E. (1994). Category interference in translation and picture naming: Evidence for asymmetric connections between bilingual memory representations. *Journal of Memory and Language, 33,* 149–174.

Kroll, J. F., Sumutka, B. M., & Schwartz, A. I. (2005). A cognitive view of the bilingual lexicon: Reading and speaking words in two languages. *International Journal of Bilingualism, 9,* 27–48.

Kroll, J. F., & Tokowicz, N. (2005). Models of bilingual representation and processing: Looking back and to the future. In J. F. Kroll & A. M. B. de Groot (Eds.), *Handbook of bilingualism: Psycholinguistic approaches* (pp. 531–553). New York: Oxford University Press.

Kuhl, P. K. (1986). Theoretical contributions of tests on animals to the special-mechanisms debate in speech. *Experimental Biology, 45,* 233–265.

Kuhl, P. K. (2004). Early language acquisition: Cracking the speech code. *Nature Reviews Neuroscience, 5,* 831–843.

Kuhl, P. K., & Meltzoff, A. N. (1982). The bimodal perception of speech in infancy. *Science, 218,* 1138–1141.

Kuhl, P. K., & Miller, J. D. (1978). Speech perception by the chinchilla: Identification functions for synthetic VOT stimuli. *Journal of the Acoustical Society of America, 63,* 905–917.

Kuhl, P. K., Tsao, F.-M., & Liu, H.-M. (2003). Foreign-language experience in infancy: Effects of short-term exposure and social interaction on phonetic learning. *Proceedings of the National Academy of Sciences, 100,* 9096–9101.

Kuhl, P. K., Williams, K. A., Lacerda, F., Stevens, K. N., & Lindblom, B. (1992). Linguistic experience alters phonetic perception in infants by 6 months of age. *Science, 255,* 606–608.

Kutas, M., & Hillyard, S. A. (1980). Reading senseless sentences: Brain potentials reflect semantic incongruity. *Science, 207,* 203–205.

Kutas, M., & Van Petten, C. K. (1994). Psycholinguistics electrified: Event-related brain potential investigations. In M. A. Gernsbacher (Ed.), *Handbook of psycholinguistics* (pp. 83–143). San Diego, CA: Academic Press.

La Heij, W. (2005). Selection processes in monolingual and bilingual lexical access. In J. F. Kroll & A. M. B. de Groot (Eds.), *Handbook of bilingualism: Psycholinguistic approaches* (pp. 289–307). New York: Oxford University Press.

La Heij, W., De Bruyn, E., Elens, E., Hartsuiker, R.,

Helaha, D., & Van Schelven, L. (1990). Orthographic facilitation and categorical interference in a word-translation version of the Stroop task. *Canadian Journal of Psychology*, *44*, 76–83.

La Heij, W., Hooglander, A., Kerling, R., & Van der Velden, E. (1996). Nonverbal context effects in forward and backward word translation: Evidence for concept mediation. *Journal of Memory and Language*, *35*, 648–665.

Lam, A. S. L., Perfetti, C. A., & Bell, L. (1991). Automatic phonetic transfer in bidialectal reading. *Applied Psycholinguistics*, *12*, 299–311.

Lambert, S. (1989). Information processing among conference interpreters: A test of the depth-of-processing hypothesis. In L. Gran & J. Dodds (Eds.), *The theoretical and practical aspects of teaching conference interpreting*. Udine, Italy: Campanetto.

Lambert, W. E. (1977). The effects of bilingualism on the individual: Cognitive and sociocultural consequences. In P. A. Hornby (Ed.), *Bilingualism: Psychological, social, and educational implications* (pp. 15–27). New York: Academic Press.

Lambert, W. E. (1981). Bilingualism and language acquisition. In H. Winitz (Ed.), *Native language and foreign language acquisition* (pp. 9–22). New York: The New York Academy of Sciences.

Lambert, W. E., Havelka., J., & Crosby, C. (1958). The influence of language-acquisition contexts on bilingualism. *Journal of Abnormal and Social Psychology*, *56*, 239–244.

Lambert, W. E., Ignatow, M., & Krauthammer, M. (1968). Bilingual organization in free recall. *Journal of Verbal Learning and Verbal Behavior*, *7*, 207–214.

Lasky, R. E., Syrdal-Lasky, A., & Klein, R. E. (1975). VOT discrimination by four to six and a half month old infants from Spanish environments. *Journal of Experimental Child Psychology*, *20*, 215–225.

Laufer, B. (1988). The concept of "synforms" (similar lexical forms) in vocabulary acquisition. *Language and Education*, *2*, 113–132.

Laufer, B. (1992). How much lexis is necessary for reading comprehension? In P. J. L. Arnaud & H. Béjoint (Eds.), *Vocabulary and applied linguistics* (pp. 126–132). Basingstoke, UK: Macmillan.

Laufer, B. (1997). What's in a word that makes it hard or easy: Some intralexical factors that affect the learning of words. In N. Schmitt & M. McCarthy (Eds.), *Vocabulary: Description, acquisition and pedagogy* (pp. 140–155). Cambridge, UK: Cambridge University Press.

Laufer, B. (2003a). The influence of L2 on L1 collocational knowledge and on L1 lexical diversity in free written expression. In V. Cook (Ed.), *Effects of the second language on the first* (pp. 19–31). Clevedon, UK: Multilingual Matters.

Laufer, B. (2003b). Vocabulary acquisition in a second language: Do learners really acquire most vocabulary by reading? Some empirical evidence. *Canadian Modern Language Review*, *59*, 567–588.

Lawson, M. J., & Hogben, D. (1998). Learning and recall of foreign-language vocabulary: Effects of a keyword strategy for immediate and delayed recall. *Learning and Instruction*, *8*, 179–194.

Laxén, J., & Lavaur, J.-M. (2010). The role of semantics in translation recognition: Effects of number of translations, dominance of translations, and semantic relatedness of multiple translations. *Bilingualism: Language and Cognition*, *13*, 157–183.

Lee, W. L., Wee, G. C., Tzeng, O. J. L., & Hung, D. L. (1992). A study of interlingual and intralingual Stroop effects in three different scripts: Logograph, syllabary, and alphabet. In R. J. Harris (Ed.), *Cognitive processing in bilinguals* (pp. 427–442). Amsterdam: Elsevier Science Publishers.

Lehtonen, M., & Laine, M. (2003). How word frequency affects morphological processing in monolinguals and bilinguals. *Bilingualism: Language and Cognition*, *6*, 213–225.

Lehtonen, M., Niska, H., Wande, E., Niemi, J., & Laine, M. (2006). Recognition of inflected words in a morphologically limited language: Frequency effects in monolinguals and bilinguals. *Journal of Psycholinguistic Research*, *35*, 121–146.

Lehtonen, M. H., Laine, M., Niemi, J., Thomsen, T., Vorobyev, V. A., & Hugdahl, K. (2005). Brain correlates of sentence translation in Finish–Norwegian bilinguals. *NeuroReport*, *16*, 607–610.

Lemhöfer, K., Dijkstra, T., & Michel, M. C. (2004). Three languages, one ECHO: Cognate effects in trilingual word recognition. *Language and Cognitive Processes*, *19*, 585–611.

Lemhöfer, K., Spalek, K., & Schriefers, H. (2008). Cross-language effects of grammatical gender in bilingual word recognition and production. *Journal of Memory and Language*, *59*, 312–330.

Lenneberg, E. H. (1967). *Biological foundations of language*. New York: Wiley.

Lenneberg, E. H., & Roberts, J. M. (1956). The language of experience: A study in methodology. *International Journal of American Linguistics, Memoir*, *13*, 22.

Leopold, W. F. (1939, 1947, 1949a, 1949b). *Speech development of a bilingual child: A linguist's record* (4 vols.). Evanston, IL: Northwestern University Press.

Levelt, W. J .M. (1989). *Speaking: From intention to articulation*. Cambridge, MA: MIT Press.

Levelt, W. J. M. (1999). Models of word production. *Trends in Cognitive Sciences, 3*, 223–232.

Levelt, W. J. M., & Maassen, B. (1981). Lexical search and order of mention in sentence production. In W. Klein & W. J. M. Levelt (Eds.), *Crossing the boundaries in linguistics. Studies presented to Manfred Bierwisch* (pp. 227–252). Dordrecht: Reidel.

Levelt, W. J. M., Praamsma, P., Meyer, A. S., Helenius, P., & Salmelin, R. (1998). An MEG study of picture naming. *Journal of Cognitive Neuroscience, 10*, 553–567.

Levelt, W. J. M., Roelofs, A., & Meyer, A. S. (1999). A theory of lexical access in speech production. *Behavioral and Brain Sciences, 22*, 1–75.

Levelt, W. J. M., Schriefers, H., Vorberg, D., Meyer, A. S., Pechmann, T., & Havinga, J. (1991). The time course of lexical access in speech production: A study of picture naming. *Psychological Review, 98*, 122–142.

Levin, J. R., Pressley, M., McCormick, C. B., Miller, G. E., & Shriberg, L. K. (1979). Assessing the classroom potential of the keyword method. *Journal of Educational Psychology, 71*, 583–594.

Levin, J. R., Shriberg, L. K., Miller, G. E., McCormick, C. B., & Levin, B. B. (1980). The keyword method in the classroom: How to remember the states and their capitals? *The Elementary School Journal, 80*, 185–191.

Levinson, S. (1996). Language and space. *Annual Review of Anthropology, 25*, 353–382.

Levinson, S. (2003). *Space in language and cognition*. Cambridge, UK: Cambridge University Press.

Léwy, N., & Grosjean, F. (1996). *A computational model of bilingual lexical access*. Unpublished manuscript. Neuchâtel University, Switzerland.

Li, P., & Farkas, I. (2002). A self-organizing connectionist model of bilingual processing. In R. R. Heredia & J. Altarriba (Eds.), *Bilingual sentence processing* (pp. 59–85). Amsterdam: Elsevier Science Publishers.

Liberman, A. M., & Mattingly, I. G. (1985). The motor theory of speech perception revised. *Cognition, 21*, 1–36.

Lichtheim, L. (1885). On aphasia. *Brain, 7*, 433–484.

Linck, J. A., Kroll, J. F., & Sunderman, G. (2009). Losing access to the native language while immersed in a second language: Evidence for the role of inhibition in second-language learning. *Psychological Science, 20*, 1507–1515.

Lisker, L., & Abramson, A. S. (1964). A cross-language study of voicing in initial stops: Acoustical measurements, *Word, 20*, 384–422.

Long, M. (2005). Problems with supposed counter-evidence to the Critical Period Hypothesis. *International Review of Applied Linguistics in Language Teaching, 43*, 287–317.

Lotto, L., & De Groot, A. M .B. (1998). Effects of learning method and word type on acquiring vocabulary in an unfamiliar language. *Language Learning, 48*, 31–69.

Lucy, J. A. (1992). *Grammatical categories and cognition. A case study of the linguistic relativity hypothesis*. Cambridge, UK: Cambridge University Press.

Lucy, J. A. (1997). Linguistic relativity. *Annual Review of Anthropology, 26*, 291–312.

Lucy, J. A., & Gaskins, S. (2001). Grammatical categories and the development of classification preferences: A comparative approach. In M. Bowerman & S. C. Levinson (Eds.), *Language acquisition and conceptual development* (pp. 257–283). Cambridge, UK: Cambridge University Press.

Lukatela, G., Savić, M., Gligorijević, B., Ognjenović, P., & Turvey, M. T. (1978). Bi-alphabetical lexical decision. *Language and Speech, 21*, 142–165.

MacDonald III, A. W., Cohen, J .D., Stenger, V. A., & Carter, C. S. (2000). Dissociating the role of the dorsolateral prefrontal and anterior cingulate cortex in cognitive control. *Science, 288*, 1835–1838.

MacDonald, M. C., Just, M. A., & Carpenter, P. A. (1992). Working memory constraints on the processing of syntactic ambiguity. *Cognitive Psychology, 24*, 56–98.

Macizo, P., & Bajo, M. T. (2004). When translation makes the difference: Sentence processing in reading and translation. *Psicológica, 25*, 181–205.

Macizo, P., & Bajo, M. T. (2006). Reading for repetition and reading for translation: Do they involve the same processes? *Cognition, 99*, 1–34.

Mack, M. (1986). A study of semantic and syntactic processing in monolinguals and fluent early bilinguals. *Journal of Psycholinguistic Research, 15*, 463–488.

MacKay, I. R. A., Meador, D., & Flege, J. E. (2001). The identification of English consonants by native speakers of Italian. *Phonetica, 58*, 103–125.

MacLeod, C. M. (1991). Half a century of research on the Stroop effect: An integrative review. *Psychological Bulletin, 109*, 193–203.

Macnamara, J. (1967). The linguistic independence of bilinguals. *Journal of Verbal Learning and Verbal Behavior, 6*, 729–736.

Macnamara, J., Krauthammer, M., & Bolgar, M. (1968). Language switching in bilinguals as a function of stimulus and response uncertainty. *Journal of Experimental Psychology*, *78*, 208–215.

Macnamara, J., & Kushnir, S. L. (1971). Linguistic independence of bilinguals: The input switch. *Journal of Verbal Learning and Verbal Behavior*, *10*, 480–487.

MacSweeney, M., Capek, C. M., Campbell, R., & Woll, B. (2008). The signing brain: the neurobiology of sign language. *Trends in Cognitive Sciences*, *12*, 432–440.

MacSweeney, M., Woll, B., Campbell, R., McGuire, P. K., David, A. S., Williams, S. C. R., et al. (2002). Neural systems underlying British Sign Language and audio-visual English processing in native users. *Brain*, *125*, 1583–1593.

MacWhinney, B. (1987). Applying the competition model to bilingualism. *Applied Psycholinguistics*, *8*, 315–329.

MacWhinney, B. (1997). Second language acquisition and the competition model. In A. M. B. de Groot & J. F. Kroll (Eds.), *Tutorials in bilingualism: Psycholinguistic perspectives* (pp. 113–142). Mahwah, NJ: Erlbaum.

MacWhinney, B. (2005). Extending the competition model. *International Journal of Bilingualism*, *9*, 69–84.

MacWhinney, B., Bates, E., & Kliegl, R. (1984). Cue validity and sentence interpretation in English, German, and Italian. *Journal of Verbal Learning and Verbal Behavior*, *23*, 127–150.

Mägiste, E. (1979). The competing language systems of the multilingual: A developmental study of decoding and encoding processes. *Journal of Verbal Learning and Verbal Behavior*, *18*, 79–89.

Mägiste, E. (1984a). Learning a third language. *Journal of multilingual and multicultural development*, *5*, 415–421.

Mägiste, E. (1984b). Stroop tasks and dichotic translation: The development of interference patterns in bilinguals. *Journal of Experimental Psychology: Learning, Memory, and Cognition*, *10*, 304–315.

Mägiste, E. (1985). Development of intra- and interlingual interference in bilinguals. *Journal of Psycholinguistic Research*, *14*, 137–154.

Mägiste, E. (1986). Selected issues in second and third language learning. In J. Vaid (Ed.), *Language processing in bilinguals: Psycholinguistic and neuropsychological perspectives* (pp. 97–122). Hillsdale, NJ: Erlbaum.

Malakoff, M., & Hakuta, K. (1991). Translation skill and metalinguistic awareness in bilinguals. In E. Bialystok (Ed.), *Language processing and language awareness in bilingual children* (pp. 141–166). New York: Oxford University Press.

Malakoff, M. E. (1992). Translation ability: A natural bilingual and metalinguistic skill. In R. J. Harris (Ed.), *Cognitive processing in bilinguals* (pp. 515–529). Amsterdam: North Holland.

Malt, B., & Sloman, S. (2003). Linguistic diversity and object-naming by non-native speakers of English. *Bilingualism: Language and Cognition*, *6*, 47–67.

Marian, V., & Spivey, M. (2003a). Bilingual and monolingual processing of competing lexical items. *Applied Psycholinguistics*, *24*, 173–193.

Marian, V., & Spivey, M. (2003b). Competing activation in bilingual language processing: Within- and between-language competition. *Bilingualism: Language and Cognition*, *6*, 97–115.

Marschark, M., Richman, C. L., Yuille, J. C., & Hunt, R. R. (1987). The role of imagery in memory: On shared and distinctive information. *Psychological Bulletin*, *102*, 28–41.

Marschark, M., & Surian, L. (1989). Why does imagery improve memory? *European Journal of Cognitive Psychology*, *1*, 251–263.

Marslen-Wilson, W. (1987). Functional parallelism in spoken word-recognition. *Cognition*, *25*, 71–102.

Martin-Rhee, M. M., & Bialystok, E. (2008). The development of two types of inhibitory control in monolingual and bilingual children. *Bilingualism: Language and Cognition*, *11*, 81–93.

Mayberry, R. I. (1993). First-language acquisition after childhood differs from second-language acquisition: The case of American Sign Language. *Journal of Speech and Hearing Research*, *36*, 51–68.

Mayberry, R. I. (2007). When timing is everything: Age of first-language acquisition effects on second-language learning. *Applied Psycholinguistics*, *28*, 537–549.

Mayberry, R. I., & Eichen, E. B. (1991). The long-lasting advantage of learning sign language in childhood: Another look at the critical period for language acquisition. *Journal of Memory and Language*, *30*, 486–512.

Mayberry, R. I., & Lock, E. (2003). Age constraints on first versus second language acquisition: Evidence for linguistic plasticity and epigenesis. *Brain and Language*, *87*, 369–384.

Maye, J., Werker, J. F., & Gerken, L. (2002). Infant sensitivity to distributional information can affect phonetic discrimination. *Cognition*, *82*, B101–B111.

McClelland, J. L., & Elman, J. L. (1986). The TRACE model of speech perception. *Cognitive Psychology*, *18*, 1–86.

McClelland, J. L., & Rumelhart, D. E. (1981). An interactive activation model of context effects in letter perception, Part 1: An account of basic findings. *Psychological Review, 88,* 375–407.

McCormack, P. D. (1976). Language as an attribute of memory. *Canadian Journal of Psychology, 30,* 238–248.

McDaniel, M. A., & Pressley, M. (1984). Putting the keyword method in context. *Journal of Educational Psychology, 76,* 598–609.

McDaniel, M. A., & Pressley, M. (1989). Keyword and context instruction of new vocabulary meanings: Effect of text comprehension and memory. *Journal of Educational Psychology, 81,* 204–213.

McDaniel, M. A., Pressley, M., & Dunay, P. K. (1987). Long-term retention of vocabulary after keyword and context learning. *Journal of Educational Psychology, 79,* 87–89.

McDaniel, M. A., & Tillman, V. P. (1987). Discovering a meaning versus applying the keyword method: Effects on recall. *Contemporary Educational Psychology, 12,* 156–175.

McDonald, J. L. (1987). Sentence interpretation in bilingual speakers of English and Dutch. *Applied Psycholinguistics, 8,* 379–413.

McDonald, J. L. (2000). Grammaticality judgments in a second language: Influences of age of acquisition and native language. *Applied Psycholinguistics, 21,* 395–423.

McDonald, J. L. (2006). Beyond the critical period: Processing-based explanations for poor grammaticality judgment performance by late second language learners. *Journal of Memory and Language, 55,* 381–401.

McDonald, J. L., & Carpenter, P. A. (1981). Simultaneous translation: Idiom interpretation and parsing heuristics. *Journal of Verbal Learning and Verbal Behavior, 20,* 231–247.

McDonald, J. L., & Heilenman, L. K. (1992). Changes in sentence processing as second language proficiency increases. In R. J. Harris (Ed.), *Cognitive processing in bilinguals* (pp. 327–336). Amsterdam: Elsevier Science Publishers.

McRae, K., De Sa, V. R., & Seidenberg, M. S. (1997). On the nature and scope of featural representations of word meaning. *Journal of Experimental Psychology: General, 126,* 99–130.

Meara, P. (1983). Word associations in a foreign language: A report on the Birkbeck Vocabulary Project. *Nottingham Linguistic Circular, 11,* 29–39.

Meara, P. (1993). The bilingual lexicon and the teaching of vocabulary. In R. Schreuder & B. Weltens (Eds.), *The bilingual lexicon* (pp. 279–297). Amsterdam-Philadelphia: John Benjamins.

Mechelli, A., Crinion, J. T., Noppeney, U., O'Doherty, J., Ashburner, J., Frackowiak, R. S., &

Price, C. J. (2004). Neurolinguistics: Structural plasticity in the bilingual brain. *Nature, 431,* 757.

Mehler, J., Dommergues, J. Y., Frauenfelder, U., & Segui, J. (1981). The syllable's role in speech segmentation. *Journal of Verbal Learning and Verbal Behavior, 20,* 298–305.

Mehler, J., Jusczyk, P. W., Lambertz, G., Halsted, N., Bertoncini, J., & Amiel-Tison, C. (1988). A precursor of language acquisition in young infants. *Cognition, 29,* 144–178.

Meisel, J. (1989). Early differentiation of languages in bilingual children. In K. Hyltenstam & L. Obler (Eds.), *Bilingualism across the lifespan. Aspects of acquisition, maturity and loss* (pp. 13–40). Cambridge, UK: Cambridge University Press.

Meisel, J. M. (2001). The simultaneous acquisition of two first languages: Early differentiation and subsequent development of grammars. In J. Cenoz & F. Genesee (Eds.), *Trends in bilingual acquisition* (pp. 11–41). Amsterdam/Philadelphia: John Benjamins.

Melson, W. H., & McCall, R. B. (1970). Attentional responses of five-months girls to discrepant auditory stimuli. *Child Development, 41,* 1159–1171.

Merton, R. K. (1968). The Matthew effect in science. *Science, 159,* 56–63.

Meuter, R. F. I., & Allport, A. (1999). Bilingual language switching in naming: Asymmetrical costs of language selection. *Journal of Memory and Language, 40,* 25–40.

Meuter, R. F. I., Humphreys, G. W., & Rumiati, R. I. (2002). Bilingual language switching and the frontal lobes: Modulatory control in language selection. *The International Journal of Bilingualism, 2,* 109–124.

Miller, N. A., & Kroll, J. F. (2002). Stroop effects in bilingual translation. *Memory & Cognition, 30,* 614–628.

Mills, D., Coffey-Corina, S., & Neville, H. J. (1997). Language comprehension and cerebral specialization from 13 to 20 months. *Developmental Neuropsychology, 13,* 397–445.

Mills, D. L., Plunkett, K., Prat, C., & Schafer, G. (2005). Watching the infant brain learn words: Effects of vocabulary size and experience. *Cognitive Development, 20,* 19–31.

Minkowski, M. (1927/1983). A clinical contribution to the study of polyglot aphasia especially with respect to Swiss–German. In M. Paradis (Ed.), *Readings on aphasia in bilinguals and polyglots* (pp. 205–232). Montreal: Didier.

Miyake, A., & Friedman, N. P. (1998) Individual differences in second language proficiency: Working memory as language aptitude. In A. F. Healy & L. E. Bourne (Eds.), *Foreign language learning:*

Psycholinguistic studies on training and retention. (pp. 339–364). Mahwah, NJ: Erlbaum.

Mondria, J. A. (2003). The effects of inferring, verifying, and memorizing on the retention of L2 word meanings. *Studies in Second Language Acquisition, 25,* 473–499.

Monsell, S. (1987). On the relation between lexical input and output pathways for speech. In A. Allport, D. MacKay, W. Prinz, & E. Scheerer (Eds.), *Language perception and production: Relationships between listening, speaking, reading, and writing* (pp. 273–311). London: Academic Press.

Monsell, S. (2003). Task switching. *Trends in Cognitive Sciences, 7,* 134–140.

Morais, J., Content, A., Cary, L., Mehler, J., & Segui, J. (1989). Syllabic segmentation and literacy. *Language and Cognitive Processes, 4,* 57–67.

Morrison, C. M., Ellis, A. W., & Quinlan, P. T. (1992). Age of acquisition, not word frequency, affects object naming, not object recognition. *Memory & Cognition, 20,* 705–714.

Morrison, C. M., Hirsh, K. W., Chappell, T., & Ellis, A. W. (2002). Age and age of acquisition: An evaluation of the cumulative frequency hypothesis. *European Journal of Cognitive Psychology, 14,* 435–459.

Morrissey, M. D. (1981). A case for "friends". *International Review of Applied Linguistics in Language Teaching, 19,* 65–68.

Moser, B. (1978). Simultaneous interpretation: A hypothetical model and its practical application. In D. Gerver & H. W. Sinaiko (Eds.), *Language interpretation and communication* (pp. 353–368). New York: Plenum.

Moser-Mercer, B. (1994). Aptitude testing for conference interpreting: Why, when and how. In S. Lambert & B. Moser-Mercer (Eds.), *Bridging the gap. Empirical research in simultaneous interpretation* (pp. 57–68). Amsterdam/Philadelphia: John Benjamins.

Moser-Mercer, B., Frauenfelder, U. H., Casado, B., & Künzli, A. (2000). Searching to define expertise in interpreting. In B. Englund Dimitrova & K. Hyltenstamm (Eds.), *Language processing and simultaneous interpreting: Interdisciplinary perspectives* (pp. 107–131). Amsterdam/Philadelphia: John Benjamins.

Munro, M. J., & Derwing, T. M. (1994). Evaluations of foreign accent in extemporaneous and read material. *Language Testing, 11,* 253–266.

Munro, M. J., & Derwing, T. M. (1995). Processing time, accent, and comprehensibility in the perception of native and foreign-accented speech. *Language and Speech, 38,* 289–306.

Munro, M. J., & Derwing, T. M. (1999). Foreign accent, comprehensibility, and intelligibility in the speech of second language learners. *Language Learning, 49,* Supplement 1, 285–310.

Murphy, S. (2003). Second language transfer during third language acquisition. *Teachers College, Columbia University Working Papers in TESOL & Applied Linguistics, 3,* 1–21.

Murre, J. M. J. (2005). Models of monolingual and bilingual language acquisition. In J. F. Kroll & A. M. B. de Groot (Eds.), *Handbook of bilingualism: Psycholinguistic approaches* (pp. 154–169). New York: Oxford University Press.

Nas, G. (1983). Visual word recognition in bilinguals: Evidence for a cooperation between visual and sound based codes during access to a common lexical store. *Journal of Verbal Learning and Verbal Behavior, 22,* 526–534.

Nation, I. S. P. (1990). *Teaching and learning vocabulary.* New York: Newbury House.

Nation, P. (1993). Vocabulary size, growth, and use. In R. Schreuder & B. Weltens (Eds.), *The bilingual lexicon* (pp. 115–134). Amsterdam/Philadelphia: John Benjamins.

Nazzi, T., & Bertoncini, J. (2003). Before and after the vocabulary spurt: Two modes of word acquisition? *Developmental Science, 6,* 136–142.

Nazzi, T., Bertoncini, J., & Mehler, J. (1998). Language discrimination by newborns: Towards an understanding of the role of rhythm. *Journal of Experimental Psychology: Human Perception and Performance, 24,* 756–766.

Nazzi, T., & Ramus, F. (2003). Perception and acquisition of linguistic rhythm by infants. *Speech Communication, 41,* 233–243.

Neely, J. H. (1991). Semantic priming effects in visual word recognition: A selective review of current findings and theories. In D. Besner & G. Humphreys (Eds.), *Basic processes in reading: Visual word recognition* (pp. 264–336). Hillsdale, NJ: Erlbaum.

Nelson, K. (1973). Structure and strategy in learning to talk. *Monographs of the Society for Research in Child Development, 38,* (1–2 Serial No. 149), 1–135.

Nelson, T. (1978). Detecting small amounts of information in memory: Savings for non-recognized items. *Journal of Experimental Psychology: Human Learning and Memory, 4,* 453–468.

Neville, H., Nicol, J. L., Barss, A., Forster, K. I., & Garrett, M. F. (1991). Syntactically based sentence processing classes: Evidence from event-related potentials. *Journal of Cognitive Neuroscience, 3,* 151–165.

Newport, E. L. (1988). Constraints on learning and their role in language acquisition: Studies of the acquisition of American Sign Language. *Language Sciences, 10*, 147–172.

Newport, E. L. (1990). Maturational constraints on language learning. *Cognitive Science, 34*, 11–28.

Nicoladis, E., & Grabois, H. (2002). Learning English and losing Chinese: A case study of a child adopted from China. *The International Journal of Bilingualism, 6*, 441–454.

Nieuwland, M. S., & Van Berkum, J. J. A. (2006). When peanuts fall in love: N400 evidence of the power of discourse. *Journal of Cognitive Neuroscience, 18*, 1098–1111.

Noble, C. E. (1952). The role of stimulus meaning (m) in serial verbal learning. *Journal of Experimental Psychology, 43*, 437–446.

Norman, D. A., & Shallice, T. (1986). Attention to action: Willed and automatic control of behavior. In R. J. Davidson, G. E. Schwartz, & D. Shapiro (Eds.), *Consciousness and self-regulation: Advances in research and theory, Vol. 4* (pp. 1–18). New York/London: Plenum Press.

Obler, L. K. (1981). Right hemisphere participation in second language acquisition. In K. Diller (Ed.), *Individual differences and universals in language learning aptitude* (pp. 53–64). Rowley, MA: Newbury.

Obler, L. K., & Albert, M. L. (1978). A monitor system for bilingual language processing. In M. Paradis (Ed.), *Aspects of bilingualism* (pp. 156–164). Columbia, SC: Hornbeam Press.

Oh, J. S., Jun, S. A., Knightly, L. M., & Au, T. K. F. (2003). Holding on to childhood language memory. *Cognition, 86*, B53–B64.

Ojemann, G. A., & Whitaker, H. A. (1978). The bilingual brain. *Archives of Neurology, 35*, 409–412.

Ojima, S., Nakata, H., & Kakigi, R. (2005). An ERP study of second language learning after childhood: Effects of proficiency. *Journal of Cognitive Neuroscience, 17*, 1212–1228.

Oller, J. W. (1972). Assessing competence in ESL: reading. *TESOL Quarterly, 6*, 313–323.

Onifer, W., & Swinney, D. A. (1981). Accessing lexical ambiguities during sentence comprehension: Effects of frequency of meaning and contextual bias. *Memory & Cognition, 9*, 225–236.

Osterhout, L., & Holcomb, P. J. (1992). Event-related brain potentials elicited by syntactic anomaly. *Journal of Memory and Language, 31*, 785–806.

Otake, T., Hatano, G., Cutler, A., & Mehler, J. (1993). Mora or syllable? Speech segmentation in Japanese. *Journal of Memory and Language, 32*, 258–278.

Otten, M., Nieuwland, M. S., & Van Berkum, J. J. A. (2007). Great expectations: Specific lexical anticipation influences processing of spoken language. *BMC Neuroscience, 8*, 89.

Padilla, P., Bajo, M. T., Cañas, J. J., & Padilla, F. (1995). Cognitive processes of memory in simultaneous interpretation. In J. Tommola (Ed.), *Topics in interpreting research* (pp. 61–71). University of Turku: Centre for Translation and Interpreting.

Padilla, F., Bajo, M. T., & Macizo, P. (2005). Articulatory suppression in language interpretation: Working memory capacity, dual tasking and word knowledge. *Bilingualism: Language and Cognition, 8*, 207–219.

Paivio, A. (1986). *Mental representations: A dual coding approach.* New York: Oxford University Press.

Paivio, A., & Desrochers, A. (1980). A dual-coding approach to bilingual memory. *Canadian Journal of Psychology, 34*, 388–399.

Pallier, C., Dehaene, S., Poline, J. B., LeBihan, D., Argenti, A. M., Dupoux, E., & Mehler, J. (2003). Brain imaging of language plasticity in adopted adults: Can a second language replace the first? *Cerebral Cortex, 13*, 155–161.

Papadopoulou, D., & Clahsen, H. (2003). Parsing strategies in L1 and L2 sentence processing: A study of relative clause attachment in Greek. *Studies in Second Language Acquisition, 25*, 501–528.

Papagno, C., Valentine, T., & Baddeley, A. (1991). Phonological short-term memory and foreign-language vocabulary learning. *Journal of Memory and Language, 30*, 331–347.

Papagno, C., & Vallar, G. (1995). Verbal short-term memory and vocabulary learning in polyglots. *Quarterly Journal of Experimental Psychology, 48A*, 98–107.

Paradis, M. (1981). Neurolinguistic organization of a bilingual's two languages. In J. E. Copeland & P. W. Davis (Eds.), *The seventh LACUS Forum* (pp. 486–494). Columbia, SC: Hornbeam Press.

Paradis, M. (1990). Language lateralization in bilinguals: Enough already! *Brain and language, 39*, 576–586.

Paradis, M. (1992). The Loch Ness Monster approach to lateralization in bilingual aphasia: A response to Berquier & Ashton. *Brain and Language, 43*, 534–537.

Paradis, M. (1994). Toward a neurolinguistic theory of simultaneous translation: The framework. *International Journal of Psycholinguistics, 10*, 319–335.

Paradis, M. (1995). Epilogue: Bilingual aphasia 100 years later: Consensus and controversies. In M. Paradis (Ed.), *Aspects of bilingual aphasia* (pp. 211–223), Oxford/New York: Pergamon Press.

Paradis, M. (1997). The cognitive neuropsychology of bilingualism. In A. M. B. de Groot & J. F. Kroll (Eds.), *Tutorials in bilingualism: Psycholinguistic perspectives* (pp. 331–354). Mahwah, NJ: Erlbaum.

Paradis, M. (2000). Generalizable outcomes of bilingual aphasia research. *Folia Phoniatrica et Logopaedia, 52,* 54–64.

Paradis, M. (2001). Bilingual and polyglot aphasia. In R. S. Berndt (Ed.), *Handbook of neuropsychology*, (2nd ed., Vol. 3, pp. 69–91). Oxford, UK: Elsevier Science Publishers.

Paradis, M. (2003). The bilingual Loch Ness Monster raises its non-asymmetric head again—or, why bother with such cumbersome notions as validity and reliability? Comments on Evans et al. (2002). *Brain and Language, 87,* 441–448.

Paradis, M. (2004). *A neurolinguistic theory of bilingualism.* Amsterdam/Philadelphia: John Benjamins.

Paradis, M., Goldblum, M. C., & Abidi, R. (1982). Alternate antagonism with paradoxical translation behavior in two bilingual aphasic patients. *Brain and Language, 15,* 55–69.

Paulesu, E., Goldacre, B., Scifo, P., Cappa, S. F., Gilardi, M. C., Castiglioni, I., Perani, D., & Fazio, F. (1997). Functional heterogeneity of left inferior frontal cortex as revealed by fMRI. *Neuroreport, 8,* 2011–2017.

Paulmann, S., Elston-Güttler, K. E., Gunter, T. C., & Kotz, S. A. (2006). Is bilingual lexical access influenced by language context? *NeuroReport, 17,* 727–731.

Pavlenko, A. (1999). New approaches to concepts in bilingual memory. *Bilingualism: Language and Cognition, 2,* 209–230.

Pavlenko, A. (2000). L2 influence on L1 in late bilingualism. *Issues in Applied Linguistics, 11,* 175–205.

Pavlenko, A. (2002). Bilingualism and emotions. *Multilingua, 21,* 45–78.

Pavlenko, A. (2005). Bilingualism and thought. In J. F. Kroll & A. M. B. de Groot (Eds.), *Handbook of bilingualism: Psycholinguistic approaches* (pp. 433–453). New York: Oxford University Press.

Peal, E., & Lambert, W. E. (1962). The relation of bilingualism to intelligence. *Psychological Monographs, 76,* 1–23.

Pearson, B. Z. (1998). Assessing lexical development in bilingual babies and toddlers. *The International Journal of Bilingualism, 2,* 347–372.

Pearson, B. Z., & Fernández, S. C. (1994). Patterns of interaction in the lexical growth in two languages of bilingual infants and toddlers. *Language Learning, 44,* 617–653.

Pearson, B. Z., Fernández, S. C., & Oller, D. K. (1993). Lexical development in bilingual infants and toddlers: Comparison to monolingual norms. *Language Learning, 43,* 93–120.

Pearson, B. Z., Fernández, S. C., & Oller, D. K. (1995). Cross-language synonyms in the lexicons of bilingual infants: One language or two? *Journal of Child Language, 22,* 345–368.

Penfield, W. (1963). *The second career.* Boston: Little, Brown & Company.

Penfield, W., & Roberts, L. (1959). *Speech and brain mechanisms.* Princeton, NJ: Princeton University Press.

Perani, D., & Abutalebi, J. (2005). The neural basis of first and second language processing. *Current Opinion in Neurobiology, 15,* 202–206.

Perani, D., Dehaene, S., Grassi, F., Cohen, L., Cappa, S. F., Dupoux, E., et al. (1996). Brain processing of native and foreign languages. *NeuroReport, 7,* 2439–2444.

Perani, D., Paulesu, E., Sebastián-Gallés, N., Dupoux, E., Dehaene, S., Bettinardi, V., et al. (1998). The bilingual brain: Proficiency and age of acquisition of the second language. *Brain, 121,* 1841–1852.

Perecman, E. (1984). Spontaneous translation and language mixing in a polyglot aphasic. *Brain and Language, 23,* 43–63.

Perfetti, C. A., Liu, Y., & Tan, L. H. (2005). The lexical constituency model: Some implications of research on Chinese for general theories of reading. *Psychological Review, 112,* 43–59.

Perfetti, C. A., & Zhang, S. (1995). Very early phonological activation in Chinese reading. *Journal of Experimental Psychology: Learning, Memory, and Cognition, 21,* 24–33.

Peterson, R. R., & Savoy, P. (1998). Lexical selection and phonological encoding during language production: Evidence for cascaded processing. *Journal of Experimental Psychology: Learning, Memory, and Cognition, 24,* 539–557.

Pettito, L. A., & Marentette, P. F. (1991). Babbling in the manual mode: Evidence for the ontogeny of language. *Science, 251,* 1493–1496.

Philipp, A. M., Gade, M., & Koch, I. (2007). Inhibitory processes in language switching: Evidence from switching language-defined response sets. *European Journal of Cognitive Psychology, 19,* 395–416.

Philipp, A. M., & Koch, I. (2009). Inhibition in language switching: What is inhibited when switching between languages in a naming task? *Journal of Experimental Psychology: Learning, Memory, and Cognition, 35,* 1187–1195.

Pinker, S. (1994). *The language instinct: How the mind creates language.* New York: William Morrow and Company.

Piske, T., MacKay, I. R. A., & Flege, J. E. (2001).

Factors affecting degree of foreign accent in an L2: A review. *Journal of Phonetics, 29,* 191–215.

Pitres, A. (1895/1953). Etude sur l'aphasie chez les polyglottes. *Revue de médicine, 15,* 873–899. [Translated in M. Paradis (Ed.), *Readings on aphasia in bilinguals and polyglots* (pp. 26–48). Montreal: Marcel Didier].

Polka, L., & Werker, J. F. (1994). Developmental changes in perception of nonnative vowel contrasts. *Journal of Experimental Psychology: Human Perception and Performance, 20,* 421–435.

Potter, M. C., So, K.-F., Von Eckardt, B., & Feldman, L. B. (1984). Lexical and conceptual representation in beginning and proficient bilinguals. *Journal of Verbal Learning and Verbal Behavior, 23,* 23–38.

Poulisse, N. (1997). Language production in bilinguals. In A. M. B. de Groot & J. F. Kroll (Eds.), *Tutorials in bilingualism: Psycholinguistic perspectives* (pp. 201–224). Mahwah, NJ: Erlbaum.

Poulisse N., & Bongaerts, T. (1994). First language use in second language production. *Applied Linguistics, 15,* 36–57.

Pressley, M., & Levin, J. R. (1978). Developmental constraints associated with children's use of the keyword method of foreign language vocabulary learning. *Journal of Experimental Child Psychology, 26,* 359–372.

Pressley, M., Levin, J. R., & Delaney, H. D. (1982a). The mnemonic keyword method. *Review of Educational Research, 52,* 61–91.

Pressley, M., Levin, J. R., Hall, J. W., Miller, G. E., & Berry, J. K. (1980). The keyword method and foreign word acquisition. *Journal of Experimental Psychology: Human Learning and Memory, 6,* 163–173.

Pressley, M., Levin, J. R., Kuiper, N. A., Bryant, S. L., & Michener, S. (1982b). Mnemonic versus nonmnemonic vocabulary-learning strategies: Additional comparisons. *Journal of Educational Psychology, 74,* 693–707.

Pressley, M., Levin, J. R., & Miller, J. E. (1981). The keyword method and children's learning of foreign vocabulary with abstract meanings. *Canadian Journal of Psychology, 35,* 283–287.

Preston, M. S., & Lambert, W. E. (1969). Interlingual interference in a bilingual version of the Stroop color-word task. *Journal of Verbal Learning and Verbal Behavior, 8,* 295–301.

Price, C. J., Green, D. W., & Von Studnitz, R. (1999). A functional imaging study of translation and language switching. *Brain, 122,* 2221–2235.

Prince, P. (1996). Second language vocabulary learning: The role of context versus translations as a function of proficiency. *The Modern Language Journal, 80,* 478–493.

Prior, A., MacWhinney, B., & Kroll, J. F. (2007). Translation norms for English and Spanish: The role of lexical variables, word class, and L2 proficiency in negotiating translation ambiguity. *Behaviour Research Methods, 39,* 1029–1038.

Raugh, M. R., & Atkinson, R. C. (1975). A mnemonic method for learning a second-language vocabulary. *Journal of Educational Psychology, 67,* 1–16.

Rayner, K., & Sereno, S. C. (1994). Eye movements in reading: Psycholinguistic studies. In M. A. Gernsbacher (Ed.), *Handbook of psycholinguistics* (pp. 57–81). San Diego, CA: Academic Press.

Read, J. (1993). The development of a new measure of L2 vocabulary knowledge. *Language Testing, 10,* 355–371.

Read, J. (2004). Research in teaching vocabulary. *Annual Review of Applied Linguistics, 24,* 146–161.

Reynolds, A. G. (1991). The cognitive consequences of bilingualism. In A. G. Reynolds (Ed.), *Bilingualism, multiculturalism, and second language learning* (pp. 145–182). Hillsdale, NJ: Erlbaum.

Richards, J. C., Platt, J., & Platt, H. (1992). *Longman dictionary of language teaching & applied linguistics.* Addison Wesley Publishing Company.

Ringbom, H. (1987). *The role of the first language in foreign language learning.* Clevedon/Philadelphia: Multilingual matters.

Rinne, J. O., Tommola, J., Laine, M., Krause, B. J., Schmidt, D., et al. (2000). The translating brain: Cerebral activation patterns during simultaneous interpreting. *Neuroscience Letters, 294,* 85–88.

Rivera-Gaxiola, M., Silva-Pereyra, J., & Kuhl, P. K. (2005). Brain potentials to native and non-native speech contrasts in 7- and 11-month-old American infants. *Developmental Science, 8,* 162–172.

Roberts, P. (1983). Memory strategy instruction with the elderly: What should memory training be the training of? In M. Pressley & J. R. Levin (Eds.), *Cognitive strategy research* (pp. 75–100). New York: Springer-Verlag.

Rodríguez, M., & Sadoski, M. (2000). Effects of rote, context, keyword, and context/keyword methods on retention of vocabulary in EFL classrooms. *Language Learning, 50,* 385–412.

Rodriguez-Fornells, A., De Diego Balaguer, R., & Münte, T. F. (2006). Executive control in bilingual language processing. *Language Learning, 56,* 133–190.

Rodriguez-Fornells, A., Lutz, T., & Münte, T. F. (2010). *Syntactic interference in bilingual naming performance is modulated by language switching: An electrophysiological study.* Manuscript submitted for publication.

Rodriguez-Fornells, A., Van der Lugt, A., Rotte, M., Britti, B., Heinze, H. J., & Münte, T. F. (2005). Second language interferes with word production in fluent bilinguals: Brain potential and functional imaging evidence. *Journal of Cognitive Neuroscience, 17,* 422–433.

Roelofs, A. (1992). A spreading-activation theory of lemma retrieval in speaking. *Cognition, 42,* 107–142.

Roelofs, A. (1997). The WEAVER model of word-form encoding in speech production. *Cognition, 64,* 249–284.

Roelofs, A., Meyer, A. S., & Levelt, W. J. M. (1996). Interaction between semantic and orthographic factors in conceptually driven naming: Comment on Starreveld and La Heij (1995). *Journal of Experimental Psychology: Learning, Memory, and Cognition, 22,* 246–251.

Rohde, D. L. T., & Plaut, D. C. (2003). Less is less in language acquisition. In P. Quinlan (Ed.), *Connectionist models of development* (pp. 189–231). Hove, UK: Psychology Press.

Rosch, E. (1975). Cognitive representations of semantic categories. *Journal of Experimental Psychology: General, 104,* 192–233.

Rosenblum, L. D., Schmuckler, M. A., & Johnson, J. A. (1997). The McGurk effect in infants. *Perception and Psychophysics, 59,* 347–357.

Rosenblum, T., & Pinker, S. A. (1983). Word magic revisited: Monolingual and bilingual children's understanding of the word–object relationship. *Child Development, 54,* 773–780.

Rosinski, R. R., Golinkoff, R. M., & Kukish, K. S. (1975). Automatic semantic processing in a picture–word interference task. *Child Development, 46,* 247–253.

Rothkopf, E. Z. (1971). Incidental memory for location of information in text. *Journal of Verbal Learning and Verbal Behavior, 10,* 608–613.

Rott, S. (1999). The effect of exposure frequency on intermediate language learners' incidental vocabulary acquisition and retention through reading. *Studies in Second Language Acquisition, 21,* 589–619.

Rubenstein, H., Lewis, S. S., & Rubenstein, M. A. (1971). Evidence for phonemic recoding in visual word recognition. *Journal of Verbal Learning and Verbal Behavior, 10,* 645–657.

Ruiz, C., Paredes, N., Macizo, P., & Bajo, M. T. (2008). Activation of lexical and syntactic target language properties in translation. *Acta Psychologica, 128,* 490–500.

Saer, D. J. (1923). The effects of bilingualism on intelligence. *British Journal of Psychology, 14,* 25–38.

Saffran, J. R. (2001). Words in a sea of sounds: The output of infant statistical learning. *Cognition, 81,* 149–169.

Saffran, J. R. (2003). Statistical language learning: Mechanisms and constraints. *Current Directions in Psychological Science, 12,* 110–114.

Saffran, J. R., Aslin, R. N., & Newport, E. L. (1996a). Statistical learning by 8-month-old infants. *Science, 274,* 1926–1928.

Saffran, J. R., Newport, E. L., & Aslin, R. N. (1996b). Word segmentation: The role of distributional cues. *Journal of Memory and Language, 35,* 606–621.

Saffran, J. R., & Wilson, D. P. (2003). From syllables to syntax: Multilevel statistical learning by 12-month-old infants. *Infancy, 4,* 273–284.

Sagarra, N., & Alba, M. (2006). The key is in the keyword: L2 vocabulary learning methods with beginning learners of Spanish. *The Modern Language Journal, 90,* 228–243.

Salamoura, A., & Williams, J. N. (1999). Backward word translation: Lexical vs. conceptual mediation or "concept activation vs. word retrieval"? *RCEAL Working Papers in English and Applied Linguistics, 6,* 31–56.

Sánchez-Casas, R. M., Davis, C. W., & García-Albea, J. E. (1992). Bilingual lexical processing: Exploring the cognate/non-cognate distinction. *European Journal of Cognitive Psychology, 4,* 293–310.

Sánchez-Casas, R., & García-Albea, J. E. (2005). The representation of cognate and noncognate words in bilingual memory: Can cognate status be characterized as a special kind of morphological relation? In J. F. Kroll & A. M. B. de Groot (Eds.), *Handbook of bilingualism: Psycholinguistic approaches* (pp. 226–250). New York: Oxford University Press.

Sandler, W., Meir, I., Padden, C., & Aronoff, M. (2005). The emergence of grammar: Systematic structure in a new language. *Proceedings of the National Academy of Science, 102,* 2661–2665.

Sanz, C. (2000). Bilingual education enhances third language acquisition: Evidence from Catalonia. *Applied Psycholinguistics, 21,* 23–44.

Schein, J. D., & Delk, M. T. Jr. (1974). *The deaf population of the United States.* Silver Spring, MD: National Association of the Deaf.

Schmitt, N., & Meara, P. (1997). Researching vocabulary through a word knowledge framework: Word associations and verbal suffixes. *Studies in Second Language Acquisition, 19,* 17–36.

Schneider, V. I., Healy, A. F., & Bourne, L. E. Jr. (1998). Contextual interference effects in foreign language acquisition and retention. In A. F. Healy & L. E. Bourne Jr. (Eds.), *Foreign language learning: Psycholinguistic studies on training and retention* (pp. 77–90). Mahwah, NJ: Erlbaum.

Schneider, V. I., Healy, A. F., & Bourne, L. E. (2002). What is learned under difficult conditions is hard to forget: Contextual interference effects in foreign vocabulary acquisition, retention, and transfer. *Journal of Memory and Language, 46,* 419–440.

Schön, D., Boyer, M., Moreno, S., Besson, M., Peretz, I., & Kolinsky, R. (2008). Songs as an aid for language acquisition. *Cognition, 106,* 975–983.

Schönpflug, U. (1997, April). *Bilingualism and memory.* Paper presented at the First International Symposium on Bilingualism. Newcastle-upon-Tyne, UK.

Schoonen, R., & Verhallen, M. (1998). Kennis van woorden: De toetsing van diepe woordkennis [Knowledge of words: The testing of deep word knowledge]. *Pedagogische Studiën, 75,* 153–168.

Schriefers, H., Meyer, A. S., & Levelt, W. J. M. (1990). Exploring the time course of lexical access in language production: Picture–word interference studies. *Journal of Memory and Language, 29,* 86–102.

Schulpen, B., Dijkstra, T., Schriefers, H. J., & Hasper, M. (2003). Recognition of interlingual homophones in bilingual auditory word recognition. *Journal of Experimental Psychology: Human Perception and Performance, 29,* 1155–1178.

Schwanenflugel, P. J. (1991). Why are abstract concepts hard to understand? In P. J. Schwanenflugel (Ed.), *The psychology of word meanings* (pp. 223–250). Hillsdale, NJ: Erlbaum.

Schwanenflugel, P. J., Harnishfeger, K. K., & Stowe, R. W. (1988). Context availability and lexical decisions for abstract and concrete words. *Journal of Memory and Language, 27,* 499–520.

Schwanenflugel, P. J., & Rey, M. (1986). Interlingual semantic facilitation: Evidence for a common representational system in the bilingual lexicon. *Journal of Memory and Language, 25,* 605–618.

Schwartz, A. I., & Kroll, J. F. (2006). Bilingual lexical activation in sentence context. *Journal of Memory and Language, 55,* 197–212.

Schwartz, A. I., Kroll, J. F., & Diaz, M. (2007). Reading words in Spanish and English: Mapping orthography to phonology in two languages. *Language and Cognitive Processes, 22,* 106–129.

Scoresby-Jackson, R. E. (1867). Case of aphasia with right hemiplegia. *Edinburgh Medical Journal, 12,* 696–706.

Scovel, T. (1988). *A time to speak: A psycholinguistic inquiry into the critical period for human speech.* Rowley, MA: Newbury House.

Sebastián-Gallés, N., & Bosch, L. (2002). Building phonotactic knowledge in bilinguals: Role of early exposure. *Journal of Experimental Psychology: Human Perception and Performance, 28,* 974–989.

Sebastián-Gallés, N., & Bosch, L. (2005). Phonology and bilingualism. In J. F. Kroll & A. M. B. de Groot (Eds.), *Handbook of bilingualism: Psycholinguistic approaches* (pp. 68–87). New York: Oxford University Press.

Sebastián-Gallés, N., Dupoux, E., Segui, J., & Mehler, J. (1992). Contrasting syllabic effects in Catalan and Spanish. *Journal of Memory and Language, 31,* 18–32.

Segalowitz, N. S., & Segalowitz, S. J. (1993). Skilled performance, practice, and the differentiation of speed-up from automatization effects: Evidence from second language word recognition. *Applied Psycholinguistics, 14,* 369–385.

Segalowitz, S. J., Segalowitz, N. S., & Wood, A. G. (1998). Assessing the development of automaticity in second language word recognition. *Applied Psycholinguistics, 19,* 53–67.

Seleskovitch, D. (1976). Interpretation: A psychological approach to translating. In R. Brislin (Ed.), *Translation: Applications and research* (pp. 92–116). New York: Gardner Press.

Service, E. (1992). Phonology, working memory, and foreign-language learning. *The Quarterly Journal of Experimental Psychology, 45A,* 21–50.

Service, E., & Craik, F. I. M. (1993). Differences between young and older adults in learning a foreign vocabulary. *Journal of Memory and Language, 32,* 608–623.

Shallice, T., McLeod, P., & Lewis, K. (1985). Isolating cognitive modules with the dual-task paradigm: Are speech perception and production separate processes? *The Quarterly Journal of Experimental Psychology, 37A,* 507–532.

Sholl, A., Sankaranarayanan, A., & Kroll, J. F. (1995). Transfer between picture naming and translation: A test of asymmetries in bilingual memory. *Psychological Science, 6,* 45–49.

Simpson, G. B. (1981). Meaning dominance and semantic context in the processing of lexical ambiguity. *Journal of Verbal Learning and Verbal Behavior, 20,* 120–136.

Simpson, G. B. (1994). Context and the processing of ambiguous words. In M. A. Gernsbacher (Ed.), *Handbook of Psycholinguistics* (pp. 359–374). San Diego, CA: Academic Press.

Singh, J. A. L., & Zingg, R. M. (1942). *Wolf-children and feral man.* Hamden, CT: Shoe String Press. [Reprinted 1966, New York: Harper & Row].

Singleton, D. (2005). The critical period hypothesis: A coat of many colors. *International Review of*

Applied Linguistics in Language Teaching, 43, 269–285.

Singleton, J. L., & Newport, E. L. (2004). When learners surpass their models: The acquisition of American Sign Language from inconsistent input. *Cognitive Psychology, 49,* 370–407.

Skuse, D. H. (1993). Extreme deprivation in early childhood. In D. Bishop & K. Mogford (Eds.), *Language development in exceptional circumstances* (pp. 29–46). Hillsdale NJ: Erlbaum.

Smith, F. (1923). Bilingualism and mental development. *British Journal of Psychology, 13,* 270–282.

Smith, M. C. (1997). How do bilinguals access lexical information. In A. M. B. de Groot & J. F. Kroll (Eds.), *Tutorials in bilingualism: Psycholinguistic perspectives* (pp. 145–168). Hove, UK: Erlbaum.

Snodgrass, J. G. (1993). Translating versus picture naming: Similarities and differences. In R. Schreuder & B. Weltens (Eds.), *The bilingual lexicon* (pp. 83–114). Amsterdam/Philadelphia: John Benjamins.

Snow, C. E., & Hoefnagel-Höhle, M. (1978). The critical period for language acquisition: Evidence from second language learning. *Child Development, 49,* 1114–1128.

Soares, C., & Grosjean, F. (1984). Bilinguals in a monolingual and a bilingual speech mode: The effect on lexical access. *Memory & Cognition, 12,* 380–386.

Solin, D. (1989). The systematic misrepresentation of bilingual crossed aphasia data and its consequences. *Brain and Language, 36,* 92–116.

Sommer, S., & Gruneberg, M. (2002). The use of Linkword language computer courses in a classroom situation: A case study at Rugby school. *Language Learning Journal, 26,* 48–53.

Spelke, E., Hirst, W., & Neisser, U. (1976). Skills of divided attention. *Cognition, 4,* 215–230.

Spivey, M. J., & Marian, V. (1999). Cross talk between native and second languages: Partial activation of an irrelevant lexicon. *Psychological Science, 10,* 281–284.

Stanovich, K. E. (1986). Matthew effects in reading: Some consequences of individual differences in the acquisition of literacy. *Reading Research Quarterly, 21,* 360–407.

Starreveld, P. A. (2000). On the interpretation of onsets of auditory context effects in word production. *Journal of Memory and Language, 42,* 497–525.

Starreveld, P. A., & La Heij, W. (1995). Semantic interference, orthographic facilitation, and their interaction in naming tasks. *Journal of Experimental Psychology: Learning, Memory, and Cognition, 21,* 686–698.

Starreveld, P. A., & La Heij, W. (1996). Time-course analysis of semantic and orthographic context effects in picture naming. *Journal of Experimental Psychology: Learning, Memory, and Cognition, 22,* 896–918.

Steinhauer, K., White, E. J., & Drury, J. E. (2009). Temporal dynamics of late second language acquisition: Evidence from event-related brain potentials. *Second Language Research, 25,* 13–41.

Sternberg, R. J. (1987). Most vocabulary is learned from context. In M. G. McKeown & M. E. Curtis (Eds.), *The nature of vocabulary acquisition* (pp. 89–106). Hillsdale, NJ: Erlbaum.

Stowe, L. A., Haverkort, M., & Zwarts, F. (2005). Rethinking the neurological basis of language. *Lingua, 115,* 997–1042.

Stroop, J. R. (1935). Studies on interference in serial verbal reactions. *Journal of Experimental Psychology, 18,* 643–662. [Available in Classics in the History of Psychology, an internet resource developed by C.D. Green; http://psychclassics.yorku.ca/Stroop/]

Su, I. (2001). Transfer of sentence processing strategies: A comparison of L2 learners of Chinese and English. *Applied Psycholinguistics, 22,* 83–112.

Sundara, M., Polka, L., & Molnar, M. (2008). Development of coronal stop perception: Bilingual infants keep pace with their monolingual peers. *Cognition, 108,* 232–242.

Supalla, T., & Newport, E. (1978). How many seats in a chair? The derivation of nouns and verbs in American Sign Language. In P. Siple (Ed.), *Understanding language through sign language research* (pp. 91–132). New York: Academic Press.

Swinney, D. A. (1979). Lexical access during sentence comprehension: (Re)consideration of context effects. *Journal of Verbal Learning and Verbal Behavior, 18,* 645–659.

Tabossi, P., Colombo, L., & Job, R. (1987). Accessing lexical ambiguity: Effects of context and dominance. *Psychological Research, 49,* 161–167.

Taft, M. (1994). Interactive-activation as a framework for understanding morphological processing. *Language and Cognitive Processes, 9,* 271–294.

Taft, M., & Forster, K. I. (1975). Lexical storage and retrieval of prefixed words. *Journal of Verbal Learning and Verbal Behavior, 14,* 638–647.

Taft, M., Hambly, G., & Kinoshita, S. (1986). Visual and auditory recognition of prefixed words. *Quarterly Journal of Experimental Psychology: Human Experimental Psychology, 38A,* 351–366.

Talamas, A., Kroll, J. F., & Dufour, R. (1999). From form to meaning: Stages in the acquisition of second-language vocabulary. *Bilingualism: Language and Cognition, 2*, 45–58.

Tan, L. H., Liu, H.-L., Perfetti, C. A., Spinks, J. A., Fox, P. T., & Gao, J.-H. (2001). The neural system underlying Chinese logograph reading. *NeuroImage, 13*, 836–846.

Tan, L. H., Spinks, J. A., Feng, C.-M., Siok, W. T., Perfetti, C. A. et al. (2003). Neural systems of second language reading are shaped by native language. *Human Brain Mapping, 18*, 158–166.

Tanenhaus, M. K., Leiman, J. M., & Seidenberg, M. S. (1979). Evidence for multiple stages in the processing of ambiguous words in syntactic contexts. *Journal of Verbal Learning and Verbal Behavior, 18*, 427–440.

Tanenhaus, M. K, Spivey-Knowlton, M. J, Eberhard, K. M, & Sedivy, J. C. (1995). Integration of visual and linguistic information during spoken language comprehension. *Science, 268*, 1632–1634.

Taylor, I. (1976). Similarity between French and English words—A factor to be considered in bilingual language behavior? *Journal of Psycholinguistic Research, 5*, 85–94.

Taylor, I., & Taylor, M. M. (1990). *Psycholinguistics: Learning and using language.* Englewood Cliffs, NJ: Prentice Hall.

Tees, R. C., & Werker, J. F. (1984). Perceptual flexibility: Maintenance or recovery of the ability to discriminate non-native speech sounds. *Canadian Journal of Psychology, 38*, 579–590.

Thierry, G., & Wu, Y. J. (2004). Electrophysiological evidence for language interference in late bilinguals. *Neuroreport, 15*, 1555–1558.

Thomas, M. H., & Wang, A. Y. (1996). Learning by the keyword mnemonic: Looking for long-term benefits. *Journal of Experimental Psychology: Applied, 2*, 330–342.

Thomas, M. S. C., & Allport, A. (2000). Language switching costs in bilingual visual word recognition. *Journal of Memory and Language, 43*, 44–66.

Thomas, S. C., & Van Heuven, W. J. B. (2005). Computational models of bilingual comprehension. In J. F. Kroll & A. M. B. de Groot (Eds.), *Handbook of bilingualism: Psycholinguistic approaches* (pp. 202–225). New York: Oxford University Press.

Tokowicz, N., & Kroll, J. F. (2007). Number of meanings and concreteness: Consequences of ambiguity within and across languages. *Language and Cognitive Processes, 22*, 727–779.

Tokowicz, N., Kroll, J. F., De Groot, A. M. B., & Van Hell, J. G. (2002). Number-of-translation norms for Dutch–English translation pairs: A new tool for examining language production.

Behavior Research Methods, Instruments, & Computers, 34, 435–451.

Tommola, J., Laine, M., Sunnari, M., & Rinne, J. O. (2000/01). Images of shadowing and interpreting. *Interpreting, 5*, 147–167.

Toro, J. M., Trobalón, J. B., & Sebastián-Gallés, N. (2003). The use of prosodic cues in language discrimination tasks by rats. *Animal Cognition, 6*, 131–136.

Treffers-Daller, J. (1998). Variability in code-switching styles: Turkish–German code-switching patterns. In R. Jacobson (Ed.), *Code-switching worldwide* (pp. 177–197). Berlin: Mouton de Gruyter.

Trehub, S. E. (1973). Infants' sensitivity to vowel and tonal contrasts. *Developmental Psychology, 9*, 91–96.

Tzelgov, J., Henik, A., & Leiser, D. (1990). Controlling Stroop interference: Evidence from a bilingual task. *Journal of Experimental Psychology: Learning, Memory, and Cognition, 16*, 760–771.

Tzelgov, J., Henik, A., Sneg, R., & Baruch, O. (1996). Unintentional word reading via the phonological route: The Stroop effect with cross-script homophones. *Journal of Experimental Psychology: Learning, Memory, and Cognition, 22*, 336–349.

Tzeng, O. J. L., Hung, D. L., & Wang, S.-Y. (1977). Speech recoding in reading Chinese characters. *Journal of Experimental Psychology: Human Learning and Memory, 3*, 621–630.

Ullman, M. T. (2001). The neural basis of lexicon and grammar in first and second language: The declarative/procedural model. *Bilingualism: Language and Cognition, 4*, 105–122.

Ullman, M. T., Corkin, S., Coppola, M., Hickok, G., Growdon, J. H., Koroshetz, W. J., & Pinker, S. (1997). A neural dissociation within language: Evidence that the mental dictionary is part of declarative memory, and that grammatical rules are processed by the procedural system. *Journal of Cognitive Neuroscience, 9*, 266–276.

Umbel, V. M., Pearson, B. Z., Fernández, M. C., & Oller, D. K. (1992). Measuring bilingual children's receptive vocabularies. *Child Development, 63*, 1012–1020.

Underwood, B. J. (1969). Attributes of memory. *Psychological Review, 76*, 559–573.

Underwood, B. J., & Ekstrand, B. R. (1967). Effects of distributed practice on paired-associate learning. *Journal of Experimental Psychology: Monograph Supplement, 73*, 1–21.

Vaid, J., & Chengappa, S. (1988). Assigning linguistic roles: Sentence interpretation in normal and aphasic Kannada–English bilinguals. *Journal of Neurolinguistics, 3*, 161–183.

Vaid, J., & Genesee, F. (1980). Neuropsychological

approaches to bilingualism. *Canadian Journal of Psychology, 34,* 417–445.

Vaid, J., & Hall, D. G. (1991). Neuropsychological perspectives on bilingualism: Right, left, and center. In A. Reynolds (Ed.), *Bilingualism, multiculturalism, and second language learning: The McGill conference in honor of Wallace E. Lambert* (pp. 81–112). Hillsdale, NJ: Erlbaum.

Van Assche, E. (2009). *Bilingual word recognition in a sentence context.* Unpublished PhD. Thesis, University of Ghent.

Van Assche, E., Duyck, W., Hartsuiker, R. J., & Diependaele, K. (2009). Does bilingualism change native-language reading? Cognate effects in a sentence context. *Psychological Science, 20,* 923–927.

Van Berkum, J. J. A., Brown, C. M., Zwitserlood, P., Kooijman, V., & Hagoort, P. (2005). Anticipating upcoming words in discourse: Evidence from ERPs and reading times. *Journal of Experimental Psychology: Learning, Memory, and Cognition, 31,* 443–467.

Van Berkum, J. J. A., Hagoort, P., & Brown, C. M. (1999). Semantic integration in sentences and discourse: Evidence from the N400. *Journal of Cognitive Neuroscience, 11,* 657–671.

Van Berkum, J. J. A., Zwitserlood, P., Hagoort, P., & Brown, C. M. (2003). When and how do listeners relate a sentence to the wider discourse? Evidence from the N400 effect. *Cognitive Brain Research, 17,* 701–718.

Van Hell, J. G., & Candia Mahn, A. (1997). Keyword mnemonics versus rote rehearsal: Learning concrete and abstract foreign words by experienced and inexperienced learners. *Language Learning, 47,* 507–546.

Van Hell, J. G., & De Groot, A. M. B. (1998a). Conceptual representation in bilingual memory: Effects of concreteness and cognate status in word association. *Bilingualism: Language and Cognition, 1,* 193–211.

Van Hell, J. G., & De Groot, A. M. B. (1998b). Disentangling context availability and concreteness in lexical decision and word translation. *The Quarterly Journal of Experimental Psychology, 51A,* 41–63.

Van Hell, J. G., & De Groot, A. M. B. (2008). Sentence context modulates visual word recognition and translation in bilinguals. *Acta Psychologica, 128,* 431–451.

Van Hell, J. G., & Dijkstra, T. (2002). Foreign language knowledge can influence native language performance in exclusively native contexts. *Psychonomic Bulletin & Review, 9,* 780–789.

Van Heuven, W. J. B., & Dijkstra, A. (2001). *The semantic, orthographic, and phonological interactive activation model.* Poster presented at the 12th Conference of the European Society for Cognitive Psychology, Edinburgh, UK.

Van Heuven, W. J. B., Dijkstra, T., & Grainger, J. (1998). Orthographic neighborhood effects in bilingual word recognition. *Journal of Memory and Language, 39,* 458–483.

Van Heuven, W. J. B., Schriefers, H., Dijkstra, T., & Hagoort, P. (2008). Language conflict in the bilingual brain. *Cerebral Cortex, 18,* 2706–2716.

Van Leerdam, M., Bosman, A. M. T., & De Groot, A. M. B. (2009). When MOOD rhymes with ROAD: Dynamics of phonological coding in bilingual visual word perception. *The Mental Lexicon, 4,* 303–335.

Van Orden, G. C. (1987). A ROWS is a ROSE: Spelling, sound, and reading. *Memory & Cognition, 15,* 181–198.

Van Orden, G. C., Johnston, J. C., & Hale, B. L. (1988). Word identification in reading proceeds from spelling to sound to meaning. *Journal of Experimental Psychology: Learning, Memory, and Cognition, 14,* 371–386.

Van Orden, G. C., Pennington, B. F., & Stone, G. O. (1990). Word identification in reading and the promise of subsymbolic psycholinguistics. *Psychological Review, 97,* 488–522.

Van Wijnendaele, I., & Brysbaert, M. (2002). Visual word recognition in bilinguals: Phonological priming from the second to the first language. *Journal of Experimental Psychology: Human Perception and Performance, 28,* 616–627.

Ventureyra, V. A. G., Pallier, C., & Yoo, H.-Y. (2004). The loss of first language phonetic perception in adopted Koreans. *Journal of Neurolinguistics, 17,* 79–91.

Vihman, M. M., Thierry, G., Lum, J., Keren-Portnoy, T., & Martin, P. (2007). Onset of word form recognition in English, Welsh, and English–Welsh bilingual infants. *Applied Psycholinguistics, 28,* 475–493.

Vingerhoets, G., Van Borsel, J., Tesink, C., Van den Noort, M., Deblaere, K., et al. (2003). Multilingualism: an fMRI study. *Neuroimage, 20,* 2181–2196.

Volterra, V., & Taeschner, T. (1978). The acquisition and development of language by bilingual children. *Journal of Child Language, 5,* 311–326.

Von Studnitz, R. E., & Green, D. W. (1997). Lexical decision and language switching. *International Journal of Bilingualism, 1,* 3–24.

Von Studnitz, R. E., & Green, D. W. (2002a). Interlingual homograph interference in German–English bilinguals: Its modulation and locus of control. *Bilingualism: Language and Cognition, 5,* 1–23.

Von Studnitz, R. E., & Green, D. W. (2002b). The cost of switching language in a semantic categorization task. *Bilingualism: Language and Cognition, 5*, 241–251.

Vosse, T., & Kempen, G. (2000). Syntactic structure assembly in human parsing: A computational model based on competitive inhibition and a lexicalist grammar. *Cognition, 75*, 105–143.

Votaw, M. C. (1992). A functional view of bilingual lexicosemantic organization. In R. J. Harris (Ed.), *Cognitive processing in bilinguals* (pp. 299–321). Amsterdam: Elsevier Science Publishers.

Vroomen, J., Van Zon, M., & De Gelder, B. (1996). Metrical segmentation and inhibition in spoken word recognition. *Journal of Experimental Psychology: Human Perception and Performance, 21*, 98–108.

Wang, A. Y., & Thomas, M. H. (1992). The effect of imagery-based mnemonics on the long-term retention of Chinese characters. *Language Learning, 42*, 359–376.

Wang, A. Y., & Thomas, M. H. (1995a). Effect of keywords on long-term retention: Help or hindrance? *Journal of Experimental Psychology, 87*, 468–475.

Wang, A. Y., & Thomas, M. H. (1995b). The effect of imagery-based mnemonics on the long-term retention of Chinese characters. In B. Harley (Ed.), *Lexical issues in language learning* (pp. 167–183). Amsterdam/Philadelphia: John Benjamins.

Wang, A. Y., & Thomas, M. H. (1999). In defense of keyword experiments: A reply to Gruneberg's commentary. *Applied Cognitive Psychology, 13*, 283–287.

Wang, A. Y., Thomas, M. H., Inzana, C. M., & Primacerio, L. J. (1993). Long-term retention under conditions of intentional learning and the keyword mnemonic. *Bulletin of the Psychological Society, 31*, 545–547.

Wang, A.Y., Thomas, M. H., & Ouellette, J. A. (1992). Keyword mnemonic and retention of second-language vocabulary words. *Journal of Educational Psychology, 84*, 520–528.

Wang, Y., Kuhl, P. K., Chen, C., & Dong, Q. (2009). Sustained and transient language control in the bilingual brain. *Neuroimage, 47*, 414–422.

Wartenburger, I., Heekeren, H. R., Abutalebi, J., Cappa, S. F., Villringer, A., & Perani, D. (2003). Early setting of grammatical processing in the bilingual brain. *Neuron, 37*, 159–170.

Weber, A., & Cutler, A. (2004). Lexical competition in non-native spoken-word recognition. *Journal of Memory and Language, 50*, 1–25.

Weber-Fox, C. M., & Neville, H. J. (1996). Sensitive periods differentiate processing of open- and closed-class words: An ERP study of bilinguals. *Journal of Speech, Language and Hearing research, 44*, 1338–1353.

Weikum, W. M., Vouloumanos, A., Navarra, J., Soto-Faraco, S., Sebastián-Gallés, N., & Werker, J. F. (2007). Visual language discrimination in infancy. *Science, 316*, 1159.

Weinreich, U. (1953). *Languages in contact: Findings and problems*. New York: Linguistic Circle of New York. [Reprinted 1974, The Hague: Mouton].

Weltens, B., De Bot, K., & Van Els, T. (1986). *Language attrition in progress*. Dordrecht: Foris.

Werker, J. F. (1989). Becoming a native listener. *American Science, 77*, 54–59.

Werker, J. F., & Byers-Heinlein, K. (2008). Bilingualism in infancy: First steps in perception and comprehension. *Trends in Cognitive Science, 12*, 144–151.

Werker, J. F., Cohen, L. B., Lloyd, V. L., Casasola, M., & Stager, C. L. (1998). Acquisition of word–object associations by 14-month-old infants. *Developmental Psychology, 34*, 1289–1309.

Werker, J. F., Fennell, C. T., Corcoran, K. M., & Stager, C. L. (2002). Infants' ability to learn phonetically similar words: Effects of age and vocabulary size. *Infancy, 3*, 1–30.

Werker, J. F., Gilbert, J. H. V., Humphrey, K., & Tees, R. C. (1981). Developmental aspects of cross-language speech perception. *Child Development, 52*, 349–355.

Werker, J. F., & Tees, R. C. (1984). Cross-language speech perception: Evidence for perceptual reorganization during the first year of life. *Infant Behavior and Development, 7*, 49–63.

Wernicke, C. (1874). *Der aphasische Symptomen-complex. Eine psychologische Studie auf anatomischer Basis*. Breslau: Cohn und Weigert.

Whitney, P. (1998). *The Psychology of language*. Boston, MA: Houghton Mifflin Company.

Wierzbicka, A. (1985). The double life of a bilingual. In R. Sussex & J. Zubrzycki (Eds.), *Polish people and culture in Australia* (pp. 187–223). Canberra: Australian National University.

Wilks, C., & Meara, P. (2002). Untangling word webs: Graph theory and the notion of density in second language word association networks. *Second Language Research, 18*, 303–324.

Wilks, C., Meara, P., & Wolter, B. (2005). A further note on simulating word association behaviour in a second language. *Second Language Research, 21*, 359–372.

Williams, S., & Hammarberg, B. (1998). Language switches in L3 production: Implications for a polyglot speaking model. *Applied Linguistics, 19*, 295–333.

Xue, G., Dong, Q., Jin, Z., Zhang, L., & Wang, Y. (2004). An fMRI study with semantic access in low proficiency second language learners. *Neuro-Report, 15*, 791–796.

Author index

Entries followed by *f* indicate a figure and *t* indicates a table.

Subject index

Entries in bold indicate glossary definitions. Entries followed by *f* indicate a figure and *t* indicates a table.